Strategic Reward Management:

Design, Implementation, and Evaluation

Robert L. Heneman

Fisher College of Business
The Ohio State University

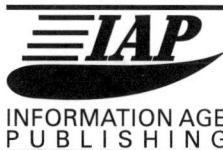

≡IAP

INFORMATION AGE
PUBLISHING

80 Mason Street • Greenwich, Connecticut 06830 • www.infoagepub.com

Library of Congress Cataloging-in-Publication Data

Heneman, Robert L.
  Strategic reward management : design, implementation, and evaluation /
Robert L. Heneman.
      p. cm.
Includes bibliographical references and index.
  ISBN 1-931576-55-6
  1. Compensation management. 2. Reward (Psychology) I. Title.
  HF5549.5.C67 H466 2002
  658.3'22–dc21
                              2002001914

✎

ISBN: 1-931576-54-8 (paper); 1-931576-55-6 (cloth)

Printed in the United States of America

To the Brausch Family

CONTENTS

Part IV. Strategic Pay Issues

Part V. From Job Evaluation to Work Evaluation

Part VI. Team Pay

Part VII. Merit Pay Revisited

Part VIII. Competency Pay

Part IX. Pay System Evaluation

Part X. Conclusions & The Future of Strategic Rewards

PREFACE

I have been very fortunate the past ten years or so to be in a position to observe and participate in the growth of strategic reward systems. The objective of this book is to summarize in readings form what I have learned. My hope is that by providing these readings in one volume, it can be used as a supplemental reader to compensation texts, as a summary of strategic reward issues for researchers, and as a reference source for practitioners to keep up to date with research and practice in this area.

As a participant/observer of the development of strategic reward systems, I bring a bias with me that is reflected in the readings. My writings in this book reflect the fact that I draw heavily upon empirical research to guide the conclusions I reach in the readings and I stay away from armchair speculation. As a result, I take positions that are not always popular. For example, based on the research, I do not advocate the wholesale abandonment of job evaluation and merit pay as has become fashionable in some compensation circles.

The WorldatWork (formerly American Compensation Association) has been extremely helpful to me in opening doors for me to be a participant/observer in strategic reward systems. I am also thankful to George Johnson at Information Age Publishing for providing me with the opportunity to publish this volume. I would like to thank Wendy Schutt and Joan Evans for doing an excellent job at helping me to prepare this volume. Lastly, I would like to thank all my coauthors that helped me write these various readings.

ACKNOWLEDGMENTS

The author and publisher wish to thank the following for permission to use copyright materials.

AMACOM, a division of American Management Association International, New York, NY for R.L. Heneman (2001). Corporate Business Strategies and Compensation Strategies. In R.L. Heneman, *Business-Driven Compensation Policies: Integrating Compensation Systems with Corporate Strategies.* New York: AMACOM, pp. 15–40; R.L. Heneman & K. Dixon (1998). How to Find, Select, and Evaluate Pay Surveys to Meet Your Organization's Needs. In R. Platt (Ed.), *Salary Survey Guidebook* (pp. 1–5). New York: AMACOM.

Elsevier Science, Greenwich, CT for M.P. Miceli & R.L. Heneman (2000). Contextual Determinants of Variable Pay Plan Design: A Proposed Research Framework. *Human Resource Management Review, 10*(3), 289–305; R.L. Heneman, K.E. Dixon, & M.T. Gresham (2000). Team Pay for Novice, Intermediate, and Advanced Teams. In M.A. Byerlein, D.A. Johnson, & S. Byerlein (Eds.), *Advances in Interdisciplinary Work Teams* (Vol. 7), Greenwich, CT: JAI Press; R.L. Heneman & C. von Hippel (1996). The Assessment of Job Performance: Focusing Attention on Context, Process and Group Issues. In D. Lewin, D.J.B. Mitchell, & M.A. Zaidi (Eds.), *Handbook of Human Resource Management,* pp.587–617. Greenwich, CT: JAI Press. R.L. Heneman, D.B. Greenberger, & J.A. Fox (2001). Pay Increase Satisfaction: A Reconceptualization of Pay Raise Satisfaction Based on Changes in Work and Pay Practices. *Human Resource Management Review.*

Human Resource Planning Society, New York, NY for D. Eskew & R.L. Heneman (1996). A Survey of Merit Pay Plan Effectiveness: End of the Line for Merit Pay or Hope for Improvement? *Human Resource Planning, 19*(2), 12–19.

Harvard Business School Press, Cambridge, MA for G.E. Ledford & R.L. Heneman (2000). Compensation: A Troublesome Lead System in Organizational Change. In M. Beer & N. Noria (Eds.) *Breaking the Code of Change* (pp. 307–322). Cambridge, MA: Harvard Business School Press.

Information Age Publishing, Greenwich, CT for R.L. Heneman, J.W. Tansky, & E.C. Tomlinson (in press). Hybrid Reward Systems for Virtual Organizations: A Review and Recommendations. In R.L. Heneman & D.B. Greenberger (Eds.), *HRM in virtual organizations.* Greenwich, CT: Information Age Publishing.

International Personnel Management Association, Alexandria, VA for R.L. Heneman (in press). Job and Work Evaluation: A Literature Review. *Public Personnel Management.*

Jossey-Bass, Inc., a subsidiary of John Wiley & Sons, San Francisco, CA for R.L. Heneman, G.E. Ledford, & M.T. Gresham (2000). The Changing Nature of Work and its Effects on Compensation Design and Delivery. In S. Rynes & B. Gerhart (Eds.), *Compensation in Organizations: Progress & Prospects* (pp. 195–240). San Francisco: New Lexington Press; R.L. Heneman & M.T. Gresham (1998). Performance-Based Pay Plans. In J.W. Smither (Ed.), *Performance Appraisal: State-of-the Art Methods for Performance Management* (Society for Industrial and Organizational Psychology Professional Practice Series) pp. 496–536, San Francisco: Jossey-Bass.

Kluwer Academic Publishers, Norwell, MA for D.J. Cohen & R.L. Heneman (1994). Ability and Effort Weights in Pay Level and Pay Increase Decisions. *Journal of Business and Psychology, 8,* 327–343. Reprinted in *Personnel Research Highlights, 1994.* Washington, DC: Office of Personnel Management, 1995; R.L. Heneman, G. Porter, D.B. Greenberger, & S. Strasser (1997). Modeling the Relationship Between Pay Level and Pay Satisfaction. *Journal of Business and Psychology, 12*(2), 147–158.

Sage Publications Limited, London, England for R.L. Heneman, C.H. Fay, & Z.M. Wang (in press). Compensation Systems in the Global Context. In D. Ones & C. Viswesvaran (pp. 77–92) *Handbook of Industrial, Work and Organizational Psychology,* London, England: Sage; R.L. Heneman & K.E. Dixon (in press). Reward System Alingment. *Compensation and Benefits Review;* R.L. Heneman & C. von Hippel (1995). Balancing Group and Individual Rewards: Rewarding Individual Contributions to the Team. *Compensation and Benefits Review, 25*(4), 63–68; R.L. Heneman & A.L. Thomas (1997). The Limited Inc.: Using Strategic Performance Management to Drive Brand Leadership. *Compensation and Benefits Review, 27*(6), 33–40; R.L. Heneman, D.E. Eskew, & J.A. Fox (1998). Using Employee Attitude Surveys to Evaluate a New Incentive Pay Program. *Compensation and Benefits Review, 28*(1), 40–44.

Swets and Zeitlinger Publishers, Lisse, The Netherlands for R.L. Heneman & G.E. Ledford (1998). Competency Pay for Professionals and Managers in Business: A Review and Implications for Teachers. *Journal of Personnel Evaluation in Education, 12*(2), 103–121.

The Association for Quality and Participation, Cincinnati, OH for G.L. Dalton, J. Stevens, & R.L. Heneman (1997). Alternative Rewards in Union Settings. *The Journal for Quality and Participation, 27*(5), 26–31.

The Free Press, a Division of Simon & Schuster, Inc., New York, NY for R.L. Heneman (2001). Merit Pay. In C. Fay (Ed.), *The Executive Handbook of Compensation* (pp. 447–464). New York: Free Press.

The McGraw-Hill Companies, New York, NY for G.E. Ledford & R.L. Heneman (2000). Pay for Skills, Knowledge, and Competencies. In L. Berger & D. Berger (Ed.), *The Compensation Handbook: A State-of-the-Art Guide to Compensation Strategy and Design* (4th ed.). New York: McGraw-Hill.

WorldatWork, Scottsdale, AZ for R.L. Heneman, C. von Hippel, D.E. Eskew, & D.B. Greenberger (1997). Alternative Rewards in Unionized Environments. *American Compensation Association Journal,* Summer, 42–55; R.L. Heneman (in press). Work Evaluation: Current State of the Art and Future Prospects. *WorldatWork Journal.*

Part I

INTRODUCTION

The contents of this book center around the management of strategic reward systems. In particular, the book focuses in on the following elements of managing a reward system: design, implementation, and evaluation. It is my belief that too much time is spent on the administration of strategic reward systems at the expense of these other activities that add more value than does administration to the organization.

Moreover, it is very important to remember that the management of reward systems takes place in a larger context that must be accommodated when designing, implementing, and evaluating strategic reward systems. This larger context includes the business environment, business strategy, and compensation strategy. Elements of the environment include the internal environment (organizational structure, business processes, HR systems) and external environment (laws and regulations, labor markets, and unions).

The collection of articles presented throughout the book is very concerned with the fit of strategic reward management with the business environment, business strategy, and compensation strategy. Research has clearly documented the importance of this "fit" to organizational effectiveness (Gomez-Mejia & Balkin, 1992). A practical illustration makes the point as well. Taco Bell was found guilty in a class action suit by current and former employees. In order to keep the number of labor hours low in a productivity formula used to grant bonuses to managers, employee time sheets failed to account for overtime hours by employees. Failure to pay attention to the legal context in designing, implementing, and evaluating a strategic reward program cost Taco Bell millions of dollars (Gatewood, 2001).

Although all of the readings in the book focus in on the management of strategic rewards in the larger business context, the readings are organized by topical area. The selection of topics is simply based on my writing interests and do not reflect the entire domain of important topics in strategic reward management.

REFERENCES

Gatewood, J.L. (2001, June 15). Taco Bell found guilty of cheating employees. *HR Executive*, p. 21.

Gomez-Mejia, L.R., & Balkin, D.B. (1992). *Compensation, organizational strategy, and firm performance*. Cincinnati, OH: South Western.

Part II

PAY AND THE CHANGING BUSINESS CONTEXT

This first part of the book provides a summary of the different types of strategic reward programs that exist. It not only describes these programs, but also lists the strengths and weaknesses of each approach based on the available research and practice descriptions. When to use these various approaches is described relative to the global business market, business and compensation strategies, and the changing nature of business processes and work in organizations. As will be shown, in recent years the number of different types of strategic reward programs has grown very large.

Heneman, R.L. , Fay, C.H., & Wang, Z.M. (in press). Compensation systems in the global context. In D. Ones & C. Viswesvaran (Eds.), *Handbook of industrial, work and organizational psychology* (pp. 77–92). London: Sage.

Heneman, R.L., Ledford, G.E., & Gresham, M.T. (2000). The changing nature of work and its effects on compensation design and delivery. In S. Rynes & B. Gerhart (Eds.), *Compensation in organizations: Progress & prospects* (pp. 195–240). San Francisco: New Lexington Press.

Heneman, R.L., & Gresham, M.T. (1998). Performance-based pay plans. In J.W. Smither (Ed.), *Performance appraisal: State-of-the-art methods for performance management* (pp. 496–536), Society for Industrial and Organizational Psychology Professional Practice Series. San Francisco: Jossey-Bass.

CHAPTER 1

COMPENSATION SYSTEMS IN THE GLOBAL CONTEXT

Robert L. Heneman, Charles H. Fay, and Zhong-Ming Wang

Source: Reprinted by permission of Sage Publications Ltd. from Heneman, R.L. , Fay, C.H., and Wang, Z.M. (in press). Compensation Systems in the Global Context. In D. Ones & C. Viswesvaran (Eds.), *Handbook of Industrial, Work and Organizational Psychology* (pp. 77–92). London: Sage.

ABSTRACT

A selective review of the compensation literature was conducted. Compensation is a multidimensional concept and topics covered include base pay, variable pay, individual incentives, ownership, and benefits. A history of compensation, a summary of the current state of knowledge, and directions for future theory, research, and practice are provided. Throughout the chapter global issues are discussed. Our goal for the chapter is to continue to invigorate compensation as an area of study in work psychology.

INTRODUCTION

Compensation (defined here as pay, benefits, and other rewards with monetary value) is by far the most costly human resource intervention in organizations. Compensation budgets of over $1 billion are not uncommon in Fortune 50 companies. As much as 80 percent of total budgets in service sector organizations are made up of compensation costs (Milkovich & Newman, 1999). Given the huge costs associated with compensation, it is surprising the small amount of attention devoted to compensation issues in the industrial psychology literature relative to other human resource interventions such as staffing and training and development. The purpose of this chapter is to selectively review the history of the study of compensation in industrial psychology, to summarize the current state of knowledge, and to offer directions for future theory, research, and practice. Throughout the chapter we will cover global issues, especially as they relate to recent developments in China. Our ultimate aim is to help to continue to invigorate compensation as an area of study in work psychology.

HISTORY OF WORK PSYCHOLOGY: CONTRIBUTIONS TO COMPENSATION

There has never been a steady stream of research with a direct focus on compensation issues from work psychology. Contributions to the compensation literature from work psychologists have been indirect rather than direct and have been sporadic rather than regular. Although indirect and sporadic, the contributions made by work psychologists have been very influential. Indirectly, the field of compensation has benefitted greatly from the efforts of work psychologists in areas such as motivation (e.g., Campbell, 1976) and criterion issues (Smith, 1976). Interestingly, the first edition of the *Handbook of Industrial and Organizational Psychology* (Dunnette, 1976) did not have a chapter on compensation. However, the chapters on motivation and criterion issues just mentioned were on the "must-read" list of compensation scholars. Motivation theory provides analysis of the processes whereby compensation decisions affect the attitudes and behaviors of employees, while the criterion problem plagues pay-for-performance plans.

Historically, the most influential work psychologist who has directly addressed compensation is Lawler. His first major work on compensation, *Pay and Organizational Effectiveness* (1971) was a major review of the micro research literature. More importantly he placed it in the context of organizational effectiveness theory showing the practical importance of compensation to organizations. While the importance of selection decisions had been pointed out in the industrial and organizational (I/O) literature (e.g., Cronbach & Gleser, 1965), Lawler provided the first major statement of the importance of compensation to organizational effectiveness.

Another major contribution of Lawler was his little known, yet highly important book *Pay and Organizational Development* (1981). This book was some 10 years ahead of the field in terms of both research and practice. In this book Lawler clearly framed the need to understand the organizational psychology of compensation decision making. That is, compensation was viewed as a powerful organizational development intervention in organizations. As such, he required that the organizational processes to deliver pay were as important or more important than the amount of pay.

Lawler was again years ahead of practice and research with his book *Strategic Pay* (1990). Influenced by the business policy literature, Lawler recognized that compensation systems not only could be integrated with the business strategies and processes in the organization, but that they should be integrated in order for organizations to have competitive advantage relative to their competitors in product and labor markets. Hence, pay systems not only needed to be framed in terms of process to be effective, but so too must they be framed in the context of the specific goals of the organization.

In his latest book, Lawler again pushes the frontier of our knowledge about compensation systems (Lawler, 2000). He argues that job-based pay systems that rely upon job descriptions and job evaluation systems are not flexible enough to adapt to the changing nature of work. Instead, pay systems should be based on people rather than jobs where people are defined by their competencies (i.e., KSAOs). It remains to be seen whether organizations will replace job-based pay systems with person-based pay systems.

In recent years, compensation has begun to receive more direct and consistent attention in the work psychology literature. The second edition of the *Handbook of Industrial and Organizational Psychology* (Dunnette & Hough, 1992) contained two chapters on compensation: one by Gerhart and Milkovich (1992) and one by Lawler and Jenkins (1992). The Frontier Series of the Society for Industrial and Organizational Psychology published an entire book on compensation topics entitled: *Compensation: Progress and Prospects* (Rynes & Gerhart, 2000). Both of these events are symbolic of the importance now being placed on compensation decision making by work psychologists.

Work psychology is not the only scholarly field investigating compensation. Economists, and particularly labor economists, have studied compensation (generally focusing on wage levels) for a much longer period than have work psychologists (e.g., Cartter, 1959; Hicks, 1934). Labor economists have developed a rich theory base to speak to some of the same issues of interest to work psychologists (e.g., criterion measurement, motivation) and others which could be, but so far have not been addressed in depth by work psychologists (e.g., perceived value of jobs, tradeoffs between different forms of compensation). Similarly, sociologists such as Treiman have considered bias and reliability problems in job analysis and job evaluation processes (Treiman, 1979; Treiman & Hartman, 1981). While work from the three fields is not integrated, work psychologists should be aware of the literature on compensation of both labor economics and sociology and make use of it in the development of psychological theory that focuses on compensation. An excellent example from work psychology where all of these fields are drawn upon is Viswesvaran and Barrick (1992).

As a result of historical developments within the field (and the influence of the literatures of labor economics, sociology, and business policy), compensation is now viewed by work psychologists as a system within the organization rather than a set of techniques. The focus has shifted away from the psychometric properties of compensation techniques to the integration of the compensation system with other organizational systems in order to achieve organizational effectiveness. It is our belief that this more macro focus to the study of compensation is going to continue, especially in light of the ongoing globalization of business practices. The next big challenge to be faced by compensation researchers and practitioners alike is how to best pay people in a global business environment.

THE CURRENT STATE OF AFFAIRS

Our focus in this chapter is the total cash compensation system in the organization as shown in Figure 1. Elements of this system include base pay (wages and salaries), variable pay, individual incentives, ownership, and benefits. Each of these elements has cash value to the employee and organization. All need to be integrated with the compensation strategy and with one another. The compensation strategy in concert with the total cash compensation system yields outcomes related to the effectiveness of the organization, including productivity, innovation, higher quality, and customer satisfaction.

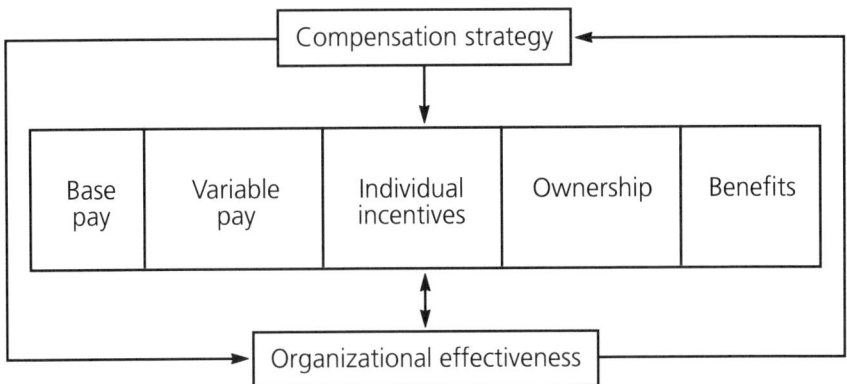

Figure 1.   Chapter framework.

We will first focus on issues that arise in the formulation and execution of compensation strategy. Next we will review the issues that arise with each element of total cash compensation. Lastly, we will review the relationship between each element of total cash compensation and organizational effectiveness criteria.

Compensation Strategy

The most important stream of research that has been developed in compensation the past 15 years is the study of pay from a strategic perspective. With this approach, the organization is the unit of analysis rather than individuals in the organization (Lawler & Jenkins, 1992). Compensation is studied from the perspective of how compensation can be used by organizations to adapt to a rapidly changing business environment (Gomez-Mejia & Balkin, 1992).

At the most general level, two steps are undertaken to make compensation systems strategic (Wright, Dyer, Boudreau, & Milkovich, 1999). First, the compensation system is aligned with the goals of the organization. Second, the compensation system is fully integrated with other human systems in the organization. Operationally, the first step is carried out by aligning each element of the compensation system with the vision and mission of the organization. The second step is achieved by integrating elements of the compensation system with the human resource goals of the organization (Heneman, 2001).

The strategic compensation process is depicted in Figure 2. As can be seen, the ultimate goal of strategic compensation decision making is to achieve a "fit" between organizational goals, compensation systems, and human resource goals. A consistent finding in the literature is that a strategic approach to compensation is associated with enhanced business performance by the organization (Becker & Gerhart, 1992).

Interestingly, it appears that of the two-stage strategic process just described, the most important step is the alignment of compensation with the business strategy rather than the integration of compensation with other human resource goals. Main effects for compensation are usually significant, while interaction effects between compensation and other human resource systems are usually nonsignificant (Gerhart, Trevor, & Graham, 1996). There are several possible interpretations to this repeated finding. First, it may be that compensation systems are so powerful that they overwhelm the effects of other human resource systems. Second, it may be the case that there has not been enough careful theoretical development regarding the interaction of compensation with other human resource systems (Heneman, 2000). Third, there may be multicollinearity in the data

Figure 2.   Strategic compensation process

due to strong correlation between the main effect for compensation and the interaction effects for compensation and other human resource system variables.

It should also be noted that business strategy sometimes has an indirect as well as direct effect on compensation decisions. Tullar (1998) conducted a study in a food and beverage distribution center where he found that the compensation strategy impacted the design of work and in turn the design of work impacted job evaluation point level assignments. In particular, business process reengineering was associated with a significant increase in Hay System job evaluation points.

Government Reform and Compensation Strategy

Compensation systems reform often has a fundamental impact on compensation strategy. In China, for example, compensation was for a long time under a centralized national system with a more institutional basic time-pay with eight levels of skills or positions. During the period between the first pay systems reform in 1956 and the nationwide readjustment in 1976, the characteristics of compensation system were universal salary grades, centralized salary operations, fixed basic wages, and equalitarian wage distribution. In the governmental and administrative departments, the pay system was reformed, changing from a wage grade system started in

1956 to a structured wage system in 1985, consisting of basic wage, position pay, tenure wage, and reward wage.

In 1983, two measures were taken to adjust the pay systems among industrial organizations in China: (1) linking pay with the firms' economic performance; (2) adopting a performance appraisal system for promotion of pay. By 1995, more than 40,000 enterprises implemented the "Position and Skill Pay" on the basis of work evaluation and actual performance. Therefore, we see a clear move from the egalitarian wage-payment system with a flat reward structure towards performance-based pay system (Wang & Feng, 2000).

When China started its economic reform in 1978, one of the important strategies in managing State enterprises was to restore the bonus system that was abolished in 1966, and to develop more effective compensation systems. The bonus systems were regarded as a supplementary gain to the basic wage and closely based on actual performance. This became the first active area in industrial and organizational psychology in China in the early and mid-1980s. Field studies on work motivation and compensation systems design were conducted in various enterprises.

Individual Differences and Compensation Strategies

In a field study, Wang (1994) found significant age differences and organizational position differences in employees' needs for the types of compensations. Intrinsic needs for technical training and satisfactory jobs were most preferred by young employees, while a bonus was more important to the middle-aged. Among the elder employees, social rewards such as an excellent worker title appeared to be more important. A more flexible and comprehensive multiple compensation structure combining social rewards with material incentives should be used in order to motivate the workforce. A field experiment was then implemented using a flexible multireward system in some departments of a steel file company. Employees who completed their production targets could choose an incentive among five alternatives: bonus, technical training, flexible working time, group vocation, and excellent worker title. Compared with the control group, the experimental group under the multi compensation system resulted in significant higher motivation and doubled productivity.

In examining the relative importance of the compensation components in recruiting, motivating and retaining local Chinese employees, Luk and Chiu (1998) found that base salary, merit pay and year-end bonus were the three most significant items among 37 components, perceived by employers, for all three levels of employees (managers, supervisors, and workers) in all three functions (attraction, motivation, and retention). Generally speaking, the fourth and fifth places were occupied by housing provision, annual leave, cash allowance, and individual bonus interchangeably.

Organizational Structure and Compensation Strategies

In a recent study on comparisons among compensation systems in administrative bureaus versus industrial organizations, Wang and Chen (2000) emphasized the structural effects of compensation management in administrative bureaus and enterprises on work motivation and performance. More than 490 management staff from 18 enterprises and 16 administrative bureaus participated in this study. The main results showed: (1) different ownership systems (state-owned enterprises, international joint ventures, township companies, and governmental offices) had different effects on compensation management, particularly human resources management practices, organizational cultures, satisfaction, and performance; (2) organizational culture had influences on the implementation of compensation systems; (3) human resource management patterns can affect compensation management systems; (4) the position levels had influences on compensation management, employees' satisfaction, and performance. In terms of compensation management, employees from enterprises showed higher pay satisfaction and compensation justice than that of governmental staff though the latter had higher organizational performance than the former. As to the cross-ownership comparison, employees from township companies showed the highest compensation satisfaction, state-enterprise employees second, and joint venture employees third.

Base Pay

The process used to establish base wages and salaries in organizations is shown in Figure 3. The results of a job analysis are used in the job evaluation and market survey process. Job evaluation is a process whereby standards are developed to assess the value of the job to the organization. Each job description is graded using a predefined set of standards. Market surveys are con-

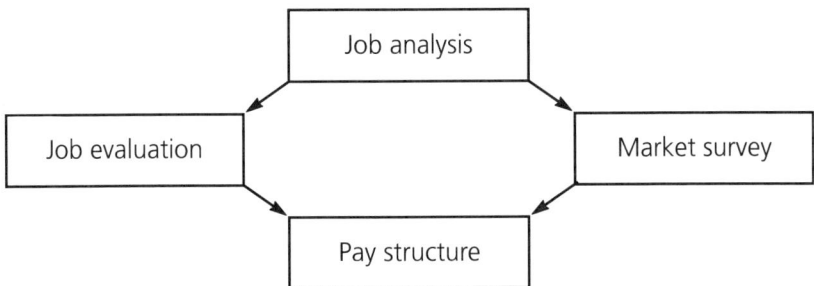

Figure 3.   Process followed to develop base pay.

ducted to assess the value of the job external to the organization. Job descriptions are used to ensure that the jobs being compared are comparable to one another. The results of the job evaluation and market survey processes are merged together to form a pay structure. The pay structure sets forth the parameter of pay levels possible for each job in the organization. The process just described has been researched over the years and several important themes emerge from this research that will now be covered.

Job Evaluation

The research over the years consistently shows that different job evaluation systems lead to different results (Collins & Muchinsky, 1993; Madigan, 1985; Treiman, 1979). That is, the rank order of jobs and subsequent pay varies as a function of the job evaluation method. The important implication here is that great care must be taken in selecting or developing a job evaluation system. Attention needs to be paid to both the reliability and validity of the system. Reliability, of course, serves as the upper bound to validity. It can be strengthened by carefully defining the job evaluation standards. However, even with a job evaluation system reliability of .9, Treiman (1979, p. 41) demonstrates that job assignment in an 18-grade pay structure will have an error of as much as Å 2.75 grades. Validity can be enhanced by carefully matching the standards to the goals of the organization (Heneman, 2001).

While the labor economics literature reports many different models that speak to job value (Wallace & Fay, 1988); work psychology has not developed extensive theory in this area. Yet, to a great extent, job value is a function of individual and group perceptions. Neither economic nor sociological theory speaks specifically to affect issues surrounding perceptions of job value.

Market Surveys

In creating a pay structure, a decision must be made as to how much weight to place on the value of the job as established internally by a job evaluation system and as established by the market value of jobs. Research indicates that greater weight is usually placed on the market value (Weber & Rynes, 1991). Increasingly, a job evaluation approach known as market pricing is being used by organizations where the sole determinant of base pay is the market value. While the heavy weighting of market survey results may seem like a good solution to the problems with job evaluation, it is not. Market surveys are plagued by measurement error and sampling error (Rynes & Milkovich, 1986). Shoddy craftsmanship of surveys results in dubious market data. For example, job titles are often used rather than job analysis to define jobs. Job titles are notoriously misleading and may create measurement error. Convenience samples are often used in selecting companies to survey leading to sampling error. In order to generate meaningful market data, careful attention needs to be given to measurement theory in designing the surveys and to sampling theory in selecting companies to survey (Heneman & Dixon, 1998).

Even when many different survey sources are used, it is unlikely that market matches will be found for all jobs in an organization. Johnson and Johnson, for example, which practices pure market pricing (i.e., no job evaluation is done) can get market rates for only about 85 percent of their jobs. Statistical models (usually multiple linear regression) utilizing job attributes are developed to estimate wages of jobs for which no market rates are available.

Pay Structures

The administrative tool used by most organizations to link market data and job evaluation judgments is the salary structure. Traditionally the typical organization had one salary structure for every broad job family (e.g., blue collar, clerical, technical, administrative). Each structure had anywhere from two to four grades for every layer of organizational hierarchy among the jobs covered.

Increasingly, organizations are reducing the number of pay grades in the organization and increasing the width of the remaining pay grades. Usually, this is done in response to changes in the business strategy where the organization needs to be made more flexible in order to more rapidly adapt to the changing business environment. By reducing the number of pay grades, employees and pay become more flexible to be in alignment with the strategy. Employee job duties are more broadly defined under this approach and base pay dispersion is more marked than under a system with many pay bands. Also, consistent with a business strategy of cost reduction, broadbanding may lead to a reduction in labor costs as fewer people are needed because employees can perform multiple duties.

Unfortunately, no analytical research has been conducted on broadbanding. The data collected to date are only descriptive in nature. The best descriptive survey to date was conducted by Abosch and Hand (1998). Their data indicate that when asked to evaluate the effectiveness of broadbanding, 70 percent of managers, 85 percent of human resource professionals, and 56 percent of employees in organizations with broadbanding rated it as effective or very effective. Broadbanding is typically used for exempt rather than nonexempt employees. There has been a considerable expansion of broadbanding to international company locations. Broadbanding is used relatively more often in Latin America than in Europe or Asia and broadbanding is expected to grow rapidly in Europe, Asia, and Latin America (Abosch & Hmurovic, 1998).

Although these initial results are promising, care must be taken in using broadbanding. Initially, broadbanding may lead to increased rather than decreased costs. Because pay grade widths are broader, the maximum amount of pay available increases and unless control points are used in the bands, usually based on market values, broadbanding can lead to runaway labor costs. As a result, there also needs to be a sound method of assessing employee contributions to the organization. A well-developed performance appraisal or competency assessment is needed to ensure that progression within pay grades is based upon "true" performance rather than error-filled ratings.

Person-Based Pay

Again, due to the need to create more flexible organizations, organizations have enacted person-based pay systems to allow employees to be more flexible in the duties they perform. Ultimately, the hope with these systems is to decrease headcount and labor costs as employees will have multiple skills and be able to perform multiple tasks. The primary theory base for person-based pay is human capital theory (Becker, 1975), which posits that most individuals decide to pursue formal education (and make other human capital investments in knowledge, skills or abilities) based on expected career returns. Conversely, job value is affected by the degree of formal education and other human capital investment required.

Skill-based pay systems are usually used for lower-level employees and provide pay increases or bonuses for mastering new skills to be used at work. Competency-based pay is usually used for professional and managerial positions. Pay is provided for competency development where competencies are defined as knowledge, skills, abilities, and other factors (e.g., personality) related to effective performance.

Both descriptive and analytical studies have been conducted on skill-based pay and the results are encouraging. Jenkins, Ledford, Gupta, and Doty (1987) reported that at least 80 percent of organizations with skill-based pay reported that their skill-based pay was at least moderately successful. An excellent study was conducted by Murray and Gerhart (1998) using a time series design. When a plant using skill-based pay was compared to a comparable plant without skill-based pay, the results indicated that the skill-based pay plant had 58 percent greater productivity, 16 percent less labor costs, and favorable quality outcomes relative to the comparison plant without skill-based pay. It should be noted that cost reductions should be expected in the long run, but not in the short run with skill-based pay. The direct and indirect start-up costs are high. Indirect costs include large training and certification expenses. Direct costs are the result of higher wages with skill-based pay.

A descriptive study of competency-based pay was conducted by the American Compensation Association (1996). The interesting finding reported here was that while competencies were being extensively used for staffing and development purposes, they are seldom being used for compensation purposes. Preliminary results of an analytical study of competencies for a large multinational food company show a relationship between competencies and business results (Heneman, Ledford, & Gresham, 2000).

Merit Pay

The links of pay increases in base salary to performance ratings continues to be a controversial issue. Although confidence in merit pay as an effective reward system has waned, it continues to be frequently used (Eskew & Heneman, 1996). For example, many companies in Japan are using merit pay to replace seniority-based systems. The major problem with merit pay seems to be that it is used as a stand-alone reward program meant to reward all aspects of performance in the organization. In order to overcome this problem, two steps need to be taken (Heneman, in press). First, generic performance standards should not be used to assess performance. Instead, performance standards should be directly tied to the business strategy of the organization. Second, merit pay plans should be used in conjunction with other reward plans such as variable pay. For example, Heneman, Eskew, and Fox (1998) document the effective use of profit sharing and merit pay in concert with one another. In the flight simulator company examined, merit pay was used as the funding gate for employees to receive a differential share of the profits.

Variable Pay

The use of variable pay plans continues to increase (Lawler, Mohrman, & Ledford, 1998). Common features to these plans include a pay-for-performance component, performance measured at the team, business unit, or organizational level, and pay in the form of a cash bonus rather than an increase to base pay (Miceli & Heneman, in press). Typical types of variable pay plans include gainsharing, goalsharing, team pay, and profit sharing (Heneman, Ledford, & Gresham, 2000). Gainsharing plans usually measure performance at the business unit level and pay for cost reductions. Goalsharing plans also usually measure performance at the business unit level and pay for cost reductions and revenue generation activities (e.g., customer service). Team pay is used for small, intact work groups (e.g., self-directed work teams). Profit-sharing measures performance at the organizational level.

Variable pay is held in high regard by management relative to base pay increases for three major reasons. First, variable pay plans are self-funding, e.g., no profit share payout is made unless there is a profit. Second, variable pay is seen to reduce the entitlement psychology inherent with increases to base pay. Pay is tied to the results of the business rather than to market or cost of living conditions. Third, pay is viewed as less of an annuity. With pay increases due to merit, for example, the merit increase is permanently built into base pay and compounds itself over time. Variable pay must be re-earned every year (or every other pay period).

A major drawback to variable pay plans is the concept of line of sight (Heneman, Ledford, & Gresham, 2000). Fashioned loosely on expectancy theory (Vroom, 1964), line of sight refers to the perceived influence that employees have over the outcomes that must be impacted to achieve a cash bonus. Profit as a performance measure, for example, has a very long line of sight that diminishes the motivational value of the reward. By contrast, measures at the individual level have a less lengthy line of sight.

Recent research has also begun to examine variable pay in international environments such as China. In China there was a long tradition of egalitarianism and the "iron rice bowl" (i.e., guaranteed employment and guaranteed pay irrespective of performance) during the 1950s through 1970s. In the early 1980s, as a reaction to the "iron rice bowl" problem in pay distribution, an individualistic piece-rate bonus system emphasizing individual performance became popular in some Chinese industries. This practice discouraged collective responsibility and weakened team effectiveness (Wang, 1990). Thus, studies of industrial/organizational psychology were carried out to compare work efficiencies between individual and group compensation systems and to provide systematic evidence for improving the structure of compensation systems in Chinese enterprises. A series of field experiments were carried out to find out the effects of workers' attributions upon performance under individual versus team reward systems in Chinese enterprises. The results showed that under the group compensation system, employees tended to attribute their performance to the team cooperation and collective efforts which may maintain or enhance work motivation, and under the individual compensation system, they more frequently attributed their performance to personal factors or task difficulty which may reduce their work motivation. An implication of this study was that a team-oriented compensation system with clear responsibility structure would be more effective in facilitating morale, cooperation, and productivity in Chinese enterprises (Wang, 1994).

Individual Incentives

Individual incentive plans also link pay to performance in the form of a cash bonus. Unlike variable pay plans, however, pay is linked to individual performance rather than to group measures of performance (e.g., piece rate, sales). As a result of using individual rather than group measures of performance, the line of sight is probably shorter for individual incentive plans than for variable pay plans. In support of the line of sight advantage of individual incentives, the research clearly shows that they have the largest impact on employee performance (Heneman et al., 1998).

A distinct disadvantage to individual incentives is that they may detract from team performance (Wageman, 1995). It is sometimes possible to overcome this disadvantage, however, when incentive pay is coupled with variable pay (Crown & Rosse, 1995) especially in those business environments where both individual and organizational business goals are emphasized (Heneman et al., 1998).

Individual incentives for CEOs have recently been an active area of study in the global context. Wang and Feng (2000), for example, completed a study recently concerning the relationship among the compensation program dimensions, compensation perception, and performance among 251 managers in Chinese companies, and attempted to build up an assessment model of compensation program characteristics for managers. The results indicated that: (1) compensation program dimensions included need dimension, goal dimension, motivation dimension, and performance regulation dimension; (2) distributive justice was more related to the goal dimension and organizational systems and procedural justice was more dependent upon the need dimension and organizational level features of compensation programs, while both kinds of justice were closely related with performance regulation dimension. Compensation perception affected managerial performance. Managers' achievement motive affected level of effort and also affected indicators of company performance directly.

Ownership

At the other end of the spectrum from individual incentives in terms of line of sight are ownership plans where employees are made stockholders. The performance measure to be influenced by employees for a reward is the value of company stock. Many factors exogenous to the company (e.g., economy), yet alone to the employee, have an impact on the value of stock. Even with the long sight of sight, there has been an explosion in the use of ownership plans in recent years (Capell, 1996).

One interesting variation on stock ownership plans is "phantom stock" used in privately held companies. Under this approach, internal stock is issued that serves as a proxy for public stock. The "stock" is based on the book value of the company rather than the market value of the stock (Tully, 1998). Although no empirical comparison has been made between phantom and regular stock ownership plans, one would expect that the line of sight would be shorter with phantom stock because it is less at the mercy of the economic market. Book value reflects indices more under the control of employees, such as cost (Heneman, Ledford, & Gresham, 2000).

Benefits

Benefits, once considered a "fringe" element in total cash compensation now constitute the second largest component (26.5 percent) of total cash compensation (U.S. Bureau of Labor Statistics, 1999). Unfortunately, while the amount spent on benefits has increased, there has not been a great deal of benefits research by psychologists. Some current issues in the benefits arena follow.

Flexible Benefit Plans

It used to be the case that most employees in one company all received the same benefits. While easy to administer, standard benefit plans often fail to provide meaningful benefits to employees, who have varying ages, needs, and lifestyles. In response to this situation, many organizations now provide choice in benefits selection by employees. That is, employees are given the opportunity to choose the benefits that best suit their needs at various stages in their lives. From a motivational point of view, flexible benefits are advantageous because they allow employees to select from a "cafeteria" of benefits plans those benefits which have positive valance for them. In turn, these benefits with positive valance are likely to be motivational (Vroom, 1964). Another advantage with flexible benefits is that they allow the company to control costs by no longer providing all benefits to all employees even if all employees didn't need certain benefits. They also enable cost control through the introduction of cost sharing with employees, either through coinsurance (e.g., increased deductibles, exclusions) or shared premium payments.

One disadvantage to flexible benefits is that employees may fail to select certain benefits critical to their well-being. As a result, most flexible benefits plans require a core set of benefits to be selected by all employees (e.g., health-care insurance). Another disadvantage of cafeteria-style plans is the huge number of benefit options that may confront the employees. For example, at one company employees were overwhelmed with over 16,000 possible benefit choices! In response, the company developed an expert system to aid employee decision making. An expert system was created to show the employees the most logical options for them to select depending upon their demographic characteristics (Bloom & Milkovich, 1999).

Cash Balance Pension Plans

Given the large costs associated with employee pension plans, many large organizations are converting their existing defined benefit pension plans to "cash balance" or "pension equity plans." As with traditional pension plans, these plans are funded by the employer, guarantee a retirement benefit that has little or no risk to the employee and are governed by the same provisions of ERISA that govern traditional defined benefit pension plans. But unlike traditional plans, the amount available upon retirement is based on earnings in a hypothetical individual account rather than on the basis of years of service. Each year an employee's cash balance account grows by (usually) some percentage of annual salary. The account also increases in value through accrued interest or in line with some index such as the CPI. Thus, cash balance plans grow over the entire career of the employee; a career average pay plan rather than a final average pay plan that is characteristic of the traditional pension (Quick, 1999). As a result, cash balance plans are advantageous to those employees that are mobile in their careers, while traditional benefit plans are advantageous to those that remain for a long period of time with an employer. More money is available to employees sooner in their careers with a cash balance plan (McNamee, 1999). The shift from traditional pension plans to cost balance pension plans by many employers may fundamentally alter the nature of the employment relationships from long-term duration to short-term duration with a corresponding decrease in employee commitment and turnover (Tsui, Pearce, Porter, & Tripoli, 1997). More research is needed on this important topic.

Employer-Based Rehabilitation

As a result of sky rocketing costs associated with workers compensation laws and the Americans with Disabilities Act, some employers are now developing early return-to-work programs. These programs help get injured employees back on the job who might otherwise be at home to recover. In essence, these programs make it possible to return to work earlier than normal to perform modified work duties while they are recovering (Growick, 1998). As such, they are more cost effective than time off for recovery because under modified work duties, the employee is able to provide some services to the company while recovering.

ORGANIZATIONAL EFFECTIVENESS

Both narrative and meta-analytical reviews of the research literature clearly show that cash compensation is correlated with individual performance (e.g., Gupta & Mitra, 1998) and organizational effectiveness (Heneman et al., 1998). In light of this convincing data, it is amazing how the "does money matter" argument continues to be advanced every decade or so. The latest iteration of this argument, the belief that money has a negative influence on behavior in work organizations, is in a book titled *Punished by Rewards* (Kohn, 1993).

While it has been clearly shown that pay does have an impact on organizational effectiveness, several themes must be kept in mind in interpreting evaluative studies associated with pay systems. First, the level of pay system effectiveness varies by measure of organizational effectiveness. For example, self-report data using rating scales of company performance completed by human resource professionals tend to report a larger impact on organizational effectiveness than do studies with "hard," archival measures of performance such as productivity and profit. Second, some pay plans are clearly more effective than others. Regardless of the measures of organizational effectiveness used, individual incentive plans have the largest impact on organizational effectiveness (Heneman et al., 2000).

Third, causality is an issue seldom addressed. In terms of compensation evaluation studies, the vast bulk of studies are correlational in nature rather than experimental. Well-designed studies like Murray and Gerhart (1998) and Petty, Singleton, and Connell (1992) are difficult to find in the literature. As a result, causality is an issue. The central question is whether highly effective organizations have the capabilities to use certain monetary reward systems or if certain monetary reward systems result in improved organizational performance.

Fourth, the research literature clearly shows that the effectiveness of pay plans varies as a function of the pay plan design features and implementation strategies (McAdams & Hawk, 1995). Psychometric properties of pay plan measures appear to be only one of many design and implementation issues that must be accounted for if a pay plan, regardless of type, is to be effective. Fifth, the evaluation studies to date are culture bound. The vast majority of studies have been conducted in the United States. The evaluation of pay plans in other countries is relatively new.

Given these caveats, Table 1 shows our collective best judgments of the impact of varying forms of total cash compensation on organizational performance. Satisfaction refers to satisfaction with the job and satisfaction with pay. These satisfaction measures are correlated with one another and are also correlated with absenteeism, turnover, and union vote (Heneman, 1985).

Table 1.   Compensation Plan Effectiveness

Plan	Organizations productivity	Employee satisfaction
Broadbanding	?	?
Person-based pay	Moderate	High
Market-based pay	?	?
Merit pay	Low	Moderate
Variable pay	Moderate	Moderate
Individual incentives	High	Low
Ownership	Low	Moderate
Flexible benefits	?	High

Sources: Barber, Dunham, and Formisano (1992); Welbourne and Gomez-Mejia (1995); Jenkins, Mitra, Gupta, and Shaw (1998); Kruse (1993); Blinder (1990); McAdams and Hawk (1995); Heneman (1992); Lawler, Mohrman, and Ledford (1998); Blasi, Conte, and Kruse (1996); Gerhart and Milkovich (1992); Lawler and Jenkins (1992); Jenkins, Ledford, Gupta, and Doty (1987); Schuster (1989); Peck (1984, 1989, 1991); O'Dell (1987); Abosch and Hand (1998).

NEW DIRECTIONS

The field of compensation has always followed the scientist-practitioner model of industrial/organizational psychology. Science and practice are intertwined in compensation decision making. Consequently, we will structure our recommendations for future directions around theory, research, and practice. Given the global context to this chapter, we have also included a separate section on global compensation.

Theory

As indicated in the historical section of this chapter, we are very pleased at the shift in the unit of analysis in the study of compensation decision making from a focus on the individual to a focus on the organization. While being pleased with this shift in the unit of analysis, much theory building needs to be undertaken with the organization as the unit of analysis. While theory building is highly advanced at the individual level in compensation (e.g., expectancy theory), theory building is at a more basic level when the unit of analysis is the organization. In building theory at the organizational level, we believe that several steps need to be taken.

A major theoretical issue is the choice of dependent variable(s). Just as the "criterion problem" has plagued theory building at the individual level, so too will the criterion problem nag at theory building at the organizational level. Clearly, organizational performance is multidimensional (Whetten & Cameron, 1994) and the task for those building organizational-level compensation models will be to carefully match the independent variables to the appropriate measures of organizational performance. The appropriate measures are likely to vary as a function of the goals of the organization (Rogers & Wright, 1998) and the goals of the compensation plan (Heneman, Ledford, & Gresham, 2000). The nomological net between the goals of the organization, goals of the compensation plan, and organizational effectiveness will need to be clearly explicated by our theories. If not, a "shotgun" empiricism approach may prevail with significant findings being a function of chance or convenience of measures available, rather than being grounded in a well-conceived nomological net.

Another major issue in theory development is the need to move away from only focusing on the outcome of the compensation plan. In order to understand the well-documented impact of compensation, focus needs to be on developing models of the under lying process whereby compensation decisions at the organizational level are translated into impacts on organizational effectiveness. In order to achieve this end, compensation should not be treated as a homogeneous construct due to the common denominator of money across all pay plan types. Instead, midrange theories need to be developed that explicate the different processes involved with different types of pay systems. By doing so, we are more likely to be able to know which measures of organizational effectiveness are likely to be impacted by each pay plan type and also be able to explain the differential effects of different pay plan types on the same measures of organizational effectiveness. Heneman (in press) suggests that new midrange theories will need to be created for this purpose to supplement grand compensation theories such as agency theory.

Research

A rich irony in the study of compensation is the increased need for the study of compensation and the reluctance of organizations to allow their compensation systems to be studied. In terms of need, many new populations (e.g., public sector, nonprofits, small companies) are using new forms of pay for the first time ever. At the same time, however, organizations are very reluctant to show their "dirty laundry" (i.e., poor-performing compensation system) in public. Ultimately, the choice not to study one's compensation system is a poor strategic choice. The state of Kentucky, for example, has forced, by law, school districts to use financial incentives (Odden & Kelley, 1997). One can envision other organizations, even in the private sector, where such legislation could be forthcoming. For example, health care would be a likely candidate. Gain-sharing plans could logically be mandated to save on escalating health-care costs. Although this example is speculative, the point is that organizations may need to be more open in sharing pay intervention data if they wish to retain control of the pay plan interventions that they prefer to implement.

While there has been a noticeable increase in the study of new forms of pay, there is also a need for the study of pay in new environments. Systematic data collected from the public sector, small companies, and nonprofits are almost nonexistent. Because this is a new area of study, especially for new pay systems, a qualitative case-study approach would be helpful to identify the facilitating factors and restraints faced by these special sectors of our economy.

Lastly, in terms of research, more longitudinal research is needed. The benefits as well as costs associated with various pay plans sometimes do not emerge when viewed within the context of cross-sectional data. For example, skill-based pay has high upfront costs in the form of both direct (pay increases) and indirect costs (training and administration). If evaluated only from a short-term perspective, the fact may be overlooked that these short-term costs for skill-based pay are overcome by increased organizational effectiveness over the long term (Murray & Gerhart, 1998).

Practice

Several recent trends in practice need to be carefully scrutinized. These trends include the broadbanding of pay ranges, the increasing emphasis on market value over job evaluation, and the use of classification systems of job evaluation to replace point-factor systems. In particular, the relationship between broadbanding and organizational effectiveness has not been documented with anything other than self-report data. Employee reactions to market pricing have never been investigated. The psychometric properties of classification systems, as opposed to point-factor systems, are not well established.

Unlike the selection area, the dollar value impact of compensation decisions has not been well documented. Utility analysis needs to be extended from staffing decision making to compensation decision making. An excellent first step has been taken in this direction by Klaas and McClendon (1996) who looked at the financial impact of competitive pay level policies for organizations. Similarly, Bloom (1999) has provided an initial study on the impact of pay dispersion on individual and group performance. Unfortunately, the setting (major league baseball) focuses on organizations that are very different from the typical work organization.

Similar studies are needed in other areas related to total compensation practice. Little is known, for example, about the attractiveness to potential employees of different mixes of components of the total compensation package, or the individual differences that might be associated with such preferences. It is likely, for example, that a compensation package with a large component of individual incentive pay would be more appealing to an applicant who believes herself to be a high performer and who has low risk aversion than a package of equal expected value consisting mostly of base pay and benefits.

Global Compensation

Changes in pay systems at the international level have tremendous implications for practice. Sweeping generalizations about the effectiveness of pay using broad measures of culture (e.g., Hofstede, 1980) have not been particularly useful. It has been shown that very specific attitudes (e.g., entitlement) rather than general cultural attitudes (e.g., power distance) are more predictive of the receptivity of different cultures to compensation plans (Meuller & Clark, 1998). Moreover, it has been argued that corporate business strategy and local labor market conditions are more likely to impact the effectiveness of pay plans than are culture-based attitudes (Bloom & Milkovich, 1999; Milkovich & Bloom, 1998).

This is not to say that significant differences in pay practices do not exist. Pay data from national surveys (including both local national and multinational firms) conducted by the Hay Group, for example, indicate different pay relationships between different job levels. The Hay job evaluation system is used in each country to provide a common metric of internal job value. Market rates for different jobs are collected in each country and pay lines are constructed. Table 2 shows that wage dispersions across jobs varies greatly from country to country. The ratio of market rates for jobs valued at 600 Hay points to those for jobs valued at 300 Hay points ranges from 1.7 to 3.1; the ratio of market rates valued at 1000 Hay points to those for jobs valued at 300 Hay points ranges from 2.2 to 6.6 (Hay Group, 1999).

However, it is possible that other approaches to defining culture (e.g., Hampden-Turner & Trompenaars, 1993; Trompenaars, 1993) may be of more use in differentiating the impact of culture on compensation systems. Trompenaars (1993), for example, notes differences in achievement- and ascription-oriented organization cultures and the impact on performance-based pay systems. This framework can be used to explain the finding of Mueller and Clarke (1998) where entitlement attitudes were found to be much more pervasive among business school students in the former Com-

Table 2.   Comparison of Market Rates for Jobs of Different Value

Country	Market rate ratio of jobs valued at 600 to jobs valued at 300 Hay points	Market rate ratio of jobs valued at 1000 to jobs valued at 300 Hay points
Argentina	2.83	5.46
Australia	1.70	2.79
Brazil	2.74	5.53
Canada	1.64	2.54
China	2.49	6.16
Columbia	2.78	6.29
France	1.90	2.97
Germany	1.85	3.22
Hong Kong	2.45	5.18
Indonesia	3.02	5.73
Japan	1.87	2.77
Malaysia	2.81	5.21
Mexico	2.88	5.96
Norway	1.53	2.17
Poland	2.57	5.38
Singapore	2.36	4.34
South Korea	2.15	3.83
Sweden	1.67	2.94
United Arab Emirates	2.38	4.32
United Kingdom	1.78	3.02
United States	1.81	3.12
Venezuela	2.96	6.58

Source: Computed from HayGroup's PayNet© Services, Country Guides, *www.haypaynet.com* Representative job titles at 300 Hay points include entry-level college graduate, foreman, and sales representative. Representative job titles at 600 Hay points include senior engineer, sales manager, and experienced professional staff. Representative job titles at 1000 Hay points include plant manager (small plant), middle/senior management, and functional directors.

munist countries of central and eastern Europe than among similar students in the United States. In contrast, a study of Russian and U.S. managers and students (Giacobbe-Miller, Miller, & Victorov, 1998) found equity/performance equally important in attitudes about pay determination except when individual need was a factor.

Cultural influence on reward allocation has been a crucial topic in the understanding of fairness and global compensation. In his review chapter on negotiation and reward allocations across cultures, Leung (1997) noticed the effects of individualism-collectivism framework on distributive behavior and proposed a contextual model which assumes that culture interacts with a number of situational variables to determine the allocation rule used. Leung, Smith, and Wang (1996) studied joint-venture hotels in the Hangzhou and Shanghai areas in China. A total of 137 Chinese managerial staff from 42 joint-venture hotels participated in the study. Procedural justice and performance-based distributive justice were found to be predictive of job satisfaction. However, unlike American results, interactional justice was not related to job satisfaction in joint ventures in China. It is possible that because of the higher acceptance of hierarchy and authority figures in Chinese organizations, the level of interactional justice required by Chinese employees from their superiors may be lower. This finding makes it clear that justice theories developed and confirmed in the United States should not be automatically assumed to be valid in different cultures. As predicted, the comparison with expatriate staff did not account for additional variance in the prediction of job satisfaction. Clearly, local staff did not regard them as a meaningful referent group for social comparison in the perception of distributive justice. In contrast, the comparison with other local staff was able to add to the prediction of job satisfaction. This finding highlights the importance of social comparison in fairness judgments of compensation systems in joint ventures. The conceptualization of distributive justice as a comparison between performance inputs and salaries is too narrow in joint ventures and needs to be broadened to include social comparison processes.

Also, senior managers showed the lowest level of perceived procedural and interaction justice. This pattern of results suggests that senior staff probably expected decision-making processes to be fairer, and interpersonal treatment received from expatriate staff more positive.

Contrary to expectation, rank did not show any effect on performance-based distributive justice. This recent finding probably reflects the fact that all levels of staff in these joint ventures are paid at a comparable level based on their performance inputs. It is interesting to note that the only significant effect involves the comparison with local employees in state-owned hotels. Middle managers reported the highest level of perceived justice, whereas senior managers and supervisors regarded their pay as less fair in comparison with local staff in other state-owned hotels.

Legal and regulatory systems differ considerably across countries in way that impact at least the benefits segment of the total compensation program. In the United States, Japan, and parts of Western Europe, for example, company pension plans account for a significant portion of typical retirement income. In Singapore, most of Latin America, France, and Italy, the typical retiree receives little or no retirement income from a company pension plan, but instead relies on government programs (Towers Perrin, 1999) and private savings. The use of perquisites varies widely from country to country and is usually driven by tax law (Moorman-Scrivener & Terry, 1996). Labor law and practice differs widely across countries and differences in governance approaches (e.g., works councils in Germany, codetermination in Sweden, joint consultation systems in Japan) and these differences impact many aspects of the rewards system (Begin, 1997; Heneman, von Hippel, Eskew, & Greenberger, 1997).

An indication of some specific differences driven by law and culture is provided in Table 3. This table shows the differences in official holidays and minimum mandated vacation days in selected countries. While companies may choose to provide more paid time off, the number of legal holidays varies from 7 to 18 days in the countries studied, and mandated minimum vacation time ranges from 0 to 30 days.

Table 3.   Comparison of Legal Holidays an Mandated Minimum Vacation Time

Country	Official holidays (days)	Legally mandated vacation (days)
Argentina	10	14
Australia	10	20
Brazil	10	30
Canada	9	10
China	7	0
Columbia	15	18
France	11	25
Germany	7–10	20
Hong Kong	17	7
Indonesia	13	12
Japan	14	10
Malaysia	14	8–16
Mexico	7	6
Norway	10	21
Poland	12	18
Russia	10	20
Singapore	11	11
South Korea	18	10 + 1/yr
Sweden	11	25
United Arab Emirates	9	30
United Kingdom	8	15
United States	10	0 *
Venezuela	13	15

Source: Computed from HayGroup's PayNet© Services, Country Guides, *www.haypaynet.com*
* No legally mandated vacation time; 10 days plus additional days based on length of service is customary.

Also for practice, there appears to be a convergence of pay plan types across countries (Gross & Wingerup, 1999). This convergence movement appears to run counter to popular opinion that pay plans must vary by country in order to be effective. For example, Milliman, Nason, Lowe, Nam-Hyeon, and Huo (1995) found a similar factor structure for performance appraisal practices across Japan, Korea, Taiwan, and the United States. Similarly, Japanese companies operating in the United States have shifted U.S. subsidiary compensation practices to conform more closely to those of their U.S. competitors, and to a lesser extent have shifted practices in the Japanese parent (Mukuda, 1999). In contrast, another survey found executive pay practices in U.S. subsidiaries of foreign firms shifted to meet U.S. standards with little or no impact on executive pay practices in the parent firm (Graskamp, 1999).

Hence, while local conditions must be recognized, core components of the compensation plan such as performance appraisal may be common across countries. As such, multinational organizations may be able to adapt a "mass-customization" strategy (LeBlanc, 1997) whereby there is a common core of compensation techniques with some alterations to the plan to meet local circumstances. That is, there is a common compensation platform across countries with some, but not total accommodations to meet local conditions.

CONCLUSION

As indicated in this selective review, large changes are taking place in the manner in which employees are compensated in organizations. Emphasis across all areas of pay is on rewarding contribution to the organization rather than membership in the organization. This focus on performance-based pay systems is gaining attention in all areas of the world, not just the United States. Given the evaluation studies conducted to date, there is reason for optimism about the results of efforts by companies to shift from a focus on membership to performance. These new pay plans do seem to have positive outcomes. Missing, however, is a fundamental understanding of why these pay systems work and under what circumstances they work. There is a large need for more and better theory development and research as to the processes whereby these pay programs work. Work psychologists can have a marked impact in developing this new body of theory and research.

30   R.L. HENEMAN, C.H. FAY, and Z-M. WANG

REFERENCES

Abosch, K.S., & Hand, J.S. (1998). *Life with broadbands*. Scottsdale, AZ: American Compensation Association.
Abosch, K.S., & Hmurovic, ? (1998, Summer). A traveler's guide to global broadbanding. *ACA Journal,* 38–46.
American Compensation Association. (1996). *Raising the bar: Using competencies to enhance employee performance*. Scottsdale, AZ: Author.
Barber, A.E., Dunham, R.B., & Formisano, R.A. (1992). The impact of employee benefits on employee satisfaction: A field study. *Personnel Psychology, 45,* 55–75.
Becker, B., & Gerhart, B. (1992). Special research forum: Human resource management and organizational performance. *Academy of Management Journal,* 39(4), entire issue.
Becker, G.S. (1975). *Human capital: A theoretical and empirical analysis, with special reference to education* (2nd ed.). New York: Columbia University Press.
Begin, J.P. (1997). *Dynamic human resource systems: Cross-national comparisons*. New York: Walter de Gruyter.
Blasi, J., Conte, M., & Kruse, D. (1996). Employee stock ownership and corporate performance among public companies. *Industrial and Labor Relations Review, 50,* 60–79.
Blinder, A.S. (Ed.). (1990). *Paying for productivity: A look at the evidence*. Washington, DC: Brookings Institution.
Bloom, M. (1999). The performance effects of pay dispersion on individuals and organizations. *Academy of Management Journal, 42*(1), 25–40.
Bloom, M., & Milkovich, G.T. (1999). A SHRM perspective on international compensation and reward systems. *Research in personnel and human resources management* (Suppl. 4, pp. 283–303). Greenwich, CT: JAI Press.
Campbell, J.P. (1976). Motivation theory in industrial and organizational psychology. In M.D. Dunnette (Ed.), *Handbook of industrial and organizational psychology* (pp. 63–130). New York: John Wiley.
Capell, K. (1996, July 22). Owens Coming plays share the wealth. *Business Week,* 82–83.
Cartter, A.M. (1959). *Theory of wages and employment*. Homewood, IL: Richard D. Irwin.
Collins, J.M., & Muchinsky, P.M. (1993). An assessment of the construct validity of three job evaluation methods. *Academy of Management Journal, 36,* 895–901.
Cronbach, L.J., & Gleser, G.C. (1965). *Psychological tests and personnel decisions*. Urbana: University of Illinois Press.
Crown, D.F., & Rosse, J.G. (1995). Yours, mine, and ours: Facilitating group productivity through the integration of individual and group goals. *Organizational Behavior and Human Decision Processes, 64,* 138–150.
Dunnette, M.D. (Ed.). (1976). *Handbook of industrial and organizational psychology*. Chicago: Rand-McNally.
Dunnette, M.D., & Hough, L.M. (1992). *Handbook of industrial and organizational psychology* (Vol. 3, 2nd ed.). Palo Alto, CA: Consulting Psychologists Press.

Eskew, D., & Heneman, R.L. (1996). A survey of merit pay plan effectiveness: End of the line for merit pay or hope for improvement? *Human Resource Planning Journal, 19*(2), 12–19.

Gerhart, B., & Milkovich, G.T. (1992). Employee compensation: Research and practice. In M.D. Dunnette, & L.M. Hough (Eds.), *Handbook of industrial and organizational psychology* (Vol. 3, 2nd ed., pp. 1009–1055), Palo Alto, CA: Consulting Psychologists Press.

Gerhart, B., Trevor, C.D., & Graham, M.E. (1996). New directions in compensation research: Synergies, risk, and survival. In G. Ferris (Ed.), *Research in personnel and human resources management* (pp. 143–203). Greenwich, CT: JAI Press.

Giacobbe-Miller, J.K., Miller, D.J., & Victorov, V.I. (1998). A comparison of Russian and U.S. pay allocation decisions, distribution judgments, and productivity under different payment conditions. *Personnel Psychology, 51*(1), 137–163.

Gomez-Mejia, L.R., & Balkin, D.B. (1992). *Compensation, organizational, strategy, and firm performance.* Cincinnati, OH: South-Western.

Graskamp. E. (1999). How foreign companies use U.S. incentive pay practices in the United States. *Compensation and Benefits Management, 15*(3), 60–63.

Gross, S.E., & Wingerup, P.L. (1999, July/August). Global pay? Maybe not yet! *Compensation and Benefits Review,* 25–34.

Growick, B.S. (1998). Employer-based rehab: Wave of the future. *Workers Compensation Cost Control, 7*(4), 1–3.

Gupta, N., & Mitra, A. (1998, Autumn). The value of financial incentives: myths and empirical realities. *ACA Journal,* 58–66.

Hampden-Turner, C., & Trompenaars, A. (1993). *The seven cultures of capitalism.* New York: Doubleday.

Heneman, H.G., III (1985). Pay satisfaction. In K.N. Rowland, & G.R. Ferris (Eds.), *Research in personnel and human resources management* (Vol. 3, pp. 115–139). Greenwich, CT: JAI Press.

Heneman, R.L. (1992). *Merit pay: Linking pay increases to performance ratings.* Reading, MA: Addison-Wesley-Longman.

Heneman, R.L. (2000). The changing nature of pay systems and the need for new midrange theories of pay. *Human Resource Management Review, 10,* 245–247.

Heneman, R.L. (2001). *Business-driven compensation policies: Integrating compensation systems with corporate strategies.* New York: AMACOM.

Heneman, RL. (in press). Merit pay. In C. Fay (Ed.), *The executive handbook of compensation.* New York: Free Press.

Heneman, R.L., Eskew, D., & Fox, J. (1998). Using employee attitudes to evaluate a new incentive program. *Compensation and Benefits Review, 18*(1), 40–44.

Heneman, R.L., & Dixon, K. (1998). How to find, select, and evaluate market surveys to meet your organizations needs. In R. Platt (Ed.), *Salary survey guidebook* (pp. 1–5). New York: AMOCOM.

Heneman, R.L., Ledford, G.E., & Gresham, M. (2000). The changing nature of work and its *effects on* compensation design and delivery. In S. Rynes & B. Gerhart (Ed.), *Compensation in organizations: Current research and practice* (pp. 195–240), Society for Industrial and Organizational Psychology Frontiers of Industrial and Organizational Psychology Series. San Francisco: Jossey-Bass.

Heneman, R.L., von Hippel, C., Eskew, D.E., & Greenberger, D.B. (1997, Summer). Alternative rewards in unionized environments. *ACA Journal,* 42–55.

Hicks, R. (1934). *Theory of wages.* New York: McMillan.

Hofstede, G. (1980). *Cultures consequences.* Newbury Park, CA: Sage.

Jenkins, D.G., Jr., Ledford, G.E., Jr., Gupta, N., & Doty, D.H. (1987). *Skill-based pay: Practices, payoffs, pitfalls, and prescriptions.* Scottsdale, AZ: American Compensation Association.

Jenkins, G.D., Jr., Mitra, A., Gupta, N., & Shaw, J.D. (1998). Are financial incentives related to performance? A meta-analysis review of empirical research. *Journal of Applied Psychology, 83,* 777–787.

Klaas, B.S., & McClendon, J.A. (1996). To lead, lag, or match: Estimating the financial impact of pay level policies. *Personnel Psychology, 49,* 121–135.

Kohn, A. (1993). *Punished by rewards.* Boston: Houghton-Mifflin.

Kruse, D.L. (1993). *Profit .sharing: Does it make a difference?* Kalamazoo, MI: Upjohn Institute.

Lawler, E.E., III (1971). *Pay and organizational effectiveness.* New York: McGraw-Hill.

Lawler, E.E., III (1981). *Pay and organizational development.* Reading, MA: Addison-Wesley.

Lawler, E.E., III (1990). *Strategic pay.* San Francisco: Jossey-Bass.

Lawler, E.E., Ill (2000). *Rewarding excellence: Pay strategies for the new economy.* San Francisco: Jossey-Bass.

Lawler, E.E., III, & Jenkins, G.D., Jr. (1992). Strategic reward systems. In M.D. Dunnette & L.M. Hough (Eds.), *Handbook of industrial and organizational psychology* (Vol. 3, 2nd ed., pp. 1009–1055). Palo Alto, CA: Consulting Psychologists Press.

Lawler, E.E. III, Mohnnan, S.A., & Ledford, G.E. (1998). *Strategies for high performance organizations.* San Francisco: Jossey-Bass.

LeBlanc, P. (1997, Spring). Mass customization. *ACA Journal,* 16–31.

Leung, K. (1997). Negotiation and reward allocation across cultures, In P.C. Earley & M. Erez (Eds.), *New perspectives on international industrial organizational psychology.* San Francisco: The New Lexington Press.

Leung, K., Smith, P.B., & Wang, Z.M. (1996). Job satisfaction in joint venture hotels in China: An organizational justice analysis. *Journal of International Business Studies, 27*(5), 947–962.

Luk, VW.M., & Chiu, R.K. (1998). Reward systems for local staff in China. In J. Selmer (Ed.), *International management in China: Cross-cultural lssues* (ch. 10). London: Routledge.

Madigan, R.M. (1985). Comparable worth judgments: A measurement properties analysis. *Journal of Applied Psychology, 70,* 137–147.

McAdams, J.L., & Hawk, E.J. (1995). *Organizational performance and rewards.* Scottsdale, AZ: American Compensation Association.

McNamee, M. (1999, October 4). Good pensions, bad sales pitch. *Business Week,* 44.

Miceli, M., & Heneman, R.L. (in press). Contextual determinants of variable pay plan design: A proposed research framework. *Human Resource Management Review.*

Milkovich, G.T., & Bloom, M. (1998). Rethinking international compensation. *Compensation and Benefits Review, 30*(1), 15–23.

Milkovich, G.T., & Newman, J.M. (1999). *Compensation* (Vol. 3., 6th ed., pp. 481–570). Palo Alto, CA: Consulting Psychologists Press.

Milliman, J.F., Nason, S., Lowe, K., Nam-Hyeon, K., & Huo, P. (1995). An empirical study of performance appraisal practices in Japan, Korea, Taiwan, and the US. *Academy of Management Best Paper Proceedings*, 182–186.

Moorman-Scrivener, S., & Terry, J., (Eds.). (1996). *International benefit guidelines 1996*. New York: William M. Mercer.

Meuller, S.L., & Clarke, L.D. (1998). Political-economic context and sensitivity to equity: Differences between the United States and the transition economics of central and eastern Europe. *Academy of Management Journal, 41*, 319–329.

Mukuda, M.K. (1999). Compensation and HR practices: Global challenges of Japanese companies. *ACA Journal, 8*(3), 61–66.

Murray, B., & Gerhart, B. (1998). An empirical analysis of a skill-based pay program and plant performance outcomes. *Academy of Management Journal, 41*, 68–78.

Odden, A., & Kelley, C. *(1997). Paying teachers for what they know and do: New and smarter compensation strategies to improve schools.* Thousand Oaks, CA: Corwin Press.

O'Dell, C.O. (1987). *Major findings from people, performance, and pay.* Scottsdale, AZ: American Compensation Association.

Peck, C. (1984). *Pay and performance: The interaction of compensation and performance appraisal.* Research Bulletin No. 155. New York: Conference Board.

Peck, C. (1989). *Variable pay: New performance rewards.* Research Bulletin No. 246. New York: Conference Board.

Peck, C, (1991). *Gainsharing for productivity.* Report No. 967. New York: Conference Board.

Petty, M.M., Singleton, B., & Connell, D.W. (1992). An experimental evaluation of an incentive plan in the electric utility industry. *Journal of Applied Psychology, 77*, 427–436.

Quick, C. (1999). An overview of cash balance plans. *Employee Benefit Research Institute Notes, 20*(7), 1–8.

Rogers, E.W., & Wright, P.M. (1998). *Measuring organizational performance in strategic human resource management: Problems and prospects* (Working Paper 98–09). School of Industrial and Labor Relations, Cornell University.

Rynes, S., & Gerhart, B. (Eds.) (2000). *Compensation in organizations: Progress and prospects.* San Francisco: New Lexington Press.

Rynes, S.L., & Milkovich, G.T. (1986). Wage surveys: Dispelling some myths about the market wage! *Personnel Psychology, 34*, 71–90.

Schuster, J.R. (1989). Improving productivity through gainsharing: Can the means be justified in the end? *Compensation and Benefits Management, 5*, 207–210.

Smith, P.C. (1976). Behaviors, results, and organizational effectiveness: The problem of criteria. In M.D. Dunnette (Ed.), *Handbook of industrial and organizational psychology* (pp. 745–776). New York: John Wiley.

Towers Perrin. (1999). *Worldwide total rewards 1998.* New York: Towers Perrin Global Resource Group.

Treiman, D.J. (1979). *Job evaluation: An analytic review.* Washington, DC: National Academy Press.

Treiman, D.J., & Hartman, H.I. (Eds.) (1981). *Women, work and wages: Equal pay for jobs of equal value.* Washington, DC: National Academy Press.

Trompenaars, A. (1993). *Riding the waves of culture: Understanding cultural diversity in business.* London: Nicholas Brealey.

Tsui, A.S., Pearce, J.L., Porter, L.W., & Tripoli, A.M. (1997). Alternative approaches to the employee-organization relationship: Does investment in employees pay off? *Academy of Management Journal, 40,* 1089–1121.

Tullar, W.L. (1998). Compensation consequences of reengineering. *Journal of Applied Psychology, 83,* 975–980.

Tully, S. (1998, October 26). A better taskmaster than the market? *Fortune,* 277–286.

U.S. Bureau of Labor Statistics. (1999). *Employer costs for employee compensation—March* 1999. USDL: 99–173. Washington, DC: U.S. Department of Labor.

Viswesvaran, C., & Barrick, M.R. (1992). Decision-making effects on compensation surveys: Implications for market wages. *Journal of Applied Psychology, 77,* 588–597.

Vroom, V. (1964). *Work and motivation.* New York: Wiley.

Wageman, R. (1995). Interdependence and group effectiveness. *Administrative Science Quarterly, 40,* 145–180.

Wallace, M.J., Jr., & Fay, C.H. (1988). *Compensation: Theory and practice* (2nd ed.). Boston: PWS-Kent.

Wang, Z.M. (1990). Human resource management in China: Recent trends. In R. Pieper (Ed.), *Human resource management: An international comparison.* Berlin: Walter de Gruyter.

Wang, Z.M. (1994). Culture, economic reform, and the role of industrial and organizational psychology in China. In H.C. Triandis, M.D. Dunnette, & L.M. Hough (Eds.), *Handbook of industrial and organizational psychology* (Vol. 4, 2nd ed., ch. 14). Palo Alto, CA: Consulting Psychologist Press.

Wang, Z.M., & Chen, Z. (2000). Compensation systems structure, justice and impact of organizational systems. In Z.M. Wang et al. (Eds.), *Research advances in human resources and organizational behavior.* Beijing: China People's University Press (in press).

Wang, Z.M., & Feng, Z.Q. (2000). CEO compensation design and its motivational mechanism. In Z.M. Wang et al. (Eds.), *Research advances in human resources and organizational behavior.* Beijing: China People's University Press (in press).

Weber, C.L., & Rynes, S.L. (1991). Effects of compensation strategy on job pay decisions. *Academy of Management Journal, 34,* 86–109.

Welbourne, T., & Gomez-Mejia, L.R. (1995). Gainsharing: A critical review end a future research agenda. *Journal of Management, 21,* 559–609.

Whetten, D.A., & Cameron, K.S. (1994). Organizational effectiveness: old models and new constructs. In J. Greenberg (Ed.), *Organizational behavior: The state of the science* (pp. 135–154). Hillsdale, NJ: Lawrence Erlbaum Associates.

Wright, P.M., Dyer, L.D., Boudreau, J.W., & Milkovich, G.T. (1999). Strategic human resources management in the twenty-first century. *Research in personnel and human resources management* (Suppl. 4). Stamford, CT: JAI Press.

CHAPTER 2

THE CHANGING NATURE OF WORK AND ITS EFFECTS ON COMPENSATION DESIGN AND DELIVERY

Robert L. Heneman, Gerald E. Ledford Jr., and Maria T. Gresham

Source: Heneman, R.L., Ledford, G.E., & Gresham, M.T. (2000) The Changing Nature of Work and its Effects on Compensation Design and Delivery. In S. Rynes & B. Gerhart (Eds.), *Compensation in Organizations: Progress & Prospects* (pp. 195–240). San Francisco: New Lexington Press. Reprinted by permission of Jossey-Bass, Inc., a subsidiary of John Wiley & Sons.

In 1966 Opsahl and Dunnette issued a challenge to the industrial and organizational (I/O) psychology research community:

> Strangely, in spite of the large amounts of money spent and the obvious relevance of behavioral theory for industrial compensation practices, there is probably less solid research in this area than in any other field related to worker performance. We know amazingly little about how money interacts with other factors or how it acts individually to affect job behavior. Although the relevant literature is voluminous, much more has been written about the subject than is actually known. Speculation, accompanied by compensation fads and fashions, abounds; research studies designed to answer fundamental questions about the role of human motivation are all too rare. (p. 94)

Considerable research in I/O psychology, as well as in sociology, industrial relations, business strategy, and labor economics, has aided our understanding of many compensation issues during the past three decades. Yet compensation topics continue to be underrepresented in I/O psychology relative to the importance of compensation to individuals and organizations. The challenge to conduct more and better research is still as relevant today as it was more than thirty years ago.

Research needs have shifted, however, due to dramatic changes in compensation practices during the past decade (Ledford, Lawler, & Mohrman, 1995). These changes are in part a response to fundamental mental changes in the nature and design of work in contemporary organizations. This chapter reviews many such changes, including the decreasing use of job descriptions and job analysis as a basis for organization design, the delayering of the organizational hierarchy, the increasing use of team-based structures, and changes in technology. In response to these forces and others, many elements of employee compensation design are changing significantly. Base design is shifting from job-based pay to person-based approaches that reward skill, knowledge, and competency. Pay for performance is increasingly based on collective (team, unit, and corporation) rather than individual performance. Spending on employee benefits is being challenged, and cafeteria-style benefits plans are now a widespread method of cost control. The overall compensation budget is being reallocated, with the ratio of variable performance-based pay to base pay increasing. Documentation of these trends can be found in ongoing surveys by the Conference Board, the American Compensation Association, and the Center for Effective Organizations (Heneman & Gresham, 1998). These changing compensation practices are part of a profile that has many names. It has been called strategic pay (Lawler, 1990), the new pay (Schuster & Zingheim, 1992), alternative rewards (McAdams & Hawk, 1994), and innovative pay systems (Wilson, 1995).

These new approaches to compensation are in need of research that helps us understand why and where they are adopted, their effectiveness, and the key design variables that explain success and failure. As in 1966, the practice of compensation has far outrun the research literature. Practitioners are not waiting for research results. There is tremendous practitioner interest, excitement, and confusion about compensation issues, and practitioners are relying on whatever information they find available. For example, at least nine trade books about new forms of compensation were published between 1990 and 1996 (Heneman & Gresham, 1998).

This chapter attempts, first, to summarize what we know about the changing nature of work and how it is affecting compensation. Second, we will outline the innovations taking place in the field of compensation and contrast those changes with traditional compensation practices. We will consider such new forms of pay as broadbanding, pay for skills and competencies, pay for team and organizational performance (variable pay), and employee ownership. Third, we will review the limited available research on the effects of these new pay systems on individual and organizational effectiveness outcomes. Finally, we will offer a framework to guide future research.

CHANGES IN THE NATURE OF WORK

Changes in the nature of work are having, and will continue to have, profound effects on the management of human resources in organizations (Cappelli et al., 1997; Howard, 1995). We will review the major changes that are likely to affect compensation strategy and practice in organizations. Such changes are a response to changing business strategies that demand more flexible, nimble organizational forms and work. In turn, these create the need for new forms of compensation. Our focus here is on five areas in which fundamental changes in the nature of work are taking place: employment relationships, technology, business strategy, organizational structure, and job design.

Changes in the Employment Relationship

The nature of the employment relationship appears to be changing in fundamental ways (Crandall & Wallace, 1997). The new employment relationship implies a change in the commitments of the parties to one another at both the institutional and psychological levels. Both have a bearing on the compensation system and will be discussed in turn.

From an institutional perspective, Tsui, Pearce, Porter, and Tripoli (1997) define four types of employment relationships: quasi-spot contracts, mutual investment contracts, underinvestment contracts, and overinvestment contracts. Although these researchers directed little attention to compensation issues, these four exchange philosophies would appear to have compensation implications. For example, a quasi-spot contract is one where the employer offers short-term economic rewards for very specific employee contributions. Traditional short-term performance incentives such as piece rate and sales commissions would seem appropriate to this type of relationship. A mutual investment contract is one where there are broad, unspecified, and open employer inducements and employee contributions. Forms of compensation that may be appropriate here include skill-based pay as an investment in human capital, stock as an incentive for long-term participation, and benefits (such as dependent care or concierge services) to allow the employee to make a high commitment to work. An underinvestment contract is one where the employee has broad and open-ended obligations to the employer while the employer provides short-term monetary rewards. An example of this type of pay system may be a sales force organized by teams, with broad and open-ended roles for team members, where pay is provided on the basis of individual commissions. Overinvestment is characterized by the employee's performing very specific job functions while the employer provides open-ended and broad-range rewards. Providing part-time, seasonal, or temporary employees with a profit-sharing check is an example of this.

The highest level of performance in the Tsui et al. (1997) study was associated with mutual investment, and underinvestment consistently produced the worst results. Perceptions of commitment, trust, and fairness were highest for overinvestment and mutual investment. Although compensation was not investigated, the results suggest that long-term incentives such as stock ownership and pay plans that invest in human capital (for example, skill-based pay) may be helpful to organizations that want to transition from quasi-spot contracts to mutual investment contracts.

At the psychological level, employees form perceptions about the employment relationship offered by the employer. In particular, they respond to the employer's collection of reward practices. The employee's understanding of these practices is referred to as a psychological contract and has two notable aspects (Rousseau, 1997) that can be related to compensation practices.

First, individuals use schemata when evaluating rewards, such that different forms of compensation may not be evaluated independent from one another. Traditionally, as evidenced in the pay satisfaction literature, pay system components (such as level, raises, structure, administration, and benefits; see Heneman & Schwab, 1985) are not considered by researchers relative to one another. Employees may apply more complicated schemata when they look at the relationship of compensation components to one another and the relationship of compensation to rewards other than compensation (such as training).

Second, psychological contracts are dynamic. Thus, changes in the nature of the institutional contract are likely to spell changes in the psychological contracts as well. For example, compensation systems may need to be modified to match the duration of the employment contract more appropriately (von Hippel, Mangum, Greenberger, Heneman, & Skoglind, 1997).

For example, organizations using temporary employees may not include them in a competency-based pay system because the investment they make in knowledge, skill, and development may be lost to a rival organization when the employees leave. But not all temporary employees are alike (von

Hippel et al., 1997). Some employees are voluntary temporaries, meaning that they desire to remain temporary, while others are involuntary temporaries, meaning that they view temporary work as a vehicle to full-time job placement. Organizations may be more likely to provide competency pay to voluntary than to involuntary temporaries because the latter are more likely to remain with the organization. Moreover, survey data indicate that pay is a more important motivator for voluntary than for involuntary temporaries (von Hippel et al., 1997).

Changes in Technology

New technology has made it easier for organizations to monitor employee performance in terms of both content and process. Regarding content, improved information systems have made it possible to monitor vast amounts of data at the individual, team, and organizational levels. Not only has the amount of data increased but so has their quality. Heightened focus on financial performance has resulted in new financial modeling techniques, such as economic value added, being used and applied to compensation systems. Similarly, heightened focus on the operational aspects of the organization through programs such as Total Quality Management (TQM) has resulted in an increased sensitivity by managers to improved operational indicators of success and the linking of these indicators to compensation through gainsharing and goalsharing plans. Although the data are better, they are not perfect. For example, the customer service construct has not been fully explicated (Cardy & Dobbins, 1994).

Regarding process, electronic technology (telephone, video, computer) has made it possible to monitor employees in remote locations and to monitor a large number of employees at the same time. This capability is increasingly important as organizations expand into world markets and as spans of control grow due to flattening of managerial hierarchies. However, electronic performance monitoring is not without its problems. For example, research reviewed by Hedge and Borman (1995) suggests that electronic performance monitoring may sensitize employees to overemphasize monitored activities while underemphasizing nonmonitored aspects.

Interestingly, economic theories such as efficiency wage theory and agency theory suggest that the new forms of performance-based compensation may produce less, rather than more, need for electronic performance monitoring (Conlon & Parks, 1990). Performance-based pay may decrease monitoring for three reasons. First, performance-based pay is usually granted in addition to pay. As total pay increases, there is more of an incentive for employees to monitor their own performance. As total compensation rises with performance and eventually exceeds the market average, employees will not be able to replace this level of total compensation in the market. As a result, there is an incentive to do well and retain one's position. Second, as will be discussed later in the chapter, performance-based pay plans are increasingly team-based. As a result, there is incentive for employees to monitor one another because payment may be dependent on the performance of the entire team. Third, some of the new performance-based pay provides equity (in the form of stock) for employees. Hence it is in the employees' best interest to act like owners in order to build the value of their equity holdings.

Changes in Business Strategy

The strategic compensation literature suggests that a major, if not the major, goal of a compensation system is to improve organizational performance. This goal is believed to be attained through the alignment of compensation components with one another and with other HR practices, as well as with organizational goals and context (Lawler & Jenkins, 1992). This perspective is in contrast to the traditional approach to compensation systems, which views the objectives of compensation systems in terms of attraction, retention, and motivation (Patten, 1977). These traditional objectives are to be achieved by influencing the expenditure, direction, and sustainability of employee effort rather than by aligning compensation systems with organizational goals. Both in practice and in research, traditional compensation systems have been focused on the performance of the individual. In contrast, strategic compensation systems focus on the performance of the entire organization.

Recent reviews have placed heavy emphasis on the importance of business strategy to compensation system design and implementation (Gomez-Mejia & Balkin, 1992; Lawler &Jenkins, 1992). The major point made in this body of literature is that components of the compensation system must be in alignment with organizational goals, in order for compensation systems to lead to improved organizational performance (Heneman & Gresham, 1998; Lawler, 1990).

An example of this new strategic focus as it relates to compensation comes from Montemayor (1996). He found that components of the pay system (compensation philosophy, external competitiveness, mix of incentive to base pay, merit pay increases, and pay administration) varied by business strategy (cost leadership, differentiation, innovation) in a sample of 280 multi-industry organizations. Alignment between business strategy and compensation system components was associated with enhanced organizational effectiveness (using perceptual measures of organizational effectiveness). Other empirical work of this type has been conducted by Gomez-Mejia and Balkin (1992).

As noted by Wright and Snell (1998), a strategic focus also implies an alignment between components of the compensations system. For example, Heneman (in press) shows how merit pay his been used in conjunction with other reward systems in organizations, such as profit sharing and competency-based pay. This added dimension of human resource strategy is often overlooked in compensation literature.

Another dimension of business strategy as it relates to compensation is the larger context in which business strategy is embedded (Hambrick & Snow, 1989). For example, Snell and Dean (1994) found in a sample of manufacturers pursuing an "integrated manufacturing" strategy that the relationship between work process used (advanced manufacturing technology, TQM, and just-in-time inventory) was not related to the use of compensation system components (individual incentives, group incentives, hourly pay, salary, seniority, skill-based pay). Relationships among these manufacturing processes and pay system components were obtained when organizational context variables (size, performance, unionization, plant location) were entered as moderators of this relationship.

Changes in Organizational Structures

New organizational structures are being formed to coordinate and integrate the work of employees. Presumably, there should be a link between structure and the compensation system because structure in part determines the type of work people perform, which in turn partly determines compensation. Unfortunately, very little empirical work has taken place in this area, with one noticeable exception: the extent to which individual, group, or individual-plus-group rewards should be used in a team-based organizational structure (see Crown & Rosse, 1995; Wageman, 1995). Although this issue is important, it ignores the fact that there are different types of teams, with different potential compensation implications. It also ignores the fact that there are new organizational structures other than teams that are also likely to have implications for organizations. Shaw and Schneier (1995) summarize three typologies of teams and suggested pay systems for each (Lawler & Cohen, 1992; Montemayor, 1994; Saunier & Hawk, 1994). Gross (1995) also provides a typology of teams and appropriate rewards. For example, spot bonuses might be more appropriate for a team of limited duration such as a task force, whereas skill-based pay might be more appropriate for an ongoing team such as a self-directed work team.

Along with differences between teams, changes have been occurring in organizational structures other than teams. Newly emerging organizational structures include virtual organizations, networks, and cellular forms. According to Crandall and Wallace (1997), a virtual organization is one where people from multiple corporate entities work together at a common site. Virtual organizations arise as a result of a variety of factors (e.g., former competitors forming alliances to control the market; new mergers of technology, markets, and opportunities; or vertical and horizontal integration) and develop in three stages: (1) telecommuting; (2) front-line model, where sales and service functions are located in the field close to the customer; and (3) cyberlink model, where organizations manage work collaboratively with customers and teams from both producers and suppliers.

Although further construct explication is required, the virtual organization does point to the need to reexamine basic compensation concepts. For example, how is equity established when multiple organizations with multiple compensation systems work on a common project? How is the effectiveness of the compensation system to be assessed when multiple organizations house differing compensation objectives?

Miles, Snow, Mathews, Miles, and Coleman (1997) differentiate between five types of organizational structures: functional, divisional, matrix, network, and cellular. Again, compensation systems may need to vary by type of structure. For example, functional and divisional structures were begun in an era (1850–1950) of product and service standardization and specialization. Traditional job evaluation methods helped promote standardization across specialized jobs. Matrix, network, and cellular organizations emerged in an era (1950–2000) when the market began to demand customized products and services. In matrix and network structures, jobs are highly interdependent. As a result, traditional job evaluation systems may not be appropriate. Instead, the team rather than the job becomes the unit of analysis, and the compensation system may need to be team-based. Currently, we are in an era of innovation that requires network structures and cellular organizations. Under these structures, work is formed into cells (such as self-directed work teams) that interact inside and outside the organization. The cell must continually transform itself to survive in the organization as innovations create new requirements of people. With the cellular structure, the focus is on the creation of new knowledge and skills. As a result, the units of analysis become the person and the team, rather than the job. Person-based pay programs (such as skill-based pay) and team-based pay would seem to be a natural fit here.

Changes in Job Design

Fundamental changes are taking place in the nature of jobs (Cappelli et al., 1997). These changes fall into several categories: number of jobs, types of jobs, and relationships between jobs. In terms of the number of jobs, several trends stand out. First, reductions in force are no longer concentrated solely in manufacturing, but have spread to the service sector as well (bank tellers, for example). Second, management positions are being eliminated, with some organizations replacing supervisors and mid-level managers with self-directed work teams. Both in theory (see Ilgen & Hollenbeck, 1991) and in practice (see Bridges, 1995; O'Neal, 1995), organizations are beginning to shift the unit of analysis from jobs to people. Instead of describing work in terms of elements, tasks, and duties, work is beginning to be defined in terms of roles and competencies. Roles refer to expected patterns of behavior for people (Naylor, Pritchard, & Ilgen, 1980); competencies refer to knowledge, skills, abilities, and other attributes of people related to effective job performance (Heneman & Ledford, 1998).

Controversy surrounds the distinction between jobs versus people as the unit of analysis for compensation decisions (Cohen & Heneman, 1994). One element of the controversy concerns the extent to which person-based systems are actually used in practice. A recent survey shows that although organizations have begun to build role- and competency-based systems for selection and development purposes; there are very few actual applications of such systems with respect to compensation (American Compensation Association, 1996). A second aspect of controversy is that the distinction between jobs and people is cloudy at a conceptual level. For example, traditional job evaluation systems, like competencies, also measure skill and effort. In addition, Cohen and Heneman (1994) found that human resource professionals use both person- and job-based attributes in compensation decision making. These considerations suggest that the distinction between person- and job-based systems may be an oversimplification. Interestingly, I/O psychologists such as Ilgen and Hollenbeck (1991) seem to be moving away from job-based to role- and competency-based explanations. At the same time, economists are beginning to move away from the person (in human capital theory) to look at the job (see Lazear, 1992).

The net result of the controversy seems to be that organizations must delicately balance the mix of job and person requirements in compensation systems. The relative balance is likely to be a function of the strategy, structure, processes, and people in organizations (Finegold, Lawler, & Ledford, 1998). Industrial and organizational psychologists should be quite helpful in this area, with expertise in both job analysis and the measurement of individual differences. In terms of relationships between jobs, traditional organizations featured clearly defined upward mobility paths for employees with promotional pay increases. However, career moves now take many avenues other than upward mobility, which sometimes results in career paths that look more like lattices than ladders (Heneman, Heneman, & Judge, 1997). Not only has the concept of promotions begun to change, but so have the rewards associated with promotions. In traditional organizations, promotions result in a new job title and a new rate of pay before demonstrating actual competence at the new job. In contrast, organizations with enriched jobs and broadbanded job classifications may not offer a new job title or provide pay increases until after the competencies on the new job have been certified as being mastered. Clearly, the message between these two systems is different, but the behavioral and attitudinal reactions to these differences have yet to be studied.

As a result of changes in business strategy, organizational structure, employment relationships, technology, and jobs, employers have begun to experiment with new types of compensation systems. Before examining the new types of compensation systems, a review of the differences in conceptual foundations between traditional and new pay systems will be presented.

Conceptual Foundations of New Pay Systems

Traditional compensation models rely on an administrative framework, wherein compensation is viewed from the perspective of the HR department (Heneman & Schwab, 1979). More recently, however, a shift has been taking place, wherein pay is increasingly viewed from a strategic perspective (Gomez-Mejia & Balkin, 1992; Lawler & Jenkins, 1992). That is, the focus has shifted away from the HR department to a focus on the business strategy of the entire organization. Differences between the administrative focus and strategic focus are shown in Table 1.

Table 1.   Pay System Focus: Administrative Versus Strategic

Administrative Focus	Strategic Focus
Job	Person
Individual	Team
Time	Output
Lag System	Lead System
Top-down	Bottom-up
Centralized	Decentralized
Static	Dynamic
Internal equity	External equity
Fixed	Variable

Traditional pay systems provide pay for the job (Milkovich & Newman, 1996). The amount paid to each job is based on an assessment of its internal and external worth. Internal worth is established through the use of job evaluation systems, while external worth is established using market surveys. A pay structure is established to set boundaries on pay, based on the results of the job evaluation and market survey. Movement takes place within the pay structure based on time spent by the individual in the job category, or by "merit."

For organizations to focus employee efforts on business results, pay systems have begun to emphasize providing pay for the mastery of knowledge and skills and for the accomplishment of individual and team goals. Pay is provided for skill and knowledge mastery to ensure that the workforce is lean, flexible, and adaptable to change (Kanfer & Heggestad, 1997). Work is organized around teams, and individual pay is supplemented with team pay to break down barriers between functional areas that may interfere with customer responsiveness. Pay is provided for output, rather than time on the job, job tasks and duties. Output may be assessed by the certification or mastery of skill and knowledge blocks, by the demonstration of behaviors critical to organizational success, or by actual output of teams and individuals (Heneman & von Hippel, 1996). That is, inputs, throughputs, and outputs are measured and rewarded. These measures closely reflect the strategy of the organization.

Measurements may be formed in response to business strategies, or business strategies may be formed as a result of compensation measurements. The former approach is referred to as a lag system, and the latter as a lead system (Lawler, 1981). One survey by the American Compensation Association (1996) of over six hundred new pay plans reported that most of these new plans operated as lead systems.

Another difference between traditional and emerging systems is that development of measures used to be conducted exclusively by the HR department, with top-down approval by management. However, with a strategic perspective, employees are more likely to be involved in these decisions (in a bottom-up approach). Kahnweiler, Crane, and O'Neill (1994) reported in a survey of employer practices that approximately 50 percent of organizations now use employees to help develop performance measures.

Organizations have also shifted from static to dynamic or "nimble" pay systems (Ledford, 1995). That is, pay systems are redesigned frequently to match changes in business strategy. Responsiveness to changes in the market is seen as a source of competitive advantage (Crandall & Wallace, 1997; Kessler & Chakrabarti, 1996). However, decentralized systems can create inequity in pay across business units. This problem is likely intensified the greater the mobility of labor across business units.

Another factor that produces internal inequity in pay is when organizations decide at the strategic level to abandon internal equity for the sake of external equity. That is, strict market pricing replaces job evaluation, and resulting inequities are blamed on the market rather than the compensation system. As this brief discussion indicates, the logic behind the new pay systems differs from that of traditional pay systems. This logic has been translated into new forms of pay that we will now consider.

NEW FORMS OF PAY

General Issues

Before considering specific reward system innovations that can increase motivation, several general issues require comment. First, reward systems have multiple objectives, many of which are not directly related to motivation (Lawler, 1971, 1981, 1990; Lawler & Jenkins, 1992). For example, one objective of almost all reward systems is to attract and retain key personnel. Reward systems can also be used to help support business strategies, for example, by controlling compensation costs or by making pay more variable in cyclical businesses. Reward systems also help define organizational structure for employees, because the levels at which performance is measured and rewarded (individual, team, plant, division, business, or corporation) draw employee attention to those levels. Reward systems can also help foster a desired organizational culture (participative, innovative, paternalistic, conservative, and so on) by rewarding, punishing, or ignoring particular patterns of behavior.

Second, any of these reward system objectives may be in conflict with motivational objectives. For example, the need for cost control may limit the incentive value of a reward system. The need to attract adequate talent in a tight labor market may lead to the overpayment of base wages and a deemphasis on performance incentives that increase motivation. Different motivational objectives may be in conflict as well. For example, reward systems may motivate short-term performance at the expense of long-term performance.

Third, most modern reward systems are multilayered. Base pay (salary or fixed wage) is usually the largest component. Benefits, including retirement, health, insurance, and education benefits, are also substantial, often exceeding 40 percent of total compensation costs in the United States (Gerhart & Milkovich, 1992). Pay for performance may include separate incentives for multiple levels of performance, including individual, team, unit, division, and corporate performance. Finally, stock ownership plans or stock options are increasingly prominent rewards that promote broad-based employee ownership in the company. Thus, important issues in reward system design are determining the relative mix of these different types of rewards for each population of employees and aligning the objectives of different components in a manner that supports business and informs rather than confuses employees.

An important concept in reward systems is line of sight. It refers to the degree to which an employee can see a clear connection between his or her behavior and a payout from an incentive system. Clear line of sight may involve a number of steps, including understanding how specific behaviors generate performance, how performance is measured in the incentive plan, and how the incentive plan provides different levels of reward for different levels of performance. This concept is clearly rooted in expectancy theories of motivation (Vroom, 1964) and helps explain why some reward systems have little direct motivational value while others have more powerful effects. For example, rewards for corporate performance (profit sharing or stock options, for example) may have a weak line of sight. Employees at the lowest levels of a large corporation may not believe they have the power to influence plan payouts because they do not see how they can affect corporate performance. By contrast, individual and small group incentives (for example, sales commissions) often have strong motivational effects.

With these concepts in mind, we will consider currently prominent innovations relevant to each component of a total reward system (base pay, benefits, pay for performance, and corporate ownership). We will focus first on describing each approach and then presenting a review of the limited research available for each approach.

Base Pay Options

Two major options in base pay design that are currently receiving widespread attention are broadbanding systems and skill-based pay systems. Broadbanding greatly simplifies job grading by revising the overall architecture of the pay system. Skill-based systems revise the basis for allocating pay within the overall architecture. Both systems are oriented more toward motivating employees to focus on long-term development, not necessarily on performance. Also, both systems promote greater flexibility in the use of human resources.

Broadbanding

Large organizations typically develop elaborate pay grade systems over time. Multiple pay grades permit firms to offer relatively frequent promotions to higher grades, to create pay distinctions that mirror the hierarchical and status distinctions in the organization, and to control salary progression within grades. Large companies often have dozens of pay grades between the lowest-paid employee and the top executives.

Broadbanding often radically reduces the number of grades in the organization (Abosch & Hand, 1994). Companies such as General Electric and Northern Telecom have recently combined grades where as few as six remain in the entire corporation or large business unit. As grades are combined, the spread between the bottom and the top of the range increases from perhaps 35 to 50 percent to as much as 300 percent. In addition, firms using broadbanding usually eliminated traditional pay tools, such as point factor job evaluation an range controls. Some firms adopting broadbanding expect that most employees will remain within one band, such as an engineering band or middle manager band, during their entire career. For example, the Materials Group of Avery Dennison, a business with annual sales of nearly $1 billion, collapsed its complex grade structure into just three bands (one each for executives, managers and nonmanagers).

Broadbanding fits the strategy, structure and culture of many firms. A company that has radically delayered in favor of flexible, lateral, team-oriented structures may find numerous grades to be anachronistic. Broadening bands can have appositive impact on motivation because it can give managers more flexibility in rewarding employee performance within a very broad band. It also encourages employees to focus on developing skills that make them more valuable, rather than chasing job evaluation points and grades. Broadbanding may reduce incidents in which employees are reluctant to take assignments that are not associated with opportunities for promotion to another pay grade. Companies adopting broadbanding often hope to reduce the time, effort and energy currently needed to manage their complex pay grade systems.

Broadbanding may also create a variety of problems. For example, once more familiar methods of cost control have been abandoned, it may not be clear how pay costs will be controlled and pay equity will be maintained. Line managers typically assume a critical variable in controlling compensation costs in broadbanding, and they may need to be evaluated partly on the basis of the effectiveness in which they perform this role. A well-developed performance management system is needed for managers to perform the cost containment role. Extensive communication is also needed in broadbanding to help employees understand how the new system works and how they can advance in it. Finally, escalating costs sometimes associated with broadbanding may lead organizations to create "control points," "pay zones," or "shadow ranges" within each broad band. In essence, these techniques simply create smaller bands within the larger bands to control costs. As a result, a large number of pay grades are re-created, though still under the guise of broadbanding. When this happens, it may appear to employees, and rightfully so, that little has changed other than the nomenclature.

The best research on broadbanding is a long-term evaluation of three pilot projects in the U.S. federal government (Schay, 1997). The study traced the effects of broadbanding experiments in three units covering thirteen thousand employees in professional, administrative, technical, and nonmanagement occupations. The units were two Navy research laboratories, the National Institute of Standards and Technology, and an Air Force logistics operation. The study found that wage costs increased somewhat because of the way the programs were managed but that the units also experienced a number of benefits. High performers were less likely to quit, and low performers were more likely to quit, than in control units; overall, pay attitudes were much more favorable in the pilot units; and organizational performance increased on several dimensions.

One benchmark survey of broadbanding practices has been conducted with about one hundred companies (Abosch & Hand, 1994). The number one reason for implementing broadbands was to "create more organizational flexibility." Less than 10 percent of the surveyed companies reported increased payroll costs associated with broadbanding, although 38 percent of the surveyed companies did not track changes in cost. Almost 77 percent of the survey respondents felt that their plan was "effective" or "fairly effective." Companies that viewed their plan as effective, versus companies that viewed their plan as ineffective, spent more time on plan development, were in manufacturing, and had had experience the plan for at least two years. These data offer some support for the concept of broadbanding, but they are limited by the self-report nature of the data collection process.

Pay for Skill, Knowledge, and Competency

The most common base pay system is job-based pay, which rewards employees for the job currently held. By contrast, skill-based pay (also termed pay for skills, knowledge-based pay, and competency-based pay), rewards employees for their repertoire of knowledge and skill (Lawler, 1990; Lawler & Ledford, 1985; Ledford, 1991). Systems that reward managers and professionals most often are called competency pay, while systems that reward lower-level employees are called skill-based pay or pay for knowledge plans. Typically, employees receive formal certification to show that they have obtained the skill before they receive additional pay. This differs from job-based pay, where the pay is attached to the job and employees receive immediate pay increases when they move to a new job even if they are not capable of performing it. In addition, skill-based pay systems usually deemphasize seniority and other factors unrelated to skill. This contrasts with the common use of maturity curves for engineers, which assume without proof that an employee becomes more valuable with greater experience.

Three types of skills are usually identified in skill-based pay systems:

- *Depth of skill* is increased knowledge of one technical specialty. Examples include the "technical ladder" for engineers, which provides opportunities for promotion based on expertise rather than hierarchical advancement, and apprenticeship systems for workers in the skilled trades.
- *Breadth of skill* is increased knowledge of a variety of tasks or jobs. For example, engineers might be rewarded for learning more than one discipline; factory workers may be rewarded for learning all jobs in their work team or factory.
- *Vertical skill* is self-management skill. For example, the Volvo Kalmar plant gave all team members a raise when they proved they could operate without a supervisor.

A skill-based pay plan can reward one, two or all three of these types of increased skill. In the typical plan, manufacturing employees are rewarded for learning breadth skills so that they can participate in self-managing work teams.

The most common type of skill-based pay system is a base pay system, which is typically found in manufacturing plants and similar environments. These systems typically divide the work of the organization into skill "blocks" that each require perhaps four to twelve months to learn. Training requirements and certification standards are identified for each block. The design is often complex and careful, since employees receive permanent base pay rewards for increases in skill.

A new but increasingly important approach to skill-based pay uses bonuses instead of base wage increases to reward skill acquisition. This approach is appropriate in situations where the knowledge base is changing quickly or is difficult to specify. It makes sense in certain kinds of high-technology work, including the work of engineers and information systems professionals, for whom the knowledge base may become obsolete in as little as five years. It may not make sense to make permanent increases to salary for obtaining knowledge that will soon be out of date.

The bonus approach can also be combined with performance management systems. All employees can have learning objectives that are similar to performance objectives and can receive bonuses that vary in size, depending on the importance and difficulty of the learning objectives. This approach has the added motivational value of using specific, challenging goals as the basis for the reward. Organizations using this approach with managers and technical professionals include Avery Dennison, Rockwell, and the U.S. military.

Data from studies of Fortune 1000 companies indicate that almost two-thirds of U.S. companies now use some form of skill-based pay with at least some employees and that the percentage of firms using it has increased more than 50 percent since 1987 (Lawler, Mohrman, & Ledford, 1998). Most companies cover relatively few employees with these plans (typically 20 percent or less), but some prominent companies go much further. Procter & Gamble pays virtually all of its manufacturing workers on skill-based pay plans, and Polaroid pays all employees on a modified competency pay plan.

Large-scale surveys (Jenkins, Ledford, Gupta, & Doty, 1992) and case studies at General Mills (Ledford & Bergel, 1991), Honeywell (Ledford, Tyler, & Dixey, 1991), and Northern Telecom (LeBlanc, 1991) suggest that success rates for skill-based pay plans are relatively high. For example, a study of ninety-six skill-based pay plans (Jenkins et al., 1992) found that two-thirds of the survey respondents believed that skill-based pay plans in their organization resulted in improved productivity, quality, output, safety, attendance, and employee-management relations. Employees also tend to have favorable attitudes about skill and competency pay plans, in part because the plans reward the additional skills and knowledge employees develop (Heneman & Ledford, 1998).

One of the authors, Gerald E. Ledford Jr., has recently completed collection of extensive data about a mature competency pay system covering managers at a well-known food processing company. The system, now six years old, covers over one thousand managers at more than forty plants and distribution and sales centers throughout the United States. The system covers all managers from first-line supervisors up to the level of the plant management team.

The system was installed at a time of great change in the company. (Indeed, it was experiencing most of the changes in the nature of work noted earlier in this chapter.) Senior management approved the new pay system as a way to facilitate and support these changes. Senior management was redefining the role of the manager and eliminating levels of management, which reduced opportunities for hierarchical advancement. So the company collapsed a number of prior pay grades for managers on the system into one broad pay band that had a range spread of approximately 300 percent. The company did not use job descriptions for managers but used three generic titles within the broadband: "resource" "senior resource" and "site resource."

Managers were rewarded not for hierarchical advancement but for their progress in developing four competencies. It was possible to receive higher pay without receiving a higher job title, deliberately downplaying the hierarchy in the system and emphasizing that value to the company rather than job or job title drove pay increases. The pay system was based on four competencies that were derived from a management analysis of the company's strategic business direction. The competencies were leveraging technical and, business systems, leading for results, building workforce effectiveness, and understanding and meeting customer needs. These competencies reflected the company's movement toward team-based systems that demanded more skill, higher motivation, and ongoing development among the workforce; the new definition of the role of the manager; and the company's quality initiative.

The research project involved an assessment of the plan based on surveys of almost seven hundred employees on the system, one survey per site completed by a senior manager, archival data (promotions and turnover), and performance rankings of twenty-one regions (each including one or more locations). The results suggested that there was a wide range of attitudes about the system and considerable variation in the level of implementation effectiveness across locations. Overall, on average, employees displayed mildly positive attitudes about the system.

The most interesting results concerned the relationship between performance and aggregated survey responses. The study measured performance at the individual level, the location level, and the region level. Individual performance was a self-rating that mirrored the company's performance appraisal rating. Location performance was a survey at the location-level survey. Region performance was based on the company's primary hard performance indicator, a composite performance score that combined indicators of productivity, cost, quality, and employee outcomes (primarily safety).

Predictor variables included a battery of indicators from the survey of managers on the competency pay system. The measures examined the degree to which the system led to increased competency, its fit with business needs, its alignment with HR systems other than pay, administrative factors, and change management issues. These variables were summated to the site level for analyses with location as the performance measure and summated to the region level in analyses with the region performance indicator.

Correlational analyses indicated that there were essentially no significant or meaningful correlations between any of the predictors and individual-level performance but that there was a relatively strong relationship between a wide range of predictors and perceived location-level success and region-level performance. The lack of relationship to individual performance is surprising, given the large N (almost 700). The most interesting results for our purposes concerned the relationship between the predictors relevant to the changing nature of work and the hard measure of performance at the region level. Region performance was strongly and significantly correlated with the level of competency acquisition in the region (.66); the degree to which competencies fit a downsized, delayered management structure in the region (.53); the degree to which competencies helped create a lean management structure (.45); the degree to which competencies helped managers understand their new roles (.59); and the degree to which competencies led managers to take responsibility for their own development (.64). These results suggest that competency pay was effective because it was integrated with the new roles and structure of the business. Competency pay was implemented as a part of the business strategy rather than as a "stand-alone" compensation program.

Additional analyses offer support for the hypothesis that the effectiveness of the competency pay system and its fit with changes in the nature of work are causally related to performance in the expected direction. Controlling for salary, promotion, and both salary and promotion had essentially no impact on the correlations, so it does not appear that more favorable attitudes on the manager survey were the result of a higher average level of rewards at locations or regions. In addition, an analysis of the hard performance data over a three-year period suggested strong causal decay. That is, predictors were strongly related to outcomes in the year of the study and in the prior year but were not strongly related to performance two years earlier.

The results of this study are encouraging for several reasons. The study examines a mature system for managers and professionals. It provides some of the first good research evidence that a competency pay system is related to hard performance outcomes at the organization level. Finally, the study indicates that changes in the nature of work at the region level are significantly related to the effectiveness of the competency pay system and its impact on performance.

The best-designed study of skill-based pay to date was conducted by Murray and Gerhart (1998), who also found positive results for skill-based pay. In comparing a treatment plant with skill-based pay to a comparable comparison plant without skill-based pay, they reported greater productivity, lower labor costs, and improved quality in the treatment plant.

Organizations seem to accrue the benefits of such a plan only if it is designed to promote one or more of the following things:

- *Employee flexibility.*   Skill-based pay may enhance cross-trained employees' ability to control and eliminate production or service delivery bottlenecks. It may also permit leaner staffing.
- *Support for high involvement.*   Skill-based pay systems are used more often and are more effective in organizations with high levels of employee involvement. The pay system gives employees incentives to learn the technical and social skills they need to manage themselves effectively. This may bring advantages such as reduced need for management positions, more effective employee problem solving, and better cooperation across departments.
- *Acquisition of critical skills.*   Certain types of employees may be attracted to join the organization and remain in it because of skill-

based pay. This is one impetus for the extensive development of skill-based pay plans in information technology groups, for example.

Skill-based pay plans also typically run into problems even when they are successful (Ledford & Bergel, 1991). In some cases, these problems are so serious that the plans fail. The most serious concern to managers is the potential for higher costs. At the outset, higher costs are almost a certainty, due to the cost of wage incentives, increased training, and certification-related expenditures. The organization adopting skill-based pay must bet that these higher costs will be offset by benefits to the organization. Unless the benefits are realized, the plan will cost more than it is worth to the organization.

In addition, skill-based pay plans can be confusing because employees must understand the range of skill blocks for which they are eligible, the training and certification requirements for the blocks, the pay rates for each block, and so on. This means that skill-based pay systems require considerable communication to motivate the acquisition of knowledge and skills properly. Certification processes may be time-consuming, and employees may object to the certification criteria as unfair or inappropriate. If the skill-based pay system rewards employees for learning skills that they do not use, either because of limited work assignments or because skill blocks become obsolete as the technology changes, the plan will escalate wages for no benefit. Finally, not all employees have the ability or desire to learn new skills. If there are too many in the workforce who do not want skill-based pay, its chances of success are slim.

One common concern of managers is that employees will become disgruntled if they "top out" and cannot continually earn increases in a skill-based pay system. Topping out is probably not a serious problem, however, perhaps because employees realize that they are better off both financially and participatively under most skill-based pay systems than they would be in other systems.

Benefit Options

Because benefits are awarded on the basis of organizational membership or attainment of particular organizational levels, they probably have little impact on productivity. For example, many employees receive insurance and retirement benefits simply because they are employees. Moreover, most benefit plans are standardized for all employees and thus may not meet their specific needs at a certain point in time.

As the cost of benefits has escalated, many organizations have struggled with how to make them more variable and how to tie them more closely to employee behavior. Retirement benefits in particular are a large corporate expense that bears essentially no relationship to individual or company performance. For example, conventional pensions reward survival in the company over a long period of time, rather than performance. Perhaps the most interesting change in the benefits arena is variable funding of retirement plans based on corporate performance.

An example of a company that has adopted such an approach as part of a broader turnaround is Owens Corning (Capell, 1996). The Rewards and Resources program now applies to all salaried employees and is being negotiated into union contracts across the company. The company is reducing its match to a retirement savings plan and replacing it with a profit-sharing contribution of up to 4 percent of pay and an annual stock bonus worth up to 8 percent, each linked to corporate performance. Employees also are guaranteed yearly option grants of 4 percent of base pay.

More common is the attempt to tailor benefits to individual needs by means of "cafeteria-style" benefit plans. These plans allow employees to tailor their choices. For example, they may want to put less money into a retirement plan and more into tuition reimbursement benefits. These plans are used by about 70 percent of Fortune 1000 companies. The limited evidence suggests that having such choice may help reduce overall costs while increasing employee satisfaction (Barber, Dunham, & Formisano, 1992; Lawler, 1990).

Variable Pay

Paying for performance is a critical and complex issue. The starting point for variable pay needs to be an analysis of the business strategy, organizational structure, and organizational culture. This analysis will indicate the types of performance that the organization needs to reward (e.g., cost, revenue, profit, customer service) and the level of analysis at which rewards should be located (team, business unit, or corporation).

Variable pay is the most common pay innovation that ties pay to performance at the team, business unit, or organizational level. There are many forms of variable pay, and variable pay plans have many names: gainsharing, profit sharing, team pay, and goalsharing are a few. Gainsharing is used by 45 percent of large U.S. firms, and profit sharing is used by 69 percent. The use of gainsharing has greatly increased over the past decade; only 26 percent of firms used gainsharing in 1987. The use of profit sharing has not increased much over the past decade (Lawler et al., 1998).

These plans have two common characteristics. First, they pay for performance through bonuses that are paid near the time that the performance occurs, and second, they pay for the performance of collectivities rather than individuals. Pay varies with performance, meaning that the organization pays out more when it can afford to and less when performance does not justify high payment. Some plans even go one step further and put pay "at risk." Under this approach, base pay is reduced to fund performance-based pay.

Successful variable pay plans seem to have two important characteristics: (1) a formula by which employees share monetarily in the performance gains of the organization and (2) structures and processes by which employees share in the creation of organizational performance gains. If the first element is not present, the plan will not motivate improved performance because there will be no line of sight—that is, no clear connection behavior, performance and reward. The plan is simply a benefit that pays at some times and not at others. The second element is the means by which employees help create improved performance, generating a pool of money in which they share. Without it, employees will not be motivated because they will have no way to influence the size of their bonuses.

A case study highlights these two points. When Hughes Electronics won a contract to install a $1 billion air defense system for Saudi Arabia, it lived up to its reputation of providing great technology late and was in danger of losing a $50 million bonus for completing the project on time. The CEO of Hughes offered the nine hundred engineers involved in the project 40 percent of the $50 million bonus to split among themselves if the project was completed on time. They came from a year behind schedule to on-time installation, and each team member earned an average of $22,000. This bonus was motivating because it was high enough to be meaningful to all employees involved with it, because it was tied to a clear but challenging goal, and because the number of employees covered by it was small enough that project members could influence the payout.

Variable pay plans have a relatively high success rate. Reviews of the literature and large-scale studies suggest that variable pay plans result in increased organizational performance in most cases; perhaps two cases out of three (Bullock & Lawler, 1984; Bullock & Tubbs, 1987; Lawler, 1988; McAdams & Hawk, 1994; Mitchell, Lewin, & Lawler, 1990; Weitzman & Kruse, 1990; Welbourne; Balkin, & Gomez-Meija, 1995). Typical benefits reported for variable pay include increased productivity, better quality, lower costs, lower absenteeism and turnover, and more favorable employee attitudes. Unlike other innovative pay plans (such as broadbanding) that typically rely on self-report data, greater confidence can be placed in the results of these studies as they often use "hard" data.

For the plan to succeed in improving performance, it must change patterns of behavior that can in turn lead to increased performance. Increases in performance may result from increased employee suggestions for improvement; greater employee effort; better and more persistent problem solving; cooperation within and between groups in the organization, greater demands on management for improved performance, and better relations between management and employees.

Of course, there are also variable pay failures. Reasons for the failure of some variable pay plans are documented by McAdams and Hawk (1994). Plans may fail either because the formula is poorly designed or because the gain-producing structures are inadequate.

There are many potential problems with variable pay formulas. For example, with respect to design issues, the hurdle for achieving a payout may be too high, especially early in the life of the plan. Employees tend to give up on plans that do not pay out in the first year or two. Conversely, if the formula makes it is too easy to achieve a payout, the plan may fail because it does not cause employees to change their behavior. In addition, there may not be enough money available in the plan to motivate a change in behavior. Convention suggests that bonus opportunities must represent 5 to 10 percent of base pay to be motivating. The greater the amount of money available, the more motivating the plan; some plans make it possible for employees to earn 25 percent or more of base pay in bonuses, although a much lower amount is typical.

The formula may be designed to reward the wrong behaviors or may not cover all the relevant behaviors and metrics. For example, a formula that rewards increased labor productivity may lead employees not only to work harder but also to increase production of scrap and waste. Payouts may also be too infrequent. From a motivational point of view, frequent payouts are desirable, although this may not be practical for an organization's accounting system or performance cycles. Still other problems can be created by omitting key groups from the plan. For example, if the plan covers only direct labor employees, support employees such as maintenance workers and material handlers may resist changing their behavior in order to make it possible for others to earn a bonus. Finally, the formula can be too inflexible. Because the formula is tailored to a particular context, the formula needs to change as the business plan it is designed to support also evolves. This suggests the need for periodic changes to the variable pay plan, which can be difficult to negotiate or gain support for.

Beyond potential problems with formula design, the structures needed to support performance improvement may be absent or poorly implemented. Most variable plans require a participative system that generates and processes employee ideas for improvement. This may be a separate system of variable pay committees; or participation may be integrated into the role of existing work teams. Whatever the particular structure, unless employees have the opportunity to suggest improvements, they are left with the sole option of working harder to achieve a payout. Inadequate training and communication about the plan and organizational performance are other common sources of problems. Employees are not motivated by a plan unless they understand it and unless they know the direction of organizational performance and how it is changing.

These considerations suggest that another essential variable is trust. Employees must trust that the formula is fair, that they will receive a payout for their efforts, and that their ideas will lead to organizational changes. If trust is very low, adoption of variable pay should be reconsidered. Relatedly, management may be a barrier to success. Employees question why things have been done in certain ways in the past and challenge management to adopt changes faster. Some managers see this as a desirable aspect of variable pay, while others are threatened by such behavior.

The design of variable pay plan formulas is complex, and it has been the subject of numerous books, manuals, and training programs (see Belcher et al., 1998). We will highlight some of the most important issues.

There are several essential principles of variable pay design. First, such plans are usually designed to be self-funding, so that the money paid out in bonuses is derived from savings that the plan itself generates. Another principle is line of sight. There are many ways of increasing line of sight in variable pay plans and therefore increasing the motivational power of these plans. Simpler measures and formulas tend to produce greater line of sight; so do more frequent payouts. Paying out to smaller units (such as teams) creates greater line of sight than paying out in a large plant or an entire company. However, competition may also be heightened between groups by paying out to smaller groups. Support processes can also be critical to creating line of sight. Considerable training and information sharing must help employees understand a plan that is not obvious to them.

Many different performance measures can be used as the basis for a variable pay formula. These range from very concrete behavioral measures (accidents, absenteeism, safety inspection ratings) to measures of unit performance (productivity, cost, quality, on-time delivery, cycle time) to measures of financial performance (return on sales or investment, profit, economic value added). The best measure for a given organization can be discovered only through analysis of the business strategy, organizational structure, and culture. The advantage of behavioral measures is that they have strong line of sight and therefore greater motivational value. For example, employees are motivated to reduce absenteeism because there is a clear connection between attendance and bonuses.

Financial performance metrics are more closely tied to the organization's ability to pay. If the organization is doing well, it can afford to pay bonuses; if it is not doing well, no bonuses are paid out. This often makes financially oriented plans attractive to managers. However, most employees often have modest control over financial performance. Whether the organization makes a high profit or achieves a high rate of return depends on market conditions, competitor behavior, capital equipment purchases, and accounting decisions that employees cannot influence.

Nevertheless, there is a clear trend in the United States toward using plans tied to the financial performance of the corporation. The Big Three automakers all offer profit-sharing bonuses, which have varied greatly with company performance in recent years. Before the Daimler-Chrysler merger, Chrysler workers earned $8,000 annually due to good performance, and General Motors workers made $300 in bonuses for 1996. (Saturn workers, on a separate plan that rewards quality and financial performance, received $10,000 each.) Intel offered employees the equivalent of at least one-third their annual salary as a bonus for good company performance in 1996. Levi Strauss is offering all employees an extra year's pay as a bonus if the company achieves a cumulative cash flow of $7.6 billion for the six-year period starting in 1996. Finally, IBM paid bonuses averaging $4,979 for all employees worldwide based on 1996 performance.

In evaluating these plans, we must recognize that they have limited motivational value, lucrative as they are, because there is little line of sight between payouts and individual behavior. However, these plans have been linked to moderate productivity increases (Weitzman & Kruse, 1990) and may also have other advantages. They offer companies a way of paying employees well when they can afford to do so and help increase employee identification with the company and its success.

Unit performance metrics are in the middle on the continuum from line of sight to ability to pay. Employees can influence them more easily than financial performance measures, but not as easily as behavior measures. An organization that shows good performance on productivity tends to make a higher rate of return over the long run, but the relationship is not perfect. A plan based on unit performance or behavioral measures may pay out handsomely even when the total organization is losing money or may not pay; out at all when the organization is making high profits. However, these metrics are the ones most often recommended in the gainsharing literature. Companies making heavy use of such metrics for unit level gainsharing plans include TRW, Dana, Hughes, and Weyerhaeuser. All cover half or more of their workforce with gainsharing plans that use such metrics.

Many organizations attempt to realize the best of both worlds, by combining different types of metrics in the same formula. For example, there may be a requirement that the organization recognize a profit before it makes payouts on unit performance or behavioral measures. These and other options protect against payouts in bad times, but at the risk of making the plan more complex and difficult to understand. The plan may also inadvertently include so many safeguards that it cannot pay out.

Gainsharing formulas also highlight the design choice of whether to pay out when the organization does better than in past (gainsharing when performance exceeds historical levels) or when the organization reaches targets that are defined by management (goal sharing). Gainsharing based on historical performance usually appears fair to employees. It also avoids employee fears of a "speed-up," a common problem in individual incentive plans such as piecework. From a motivational perspective, goal sharing is attractive because it takes advantage of the motivational power of specific, challenging goals. Goal sharing may also be the most practical approach in some situations. Historical data may be unavailable, as in a new plant, or may be irrelevant, as in the case of an organization that must perform at a much higher level than in the past to stay in business. Management-set targets are very flexible and can change annually to reflect new business directions and emphases.

Managers can determine the suitability of any particular formula only through an analysis of the needs of the organization. Different plans are appropriate to different settings. Also, we again emphasize that the support processes and structures are at least as important to success as the specifics of the formula itself.

Ownership Options

There are two primary ways in which companies offer opportunities for equity participation: employee stock ownership plans (ESOPs) and stock options. These plans have many of the same advantages and motivational problems as corporate profit sharing but are even more complex from the individual employee's standpoint. A wave of ESOP adoptions during the 1980s in the United States resulted from favorable tax legislation. Almost two-thirds of Fortune 1000 firms in the country have such plans, and one-third cover all employees with them (Lawler, Mohrman, & Ledford, 1998). Although it is possible to construct ESOP plans that have motivational value, especially in small companies, most are designed in ways that greatly mitigate motivational effects (Lawler & Jenkins, 1992). Most ESOP plans are part of the retirement system, meaning that any reward is very remote from the employee's point of view. In addition, employees typically are not allowed control of their shares until they retire, meaning that they cannot vote as a shareholder on corporate governance issues.

During the past few years, there has been an explosion in the use of broad-based stock options (Capell, 1996). These plans have become a standard part of pay packages in the high-technology sector, and high-tech firms often have serious recruitment and retention problems if they cannot offer stock options. The rewards for these plans can be spectacular in successful companies. Microsoft offers below-market base pay but stock options so lucrative that fully half of the workforce-and virtually all employees with more than five years' tenure-own over $1 million in company stock. PepsiCo was one of the first companies outside the high-technology sector to offer stock options to all employees, and options now cover millions of workers in the American economy in companies such as Monsanto, Starbucks, and Delta Air Lines. A recent survey indicates that the vast majority of Fortune 1000 firms use stock options, and 20 percent cover half or more of the workforce (Lawler et al., 1998).

Appealing as stock options and ESOP plans may be from the standpoint of employees who have been made wealthy by such plans, they have questionable motivational value. Few of Microsoft's twenty-eight thousand employees below the executive level can have a significant effect on the firm's stock performance. Not only is there low line of sight to company performance, there is no line of sight to the macroeconomic, international, financial, and market forces far beyond the company's boundaries that influence stock prices. In addition, employees often find the *meaning* of stock options very difficult to understand. An administrative employee at a leading biotechnology firm allowed $750,000 in stock options to expire because she did not understand how the plan worked. Once this happened, the company was legally powerless to correct the problem.

Privately held organizations, which do not have publicly traded stock, sometimes use "phantom stock." They issue internal stock to serve as a proxy for public stock. The phantom stock's value is based on the book value of the organization and is not the same as phantom stock for executives, defined as stock price appreciation plus dividends. By comparison, the value of publicly traded stock is its market. Although there have been no formal empirical studies of phantom stock plans, the theory of line of sight would suggest that phantom stock plans are more likely to be successful at motivating employee performance because book value reflects criteria (such as cost) more under the employees control than market value, which is at the mercy of market conditions as well as company performance. Major companies with phantom stock plans include Kino's and Mary Kay (Tully, 1998).

The empirical evidence on employee stock ownership plans has been reviewed in two places. Conte and Kruse (1991) looked at the impact of ESOP plans on organizational effectiveness. The results suggest that ESOPs are not likely to have an impact on employee productivity. This result should not be surprising, given that the actual intent of most ESOP plans is to raise capital, not to raise labor productivity. The evidence on public stock ownership plans has been reviewed in meta-analysis by Ben-Ner and Jones (1995), who found that although ownership does affect productivity, it is dependent on the extent of participation in decision making that accompanies ownership.

FUTURE RESEARCH

The new forms of pay reviewed here invite new advancements in compensation theory and research. Suggestions for future research follow and are summarized in Figure 2.

Changes in Pay Practices

Further theory development is crucial if we are to understand the new forms of pay. While categorization schemes such as the one shown in Figure 1 may be helpful from a heuristic perspective to show differences in pay system characteristics, theory development and application are needed to achieve an understanding of how these systems operate and the impact they have on individual and organizational outcomes.

One approach to the study of the new pay is to look at the effects of the components of these systems in terms of main effects and interactions. To do so, careful construction of theory is needed to guide an examination of the synergistic effects between compensation components and changes in the nature of work (Delery & Doty, 1996; Gerhart, Trevor, & Graham, 1996). Thoughtful theoretical development is in direct contrast to a "shotgun empiricism" approach, wherein all available interactions are tested and then the significant interactions are given a post hoc explanation. Unfortunately, shotgun empiricism seems to dominate the current literature on "bundles" of human resource activities, including pay.

There is a growing theoretical base to draw on to guide compensation research in this era of new pay forms. New theory bases include organization justice (Welbourne et al., 1995), tournament theory (Becker &

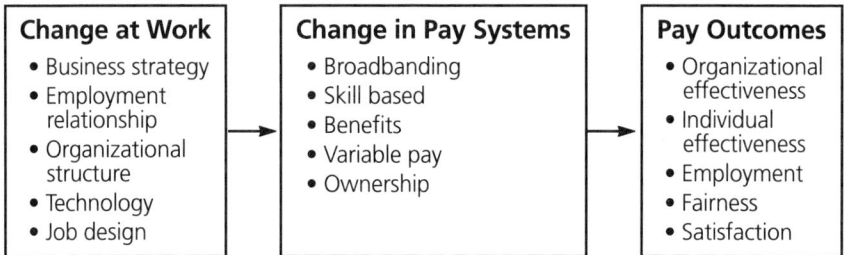

Change at Work	**Change in Pay Systems**	**Pay Outcomes**
• Business strategy • Employment relationship • Organizational structure • Technology • Job design	• Broadbanding • Skill based • Benefits • Variable pay • Ownership	• Organizational effectiveness • Individual effectiveness • Employment • Fairness • Satisfaction

Figure 2.   Future research agenda.

Huselid, 1992), agency theory (Conlon & Parks, 1990; Parks & Conlon, 1995), resource-based view of the firm (Barney & Wright, 1998), and population ecology (Welbourne & Andrews, 1996). As noted by Heneman (1992) and by Gerhart and Milkovich (1992), we are more likely to improve our knowledge of compensation systems if we adapt these theories to study compensation systems, rather than using compensation systems to study these theories. An excellent example here is Murray and Gerhart (1998), who used the job characteristics model and expectancy theory to study skill-based pay, rather than using skill-based pay to test expectancy theory and the job characteristics model.

Specific compensation problems need theoretical guidance to resolve them. For example, there are conflicting findings regarding the benefits and drawbacks of individual versus group rewards Wageman (1995) reported in a study of intact work groups at Xerox that group performance was better when the pay plan was based on either group or individual performance rewards rather than a combination of group and individual rewards. Crown and Rosse (1995) found that for sports teams, a combination of group and individual performance goals resulted in better group performance than individual goals alone, but combined group and individual goals resulted in less effective group performance than group goals alone.

To resolve the conflicting findings regarding the utility of group and individual reward systems, theoretical concepts such as free riding and social loafing may need to be examined. Wagner (1995) found that social loafing and free riding were less likely in groups characterized by high collectivism, small group size, high accountability to the group, and low shared responsibility. Such groups may have less need for individual rewards to supplement group rewards.

Pay Outcomes

A common approach to studying pay outcomes is to use managerial or human resource ratings of pay plan and organizational effectiveness. For example, for a survey of over six hundred pay plans, the department variables used were human resource professional's judgments regarding business performance, managerial perceptions, and employee perceptions (McAdams & Hawk, 1994). Though potentially suggestive of the likely outcomes associated with pay plans, these perceptual measures are clearly both deficient and potentially contaminated. They fail to tap actual business performance, employee perceptions, and managerial perceptions. Should these types of measures be abandoned? The answer is probably no because in some studies it is not possible to gather additional outcome measures, and these data do provide a start to our understanding of pay systems. Also, perceptual measures are sometimes correlated with more objective measures (Delaney & Huselid, 1996; Montemayor, 1996).

An obvious solution to the use of perceptual measures is to use operational (productivity) and financial (profit) outcome measures. Unfortunately, this obvious solution is not without limitations as well. Measures of this type are contaminated by many factors (technology, the business cycle) other than compensation. In addition, the reliability of productivity measures is only about .60, as shown by Heneman (1986) in a meta-analysis. A final problem is that these measures are sometimes available only at the corporate level, whereas pay plans often cover employees only at the business-unit level. As a result, the amount of variance explained using these measures may be very small and insignificant. More proximal operational measures are more likely to be affected by compensation systems, but they also suffer from measurement problems as well. For example, Cardy and Dobbins (1994) document the low reliability of customer service measures.

Given the problems associated with both subjective and objective measures, two steps seem appropriate. First, multiple measures of pay plan effectiveness should be used, since organizational effectiveness is rarely a unidimensional construct anyway (Whetten & Cameron, 1994). Second, when compensation theory is tested, corrections for attenuation in the dependent variable should be applied.

Along with the use of both subjective and objective measures, the use of new measures is to be recommended. Creative and important examples follow. Gerhart, Trevor, and Graham (1996) recommended that the financial risk involved with pay plans be studied, as well as the survival of pay plans. Reported reasons for pay plan termination include lack of performance against payout measures, management changes, change in market conditions, change in business strategy, lack of acceptance by employees and management, and cost of the plan (McAdams & Hawk, 1994). As noted earlier, a strategic view of human resources suggests that the relationship between human resource activities be linked with one another as well as with the business strategy.

Three studies serve as examples of the need to look at the effects of the compensation system on other human resource systems (such as staffing). First, Cable and Judge (1994) examined preferences for various pay systems in the job search decisions of college students. Organizations were perceived as more attractive places to work when flexible benefits, high proportions of base pay to variable pay, and individual rather than group rewards were offered. These effects were reported after controlling for pay level. The results suggest that the new pay programs reviewed in this chapter may not always be acceptable to college students. Le Blanc and Mulvey (1998) report similar pay preferences for a more general population. Second, Gerhart and Trevor (1996) examined layoffs as a function of the type of pay plan used. It was shown that organizations that value employment stability have a greater tendency to use variable pay.

Another set of dependent variables to be explored are process variables. Recent research by Snell and Youndt (1995) indicates that the control of processes is at least as important as the control of outcomes to the economic performance of the firm. Kessler and Chakrabarti (1996), for example, suggest that "innovation speed is an important process variable needed for organizations to adapt to changing business environments. Reward systems are viewed as facilitating the speed at which products are developed. It is hypothesized that speed is likely to be changed by group reward systems that promote the exchange of information and ideas.

Changes in Work and Changes in Pay Practices

A question of strategic importance to compensation professionals is how compensation plans can be designed that help organizations adapt to changes in work and business environments. Concepts bandied about in discussing this issue include "fit," "flexibility," and "organizational learning." Two important articles provide some theoretical guidance in this area.

Wright and Snell (1998) argue that both fit and flexibility are required of human resource activities if they are to add value to the firm. *Fit* refers to the development of a formal organizational strategy and structure, with specification of the employee competencies to fulfill that strategy and structure. Pay systems can be used to motivate the acquisition and demonstration of competencies in alignment with the business strategy. *Flexibility* refers more to the development of individual competencies in the organization such that the organization can adapt to the changing business environment. If an organization has the needed competencies to adapt to the changing business environment, it is likely to gain advantage over organizations without such competencies. Competency- and skill-based pay systems, especially those that constantly update competency and skill blocks, are likely to develop human resources in the organization that can readily adapt to the changing business environment.

The need for flexibility points to the need for organizations to be able to learn in order to adapt to the business environment. Snell, Youndt, and Wright (1996) show how strategic human resource management activities can contribute to organizational learning. In brief, reward systems need to help develop or reinforce the three major components of organizational learning: creating knowledge, transferring knowledge, and institutionalizing knowledge. At the creation stage, competency-based pay could be used. At the transferring stage, team-based pay might be used to facilitate the sharing of learning. In the institutionalizing stage, employee ownership plans might be used to facilitate the retention of knowledge.

Changes in Pay Practices and Outcomes

There is a critical need for more and better studies that examine the impact of pay systems on individual and organizational outcomes. However, increasing the number of studies is problematic for a number of reasons. First, gaining access to data in organizations with new pay plans is difficult. Organizations usually only want to share successes (see Petty, Singleton, & Connell, 1992, for a notable exception), which poses a restriction-of-range problem. Moreover, the problem is exacerbated by the fact that organizations are unlikely to share the results of very successful plans because they are a potential source of competitive advantage to the organization (Cappelli & Crocker-Hefter, 1995). Even when organizations are willing to share, data collection may not be possible in some cases for university researchers. To protect human subjects, university review committees may, for example, preclude the researcher from matching up demographic and attitudinal data about the employee with pay and outcome measures. Even if permitted, it may be required to be on a voluntary basis, which creates a potential sampling bias.

A final problem has to do with the research design process: Providing meaningful findings is difficult without a control group or time-series data. For obvious reasons, it is often impossible to have a control group with pay interventions, and time-series data may take considerable time given the newness of these plans and their ongoing refinement, which may further confound the data.

Although these problems exist and are likely causes of the limited number of published studies on compensation relative to other industrial and organizational psychology topics, they are not insurmountable. Anonymity can be guaranteed in order to cushion the revelation of negative findings by organizations. If pay plans truly are a source of competitive advantage, organizations should not be able to obtain identical results simply by copying the pay practices of a competitor. A successful plan will fit the unique circumstances of each organization. University review committees can be shown that the benefits of the research outweigh the costs of losses of confidentiality. Steps can be taken to ensure that confidentiality is breached only by the researchers and not by others. Journal editors and reviewers can be sympathetic to internal validity threats and carefully trade off the need for well-designed research against the need for knowledge about new compensation plans. New outlets, such as the Scientist Practitioner Forum at *Personnel Psychology*, may be more responsive to this trade-off than traditional I/O psychology outlets.

With regard to better research, three issues are salient. First, pay plans should not be treated as homogeneous constructs. For example, not all employee ownership plans are alike (Ben-Ner & Jones, 1995). These various components of pay plans need to be assessed in terms of their independent and combined effects. Ben-Ner and Jones point out, for example, that the separate and combined impact of financial participation and participation in decision making is not well understood in employee ownership plans.

Second, given the heterogeneity of pay plans under the same name, specific theories need to be developed for specific pay plans rather than grand theories that are applicable across all pay plans. This has been done for merit pay (Heneman, 1990), employee ownership (Pierce, Rubenfeld, & Morgan, 1991), and skill-based pay (Murray & Gerhart, 1998). Other forms of the new pay similarly need theoretical development.

Third, the cognitive revolution in psychology has provided great insight into performance appraisal, which is a closely allied subject of compensation systems. One would suspect that cognitive psychology would be useful in understanding compensation decision making. We should note two examples of inroads in this area. Henderson and Fredrickson (1996) found that executive compensation is in part a function of the cognitive demands placed on the executive by the organization. Bazerman, Lowenstein, and White (1992) report using a cognitive approach to explore the inconsistent manner in which interpersonal comparisons are made when making pay allocation decisions.

CONCLUSION

Organizations spend huge sums of money on compensation. It is not uncommon for labor costs to make up 70 percent or more of the total budget in service sector organizations. It is hardly surprising, then, that decision makers in organizations are carefully monitoring the utility of dollars spent on compensation to see to what extent compensation programs are contributing to organizational effectiveness. We are encouraged by the fact that organizations are experimenting with new forms of pay that may show a better return on investment than has been the case with traditional pay programs. The time is ripe for academics to capitalize on the attention executives are giving to pay systems by conducting meaningful theory-driven research in field settings.

Concurrently, theory is being developed in academic settings that is highly relevant to the study of these new pay systems. Newer theories come to us from business strategy, which focuses on human resource practices as a source of competitive advantage for organizations; from cognitive and social psychology, which offers important perspectives on decision making by individuals and teams; and from economics, which looks at the relationship between the owner (principal) and employee (agent) in compensation decision making.

Our hope is that the current opportunities in the field can be coupled with the advancement of theory in the academy. Sound practice and theory go hand in hand. We would like to see a new generation of compensation scholars address the effects of the changing nature of work on compensation. We now have a good start on developing a descriptive body of knowledge regarding these new pay practices. Professional associations, especially the American Compensation Association, and compensation consulting firms have led the way.

However, as was true for Opsahl and Dunnette (1966) as they reviewed research on traditional pay systems more than thirty years ago, we need more analytical work in compensation based on sound theory to show when and why innovative pay plans work. This next step should increase organizational effectiveness, because we will know not only that pay programs work but also, more important, *why* they work. Although we need to focus on the organizational outcomes associated with new pay plans, we must also devote attention to the study of the processes that lead to these outcomes.

REFERENCES

Abosch, K.S., & Hand, J.S. (1994). *Broadbanding design, approaches, and practices.* Scottsdale, AZ: American Compensation Association.

American Compensation Association. (1996). *Raising the bar: Using competencies to enhance employee performance.* Scottsdale, AZ: Author.

Barber, A.E., Durham, R.B., & Formisano, R.A. (1992). The impact of employee benefits on employee satisfaction: A field study. *Personnel Psychology, 45,* 55–75.

Barney, J.B., & Wright, P.M. (1998). On becoming a strategic partner: The role of human resources in gaining competitive advantage. *Human Resource Management, 37,* 31–46.

Bazerman, M.H., Lowenstein, G.F., & White, S.B. (1992). Reversals of preference in allocation decisions: Judging an alternative versus choosing among alternatives. *Administrative Science Quarterly, 37,* 220–240.

Becker, B.E., & Huselid, M.A. (1992). Direct estimates of SD, and the implications for utility analysis. *Journal of Applied Psychology, 77,* 227–233.

Belcher, J.G., Jr., Butler, R.J., Cheatham, D.W., Goberville, G.J., Heneman, R.L., & Wilson, T.B. (1998). *How to design variable pay.* Scottsdale, AZ: American Compensation Association.

Ben-Ner, A., &Jones, D.C. (1995). Employee participation, ownership, and productivity: A theoretical framework. *Industrial Relations, 34,* 532–554.

Bridges, W. (1995) *Jobshift: How to prosper in a workplace without jobs.* Reading, PA: Addison-Wesley.

Bullock, R.J., & Lawler, E.E., III. (1984). Gainsharing: A few questions and fewer answers. *Human Resource Management, 23,* 23–40.

Bullock, R.J., & Tubbs, M.E. (1987) . A case meta-analysis of gainsharing plans as organizational development interventions. *Journal of Applied Behavioral Science, 26,* 383–404.

Cable, D.M., & Judge, T.A. (1994). Pay preference and job search decisions: A person-organization fit perspective. *Personnel Psychology, 47,* 317–348.

Capell, K. (1996, July 22). Owens Corning plays share the wealth. *Business Week,* 82–83.

Cappelli, P., Bassi, L., Katz, H., Knoke, D., Osterman, P., & Useem, M. (1997) . *Change at work.* New York: Oxford University Press.

Cappelli, P., & Crocker-Hefter, A. (1995). Distinctive human resources are firms' core competencies. *Organizational Dynamics, 24,* 7–22.

Cardy, R.L., & Dobbins, G.H. (1994). *Performance appraisal: Alternative perspectives.* Cincinnati, OH: South-Western.

Cohen, D., & Heneman, R.L. (1994). Ability and effort weights in pay level and pay increase decisions. *Journal of Business and Psychology, 8,* 327–343.

Conlon, E.J., & Parks, J.M. (1990). Effects of monitoring and tradition on compensation arrangements: An experiment with principal-agent dyads. *Academy of Management, Journal, 43,* 603–622.

Conte, M.A., & Kruse, D.L. (1991). ESOPs and profit-sharing plans: Do they link employee pay to company performance? *Financial Management, 20,* 91–100.

Crandall, N.F., & Wallace, M.J., Jr. (1997). Inside the virtual workplace: Forging a new deal for work and rewards. *Compensation and Benefits Review, 29,* 27–36.

Crown, D.R, & Rosse, J.G. (1995). Yours, mine and ours: Facilitating group productivity through the integration of individual and group goals. *Organizational Behavior and Human Decision Processes, 64,* 138–150.

Delaney, J.T., & Huselid, M.A. (1996) . The impact of human resource management practices on perceptions of organizational performance. *Academy of Management Journal, 39,* 949–969.

Delery, J.E., & Doty, D.H. (1996). Modes of theorizing in strategic human resource management: Tests of universalistic, contingency, and configurational performance predications. *Academy of Management Journal, 39,* 802–835.

Finegold, D., Lawler E.E., III, & Ledford, G.E., Jr. (1998). Competencies, capabilities, and strategic organizational design. In A.M. Monrman Jr., J.R. Galbraith, & E.E. Lawler III (Eds.), *Tomorrow's organization: Crafting winning capabilities in a dynamic world.* San Francisco: Jossey Bass.

Gerhart, B., & Milkovich, G.T. (1992). Employee compensation: Research and practice. In M.D. Dunnette & L.M. Hough (Eds.), *Handbook of industrial and organizational psychology* (2nd ed., Vol. 3, pp. 481–570). Palo Alto, CA: Consulting Psychologists Press.

Gerhart, B., & Trevor, C.O. (1996). Employment variability under different managerial compensation systems. *Academy of Management Journal, 39,* 1692–1712.

Gerhart, B., Trevor, C.O., & Graham, M.E. (1996). New directions in compensation research: Synergies, risk, and survival. *Research in Personnel and Human Resources Management, 14,* 143–203.

Gomez-Mejia, L.R., & Balkin, D.B. (1992). *Compensation, organizational strategy, and firm performance.* Cincinnati, OH: South-Western.

Gross, S.E. (1995). *Compensation for teams.* New York: AMACOM.

Hambrick, D.C., & Snow, C.C. (1989). Strategic reward systems. In C.C. Snow (Ed.), *Strategy, organization design, and human resource management* (pp. 333–367). Greenwich, CT: JAI Press.

Hedge, J.W., & Borman, W.C. (1995). Changing conceptions and practices in performance appraisal. In A. Howard (Ed.), *The changing network of work* (pp. 451–484). San Francisco: Jossey Bass.

Henderson, A.D., & Fredrickson, J.W. (1996). Information-processing demands as a determinant of CEO compensation. *Academy of Management Journal, 39,* 575–606.

Heneman, H.G., III, Heneman, R.L., & Judge, T. (1997). *Staffing organizations* (2nd ed.). Burr Ridge, IL: Irwin.

Heneman, H.G., III, & Schwab, D.P. (1979). Work and rewards theory. In D. Yoder & H.G. Heneman Jr. (Eds.), *ASPA handbook* of *personnel and industrial relations* (pp. 6.1–6.22). Washington, DC: Bureau of National Affairs.

Heneman, H.G., III, & Schwab, D.P. (1985). Pay satisfaction: Its multidimensional nature and measurement. *International Journal of Psychology, 20,* 129–141.

Heneman, R.L. (1986). The relationship between supervisory ratings and results-oriented measures of performance: A meta-analysis. *Personnel Psychology, 39,* 811 826.

Heneman, R.L. (1990). Merit pay research. In G.R. Ferris & K.M. Rowland (Eds.), *Research in personnel and human resources management* (Vol. 8, pp. 203–263). Greenwich, CT: JAI Press.

Heneman, R.L. (in press). Merit pay. In C.H. Fay (Ed.), *The executive compensation handbook.* New York: Free Press.

Heneman, R.L., & Gresham, M.T. (1998). Linking appraisals to compensation and incentives. In J.W. Smither (Ed.), *Performance appraisal: State-of-the art methods for performance management* (pp. 496–536). San Francisco: Jossey Bass.

Heneman, R.L., & Ledford, G.E., Jr. (1998). Competency pay for managers and professionals: Implications for teachers. *Journal for Personnel Evaluation in Education, 2,* 103–121.

Heneman, R.L., & von Hippel, C. (1996). The assessment of job performance: Focusing attention on context, process and group issues. In D. Lewin, D.J.B. Mitchell, & M.A. Zaidi (Eds.), *Handbook of human resource management* (pp. 587–617). Greenwich, CT: JAI Press.

Howard, A. (1995). A framework for work change. In A. Howard (Ed.), *The changing nature of work* (pp. 3–44) . San Francisco: Jossey Bass.

Ilgen, D.R., & Hollenbeck, J.R. (1991) . The structure of work: Job design and roles. In M.D. Dunnette & L.M. Hough (Eds.), *Handbook of industrial and organizational psychology* (2nd ed., Vol. 2, pp. 165–208). Palo Alto, CA: Consulting Psychologists Press.

Jenkins, G.D., Jr., Ledford, G.E., Jr., Gupta, N., & Doty, D.H. (1992). *Skill-based pay: Practices, payoffs, pitfalls, and prescriptions.* Scottsdale, AZ: American Compensation Association.

Kahnweiler, W.M., Crane, D.P., & O'Neill, C.P (1994, Spring). Employee involvement in design in and managing pay systems. *American Compensation Association Journal,* 68–81.

Kanfer, R., & Heggestad, E.D. (1997) . Motivational traits and skills: A person-centered approach to work motivation. In L.L. Cummings & B.M. Staw (Eds.), *Research in organizational behavior* (Vol. 19, pp. 1–56). Greenwich, CT: JAI Press.

Kessler, E.H., & Chakrabarti, A.R (1996). Innovation speed: A conceptual model of context, antecedents, and outcomes. *Academy of Management Review, 21,* 1143–1191.

Lawler, E.E., III. (1971). Corporate profits and employee satisfaction: Must they be in conflict? *California Management Review, 14,* 46.

Lawler, E.E., III. (1981). *Pay and organizational development.* Reading, MA: Addison-Wesley.

Lawler, E.E., III. (1988) . Pay for performance: Making it work. *Personnel,* 65, 22–27.

Lawler, E.E., III. (1990). *Strategic pay: Aligning organizational strategies and pay systems.* San Francisco: Jossey Bass.

Lawler, E.E., III, & Cohen, S.G. (1992, Autumn). Designing pay systems for teams. *American Compensation Association Journal,* 6–18.

Lawler, E.E., III, & Jenkins, G.D., Jr. (1992). Strategic reward systems. In M.D. Dunnette & L.M. Hough (Eds.), *Handbook of industrial and organizational psychology* (2nd ed., Vol. 3, pp. 1009–1055). Palo Alto CA: Consulting Psychologists Press.

Lawler, E.E., III, & Ledford, G.E., Jr. (1985). Skill-based pay: A concept that's catching on. *Personnel, 62,* 30–37.

Lawler, E.E., III, Mohrman, S.A., & Ledford, G.E., Jr. (1998). *Strategies for high-performance organizations.* San Francisco: Jossey-Bass.

Lazear, E.P. (1992). The job as a concept. In W.J. Bruns Jr. (Ed.), *Performance measurement, evaluation, and incentives* (pp. 183–215). Boston: Harvard Business School Press.

Le Blanc, P.V. (1991). Skill-based pay case number 2: Northern Telecom. *Compensation and Benefits Review, 23,* 39–56.

Le Blanc, P.V., & Mulvey, P.W. (1998). How American workers see the rewards of work. *Compensation and Benefits Review, 30,* 24–28.

Ledford, G.E., Jr. (1991) . Three case studies on skill-based pay: An overview. *Compensation and Benefits Review, 23,* 11–23.

Ledford, G.E., Jr. (1995). Designing nimble reward systems. *Compensation and Benefits Review, 27,* 46–54.

Ledford, G.E., Jr., & Bergel, G. (1991) . Skill-based pay case number 1: General Mills. *Compensation and Benefits Review, 23,* 24–38.

Ledford, G.E., Jr., Lawler, E.E., III, & Mohrman, S.A. (1995). Reward innovations in Fortune 1000 companies. *Compensation and Benefits Review, 27,* 76–80.

Ledford, G.E., Jr., Tyler, W.R., & Dixey W.B. (1991) . Skill-based pay case number 3: Honeywell ammunition assembly. *Compensation and Benefits Review, 23,* 57–T7.

McAdams, J.L., & Hawk, E.J. (1994) . *Organizational performance and rewards.* Scottsdale AZ: American Compensation Association.

Miles, R.E., Snow, C.C., Mathews, J.A., Miles, G., & Coleman, H.J. Jr., (1997). Organizing in the knowledge age: Anticipating the cellular form. *Academy of Management Executive, 11,* 7–20.

Milkovich, G.T., & Newman, J.M. (1996). *Compensation* (5th ed.). Burr Ridge, IL: Irwin.

Mitchell, D.J.B., Lewin, D., & Lawler, E.E., III. (1990) . Alternative pay systems, firm performance, and productivity. In A.S. Blinder (Ed.), *Paying for productivity: A look at the evidence* (pp. 15–94). Washington, DC: Brookings Institution.

Montemayor, E.F. (1994, Summer). A model for aligning teamwork and pay. *American Compensation Association Journal, 18–25.*

Montemayor, E.F. (1996). Congruence between pay policy and competitive strategy in high-performing firms. *Journal of Management, 22,* 889–908.

Murray, B.C., & Gerhart, B. (1998) . An empirical analysis of a skill-based pay program and plant performance outcomes. *Academy of Management Journal, 41,* 68–78.

Naylor, J.C., Pritchard, R.D., & Ilgen, D.R. (1980). *A theory of behavior in organizations.* Orlando, FL: Academic Press.

0'Neal, S. (1995, Autumn). Competencies and pay in the evolving and world of work. *American Compensation Association Journal,* 72–79.

Opsahl, R.L., & Dunnette, M.D. (1966). The role of financial compensation in industrial motivation. *Psychological Bulletin, 66,* 94–118.

Parks, J.M., & Conlon, E.J. (1995). Compensation contracts: Do agency theory assumptions predict negotiated agreements? *Academy of Management Journal, 38,* 821–838.

Patten, T.H., Jr. (1977). *Pay.* New York: Free Press.

Petty, M.M., Singleton, B., & Connell, D.W. (1992). An experimental evaluation of an incentive plan in the electric utility industry. *Journal of Applied Psychology, 77,* 427–436.

Pierce, J.L., Rubenfeld, S.A., & Morgan, S. (1991). Employee ownership: A conceptual model of process and effects. *Academy of Management Journal, 16,* 121–144.

Rousseau, D.M. (1997). Organizational behavior in the new organizational era. *Annual Review of Psychology, 48,* 515–546.

Saunier, A.M., & Hawk, E.J. (1994). Realizing the potential of teams through team-based rewards. *Compensation and Benefits Review* [Special issue], 24–33.

Schay, B. (1997) . Paying for performance: Lessons learned in fifteen years of federal demonstration projects. In H. Risher & C.H. Fay (Eds.), *New strategies for public pay: Rethinking government compensation* (pp. 253–272). San Francisco: Jossey-Bass.

Schuster, J.R., & Zingheim, P.R (1992). *The new pay.* San Francisco: New Lexington Press.

Shaw, D.G., & Schneier, C.E. (1995). Team measurement and rewards: How some companies are getting it right. *Human Resource Planning* 19, 201–220.

Snell, S.A., & Dean, J.W., Jr. (1994). Strategic compensation for integrated manufacturing: The moderating effects of jobs and organizational inertia. *Academy of Management Journal, 37,* 1109–1140.

Snell, S.A., &Youndt, M.A. (1995). Human resource management and firm performance: Testing a contingency model of executive controls. *Journal of Management, 21,* 711–737.

Snell, S.A., Youndt, M.A., & Wright, P.M. (1996). Establishing a framework for research in strategic human resource management: Merging resource theory and organizational learning. In G.R. Ferris (Ed.), *Research in personnel and human resources management* (Vol. 14, pp. 61–90). Greenwich, CT: JAI Press.

Tsui, A.S., Pearce, J.L., Porter, L.W, & Tripoli, A.M. (1997) . Alternative approaches to the employee-organization relationship: Does investment in employees pay off? *Academy of Management Journal, 40,* 1089–1121.

Tully, S. (1998, October 26). A better taskmaster than the market? *Fortune,* 277–286.

von Hippel, C., Mangum, S.L., Greenberger, D.B., Heneman, R.L., & Skoglind, J.D. (1997). Temporary employment: Can organizations and employees both win? *Academy of Management Executive,11,* 92–103.

Vroom, V.H. (1964). *Work and motivation.* New York: Wiley.

Wageman, R. (1995). Interdependence and group effectiveness. *Administrative Science Quarterly, 40,* 145–180.

Wagner, J.A., III. (1995). Studies of individualism-collectivism: Effects on cooperation in groups. *Academy of Management Journal, 38,* 152–172.

Weitzman, M.L., & Kruse, D.L. (1990) . Profit sharing and productivity, In A.S. Binder (Ed.), *Paying for productivity: A Look at the evidence* (pp. 95–142). Washington, DC: Brookings Institution.

Welbourne, T.M., & Andrews, A.O. (1996). Predicting the performance of initial public offerings: Should human resource management in the equation? *Academy of Management Journal, 39,* 891–919.

Welbourne, T.M., Balkin, D.B., & Gomez-Mejia, L.R. (1995). Gainsharing and mutual monitoring: A combined agency-organizational justice interpretation. *Academy of Management Journal, 38,* 881–899.

Whetten, D.A., & Cameron, K.S. (1994). Organizational effectiveness: Old models and new constructs. In J. Greenberg (Ed.), *Organizational behavior: The state of the science* (pp. 135–154) . Mahwah, NJ: Erlbaum.

Wilson, T.B. (1995). *Innovative reward systems for the changing workplace.* New York: McGraw-Hill.

Wright, P.M., & Snell, S.A. (1998). Toward a unifying framework for exploring fit and flexibility in strategic human resource management. *Academy of Management Journal, 23,* 756–772.

CHAPTER 3

PERFORMANCE-BASED PAY PLANS

Robert L. Heneman and Maria T. Gresham

Source: Heneman, R.L., & Gresham, M.T. (1998). Performance-Based Pay Plans. In J.W. Smither (Ed.) *Performance Appraisal: State-of-the Art Methods for Performance Management* (pp. 496–536), Society for Industrial and Organizational Psychology Professional Practice Series. San Francisco: Jossey-Bass. Reprinted by permission of Jossey-Bass, Inc., a subsidiary of John Wiley & Sons.

A revolution is taking place in compensation and incentive systems. Many organizations today are reengineering their compensation and incentive systems to link pay to achieving organizational strategies. New pay-for-performance plans are used to compensate employee performance at all levels in the organization. These new reward systems are now referred to as *alternative rewards* (McAdams & Hawk, 1995), the *new pay* (Schuster & Zingheim, 1992), and *strategic pay* (Lawler, 1990). In this chapter they will be collectively be referred to as *performance-based pay plans*.

The purpose of this chapter is to show how organizations can most effectively make the link between performance appraisal and compensation and incentive systems. This requires an understanding of the need for performance-based pay, the compensation context, types of reward systems, design issues, and implementation issues. Each of these topics will be addressed in turn.

THE NEED FOR PERFORMANCE-BASED PAY

Although there has been explosive growth in performance-based pay plans (Lawler, Mohrman, & Ledford, 1995), not all employees prefer pay increases based on performance. For example, research has shown that exempt employees tend to be more in favor of performance-based pay plans than nonexempt employees. Nonexempt employees tend to favor pay based on seniority and cost of living (Heneman, 1992). As a result, a critical starting point for the linking of pay to performance is to assess whether this concept is a viable method of pay for organizations.

The thesis of this chapter is that pay-for-performance plans are not only desirable but are a necessity in most organizations. Traditional pay plans, which reward people for the value of their job and time in the job, are a huge expenditure for organizations, but have not been a source of above-average returns. Traditional pay plans simply reward employees for the status quo as depicted in job descriptions that are often static and fail to capture behaviors outside the boundaries of the job that are critical to organizational effectiveness (Ilgen & Hollenbeck, 1991). Incentives have traditionally been provided only to a small and elite portion of the labor force, usually executives and sales representatives. As competition in product and service markets intensifies in domestic and international markets, bureaucratic organizations that perpetuate the status quo are finding it very difficult to compete (Lawler, 1990). For a company to gain a competitive advantage, employees must be empowered to be more flexible in their jobs. The accomplishment of results must be emphasized over mere participation in activities, and there must be continual upgrading of employee knowledge, skills, abilities, and competencies. It is our contention that these objectives are more likely to be met with performance-based pay plans than with traditional pay plans.

It should be noted that the use of performance-based pay plans often requires some fundamental changes in the way organizations are managed. Operational and financial information previously reviewed only by management may need to be shared with employees. Along with open information, management may need to empower employees to make decisions previously made by management such as deciding which performance standards are to be used to assess performance. Management may also need to provide much more support to employees in the form of training and development opportunities for employees to be successful in a performance-based environment.

Opponents of pay-based reward systems point to many flaws with performance-based pay plans, suggesting that they may actually detract from organizational effectiveness. While these flaws are very interesting and certainly do arise upon occasion, empirical research usually shows little support for these positions. Criticisms of performance-based pay plans and rebuttals to these claims are shown in Table 1.

Table 1. Criticisms of Performance Based Pay

Criticism	Empirical Rebuttal
• Performance-based pay doesn't work in other cultures.	• Performance-based pay has been used for years in Russia (Gaga & Kaz, 1996) and is now being tried in Japan (Pollack, 1993).
• Performance-based pay doesn't work with unionized employees.	• About 25 percent of union contracts have performance-based pay clauses (Heneman, von Hippel, Eskew, & Greenberger, 1996).
• Performance-based pay leads to decreased intrinsic motivation (Deci, 1972; Kohn, 1993).	• Performance-based pay does not decrease intrinsic motivation (Scott, Farh, & Podsakoff, 1988; Montemayer, 1995; Podolske, 1996; Eisenberger & Cameron, 1996).
• Individual performance-based pay is inconsistent with total quality management (Deming, 1986).	• TQM organizations see greater rather than less importance for individual performance-based pay (Risher, 1992; Knouse, 1995).

In conclusion, the preponderance of current research suggests that the concept of pay-for-performance has an important role to play in the operation of organizations. Later in this chapter, this conclusion will be further bolstered by reviewing the research literature on the effectiveness of various plans. While we support the concept of pay-for-performance, we are very aware that the implementation of this concept is very difficult. Our hope is that we can show the important steps needed to use these plans successfully. There have been highly publicized cases where pay for-performance plans have had devastating consequences when not properly designed and implemented (Wright, 1994). Notable examples here include Sears and Salomon Brothers. At Sears, quotas with incentives were set for mechanics to complete a certain number of jobs in a day. It appears that mechanics cut corners to save time, resulting in poor quality repairs (Lorant, 1992). At Salomon Brothers, a performance-based pay system with limitless bonuses pitted executives against each other and may have promoted unethical behavior (Norris, 1991). Although horror stories like these do occur, the preponderance of the empirical evidence points to success with performance-based pay plans.

PAY CONTEXT

The fundamental building block in traditional pay systems is the job (Ash, Levine, & Sistrunk, 1983). The process of job analysis is used to define the job and the job is summarized in a job description that lists the duties and responsibilities of the job and a job specification that lists the knowledge, skills, abilities, and other factors required to perform the job. Wages and salaries are determined on the basis of the value of the job. In turn, the magnitude of the wage or salary determines the size of the benefits and incentives received. Value is established by assessing the internal value of the job through a process known as job evaluation and by assessing the external value of the job through market surveys (Milkovich & Newman, 1996). Hence, under a traditional plan, the job directly determines direct pay and indirectly determines benefits and incentives received.

Another fundamental building block in a traditional pay system is a pay range that spells out the minimum, midpoint, and maximum pay rates for each collection of jobs with similar value to the organization known as a pay grade. The minimum value is the lowest wage or salary that the organization will pay to people holding a particular job. The range is designed such that the legally required minimum wage is paid, but also so that the job holder is being equitably paid relative to others in different pay grades. The midpoint is usually set at or around the market average to make the jobs in the pay grade competitive with the external market. The maximum of the pay range is the maximum level that the organization is willing to pay for the contribution of this job to the organization. Even if a person has above-average credentials, the maximum he or she can earn is at this level because the duties performed only add so much value regardless of the job holder, and the organization.

In traditional organizations, movement within a pay grade is based on seniority. Each year on the job, a permanent pay increase is granted based upon position in range. Employees near the bottom of the pay range receive a larger pay adjustment than employees at the top of the pay range. Employees at the bottom of the range receive more so that they move up to the market average quickly and do not leave the organization for a job at another organization paying at the market average. Employees at the top of the pay range receive smaller increases so that they do not exceed the maximum of the pay grade.

In terms of individual pay increases, performance assessment can be used in addition to, or in replacement of, seniority as the basis to determine movement in the pay range. The better the performance of the individual, the better the pay increase or bonus. As with seniority, however, for purposes of retention and cost minimization, good performers lower in the pay grade may receive larger increases than good performers higher in the pay grade.

Performance-based pay systems provide an additional fundamental building block to the pay system. The building block is an *assessment of performance* that in turn can influence the size of the pay budget and the method used to determine pay increases. In terms of the budget, performance of the organization can increase the size of the budget available for pay increases in a given year. In effect this budget may increase the levels of the minimum, midpoint, and maximum wages of the pay range. In turn, employees are eligible for larger raises. If the organization does not want to incur any additional fixed costs in the budget, then good performance by the organization can he passed along in the form of a one-time bonus to employees that does not become a permanent addition to their wage or salary.

Performance-based pay systems also challenge the building blocks of traditional pay systems in several ways. First, pay may be increased on the basis of accomplishments not spelled out in the traditional job description. For example, someone may receive an increase or a bonus on the basis of being a member of a cross-functional task force. Second, pay may be increased on the basis of the mastery of new skills or competencies not spelled out in the traditional job description. Third, pay may be allocated on the basis of team accomplishments rather than individual accomplishments. Fourth, pay may be allocated on the basis of the results that are produced rather than the activities undertaken. Fifth, pay may be allocated on the basis of cost savings or organizational improvements. Finally, pay increases may be in the form of bonuses, benefits, or nonmonetary rewards rather than wage or salary adjustments. Moreover, these payouts may be more substantial in size than usual because they are not part of the base wage or salary and do not therefore push the base pay near or above the maximum pay level for the pay range.

In short, performance-based pay plans force organizations to clearly define effective performance and to determine what factors are likely to lead to effective performance (Campbell, 1990). Rewards are then provided for the accomplishment of those outcomes that constitute effective performance and the successful development of those factors that are likely to lead to the accomplishment of these outcomes. As will be seen in the next section, organizational results that are rewarded include so-called hard measures of performance such as costs, revenues, and profits. Factors that lead to these results and may also be rewarded include critical behaviors such as customer service, teamwork, and attention to quality, as well as underlying capabilities such as skills and knowledge. These criteria are very different from the traditional criteria of job duties and seniority. They serve as additions to duties and seniority in order to motivate improved performance. They do not always replace duties and seniority because duties and seniority may be needed to build equity, commitment, and retention in the organization.

TYPES OF PAY AND PERFORMANCE PLANS

A multitude of different pay and performance plans exist. As shown in Table 2, they vary along two dimensions: performance measure and measurement level. *Performance measure* refers to the type of measurement that is used by the organization to assess the contribution of the employee to the organization. *Measurement* refers to the level at which employee performance is measured. At the individual level, the performance directly attributed to the employee is measured. At the team or group level, performance attributable to the entire work group is measured. At the organizational level, performance attributed to the entire organization is assessed. Parenthetically it should be noted that pay is given the individual even if performance is measured at the group organization level.

Table 2.   Performance-Based Pay Plan Typology

| | Measurement Level | | |
Performance Measure	Individual	Group	Organization
Behaviors	• Merit pay	• Team-based merit pay	
Knowledge and Skills	• Skill-based pay • Competency-based pay		
Output	• Piece-rate pay	• Group incentives	
Time Savings	• Standard hour plan	• Standard hour plan	• Gainsharing: Improshare
Cost Reduction and Revenue Enhancement	• Employee suggestion systems	• Team recognition	• Gainsharing: Scanlon Plan • Gainsharing: Ruckers Plan • Gainsharing: Goalsharing
Sales	• Commissions	• Sales teams	
Profit			• Profit sharing • Stock ownership • Executive pay

Plan types corresponding to the level of each dimension are entered into the cells in Table 2. These are pure types of each plan that are helpful for illustrative purposes. In reality, many of these pure plan types are being blended together, as will be discussed in a later section.

A brief description and analysis of each plan will be presented based in part on materials from the American Compensation Association (1996a). The operational details of the various plans are spelled out in the body of literature listed in Table 3.

Table 3.   Sources of Detailed Descriptions of Pay Plan Types

Author (Date)	Book Title
Belcher (1991)	Gainsharing
Graham-Moore and Ross (1990)	Gainsharing
Gross (1995)	Compensation for Teams
Heneman (1992)	Merit Pay: Linking Pay Increases Performance Ratings
McAdams (1996)	The Reward Plan Advantage
Milkovich and Newman (1996)	Compensation
Nelson (1994)	1001 Ways to Reward Employees
Schuster and Zingheim (1992)	The New Pay
Wilson (1995)	Innovative Reward Systems for the Changing Workplace

Merit Pay

Merit pay has been referred to as the "grandfather" of all pay-for-performance plans (Milkovich & Newman, 1996). Over 80 percent of organizations use some form of merit pay (Peck, 1984.) Merit pay provides a pay increase to employees for their individual behavioral contributions to the organization. Performance is usually assessed on an annual basis using a multidimensional graphic rating scale. Occasionally, more advanced measures of employee behaviors such as Behavioral Observation Scales (BOS) or Management by Objectives (MBO) are used. Once merit pay ratings have been generated and an overall score for each employee determined; the rater then uses a merit pay matrix to make a pay increase decision for each employee. A merit pay matrix shows the range of pay increase percentages that can be granted for each level of performance and each position in the pay range. The pay increase is granted as a percentage of base pay. The increase can be granted as a permanent base pay increase or as a lump-sum bonus not built into base pay. Average merit pay increases are usually set at the level of the cost of living or the level of the average pay increase for unionized employees. In the 1990s, average merit increases have been about 3 percent to 4 percent.

Merit pay works well when behaviors that contribute to the effective functioning of the firm are rewarded. Behaviors critical to organizational effectiveness include innovation, empowerment, and customer service. Behaviors rather than results are especially important to measure when the results are outside of the control of employees. Employees would be unfairly penalized, for example, in a retail establishment when sales declined as a function of a decline in the economy rather than poor sales behaviors.

Merit pay plans have been criticized because they may promote an entitlement culture and because they fail to differentiate between high and low performers. The perception of merit pay systems is multidimensional, consisting of performance assessments and merit pay allocation. Fairness in performance assessments and the distribution of merit pay is important if merit pay systems are to work effectively (Montemayer, 1994). To prevent problems, organizations must be willing to grant no increase to employees who are not performing up to standard. By doing so, a pay increase is not automatic and additional money can be allocated to high performers to distinguish their contributions.

Team-Based Merit Pay

Another criticism of merit pay is that it leads to competition rather than cooperation. Employees are pitted against one another to compete for a limited fund. Paying for individual performance strikes some companies as too difficult. In response, team-based merit pay has supplemented traditional merit pay plans by making teamwork a performance standard that is now evaluated by team members and the supervisor. By including the teamwork criterion in individual performance appraisals, individuals cannot reach for their own goals at the expense of others. Dimensions of teamwork that have been identified by a review of the psychological literature (Stevens & Campion, 1994) and case studies in industry (Katzenbach & Smith, 1993) include dedication to a common purpose, sense of mutual accountability, mutual respect and support, technical and functional expertise, collaborative problem-solving skills, interpersonal skills, cooperation, trust-based relationships, conflict resolution, communications, goal setting and performance management, and planning and task coordination (Heneman & von Hippel, 1995). Team-based merit pay is combined with individual merit pay by adding criteria such as these to the evaluation form to supplement individual criteria such as output quality and quantity. An example of this approach is Johnsonville Foods, where the coach (supervisor) and job incumbent evaluate the job incumbent's contribution to groups, communication, willingness to work together, and attendance and timeliness at group meetings (Stayer, 1990). Other organizations such as AT&T, Xerox, and Motorola use a 360-degree review process to assess the evaluations of the individual to the team. That is, peers are used along with the job incumbent and supervisor to assess team contributions.

Skill-Based Pay

The focus of skill-based pay is on the underlying ability, skill, and knowledge possessed by employees rather than their manifest behavior. Pay increases are based upon skill mastery. Administer such a program requires the organization to define the skills required of employees in certain positions. Skill sets are described with great precision rather than relying upon general skill designations such as education levels or experience levels. Skill sets are also very job specific. Peers and supervisors are usually used to certify that the employee has mastered the required skills. Skill certification should include not only the mastery of knowledge but successful demonstration of that knowledge back on the job. Once the skill has been certified, a pay increase is granted.

Skill-based pay is used by organizations to enhance organizational learning and to promote flexibility. Employees learn new and better methods of conducting their work and become cross-trained so that they can pitch in and do whatever work is required even if it is outside their traditional job descriptions.

A major problem with skill-based pay is the substantial expense associated with this plan in the form of direct costs (increased pay) and indirect costs (training). The skill-based pay system may enhance flexibility in the workforce. However, higher labor costs may ensue if most or all employees are certified to receive top pay. Employers can avoid this possibility by controlling the rate at which employees can be certified, requiring that new skills must be used on the current job, or hiring fewer people. Skill-based pay only makes financial sense when the efficiencies of flexibility outweighs the increased costs.

Early examples of skill-based pay plans can be found at General Mills, Northern Telecom, and Honeywell (Ledford, 1991). General Mills put its plan in at a new manufacturing facility with continuous process technology and a high level of employee involvement. Skill blocks were formed based on steps in the production process. Ratings of skill mastery were obtained by peers. Northern Telecom used skill-based pay for service technicians. Skill blocks were developed for specific job families. Skill block mastery was certified by supervisors, a management review committee, and human resources. Honeywell used skill-based pay in a new assembly plant with high-involvement work practices. Generic skill sets were developed across different work areas. Skill mastery was assessed by supervisors with input from team leaders, engineers and peers. The wide range of skill-based pay practices can be seen from these examples.

Competency-Based Pay

Skill-based pay has been extended to competency-based pay. In addition to rewarding the acquisition of knowledge, skills, and abilities as with skill-based pay, competency-based pay also rewards other underlying attributes of performance including motivation and personality traits. Caution must be exercised with this approach due to the difficulty of measuring motivation (Lawler, 1996) and the legal problems associated with the measurement of employee traits for purposes of performance appraisal (Nathan & Cascio, 1986). It is, however, an important advancement in performance-based rewards because performance is actually modeled in terms of its determinants (Campbell, 1990). That is, job performance is broken down into its basic components rather than simply being viewed as an end result. Components of job performance include declarative knowledge (facts, principles, goals, self-knowledge), procedural knowledge and skills (cognitive, psychomotor, self-management, interpersonal), and motivation (choice to perform, level of effort, persistence of effort) (Campbell, 1990). Many performance-based reward systems simply measure end results and hope that employees know how to get there. Competency pay directs employees how to achieve results rather than assuming that the paths to success are readily apparent. As a starting point, firms are developing competency dictionaries to guide organizations on the development of competencies associated with organizational effectiveness. However, Zingheim, Ledford, and Schuster (1996) and Lawler (1996) suggest that while dictionaries are helpful, it is the definitions of those competencies that are specific to the business strategy of the organization that help a firm achieve a competitive advantage. Highly successful companies develop their own competency sets consistent with their strategic plans. For example, the Limited is a $10 billion retailer of specialty items. One of the competencies assessed at the Limited is "fashion sense." This competency is defined in very specific behavioral terms appropriate to the culture and history of the organization. This type of approach helps organizations derive sustained competitive advantage because the competencies are not easily imitated by other companies (Barney, 1991).

Piece-Rate Pay

Under this plan, pay is provided for individual output above a pre-defined standard. Pay increases are in the form of a pay bonus rather than a permanent adjustment to base pay. Output is usually determined on the basis of individual productivity where productivity is defined by output divided by input. In manufacturing, productivity may be measured, for example, as parts produced divided by number of hours for each employee. In the service sector, a bank for example, productivity may be assessed as number of checks processed divided by number of hours for each employee. If productivity enhancement is the organizational goal, piece-rate systems align as an appropriate reward system assuming that individual productivity can be assessed and that employee effort, more than technology, influences productivity. Problems do exist with piece-rate plans. They may discourage quality because the amount of output rather than the quality of output is counted. Teamwork may also be jeopardized because employees compete against another to receive the largest reward. Time spent on assisting others in being productive detracts from one's own productivity, and as a result piece-rate pay plans can have a dampening effect on teamwork.

Standard Hour Plan

This approach sets pay standards based on the time per unit of output. Standard hour plans place the incentive rate based on the completion of a task in some expected time period (Wagner & Hollenbeck, 1992). If tasks can be completed in less than the designated time, then employees will receive a higher hourly wage than those employees who do not complete the tasks in less than the designated time. Task completion can be measured at the individual or group level. Standard hour plans are more suitable for complex, nonrepetitive tasks that require numerous skills for completion (Milkovich & Newman, 1996).

Group Incentives

When work is designed such that the group produces an identifiable output and where it is difficult to assess the contribution of individual team members, then group incentives can be offered for output. As with piece-rate pay, incentives are paid out for production above a certain standard. The incentive is usually divided up equally among group members. This approach works well if it can be assumed that all members of the team contributed equally to the final point of service.

Suggestion Systems

Under this approach rewards are offered to individual employees for individual suggestions that produce actual cost savings. Rewards are also sometimes provided for new products or services that enhance revenues, but these rewards are built into suggestion systems far less frequently than are rewards for cost-reduction suggestions. Rewards are usually a fixed amount per successfully implemented suggestion or a percentage of the labor cost savings. Suggestions are usually reviewed by top management or an appointed committee. These plans would seem to motivate individuals to carefully guard their ideas lather than share them with others and this may be a problem in team-based environments. Criteria for selecting winning suggestions must be clearly stated so that employees understand, for example, why a money saving idea that conflicts with the mission statement may win nothing.

Team Recognition Plans

Suggestion systems can be elevated to the team level, where teams of employees compete against one another for rewards. In some organizations with team recognition plans a monetary prize is offered; in most, a nonmonetary recognition award is offered. Rewards are usually granted on the basis of the team that comes up with a more efficient way to produce their product or service. Unlike employee suggestion systems, the team is given the reward rather than the individual. Both individual suggestion systems and team recognition plans motivate employees to think outside the confines of the job description.

Gainsharing

An organizational-level pay intervention that takes many forms is known as gainsharing. There have been several generations of these plans, with each generation emphasizing different performance measures (Wallace, 1990). The first generation consisted of Scanlon and Ruckers plans, both of which provided rewards for cost savings. Second generation plans— known as Improshare—emphasized time savings. Third-generation plans, sometimes called goalsharing, performance sharing, and win sharing, emphasized revenue enhancement along with cost or time savings. Cost savings were also expanded to include costs other than labor (for example, materials). Revenue enhancement measures include customer service and quality. As can be seen by the measures used, earlier plans emphasized the reduction of inputs to increase productivity (the ratio of outputs to inputs). Later plans emphasized the reduction of inputs and the increase of outputs in the form of revenues. One of the desirable features of these plans is that they can pay for themselves. Bonuses are not allocated unless productivity increases.

Productivity is enhanced under these plans by joint committees of employees (labor union representatives in unionized organizations) and managers. These committees solicit suggestions from employees on ways to decrease costs (and increase revenues in plans that deal with both sides of the ratio), screen the suggestions for the best ones, help implement the suggestions, and administer the pay system. Hence there is a heavy component of employee empowerment in these reward plans. Payouts under these plans are set such that both employees and management gain. Cost savings and increased revenues are split between the parties so that employees' efforts are rewarded and management can reinvest money in the organization for further improvements.

Equal percentage payouts are usually granted to employees regardless of individual contributions in terms of suggestions or committee participation. This approach is intended to foster a spirit of teamwork and camaraderie among employees. It may also, however, foster feelings of resentment and inequity on the part of those employees whose individual contributions are the greatest. Corning Technologies presents an excellent example of a third-generation gainsharing plan (Altmansberger & Wallace, 1995). Labeled *goalsharing*, it was implemented in partnership with the American Flint Glass Workers Union (AFGWU), AFLCIO, and other unions. The plan was first instituted in 1988 to improve quality, and it now covers fifteen thousand manufacturing and nonmanufacturing employees. It consists of sixty different goalsharing plans. Plans vary by performance measure. For example, the first plan initiated bases payouts on cost per unit, process loss, quality, and customer service. Both attitudinal and financial data gathered by Corning Technologies suggest that the plan has had a positive impact.

Sales Commissions and Team Sales Plans

Traditional sales plans are very similar to piece-rate pay plans. Sales outputs are rewarded with a commission. Sales outputs include new accounts, revenues, and profits. There are two problems with traditional sales commissions. First, making the sale becomes more important than customer service if sales quantity is rewarded rather than sales quality. In response to this situation, an educational distribution company established sales teams consisting of sales people, support staff, and customers. The teams design—with management input—measures of both sales quantity and quality to be rewarded. By using this approach, a premium is placed on customer service. In the absence of an emphasis on customer service, long-term customer retention is a problem.

A second problem with traditional sales commissions is that sales output measures tend to be contaminated. For example, some products sell better than others and some sales territories have better customers than others. As a result, care must be taken to adjust the sales output standards for sales representatives to reflect the demand for their products or services and to reflect the territory they serve relative to other sales representatives.

Profit Sharing and Stock Sharing

The profit sharing approach is a group incentive pay plan that uses profitability as the standard for organizational-level incentives. There are three primary types of profit sharing plans. First, full payment plans allocate rewards to employees soon after profits have been determined. Second, deferred payment plans credit an employee's account, paying cash at the time of retirement. Finally, some plans involve a combination of the immediate and deferred methods. Employee stock ownership plans are not considered performance-based pay plans because they reward membership in the organization rather than performance.

Stock-sharing is another approach to group incentive-based pay created through employee stock ownership plans. Providing employees with the ability to buy company stock at a reduced rate per share is one method of stock sharing.

Under profit sharing and stock sharing, rewards are distributed to employees on the basis of the financial performance of the entire organization. Financial measures of performance of the firm include returns on assets, economic value-added formulas, and earnings per share. With profit sharing, cash rewards are distributed on an annual basis. With stock sharing, stock is distributed as a reward.

A goal of both approaches is to foster employee identification with the goals of the organization at large. Profit sharing fosters identification with short-term organizational goals, while stock sharing fosters identification with long-term interests of the organization. The downside to both of these plans is that the "line of sight," especially for lower-level employees, is unclear between individual employee behavior and organizational performance. Consequently, the motivational value of these reward programs may be diminished.

To improve the line of sight at 3M, profit sharing for manages is a tiered system where profit is measured not only at the organizational level but at the division and group levels as well (Milkovich & Newman, 1996). Other methods to shorten the line of sight include providing employees with financial data, the training needed to interpret financial data, and the authority to act on financial data. In the absence of these important steps, employees may become very frustrated with profit sharing because it asks them risk their bonus on factors outside their control.

Executive Pay

Profit sharing and stock sharing for the top level of the organization form what is known as executive pay. While cash bonuses are issued for successful organizational performance under this plan, most of the reward is issued in the form of company stock in order to ensure that executives' activities are consistent with the shareholders' interest, and to encourage executives to tend to the long-term performance of the organization. The line-of-sight problem previously described is less of an issue with executives as they make strategic decisions, which indeed influence organization performance and shareholder value. It should be noted, however, that the line-of-sight problem does not disappear with executive pay. Many factors, such as the state of the economy, still lie outside the control of executives. As a result, boards of directors might consider evaluating executive performance on the basis of individual behavior (much like merit pay plans), as well as organizational results. Behaviors evaluated might include development and execution of strategic and operational plans. Interestingly, a recent development is the use of stock options for members of the board of directors. Traditionally, cash bonuses have been provided, but increasingly stock is being issued to ensure that the long-term interests of the company are represented by the board.

PAY AND PERFORMANCE PLAN EFFECTIVENESS

Many empirical studies and literature reviews have been conducted on the effectiveness of pay and performance plan effectiveness. This literature is summarized in Table 4. Several important general themes emerge from this literature. Unlike other areas of human resource research, a large number of studies have been amassed on the impact of performance-based plans on actual productivity. In general, the results are very impressive for

Table 4.   Evaluation of Various Performance-Based Pay Plans

Plan	Frequent of Use	Average Productivity Increase	Attitudinal Reactions	Benchmark Companies
Merit pay	Large and declining	Too few studies to tell	Positive pay satisfaction and job satisfaction	Hewlett-Packard, Motorola
Piece-rate and sales	Moderate and steady	Large	Few studies, mainly case studies; dated	Lincoln Electric
Gainsharing	Small and rapidly increasing	Moderate	Positive job satisfaction	Herman Miller, General Electric
Profit sharing and stock ownership	Small and moderately increasing	Small	Too few studies to tell	3M, PepsiCo
Skill-based pay and competency-based pay	Small and moderately increasing	Too few studies to tell	Positive employer reactions; employee reactions unknown	Procter & Gamble

Sources: Kruse (1993); Blinder (1990); McAdams and Hawk (1995); Heneman (1992); Lawler, Mohrman, and Ledford (1995); Welbourne and Gomez-Mejia (1995); Blasi, Conte, and Kruse (1996); Gerhart and Milkovich (1992); Lawler and Jenkins (1992); Jenkins, Ledford, Gupta, and Doty (1992); Schuster (1989); Peck (1989, 1991); O'Dell (1987).

the magnitude of the impact of performance-based pay relative to other human resource interventions such as employee empowerment (Locke, Feren, McCaleb, Shaw, & Denny, 1980).

Actual productivity gains associated with each type of plan seem to vary by the purpose of the pay plan type. Productivity gains are substantial (averaging around 20 percent) for plans such as piece-rate that emphasize specific short-term results. Plans that are designed to foster identification with the organization, such as profit sharing, have smaller productivity gains (averaging around 5 percent). Plans such as gainsharing that have specific goals at the business unit level (and thus attempt to motivate individual performance through the group) have moderate productivity gains (averaging about 10 percent). Unfortunately, the most frequently used performance-based pay plan, merit pay, has undergone too few studies to allow us to reach any meaningful conclusions regarding productivity. A similar problem exists with the most recent innovations in performance-based pay, skill-based and competency pay.

With the exception of merit pay and to a lesser extent gainsharing, there is very little data available on employee reactions to performance-based pay. Merit pay has repeatedly been shown to be related in a positive manner to both job and pay satisfaction. Gainsharing has been repeatedly shown to be positively related to job satisfaction, but for the most part is missing data on the relationship with pay satisfaction. Very few studies have looked at employee reactions to piece-rate pay, profit sharing, and stock sharing. Only employer perceptions, which are favorable, have been reported for skill-based and competency-based pay. This summary of attitudinal data points to the crying need for additional research. Perhaps employers could band together in a consortium to further explore reactions to performance-based pay plans. An excellent model to follow here is the Mayflower group, a consortium of employers that has built a large descriptive database on employee attitudes across organizations (Johnson, 1996). Development of a database such as this for attitudinal reactions to pay would provide organizations with norms to compare themselves against. Such an effort is important as employee reactions toward pay have been shown to be related to absenteeism, turnover, and union vote (Heneman, 1985).

In terms of frequency of use, many employers appear to have become disillusioned with merit pay. Factors that may contribute to this disillusionment include small merit budgets (3 percent to 4 percent) in recent years, the use of poorly developed rating instruments, and the treatment of pay increases under traditional merit plans as a fixed rather than variable cost. On the other hand, gainsharing has taken off in popularity. The increased popularity of these plans may be due to the increased use of teams in organizations and to the emphasis in many of these plans on cost reductions.

Overall, it is difficult to say whether performance-based pay plans affect attitudes, productivity, or both attitudes and productivity. Unfortunately, within any of the pay plan types, researchers have focused on either attitudes or productivity. Future researchers and organizations evaluating the effectiveness of their performance-based pay plans need to gather both sets of evidence. We hope that this can become the norm as newly created performance-based pay plans are more frequently used and evaluated.

DESIGN ISSUES

Integration with Business Strategy and Organizational Culture

When designing a reward plan, careful consideration must be given to matching the reward plan with the objectives of the business and the culture of the organization. As can be seen in Figure 1, business strategy and organizational culture affect the selection of performance criteria. These criteria reflect the goals that the organization strives toward, and the culture needed to meet these organizational goals.

The reward plan must also be consistent with these factors. Plans that match with various business objectives are shown in Table 5. Plans consistent with different cultures are shown in Table 6. Culture refers to the shared set of beliefs and values held by members of the organization (Ott, 1989). Traditional cultures emphasize top-down decision making, vertical communications, and clearly defined jobs while involvement cultures emphasize shared decision making, lateral communications, and loosely defined roles (Lawler, 1990).

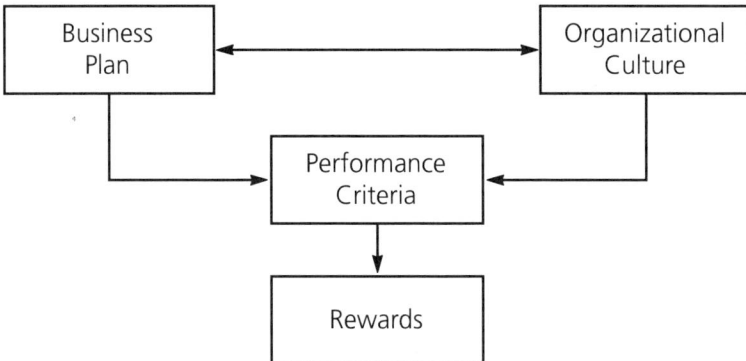

Figure 1.   Reward plan design model.

Table 5.   Matching Reward Plans with Business Objectives

Business Objective	Reward Plan
Employee development	Competency-based pay Skill-based pay
Customer service	Merit pay Competency-based pay Gainsharing
Productivity: Individual	Piece-rate Sales Standard hour
Productivity: Group	Gainsharing Standard hour Group incentives
Teamwork	Team recognition Team sales Team-based merit pay Gainsharing
Quality	Merit pay Gainsharing Competency-based pay
Profit	Executive pay Profit or stock sharing
Cost reduction and Revenue enhancement	Gainsharing Employee suggestion systems

Table 6.   Matching Reward Plans with Organizational Culture

Plans for Traditional Cultures

- Merit pay
- Piece-rate pay
- Standard hour plans
- Sales commissions
- Employee suggestion systems
- Executive pay

Plans for Involvement Cultures

- Team-based merit pay
- Team recognition plans
- Gainsharing
- Profit sharing
- Executive pay
- Stock sharing
- Skill-based pay
- Competency-based pay
- Team sales and recognition
- Group incentives

Ameritech offers an excellent example of linking performance criteria to the business plan (Heneman & von Hippel, 1996). Core competencies of the business, spelled out in the business plan, are taken directly from the business plan and then used to establish performance criteria for evaluating employees on each competency. For example, customer service is a core business competency. In turn, it is used to establish dimensions of customer service performance such as "Personalizes Customer Contacts." Ultimately, behavioral indicators of each performance dimension serve as performance criteria for customer service representatives. For example, behavioral indicators of personalized customer contact include "Treats each customer as an individual with individual needs," "Incorporates customer information in conversations," and "Recognizes different personality types and responds appropriately."

Several organizations are known for having appraisal and reward systems tied to the culture of the organization (Heneman, Waldeck, & Cushnie, 1996). Performance standards at US West and Levi Strauss, for example, are based on diversity criteria and in turn these criteria are related to the respective business plans (Mitchell & O'Neal, 1994). At Hoechst Celanese, performance relative to diversity criteria is also used to determine pay increases (Rice, 1994).

The absence of a match between the reward system, culture, and business objectives can create problems (Lawler & Jenkins, 1992). For example, organizations with a traditional culture that want to improve productivity through team-based pay may be in, for a shock. Productivity gains hoped for with teams may not be instantaneous because an involvement culture is needed for teams to work. While team-based pay can be used to change the culture, it will take time. An example of an organization with a critical alignment of the business plan, culture, and reward system is Time Warner Cable in Columbus, Ohio. The senior author of this chapter was brought in at a transitional time in the company, when it was shifting from a traditional culture to an involvement culture to be more responsive to customer and employee needs. A new mission statement was developed that stated: "We are committed to becoming the premier multimedia company through our collective talents, quality service, innovation, and technology." To emphasize employee talents, a skill-based pay plan was put in place. To deliver quality service, innovation, and technology, team-based pay was used. To ease the transition from a traditional to employee involvement culture, the merit pay system was retained. As a result of these innovations and others, Warner Cable is one of the most profitable groups in the Time Warner cable system network.

This example from Time Warner also shows the reward system being used as a lag system (Lawler, 1981). That is, the reward system was used to reinforce the shift from a traditional to involvement culture. In other organizations, according to Lawler, the reward system is used as a lead system to move the culture from traditional to innovative. That is, the reward system is developed to bring about a change in the culture. In essence, pay as a lead system provides shock therapy to the organization to free it from the traditional culture. An example of a lead system is the educational system in Kentucky, which shifted from a time-in-grade pay system to a gainsharing plan where pay increases are based on improvements in student achievement scores at the school level. This approach was mandated by Kentucky state law (Odden & Kelley, 1997).

Performance-based pay plans should only be used for organizational change under limited circumstances. There should be a perceived need for change in the existing reward system and there must be the resources needed to bring about a change (Lawler, 1991). For example, in 1984 Baker Supermarket was rapidly losing market share to other grocery chains entering the Omaha market. As a result, management met with its seventeen hundred employees to communicate the urgency of the situation. Employees concerned about the situation (and the security of their jobs) asked how they could increase their productivity. Management and employees held a series of meetings to identify areas of operations in which sales might be increased. Once these ideas were communicated, employees had a better understanding of how to improve their performance, and profitability improved. ("Case History . . . ," 1986).

A final strategic consideration is the need for performance criteria to guide the selection of reward systems rather than using reward systems as a guide to the selection of performance criteria. Performance-based reward plans are popular these days and receive considerable publicity. As a result, a senior executive may say, "We should consider using a profit sharing plan like I read about in our trade association magazine." The human resource manager is likely to receive this suggestion as a command and look for profit measures (such as return on assets or economic value added) to guide pay decisions. A better approach would be for the human resource manager to say to the executive, "Do you realize that profit sharing conflicts with our corporate goal of increasing market share? What we really need to focus on is customer service to improve market share. Perhaps we should consider using competency-based pay to be consistent with our performance measure (customer service) and our corporate goal (market share)?"

The point being made in the previous example is that the performance measurement system needs to be developed prior to the pay mechanism. One only need look to the federal government for a case study on the problems that can arise when the pay mechanism is developed prior to the performance measurement system. The Civil Service Reform Act of 1978 shifted the basis of pay in the federal government from seniority to merit. This change was done with little consideration given to performance measurement and the plan led to very unfavorable reactions by all those employees affected, as documented in many studies (Perry, 1988).

Unfavorable reactions under this type of system change are very predictable from a fairness perspective (Greenberg, 1987). Performance standards should always be spelled out in advance of rewards so that employees know what is expected of them. In the case of the federal government, performance standards were never made clear due to the absence of a well-developed appraisal system. As a result, employees were not clear about what was expected of them and in turn, were unsure how to influence their pay.

Motivational Considerations

Rewards will have more motivational influence when the employee recognizes a direct relationship between activities, performance, results achieved, and rewards gained. A primary concern in the design of reward systems is how well the plan will work in motivating employees. The theory base behind this design consideration is *expectancy theory* (Heneman, 1992). According to this theory, a reward plan needs to have the following motivational properties: expectancy, instrumentality, and valence. *Expectancy* means that employees must see a link between their efforts and performance. *Instrumentality* means that performance must be seen as being linked to outcomes or consequences. *Valence* means that the outcomes or consequences must be attractive to employees. There are many outcomes other than cash that may have as much positive valence as cash, or more. Time off, for example, is often critical to employees and may be viewed as being more attractive than cash.

An important strategic decision that organizations must make in designing reward systems is how to best influence these motivational properties of expectancy, instrumentality, and valence. There are currently four major motivational philosophies to guide these decisions, as shown in Table 7.

The pure pay perspective is based on reinforcement theory and suggests that pay should be made contingent on specific and observable measures of performance (Heneman, 1992). Under this approach, performance must be very clearly defined for employees and a direct link made to their pay. If performance is not clearly defined, then undesirable consequences may occur. For example, if performance is solely defined as output, then quality may suffer. A pure pay perspective lends itself to the use of performance-based reward plans with countable indicators of performance as in a piece-rate pay plan. It should be noted that a pay plan of this type may need to be supplemented with a merit pay plan to compensate for the undesirable consequences of measuring countable indicators only. For example, at Lincoln Electric, merit pay is used along with piece-rate pay to reinforce both quantity and quality.

Table 7.   Matching Reward Plans with Motivational Philosophies

Motivational Philosophy	Reward Plan
Pure pay	Piece-rate
	Sales commissions
	Standard hour plan
	Executive pay
	Group incentives
Employee development	Skill-based pay
	Competency-based pay
	Merit pay
Participation	Profit sharing
	Stock sharing
	Gainsharing
	Employee suggestion plans
	Merit pay
Teamwork	Team-based merit pay
	Gainsharing
	Team-based sales
	Team recognition
	Group incentives

The employee development perspective is based on human capital theory (Becker, 1996). It suggests that rather than specifying outcomes for employees to pursue, inputs or human capital should be emphasized. Human capital consists of knowledge, skills, and abilities. From this perspective, pay should be provided for capabilities rather than results to serve as a motivational factor. The employee development perspective is used when the organization wishes to emphasize flexibility in its workforce. That is, it wants employees who are qualified to perform whatever work is needed at a particular time. A company with this perspective sees no need to shut down an assembly line when a stoppage occurs, for example, or to call in a specialist to fix it. Instead, employees on the line should have the competencies needed to immediately repair the line and keep the product moving. Thus, although it may seem unusual to pay for capability rather than actual results, it can be seen from this example how capabilities can be directly related to business results. Moreover, to make the link between capabilities and results even more clear, some organizations like Westinghouse define competencies in terms of observable behaviors and results.

The participation perspective suggests that employees should become active participants in decisions that affect the business and have traditionally been decided by managers (Lawler, 1995). Some pay plans like gainsharing make employee participation a cornerstone of they pay plan. Other reward plans like piece-rate pay rely on subject matter experts, involving industrial engineers and executives to make decisions. The motivational value from plans with participation is believed to come from the process of participation as well as the amount of pay received. Participation is motivational to employees because it gives them a sense of ownership to the work process as they have input into how it is to be best accomplished. That is, they can see a relationship between their efforts and company performance. Participation also helps the employees feel that the pay system is a fair one. Research has shown that in terms of pay fairness, not only is the amount of pay that people receive important, but so too is the manner in which the amount of pay was determined (Folger & Konovsky, 1989). Pay decisions are more likely to be viewed as fair when employees have input into the process used to determine pay increases than when pay decisions are unilaterally decided by management. Input might include, for example, employees and managers jointly setting performance standards.

A teamwork perspective suggests that employees are energized by their work with others (Gross, 1995). Team members work with one another to advance their collective aims and issue sanctions to group members who fail to comply. Under this approach the social aspects of work are believed to be motivating to people. To emphasize the importance of social-interactions, rewards are offered. This approach differs from the participation philosophy in that participation can be used regardless of whether work is designed for individuals or collections of individuals to perform.

As shown in Table 7, reward plans lend themselves to different motivational philosophies. Design teams need to fully consider these perspectives and their implications when designing the reward plan. Also, they need to consider these perspectives regarding their own functioning. Research has shown that a participatory approach to pay plan design seems to work best (McAdams & Hawk, 1995). A design team needs to have representation from all business units and levels of the organization for the results of its work to be acceptable to all those affected. Special expertise is also needed, including help from finance, operations, and human resources.

Performance Measurement Levels

Many performance constructs, productivity as an example, can be measured and rewarded at the level of the individual, group, or organization. The levels selected are of primary concern in the design of performance-based pay plans because there are distinct virtues and problems with measures at each level.

Measurement at the individual level has the distinct advantage of usually being under the control of the individual. As a result, it strengthens by expectancy and instrumentality links. The downside, however, is that employees may become so engrossed in their individual accomplishments that they ignore the larger goals of their team and organization.

Group- or team-level performance measures have the advantage of putting the goal of the team before that of the individual. This approach is often advocated in team environments. Unfortunately, some employees may take advantage of this system by "social loafing" or "free riding" (Heneman & von Hippel, 1995). That is, some employees may not put forth their best efforts because others in the group will carry the slackers to group goal accomplishment through their own extra-hard efforts.

When performance is measured at the organizational level, an important advantage is that the measures of performance are closely related to the goals of the organization. Hence, they fulfill the goal of many reward plans to bring employee goals in alignment with organizational goals. Unfortunately, however, in many circumstances these organizational-level measures of performance are outside the control of individual employees, which may weaken expectancy perceptions needed for employee performance.

Given the strengths and weaknesses of performance measures at each level and the fact that many organizations have business goals at each level, an argument can be made that there should be multiple performance-based pay plans. In this fashion, the weaknesses of one plan may be offset somewhat by the strengths of another plan and multiple business goals may be accomplished. A combined reward strategy of this nature is used by Lincoln Electric, where financial rewards are provided for individual, group, and organizational performance measures (Perry, 1990). This plan has been successfully used at Lincoln Electric for over eighty years.

Rigorous empirical assessment of the combined reward strategy has produced mixed results. On one hand, Wageman (1995) found that with intact work teams at Xerox, combining individual and group pay led to deleterious effects on group performance. The groups performed better as a group when the pay plan was based on group or individual performance rewards rather than a combination of group and individual rewards. On the other hand, Crown and Rosse (1995) found in a study of sports teams that a combination of group and individual performance goals resulted in better group performance than did individual performance goals alone, but that the combined group and individual goals resulted in less effective group performance than did group goals alone. Unfortunately, neither study measured the impact of these approaches on individual performance.

The results of these two studies and the Lincoln Electric case suggest that it is possible to successfully use a combined reward strategy, but that to do so may require considerable time and that the attempt may not be appropriate in all situations. Considerable time may be required because in many organizations, employees have grown accustomed to pay increases based on individual or group performance rather than individual and group performance combined. Not all situations lend themselves to a combined plan (Lawler, 1990). Some do, of course. For example, baseball teams have both group and individual business objectives-that is, winning games and maintaining the players' own batting averages and other statistics. A combined plan may make sense for organizations that have both group and individual goals. Other settings, such as process manufacturing, may only have group output goals. In this environment, combined group and individual rewards may not make sense.

Organizations might also consider integrated individual and group reward plans instead of combined individual and group reward plans. Under this approach, often called team-based merit pay, a group-level outcome such as teamwork is measured at the individual level in terms of critical incidents that reflect desired behavior on the part of the individual (Heneman & von Hippel, 1995). In the case of teamwork, individual behaviors that are consistent with being a good team player are measured. Organizations using this approach include Motorola, Hewlett-Packard, and Levi Strauss (Shaw & Schneier, 1995). This approach led to higher group performance than did a combined plan in the Crown and Rosse (1995) study. Team-based merit pay plans keep more of the focus on the individual than do combined plans. As a result, they might be used to help individual-based reward organizations make the transition toward becoming more group focused.

IMPLEMENTATION ISSUES

The Achilles heel of many pay-for-performance plans is the implementation stage. Issues of implementation that must be considered prior to the pay plan intervention include measurement, fairness, and communications. Each of these issues will be addressed in turn.

Measurement

Pay-for-performance plans are highly dependent upon the measures of performance that are used. If the measures used are not reliable and valid, then the organization may incur large costs as a result of rewarding employees for factors not related to the effectiveness of the organization. In addition, employees are unlikely to be motivated because reliable and valid measures are needed for employees to perceive the expectancy and instrumentality links necessary for employee motivation.

It is sometimes mistakenly assumed that valid measures refer to those indexes that the organization currently measures. While these measures may be convenient, they are not necessarily valid because they may have no relationship to the business plan. Instead, for example, they may be collected as part of an off-the-shelf applications package. The data collected by this package may have been put together without regard to the specific goals of any one particular organization.

It is also sometimes mistakenly assumed that countable indicators of performance are more objective and hence more valid. Absenteeism, for example, can be a count of employees who are not at work. There are two potential problems with this count. First, the count may not be consistently made. Recorders may apply different standards (for example, excused versus unexcused) in counting absences. Second, concentrating on countable, objective indicators may lead an organization to overlook less countable but equally important indicators of performance, such as customer service.

For performance measures to be valid, they must be consistent with the business plan of the organization and be measured in a consistent and reliable manner. Methods to improve the reliability and validity of performance measures include the use of a mission statement and job analysis to develop performance measures, participation by employees in scale development, rater training, and the use of multiple raters (Heneman, 1992).

Fairness

More reliable and valid measures of performance are likely to lead to greater perceptions of fairness by employees. In turn, perceptions of fairness are likely to lead to employee acceptance of the new pay plan and a greater willingness to act in accordance with the plan. A survey of Fortune 100 firms by Bretz, Milkovich, and Read (1992) indicated that the most crucial issue organizations faced in terms of their performance appraisal systems was the fairness in how the system was used.

Fairness has two components: distributive justice and procedural justice (Greenberg, 1987). *Distributive justice* refers to the fairness of the outcome associated with the performance-based pay plan (for example, size of bonus), while *procedural justice* refers to the fairness of the procedures used to determine the outcomes (for example, performance ratings). As noted earlier, research has shown that it is not only the amount of money that is important in determining pay satisfaction, it is also the procedures used to establish pay (Folger & Konovsky, 1989). To increase the perceived procedural justice of a performance-based pay plan, the following steps can be taken (Heneman, 1992):

- Have employees participate in pay plan design.
- Create an appeals system.

- Use reliable and valid performance measures.
- Train raters to eliminate rating errors.
- Follow laws and regulations.
- Use a written policy and procedure for pay decisions.
- Send out a periodic newsletter.

For a more detailed review of issues and recommendations concerning fairness and appraisal, please see Chapter Six in this book.

Communications

An excellent example of a newsletter comes from McDonnell Aircraft Company (Handshear, 1988, supplemented by personal communication from N. A. Handshear, 1989). Known originally as *Merit Review News*, it was issued to all employees on a periodic basis to update them on the merit pay program at McDonnell Aircraft.

Topics included discussion of the size of the merit budget, range movement, and performance review guidelines. Surveys of employees' reactions at McDonnell and those of compensation professionals outside McDonnell were very positive. As a result, the newsletter was expanded to include more detail on the merit, pay guidelines and to include other compensation topics like the bonus plan. A more formal survey of this plan several years later indicated that employees who were familiar with the newsletter saw their pay as being more fair, were more committed to the organization, and were less likely to leave their jobs than employees that were not familiar with the newsletter (McCarty-Kilian 1992).

Pay Secrecy

One issue regarding the communication of performance-based pay-plans is how much information should be revealed to employees about their performance and pay and the performance and pay of other employees. Plans can range from being very closed (employees are only told their performance ratings and pay raises), to very open (employees are told everyone's performance ratings and pay raises).

The research on which approach is best is mixed (Heneman, 1992). On one hand, secrecy may result in supervisors doing a better job at differentiating among employee performance levels. On, other hand, employees axe less likely to be satisfied with secrecy, because they have a tendency to overestimate the rewards of others. Confronted with this mixed evidence, most organizations take a middle ground and let employees know the average ratings and raises, as well as the range of ratings and raises around that average, rather than letting employees know the specific figures for each employee.

Split Reviews

General Electric pioneered a concept in the 1960s known as split reviews (Meyer, Kay, & French, 1965). Under a split review, the performance review for purposes of development is separated from the performance review for purposes of pay raises. In essence, two reviews are conducted: one for pay and one for development. This split is done so that the supervisor is not required to be a coach and judge in the same session. This practice was carried out at General Electric for many years and many other organizations adopted this model.

Interestingly, Lawler, Mohrman, and Resnick (1984) returned to General Electric many years later and found that employees were not supportive of split reviews. Employees wanted pay discussed in their reviews and felt that it was not being done enough. Although it is difficult to be a coach and evaluator, it appears that supervisors should play both roles in appraisals. Employees are more likely to be satisfied (Dorfman, Stephan, & Loveland, 1986; Giles & Mossholder, 1990; Prince & Lawler, 1986) and may also be more motivated because it is easier for the employee to establish instrumentality perceptions when both topics are discussed at the same time.

In those organizations using 360-degree review systems, caution needs to be exercised in combining developmental and evaluative reviews. Recent research by the American Compensation Association (1996b) suggests that most organizations with competency models are using them for the purposes of selection and development rather than for purposes of selection, development, and compensation combined. A story from a compensation director of a large manufacturing firm illustrates why it may be advisable to couple pay with performance in a 360-degree review environment only after employee reactions to the 360-degree review process are favorable. The story goes that for a research and development facility with scientists, a 360-degree feedback process was hastily implemented for pay decisions. It immediately failed because the appraisal system was brand new and not well thought out. The scientists worked in teams. Each team got together at a remote site and set up a circle of chairs in a room. The person being evaluated sat in the middle and was grilled by the other team members. Needless to say, this procedure did not conform to the principles of a sound performance appraisal system. Coupling pay increases to this poorly developed performance appraisal system further sensitized employees to problems with the appraisal system.

SUMMARY AND CONCLUSION

Performance appraisal is only one component of the performance management process. Another important component of the performance management process is the linkage between performance judgments and rewards. Prior to the publication of this book, previous books on performance appraisal have devoted very little attention to the reward system. As demonstrated in this chapter, rewards can and should be viewed as an integral part of the performance management process. Reward systems have been shown to be related to individual and organizational effectiveness. A detailed summary of the conclusions reached for practice in this chapter is shown in Table 8. They are grouped by general principles, which list practices having wide scale applicability, and by contingency considerations, which list practices that need to be adapted to local circumstances.

Table 8.   Summary of Recommended Reward Practices

General Principles

- Performance-based pay plans have been shown to be effective in many different organizational settings.
- There has been a rapid increase in the use of performance-based pay plans by organizations.
- Performance-based pay plans are more likely to be motivational when they help employees clearly see links between their effort and performance and between their performance and rewards.
- Performance-based pay plans are more likely to be effective the more reliable and valid their measures of performance.
- Performance-based pay plans are more likely to be effective the more that employees consider the outcomes of the reward process and the procedures used to determine the outcomes to be fair.
- Pay increase parameters (minimum, average, maximum) and not individual pay increases should be communicated to employees.
- Employees are more likely to be satisfied with performance reviews when a discussion of their performance and pay is conducted in the same session than when their performance and pay are discussed in two separate sessions.

Contingencies to Consider

- Exempt employees are more likely than nonexempt employees to prefer performance-based pay plans.
- The attractiveness of different forms of rewards for employees (for example, bonus pay versus time off) varies by individual.
- The selection of the most appropriate performance-based reward plans depends upon the business objectives, culture, and motivational philosophy of the organization.
- The type of pay plan used is determined by the types of performance measures used and the level of performance measurement.
- The strengths and weaknesses of performance-based pay plans depend on the type of pay plan used.

ACKNOWLEDGMENT

The authors would like to thank Jim Smither and Sara Rynes for their helpful comments on an earlier version of this chapter.

REFERENCES

Altmansberger, H.N., & Wallace, M.J., Jr. (1995, Winter). Strategic use of goalsharing at Corning. *ACA Journal,* 64–73.

American Compensation Association. (1996a). *Certification course 12: Alternative reward systems: improving productivity and competitiveness.* Scottsdale, AZ: Author.

American Compensation Association. (1996b) . *Raising the bar: Using competencies to enhance employee performance.* Scottsdale, AZ: Author.

Ash, R.A., Levine, E.L., & Sistrunk, F. (1983). The role of jobs and job-based methods in personnel and human resources management. In K. Rowland & G. Ferris (Eds.), *Research in personnel and human resources management* (Vol. 1, pp. 45–84). Greenwich, CT: JAI Press.

Barney J.B. (1991). Firm resources and sustained competitive advantage. *Journal of Management, 17,* 99–120.

Becker, G.S. (1996, March 11). Human capital: One investment where America is ahead. *Business Week,* p. 18.

Belcher, J.G., Jr. (1991). *Gainsharing.* Houston, TX: Gulf.

Blasi, J., Conte, M., & Kruse, D. (1996). Employee stock ownership and corporate performance among public companies. *Industrial and Labor Relations Review, 50,* 60–79.

Blinder, A.S. (Ed.). (1990). *Paying for productivity: A look at the evidence.* Washington, DC: Brookings Institution.

Bretz, R.D., Jr., Milkovich, G.T., & Read, W. (1992). The current state of performance appraisal research and practice: Concerns, directions, and implications. *Journal of Management, 18,* 321–352.

Campbell, J.P. (1990) . Modeling the performance prediction problem in industrial and organizational psychology. In M.D. Dunnette & L.M. Hough (Eds.), *Handbook of industrial and organizational psychology* (Vol. 1, 2nd ed., pp. 687–732). Palo Alto, CA: Consulting Psychologists Press.

Case history: Employee feedback helps bottom line. (1986). *Small Business Report, 11,* 98.

Crown, D.F., & Rosse, J.G. (1995) . Yours, mine, and ours: Facilitating group productivity through the integration of individual and group goals. *Organizational Behavior and Human Decision Processes, 64*(2), 138–150.

Deci, R.L. (1972). The effects of contingent and noncontingent rewards and controls on intrinsic motivation. *Organizational Behavior and Human Performance, 8,* 15–31.

Deming, W.E. (1986). *Out of the crisis.* Cambridge, MA: MIT Center for Advanced Engineering Study.

Dorfman, P.W., Stephan, W.G., & Loveland, J. (1986) . Performance appraisal behaviors: Supervisor perceptions and subordinate reactions. *Personnel Psychology, 39,* 579–597.

Eisenberger, R., & Cameron, J. (1996). Detrimental effects of reward: Reality or myth? *American Psychologist, 51,* 1153–1166.

Folger, R., & Konovsky, M.A. (1989). Effects of procedural and distributive justice on reactions to pay raise decisions. *Academy of Management Journal, 32,* 115–130.

Gaga, U.A., & Kaz, M.S. (1996, November-December). The post-privatization period: A look at personal motivation systems for Russian enterprises. *American Compensation Association News,* 8–11.

Gerhart, B., & Milkovich, G.T (1992) .Employee compensation: Research and practice. In M.D. Dunnette & L.M. Hough (Eds.), *Handbook of industrial and organizational psychology* (Vol. 3, 2nd ed., pp. 10091055). Palo Alto, CA: Consulting Psychologists Press.

Giles, W.F., & Mossholder, K.W. (1990). Employee reactions to contextual and session components of performance appraisal. *Journal of Applied Psychology, 75,* 371–377.

Graham-Moore, B., & Ross, T.L. (1990). *Gainsharing.* Washington, DC: Bureau of National Affairs.

Greenberg, J. (1987). A taxonomy of organizational justice theories. *Academy of Management Review, 12,* 9–22.

Gross, S.E. (1995). *Compensation for teams.* New York: AMACOM.

Handshear, N.A. (1988, May). News preferred over mystery-members favor *Merit Review News. American Compensation Association News,* 10.

Heneman, H.G., III. (1985). Pay satisfaction. In K.M. Rowland & G.R. Ferris (Eds.), *Research in personnel and human resource management* (Vol. 3, pp. 115–139). Greenwich, CT: JAI Press.

Heneman, R.L. (1992). *Merit pay: Linking pay increases to performance ratings.* Reading, MA: Addison Wesley Longman.

Heneman, R.L., & von Hippel, C. (1995). Balancing group and individual rewards: Rewarding individual contributions to the team. *Compensation and Benefits Review, 27*(4), 63–68.

Heneman, R.L., & von Hippel, C. (1996). The assessment of job performance: Focusing attention on context, process and group issues. In D. Lewin, D.J.B. Mitchell, & M.A. Zaidi (Eds.), *Handbook of human resource management* (pp. 587–617). Greenwich, CT: JAI Press.

Heneman, R.L., von Hippel, C., Eskew, D.E., & Greenberger, D.B. (1996). Strategic rewards in unionized environments. *ACA Journal.* **Vol # & page #s?**

Heneman, R.L., Waldeck, N., & Cushnie, M. (1996) . Diversity considerations in staffing decision making. In E.E. Kossek & S. Lobel (Eds.), *Managing diversity: Human resource strategies for transforming the workplace* (pp. 74–101). Cambridge, MA: Blackwell.

Ilgen, D.R., & Hollenbeck. J.R. (1991) . The structure of work: Design and roles. In M.D. Dunnette & L.M. Hough (Eds.), *Handbook of industrial and organizational psychology* (Vol. 2, 2nd ed., pp. 165–208). Palo Alto, CA: Consulting Psychologists Press.

Jenkins, G.D., Ledford, J., Jr., Gupta, N., & Doty, D. (1992). *Skill-based pay: Practices, payoffs, pitfalls, and prescriptions.* Scottsdale, AZ: American Compensation Association.

Johnson, R.H. (1996). Life in the consortium: The Mayflower Group. In A.I. Kraut (Ed.), *Organizational surveys: Tools for assessment and change* (pp. 285–309). San Francisco: Jossey-Bass.

Katzenbach, J.R., & Smith, D.K. (1993). *The wisdom, of teams.* New York: HarperCollins.

Knouse, S.B. (1995). *The reward and recognition process in total quality management.* Milwaukee: ASQC Quality Press.

Kohn, A. (1993). *Punished by rewards.* Boston: Houghton-Mifflin.

Kruse, D.L. (1993) . Profit *sharing: Does it make a difference?* Kalamazoo, MI: Upjohn Institute.

Lawler, E.E., III. (1981). *Pay and organizational development.* Reading, MA: Addison Wesley Longman.

Lawler, E.E., III. (1990). *Strategic pay.* San Francisco: Jossey-Bass.

Lawler, E.E., III. (1995). The new pay: A strategic approach. *Compensation and Benefits Review, 27,* 14–22.

Lawler, E.E., III. (1996). Competencies: A poor foundation for the new pay. *Compensation and Benefits Review, 28*(6), 20–26.

Lawler, E.E., III, &Jenkins, G.D., Jr. (1992). Strategic reward systems. In M.D. Dunnette & L.M. Hough (Eds.), *Handbook of industrial and organizational psychology* (Vol. 3, 2nd ed., pp. 1009–1055). Palo Alto, CA: Consulting Psychologists Press.

Lawler, E.E., III, Mohrman, S.A., & Ledford, G.E., Jr. (1995). *Creating high performance organizations: Practices and results of employee involvement and TQM in Fortune 1000 companies.* San Francisco: Jossey Bass.

Lawler, E.E., III, Mohrman, A.M., Jr., & Resnick, R.M. (1984). Performance appraisal revisited. *Organizational Dynamics, 12,* 20–35.

Ledford, G.E., Jr. (1991). Three case studies on skill-based pay: An overview. *Compensation and Benefits Review, 23*(2), 11–23.

Locke, E.A., Feren, D.B., McCaleb, V.M., Shaw, K.N., & Denny, A.J. (1980). The relative effectiveness of motivating employee performance. In K.D. Duncan, M.M. Gruneberg, & D. Wallis (Eds.) *Changes in working life* (pp. 363–388). New Wiley.

Lorant, R. (1992, June 27). Mechanic sues Sears for firing. *Wisconsin State Journal,* p. Al.

McAdams, J.L. (1996). *The reward plan advantage: A manager's guide to improving business through people.* San Francisco: Jossey Bass.

McAdams, J.L., & Hawk, E.J. (1995). Organizational *performance and rewards.* Scottsdale, AZ: American Compensation Association.

McCarty-Kilian, C. (1992). Using *a corporate newsletter to communicate pay information: A study of pay fairness.* Unpublished doctoral dissertation, Ohio State University, Columbus.

Meyer, H.H., Kay, E., & French, J.R.P. (1965). Split roles in performance appraisal. *Harvard Business Review, 43,* 123–129.

Milkovich, G.T., & Newman, J.M. (1996). *Compensation.* Burr Ridge, IL Irwin.

Mitchell, R., & O'Neal, M. (1994, August 1). Managing by values. *Business Week,* pp. 46–52.

Montemayer, E.F. (1994, Winter). Aligning pay systems with market strategies. *ACA Journal,* 44–53.

Montemayer, E.F. (1995). Book review of A. Kohn, *Punished by rewards. Personnel Psychology, 4,* 941–948.

Nathan, B.R., & Cascio, W.F. (1986). Technical and legal standards. In R.A. Berk (Ed.), *Performance assessment: Methods and applications* (pp. 1–50). Baltimore, MD: Johns Hopkins University Press.

Nelson, B. (1994). *1001 ways to reward employees.* New York: Workman.

Norris, F. (1991). Look out for number one. *New York Times,* pp. Al, C5.

Odden, A., & Kelley, G. (1997). *Paying teachers for what they know and do.* Thousand Oaks, CA: Corwin Press.

O'Dell, C.O. (1987). *Major findings from people, performance, and pay.* Scottsdale, AZ: American Compensation Association.

Ott. J.S. (1989). *The organizational cultural perspective.* Florence, KY Dorsey Press.

Peck, C. (1984) . *Pay and performance: The interaction of compensation and performance appraisal.* Research Bulletin No. 155. New York: Conference Board.

Peck, C. (1989). *Variable pay: New performance rewards.* Research Bulletin No. 246. New York: Conference Board.

Peck, C. (1991). G*ainsharing for productivity.* Report No. 967. New York: Conference Board.

Perry, J.L. (1988). Making policy by trial and error: Merit pay in the federal service. *Policy Studies Journal, 17*(2), 389–405.

Perry, T.A. (1990). Staying with the basics. *HR Magazine, 35*(11) , 73–76.

Podolske, A. (1996) . Tools for defending pay for-performance against the skeptics. In *Pay-for-performance report* (pp. 1, 12–14). New York: Institute for Management and Administration.

Pollack, A. (1993, October 2). Japanese starting to link pay to performance. *New York Times,* p. Al.

Prince, J.B., & Lawler, E.E., III. (1986). Does salary discussion hurt the developmental performance appraisal? *Organizational Behavior and Human Decision Processes, 37,* 357–375.

Rice, F. (1994, August 8). How to make diversity pay. *Fortune,* pp. 79–86.

Risher, H. (1992). Paying employees for quality. In *Perspectives in total compensation.* Scottsdale, AZ: American Compensation Association.

Schuster, J.R. (1989). Improving productivity through gainsharing: Can the means be justified in the end? *Compensation and Benefits Management, 5,* 207–210.

Schuster, J.R., & Zingheim, P.R (1992). *The new pay.* San Francisco: New Lexington Press.

Scott, W.E., Jr., Farh, J.L., & Podsakoff, P.M. (1988). The effects of "intrinsic" and "extrinsic" reinforcement contingencies on task behavior. *Organizational Behavior and Human Decision Processes, 41,* 4–425.

Shaw, D.G., & Schneier, C.E. (1995). Team measurement and rewards: How some companies are getting it right. *Human Resource Planning, 18,* 34–49.

Stayer, R. (1990). How I learned to let my workers lead. *Harvard Business Review, 68*(6), 65–72.

Stevens, M.J., & Campion, M.A. (1994). The knowledge, skill, and ability requirements for teamwork: Implications for human resource management. *Journal of
Management, 20,* 503–530.

Wageman, R. (1995). Interdependence and group effectiveness. *Administrative Science Quarterly, 40,* 145–180.

Wagner, J.A., III, & Hollenbeck, J.R. (1992). *Management of organizational behavior.*
Upper Saddle River, NJ: Prentice Hall.

Wallace, M.J. (1990). *Reward and renewal: America's search for competitive advantage
through alternative pay strategies.* Scottsdale, AZ: American Compensation Association.

Welbourne, T., & Gomez-Mejia, L.R. (1995). Gainsharing: A critical review and a
future research agenda. *Journal of Management, 21,* 559–609.

Wilson, T.B. (1995). *Innovative reward systems for the changing workplace.* New York:
McGraw-Hill.

Wright, P.M. (1994). Goal-setting and monetary incentives: Motivational tools that
can work too well. *Compensation and Benefits Review, 26*(3), 41–49.

Zingheim, P.K., Ledford, G.E., Jr., & Schuster, J.R. (1996, Spring). Competencies
and competency models: Does one size fit all? *ACA Journal,* 56–65.

Part III

PAY IN NEW BUSINESS ENVIRONMENTS

Strategic reward systems have traditionally been for executives and sales personnel in private sector companies. Today, however, strategic reward programs must be managed for a wide range of different types of employees in a wide range of different business environments. New business environments in this section include temporary employees in virtual organizations, unionized employees, and public and private school teachers. Strategic reward programs have not only grown in the number of types of programs as shown in the second part of this book, but also in the number of applications as shown in this third part of the book.

Heneman, R.L., Tansky, J.W., & Tomlinson, E.C. (in press). Hybrid reward systems for virtual organizations: A review and recommendations. In R.L. Heneman & D.B. Greenberger (Eds.), *HRM in virtual organizations*. Greenwich, CT: Information Age Press.

Heneman, R.L., von Hippel, C., Eskew, D.E., & Greenberger, D.B. (1997, Summer). Alternative rewards in unionized environments. *American Compensation Association Journal,* 42–55.

Dalton, G.L., Stevens, J., & Heneman, R.L. (1997). Alternative rewards in union settings. *The Journal for Quality and Participation, 27*(5), 26–31.

Heneman, R.L., & Ledford, G.E. (1998). Competency pay for professionals and managers in business: A review and implications for teachers. *Journal of Personnel Evaluation in Education, 12*(2), 103–121.

CHAPTER 4

HYBRID REWARD SYSTEMS FOR VIRTUAL ORGANIZATIONS:

A Review and Recommendations

Robert L. Heneman, Judith W. Tansky, and Edward C. Tomlinson

Source: Heneman, R.L., Tansky, J.W., & Tomlinson, E.C. (in press). Hybrid Reward Systems for Virtual Organizations: A Review and Recommendations. In R.L. Heneman & D.B. Greenberger (Eds.). *HRM in Virtual Organizations.* Greenwich, CT: Information Age Press. Reprinted with permission from Information Age Publishing.

ABSTRACT

This chapter addresses the unique compensation needs of virtual organizations. A review of the literature suggests that various forms of virtual organizations may require tailored reward systems. We present different reward system strategies to accommodate the special needs of horizontal organizations, network organizations, alliances, and cellular organizations. Implications for future research and practice are discussed.

INTRODUCTION

Competitive pressures in the economic landscape have heralded radical transformations in the substance and character of the modern organizational structure. Traditional forms of arranging the corporation have been based on standardized principles and rigid reporting relationships to maximize efficiency and ensure consistency (Robbins, 1990). However, new organizational formats (referred to here as virtual organizations) have evolved in response to the increased demand for flexibility and innovation in the marketplace (Heneman, Ledford, & Gresham, 1999; Miles et al., 1997). Although the concept of virtual organizations is fairly new, compensation researchers and practitioners alike must rise to the challenge of developing new reward systems designed to keep step with this more fluid structure.

The purpose of this chapter is to focus on reward systems for virtual organizations, and toward this end we will specifically address three objectives. The first objective is to review the literature that has already been written. One omission in the current literature is a recognition of the fact that various forms of virtual organizations may require unique reward systems. That is, different types of reward systems are needed depending upon whether the organizational design is a horizontal organization, network organization, alliance, or cellular organization. The second objective of this chapter is to emphasize the fact that the concept of virtual organizations is inherently heterogeneous in nature. As such, "one size fits all" reward system prescriptions for virtual organizations are not appropriate. The third and final objective is to point out important implications for research and practice based on the first two objectives of this chapter.

LITERATURE REVIEW

Virtual organizations consist of people from multiple corporate entities that join forces to accomplish work (Crandall & Wallace, 1997). Such organizations have evolved to meet the demands of increased flexibility, integration, and synergism in the marketplace (Heneman, Ledford, & Gresham, 1999), and can take a variety of specific formats. The most common virtual organizations are horizontal organizations, network organizations, alliances, and cellular organizations (each of which will be described in further detail below). The inherent variety in such virtual organizational structures suggests the need for carefully tailored compensation systems that dovetail on the unique features of each specific form.

The current literature on reward systems in virtual organizations can be described as follows. First, as one would expect, there is a very small number of articles that have been published, leaving very little guidance for researchers and practitioners. Second, the existing literature is very descriptive and prescriptive in practitioner sources and theoretical in academic sources. Empirical studies either of a descriptive or analytical nature are virtually nonexistent. Third, most of the work is organized by contrasting traditional compensation practices with compensation practices in virtual organizations. Fourth, the literature can and for purposes of this chapter will be organized using the following categories: base pay, incentives, equity, benefits, indirect rewards, and pay system management.

Base Pay

Base pay refers to the amount of wages or salaries provided to employees for their services. Traditionally, in bureaucratic organizations, base pay is determined on the basis of job evaluation and market surveys (Milkovich & Newman, 1999). Job evaluation systematically compares a focal job to other jobs or to written standards in terms of the value of the jobs to the company. This systematic comparison results in grades of jobs and ensures internal equity in the company. In order to establish external equity, internal jobs are compared to comparable jobs in the labor market through the process of market surveys.

Relative to organizational structure, the theory behind traditional pay systems is straightforward. Bureaucratic organizational structures are formed in response to stable labor and product markets in order to provide products and services in the most consistent manner. Consistency is maintained by paying people for consistently performing the activities described in a job description.

As business environments have become more turbulent, more flexible forms of organizational structures such as virtual organizations have become necessary in order to adapt to the changing business environment. Flexibility rather than consistency is needed to respond to changing consumer and employee preferences (Cantoni, 1997). In this new environment, employees need to be rewarded for flexibility in job assignments rather than for consistently performing the same duties specified in a job description. Consequently, new forms of compensation need to be developed to reward flexibility (Klaas, 2000). Our literature review identified new forms of base pay that emphasize flexibility including person-based pay (Crandall & Wallace, 1998; Tucker, 1995), broadbanding (Tucker, 1995), and classification (IBM study).

Person-based pay approaches, in comparison to traditional job evaluation, shift the unit of analysis from the job to the job incumbent. In particular, emphasis is placed upon the competencies of the person.

Competencies include knowledge, skills, abilities, and other observable attributes of the person that are related to successful performance (Ledford & Heneman, 2000). Other attributes may include interests and attitudes. A common theme among competencies selected for compensation purposes is the need for flexibility. Knowledge may be emphasized because more knowledgeable people are more likely to be able to adapt to change. Innovation and creativity may be emphasized for a similar reason or because the long term competitiveness of the firm depends on new ideas and products.

Although the logic for using competencies for base pay decisions is straightforward, it is not used very often by companies (American Compensation Association, 1996). It is instead used more often for developmental purposes in organizations. One major reason for the limited use of competencies in base pay decisions is the difficulty of pricing competencies in the external market even with the use of wage and salary surveys. Although technology in the compensation profession may eventually help to overcome this obstacle to competency-based pay, it is a very difficult approach to use in virtual organizations.

One notable exception to the limited use of competencies in organizations is the use of skill-based pay plans where skills alone serve as the building block for competency assessment. These types of plans seem to work well in manufacturing settings. Murray and Gerhart (1998) reported that skill-based pay in a manufacturing plant versus a comparable plant without skill-based pay resulted in greater productivity, lower labor costs, and improved quality.

Along with person-based pay, the flexibility needed in virtual organizations can be emphasized with broadbanding. Traditional job evaluation approaches often resulted in very rigid pay hierarchies. A limited number of jobs were captured by a pay grade with very small dollar differences within and between pay grades. This approach did yield consistent pay decisions for internal equity measures, but it is called into question when organizations need people flexible enough to be responsible for work performed across pay grades.

Broadbanding provides the flexibility needed by virtual organizations. In a broadbanded system there are a small number of pay grades with large dollar amounts within and between pay grades. Jobs that are similar to one another (e.g., occupation) are grouped together into one large band. As a result, there is more room to accommodate individual differences in work performed, seniority, and contributions to the firm (e.g., performance, skill) within the same job title and pay band.

The broadbanding approach is now used extensively in companies and the descriptive evidence suggests that these plans are effective, at least in the opinion of HR survey respondents. Unfortunately, there are no analytical studies of the effectiveness of broadbanding using experimental, quasi experimental, or time series designs. A common concern voiced about broadbanding is that it may raise internal equity issues (Klaas, 2000). Also, if there is not a sound system of performance management in place, broadbanding may lead to an unwanted escalation in labor costs (Heneman, 2001).

Classification systems represent another approach to provide more flexibility in base pay determination. With this approach, job evaluation is still used to maintain consistency for internal equity, but the method of job evaluation is less rigorous and cumbersome than other traditional job evaluation methods (e.g., point-factor system). As such, it is a compromise between person based pay systems and broadbanding on one hand, and traditional job evaluation on the other, as shown in Table 1.

Table 1. Flexibility, Rigor, and Internal Equity in Work Evaluation

Work Evaluation Approach	Flexibility	Rigor	Internal Equity
Person-Based	High	Moderate	Moderate
Broadbanding	High	Low	Low
Classification	Moderate	Moderate	Moderate
Traditional Job Evaluation	Low	High	High

Historically, classification has primarily been used in the public sector. More recently, however, it is also being used by private sector companies such as IBM to promote a more flexible system.

Incentives

The norm for incentive pay in traditional bureaucratic organizations has been merit pay (Heneman, 1992). With this approach, permanent pay increases are made to base salary based upon ratings of employee performance. Three trends have rendered this approach obsolete for virtual organizations. First, virtual organizations often are newer organizations that do not have the capital available for permanent base pay increases. Capital must instead be diverted to startup costs. Second, technology has improved such that there are more measures of performance than ever before. Rather than relying on ratings of quality and quantity of performance, organizations often have actual measures of quality and quantity available to them. Third, employees may report to multiple companies. Hence, the traditional merit pay practice of having the immediate supervisor of one company make ratings of employees may no longer work. Three new approaches to performance measurement and incentive pay deal with these issues in virtual organizations: variable pay, 360-degree reviews, and balanced scorecards.

Variable pay refers to cash bonuses that are linked to individual employee performance, (e.g., MBO), team performance, (e.g., team pay), business unit performance (gainsharing), or organizational performance (e.g., profit sharing). With variable pay, cash is in the form of a bonus so it does not have the compounding cost effect of permanent pay increases. Also, performance is usually defined in the form of performance indicators under the control of employees.

Performance evaluations conducted by multiple evaluators as referred to as 360-degree reviews. Sources of these evaluators include the job incumbent, immediate supervisor, coworkers, subordinates, and customers or other external parties. These parties may come from one organization or multiple organizations as in the case of alliances. This approach to evaluation is more likely to lead to comprehensive evaluations than traditional reviews by the immediate supervisor only, because in virtual organizations, employees may be working in remote cities, have multiple bosses, and multiple work locations.

The concept of a balanced scorecard was developed by Kaplan and Norton (1996) and refers to a multidimensional set of performance dimensions to evaluate employee performance. An example of a balanced scorecard is shown in Table 2.

Table 2.   Balanced Scorecard

		Results		
Performance Standards	*Weight*	*Below*	*Meets*	*Exceeds*
Financial Goals				
Operational Goals				
Customer Service Goals				
Employee Satisfaction Goals				

This approach suggests that as with 360-degree reviews, employees must be held accountable to multiple standards of performance. By looking at "hard" measures of performance (e.g., financial and operations measures) and "soft" measures of performance (e.g., customer service and employee satisfaction), we are likely to capture more of the performance construct. Research has shown that hard and soft measures only correlate about .60 with one another (Heneman, 1986). That is, only 36 percent of the performance variance is shared by hard and soft measures. Moreover, as people in virtual organizations learn to function effectively in these new organizational structures, how a person performs (e.g., customer service) is as important to reward as what they accomplish (e.g., financial results). Both the 360-degree feedback method and the balanced scorecard method imply a pay adjustment based on the performance review; these particular review methods can be especially valuable tools in managing effective performance in virtual organizations.

Equity

In traditional organizations, turnover was minimized by providing lifetime employment. In virtual organizations where, as the name implies, the organizations may only survive a limited time span, turnover is minimized with the granting of stock options. These options, which provide ownership or equity in the company, were traditionally given only to executives but are increasingly being granted to all levels of employees. Stock options are also being used in companies that are not publicly traded. These stocks are sometimes referred to as "phantom" stocks. Payout is based on a measure of book value of the company rather than the market value of the company. As such, a book value measure becomes a "proxy" for market value.

Although some employees have become rich from stock options, many have seen these options go "underwater" which means the purchase value of the stock is higher than the value of the stock when cashed out. Hence, the perceived value of stock is very heavily dependent upon the current status of the business cycle (Platten & Weinberg, 2000).

Benefits

Under traditional pension plans, the amount received upon retirement was heavily dependent upon the years of tenure in the company. As virtual organizations tend to imply a short-term duration with any one employer, employees are increasingly looking for portability in pensions (Crandall & Wallace, 1998). In order to facilitate portability, employers have created cash-balance pensions that minimize the premium paid for tenure with one organization (Burlingame & Gulotta, 1998). Although cash balance plans may be desirable for more junior employees in virtual organizations, they may present problems when trying to attract talented senior employees to spin-off virtual organizations from large, established firms. The cost of cash balance plans to the organization is usually less (Oppel, 1999) than the more traditional type (i.e., defined benefit and defined contribution), so some virtual organizations with high capital needs may not be able to afford to continue to offer traditional benefit plans to long-tenured employees. With a mandatory shifting of all employees to cash-balance plans, virtual organizations risk losing the services of long-tenured employees from the core company. Whenever possible, employers that shift from traditional to cash balance plans should give employees a choice as to whether to participate (McNamee, 1999).

Indirect Rewards

Indirect rewards typically include three categories of rewards: development, recognition, and the work environment. Development can take many forms, including training, mentoring, visibility, professional growth and promotion. Elements of recognition include time-off, gifts, awards, praise, and job assignments (such as job enlargement and/or job enrichment [Hackman & Oldham, 1976]). The work environment includes physical space (e.g., offices) and the psychological meaningfulness of work.

Along with monetary rewards that are directly visible to employees, non-monetary or indirect rewards play an important role in virtual organizations. Non-monetary rewards are also important because they become a symbol of the culture of the organization. They also have value to the firm because they sometimes have costs associated with them that are less than direct monetary rewards. This smaller cost is important to virtual organizations with high capital needs.

Little is known about the effectiveness of indirect (non-monetary) rewards. One exception is the psychological meaningfulness of work. Research has shown that the psychological dimensions of work are correlated with job satisfaction (Fried & Ferris, 1987; Loher, Noe, Moeller, & Fitzgerald, 1985). However, recent surveys have shown that in team pay environments, development and recognition are as important or even more important to employees than direct pay (Tonkin & Ellis, 1997).

It would appear that organizations need to pay more attention to indirect rewards. One promising method to do so is to build psychological rewards associated with work into job analysis as reminded by Heneman and Heneman (1994) and shown in Table 3. Wherever possible, we suggest that it is always appropriate to use indirect rewards in the workplace, regardless of the type of organizational structure.

Pay System Management

In traditional organizations, pay systems were often designed and implemented so long ago (e.g., 40 year old job evaluation system) that employees trust the system in place. In a "new" virtual organization, with a brand

Table 3. Rewards and Job Analysis Administrative Assistant Example

Reward	Dimension	Amount	Differential	Reward Characteristics Stability
1. Starting pay	A. Individual pay (extrinsic)	$2,000/month minimum	May exceed minimum, depending on KSAO's	Changes according to market conditions
2. Pay raises	A. Individual pay (extrinsic)	Typically, 2–3%	Across the board (same % for all)	Range from 0% to 10%, annually
3. Bonuses	A. Individual pay (extrinsic)	2.5% average	Range from 0% to 10%, depending on performance	Will vary each year, depending on size of bonus pool
4. Doing different tasks	B. Skill variety (intrinsic)	0 = 4.8*	SD = .73*	Frequent change
5. Using complex skills	B. Skill variety (intrinsic)	0 = 3.9*	SD = 1.54*	No recent changes; none anticipated
6. Doing simple and repetitive tasks	B. Skill variety (intrinsic)	0 = 5.4*	SD = .37*	Will continue to be part of job

Note: * Rating scale (1–7) values, based on the three skill variety items from the Job Diagnostic Survey (JDS).

new pay system or a changed pay system, several issues can arise. First, there may be a lack of trust in the new pay system especially if employees have not been involved in the design and implementation of the pay system. Distrust may stem from the pay system being new or because it is different from traditional systems. Hence, participation in decision-making concerning the compensation system would appear to be essential in virtual organizations.

Second, there may be differences not only in pay but also in the pay systems of employees working side by side. This is especially true in the case of alliances as a form of virtual organization where the alliance may have employees from different companies with different pay systems working with one another. In order to manage this issue, virtual organizations must be very attentive to internal equity issues when designing pay systems. Not only must actual pay systems be made comparable to one another, but also employee perceptions of the comparability are important and necessary. Organizational surveys would be an important component of this process to monitor employee perceptions.

VIRTUAL ORGANIZATION FORMS AND HYBRID REWARD SYSTEMS

There is no one agreed upon definition of virtual organizations. As a result, organizations and researchers must wrestle with a variety of different types of organizational structures that might fall under the virtual organization category label. The purpose of this section of the chapter is to delineate the various forms of virtual organizations and, based on the previous literature review, indicate the types of hybrid reward systems that might be appropriate for each form of virtual organization.

Horizontal Organizations

Horizontal organizations are structured such that teams are used to facilitate horizontal processes in organizations. Bureaucracy, which tends to emphasize vertical processes, is minimized. In short, horizontal organizations are so named because they operate independent of the traditional bureaucracy. There are two types of horizontal organizations: intact work teams and temporary work teams.

Intact Work Teams

In an organization with intact work teams, work is organized on the basis of permanent teams. An auto manufacturer, for example, may have a series of teams organized around various car components (e.g., engine, drive train, etc.). Employee skill levels are critical in this type of environment because model changes occur frequently and also because employees are expected to perform multiple tasks. In this type of production environment, where skills are highly valued, skill-based pay would lend itself well to an intact work team structure. Team-based and/or business unit variable pay might also be useful in fostering group cohesion and morale. 360-degree reviews might be used to certify skill mastery by team members; balanced scorecards might be useful to give team members insight as to how they are performing on several relevant dimensions. Because the impact of any one team on overall organizational performance is low, the level of stock and profit to be allocated to a team should also be low. Instead, variable pay should be offered for operational results under the team's control. It is recommended that a defined benefits retirement plan (contribution of benefits) be provided to retain employees that are learning fairly company specific skills. Indirect rewards in the form of recognition may help increase intrinsic motivation and retain employees.

Temporary Work Teams

Temporary work teams are defined by a collection of people that come together to pursue common goals for a specified period of time and then disband. Hence, they are temporary rather than permanent. Examples include tasks forces and new product development teams.

An example of a new product development team is shown in Figure 1 and will be used to further describe this virtual form. New product development teams are often cross-functional in nature. These teams comprise the brightest and hardest working from each of the functional areas. Often, in areas such as information technology, they represent the core capability of the company; that is, if new and innovative products and services are not brought to market in a timely manner, the company will falter. These teams are highly dependent upon operations teams that ensure the product or service developed by the new product development team performs up to specifications.

With this form of virtual organization, the emphasis is more on results than skill development. Results must be achieved by the new product development for the organization to survive and these results are under the control of the new product development team. Because the performance of

```
┌─────────────────────────────────────┐
│          Management Team            │
└─────────────────────────────────────┘
```

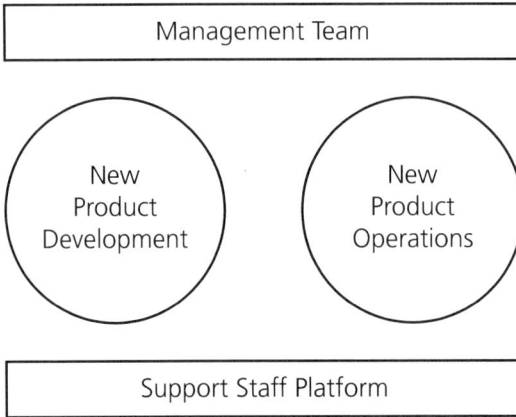

```
┌─────────────────────────────────────┐
│        Support Staff Platform       │
└─────────────────────────────────────┘
```

Figure 1.   New product development teams.

the new product operations team is highly dependent upon well-designed products or services from the new product development team, stock as well as variable pay should be used so that the two different types of teams are interdependent upon one another (e.g., team pay or gainsharing). In small or start-up companies it might be possible to achieve the same outcomes with some type of profit sharing plan. Performance review methods such as 360-degree feedback and the balanced scorecard approaches can provide meaningful insight into managing the complex interdependence among and within teams.

Again, a defined benefits plan may help retain these brightest and hardest working individuals. These are the types of individuals who also may value indirect rewards such as professional development, mentoring and job assignments.

Network Organization

In a network organization, core functions in which the organization has competitive advantage are retained in the organization while non-core functions are outsourced. As an example of a network organization, Figure 2 shows a network organization for a consulting firm. Because of the outsourced functions, the reward system must focus on aligning the interests of the outsourced firms with the interests of the consultants. To do so, emphasis must be placed upon variable pay and to a lesser degree, profit sharing to make this alignment happen. Performance review methods such as 360-degree feedback and the balanced scorecard approaches can provide meaningful insight into managing the complex interdependence among and

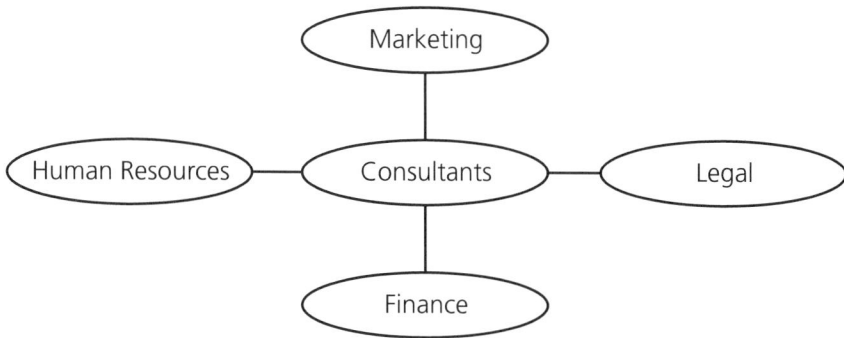

Figure 2.   Network organization

within teams. Stock should be at a minimum for the outsourced firm because the outsourced firms are not owners and they will dilute the stock available for the consultants taking the risk in this relationship.

Cash balance benefits should be used, especially for the outsourced firms where employees may continuously turnover. However, defined benefit programs may be appropriate when there is an identifiable "core" group of employees that the firm wishes to retain. Indirect rewards such as training, visibility, gifts, praise, job assignments and physical space may be used to establish the culture and to motivate individuals, particularly in the outsourced firms.

Alliances

Organizations partner together in order to become the "best product or service and lowest cost" provider; hence, the best element of each organization is combined. An example of an alliance is shown in Figure 3. TIA is the alliance and it is formed with three organizations: Bank One, AT&T, and IBM. In order to provide outstanding financial services, Bank One provides the business, AT&T brings the network, and IBM brings the information technology.

In order to align the interests of the parties together, profit sharing and variable pay should be used. Performance review methods such as 360-degree feedback and the balanced scorecard approaches can provide meaningful insight into managing the complex interdependence among and within teams. Stock is difficult to offer because there are three different "owners" of the alliance. As a substitute for stock however, phantom stock could be created whereby a book value proxy is created to substitute for the market value of the company.

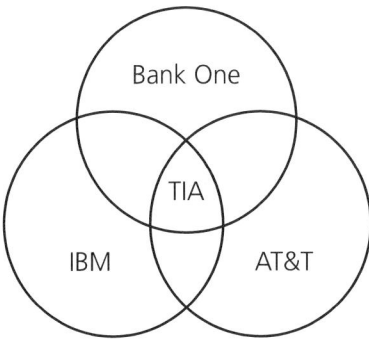

Figure 3.   Alliance

Due to the interaction required of the various firms and the reduced costs involved, cash balance benefits may be used along with a strong emphasis on indirect rewards. For example, job assignments and the psychological meaningfulness of the work may help the integration of the companies to better produce and service customers. Awards, gifts, praise and visibility may also be enticement to increase motivation.

Cellular Organizations

A cellular organization is very similar to an alliance. However, unlike an alliance, the boundaries of customers, suppliers, outsourcers, and other organizations axe blurred and blended. The organization is like a cell in that it is living and adaptive (Miles et al., 1997), and is usually temporary in nature. As shown in Figure 4, the structure is so named because the form even resembles a cell under the microscope.

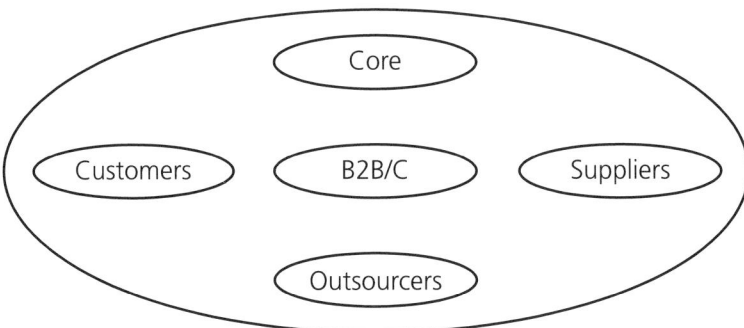

Figure 4.   Cellular organization

Again, as with networks and alliances, alignment of the parties' interests is an issue. Because the boundaries of the various organizations are blurred, it is very difficult to use variable pay; that is, performance attributable to each part of the cell is uncertain. When this is the case, high emphasis needs to be placed upon profit sharing in order to align interests. Performance review methods such as 360-degree feedback and the balanced scorecard approaches can provide meaningful insight into managing the complex interdependence among and within teams. Stock can be used as well if ownership is well understood. If not, then phantom stock can be used. As with networks and alliances, cash balance benefits should be used along with heavy emphasis on indirect pay. The former recognizes the temporary nature of the organizational structure while the latter recognizes the need to build an identifiable culture across the various constituents' part of the structure.

Because of the blurred boundaries between the organizations, skill-based pay is needed to develop "soft" skills to deal with the ambiguity of the structure. These soft skills might include self-management, conflict management, and stress management.

Summary

As can be seen in this section, not all forms of virtual organizations warrant the same reward systems. Differences in hybrid systems for various forms of virtual organizations are summarized in Table 4.

Table 4.   Recommended Pay Components by Virtual Organization Form

| | Virtual Organization Form | | | | |
| | Horizontal | | | | |
Pay Component	Intact Team	Temporary Team	Network	Alliances	Cellular
Skill Based Pay	High	Low	Low	Low	High
Variable Pay	Mod	High	High	Mod	Low
Stock	Low	Mod	Low	Mod	High
Profit Sharing	Low	Mod	Mod	High	High
Indirect Rewards	Mod	Mod	High	High	High
Defined Benefits	High	High	None	None	None
Cash Balance Benefits	None	None	High	High	High

IMPLICATIONS

Given the newness of virtual organizations and the limited amount of literature to draw upon, there are important implications for where we go next with rewarding people. Recommended action steps will be grouped by research and practice. However, we believe that development in pay systems for virtual organizations will be best served by the interchange between research and practice.

Research

Several related areas are in need of immediate research attention. First, research is needed with the organization as the unit of analysis to study the effectiveness of various reward systems in alternative virtual organization forms. Work has already been conducted on mechanistic versus organic organizations (Gomez-Mejia & Balkin, 1992) and it needs to be expanded to look at various organizational forms within the organic category.

Second, given the newness of these virtual organization forms and compensation practices, rigorous case study research is needed as well. Rigorous case study research has a long history in human resources and industrial relations. More of this type of research is now needed in the new economy. Crandall and Wallace (1998) present an excellent start in this area.

Third, as pay systems become more fluid (e.g., broadbanding) in virtual organizations, internal equity issues are likely to arise. It would appear that the units that are being "counted" for pay purposes (e.g., skills, seniority, performance) may not be clear to employees. As a result, distributive and procedural equity issues are likely to arise. These potential problems with new organizational structures and new compensation systems seem to have been ignored in the literature. While equity issues have been heavily researched in traditional organizations, they deserve another look in virtual organizations.

Practice

Pay practices in virtual organizations need to be rethought both in terms of content and process. In terms of content, care must be taken in selecting the appropriate pay components for various forms of virtual organizations. Popular pay plans, especially stock options, are touted as a panacea in the press. As shown here, stock options, as well as other new forms of pay, must be carefully matched with the organizational structure in order to be effective.

In terms of process, employee participation in decision-making is absolutely crucial with the hybrid pay forms being used in virtual organizations. Participation by employees should be included in pay plan design, implementation, and administration. By involving employees, they are more likely to understand the pay system, trust it, and be willing to act upon it to further the goals of the organization. This lesson for pay systems was pointed out years ago by Lawler (1981), but now seems to have particular salience for virtual organizations.

CONCLUSION

The new reality of the workplace necessitates the *interdependence* of jobs, thus rendering traditional paradigms nearly obsolete (e.g., bureaucratic structures). Reward systems have fortunately evolved over the years to accompany this transformation in work. As a result, organizations have many options to consider when developing a pay system for a virtual organization. The key to this process, however, is to carefully match the appropriate reward system to each type of virtual organization structure. As shown in this chapter, there is no one universal best practice when it comes to reward systems in virtual organizations.

REFERENCES

American Compensation Association. (1996). *Raising the bar: Using competencies to enhance employee performance.* Scottsdale, AZ: Author.

Burlingame, H.W. & Gulotta, M.J. (1998, November/December). Cash balance pension plan facilitates restructuring the workforce at AT&T. *Compensation and Benefits Review.*

Cantoni, C.J. (1997). Learn to manage pay and perform like an entrepreneur. *Compensation and Benefits Review.*

Crandall, N.F., & Wallace, M.J., Jr. (1998). *Work and rewards in the virtual workplace.* New York: AMACOM.

Crandall, N.F., & Wallace, M.J., Jr. (1997). Inside the virtual workplace: Forging a new deal for work and rewards. *Compensation and Benefits Review, 29,* 27–36.

Fried, Y., & Ferris, G.R. (1987). The validity of the job characteristics model: A review and meta-analysis. *Personnel Psychology, 40,* 287–322.

Gomez-Mejia, L.R., & Balkin, D.B. (1992). *Compensation, organizational strategy, & firm performance.* Cincinnati, OH: South-Western.

Heneman, R.L. (2001). *Business-driven compensation policies.* New York: AMACOM.

Heneman, H.G., III, & Heneman, R.L. (1994). *Staffing organizations.* Madison, WI: Mendota House and Austen Press.

Heneman, R.L., Ledford, G.E., Jr., & Gresham, M.T. (1999). The effects of changes in the nature of work on compensation. In S. Rynes & B. Gerhart (Eds.), *Com-*

pensation in organizations: Progress and prospects. San Francisco: New Lexington Press.

Heneman, R.L. (1992). *Merit pay*. Reading, MA: Addison-Wesley.

Heneman, R.L. (1986). The relationship between supervisory ratings and results-oriented measures of performance: A meta-analysis. *Personnel Psychology, 39,* 811–826.

Kaplan, R.S., & Norton, D.P. (1996). *The balanced scorecard*. Boston: Harvard Business School Press.

Klaas, B.S. (2000). Compensation in the jobless world. *Human Resource Management Review*.

Lawler, E.E., III (1981). *Pay and organizational development*. Reading, MA: Addison Wesley.

Ledford, G.E., & Heneman, R.L. (2000). Pay for skills, knowledge, and competencies. In L. Berger & D. Berger, (Eds.) *The compensation handbook: A state-of-the-art guide to compensation strategy and design* (4th ed.). New York: McGraw-Hill.

Loher, B.T., Noe, R.A., Moeller, N.L., & Fitzgerald, M.P. (1985). A meta-analysis of the relation of job characteristics to job satisfaction. *Journal of Applied Psychology, 70,* 280–289.

McNamee, M. (1999, October 4). Good pensions, bad sales pitch. *Business Week*, p. 44.

Miles, R.E., Snow, C.C., Mathews, J.A., Miles, G., & Coleman, H.J. Jr. (1997). Organizing in the knowledge age: Anticipating the cellular form. *Academy of Management Executive, 11,* 7–20.

Milkovich, G.T., & Newman, J.M. (1999). *Compensation* (6th ed.). Boston: Irwin McGraw-Hill.

Murray, B.C., & Gerhart, B. (1998). An empirical analysis of a skill-based pay program and plant performance outcomes. *Academy of Management Journal, 41,* 68–78.

Oppel, R.A., Jr. (1999, August 20). Companies cash in on new pension plan. *New York Times*, pp. C1, C16.

Platten, P., & Weinberg, C.R. (2000, January/February). Shattering the myths about dot.com pay. *Compensation and Benefits Review*, pp. 21–27.

Robbins, S.P. (1990). *Organization theory: Structure, design, and applications* (3rd ed.). Engelwood Cliffs, NJ: Prentice-Hall.

Tonkin, L.A.P., & Ellis, C.M. 91997). Team performance and rewards: Building responsibility for results. *Target, 13,* 1–4.

Tucker, S.A. (1995). The role of pay in the boundryless organization. *ACA Journal, 4*(3), 48–59.

CHAPTER 5

ALTERNATIVE REWARDS IN UNIONIZED ENVIRONMENTS

Robert L. Heneman, Courtney von Hippel, Don E. Eskew, and David B. Greenberger

Source: Heneman, R.L., von Hippel, C., Eskew, D.E., & Greenberger, D.B. (1997, Summer). Alternative Rewards in Unionized Environments. *American Compensation Association Journal*, pp. 42–55. Reprinted from ACA Journal, Summer 1997, with permission from WorldatWork (formerly American Compensation Association); 14040 N. Northsight Blvd., Scottsdale, AZ 85260; phone (877) 951-9191; fax (480) 483-8352; www.worldatwork.org. (copyright) 1997 WorldatWork. Unauthorized reproduction or distribution is strictly prohibited.

A strategic decision that must be reached in unionized work environments is what type of reward systems to use. An essential part of this decision-making process is knowing what types of reward systems are acceptable to unions and thus likely to be agreed upon in the collective bargaining agreement. To provide guidance in. this area, a framework has been developed to show the conditions under which various alternative reward strategies are likely to be acceptable to unions (see Figure 1). Components of the framework include:

- External influences.
- Organizational dynamics.
- Performance measures.
- Collective bargaining.
- The pay system.

> An alternative reward strategy uses direct compensation plans that are alternatives to paying employees based on time on the job, with the organization or since degree, or to granting base pay increases that are related to the value of the specific job held. Plans covered by this definition include lump sum merit pay, piece-rate pay, skilled-based pay, gainsharing, goalsharing, profit sharing and stock sharing.
>
> *Source:* ACA Certification Seminar C12, "Alternative Rewards Systems—Improving Performance and Competitiveness"

Figure 1. Definition of alternative rewards

About 150 unionized firms and 350 nonunionized firms in both manufacturing and service provided data for this study. Some results of the study are:

- Unionized organizations are more likely to use skill-based pay, gainsharing, goalsharing and stock sharing than nonunionized organizations.
- Unionized organizations are more likely to design alternative reward plans with objective, group-based performance measures. Nonunionized organizations are more likely to use subjective, individual performance measures.
- Unionized organizations are more likely to base performance standards on historical standards. Nonunionized organizations are less likely to do so.
- Unionized organizations are more likely to provide payouts to employees in equal pay amounts. Nonunionized organizations are more likely to provide different pay amounts based on individual employee performance.

ALTERNATIVE REWARDS AND THE
BUSINESS ENVIRONMENT

Increasingly, organizations are shifting away from traditional pay systems, which reward people for time in the job and number of hours worked, toward alternative reward strategies which reward employees for their performance (Lawler, Mohrman, & Ledford, 1995). The reason for this shift in pay preferences by organizations is due in part to the mounting evidence showing that alternative reward strategies are associated with improved organizational effectiveness (McAdams & Hawk, 1994). While alternative reward strategies are effective in some situations, they may not work in all. Alternative rewards need to be carefully matched both to the internal business environment (e.g., culture) and to the external business environment (e.g., customers) (Lawler, 1990).

One important factor connected to the external business environment is the presence or absence of a union. According to the National Labor Relations Act of 1935 (NLRA), if a work force is represented by a union, then management must bargain collectively with union officials over wages (financial rewards, as well as benefits and base pay), hours and working conditions.

Management must carefully design reward systems that are likely to be acceptable to a union or unions that are present in the organization. Understanding how union members view alternative rewards and how NLRA operates is necessary to design, administer and use alternative reward strategies to improve organizational effectiveness. This understanding also helps management keep the reward system from being a source of grievances and/or labor actions.

In the absence of an acceptable reward system, a union may refuse to allow a reward system other than one based on seniority in the organization. Alternatively, a union may accept the reward system to gain some other concession from management but then file a large number of grievances over the implementation of the plan. Either an impasse or, more likely, a large number of grievances can have a negative impact on the execution of alternative reward strategies.

Only about 20 percent of U.S. collective bargaining agreements have alternative reward system clauses agreed upon by labor and management (McAdams & Hawk, 1994; U.S. Department of Labor, 1981). However, without an alternative reward system, a unionized organization may not be as effective. A 1994 study of manufacturing firms showed that while alternative reward plans add to the organizational effectiveness of unionized organizations, their impact is greater in comparable nonunionized organizations (Cooke, 1994).

Unfortunately, there is little information on alternative reward practices in unionized organizations to guide decision makers on how best to use alternative rewards. One study summarized the research on traditional pay plans in unionized environments but did not review alternative rewards (Balkin, 1989). Another study looked at the use of many human resources strategies in unionized settings, including alternative rewards, but did not provide much detail on alternative rewards and was limited only to manufacturing organizations (Ng & Maki, 1994).

This paucity of information is unfortunate because, even though the level of unionization is declining in this country, many large organizations in industries such as the automobile industry must still bargain collectively with a union. Compensation practices in unionized firms have important implications for organizations that wish to remain nonunion. The objective of this study is to provide strategic decision makers in organizations with information on how to approach the use of alternative rewards in unionized environments.

A DIAGNOSTIC FRAMEWORK AND PROPOSITIONS

Figure 2 presents a framework to help strategic decision makers understand when unions will most likely accept an alternative reward system as part of the collective bargaining agreement. For an alternative reward plan to be accepted, union officials and union members need to endorse the plan and ratify the agreement before it is put into practice.

It should be noted that acceptance of the plan by the union does not necessarily mean that it favors the plan. There are several reasons why unions may grudgingly accept a reward plan:

- Union members want to preserve union jobs.
- Agreeing to the plan means gaining concession from management on another issue.
- Union members lack the bargaining power needed to convince management not to use alternative rewards. (Bargaining power refers to the ability of Party A to influence Party B to act in a manner consistent with the goals of Party A.)

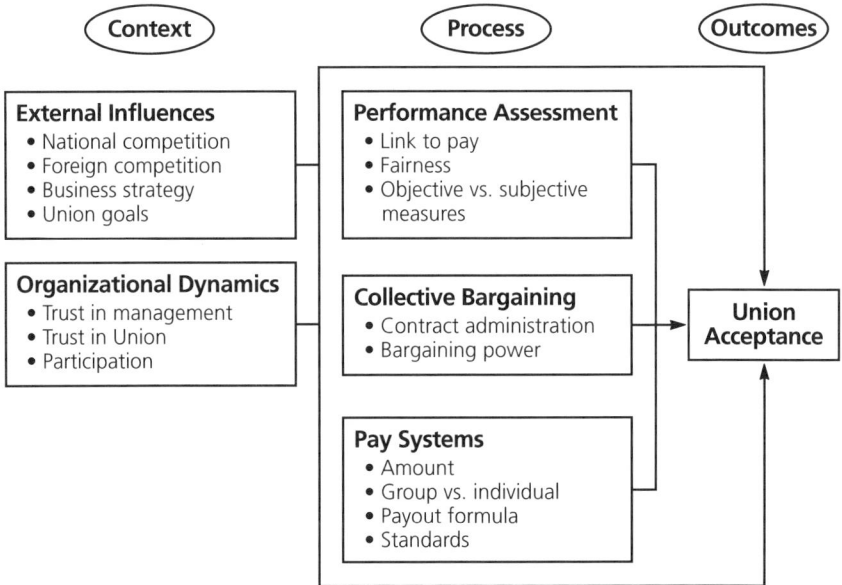

Figure 2.   Diagnostic framework for alternative rewards in unionized settings

Both the context and process must be favorable for an alternative reward system to be accepted. The context consists of external influences and organizational dynamics. The process consists of performance assessment, collective bargaining and the pay system.

REWARD SYSTEM CONTEXT

Context refers to forces inside and outside the organization that can influence the use of rewards in a unionized setting. There are two categories of context variables that affect union acceptance of an alternative reward system: external influences and organizational dynamics.

External Influences

External circumstances constrain what unions can accomplish for their members. Two external constraints placed on organizations and unions are national and foreign competition. Because of heightened competition during the past decade, organizations and unions are striving to produce better products with greater efficiency. Unions may be more willing to consider alternative reward plans if those plans are viewed as an economic necessity. For example, intense national and foreign competition may lead corporate management and union leaders to realize that increased production and efficiency are necessary not only to achieve production goals but also to survive.

Several studies provide support for this idea. One study showed that union leaders are more likely to cooperate with management when the organization is at risk of dissolution, something that could occur if an organization loses its competitiveness (Hammer & Stern, 1986). Another study found that cooperation among several organizations and their unions was stimulated by adverse competitive situations (Schuster, 1983). It has been proposed that when a company is in a "crisis situation"—perhaps caused by extreme competition—alternative reward systems already in place will be revised to address the situation (e.g., competition may force union members to accept higher gainsharing standards) (Slichter et al., 1960).

Unions tend to be more receptive to incentive plans than to wage concessions when facing severe competitive pressures (Cardinal & Helburn, 1987). Another reasonable argument is that under severe economic competition, unions may be more receptive to pay at risk plans. With pay at risk plans, an opportunity exists to earn back or even to exceed the amount of wage placed at risk. In contrast, lost wages cannot be re-earned with a wage concession plan. Also, unions and management seek higher levels of cooperation when they have a common problem that cannot be solved by traditional means (Kochan & Dyer, 1976). If alternative rewards are tied to more targeted work goals for increased competitiveness, employee outcomes from these incentives might be more favorable.

It may also be argued that unions will react differently to foreign competition than to national competition. One way that organizations can gain competitive advantage in their markets is to compete on the basis of price. One way to be able to offer lower prices is to reduce wages. In a national market, the threat of reduced wages can be countered by attempts to organize the entire industry (Fossum, 1992). By organizing the entire industry, wages are taken out of competition by the standardization of wage rates. In international markets, however, it is much more difficult to take wages out of competition by organizing workers across national borders. As a result, unions may be more accepting of increased productivity through incentive wage plans to counter the threat of reduced wages.

While some firms react to their environment through the use of alternative reward strategies, other firms are proactive in the use of alternative reward systems. They base the systems on business strategy. It is desirable for organizations to set a compensation policy that is in agreement with the overall strategy of the organization (Gomez-Mejia & Balkin, 1992). Business strategy is important to unions, and successful unions of the future must be involved with top management in the setting of strategy (Kochan, Katz, & McKersie, 1986; Kochan & Weaver, 1991).

An argument can be made that union members will have a more difficult time accepting union agreement of a reward system when that system is part of a proactive business strategy. This lack of acceptance is a result of the traditional exclusion of union members from strategy formulation. Union members are skeptical of labor-management cooperation in the setting of long-term goals (Lewin, 1987).

The concept of a business strategy may suggest to unions that there is a predetermined plan to implement policies and procedures that unions have historically rebelled against (e.g., subjective performance appraisal). Finally, business strategy may be seen by the union as a management policy that is more or less dictated to employees. Only in relatively few organizations has the union been treated as a partner in the formulation of business strategy (Lawler & Mohrman, 1987). Unlike competitive market pressures, strategy may be viewed as something that is forced upon workers rather than as a pressure that must be faced for job survival and seen as a rationale to undermine the union (see Figure 3).

Implicit in the following propositions is the idea that the level of competition has a critical impact on plan acceptance. Extreme or severe competition when union members' jobs or pay are at stake is more likely than light competition to motivate union acceptance of the plan. Also, severe competition is more likely to motivate management to include the union in business planning efforts.

- When the major reason for the institution of an alternative reward system in a unionized setting is national competition, there will be more union acceptance of that system than when national competition is not a major reason for the implementation of the implementation of the system.
- When the major reason for the institution of an alternative reward system in a unionized setting is foreign competition, there will be more union acceptance of that system than when foreign competition is not a major reason for the implementation of the system.
- Greater union acceptance for an alternative reward system will occur when foreign competition, rather than national competition, is a major reason for the implementation of the system.
- Union acceptance of an alternative reward plan is more likely when there is greater participation of the union in the formulation of business strategy.

The goals of the union as well as goals of the company also have a bearing on the acceptance of. alternative reward strategies. Job security is a primary concern of unions (Fossum 1992). A pay plan that is likely to preserve jobs is also likely to be more acceptable to the union.

Unions sometimes are fearful of alternative reward plans because if the plans are successful and increase productivity, fewer employees may be needed. Unions are more likely to accept an alternative reward plan in a contract when it is coupled with a job-security provision. The following proposition suggests that management should commit to a strategy of redeployment when alternative rewards lead to work elimination. This type of strategy is only possible for growing rather than shrinking organizations.

- Alternative reward plans are more likely to be acceptable to unions when they do not threaten the union's goal of job security for union members.

Figure 3.   How external influences affect union acceptance of alternative reward plans.

Organizational Dynamics

Whether the implementation and administration of an alternative reward system is successful depends on the information, knowledge and power relationships of all involved (Lawler, 1990; McMahan & Lawler, 1995). This broad category of relationships is labeled as organizational dynamics in the alternative reward framework. It embraces the attitudes of union members toward the major players who implement and administer the incentive pay plan.

Several hypotheses concerning organizational dynamics can be formulated from various studies (Barkin, 1948, 1970; Lawler & Mohrman, 1987). A major factor influencing organizational dynamics is trust in management, which has always been a concern of unions. This can be a key variable in determining union members' outcomes from incentive pay systems. Union members' reactions to an incentive agreement depend heavily on workers' perceptions of management control, management expectations and administration (Barkin, 1948, 1970). One study has proposed that the results of an incentive system depend on "the character of union-management relations" (Slichter et al., 1960).

If unions have little trust in management intentions, they may be concerned that incentives will take away from union members (Wildstrom, 1986). Unions also may believe that incentive programs are political tools used by management to gain more control over workers (Heneman, 1992). Basic cooperation mechanisms such as trust, fair dealing and mutuality must exist for management-labor programs to be implemented successfully (Voos, 1989). If trust in management is low, acceptance of the reward system by the union is unlikely.

The trust that union members have in the union also may play a role in the acceptance of the reward system. Consideration of its members' needs should be paramount for the union (Freeman & Medoff, 1979). How the union implements policy may affect how union members respond to the incentive system (Slichter et al., 1960). Union members may also rely on the "instrumental" relationship with their union to determine their perceptions toward union representatives (Brett, 1980). Rewards that the union secures for union members inspire loyalty. If numbers trust their union representatives to increase rewards, then acceptance of a reward system in the collective bargaining agreement is more likely.

Actions by national unions can affect perceptions of trust as well. For many unions, goals and practices pertaining to compensation are important and could ultimately influence decisions (Strauss, 1977). For example, national union policy could dismiss efforts at implementing incentive pay, even if local chapters view incentive pay as favorable. National boards and policy makers do influence wage decisions and, in some cases, "affirm" or "veto" decisions and agreements made at the local level (Fiorito & Hendricks, 1987). Outcomes from inventive systems at the local union level may depend on union policy at the national level and on how active the national body has been in shaping collective bargaining agreements to include incentive clauses.

A second variable in the organizational dynamics category is union participation in decision making. Research has shown that unions favor union representation and participation in an organization's decision making and are dissatisfied when they are not granted that participation (Gaertner & Gaertner, 1987). Various studies have also shown that productivity increases when cooperative labor-management programs are operating in organizations (Cooke, 1989; Cooke & Meyer, 1990; Schuster, 1983; Voos, 1987, 1989). Another study suggests that union involvement with incentive systems is a critical factor in members' reactions to such systems (Barkin, 1948). In unionized settings, employee participation in the creation and implementation of incentive plans increases acceptance of those involved (McMahan & Lawler, 1995). This suggests that the more the union is involved with corporate decisions and the administration of agreements such as reward programs, the more favorably union members will react to such agreements.

Individuals commonly join unions for the sense of participation in decision making that leads to a sense of control and influence (Alutto & Belasco, 1974; Hammer & Berman, 1978), especially the ability to negotiate with management (Hammer & Berman, 1978; Leigh, 1986). It can be theorized

The first proposition listed here may be moderated by the level of competition faced by the company. The greater the level of competitive threat, the less important trust may be to the acceptance of the reward strategy. Faced with a competitive threat, labor may be more likely to see the actual need for an alternative reward strategy, rather than simply trusting management that it is the "right thing to do."

- When union representatives' trust in management is high, union acceptance of the alternative reward system will be more favorable than when trust in management is low.
- When union representatives' trust in the union is high, union acceptance of the alternative reward system will be more favorable than when trust in the union is low.
- When participation in formal decision making by. unions is high within the organization, union acceptance of the alternative reward system will be more favorable than when participation is low.

Figure 4.   How organizational dynamics affect union acceptance of alternative reward plans.

that unions see participation as a means of personal control (Greenberger & Strasser, 1986). When union members actively participate in the formulation and maintenance of reward strategies, this participation should lead to a greater union acceptance of the alternative reward plan (see Figure 4).

REWARD SYSTEM PROCESS

Process refers to the administrative aspects of the reward system. Within the diagnostic framework, process consists of three categories of variables: performance assessment, collective bargaining and the pay system.

Performance Assessment

Performance assessment is fundamentally connected to any reward system. Not all unionized businesses, however, have performance-based reward systems. In a reward system, pay is tied to performance to motivate improved performance. While assessments are necessary and are ideally in the worker's best interests, they are disliked by many involved because they rely ultimately on human judgment (Lawler, 1990). Judgments must be made about the standards used to gauge performance and the desired level of employee performance relative to the standards (Heneman & von Hippel, 1997). For performance assessments to be accepted, they must be seen as accurately portraying the results attained and the effort put forth by those being appraised. Assessments must reflect actual performance to work effectively in reward systems.

Perceptions of performance assessments are not always favorable in unionized settings. There is sometimes an assumption that evaluations are not conducted fairly for those receiving them. Unions have generally resisted merit pay plans because of the presupposed subjectivity of evaluations (Freeman, 1982), unless they are used for developmental rather than reward discussions (Ng & Mild, 1994). Another major reason for opposition is that union members feel they are in competition with each other when their individual performance is evaluated (Balkin, 1989; Freeman, 1982). A study looking at U.S. government employees found that union employees were significantly less satisfied with their performance evaluations than nonunion employees (Gaertner & Gaertner, 1987). For union representatives to accept the tie between appraisals and incentives, measures should be as objective as possible (Balkan, 1989). Two key factors that may greatly influence reactions and outcomes in these reward system agreements are perceived fairness and the types of assessments made (see Figure 5).

- When performance assessments are seen as fair, union acceptance of the reward plan is more likely than when appraisal systems are seen as unfair.
- When performance assessments are seen as objective, union acceptance of the reward plan is more likely than when appraisal systems are seen as subjective.

Figure 5.   How performance assessment affects union acceptance of alternative reward plans.

Performance assessments are more likely to be seen as more objective in some alternative reward plans than in others (see Figure 6). For example, formula-driven plans such as gainsharing and profit sharing are more likely to be seen as objective than merit pay plans that are less-formula driven and more at the discretion of managerial ratings. As another example, the objective-setting process may be seen as unfair when there is no employee participation with management in the setting of objectives.

Performance assessments are more likely to be seen as fair when:
- Reliable and valid performance measures are used.
- Training is provided on how to measure performance.
- Assessment decisions can be appealed.
- Laws and regulations are followed.
- Managers are held accountable for their assessment.
- Employees participate in the development of performance standards (Heneman 1992).

Figure 6.   Making performance assessment "fair."

Collective Bargaining

Also important to alternative rewards is the contract that specifies incentive standards. The basic standards of the alternative reward plan agreement must be set through collective bargaining to comply with NLRA. The contract provided by this process should establish the rules and procedures for the reward system. However, collective bargaining agreements do not always adequately explain who will evaluate performance, how increases will be given, how grievances should be handled and what will be considered adequate performance for subsequent rewards. These are all potential administrative problems and are of critical interest to unions.

A union's acceptance of an incentive agreement is related to the proposed and actual system (Barkin, 1948, 1970). Because of these concerns, the contract clause on rewards should address all phases of evaluation, work standards, procedures for determination of increases and problem-solving procedures for union representatives.

Unions can also be wary of reward agreements for several other administrative reasons (Barkin, 1970). Unions may wish to avoid reward systems altogether because they do not want to deal with the intricacies of implementing the system. Union representatives need to feel that they will be allowed to assist in the administration of the program, be able to monitor the program and be given the freedom to communicate information about the program to their members (Barkin, 1948). If management has a history of not addressing these issues, union representatives may hinder the acceptance of the contract or raise unexpected problems during the administration of the contract.

Also related to the administration of incentive plans is how reward system decisions are made. An important concept in the administration of such plans is procedural justice, which is concerned with the fairness of the procedures used to make decisions (Greenberg & Folger, 1983). When individuals believe the procedures used to make a decision are fair, they are more likely to believe that the outcomes of that decision are fair (Folger & Greenberg, 1985; Greenberg, 1987).

If union members believe that the procedures used to determine and support increases are fair (performance evaluations, statistical formulas, grievance procedures and timely resolution of grievances, and adequate union representation in the administration of the agreement), they will be more likely to consider the system fair. One study has demonstrated that union members' evaluations of grievance procedures are more important than the pay outcomes they received from that system (Fryxell & Gordon, 1989) (see Figure 7).

- When the administration of the alternative reward plan is seen as fair, the union is more likely to accept the reward system than when the administration of the alternative reward plan is seen as unfair.
- When union representatives are satisfied with the administration of the grievance system, union acceptance of the alternative reward plan is more likely than when representatives are dissatisfied with the administration of the alternative reward plan.
- Alternative reward plans are more likely to be acceptable to unions when unions have less bargaining power than management.

Figure 7.   How collective bargaining affects union acceptance of alternative reward plans.

In addition to the administration of the contract, another facet of collective bargaining as it relates to alternative rewards is the bargaining power of labor and management. Unions may reluctantly concede to an incentive pay clause in the contract because they are forced to do so by management. Unions have less power when they represent low-skilled workers and when they do not represent all the workers in a geographic area (Fossum, 1992). Unions may concede an incentive clause to management to persuade management to offer the union a concession on another issue (e.g., job security).

The Pay System

The amount of pay increases from an incentive plan is directly linked to union acceptance of reward systems. Union members need to see that the system in place is providing rewards that are at least equal to other reward systems that could have been bargained. With the likely problems of administration and resistance to performance evaluations under a reward system, the union members' ultimate evaluation of the system may rest on the actual rewards earned. They have to be certain that the reward system is not a ruse to lessen the amount of rewards.

Whether incentives are provided to groups or individuals will likely influence the union's reaction to the system. Paying individual rewards to union members for increased performance poses problems to unions. Two basic problems have been described in connection with individual evaluations. Individual rewards may lead to employee competition, which is a concern of union representatives (Balkin, 1989; Freeman, 1982), and evaluations are perceived as subjective in nature (Freeman, 1982).

There are several additional reasons why group, rather than individual, rewards may be viewed as more desirable by union members:

- *Group rewards do not pit member against member.* Rather, they fit more closely with the union desire of group representation and group benefits.
- *Group rewards fit more closely with predicted compensation practices of the future, both in unionized and nonunionized environments.* Population demographics, technology and new types of jobs will demand changes in the future that are predicted to be best rewarded by group and team incentives, rather than by individual compensation (Deckop & Mahoney, 1989).
- *Administering group plans may be easier than administering individual incentive agreements.* In large group plans (e.g., profit sharing, gainsharing), more quantifiable, exact standards may be used to reward

group productivity rather than the more subjective measures that are often associated with individual evaluation (e.g., merit pay).

While individual pay incentives may be used successfully in certain organizations, group plans will be more acceptable to unions than individual plans. One exception may be profit-sharing plans. One survey of manufacturers found some evidence of union resistance to these plans (Ng & Maki, 1994).

One might also argue that the specific characteristics of the incentive plan influences the outcomes of these plans. While studies have found virtually no differences in employee reactions to incentive plan characteristics between unionized and nonunionized firms (Cardinal & Helburn, 1987), two characteristics are likely to stand out:

- *The payout formula for distributing rewards.*   For solidarity to prevail among union members, the members are likely to prefer that an equal-dollar payout go to each member rather than a different amount going to each member based on individual performance.
- *The standard used to gauge the level of performance needed to trigger a payout to employees.*   Union members are likely to prefer the standard be based on historical output standards rather than standards based on management discretion. Standards based on a historical basis may be seen as more attainable and less subject to a "ratcheting up of standards" used by past managers (see Figure 8).

- The larger the payout to union members from an incentive pay plan, the greater the likelihood of union acceptance of the incentive pay plan.
- Union acceptance of group-based alternative reward plans is likely to be higher than union acceptance of individual-based alternative reward plans.
- Union acceptance is likely to be greater when expected performance levels are based on historical standards rather than management discretion.
- Union acceptance will be greater when equal dollar payouts are given, rather than differential payments based on individual employee performance.

Figure 8.   How the pay system affects union acceptance of alternative reward plans.

COMPARING UNIONIZED AND NONUNIONIZED FIRMS

Few empirical studies have been conducted to examine systematic differences in alternative reward practices between unionized and nonunionized organizations. Those studies that have been conducted are now dated. Clearly, more research is needed.

A descriptive empirical study was conducted to see if, consistent with the diagnostic framework, there are systematic differences in the use of alternative rewards by unionized and nonunionized firms. The expected outcome was that for those organizations with strategic rewards, the unionized organizations would rely primarily upon objective measures of performance and group rewards, while the nonunionized organizations would rely upon subjective measures of employee performance and individual rewards. It was also expected that payouts would be distributed equally in unionized settings and distributed by individual performance in nonunionized settings, and that the performance standards used to determine payouts would be based on a historical standard in unionized settings.

Data were collected as a portion of a large research project sponsored by ACA and conducted by the Consortium of Alternative Rewards Strategies Research (CARS) (McAdams & Hawk, 1994). Senior level human resources and financial professionals responded to a survey of alternative reward practices for 2,300 pay plans. Of the 663 surveys returned, 500 were usable in the study, with 350 nonunion pay plans and 150 union pay plans represented. Approximately 60 percent of the pay plans were in manufacturing organizations, and approximately 40 percent were in service organizations.

Each variable investigated in the analysis was assessed using a one-item measure. Each item asked about the presence or absence of a particular practice for various nonmanagement occupational groups. The data were separated into unionized and nonunionized organizations. A chi-square test was used to compare differences between unionized and nonunionized organizations. This test determines whether the difference between the proportion of alternative reward plans used by unionized organizations and the proportion of alternative reward plans used by nonunionized organizations is greater than the difference expected on the basis of chance. The statistical significance of the relationship was averaged across occupations because there were few differences, and the literature reviewed offers little guidance on expected differences in alternative reward practices by occupation.

The results of the analysis are shown in Table 1. Results were in the expected direction for the most part and tend support to the relevant propositions in the diagnostic framework. Group-level performance measures were used more often in unionized firms; individual-level performance measures were used more often in nonunionized firms. Consistent with these results, gainsharing, goalsharing and stock sharing were used more frequently in unionized settings. No differences between unionized and nonunionized organizations were found for the use of merit pay or profit-sharing plans. Merit pay and profit sharing were used about the same in both settings. Piece-rate systems were used about the same amount in both settings, while skill-based pay was used more in unionized settings. In terms of the administration of strategic reward plans, historical standards and equal-dollar payouts were used more frequently in unionized environments as was predicted.

Table 1.   CARS Study Results: Unionized vs. Nonunionized Environments

Variable	Environment Used More Often In
Individual-level performance measures	Nonunionized
Group-level performance measures	Unionized
Piece rate	Equal
Merit pay	Equal
Skill-based pay	Unionized
Gainsharing	Unionized
Goalsharing	Unionized
Stock sharing	Unionized
Profit sharing	Equal
Same dollar payout to each employee	Unionized
Differential payout to each employee based on performance	Nonunionized
Standards based on historical averages	Unionized

HOW ALTERNATIVE REWARDS ARE USED IN UNIONIZED SETTINGS

Contrary to popular belief, alternative reward strategies can be used in unionized settings. In the study conducted, there were 150 unionized organizations with alternative reward plans. Hence, strategic decision making should not a priori rule out the use of an alternative reward system in a unionized organization or in a unionized business unit of an organization with both unionized and nonunionized business units.

While alternative reward plans are used in both unionized and nonunionized organizations, decision makers should not assume that different types of alternative reward plans are equally applicable in both unionized and nonunionized organizations. Unionized firms tended to use skill-based pay, gainsharing, goalsharing, and stock sharing more often than nonunionized organizations. Piece-rate, merit pay, and profit-sharing plans are used at about the same rate in unionized and nonunionized organizations.

Organizations that want to introduce alternative rewards may be more likely to gain acceptance by the union with skill-based, gainsharing, goalsharing and stock-sharing plans. To "sell" these plans to unions, management can use the results of this study to benchmark plans that seem to be used by unionized organizations. In contrast, merit pay, piece rate and profit-sharing plans may be more difficult to sell to unions because they are not unique to unionized environments.

Unionized firms reported using plans based on objective, group-based performance measures while nonunionized organizations reported using plans based on subjective, individual-based measures of performance. Reports about the use of some of the specific alternative reward plans (skill-based, merit pay, piece rate and profit sharing) seem to deviate from these general findings in reasonable and informative ways.

The greater acceptance of skill-based pay in unionized organizations than in nonunionized organizations is an interesting one. Skill-based pay uses performance measures at the individual level. One might assume that unions would react negatively to these plans. They did not, perhaps because skill assessment is more objective than merit assessment. Skill assessment relies on the measurement of more countable indicators of performance (e.g., number of items correctly filled out on a test) while merit measures may use vague personality standards (e.g., "ingenuity"). Unions may also be comfortable with skill-based pay plans because they are similar to apprenticeship programs that traditionally are used in unionized settings.

Surprisingly, merit pay was used at the same rate in the unionized sector as in the nonunionized sector, even though it is usually considered an individual reward plan. Perhaps the use of merit pay by unionized firms has to do with the increased use of team-based standards in merit-pay systems. Merit pay can be used as a measure of group as well as individual performance (Heneman & von Hippel, 1995). Alternatively, but more likely, the ratio is due to the decline in the use of merit pay in nonunionized organizations.

Although piece-rate pay is used equally in unionized and nonunionized organizations, this finding is surprising given that piece rate is an individual pay plan. One explanation for it being somewhat acceptable to unions is that it is an objective measurement of performance. Also, as with merit pay, pieces produced can be measured at the group as well as individual level.

Profit sharing was not used more frequently by unionized organizations. There are several possible explanations for this finding:

- *Profits can be measured in a subjective manner.* Because there are many different ways to measure profits, unions may be skeptical that management will use the "correct" measure to reward employees.
- *Unions may be skeptical about the ability of employees to influence this measure.* Profits are often subject to external influences in the business environment.
- *Profit sharing is likely to reward managers as well as employees.* Unions may be reluctant to accept this dependency even though it is a group-based plan (i.e., they may be hesitant to have their pay based in part on the performance of management).

Regardless of the type of pay plan used, the procedures used to make reward decisions are also important as procedural justice theory would predict (Greenberg, 1987). Acceptance is likely to be greater when union solidarity is preserved with equal-dollar payouts and when standards are attainable based on historical averages. If history is not used as a guide and if differential payouts are made on the basis of performance, union acceptance is unlikely because the reward system is less likely to be seen as fair.

Additional research is needed in three areas to substantiate the propositions tested in this study using the CARS data:

- *Only a small subset of the propositions could be tested using the CARS data.* Additional data need to be gathered that lend themselves to the testing of the other propositions.
- *The study looked at differences between unionized and nonunionized organizations.* A better design to test the propositions is to compare the alternative reward practices in unionized settings where an alternative reward strategy has been accepted with unionized settings where alternative reward plans have not been accepted. To the best of the authors' knowledge, these data have not been collected by researchers to date. One study looked at the impact of the presence or absence of alternative reward plans in unionized and nonunionized organizations but did not look at specific alternative reward practices (Cooke, 1994).
- *The presence of an alternative reward plan was used as a proxy for union acceptance of such a plan.* A more direct measure would be to survey the preferences of union members for various alternative reward strategies.

Given these concerns, the results of the empirical study presented here should be treated as suggestive and need to be further confirmed with additional research. The results do, however, provide some additional support for the framework when viewed in conjunction with the literature review.

GAINING UNION ACCEPTANCE

In making decisions about the effective development of human resources in organizations, attention must be directed toward environmental contingencies that moderate the usefulness of various HR strategies.

One important environmental contingency is the presence or absence of a labor union. If a union is present, care must be taken to think carefully about what types of reward systems are likely to be acceptable to the union and under what conditions. In designing and implementing reward systems, attention must not only be given to the strategic needs of the business but also to the goals of union members as well. In the absence of union acceptance, a labor agreement may not be reached in the collective bargaining process or, if reached, it may not be ratified by the rank-and-file union members.

Conditions that favor and hinder alternative rewards in unionized settings, based on the diagnostic framework, literature reviewed and CARS data tested, are summarized in Table 2. Consistent with previous research, a "new" management is required for reward systems to be accepted by unions (Lawler & Mohrman, 1987). Management should be:

- Open to new forms of pay such as skill-based pay.
- Willing to share information openly about the competitive position of the organization with the union.
- Willing to minimize discretionary judgment by management regarding performance assessment and rewards.
- Willing to involve union representatives of employees in some decision-making processes traditionally reserved for management (e. g., strategic planning).

Table 2.   Forces For and Against Union Acceptance of Alternative Rewards

Forces For	Forces Against
Domestic and international competition	Competitive advantage
Union participation in strategic planning	Management-dominated strategic planning
High employee trust in management and union	Low employee trust in management and union
Employee participation in pay plan decisions	No employee participation in pay plan decisions
Objective and fair performance assessment	Subjective and unfair performance assessment
Fair pay and grievance systems	Unfair pay and grievance systems
Large reward budget	Small reward budget
Group-based reward plans	Individual-based reward plans

Table 2.   Forces For and Against Union Acceptance of Alternative Rewards (Cont.)

Forces For	Forces Against
Standards based on historical record	Standards based on management discretion
Payout to employees in equal amounts	Payout to employees based on individual performance

By taking these steps, union acceptance of strategic reward systems is likely to improve.

ACKNOWLEDGMENTS

The authors wish to thank the Consortium for Alternative Reward Strategies Research (Jerry L. McAdams, CCP, and Elizabeth J. Hawk, CCP, Principal Investigators) for the data used in this study. Funding for this study came from the Center for Labor Research at The Ohio State University. The views presented in the article are not necessarily the views of the Consortium or the Center for Labor Research. The authors would also like to thank Nancy Waldeck for her assistance in collecting data.

REFERENCES

Alutto, J.A., & Belasco, J. (1974). Determinants of attitudinal militancy among nurses and teachers. *Industrial and Labor Relations Review, 27*, 216–227.

Balkin, D.B. (1989). Union influences on pay policy: A survey. *Journal of Labor Research, 10*, 299–310.

Barkin, S. (1948). Labor's attitude toward wage incentive plans. *Industrial and Labor Relations Review, 1*, 553–572.

Barkin, S. (1970, January). Wage incentive problems in arbitration. *Labor Law Journal*, 22–27.

Brett, J.M. (1980). Why employees want unions. *Organizational Dynamics, 8*, 47–59.

Cardinal, L.B., & Helburn, I.B. (1987). Union versus nonunion attitudes toward share agreements. In *Proceedings of the 39th Annual Meeting of the Industrial Relations Research Association* (pp. 167–173). Madison, WI: Industrial Relations Research Institute.

Cooke, W.N. (1994). Employee participation programs, group-based incentives, and company performance: A union-nonunion comparison. *Industrial and Labor Relations Review, 47*, 594–609.

Cooke, W.N. (1989). Improving productivity and quality through collaboration. *Industrial Relations, 28*, 299–319.

Cooke, W.N., & Meyer, D.G. (1990). Union management cooperation: Choice, implementation, and effects. In *Proceedings of the 43rd Annual Meeting* of the

Industrial Relations Research Association (pp. 385–389). Madison, WI: Industrial Relations Research Institute.

Deckop, J.R., & Mahoney, T.A. (1989). Workforce 2000: Compensation implications. In *Proceedings* of *the 42nd Annual Meeting* of *the Industrial Relations Research Association* (pp. 507–517). Madison, WI: Industrial Relations Research Institute.

Fiorito, J., & Hendricks, W.E. (1987). The characteristics of national unions. In *Advances in industrial and labor relations* (Vol. 4, pp. 1–42). Greenwich, CT: JAI Press.

Folger, R., & Greenberg, J. (1985). Procedural justice: An interpretive analysis of personnel systems. In K. Rowland & G. Ferris (Eds.), *Research in personnel and human resources management* (Vol. 3). Greenwich, CT: JAI Press.

Fossum, J.A. (1992). *Labor relations: Development, structure, process* (5th ed.). Homewood, IL: Irwin.

Freeman, R.B. (1982). Union wage practices and wage dispersion within establishments. *Industrial and Labor Relations Review, 36,* 3–21.

Freeman, R.B., & Medoff, J.L. (1979). The two faces of unionism. *Public Interest, 57,* 69–93.

Fryxell, G.E., & Gordon, M.E. (1989). Workplace justice and job satisfaction as predictors of satisfaction with union and management. *Academy of Management Journal, 32,* 851–866.

Gaertner, G.H., & Gaertner, K.H. (1987). Union membership and attitudes toward participation in determining conditions of work in the federal government. *Human Relations, 40,* 431–444.

Gaertner, G.H., Gaertner, K.H., & Akinnuis, D.M. (1984). Environment, strategy, and the implementation of administration change: The case of civil service reform. *Academy of Management Journal, 27,* 525–543.

Gomez-Mejia, L.R., & Balkin, D.B. (1992). *Compensation, organizational strategy, and firm performance.* Cincinnati, OH: SouthWestern Publishing.

Greenberg, J. (1987). Reactions to procedural justice in payment distributions: Do the means justify the ends? *Journal of Applied Psychology, 72,* 55–61.

Greenberg, J., & Folger, R. (1983). Procedural justice, participation, and the fair process effect in groups and organizations. In P.B. Paulus (Ed.), *Basic group processes* (pp. 235–256). New York: Springer-Verlag.

Greenberger, D.B., & Strasser, S. (1986). The development and application of a model of personal control in organizations. *Academy of Management Review, 11,* 164–177.

Hammer, T.H., & Berman, M. (1978). The role of noneconomic factors in faculty union voting. *Journal of Applied Psychology, 63,* 415–421.

Hammer, T.H., & Stern, R.N. (1986). A yo-yo model of cooperation: Union participation in management at the rath packing company. *Industrial and Labor Relations Review, 39,* 337–349.

Heneman, R.L. (1990). Merit pay research. In K.M. Rowland & G. Ferris (Eds.), *Research in personnel and human resources management.* Greenwich, CT: JAI Press.

Heneman, R.L. (1992). *Merit pay: Linking pay increases to performance ratings.* New York: Addison-Wesley.

Heneman, R.L., & von Hippel, C. (1997). The assessment of job performance: Focusing attention on context, process, and group issues. In D.J.B. Mitchell & M.A.

Zadi (Eds.), *Handbook of human resource management* (pp. 587–617). Greenwich, CT: JAI Press.

Heneman, R.L., & von Hippel, C. (1995). Balancing group and individual rewards: Rewarding individual contributions to the team. *Compensation & Benefits Review, 27*(4), 63–68.

Kochan, T.A., & Dyer, L. (1976). A model of organizational change in the context of union-management relations. *Journal of Applied Behavioral Science, 12,* 59–78.

Kochan, T.A., Katz, H.C., & McKersie, R. (1986). *The transformation of American industrial relations.* New York: Basic Books.

Kochan, T.A., & Weaver, K.R. (1991). American unions and the future of worker representation. In G. Strauss, D.G. Gallagher, & J. Forito (Eds.), *The state of the unions* (pp. 262–386). Madison, WI: Industrial Relations Research Association.

Lawler, E.E., III. (1981). *Pay and organizational development.* Reading, MA: Addison-Wesley.

Lawler, E.E., III. (1990). *Strategic pay.* San Francisco: Jossey-Bass.

Lawler, E.E., III, & Mohrman, S.A. (1987). Unions and the new management. *Academy of Management Executive, 1,* 293–300.

Lawler, E.E., III, Mohrman, S.A., & Ledford, G.E., Jr. (1995). *Creating high performance organizations: Practices and results in the fortune 500.* San Francisco: Jossey-Bass.

Leigh, D.E. (1986). Union preferences, job satisfaction, and the unionvoice hypothesis. *Industrial Relations, 25,* 65–71.

Lewin, D. (1987). Industrial relations as a strategic variable. In M.M. Kleiner, R.N. Block, M. Roomkin, & S.W. Salsburg (Eds.), *Human resources and the performance of the firm.* Madison, WI: Industrial Relations Research Association.

McAdams, J.L., & Hawk, F.J. (1994). *Organizational performance & rewards: 663 experiences in making the link.* Scottsdale, AZ: American Compensation Association.

McMahan, G.C., & Lawler, E.E., III. (1995). Effects of union status on employee involvement: Diffusion and effectiveness.In *Research in organizational change and development* (Vol. 8, pp. 47–76). Greenwich, CT: JAI Press.

Ng, L., & Maki, D. (1994). Trade union influence on human resource management practices. *Industrial Relations, 33,* 121–135.

Schuster, M. (1983). The impact of union management cooperation on productivity and employment. *Industrial and Labor Relations Review, 36,* 415–430.

Slichter, S.H., Healy, J.J., & Livernash, E.R. (1960). *The impact of collective bargaining on management.* Washington, DC: The Brookings Institution.

Strauss, G. (1977). Union government in the U.S.: Research past and future. *Industrial Relations, 16,* 215–242.

U.S. Department of Labor. (1981). *Characteristics of major collective bargaining agreements.* Washington, DC: U.S. Department of Labor.

Voos, P.B. (1987). Managerial perceptions of the economic impact of labor relations programs. *Industrial and Labor Relations Review, 40,* 195–208.

Voos, P.B. (1989). The influence of cooperative programs on union-management relations, flexibility, and other labor relations outcomes. *Journal of Labor Research, 10,* 103–117.

Wildstrom, S.H. (1986). Reagan's bombshell for civil servants: Merit pay. *Business-Week,* p. 61.

CHAPTER 6

ALTERNATIVE REWARDS IN UNION SETTINGS

Glenn Dalton, Jennifer Stevens, and Robert Heneman

Source: Dalton, G.L., Stevens, J., & Heneman, R.L. (1997). Alternative Rewards in Union Settings. *The Journal for Quality and Participation, 27*(5), 26–31. Reprinted with the permission of The Association for Quality and Participation from Volume 27, Number 5, 1997 issue of *The Journal for Quality and Participation,* Cincinnati, Ohio. Copyright © 1997. All rights reserved. For more information contact AQP at 513-381-1959 or visit www.aqp.org.

Increasingly, companies and unions are looking for collaborative ways to enhance organizational performance improvement efforts. They are partnering on quality initiatives, reengineering work processes, creating team-based work systems, and upgrading their technological capabilities.

As these initiatives begin to transform the way "core workers" (employees who make and deliver products and services) perform their jobs, organizations and unions are recognizing the need to make commensurate changes to their reward systems.

To some extent, most companies have redesigned their rewards programs to "pay for performance" for their executives, managerial staff, and in some cases, their salaried and hourly nonunion workforces. Relatively little has been done on a broad scale with their organized employees. But in this age of increasing global competition, some companies and unions are striving to address this misalignment in work and rewards through gain sharing, goal sharing, and other types of variable pay plans. They also are expanding the application of skilled-based systems outside the maintenance area. Together, companies and unions are searching for a win-win approach, where both the company and its employees can reap the benefits of improved organization performance.

REWARDS AT WORK

To assess the dynamics of alternative reward programs in union environments, Sibson & Company, in partnership with Ohio State University, conducted an in-depth study of five unionized manufacturing, mining, and utility companies with alternative reward programs, which include group incentive and skill-based systems.

Overall, union and management leadership considered most of the alternative reward programs in the study to be successes. The plans contributed to increased productivity and quality, encouraged greater employee understanding about the business, and in some cases, helped to forge better relationships between management and union representatives. Whether the industry was mining or manufacturing, whether the facilities were large or small, there were certain factors that enabled the successful design, implementation, and ongoing operation of these plans.

The degree to which these five factors were present—*a cooperative relationship; joint development; effective communications; flexibility; and setting achievable goals*—influenced an individual plan's success. If the company did not address one or more of these factors, the risk of failure increased substantially.

Interestingly, most plans in the survey were group-incentive plans, as opposed to person-based skill or competency programs. Although the sample size is small, it is fairly representative of unionized companies. In general, group incentive plans are easier and faster to design and implement because they have fewer components and do not require assessing and paying for individual performance. These factors represent substantial trust, equity, and fairness issues for most companies and unions.

CASE STUDY RESULTS

BHP Copper

Background: In 1989, after a long history of turbulent labor-management relations, BHP Copper, then Magma Copper in Arizona and its nine unions formed a partnership that many credit with helping to save the business. The Joint Union Management Cooperating Committee (JUMCC) began overseeing key labor-management relations and spearheading the new labor-management approach for approximately 3,500 represented employees at BHP's smelter (BHP Metals) and its San Manuel and Pinto Valley mines in Arizona.

Besides beginning a problem solving, contract-negotiation process, and the parties developed gainsharing plans for the three locations. The company committed to the plans for the first five years of a historic 15-year contract. The status of the San Manuel plant was particularly critical because plant officials needed to dramatically reduce operating costs and substantially increase the mine's output. If that was not accomplished, capital investments would no longer be feasible for an additional mining area, and the mine would close prematurely.

Plan Design and Structure: JUMCC formed a gain-sharing Oversight Group, consisting of union and management leaders, to coordinate the design and implementation of gain-sharing plans. At each location, the Oversight Group appointed a design team to recommend a plan design to the Oversight Group; the Oversight Group, in turn, sought senior management's final approval. Each facility appointed two full-time "gainshare coordinators"—one management and one union—to oversee the plan's daily administration.

Eventually, gain-share coordinators also administered an elaborate team-based suggestion program, which encouraged groups of employees to submit improvement ideas that, if implemented, allowed group members to receive individual awards of up to $2,000 out of the gain-share pool's funds for the period.

With increasing reliance on the gain-share plans as the cornerstone of the union-management relationship, the plans evolved into a design including three components: the traditional gain-sharing program, the suggestion program, and a profit-sharing program. To encourage the formation and operation of teams within the organization, coordinators created the suggestion program and funded it by changing the sharing formula from 60 percent company and 40 percent employees to 35, 40, 5 percent with the suggestion awards funded by the 5 percent reduction in the company's share. If, however, the gainsharing plan generated no pool, no suggestions awards were made. The profit-sharing component provided for payouts based on overall company profits. All of these provisions were outside the contract and not subject to the grievance and arbitration procedures.

Outcome: Despite having very similar designs, the plans at each location have had extremely varied histories, with dramatic swings in operational performance and payouts. For example, in its early years, the San Manuel plan paid quarterly payouts of 15 to 20 percent of wages as performance soared. In recent years, however, the plan has generated relatively small or no payouts as mine performance consistently fell short of performance targets. Ultimately, the company and the unions pronounced the plan a "breakdown," a contractual condition in which both parties declare that the plan is no longer achieving the objectives for which it was designed.

The opposite, however, occurred with the plan at BHP Metals. In the early years, failure to meet performance targets produced small or no payouts. But recent payouts have been consistently in the double digits, exceeding 20 percent on occasion. Considerable disputes exist, however, as to whether Metals' performance warrants this level.

Although the plans in each location have virtually identical designs, they have each taken a different approach to setting targets and associated payout levels. For example, Metals paid out over 10 percent of wages for achieving budgeted performance levels, while San Manuel didn't pay out any award until they exceeded budgeted levels. The huge disparity in payouts among locations underscores the need to clearly establish a consistent target-setting philosophy within an organization. Although BHP and its union leaders worked hard to ensure that overall plan mechanics and structures were virtually identical, they did not develop a process for aligning performance levels and payout amounts across various locations within the business.

And yet, despite such problems, management and union leadership believe that the plans have played major roles in not only the company's significant performance gains, but also in the dramatic improvements in union-management relations. Both parties remain committed to refining their gain-sharing plans. Their approaches to improving them are ongoing and vary by location, from a complete redesign (San Manuel), to significant adjustments (Pinto Valley), to relatively minor adjustments (Metals).

Metal Manufacturing Company

Background: Historically, this company has had a strong union presence with a traditional management structure. One can plant, purchased in 1994, had a simple gainsharing plan based on the plant's operational results. Meanwhile an extrusion plant had no prior incentive system. The company's financial department developed the incentive plans and implemented them at both plants during the 1993–1994 operating period. As its main objective, the company sought to enhance its ongoing cost reduction and increased productivity efforts. Ultimately, management wanted employees to embrace these goals and focus their activities on achieving them.

Plan Design and Structure: The company believed that because the two plants are cost centers, a gainsharing system was the best alternative. Eighty percent of the plan is based upon cost-reduction measures, which includes every line item within operations. This was implemented to prevent not only the selective categorization of costs but also to reinforce the importance of cost cutting. The remaining 20 percent is based upon quality and safety measures, which each plant determines individually. There is a payout cap of S percent of an employee's salary.

Management is very sensitive to employee concerns. It maintains a positive relationship with union members, who are heavily involved in overseeing the gain-sharing system. During the design process, management and union representatives agreed on the conditions of the plan. In addition to a corporate committee that oversees the plan, divisional teams also act as liaisons for communication purposes. Each committee is equally represented by union and management. Finally, a gain-sharing coordinator has been appointed for each division to oversee each plant.

Outcome: The effectiveness and perceptions of the system have been very different between the two plants. The management of the extrusion plant adopted the system's philosophy and fosters a positive work environment. The plant focuses on developing a team-based work system with employee quality training. In addition, continual training and education around business plans and objectives are priorities for the plant. Overall, management and employees believe the plan has been successful, as evidenced by the plant saving 11 times the amount it has paid out in incentives.

Meanwhile, the management at the can plant is less supportive of the current gain-sharing plan. Specifically, they believe the plan does not allow employees to directly influence results or realize the true relationship between their level of contribution and their rewards. Virtually no communication exists about the targets and the plant's performance, and, as a result, employees widely discount the plan.

From a financial perspective, the plan has been mildly successful, which has pleased management. There has been, however, some contention regarding the gain-sharing cap. Although the union participated in the design, the employees now view the cap as an artificial glass ceiling that limits the opportunity to reward high-performance levels.

Valve Manufacturer

Background: This Midwestern plant has a long history with incentive pay, starting with an individual incentive plan implemented in the 1950s. Currently, 550 bargaining unit employees are covered by a group-incentive plan that was introduced in 1989. The impetus for the group-incentive plan focused on two key factors. First, changing work standards and business needs made the individual incentive plan no longer feasible. The company needed to find a suitable alternative. Second, the organization needed to focus employees on the critical success factors necessary for creating long-term business success. Based on these factors, a group-incentive plan was the most logical choice.

Plan Design and Structure: The local management team approached the union about the group-incentive plan. Both parties agreed to jointly design the plan and formed a team of six union representatives and six management representatives. Although the team received some coaching from a consultant, the group essentially completed the design on their own because the management team had previous experience with these types of plans. The group made it a priority to obtain input from employees on the plan, and because of that, the entire design process took one year.

Employees overwhelmingly approved the plan, which has been very successful. The plan is in the union contract, and although the union wanted to annually negotiate the plan, the company would not agree to that condition. A panel of three management and six union employees meet monthly to review the plant's performance versus the critical success factors measured in the plan. The critical success factors are reviewed yearly to ensure they are still the areas on which the business should be focusing.

Outcome: Employees and management find the plan resulting from the joint management-union design process very effective. The team identified five critical success factors: cost of sales, inventory, lead time, customer satisfaction, and safety. Past performance establishes the goals for each measure. Employees are paid monthly on the number of hours they worked, but also based on the plant's performance versus the goals and its equivalent profit contribution.

In the original plan design, the goals set for each measure remained the same, even as performance increased significantly. To get the union to agree to raising the goals each year, after a certain level of performance was achieved, they negotiated a feature in the plan where the company pays employees a lump-sum amount at the end of each year, based on the amount the goal was increased. During the last contract negotiation, the company wanted to implement a rolling average for the goals to avoid this practice, but the union would not agree. A transition factor used in the payout formula-which ensured employees would not earn less than they did on the individual incentive plan-added another key design element.

Several factors indicate that the plan has been successful. Employees have a much better understanding of the business and how they affect the plant's performance. They are keenly interested in the plant's performance compared to the critical measures. They also understand that they cannot continue to work significant overtime and still meet the plan's performance targets. Employees now recognize that they can work fewer hours and earn more money-a significant shift in thinking, as the traditional way to earn additional compensation was overtime work.

The plan has also helped the company through a significant downsizing period; from 1989 to 1997, the company reduced employees to 550 from 1,000. The company now maintains the same level of sales volume with SO percent fewer people.

A Food Processing Plant

Background: Since the mid 1980s, three of the company's potato processing-plants have emphasized employee involvement through the introduction of teams, productivity work groups, and employee-suggestions programs. These programs were very successful but were never linked to any direct financial rewards. Encouraged by the positive business results created by these employee-involvement efforts, management believed a group-incentive plan would effectively complement existing programs and decided a gain-sharing plan was the best option.

Plan Design and Structure: Management designed the gainsharing plan at the division level, with a minimal amount of input from employees. The management team included several human resources managers, some line-management representatives, and the division vice president. This small management team completed the plan design in a relatively short time period. At each plant, the management team formed a gainsharing committee to communicate the plan's purpose and objectives and to provide progress reports on the plant's performance and payout levels. Management led the committees, which included some hourly employees, team leaders, and supervisors. Since the plan was implemented, however, these committees have met very irregularly.

Outcome: The plan began at all three plants on July 1, 1990 and enjoys minimal success, with plan payouts ranging from 0 to5 percent. These payouts are paid twice annually. Management does not participate in the gain-sharing plan because they are under a separate profit-sharing plan, which historically has paid up to 12 percent of their salaries.

During periods when payouts have not occurred, employees find the target-setting process-operated solely by management-flawed. Errors by management in calculating plant productivity has further broken down the plan's credibility. The plan's key performance measure is "pounds of quality processed potatoes per standard man-hour worked," so an unforeseen, low-quality potato harvest greatly reduces performance and prevents employees from earning a payout.

The gain-sharing committees would like more input into this goal-setting process and problem-solving in general, but their role continues to focus solely on communication. Although the plan is included in the union contract, it includes an article that clearly specifies that no aspect of the plan is negotiable. The plan also falls outside the parameters of the normal grievance process.

Many feel that the lack of union and employee involvement in the plan's design and ongoing administration have contributed to the plan's low level of success.

Cinergy Corporation

Background: Cinergy's Cincinnati plant produces and supplies electricity to transmission systems and employs 1,800 people at its east-side and west-side locations in the Cincinnati area. The International Brotherhood of Electric Workers represents about 1,350 of these 1,800.

Approximately 900 union employees work under a pay-for-skill model, which was mandatory at the west-side location but optional at the east-side location. Most unionized employees, however, work under the pay-for-skill model, due to the opportunity accorded them to increase their compensation level.

Faced with heightened competition from deregulation, the company reengineered its work processes and replaced its singular-skills model with a multiple-skills model. It changed its rigid, narrow job classifications to competency-based disciplines coupled with a skill-based pay plan. Cinergy also lifted a six-year hiring and promotion freeze, during which more than 200 employees left the company, primarily because of retirement. A skill-based plan, managers say, allowed employees to move up the pay scale without receiving a promotion.

Plan Design and Structure: Designing and implementing the compensation plan has involved a conceptual design, a redesign, and an ongoing assessment phase. The two designing phases took one year, and the final skill-based pay model, which began last January, required approval from both management and union leaders. Because the model is part of the union contract, it is subject to normal grievance and arbitration procedures.

Prior to the multiple-skill model, changing a motor and conducting a test run often required an electrician, mechanic, and instrument operator. With the implementation of the model, however, the task now requires only one or two employees.

According to the new model, compensation is adjusted when an employee demonstrates with knowledge and performance tests that they possess the required skills to reach the next level. Typically, an employee receives a bonus for passing the tests, as well as a raise. To learn the necessary skills, employees either may attend training sessions or read curriculum materials provided by the company.

Outcome: The company selected two groups of employees from two different plants to assess the plan. Objective knowledge-based tests and subjective performance-based tests assess employees who fall under the skill-based pay plan. Results from these pilot studies help develop similar tests for other plants. In addition, subject-matter experts and current employees have contributed their knowledge and skills to establish cut-off scores and assess the validity of the evaluation instruments.

Although the compensation plan is new, company officials say that paying for skills has been very effective. The plan makes better use of employee time and uses more competencies with its team-based approach. This approach involves teaming a manager with a union employee and each partnership oversees either a production or support team, making joint decisions. Previously, a supervisor functioned alone in the role, with higher-level decision-making left to upper management. Although management and unions like the plan, some employees feel threatened by it. They don't like the skill qualification process, testing requirements, and the absence of promotions. Previously, seniority was linked to promotions. Under the new plan, each employee can increase their compensation by showing they have a certain level of skills. To ease employee concerns, management and the unions have offered regular presentations about the new pay system. As a result, these concerns axe quickly diminishing.

With increasing competition, cost pressures, and customer demands, many more unionized organizations will be searching for ways to increase employee involvement in the business through alternative-reward programs. The insights and lessons from these case studies provide some important direction for other companies and unions when embarking on this challenging and significant endeavor.

ACKNOWLEDGMENTS

The authors wish to acknowledge the contributions of Sibson & Company's Garrett Sheridan, Michelle Tylka, John Treaty, Michael Mo and Laura Dunn. They also acknowledge the contributions of Kevin Boyle.

CHAPTER 7

COMPETENCY PAY FOR PROFESSIONALS AND MANAGERS IN BUSINESS:

A Review and Implications for Teachers

Robert L. Heneman and Gerald E. Ledford, Jr.

Source: Heneman, R.L., & Ledford, G.E. (1998). Competency Pay for Professionals and Managers in Business: A Review and Implications for Teachers. *Journal of Personnel Evaluation in Education,* *12*(2), 103–121. Permission to reprint granted from the *Journal of Personnel Evaluation in Education* and Swets & Zeitlinger Publishers. Reproduction is confined to the purpose for which the permission is hereby granted.

ABSTRACT

This article describes the use of a form of pay for knowledge and skills used for professional workers in the private sector known as competency-based pay. The definition of competencies, their assessment, and their link to pay are discussed, along with the relation of competencies to organizational performance and human resource management strategy. The relatively small amount of existing empirical research is reviewed, and two case studies of the use of competency-based pay are presented. The article concludes by summarizing lessons for education from private-sector experience, which include the need to link the competencies paid for to the capabilities the organization needs to fulfill its mission, the importance of measuring competencies in behavioral and observable terms, and the need to integrate competencies into all phases of the human resources management process, including staffing and development as well as compensation.

INTRODUCTION

Research on teacher skill, knowledge, and competency is decades old. Work on competency-based education models dates to the 1960s and this work led to job assessment models for certification in the 1970s and 1980s. The development of competency models often was followed by attempts to link pay systems—as well as other human resource systems-to the demonstration of critical competencies by teachers. However, attempts to encourage the development of teacher competencies through merit pay, career ladders, and other means have been limited and ineffective (Odden & Kelley, 1997). Many efforts failed to take into account the whole range of human resource functions (training, role descriptions, selection, performance appraisal, careers, promotion, and termination) in addition to pay. A notable exception was the work of the Joint Committee on Standards for Educational Evaluation (1988), which offered guidelines on how to develop standards for a wide range of human resource assessments in educational settings. During the 1990s, extensive effort has led to the development of the PRAXIS, INTASC, and National Board for Professional Teaching Standards models that are discussed by other articles in this issue. The new systems again raise the question of whether pay can be linked effectively to the demonstration of competencies included in the models.

In the private sector, interest in competencies has grown steadily over the last thirty years. Fundamental changes in the nature of work have been the spur for these developments. Jobs-that is, discrete, stable collections of well-defined tasks-are evolving into fluid roles and broad assignments. Constant change has led to the need for completely different technical and social skills as business has become more complex, more global, and more oriented toward change rather than stability. Companies are experimenting with ways of organizing human resource systems such as staffing, development, and compensation around competencies (Lawler, 1994; Lawler & Ledford, 1992). These systems differ greatly from traditional human resource systems, which are defined by the language of the well-defined job (Ash, Levine, & Sistrunk,1983). Competency-based systems define work in the language of the person. Work is described by the knowledge, skills, abilities, and other characteristics of the person performing work (Spencer & Spencer, 1993).

Competency systems in education have developed independently of those in business; however, competency-based education models from the late 1960s and early 1970s have been an importance influence on the development of British national standards for such professions as accounting (Finegold, Lawler, & Ledford, in press). The purpose of this article is to review developments related to competencies and competency pay in the private sector and to consider how these may be relevant to educational organizations. In particular, we examine the appropriateness of competency pay, review models and methods used to determine competencies, show how competencies are linked to pay, and review literature on the use and effectiveness of competency pay.

A theme in this article is that competency pay cannot be effective in isolation. Competency definitions must be deeply rooted in organizational needs and must be reinforced by a wide variety of human resource systems in addition to pay. This is consistent with some prior thinking and experience in the field of education (e.g., the Joint Committee on Standards for Educational Evaluation, 1988; Mohrman, Mohrman, & Odden, 1996).

THE COMPETENCY CONCEPT

The concept of competencies for managers and professionals, especially as it relates to pay decisions, is controversial (Hofrichter & Spencer, 1996; Lawler, 1996). While there is agreement about the desirability of competent managers and professionals, there is disagreement about the definition of competencies and the importance of being competent versus producing measurable results. Both of these issues are reviewed, followed by a discussion of when competencies seem appropriate to use for pay decisions.

Definition of Competencies

Here we define *competencies* as demonstrable characteristics of the person-including knowledge, skills, and behaviors-that enable performance (Ledford, 1995b). This means that competencies are portable, since they are characteristic of individual employees rather than the job. They also must be verifiable, an important characteristic for purposes of pay system design. Finally, competencies enable superior performance but are not direct indicators of performance. This means that a competency pay system will not be a complete pay system; some means of paying for performance in addition to paying for competencies is necessary.

Definitions of competency are surprisingly controversial. While most would agree that competencies include knowledge, skills, and abilities, there is wide disagreement as to whether other characteristics of the person represent competencies. Even if other characteristics are included in the definition, there is little agreement as to which other characteristics represent competencies. Other characteristics may include motives, general disposition, attitudes, values, and self-image (Spencer & Spencer, 1993). It is plausible, for example, that teacher competency may be related to such individual traits as sociability, intelligence, and extroversion.

The other category is controversial as a basis for pay decisions in business organizations for two reasons (Lawler, 1996). First, the ability of organizations to measure these characteristics in a reliable and valid manner is suspect. One need only look at the measurement problems associated with some merit pay plans to see the lack of attention paid by some businesses to measurement issues in the reward context (Heneman, 1992). Second, the measurement of these characteristics may be at odds with court interpretations of employment laws such as the Civil Rights Act. American companies used psychological tests of individual traits, such as personality characteristics and intelligence, extensively for such purposes as personnel selection and appraisal until the 1970s. Court rulings that unvalidated psychological tests were illegal as a basis for discrimination led most firms to abandon their use. Historically, the courts have frowned especially on the assessment of traits for appraisal and reward purposes (Field & Honey, 1982). Although the courts currently may hold traits in a less negative light (Werner & Bolino, 1997), we cannot recommend that organizations adapt the other category for managers and professionals. Measurement issues still exist, and poor psychometric properties for competency measures are likely to produce inaccurate pay decisions. An unvalidated system that discriminates against protected classes, even inadvertently, puts the organization in legal jeopardy. We are pessimistic about whether trait-based systems used in teacher pay decisions can avoid the measurement, validity, and discrimination problems that afflict trait-based pay systems generally.

From a theoretical perspective the omission of other categories is problematic, especially when motivation, a key determinant of performance, is omitted. Campbell, McCloy, Oppler, and Sager (1993) developed a comprehensive model of performance that suggests that performance is a function of declarative knowledge (facts, principals, goals, and self-knowledge), procedural knowledge and skills (cognitive, psychomotor, self-management, interpersonal), and motivation (choice, level, persistence). We refer to these concepts later in this article. Clearly, more research is needed to determine the extent to which these fundamental constructs can be successfully operationalized in the context of competency pay. For example, although the frame of reference applied by compensation decision makers includes motivation, this construct has not been measured directly as a part of formal compensation systems (Cohen & Heneman, 1994).

Importance of Competencies

Traditionally, managers and professionals have been paid based on their education (for example, maturity curves and most teacher pay scales) or their results (for example, management by objectives). Flaws with both approaches suggest a need for competency pay. A maturity curve pays based on type of degree and years since degree. Most teacher pay systems are even simpler, offering increased salary for teachers who have earned advanced degrees (Odden & Kelley, 1997). While easy to administer, this approach certifies only mastery of declarative knowledge. Declarative knowledge may become obsolete over time and fails to capture procedural knowledge often required for success. Results-oriented systems, like management by objectives, pay for accomplishments on countable measures of performance, such as cost, revenue, and profit. Results-oriented measures are limited by the fact that they may be both deficient and contaminated (Heneman, 1986). They may be deficient because they may overlook softer or less countable indicators of performance, such as interpersonal skills. They may be contaminated because they may be outside the control of the individual. In schools, for example, the quality of the student body and the level of parental involvement influence pupil performance but are not under teachers' control.

Competencies help fill the void when the focus is solely on education or results. In particular, competencies are very specific measures of declarative and procedural knowledge rather than general measures of declarative knowledge. Also, many competencies are under the control of the individual. Such competencies may include the personal and interpersonal skills needed to successfully achieve the desired results. Competencies are an important supplement to traditional reward systems for managers, which emphasize achievement only. Dysfunctional results can occur when the focus is solely on the achievement of results. For example, at Solomon Brothers, a results-based pay system with limitless bonuses led to unethical behavior (Norris, 1991), and at Sears, mechanics cut corners on repairs in order to meet the time quotas with their bonus plan (Lorant, 1992). A reward system focusing partly on competencies helps to balance the emphasis on performance with an emphasis on development and work processes.

Appropriateness of Competencies

Although we note the positive features of competencies for managerial and professional reward systems, they are certainly not appropriate in all situations. The degree of emphasis placed on competencies versus results depends on several factors (Sibson & Co., 1997). Competencies seem to be most appropriate in dynamic business environments where work roles are very flexible, results are achieved through knowledge, and employees are empowered. An emphasis on results is more appropriate in static business environments where work roles are fixed, results are achieved through consistent execution of repetitive tasks, and employees have little discretion in performing their work (Lawler & Ledford, 1992). Clearly, teaching better fits the former than the latter set of conditions.

Competency Models

The first step, and most critical one, in paying for competencies is to develop a competency model. A competency model offers a conceptual basis for identifying competencies, defines critical competencies, and provides standards for competency assessment.

Types of Competencies

Competencies vary along a number of dimensions. Here we consider three dimensions. First, competencies can be general or specific to the organization (Ledford, 1995b). General competencies are common across businesses, while specific competencies are specific to a particular business. Organizations may be reluctant to develop general competencies because they are easily transferable to their competitors. On the other hand, general competency systems may be easy to design and implement but may not adequately meet the specific needs of the organization. Second, competencies can be basic or advanced. Organizations usually select people to ensure that they have the basic knowledge, skills, and abilities to learn more advanced competencies. In the field of education, the PRAXIS and INTASC certification systems are oriented more toward assessing the competencies of prospective or new teachers, while the National Board for Professional Teaching Standards certification is oriented toward advanced teachers.

Third, advanced competencies can be either role-based or organization based. Role-based competencies are defined by the expectations surrounding the completion of assignments. Usually these competencies are determined by position in the organizational structure. Organization-based competencies are the expectations of the wider organization held for people in all positions within the organizational structure. Usually, they are based on the vision and mission of the organization. In schools, for example, role competencies may apply to teachers, while organizational competencies may apply to administrators as well as teachers.

Businesses that adopt competency systems usually do so to seek competitive advantage. An interesting question is whether competition might motivate the adoption of competency-based systems in schools. The answer probably is "Yes, to some extent." Clearly, there is competition between public and private schools and, to a lesser degree, between and within public school districts. Indeed, high-profile innovations in several states have attempted to increase competition by rewarding schools that perform better than their peers. Nevertheless, competitiveness is a less dominant force in public school systems than in the business sector because public school systems have discrete geographic territories, mostly captive student populations, and the virtual certainty that enough public funding will be provided to enable the system to survive. However, the different level of competition in public schools has one positive effect. School systems tend to be less reticent than businesses about sharing human resource innovations because they have less fear of losing trade secrets that confer competitive advantage.

Organizations seeking a competitive advantage from competency systems invest most heavily in developing competencies that are difficult for their competitors to imitate (Barney, 1986). Competency models providing competency advantage also should emphasize specific and advanced competency types (Zingheim, Ledford, & Schuster, 1996). Examples of competencies that seem to be appropriate for professionals and managers include fostering organizational learning, innovation, and entrepreneurship (Lado & Wilson, 1994). Research (Cofsky, 1993), reviews of the literature (Spencer & Spencer, 1993), and other work (Tucker & Cofsky, 1994) indicate that interpersonal influence, political skills, motivation, customer-service orientation, and leveraging technical information are competencies associated with professional and managerial success. On the other hand, many pay-based competency models appear to be very general and basic. Consequently, they are easy to imitate and likely to produce a small return on investment because they do not provide a source of competitive advantage. Their advantage lies in the comfort of using competency systems that are similar to those of other organizations and design and implementation that are faster than is the case in a customized system.

Sources of Competencies

The most popular sources of competencies are dictionaries with lists of predefined competencies available from consulting firms and the government. Examples include the McBer/Hay dictionary, *Career Architect* from Drake Beam and Morin, *Profiler* from Personnel Decisions International, *Prospector* from the University of Southern California, and *O*Net* and the

National Skills Standard system from the U.S. government. Most of the dictionaries have been created for purposes of employee development rather than for purposes of compensation. Adopting these systems off the shelf for pay purposes is likely to be problematic. On the other hand, they are ready-made, quick, and easy to use. Organizations that must quickly move up to industry standards to succeed may be forced to rely on a dictionary approach. In the field of education, some have urged the use of the PRAXIS, INTASC, or National Board certifications as a basis for competency pay, albeit in some cases with local modifications based on local needs (e.g., Conley & Odden, 1995; Mohrman, Mohrman, & Odden, 1996; Odden & Kelley, 1997).

Another approach is to develop customized competencies for a particular organization. Under this approach, competencies are specifically defined for a particular organization. The advantage of this approach is that time and unique competencies can be used to guide the organization forward. The downside, of course, is the time and cost to develop competencies. In most organizations, this process takes a year or more (American Compensation Association, 1996). There are some indications that organizations tend to build competency pay systems around a handful of social competencies, such as communication skills and team orientation, that are fashionable but probably not the result of a customized analysis of unique organizational needs (Zingheim, Ledford, & Schuster, 1996). There are some examples of school districts that have developed customized competencies systems, with mixed results (Conley & Odden, 1995).

COMPETENCY ASSESSMENT

Emerging from the practice and research literature is a prototype process to assess competencies. The first step is the creation of competency standards. Attention here needs to be focused on three sets of standards-national competencies, individual competencies, and core competencies (Finegold, Lawler, & Ledford, in press). National competencies are those general and basic competencies applicable across a multitude of organizations and available from government agencies, professional associations, and even consulting firms. More often than not, these standards are used for the purpose of selection rather than for the purpose of pay. Sometimes, however, organizations may be in labor markets where they cannot find people with these talents, and they may need to develop pay systems to reward existing employees for mastery of general and basic skills.

Individual competencies are more specific and advanced competencies are required by the business to succeed. These competencies are often identified by subject-matter experts internal to the organization. Subject-matter experts create lists of behaviors that are believed to separate effective from ineffective performers in the organization. This approach originated with the critical incident technique (Flanagan, 1954) for purposes of performance appraisal (Latham & Wexley, 1994) and has now been refined into behavioral event interviewing (Spencer & Spencer, 1993).

A potential problem with individual competencies is that the sum of performance at the individual level may not sum to effective performance at the corporate level (Finegold, Lawler, & Ledford, in press). Hence, attention must also be given to core competencies in the creation of standards. Here we define core competencies as those aspects of the business believed to have the greatest strategic value to the business (Prahalad & Hamel, 1990; Marino, 1996). These core competencies are measured at the level of the organization rather than at the level of the individual. Often they are explicit or implicit in vision, mission, values, and aspiration statements. Increasingly, core competencies are viewed as human capital rather than financial capital (Capelli & Crockner-Hefter, 1996). Individual competencies must be validated against these core competencies of the business if competencies are going to help a business achieve competitive advantage.

Another important aspect of standards development is the use of employees in formulating standards for defining competency content and for measuring the use of competencies in the workplace (Heneman & von Hippel, 1996). When employees are involved in the setting of standards, they are more likely to see the system as valid (Friedman & Cornelius, 1976) and be more satisfied (Silverman & Wexley, 1984) than when they are not involved. The lack of participation in standard development is a source of concern for competency pay systems that are based on standard dictionaries established at the national level. On the other hand, national standards may facilitate implementation if they have been well institutionalized. Also, from the employee perspective, competency dictionaries are desirable because they apply to multiple employers in the labor market.

The second step of competency assessment is to attach rating scales to the performance standards. Fortunately, because competencies are most often measured as manifest behaviors, previous research in performance appraisal is very helpful for this step. Competencies can be assessed using Behaviorally Anchored Rating Scales (BARS) that use a Thurstone scaling methodology. Competencies also can be assessed by Behavioral Observation Scales (BOS) that use Liken scales. Latham and Wexley (1994) indicate a preference for BOS based on psychometric, legal, and user-reaction criteria. Unfortunately, competencies often seem to be measured using trait labels and graphic rating scales. This approach often leads to disastrous results with merit pay programs (Heneman, 1992), and a similar fate is likely to await competency pay programs that do not devote the time necessary to develop behavioral measures with sound psychometric properties.

The third step in the process of competence assessment is the selection and training of raters. Increasingly, organizations are using multirater or 360 degree review procedures (Heneman & von Hippel, 1996). Under this approach, ratings come not only from immediate supervisors but also from the job incumbent, peers, subordinates, and customers. While this approach appears to work well for developmental reasons, caution must be exercised when using this approach for reward decisions. Raters need to be carefully trained, and conditions need to be set to minimize the chances of rating errors (Heneman & von Hippel, 1996). Unfortunately, some organizations with competency pay fail to take these precautions, and the competency assessment becomes compromised by political issues (Longnecker, Sims, & Gioia, 1987).

The fourth step in the competency assessment process is validation. Validation studies help assure policy makers that the competency system rewards behaviors that indeed are associated with effective performance. In addition, validation studies offer legal protection in case the competency system discriminates against protected groups. In actual practice, however, empirical validation procedures are infrequently used by businesses that attempt to manage competencies (American Compensation Association, 1996). When validation is done, it is usually by large rather than small organizations, and a content validation strategy is usually used with competencies being identified by job incumbents. Moreover, the validation step may be omitted due to the changing nature of competencies. By the time a validation study is conducted, a new set of competencies may be needed by the organization for strategic advantage (Ledford, 1995a). Some competencies may be more stable than others and these are more likely candidates for validation work. Possible avenues for validation research include assessing reliability, correlating ratings with business results, surveying employee reactions to competencies, and undertaking construct validation procedures.

Although there has been some research validating competency models used for such purposes as selection and development (Spencer & Spencer, 1993), we found no empirical studies of the validity of competency models developed for pay purposes. A notable validity study for purposes other than pay is by Spreitzer, McCall, and Mahoney (1997). They assessed the construct validity of a model developed to assess the early identification of executive potential. To do so, they undertook an elaborate content, concurrent, and predictive validity study using ratings from over 800 executives in twenty-one countries. Although there were methodological problems such as common method bias for some of the data, the results were very promising. Another notable exception is the work of Borman and Brush (1993). They reviewed the literature on managerial performance and developed a taxonomy of managerial performance requirements based on twenty-six empirical studies. Using subject-matter experts, the dimensions of managerial performance identified in these studies were collapsed into eighteen dimensions using inductive and empirical procedures.

It should be noted that so far, few businesses using skill-based pay have faced discrimination, and other legal charges (Jenkins, Ledford, Gupta, & Doty, 1992). This probably is due, in part, to the high level of employee involvement that typically is used to develop such pay plans. Also, these plans tend to be face valid—that is, they seem sensible to employees who are on these plans. Certainly, school systems should bear these lessons in mind by involving teachers in the design process and by using competencies that appear obviously related to teacher effectiveness.

Although these steps probably offer some legal prophylaxis, it should be remembered that competencies with face validity are not necessarily valid in a legal or predictive sense. Teachers and administrators may firmly but wrongly believe that certain competencies are related to teaching performance. For example, authorities have tried for decades to specify the one best way to teach—that is, the way that intuitively seems obviously related to performance—even though effective teaching styles may be highly variable and context specific.

Formal validation is likely to be an important step in educational organizations. Teacher competencies probably do not change rapidly, facilitating such studies. Moreover, public organizations tend to face considerable risk of litigations, and the protection afforded by validity studies can be valuable. However, educational organizations cannot escape the possibility of legal liability if their competency systems discriminate against protected groups and appropriate evidence of validity is unavailable. It should be noted that basing competency pay on the available national certification standards (PRAXIS, INTASC, and National Board certifications) is no guarantee of legal protection. Other articles in this volume explore the state of validity research on these certification processes, but we may summarize the findings by saying that validity research on all of these processes is still at a very early stage.

LINKING COMPETENCY ASSESSMENT TO PAY

Three major issues arise when linking competency assessment to pay: the pay form must be determined, a pay structure must be constructed, and market value must be assessed.

The first choice is whether to add competency pay to the base wage (salary) or to pay it in the form of a one-time bonus. The bonus option is rarely considered in the education literature that discusses pay for skills or competencies. (One plan that does reward competencies with bonuses is the

Douglas County, Colorado, skill-pay system.) Base-pay systems are typical, and employees usually prefer the permanent increase in pay they provide. However, bonuses are attractive in several situations. First, if employee pay is already high relative to the market or relative to the resources available, bonuses may be the only way to provide a meaningful incentive for new behaviors. Second, bonuses are desirable when the competencies that employees must absorb are changing rapidly because the organization need not offer a permanent wage increase for skills with temporary value. Bonuses have other advantages as well. Bonus plans are simple to administer. Also, one-time bonuses can be larger-thus offering a larger immediate incentive-than base-pay increases, which usually must be conservative because of the annuity effect of increases in base pay.

Second, a pay structure is necessary, especially in base-pay systems. Competency pay can be blended into existing pay structures, or a new pay structure can be created to accommodate competency pay. The pay structure sets limits on the amount of pay. If combined with merit pay, competencies can be used as the performance criteria to evaluate performance for purposes of a pay increase or lump-sum bonus.

Many pay structures have pay ranges for each pay grade. Because the distance between the minimum pay level and maximum pay level within each grade is small, usually around 40 per cent, it may be difficult to use competencies to move employees' pay within the pay grade on the basis of competency mastery. Consequently, broadbanding is often used with competency pay. Under this approach, the number of pay grades is reduced, and the distance between the minimum and maximum is increased. Movement within the broad band is then based on mastery of competency sets rather than on performance. For example, the team leader, lead person, and supervisor pay grades may be collapsed into a broad band known as *management*. Director, manager, and vice president pay grades may be collapsed into a broad band known as *executive*. Progression within each band may be based on mastering competency sets such as technical expertise, coaching, and strategy. Competency sets may be basic for the management grade and advanced for the executive grade.

Broadbanding represents a significant departure from traditional models for teacher pay. Pay is no longer directly bound by a matrix of degrees and years of experience. Under traditional models of teacher pay, degree and years experience are signals of likely competence on the job. Broadbanding allows for competencies to be measured directly and does not equate professional credentials with competencies.

It is difficult to price the market values of competencies. Market surveys report the value of jobs rather than the value of competencies that individuals have mastered. Nevertheless, it is critical to approximate market value to establish control points in the structure. In the absence of market control, competency pay can lead to excessive costs. To establish market value, usually some sort of benchmark procedure is used. For example, for the previous example of the executive pay band, we might establish the maximum for the band by looking at the maximum pay rates for executive jobs in our surveys. The minimum may be established by looking at the minimum pay rates for manager jobs in our surveys. A more precise procedure to establish market value is to survey the amount paid in the market for competencies rather than job. Unfortunately, market surveys of this nature are only in their infancy, and more crude job-based surveys must be used.

One method that could be developed to translate job-based market survey data into person-based market values is to use a synthetic market-value approach. This procedure first requires the identification of competencies for a particular position. For example 30 percent of the team leader position may require managerial competencies, and 70 percent may require technical competencies. Next, job-based survey data would be examined to find the market value of jobs with similar managerial competencies and technical competencies. Lastly, the market value of the team leader would be the sum of the market value for jobs with similar managerial competencies multiplied by 30 per cent plus the market value for jobs with similar technical competencies multiplied by 70 percent.

EMPIRICAL RESEARCH

Given how recent competency pay plans have been established, there is very little research available to guide competency pay efforts. As will be shown, most of the research is descriptive in nature. It is organized around two themes-practices and effectiveness.

Practices

The American Compensation Association (1996) sponsored a survey of competency management practices, covering all human resource practices including pay. The survey was sent to 19,016 North American companies. Of these, 1257 respondents indicated that they had or were developing competency systems, and 217 companies agreed to complete a detailed survey. Only fifty-four organizations reported using competency pay practices. Most respondents were in large organizations with about an even mix of manufacturing and service organizations.

Competencies assessed most frequently included performance behaviors and personal attributes. Also frequently assessed, but less frequently than performance behaviors and personal attributes, were technical skills and knowledge. Although personal attributes were used, only one company had faced a legal challenge. The number of competencies assessed ranged from less than five to more than thirty. The modal category was the assessment at five to nine competencies. Often 360 degree feedback is used, but many require the manager to interpret and feedback the data.

In terms of specific pay practices, about 30 percent of organizations use broad bands for managerial and professional positions. About 70 percent of managers and professionals are covered by competency pay in the average company with competency pay. Competencies are usually used to assess position within the pay grade. The form of pay is usually an adjustment to base pay rather than a bonus. Competency pay usually follows from prior experience in the organization with the use of competencies for other purposes, such as development or selection.

The data from this study make very clear that competency pay is being used very cautiously in business. While it is common to use competency pay for managers and professionals in those firms with competency pay, the absolute number of companies with competency pay is very small. When it is used, it is usually developed after other competency-based human resource applications such as performance management, staffing, and training have been developed. Soft attributes are measured more often than technical knowledge and skill.

Effectiveness

The same survey from the American Compensation Association (1996) reported on the perceived effectiveness of competency models. It did not report on the perceived effectiveness of competency pay, probably because of the small number of organizations with competency pay responding to the survey. A majority of respondents with competency models in their organization for more than a year perceived the result as favorable in terms of goal accomplishment. Many were uncertain of the result, and very few respondents indicated that the competency model had no effect or negative results. Although these data are suggestive, they are limited by their self-report nature.

Considerable prior work on skill-based pay is relevant to the issue of the effectiveness of competency pay. These plans typically reward the demonstration of technical competencies for employees at the bottom of the organizational hierarchy, such as factory workers. Large-scale survey studies (Jenkins, Ledford, Gupta, & Doty, 1992) suggest that these plans have a high success rate. Several available case studies (Ledford & Bergel, 1991; Ledford, Tyler, & Dixey, 1991) are also encouraging.

An unpublished study by Murray and Gerhart (1997) is more experimental in nature. They examined the effectiveness of a skill-based pay plan in manufacturing. They compared the output of two comparable auto parts manufacturers—one with skill-based pay and the other without. Outcomes were measured over thirty-seven months. Productivity and quality were higher at both, while labor costs were lower at the plant with skill-based pay.

Another interesting unpublished study is by Mericle and Kin (1996). They surveyed the effectiveness of skill-based pay for 227 employees in a unionized manufacturing firm. Effectiveness was measured as actual skill acquisition, based on company records. The results indicated that about 90 percent of the respondents had mastered one or more of the six skill sets since plan inception in 1991. Greater skill acquisition took place when employees were more educated, had more knowledge of how the plan worked, and had higher pay satisfaction. Skill acquisition also increased when employees were younger, had a lower level of commitment to the union, and had less experience with workplace innovations. Although the type of competency pay and type of occupation again bound these results, the results again show that competency pay can be related to hard outcomes. In addition, they raise the important possibility that competency pay is moderated not only by pay plan characteristics but by individual difference variables as well.

Skill-based pay plans typically apply to factory workers and others at lower levels of the hierarchy, whereas the label competency pay is more often applied to systems for professionals and managers. Although the results of skill-based pay research are encouraging, we need data directly relevant to competency pay systems for managers and professionals such as teachers. Skill-based pay tends to measure more hard outcomes, such as procedural knowledge, while competency pay typically measures softer outcomes, such as interpersonal skills. Hence, the generalizability of results from skill-based pay to competency pay is open to question. In the teaching profession, the critical issue is to identify both hard and soft competencies that are related to student learning.

CASE STUDIES

Given the limited empirical evidence on competency pay and the limited use of competency pay for managers and professionals, we thought that it might be interesting to report on two case studies. The authors have been personally involved with these systems. The two companies are the Limited, Inc. and a major food processor.

The Limited, Inc.

A full version of the Limited case study is presented in Heneman and Thomas (1997). A brief synopsis follows. The Limited is a $9 billion retailer of specialty brands. Its eighteen business units include well-known brands, such as Victoria's Secret, Henri Bendel, Limited, and Abercrombie and Fitch. Its over 6,000 stores employ over 33,000 employees. Over the past nine years, the Limited has grown rapidly from a $400 million business to a $9 billion business. Because of this growth, the focus has been in the achievement of results such as sales, market share, and growth. Two years ago, senior management became aware that to manage this large enterprise, emphasis would also need to be placed on developing leadership competencies to supplement the entrepreneurial focus on results.

To focus management attention on leadership competencies, a competency model was established for the top 500 managers in the company. Developing the Limited's competency model took two years, a long time frame that permitted ample manager participation in the development of competency standards. The company's model consisted of eight competency sets, and each set was further defined by one to five subdimensions. Each subdimension was anchored by critical incidents of performance ranging from highly effective to ineffective. Supervisors rated subordinates on the competencies included in the model.

An example of a competency set in the model was *thinking skills*. Two subdimensions captured this competency: (1) analysis and decision making and (2) visionary thinking. A critical incident for analysis and decision making was "Makes timely decisions." This incident was anchored with a rating scale ranging from "Towering strength = Consistently makes timely decisions that balance systematic analysis with decisiveness" to "Ineffective/ Needs Improvement = Makes snap judgments and decisions without necessary information or delays too long on decisions." Although this particular competence is somewhat general, more specific competencies, such as *fashion sense*, were included as well. All competencies were defined by specific, observable behaviors to ensure appropriate rating.

The competency model was first developed for staffing, performance management, and development purposes. The performance management system was pilot tested in several business units before implementation. Survey data were gathered on user reactions to the new system, and they were used to modify the system before implementation across all the business units. Currently, the competency is being used for all business units. Work is now underway to use it for purposes of compensation decision making. Merit pay increases and stock options will now be based on competency mastery as well as the achievement of bottom-line results. Currently, the system is being extended to professional employees as well.

Experiences at the Limited reinforce some of the points in the prior literature. On the positive side, competencies helped managers to learn how to lead the organization toward the accomplishment of results. It is very difficult to achieve competitive advantage by solely focusing on the achievement of goals. The path to the goal can be established with the development of competency standards. In addition, participation in the development of standards was very helpful in gaining user acceptance of the new systems. This acceptance may not have been achieved had an off-the-shelf system been installed. On the negative side, and again consistent with the literature, the Limited has devoted little attention to the systematic evaluation of the new system either in terms of validity or effectiveness. While no news may be good news, a more proactive approach to evaluation might help them to further develop the system before cascading it down to other levels in the organization.

Issues not covered in the literature have arisen at the Limited, as well. Questions have arisen as to whether the same competency standards can be applied across different types of managerial jobs and different business units. The intent of the system was to have a common set of standards to promote labor mobility between managerial positions and to have a common yardstick to make administrative decisions. This approach may conflict with the need to develop specific standards that are unique to the various assignments and divisions. This tradeoff represents an important strategic consideration that large organizations must consider. In some settings, a compromise may be reached where there are a core set of competencies for all positions and divisions and a specific set of competencies for each position and division.

Another important point brought out by the Limited case study is the role that competencies can play in bringing about organizational change. Competencies could have been treated at the Limited as a job analysis project sponsored by the human resources department. The impact of this approach on bringing about change in the organization would more than likely be negligible. The process used to develop a competency system at the Limited helped to transform the organization. Top management first applied this process to themselves, which clearly established the importance of competencies. Top management helped design the system, which gave ownership of the system to management rather than to the human resource department. The system was tied directly to the business plan to emphasize the business need for competencies. The system is being linked to merit pay and to stock options to show the rewards associated with participation in the process. Managers were provided extensive training on how to use the system so that it was properly implemented.

Food Processor

The second author has recently completed the collection of extensive data about a mature competency pay system covering managers at a well-known food processing company (which we here call "FoodCo"). The system, now five years old, covers over 1,000 managers at over forty plants and distribution and sales centers throughout the United States. The system covers all managers from first-line supervisor up to the level of the plant management team. The system was installed at a time of great change in the company. Senior management was redefining the role of the manager and eliminating levels of management, which reduced opportunities for hierarchical advancement. Senior management approved the system as a way to facilitate and support these changes. It collapsed a number of prior pay grades into one broad pay band for managers on the system. There were three titles within this band-resource, senior resource, and site resource. Managers were rewarded not for hierarchical advancement but for their progress in developing four competencies. These were leveraging technical and business systems, leading for results, building workforce effectiveness, and understanding and meeting customer needs. The emphases on developing subordinates and meeting customer needs were relatively novel in the company.

The research project involved an assessment of the plan based on surveys of almost 700 employees on the system, one survey per site completed by a senior manager, archival data (promotions and turnover), and performance rankings of twenty-one regions (each including one or more plants). The results suggested that there was a wide range of attitudes about the system and considerable variation in the level of implementation effectiveness across locations. Overall, employee attitudes on average were mildly positive about the system.

The most interesting results concerned the relationship between hard rankings of performance and aggregated survey responses. The company uses a composite ranking that combines hard indicators of productivity, cost, quality, and employee outcomes. For both 1996 and year-to-date 1997 rankings, the correlations with design and implementation factors measured on the surveys were strong, in a number of cases ranging from 0.30 to 0.47. These correlations are very strong when viewed in the context of compensation research, where typically correlations range between .00 and .20 when studies relate pay practices to hard indicators of productivity, cost, quality, and employee outcomes. For example, the correlation between senior manager ratings of the degree of ongoing communication about the competency pay system and 1997 performance ranking was .47. Other key success factors included amount of money available under the system (.41), and degree to which the system was tailored to meet local needs (.35). The correlations between performance rankings and aggregated employee attitudes were similarly high. The strongest predictors of 1997 performance ranking were alignment of the competency pay system with training and development practices (.42), fairness of the system (.39), communication about the system (.39), and fairness of competency appraisals (.37). Preliminary analyses indicated that the high correlations are not the result of statistical artifacts, such as aggregation effects, and the results cannot be explained away by any higher level of pay or promotion in the more "successful" regions.

The results of this study are extremely encouraging for several reasons. The study examines a mature system for managers and professionals. It provides some of the first good research evidence that a competency pay system is related to hard performance outcomes at the organization level. Finally, the study points to a number of design and implementation factors that have implications for action as the company attempts to improve the system in the future.

CONCLUSIONS AND IMPLICATIONS FOR TEACHERS

Competency models are being used extensively in business. They are being used to develop business strategies based on people rather than capital. Also, they are being used to develop person-based rather than job-based human resource systems. Ultimately, they represent an attempt to link organizational and individual goals. Unlike previous attempts to link organizational and individual goals that emphasized the accomplishment of results, competency models place the focus on knowledge and skills that are under the control of employees and measured by observable behaviors.

Competency models have primarily been developed for the purpose of employee development rather than for the purpose of pay and have primarily been developed for nonexempt employees rather than managers and professionals. Increasingly, however, employers are beginning to experiment with competency pay for professionals and managers.

Conclusions reached in the business literature on competency pay for professionals and managers just reviewed clearly support conclusions in the education literature on competency pay for teachers (Conley & Odden, 1995; Kelley, 1997; Mohrman, Mohrman, & Odden, 1996; Odden & Kelley, 1997). In particular, several messages stand out. First, unlike merit pay, competency pay is not a "one size fits all" type of pay plan. It must be carefully matched to the goals, culture, and political realities of the organization. Competency pay should be viewed as one pay delivery along with others such as school bonuses and individual incentives. Second, there is often a tradeoff between developing competencies at the local versus national level. At the local level, acceptance can be gained by teacher participation in the development process. At the national level, while the level of participation may be reduced, greater care can be taken to ensure reliable and valid measures are created. To resolve this dilemma, a strategy used by business is to use "mass-customization" (LeBlanc, 1997), where a core set of competencies are established at a central level and supplemental competencies are established at the local level. From our perspective, both participation and measurement are vital components. Third, care must be taken to avoid the use of competencies that have little meaning. Competencies may have little meaning because they fail to be tied to the core capabilities of the organization or because they fail to measure competencies in behavioral and observable terms. Competency pay systems with meaningless competencies are poorly developed merit pay plans in disguise.

Our review raises two issues that need to be kept in mind by educational institutions considering competency pay-the importance of process and the relationship of competencies to other components of organizational effectiveness. In terms of process, it is very clear that meaningful competencies by themselves add little value to improving organizational effectiveness. Experiences by business with performance appraisal and by educational organizations with merit pay and differentiated staffing points to the importance of how competencies are developed and used. Competencies must be fully integrated into all phases of human resources (staffing, development, compensation) rather than be a stand-alone product for purposes of pay decisions. Merit pay was often developed as an isolated human resource practice, and in many cases it failed because it was not created in the context of human resource goals for the organization. The Joint Committee's work (1988) again illustrates how competencies might be applied consistently across a variety of human resource systems.

Another important process issue has to do with the commitment of resources to a competency pay system. The design, administration, implementation, and evaluation of these plans is costly. Training, for example, plays a critical and expensive role here. Care must be taken to ensure that assessors are using the competencies in a reliable manner. The form itself can only contribute so much toward this end. Judgment must be applied, and safeguards must be established, including training, to ensure accurate and reliable assessments. Obviously, this is no small hurdle in a politically charged educational setting.

A second important lesson from business is the fact that competency models are more than simply human resource systems. They also impact other important systems in the organization that are related to organizational effectiveness. An example of another system is the strategy of the organization. Competencies must be consistent with the core competencies and capabilities of the entire organization. If these competencies are to be useful, they must be unique to the culture of the organization such that they add value that cannot be found elsewhere. As another example, competencies of the organization need to be consistent with the structure of the organization. Work in the organization must be structured in ways that facilitate the development of core competencies and capabilities. Large bureaucracies have for years, for example, hindered movement toward site-based reform. Finally, systems of the organization must be in alignment with one another. In order for employees and organizational goals to link together, strategy, structure, process, people, and rewards must be aligned with one another. Just as the pay system cannot operate independent of other human resource systems, so too must competency models be in alignment with other systems of the organization.

ACKNOWLEDGMENT

Presented at the Consortium for Policy Research in Education conference on Assessing Teachers' Knowledge and Skills: Implications for Incentives and Compensation, Chicago, September 18–19, 1997.

REFERENCES

American Compensation Association. (1996). *Raising the bar.* Scottsdale, AZ: Author.

Argyris, C., & Schon, D.A. (1978). *Organizational learning.* Reading, MA: Addison-Wesley.

Ash, R.A., Levine, E.L., & Sistrunk, F (1983). The role of jobs and job-based methods in personnel and human resources management. In K. Rowland & G. Ferris (Eds.), *Research in personnel and human resources management* (Vol. 1, pp. 45–84). Greenwich, CT: JAI Press.

Barney, J.B. (1986). Organizational culture: Can it be a source of sustained competitive advantage? *Academy of Management Review, 11,* 656–665.

Borman, W.C., & Brush, D.H. (1993). More progress toward a taxonomy of managerial performance requirements. *Human Performance, 6,* 1–21.

Campbell, J.P., McCloy, R.A., Oppler, S.H., & Sager, C.E. (1993). A theory of performance. In N. Schmitt & W.C. Borman (Eds.), *Personnel selection in organizations* (pp. 35–70). San Francisco: Jossey-Bass.

Capelli, P., & Crocker-Hefter, A. (1996, Winter). Distinctive human resources are firms' core competencies. *Organizational Dynamics,* pp. 7–22.

Cofsky, K.M. (1993, November/December). Critical keys to competency-based pay. *Compensation and Benefits Review,* pp. 46–52.

Cohen, D., & Heneman, R.L. (1994). Ability and effort weights in pay level and pay increase decisions. *Journal of Business and Psychology, 8,* 327–343.

Conley, S., & Odden A. (1995). Linking teacher compensation to teacher career development. *Educational Evaluation and Policy Analysis, 17,* 219–237.

Field, H.S., & Honey, WH. (1982). The relationship of performance appraisal characteristics to verdicts in selected employment discrimination cases. *Academy of Management Journal, 25,* 392–406.

Finegold, D., Lawler, E.E., III, & Ledford, G.E., Jr. (In press). Competencies, capabilities, and strategic organization design. In S.A. Mohrman, J. Galbraith, & E.E. Lawler III (Eds.), *Tomorrow's organization: Creating winning competencies.* San Francisco: Jossey-Bass.

Flanagan, J.L. (1954). The critical incident technique. *Psychological Bulletin, 51,* 327–358.

Friedman, B.A., & Cornelius, E.T., III (1976). Effect of rater participation in scale construction on the psychometric characteristics of two rating scale formats, *Journal of Applied Psychology, 61,* 210–216.

Gupta, N., Ledford, G.E., Jr., Jerkins, G.D., Jr., & Doty, D.H. (1992). Survey-based prescriptions for skill based pay. *ACA Journal, 1*(1), 50–61.

Heneman, R.L. (1986). The relationship between supervisory ratings and results-oriented measures of performance: A meta-analysis. *Personnel Psychology, 39,* 811–826.

Heneman, R.L. (1992). *Merit pay: Linking pay to performance ratings.* Reading, MA: Addison-Wesley.

Heneman, R.L., & Thomas, A.L. (1997). The Limited, Inc.: Using strategic performance to drive brand leadership. *Compensation and Benefits Review, 27*(6), 33–40.

Heneman, R.L., & von Hippel, C. (1996). The assessment of job performance: Focusing attention on context, process, and group issues. In D. Lewin, D.J.B. Mitchell, & M.A. Zaidi (eds.), *Handbook of human resource management* (pp. 587–617). Greenwich, CT: JAI Press.

Hofrichter, D.A., & Spencer, L.M., Jr. (1996, November/December). Competencies: The right foundation for effective human resource management. *Compensation and Benefits Review,* pp. 20–26.

Jerkins, G.D., Jr., Ledford, G.E., Jr., Gupta, N., & Doty, D.H. (1992). *Skill-based pay: Practices, payoffs, pitfalls, and prospects.* Scottsdale, AZ: American Compensation Association.

Joint Committee on Standards for Educational Evaluation. (1988). *The personnel evaluation standards.* Newbury Park, CA: Sage.

Kelley, C. (1997). Teacher compensation and organization. *Education Evaluation and Policy Analysis, 19,* 15–28.

Lado, A.A., & Wilson, M.L. (1994). Human resource systems and sustained competitive advantage: A competency-based perspective. *Academy of Management Review, 19,* 699–727.

Latham, G.P., & Wexley, K.N. (1994). *Increasing through performance appraisal* (2nd ed.). Reading, MA: Addison-Wesley.

Lawler, E.E., III. (1994). From job-based to competency-based organizations. *Journal of Organizational Behavior, 15,* 3–15.

Lawler, E.E., III. (1996, November-December). Competencies: A poor foundation for the new pay. *Compensation and Benefits Review,* 20–26.

Lawler, E.E., III, & Ledford, G.E., Jr. (1992). A skill-based approach to human resource management. *European Management Journal, 10,* 383–391.

LeBlanc, P. (1997, Spring). Mass customization: A reward mosaic for the future? *ACA Journal,* pp. 16–31.

Ledford, G.E., Jr. (1995a). Designing nimble reward systems. *Compensation and Benefits Review, 27*(4), 46–54.

Ledford, G.E., Jr. (1995b). Paying for the skills, knowledge, and competencies of knowledge workers. *Compensation and Benefits Review, 27*(4), 55–62.

Ledford, G.E., Jr., & Bergel, G. (1991). Skill-based pay case number 1: General Mills. *Compensation and Benefits Review, 23*(2), 24–38.

Ledford, G.E., Jr., Tyler, W .R., & Dixey, WB. (1991). Skill-based pay case number 3: Honeywell ammunition assembly plant. *Compensation and Benefits Review, 23*(2), 57–77.

Longnecker, C.O., Sims, H.P., & Gioia, D.A. (1987). Beyond the mask: The politics of employee appraisal. *Academy of Management Executive, 1,* 183–198.

Lorant, R., (1992, June 27). Mechanic sues Sears for firing. *Wisconsin State Journal,* p. B1.

Marino, K.E. (1996). Developing consensus on firm competencies and capabilities. *Academy of Management Executive, 10,* 40–51.

Mericle, K., & Kim, D. (1996). *Assessing correlates of pay satisfaction and skill acquisition under skill-based pay systems.* Unpublished manuscript, University of Wisconsin.

Mohrman, A.M., Mohrman, S.A., & Odden, A.R. (1996). Aligning teacher compensation with systematic school reform: Skill-based pay and group-based pay performance rewards. *Educational Evaluation and Policy Analysis, 18,* 51–71.

Murray, B., & Gerhart, B. (1997). *An empirical analysis of a skill-based pay program and changes in organizational outcomes.* Unpublished manuscript, University of Texas at San Antonio.

Norris, F. (1991, November 12). Look out for number one. *New York Times,* pp. A1, C5.

Odden, A., & Kelley, C. (1997). *Paying teachers for what they know and do.* Thousand Oaks, CA: Corwin Press.

Prahalad, C.K., & Hamel, G. (1990, May-June). The core competence of the corporation. *Harvard Business Review,* pp. 79–91.

Sibson & Co. (1997). *Why link competencies to pay.* Raleigh, NC: Author.

Silverman, S.B., & Wexley, K.N. (1984). Reactions of employees to performance appraisal interviews as a function of their participation in scale development. *Personnel Psychology, 37,* 703–710.

Spencer, L.M., Jr., & Spencer, S.M. (1993). *Competence at work.* New York: Wiley.

Spreitzer, G.M., McCall, M.W, Jr., & Mahoney, (1977). Early identification of international executive potential. *Journal of Applied Psychology, 82,* 6–29.

Tucker, S.A., & Cofsky, K.M. (1994, Spring). Competency-based pay on a banding platform. *American Compensation Association Journal,* pp. 30–45.

Werner, J.M., & Bolino, M.L. (1997). Explaining U.S. Court of Appeals decisions involving performance appraisal: Accuracy, fairness, and validation. *Personnel Psychology, 50,* 1–24.

Zingheim, P., Ledford, G.E., Jr., & Schuster, J. (1996). Competencies and competency models: One size fits all? *ACA Journal, 5*(1), 56–65.

Part IV

STRATEGIC PAY ISSUES

I n this part of the book, specific issues related to aligning strategic reward programs within the business context are discussed. Emphasis is placed on matching reward programs with business and compensation strategies, organizational structure, organizational culture, organizational change, and the external environment of the business. The major point made in this part of the book is that a careful fit must be made between the reward program and business context in order for the reward program to be effective.

Heneman, R.L. (2001). Corporate business strategies and compensation strategies. In R.L. Heneman, *Business-driven compensation policies: Integrating compensation systems with corporate strategies* (pp. 15–40). New York: AMACOM.

Miceli, M.P., & Heneman, R.L. (2000). Contextual determinants of variable pay plan design: A proposed research framework. *Human Resource Management Review, 10*(3), 289–305.

Heneman, R.L., & Dixon, K.E. (in press). Reward system alingment. *Compensation and Benefits Review.*

Heneman, R.L., & Dixon, K. (1998). How to find, select, and evaluate pay surveys to meet your organization's needs. In R. Platt (Ed.), *Salary survey guidebook* (pp. 1–5). New York: AMACOM.

Ledford, G.E., & Heneman, R.L. (2000). Compensation: A troublesome lead system in organizational change. In M. Beer & N. Noria (Eds.) *Breaking the code of change* (pp. 307–322). Cambridge, MA: Harvard Business School Press.

CHAPTER 8

CORPORATE BUSINESS STRATEGIES AND COMPENSATION STRATEGIES

Robert L. Heneman

It is essential to have the corporate business strategy in hand before developing a new compensation system or revising an existing one. Most often, the corporate business strategy is readily available. Sometimes, however, while the corporate business strategy has been established, it may be difficult to locate. Other times, it may need to be formulated. Strategy formulation is especially likely to take place in lower levels of the organization. There may be a corporate plan, for example, that has little specific direction for a specific division or plant of the company. Under these circumstances, a local business strategy may need to be formulated prior to work on a compensation system. In this chapter, sources of strategies will be discussed along with strategy formulation.

Once the corporate business strategy has been formulated, it must be translated into a specific compensation strategy; this process will be shown in this chapter. Also, several case studies will be provided to show how this step is taken by organizations. An important point to bear in mind throughout the chapter is that generic compensation strategies, just like generic business strategies, are unlikely to be effective. They must be tailor-made to the needs of the business.

BUSINESS STRATEGY TYPES

Organizations seek to develop a unique approach to their product or service that competitors will have a difficult time imitating. If the strategic approach taken by a company is easily imitated by its competitors, then the strategy is not a source of competitive advantage because others can take the same steps (Barney, 1997). Categories of business strategies whereby companies seek to develop unique capabilities follow.

Customer Service

Both service sector organizations and, increasingly, manufacturing sector companies are attempting to differentiate their services and products on the basis of customer service. Good customer service can be defined in terms of several factors (Parasuam, Zeitmal, & Berry, 1998; Schneider & Bowen, 1995). One factor is a tangible outcome that customers receive from service agents, such as a timely response to customer concerns. Another dimension is reliability and the degree to which quality customer service is delivered on repeated business. Responsiveness refers to the extent to which customer demands are met. Empathy refers to the extent to which the service agent is empathetic toward the needs of the customers. Assurance refers to the extent to which promises made by the service agent to the customer are acted upon by the service agent.

Quality

Some organizations compete on the basis of the quality of their product or service. Often a total quality management program (TQM) is used to deliver high quality products and services (Lawler, Mohrman, & Ledford, 1998). In order to deliver high quality products and services, organizations rely on several sets of activities in a TQM program. First, statistical process control is used to measure the extent to which there are defects in the products and services being provided that need to be corrected. Second, constant contact is made with the customers to ensure that the product or service meets their specifications. Third, process reengineering often takes place to ensure that business processes are in alignment with the quality objectives. Fourth, decision making is pushed down in the organization. Employees are empowered to make decisions normally made by supervisors in order to be more responsive to the customer's specifications.

Innovation and Time to Market

Another way to differentiate oneself from the competition is to have innovative products and services that others would have a difficult time reverse engineering to produce a similar product or service. This requires that the organization be capable of learning how to be innovative on a repeatable basis. One innovation alone is unlikely to lead to competitive advantage over time. Moreover, good ideas must be brought to market quickly. In order for organizations to develop the learning capabilities needed for ongoing innovation, several key elements must be in place (Snell, Youndt, & Wright, 1996). First, there must be a system in place to create new products or services. For example, cross-functional product development teams may be used. Second, there must be a knowledge transfer system. That is, learning in one part of the organization must be transferred to other parts of the organization. Some organizations, like General Electric, for example, have a Chief Learning Officer to make sure this transference of knowledge takes place. Third, knowledge must be institutionalized so that it can be used on a repeated basis. Expert systems are sometimes created to capture the knowledge base in an automated information system.

Productivity

By definition productivity refers to output divided by input. In order to be more productive than a competitor, one must increase output, decrease input, or do both. Output refers to the product or service provided, while input refers to the human capital used to deliver the product or service to the customer. Output can be increased by providing a high quality product or service. Input can be decreased by decreasing the number of people needed to produce a product or service. In order to accomplish a decrease in the number of employees needed, more qualified employees are needed to do more of the work and to develop more efficient ways to produce the product or service.

Cost

Perhaps the most obvious way to compete is to reduce costs, so that customers purchase from you rather than from a competitor with a higher price. Obviously, the approach is easy to imitate and may lead to "price warfare," eventually diminishing the quality of the product or service.

Financial

Another way to compete is by doing more with the capital in your organization than others do. The consulting firm of Stern Stewart uses an economic value-added (EVA) model to guide the corporate strategy of its clients. EVA is defined as the return to capital minus the cost of capital. Essentially, it gauges the extent to which the company is generating returns on capital invested in the organization above and beyond alternative investments of the same amount of capital in some financial vehicle other than the organization.

Human Capital

Traditionally, labor has been viewed as a cost to the organization. Increasingly, however, labor is being viewed as a source of revenue generation as well. For example, Sears has shown that the employment relations climate at Sears is related to the bottom line of the business (Rucci, Kirn, & Quinn, 1998). In particular, it has found that employee attitudes toward work are positively correlated with customer service ratings. In turn, customer service ratings are positively correlated with revenue growth at Sears.

Balanced Scorecard

Very few organizations have a pure business strategy of competing solely on the basis of customer service, quality, innovation, productivity, cost, financials, or human capital. Most organizations compete on multiple fronts and compete on the basis of more than one of these factors. Moreover, the "mix" of strategic factors that are emphasized by companies may shift over time in response to the market. An important concept that captures the actual complexities of business strategies just described is the balanced scorecard approach (Kaplan & Norton, 1996).

A balanced scorecard approach implies that multiple strategies are pursued by firms at any one point in time and that the relative "balance" or weight of these strategies may change over time. Hence, a balanced score-card approach to business strategy will list the strategies to be pursued over a period of time and also specify the relative weight of each strategy. Another way for an organization to be unique relative to its competitors is to have a unique blend of business strategies with synergy between the strategies.

SOURCES OF BUSINESS STRATEGIES

As previously indicated in this chapter, business strategies are often readily available in organizations. A brief description of business strategy docu-ments follows.

Vision Statement

A vision statement is a statement of what the organization ultimately hopes to achieve. As such, it is sometimes called an "end-point" vision. Vision statements take various forms and lengths. Some vision statements are very broad, far-reaching philosophical statements. Others are very short with a specific measure of success (e.g., "be a $12 billion retailer by 2002"). A vision statement is sometimes referred to as an aspiration state-ment, as in "here is what we aspire to be."

Mission Statement

The mission statement describes the core capabilities of the company. Often embodied in the mission statement is the extent to which the com-pany is "known" for customer service, quality, innovation, productivity, cost, financials, human capital, or some combination of these factors. For example, a company that views itself as "leaders in new product develop-ment" is likely to be pursuing a strategy of innovation. Other statements, such as "lowest cost manufacturer," may be much more self-evident.

Values

A values statement spells out the beliefs of senior management as to how business should be conducted by the business enterprise. Embodied in a values statement are likely to be beliefs about diversity, teamwork, customer service, ethics, and integrity. It is a guide to how business is to be conducted rather than what is to be achieved.

Critical Success Factors

Critical success factors list the events that must take place in order for the business to be successful. These events may include the development of core capabilities by the company as well as factors outside the company that need to take place (e.g., acquisitions).

Operational Plans

Operational plans are detailed action plans that spell out specific business goals for each unit in the business as they relate to the larger mission, vision, values, and critical success factors.

CASCADING GOALS IN BUSINESS PLANNING

Not only may the corporate entity in a business have a vision, mission, values, critical success factors, and operational plans, but so too may each business unit within the organization. The business unit may be a division of the company, a department, a plant, a sector, a geographic region, or a work team. It is critical that these strategic plans at the business unit be in alignment with the strategic plans at the corporate level. That is, the strategic plans should naturally cascade down from one level to the next. Both corporate and business unit strategic documents need to be obtained prior to compensation strategy formulation. Discrepancies need to be resolved prior to compensation strategy formulation as well.

STRATEGY FORMULATION

Well-formulated business strategy is least likely to be found at the business unit level. In the absence of this information, the local business unit needs to go through a strategic planning process prior to the development of a new compensation system or the redesign of an existing system. The typical process followed is shown in Figure 1. This process is usually undertaken by senior management with the aid of a consultant.

```
┌─────────────────────┐
│    SWOT Analysis    │
└─────────────────────┘
           │
           ▼
┌─────────────────────┐
│       Vision        │
└─────────────────────┘
           │
           ▼
┌─────────────────────┐
│       Mission       │
└─────────────────────┘
           │
           ▼
┌─────────────────────┐
│  Operational Plans  │
└─────────────────────┘
```

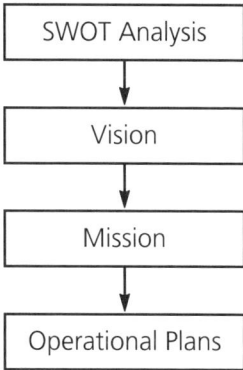

Figure 1.   Business strategy formulation process

The first step in the process is to conduct a SWOT analysis. Emphasis here is upon identifying strengths and weaknesses internal to the organization and identifying opportunities and threats external to the organization that are faced by the organization. This step usually requires amassing considerable internal and external data to make these assessments.

Based on this SWOT analysis, a path to the future is determined by focusing on facilitating forces (i.e., strengths and opportunities) and by avoiding or changing restraining forces (i.e., weaknesses and threats). This assessment of the facilitating and restraining forces in the SWOT analysis leads to a vision statement. If done properly, it is an honest assessment of what the organization can expect to deliver on given the forces shown in Figure 2.

The SWOT analysis, along with the vision, helps produce a mission statement. The mission statement describes the core capabilities that must be present in order to take advantage of strengths and opportunities and to counteract weaknesses and threats. The mission statement captures not only current capabilities, but also capabilities that can be realistically developed by the organization as a part of its balanced scorecard strategic portfolio.

	Forces	
Location	Strengths	Weaknesses
Internal	Strengths	Weaknesses
External	Opportunities	Threats

Figure 2.   A SWOT analysis as the basis for vision and mission

Lastly, operational plans are developed to capitalize on current strengths and to develop new capabilities that can be used to exploit opportunities faced by the company and to thwart weaknesses and threats that may detour the accomplishment of the organizational mission. Operational plans are usually very detailed and lengthy relative to the other strategic planning documents and are most subject to change in the short run. As a result, designing compensation policies around this short-term document alone is likely to be a futile effort.

COMPENSATION STRATEGY

As described in the previous chapter and shown in Figure 3, the formulation of compensation strategy is dependent upon business strategy and other forces. Given that the relationship between these other forces and compensation strategy is fairly well defined elsewhere in the literature, the focus here will be on the less well-defined link between business strategy and compensation strategy. Compensation strategy can be subdivided into five segments, as shown in Figure 4. A checklist of compensation strategy issues to consider is shown in Figure 5 for each segment. Each issue will be described in turn.

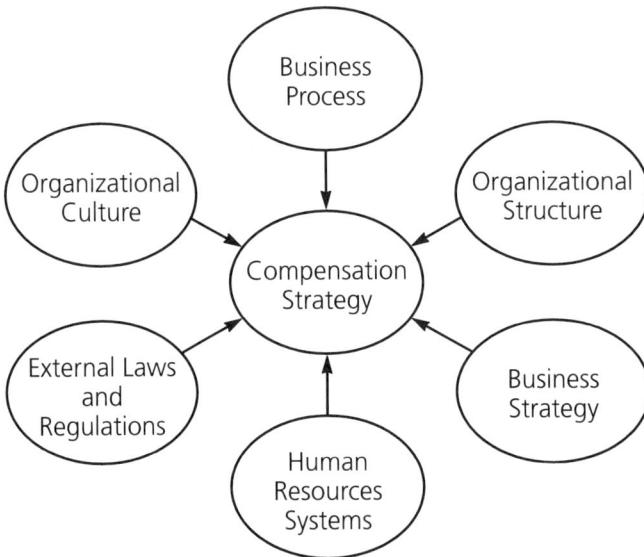

Figure 3.   Forces influencing compensation strategy

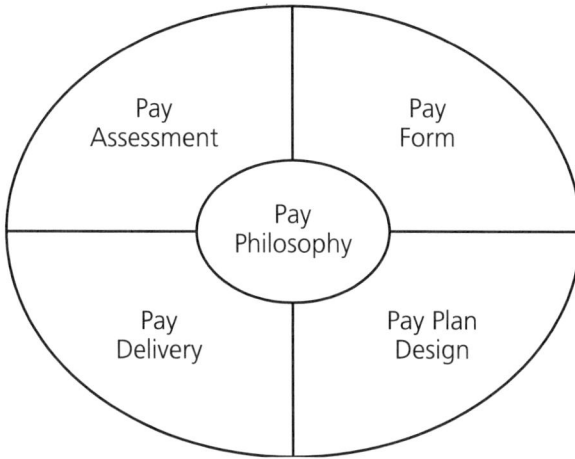

Figure 4.   Compensation strategy segments

Pay Philosophy
- ☐ Internal vs. External Equity
- ☐ Lead vs. Lag Market
- ☐ Attraction vs. Retention

Pay Assessment
- ☐ Job vs. Person
- ☐ Results vs. Behaviors
- ☐ Seniority vs. Performance
- ☐ Education vs. Skills

Pay Form
- ☐ Monetary vs. Nonmonetary
- ☐ Fixed vs. Variable
- ☐ Individual vs. Team

Pay Delivery
- ☐ Narrow vs. Broad Pay Bands
- ☐ Small vs. Large Pay Band Overlap
- ☐ Open vs. Closed Pay Communications

Pay Plan Design
- ☐ Participative vs. Non participative
- ☐ Centralized vs. Decentralized
- ☐ Static vs. Dynamic
- ☐ Lead vs. Lag

Figure 5.   Compensation strategy checklist

Pay Philosophy

The cornerstone to compensation strategy is the compensation philosophy of the company. This segment of the compensation strategy articulates fundamental beliefs about the goals of all components of the compensation system relative to the business strategy.

Internal vs. External Equity

The first fundamental issue to have a bearing on all compensation decision making is the extent to which internal versus external equity is to be stressed in the organization. In an ideal world, both internal and external equity would be emphasized and be in sync with one another. Frequently, however, internal equity and external equity strategies are not in perfect alignment with one another; thus, one or the other must be emphasized. An internal equity strategy determines the value of the job and/or person based on value added to the company as assessed by a job or person evaluation system. An external equity strategy determines the value of the job or the person on the basis of the market as assessed by a market survey.

Organizations that place an emphasis on financials, cost, customers, or innovation as a business strategy are more likely to follow an external equity strategy because it is consistent with the business philosophy of setting product service prices at the market value. Organizations that emphasize quality are also more likely to use an external equity strategy because of the large administrative steps and costs associated with an internal equity strategy that may be inconsistent with a total quality management philosophy. Organizations that follow productivity as a human capital business strategy are likely to adopt an internal equity compensation strategy because of the intrinsic value of human capital to the company's business strategy.

A cautionary note is in order for companies that follow an external equity strategy. The assumption is that organizations have perfect market information. In many situations perfect market information is not available for reasons spelled out in Chapter 5 of this book. Hence, many companies opt to pursue both internal and external equity strategies.

Lead vs. Lag Market

When external equity is to be considered, as it most often is, a decision must be made whether to lead, lag, or match the market. The approach to be taken may be uniform for the entire company or vary by business unit or by occupation. By leading the market, the hope is that one can attract higher quality employees to the organization and retain existing staff. Attraction and retention are maximized because alternative employment opportunities in the market pay less. Although labor is more costly with a lead policy, the hope is that these additional costs will be paid for by more productivity from higher quality personnel attracted to the organization and by lower turnover costs. The philosophy of a lag policy is to pay less than the market average for labor in hopes of having lower labor costs and more profits. A compromise position is to match the market and compete on grounds other than labor costs.

Organizations with cost-driven business strategies are most likely to follow a lag policy for obvious reasons. Companies that place a premium on human capital with their business strategy are more likely to follow a lead policy to differentiate themselves from their competitors on the basis of labor quality. Organizations that emphasize total quality management (TQM) may also use a lead policy in order to attract talented people who do not need monitoring (e.g., performance appraisals). More efficient systems can be built without the administrative burden and cost associated with a performance monitoring system. Firms following the other business strategies are likely to follow a match the market philosophy.

Attraction vs. Retention

Organizations have a finite budget to be used for compensation. Tough decisions have to be made regarding the allocation of these dollars. One such decision is whether to devote more money to attracting the best talent available than to retaining current personnel. Customer- and quality-focused organizations must meet the demands of the customer immediately and don't have the luxury of waiting to attract better customer service-oriented employees so they are likely to emphasize retention. Innovative organizations are more likely to need to go to the outside market for employees with skill sets that are not available in-house. Cost-focused organizations are likely to put greater emphasis on attraction because there are usually fewer new entrants to the organization to be paid than there are current employees to be paid. Productivity-, financial-, and human capital-focused organizations are likely to maintain a balance between the two objectives.

Pay Assessment

In determining the amount to pay each employee, an assessment must be made of the value that the person adds to the organization. Both human capital and job characteristics can be used to make these assessments. Several hotly debated topics often accompany this segment of compensation strategy.

Job vs. Person

A very fundamental issue faced by compensation decision makers is how much emphasis to place on the job that the person holds versus how much emphasis to place on the different human capital characteristics that the person brings to the job in deciding rates of pay. Traditionally, major emphasis has been placed upon the job rather than the person. Elaborate job-based systems with job descriptions, job classifications, and job evaluation systems are commonplace in organizations. Increasingly, however, organizations are attempting to become more internally flexible to meet market demands, and, in doing so, some organizations are beginning to place more emphasis on the person than the job. Organizations with a person-based focus are more likely to have innovation, quality, and human capital as corporate business strategies. Flexibility is extremely important for the accomplishment of these business strategies. Organizations that are pursuing a low-cost or financial business strategy usually do not follow a person-based assessment strategy because the costs of this type of approach can be high. For example, the start-up costs of a skill-based pay system are quite large. Productivity-driven organizations are more likely to follow a job-based compensation strategy because it is easier and more relevant to build this kind of accounting system.

Results vs. Behaviors

Another decision-making point is whether to assess the results people achieve or to assess the behaviors expected to lead to the results. In organizations that emphasize productivity as a business strategy, usually both results and behaviors are emphasized. Results focus on the output side of the productivity ratio and behaviors on the input side of the productivity ratio. Financial- and cost-driven companies most often focus on a results-based compensation strategy so that people "pay for themselves." Organizations driven by customer service and human capital tend to favor behaviors because they are so crucial to the delivery of exemplary service. Quality-based organizations most often focus on results rather than on behaviors because this philosophy is consistent with the team philosophy of the importance of the overall system results rather than people's behavior within the system.

Seniority vs. Performance

Outside customer-driven organizations in the public and nonprofit sectors, it is becoming rare for an organization to emphasize seniority over performance. Whether performance is measured by behaviors or results is debatable, but the need to focus on performance is a part of most companies' compensation strategy regardless of the business strategy. The need to consider this issue in formulating a compensation strategy cannot be stressed enough. The importance of seniority versus performance needs to be clearly articulated rather than be implicit in the compensation policy because many employees still feel that the "fair" thing to do is to reward them for their years with the company. Action steps must be taken by companies to change that philosophy, and these steps are far more likely to be taken if the seniority versus erformance tradeoff is explicitly addressed in the compensation strategy.

Education vs. Skills

A fundamental distinction exists between education and skills. Education refers to the mastery of declarative knowledge, while skills refers to the mastery of procedural knowledge. Education is usually obtained by taking courses in an educational setting, while skills are usually obtained through on-the-job experience. A low-cost business strategy is often associated with an education compensation strategy. To minimize costs, education is to be obtained off the job and paid for by the incumbent. Organizations that have a quality-based business strategy are likely to put more emphasis on skills that are specific to their business environment. In terms of business strategies other than quality or cost, organizations are likely to have a mix of education and skill assessment as part of their compensation philosophy. Increasingly, however, the emphasis is on education over skills, so that employees have the breadth of knowledge needed to add value to the firm as it changes over time. As with seniority, this is a very sensitive issue with employees and should be explicitly addressed in the compensation strategy.

Pay Form

Although the amount of money available for compensation in a company is finite, the form that pay merit takes can vary. Variance in pay form is also a function of the type of business strategy.

Monetary vs. Nonmonetary

Some forms of pay, such as recognition, are social in nature, cost the organization very little, and are labeled nonmonetarv rewards. Other forms of pay are more direct, are very costly to the organization, and are referred to as monetary rewards. Obviously in a cost-driven business, emphasis is likely to be on nonmonetary rewards. Organizations driven by an innovation strategy are likely to place at least equal emphasis on nonmonetary versus monetary rewards in the spirit of providing creative rewards for creative people. Human capital-driven organizations are also likely to focus on both forms of compensation to emphasize the importance of human capital to the business strategy. Organizations with a focus on quality often stress nonmonetary rewards as a way to celebrate new process innovations that provide a higher quality product. Traditionally, customer service-driven organizations have used nonmonetary rewards to honor excellence in customer service (e.g., an employee of the month plaque displayed in the lobby). Finance-driven organizations tend to focus on monetary rewards given the importance of capital to their business strategy. Productivity-based organizations tend to focus on monetary rewards because this form of pay is consistent with their accounting, and measurement system.

Fixed vs. Variable

A fixed pay system implies that pay increases are across-the-board based on membership in the organization, and/or built into base pay. A variable pay system implies that pay increases are based on performance and/or are in the form of a cash bonus. Increasingly, all organizations regardless of their business strategy are moving toward variable pay systems. Most likely to develop this philosophy are organizations with a cost- or finance-driven business strategy. Increased costs are to be incurred only if the business prospers. Other companies are also likely to follow a variable pay strategy, but for different reasons. Those that focus on innovation and human capital are more likely to provide nay in a variable term because of its motivational properties. Quality- and productivity-based organizations are also likely to use variable pay because the performance measures used often are based on the metrics used by the business to gauge business strategy success. Customer driven organizations, especially in the public and nonprofit sectors, continue to rely upon fixed pay systems. These pay systems (e.g., across-the-board increases, cost-of-living increases, merit pay) are used to buy the loyalty of employees to the organization. Although they are usually not well paid relative to the market, they can always count on a pay increase each year. With this loyalty to a nonprofit organization, such as a nonprofit counseling agency, may come loyalty by the customer to the nonprofit service deliverer, such as a particular counselor.

Individual vs. Team

Pay can be given for individual accomplishments or for team (collective) accomplishments. Traditionally in the United States, pay has been allocated to individuals, rather than to teams. However, with the advent of team-based work systems like self-directed work teams in the United States, a part of compensation is increasingly being used for team pay rather than solely for individual pay. Team-based work systems are likely to be found in organizations with business strategies that emphasize quality and innovation. Hence, they are likely to have a team-based pay strategy. Firms pursuing other business strategies are less likely to have team-based pay systems.

Pay Delivery

Different forms of pay can be delivered using different vehicles. Different types of pay delivery vehicles need to be incorporated into the compensation strategy because they again vary by type of business strategy.

Narrow vs. Broad Pay Bands

The outside parameters of pay bands are defined by the minimum to be paid and the maximum to be paid for people who fall in a particular pay band. The maximum is usually set based on the maximum value of the job to the company as determined by a job evaluation system. Narrow pay bands help organizations minimize their costs. For example, someone in a clerical position in a university may have a Ph.D. but still be paid a low wage rate relative to professionals with a Ph.D. because the value of a clerical job to the university is low relative to the value of a professional job that actually requires a Ph.D. As a result, using narrow pay bands as a compensation strategy goes well with low-cost strategy employers. For similar reasons, narrow pay bands are prevalent with financially driven institutions. Because of the dampening motivational effects of narrow pay bands on bright people in low grades, organizations that pursue innovations, customer service, productivity, and human capital as business strategies tend to favor broad bands as a compensation strategy. Broad bands reward employees for performing outside the scope of their narrowly defined job duties, and they do not bump up against the maximum of the pay grade as quickly; hence broad bands may be more motivational as well as costly.

Small vs. Large Pay Band Overlap

The amount of overlap between pay bands has important implications for the development of human resources in organizations. A small amount of overlap communicates to employees in the organization that advancement is determined by developing new skills and acquiring more education so that they can move up to the next pay grade in the pay structure-one that requires a higher level of skill and/or education to receive higher levels of pay. In other words, a premium is placed upon promotion. On the other hand, a large amount of overlap between pay bands communicates the message that while one does not necessarily have the skills or education to advance, the person can nevertheless earn as much as or more than someone in adjacent pay grades by virtue of hard work and effort that result in solid business results.

Firms that emphasize quality, cost, financials, innovation, and productivity in their business strategy tend to have very flat organizations with fewer promotional opportunities. It is very difficult to retain quality personnel unless there is a large amount of overlap in pay grades. In order to successfully compete by quality, cost, financials, innovation, or productivity, human resources need to multitask for the organization to be effective; a large amount of overlap allows employees the room to be rewarded for the effort required to perform multiple tasks with the same level of value to the organization. Companies that compensate on the basis of human capital are more likely to have less overlap in pay grades in order to motivate upward movement in the pay structure. Employees are motivated to acquire new skills so that they can do higher structured work rather than do more tasks at the same level of complexity. A similar objective can also be achieved by having a large amount of pay band overlap along with a skill band pay system.

Open vs. Closed Pay Communications

The amount of detail about the compensation system revealed to employees can also vary by business strategy. A very closed system might, for example, reveal to each employee only his or her own pay and discipline employees for talking with other employees about the pay levels. A very open system would be one in which each employee knows every other employee's pay amounts. Traditionally, most compensation systems have been more closed than open. Increasingly, however, organizations are opening up the pay systems. More openness is especially likely to be found in companies with a human capital business strategy. In order to retain highly talented employees, no secrets are kept so that turnover does not take place as a result of hearsay. Closed compensation systems are most common in firms with a low-cost business strategy. The hope here is to minimize turnover by ay amounts. Traditionally, most compensation systems have been more closed than open. Increasingly, however, organizations are opening up the pay systems. More openness is especially likely to be found in companies with a human capital strategy. In order to retain highly talented employees, no secrets are kept so that turnover does not take place as a result of hearsay. Closed compensation systems are most common in firms with a low-cost business strategy. The hope here is to minimize turnover by keeping employees ignorant about just how low their pay levels are. Organizations following business strategies other than cost or human capital are likely to pursue a midrange strategy that is neither too open nor too closed. Under this type of compensation strategy, data are not released about individual pay levels. However, pay ranges are made public as well as averages within the pay range.

Pay Plan Design

Compensation strategy includes not only the amount and process to be paid, but also the processes that were used to reach these decisions. Processes that need to be considered in the compensation strategy follow.

Participative vs. Nonparticipative

In a participative pay plan design, both employees and managers become involved in the design of the system. It is a method of empowering employees to perform roles previously performed only by management. In a nonparticipative pay plan design, only senior management is involved in designing compensation programs. A participative pay plan design strategy requires that an empowered work force already be in place. Usually, this type of work design system is found in organizations that emphasize productivity, innovation, customer service, quality, and human capital, An empowered work force is seen as a means to each of these business strategy ends. One is less likely to find participative decision making being used with employees in cost- and financially-driven organizations. More emphasis is placed on capital than on people with these business strategies, and financial matters, including compensation, are treated at the senior management level.

Centralized vs. Decentralized

The design of compensation strategy can take place at the corporate level or at the business unit level. In recent times, more and more organizations have experimented with developing compensation strategy at the business unit level; historically, compensation strategy has been formulated at the corporate level. Decentralized systems seem to work well only under specific business strategies. In particular, they tend to work with companies focused on quality and innovation. Under these business strategies, other business strategies are also often localized, so it is logical to link the pay system as well to decentralized strategy formulation. In most organizations, however, especially in cost- and financially-driven ones, most finances including compensation are controlled at the corporate level. Also, in many organizations, labor migrates from business unit to business unit, and different pay plans at different locations for the same work performed may be perplexing to employees. Organizations with productivity, human capital, and customer-driven business strategies are likely to develop strategic compensation plans at both the corporate and business unit levels. To do so allows for standardization across plans while allowing modifications for local circumstances. This compromise approach is sometimes referred to as "mass customization" and is likely to be used more often by companies in the future (LeBlanc, 1997).

Static vs. Dynamic

Temporal aspects of pay systems are important to compensation strategy as well as to the content of the pay system (Ledford, 1995). Organizations change their business strategies more frequently than ever before, and the question becomes how often should the compensation system change to reflect these changes? Too frequent change may undermine the credibility of the compensation strategy, while too infrequent change may undermine the business strategy. Experience suggests that significant business changes must occur for the compensation system to change. These changes in business strategy are most likely to take place in organizations pursuing an innovation strategy.

Lead vs. Lag

Compensation strategies can either lead or lag the business strategy (Ledford & Heneman, in press). A lead compensation strategy is used to show to employees the importance of subsequent business strategy changes. A lag compensation strategy is designed to reinforce the change in business strategy. As with very dynamic compensation strategies, lead compensation systems seem to work in very limited circumstances. Once again, organizations with a very innovative business strategy might use a lead compensation strategy to make the impending business strategy change more salient to employees.

CONTINGENCY FACTORS

The matching of business strategy to compensation strategy is a delicate task. Some general observations were made in the previous section on which compensation strategies seem to be the most logical for various business strategies. These are simply observations based on personal experiences of the author and are not grounded in research data because the data to substantiate these observations remains to be collected. Moreover, the relationship is often more complex than the pure strategies match portrayed. In particular, other contingencies must be considered along with business strategy in the formulation of compensation strategy, as they may modify the relationship between business strategy and compensation strategy. These contingency factors are shown in Figure 6, along with a summary of business and compensation strategies.

An example will help point out the importance of these contingencies in strategic compensation decision making. Take the case of the observation that participation in decision making is often used with quality-based business strategies. Although in general this may be true, it is only a starting point for compensation strategy discussions. Consideration must also

Business Strategy	Compensation Strategy	Contingencies
Customer Service		
Quality	Pay Philosophy	Human Resources Systems
Innovation and Time to Market	Pay Assessment	Organizational Structure
Productivity	Pay Form	Business Processes
Cost	Pay Delivery	Organizational Culture
Financial	Pay Plan Design	Laws and Regulations
Human Capital		

Figure 6.   Contingency factors to consider

be given to the contingency factors. A participative compensation strategy may not fit in a quality-based organization that is very hierarchical in terms of structure, that has a command and control cultural orientation, is very statistically driven in terms of business process, and is subject to unfair labor practice charges under the National Labor Relations Act for the use of company organized teams to decide benefits to be offered. Performance-based pay plans do not work well when staffing decisions are based upon seniority rather than performance. Business strategy should weigh heavily in compensation strategy formulation, but certainly it cannot be used independently of these contingency factors.

CASE STUDIES

There is no mechanical algorithm to decide the compensation strategies on the basis of business strategy. The process is as much, or maybe even more, art than science. To solidify some of the points in this chapter, several cases will be presented to show the link between business strategy and compensation strategy.

Case 1: Law Firm

H, L, and C is a full-service law firm located in the Midwest and southeast. It started as a very small law firm twenty-five years ago and has now grown to be the eighteenth largest firm in the country. In order to successfully compete, small law firms are becoming very specialized boutiques or are being merged and acquired by other firms to become full-service law firms, as is the case with H, L, and C.

H, L, and C aspires to be a nationally recognized firm offering full service to large clients. Currently, it is regional in scope. The business strategy of H, L, and C is multifaceted and as such has a balanced scorecard emphasis to it. One facet of the firm's business strategy is to be very active in the communities at large that it serves. The firm wants to have a very visible presence so that people are aware of its services and reputation by word of mouth rather than by media. As a result, members of the firm are very active in professional associations, employer associations, and community service boards. A second facet of the business strategy is to have a highly talented staff in each practice area. No location has a resident expert in each practice area, but there must be a highly regarded expert in the firm available to provide guidance in all geographic areas. A third facet of the firm's strategy is to be very well managed and make extensive use of virtual technology to coordinate services across regions.

The compensation strategy was developed in response to the business strategy. While billable hours serve as the common denominator for determining value of the attorneys, monetary value is also placed on community involvement, firm management, professional development, teamwork, and the development of new clients. Community involvement is seen as a long-term performance strategy, while the development of new clients is seen as a short-term performance strategy. Professional development is important to reward in order to develop in-house expertise. Teamwork and firm management are needed to coordinate services in a virtual environment. Compensation decision making is kept at the equity partner level, and profits are shared with all associates, including nonattorneys. Profits are shared to facilitate shared services, and decision making is retained at the equity partner level to be consistent with the previous cultures at the firms acquired over time to form H, L, and C.

Case 2: Implement Dealer

The Jacobs companies are located in Ohio and Arizona. They have a dealership network in each state and provide and service heavy operating equipment for road construction. They are family owned and have been in business for more than 100 years. The vision of the family is to become the largest dealership in both Ohio and Arizona. To achieve this vision will be difficult, because in recent years there has been a large influx of foreign competition in the market. Margins on products have been drastically reduced from about 20 percent to 6 percent, making cost issues a major concern. The Jacobs family believes that its major source of competitive advantage is its people, many of whom have been with the company for more than thirty years. The company takes great pride in the values developed over the years with the family and believes that this has fostered a feeling of loyalty by the workforce. In order to continue to grow, new skills (e.g., customer service, technical expertise) will need to be developed in the workforce, and work will need to be organized in a more efficient manner to reduce costs.

The business strategy is based upon a set of core values. One set of core values emphasizes high performance as defined by being creative and proactive, providing legendary service, developing superior skills, and routinely accomplishing business objectives. Another set of core values emphasizes business ethics and includes honesty, integrity, and fairness in all business relationships, including the employment relationship. A final set of core values is labeled commitment and includes having a caring attitude, sharing wealth with employees, and being loyal to the company.

The compensation strategy draws directly upon these core values. One important current objective to be met as a part of the high performance value is the reduction of cost. Pay supplemental to base pay is offered for cost minimization at the business unit level. Also, supplemental pay is part of the compensation strategy for improvements in product and service quality objectives. In order to foster loyalty to the company, there has never been a layoff at the Jacobs Family Company. In order to avoid layoffs, staffing levels are kept low and base wages are targeted below the market. Variable pay is used to make up the difference in market levels, and base wage savings are researched for downturns in the economy so that layoffs do not need to take place. Many nonmonetary rewards are used to recognize the importance of the "extended family members" to the organization. Tuition reimbursement is provided to reward loyalty to the company and to build new skills in the workforce.

Case 3: Gourmet Rice Meal Manufacturer

Mealsolutions is a billion-dollar manufacturer of gourmet rice meals. It has developed many types of packaged meals that can be served with rice. The market is a very competitive one, and the company has decided to specialize in the high end of the market and hopes to become the number-one seller of gourmet meal solutions.

In order to accomplish this mission, Mealsolutions has had to undertake a massive restructuring of the business. Low-margin products have been discontinued and the labor force has been reduced. A new senior executive team has been assembled to guide the company back to profitability.

Several strategic directives were formed by the new senior executives to guide the transformation of Mealsolutions. First, they would create a vast knowledge base of customer preferences. Second, they would create an integrated business to deliver value to the customer. Third, they would grow a highly talented workforce that was committed to continuous improvement. Fourth, they would share the business results with employees. Fifth, they would meet the highest possible quality standards.

As can be seen from the business strategy, the business strategic focus is on a blend of customer service, quality, and human capital. As a result, the compensation strategy developed to support this strategy. One strategy was to share financial success with employees as shareholders in the company. Another was to ensure that the compensation system was equitable, open, and understood by all associates. In addition, employees were to receive compensation commensurate with their level of responsibility and contribution to the company. Rewards were to be based on business results. Lastly, employees were to be given choices from a compensation "menu."

REFERENCES

Barney, J. (1997). *Gaining and sustaining competitive advantage*. Reading, MA: Addison-Wesley.

Kaplan, R.S., & Norton, D.P. (1996). *The balanced scorecard*. Boston: Harvard Business School Press.

Lawler, E.E., III, Mohrman, S.A., & Ledford, G.E., Jr. (1998). *Strategies for high performance organizations*. San Francisco: Jossey-Bass.

LeBlanc, P.V. (1997, Spring). Mass customization: A rewards mosaic for the future? *ACA Journal*, pp. 16–32.

Ledford, G.E., Jr. (1995, July-August). Designing nimble reward systems. *Compensation and Benefits Review*, pp. 46–54.

Ledford, G.E., Jr., & Heneman, R.L. (In press). Compensation: A troublesome lead system in organizational change. In M. Beer & N. Noria (Eds.), *Breaking the code of change*. Cambridge, MA: Harvard Business School Press.

Parasuam, P., Zeitmal, V.A., & Berry, L.L. (1998). SERVQUAL: A multiple item scale for measuring consumer perceptions of service quality. *Journal of Retailing, 64*, 13–37.

Rucci, A., Kirn, S., & Quinn, R. (1998, January-February). The employee-customer-profit chain at Sears. *Harvard Business Review*, pp. 82–97.

Schneider, B., & Bowen, D.E. (1995). *Winning the service game.* Boston: Harvard Business School Press.

Snell, S.A., Youndt, M.A., & Wright, P.M. (1996). Establishing a framework for research in strategic human resource management: Merging resource theory in organizational learning. In G.R. Ferris & K.M. Rowland (Eds.), *Research in personnel and human resources management* (pp. 61–90). Greenwich, CT: JAI Press.

CHAPTER 9

CONTEXTUAL DETERMINANTS OF VARIABLE PAY PLAN DESIGN:

A Proposed Research Framework

Marcia P. Miceli and Robert L. Heneman

Source: Reprinted from *Human Resource Management Review, 10*(3). Miceli, M.P. & Heneman, R.L. Contextual Determinants of Variable Pay Plan Design: A Proposed Research Framework, pp. 289–305. Copyright © 2000, with permission from Elsevier Science.

ABSTRACT

Increasingly, organizations are using variable pay plans to reward employees for the results that they achieve. Current discussion of variable pay focuses on variable pay plan design mechanics, with insufficient attention given to contextual variables that may affect variable pay plan design. We offer a preliminary framework for examining the contextual determinants of variable pay plan design. Components of the framework include characteristics of the environment, characteristics of the organization, and the organization's pay strategies. Propositions for future research are offered.

INTRODUCTION

Academic and practitioner interest in variable pay—a method of rewarding employees for the results they achieve in organizations—is increasing. Evidence of this increased interest comes in at least three forms. First is the recent appearance of reviews of research on different types of variable pay plans, including gainsharing (Welbourne & Gomez-Mejia, 1995), profit sharing (Weitzman & Kruse, 1990), and team pay (DeMatteo, Eby, & Sundstrom, 1998). Second, as shown in a survey of Fortune 1000 companies, the current and planned use of variable pay has increased markedly (Lawler, Mohrman, & Ledford, 1995). Third, practitioner books (e.g., Belcher, 1996) and training programs (e.g., Belcher et al., 1998) on variable pay are proliferating.

The focus in this new area of compensation theory and practice has been on the mechanics of variable pay plan design. One objective of this article is to broaden this line of inquiry to include a discussion of the context in which variable pay takes place. We propose that variable pay plan design is a function of the organization in which the pay plan is located and the environment in which that organization operates. The wide variety of variable pay plan designs in use suggests that there is as yet no agreement as to "one best approach" to variable pay design. Therefore, a second objective is to provide preliminary logic suggesting circumstances under which different variable pay plan components may be most appropriate or useful.

VARIABLE PAY DEFINED

One theme emerging from the growing body of knowledge is that the term "variable pay" refers to a hybrid combination of gainsharing, profit sharing, and team pay. Increasingly, it is difficult to find "pure" forms of gainsharing, profit sharing, and team pay. The lines of demarcation between these "pure" plans are decidedly blurred in both theory (Heneman, Ledford, & Gresham, in press) and actual pay practice (McAdams & Hawk, 1994). Perhaps because of this complexity, "variable pay" has been defined in different ways. Three examples follow.

> Variable pay is any form of direct pay that is not folded into base pay and that varies according to performance. (Schuster & Zingheim, 1992, p. 154)

> An alternative compensation system that ties pay to business outcomes and supports a participative management process. Cash payments are based on a predetermined measure or measures of group or organizational outcomes. (Belcher, 1996, p. 10)

> This is compensation received in addition to base pay, and it varies depending on the performance of the individual, team, company, etc. By its very nature, it

is not guaranteed, although many organizations have allowed such programs to become entitlements, like base pay. Variable pay is usually received in a lump-sum check, and does not become part of base pay. Variable pay can also take the form of case payments or equity related investments. (Wilson, 1995, p. 53)

The two themes common to these three definitions are that variable pay provides case payments in the form of a bonus, and that it is tied to a measure of tem, business unit, or organizational measures of performance. The authors do not clearly agree as to whether payment made in non-cash forms, such as stock options, would be considered variable pay. Nor do they agree as to whether plans rewarding performance measured strictly at the individual level, i.e., individual incentive plans, constitute variable pay plans. Because there appears to be less of a consensus on these two factors, we will exclude stock plans and individual pay-for-performance plans from our definition of variable pay plans.

DIMENSIONS OF VARIABLE PAY DESIGN

Pay plans vary as to pay basis, design, and administration (Gomez-Mejia & Balkin, 1992). Thus, studies of variable pay could focus on either processes or outcomes. Processes encompass who "championed" the plan when it was designed and "sold," how opportunities for participation are utilized, how the appeal procedure is operated, how performance feedback is provided, and so on.

However, because of the current interest in design features, and because most of the pay literature defines pay plan characteristics in terms of outcome rather than process variables, the focus here will primarily be on outcome characteristics. Figure 1 provides a preliminary attempt to classify some important characteristics and their variations. They include the performance measures selected, such as costs or revenues; and the level of measurement, such as the team, business unit, or organization. Other characteristics are the payout formula, which may be pre-specified or discretionary and vary as to basis (e.g., based on financial goal achievement vs. customer service ratings); the type and frequency of payout (e.g., based on accomplishment of milestones or regularly by time); and the amount of payout (in absolute terms) and leverage (in relative terms), i.e., the ratio of variable pay to total pay.

Our propositions attempt to link some of these characteristics to contextual variables. Because of the state of existing research, and because of space limitations, not all characteristics are explored to the same extent. It is hoped that this article will stimulate more development of propositions as well as empirical work.

- performance measures
- level of performance measure
- payout formula
- amount of payout
- type of payout
- frequency of payout
- leverage

Figure 1.   Variable pay design characteristics

A PRELIMINARY FRAMEWORK

In Figure 2, we present a preliminary framework for linking certain pay plan characteristics, as shown in Figure 1, to contextual variables. Classifying a wide variety of variables into a few categories, we propose that the organization's environment influences plan characteristics through its

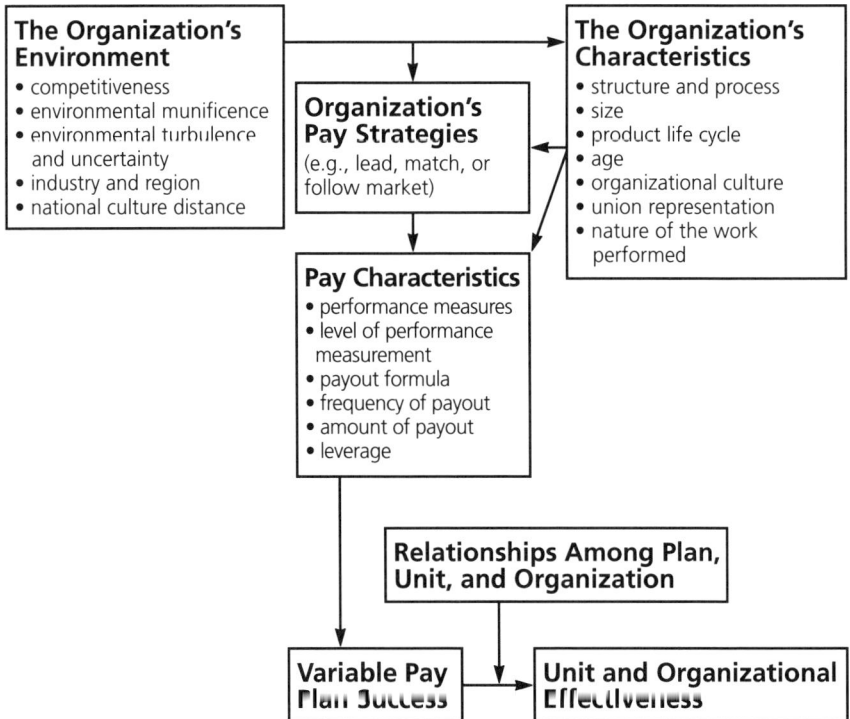

The Organization's Environment
- competitiveness
- environmental munificence
- environmental turbulence and uncertainty
- industry and region
- national culture distance

Organization's Pay Strategies
(e.g., lead, match, or follow market)

The Organization's Characteristics
- structure and process
- size
- product life cycle
- age
- organizational culture
- union representation
- nature of the work performed

Pay Characteristics
- performance measures
- level of performance measurement
- payout formula
- frequency of payout
- amount of payout
- leverage

Relationships Among Plan, Unit, and Organization

Variable Pay Plan Success

Unit and Organizational Effectiveness

Figure 2.   A preliminary model of the context of variable pay design

effect on pay strategies, and through its effect on organization characteristics. Because strategies can be manifested in intentions, managerial actions, or both (Gerhart & Milkovich, 1992), we propose that pay strategies, as well as the organization's characteristics, directly influence plan characteristics.

We focus in this article on predicting plan characteristics, rather than on predicting their consequences, such as plan success or organizational effectiveness. However, one can reasonably ask why plan characteristics matter, and thus, the tie to organizational effectiveness seems critical and must be addressed at least in a general way.

Following some prior research (Balkin & Gomez-Mejia, 1987), predictions of plan success would follow the same logic as predictions regarding the choice of plan characteristics. That is, the contingency theory of compensation strategy holds that the effectiveness of a compensation strategy depends on the fit among environment, organization, and strategy (Balkin & Gomez-Mejia, 1987; Lawler, 1990). Thus, the more rational the decision-makers, then the greater the extent to which plan characteristics reflect a good fit, and consequently, the more effective the plan. The extent to which the plan's success influences the effectiveness of the unit or organization in which it is operated may depend on the relationships among the plan, the unit, and the larger organization. For example, if a plan covers all employees in an organization and payouts represent a significant proportion of total pay, then, all other factors being equal, the plan will have greater impact or organizational success than will a small-payout plan covering only a small group of employees.

Some empirical research supports a contingency view of environment, organization, plan design, plan success, and organization effectiveness. For example, in one study (Balkin & Gomez-Mejia, 1987) firms in early growth stages were more likely to use larger pay incentives to attract highly qualified employees despite low capital, and they also found these incentives to be more effective than did firms in more mature stages. In another study, foreign subsidiary effectiveness declined as the incentive-fixed pay mix deviated from "ideal profiles" (Roth & O'Donnell, 1996).

On the other hand, empirical research has not consistently shown support for a contingency theory of variable pay plan effectiveness. That is, the interactions between independent variables predicting pay plan effectiveness are usually insignificant while the main effects of these independent variables are significant (Gerhart, Trevor, & Graham, 1996).

One interpretation of these findings is that there are universal "best (pay) practices" regardless of the characteristics of the organization and its environment. Another interpretation of these findings is that there needs to be more careful theory development to specify the most important interacting variables. Much of the previous research appears to have selected interaction terms on the basis of data availability rather than the basis of sound theoretical arguments. Further, there is little theory or empirical research explaining why organizations do not universally adopt these "best practices." Our purpose here is not to resolve the debate, which clearly requires empirical testing. Rather, we attempt to specify theory more carefully to facilitate this testing.

Three limitations must be made explicit. First, given the state of the literature, our framework is preliminary and incomplete; for example, every factor that could be important in determining plan characteristics or plan success has not been identified. Second, because our focus is on the characteristics of variable pay, we do not deal extensively here with the consequences of plan success or failure, including the plan's impact on organizational functioning. Third, compensation systems should not be treated in isolation; rather they should be viewed as a part of broader HR systems, in which other elements could harmonize or be at odds (Becker & Huselid, 1996). Research shows that plans are more likely to affect organization performance when they are bundled with other incentives; alignment gives greater power to influence performance (Gomez-Mejia & Balkin, 1992). However, strictly for ease of communication and to conform to space limitations, we will deal here only with variable pay.

We now discuss each category of potential predictors in more depth. We approach these in the order in which they appear in Figure 2, rather than the order in which plan characteristics have been described, since each may affect several aspects of plan characteristics.

SOME PREDICTORS OF VARIABLE PAY PLAN CHARACTERISTICS

The Organization's Environment

As shown in Figure 2, the organization's environment affects plan characteristics indirectly through its impact on the organization's pay strategies. The environment may also affect other organization characteristics, which in turn affect pay strategies, and ultimately, plan characteristics. Several aspects of the environment that are relevant to pay include competitiveness, environmental munificence, environmental turbulence and uncertainty, industry and region, and national culture distance.

Competitiveness. According to "standard economic theories of competitive markets" (neoclassical models) such as human capital theory (Becker, 1975) and compensating wage differentials theory (Smith, 1937), employers are price (wage) takers (Gerhart & Milkovich, 1992, p. 488). In a purely competitive world, goals are largely irrelevant, because managers would have little freedom to design pay structures to support varying goals, in competitive labor and product markets (Katz, 1987). Employers who must hire from highly competitive labor markets would be forced to offer higher overall pay rates, including incentives, to attract employees (Jereski, 1996).

However, the product market also plays an important role; employers would not have unlimited capacity to set high pay. If workers are interchangeable, employers who offer generous pay would be undercut over the long run by product market competitors who pay less, and employers who cut too far would be unable to attract employees.

Since the ability to pay is a function of the productivity of the organization (Mitchell, 1997), employers in a competitive market generally prefer highly "leveraged" pay systems (Gomez-Mejia & Balkin, 1992). That is, organizations could use plan payouts, which are at risk, to offset low wages and salaries, which are assured. The higher the ratio of incentives relative to wages and salaries during the same period, the more highly leveraged the system. Payouts could be more easily reduced than base pay when productivity levels decline (Klaas & Ullman, 1995). Thus, conditions in some markets may constrain employers into "follower" roles. At the extreme, such organizations could not choose pay strategies and would adopt the same plans that competitors adopted.

Proposition 1.   The more competitive the market conditions, the greater the match between the characteristics of an employer's variable pay plan and those of benchmark employers' plans.

Environmental Munificence.   Citing other research (Dess & Beard, 1984), Klaas and Ullman (1995, p. 288) defined environmental munificence as the "degree to which resources needed by firms in an environment are abundant or scarce." Greater environmental munificence may provide greater freedom to adopt varying pay strategies and varying plan features. Where market conditions conform less to the assumptions of the neoclassical model, employers may have greater freedom to adopt alternative pay goals, and (if rational) pay designs consistent with them (Gerhart & Milkovich, 1990, 1992). Apparently, deviation from these assumptions is common; many authors agree that organizations have "considerable discretion in choosing compensation strategies" for their managers (Stroh, Brett, Baumann, & Reilly, 1996, p. 752) and other employees. Where environmental munificence is high, managers may perceive the organization is insulated from product cost competition, and see less need to leverage pay (Klaas & Ullman, 1995).

Proposition 2.   There will be an inverse relationship between environmental munificence and the size of variable pay relative to total pay.

Environmental Turbulence and Uncertainty.   Citing environmental change pressures of global competition and rapid technological advances, former U.S. Labor Secretary Robert Reich proposed that organizations emphasizing high volume could better afford predictable fixed costs than could an organization shifting to "high value" strategies (Overman, 1998). Thus, he proposed that as turbulence increases, employers prefer sharing this risk with employees. Organization-wide plans using a profit-sharing formula serve as a shock absorber (Gomez-Mejia & Balkin, 1992). When environmental turbulence affects the entire organizations, it makes little sense to segment portions of the organization for coverage. Thus, the following proposition is given.

Proposition 3.   Environmental turbulence will be associated with variable pay plans that (a) are organization-wide and (b) utilize profit-sharing formulas.

Turbulence is of course related to uncertainty about outcomes or events, i.e., risk (Bloom & Milkovich, 1998). Agency theory (Fama & Jensen, 1983; Jensen & Meckling, 1976) provides a basis for understanding the role of uncertainty in incentive plan design. Essentially, agency theory proposes that an employer (the principal) contracts with an employee (agent) to perform behaviors or to bring about outcomes that serve the employer's interests. Since doing so does not necessarily serve the agent's best interests, a compensation system must be devised to align these interests.

One system would specify, monitor, and reward desired *behavior.* Desired behavior entitles one to continued employment at a standard salary or wage; its absence leads to dismissal. For example, a retail sales clerk might receive a certain hourly wage as long as she or he rang up sales correctly using the cash register (Eisenhardt, 1988). Another system would specify and reward a desired *outcome.* For example, an insurance agent would receive a commission after a policy premium is paid. The supervisor does not monitor closely what behaviors the agent uses to get the sale.

How agency theory would classify pay systems that fall somewhere in between is unclear. For example, the sales clerk's job knowledge or customer service can be judged by a supervisor, and higher performing clerks could receive higher salaries through merit pay. Some authors consider merit pay plans to be outcome-based compensation (e.g., Banker, Lee, Potter, & Srinivasan, 1996). However, merit pay plans require considerable monitoring and subjective judgments, like behavior-based systems. Rather than assume that all incentive plans are outcome-based, researchers should consider the extent to which the incentive plan may have behavior-based system features.

Generally, employees have greater control over behaviors than outcomes, which could be affected by economic downturns, the weather, the introduction of a new competitor, etc., which cannot be predicted. Thus, there is risk associated with uncertainty (Eisenhardt, 1988), the bearing of which is within the role of owners (Fama & Jensen, 1983). Employees require greater compensation if the employer does not assume all of the risk (Eisenhardt, 1988). This is true even though there is upside risk, e.g., an economic upturn, because agents are risk averse (Eisenhardt, 1989).

Where environmental uncertainty is high, incentives are very risky, and since employees cannot easily control outcomes, they will prefer salaries to incentives (Eisenhardt, 1988). Thus, employers may choose instead to invest in the behavior focused-monitoring system rather than an outcome-driven system. This suggests that organizational performance uncertainty is *negatively* related to the use of incentives (measured dichotomously), but no relationship was found in a study of retail selling incentives (Eisenhardt, 1988).

Alternatively, perhaps turbulence is associated with higher levels of *total* pay. Environmental turbulence may engender organizational turbulence (due to downsizings, acquisitions, etc.) as organizations attempt to respond to changing conditions. Under high turbulence, the principal theoretically must pay a risk premium to induce the agent to assume more risk. However, no relationship was found between organizational turbulence and total pay of managers (Stroh et al., 1996). This outcome could be seen as consistent with the neoclassical model, which proposed that in risky occupations, employees face an "unfair lottery" (Smith, 1937), in which average pay is not necessarily high in risky occupations. For example, while Harrison Ford may make millions each year, the average pay of all actors is meager. Payoffs for the most successful are huge but not high enough when spread over many "starving artists" to raise the average.

A third alternative is that employers could offer a larger potential payoff or a higher probability of payoff within incentive plans to offset the risk. Further, the company may devise and formalize plan payout formulas to provide greater assurances to employees. In one study, managers in highly turbulent organizations received a *higher* proportion of their pay in the form of incentives (Stroh et al., 1996). However, in another (Bloom & Milkovich, 1998), in general business risk was *negatively* related to the proportion of incentive pay for managers, though different measures of risk produced differing results.

A fourth alternative is that the risk-compensation takes the form simply of higher base pay. Some support for this hypothesis was found in a sample of managers (Bloom & Milkovich, 1998), though the findings varied depending on the measure of risk. It seems premature to conclude that agency theory is incorrect regarding the need for a risk premium. Instead, it may be insufficient to explain premiums fully. These disparate, and incomplete, findings suggest that employers pay a premium but that it does not take the same form in every case. It may be that industry or other factors will determine the form, for reasons already described. For example, organizations in turbulent environments may pay a premium in the form commonly used by other employers at the time of plan inception. Thus, we propose the following.

Proposition 4.   The greater the environmental or organizational turbulence, the larger the risk amount of variable pay and the larger the ratio of variable to base pay.

Industry and Region.   The institutionalization perspective (Eisenhardt, 1988) suggests that firms adopt pay practices common in their industry (Taras, 1997). From this perspective, patterns of organizational practice evolve over time and become legitimated within an organization (Pfeffer, 1982). Structures and processes tend to reflect the environmental conditions that existed at the time of organizational founding (Eisenhardt, 1988). In other words, new organizations obtain common or best practice benchmarks and try to match them. For example, incentive plans are common in the computer technology industry (Jereski, 1996). In one study, smaller high tech firms had a greater incentive component than similar non-high tech firms (Balkin & Gomez-Mejia, 1987) and incentive plans were more effective in such firms. Other research has also demonstrated industry effects (e.g., Delaney & Huselid, 1996) and mimetic tendencies (Taras, 1997), though a complete explanation as to why remains elusive.

Similarly, the firm's location affects the adoption of variable pay plans (Gomez-Mejia & Balkin, 1992). Incentive plans are common in firms in the western region of the United States, and region was found to be the best predictor of plan adoption (Cheadle, 1989) because of the mimetic effect resulting from institutionalization or simply the need to be competitive for workers. It seems reasonable to extend this reasoning to variable pay plan features since simply having a plan does not necessarily match the competition.

Proposition 5.   Variable pay plan characteristics will be similar to those dominant in the industry or region.

National Cultural Distance.   The culture of the nation in which an organization operates can affect human resource systems (Jackson & Schuler, 1995). Agency theory has implications for incentive plans in foreign subsidiaries of organizations. Specifically, it suggests that the difference between the cultures of a parent organization and a foreign subsidiary will affect the pay mix, i.e., the proportion of total pay paid in the form of incentives

(Roth & O'Donnell, 1996). As distance increases, monitoring becomes more and more difficult because information about the agents' performance becomes more difficult and expensive to attain. In a study of the measuring and medical instruments industries, the incentives proportion paid to subsidiary managers and other employees increased with cultural distance (Roth & O'Donnell, 1996). Research is needed to determine whether this generalizes to other industries.

Proposition 6. The greater the cultural distance between the parent and the subsidiary, the higher the proportion of pay paid in the form of variable pay to subsidiary employees.

The Organization's Pay Strategies

Environmental factors may give employers more actual or perceived latitude to select optimal pay strategies and a greater actual or perceived need to do so. Organization characteristics may also influence plan characteristics through their effects on pay strategies, as will be discussed later.

In some environments and organizations, employee differences are important, and pay level policies reflect this (Werner & Tosi, 1995). For example, developing and patenting drugs that address common health problems such as depression (e.g., Prozac) have made pharmaceutical firms such as Eli Lilly very profitable. If ability varies considerably among scientists, it is critical for Eli Lilly to attract the best so that a competitor does not get the patent first. Firms that aim to attract and retain employees who have high ability and expend high effort will adopt an "employer-of-choice" strategy (Klaas & Ullman, 1995, p. 297). In such firms, both (a) contingent payouts and (b) wages and salaries may be generous. Since this approach would be relatively costly to implement, determining whether its effectiveness outweighs its cost would be important.

Efficiency wage theory proposes that some employers pay higher wages than do labor market competitors, in order to gain greater organizational efficiency over the long run, for at least four potential reasons reviewed elsewhere (Campbell, 1993; Heneman, 1992; Kidwell & Bennett, 1993; Yellen, 1984). First, in efficient labor markets, higher paying employers can attract and retain more highly qualified people. Second, "efficiency wage theory explicitly posits that, by paying above average levels of pay, incumbent employees now have something additional to lose if they are terminated for poor performance, because by definition their 'next-best' job opportunity pays lower wages" (Becker & Huselid, 1996, p. 4). Third, this will reduce "shirking" and consequently, the need to supervise closely and (fourth) the attendant costs of doing so (Heneman, 1992; Yellen, 1984).

There is some evidence of differing pay strategies where measures of actions regarding managerial pay are used; the findings have been interpreted as supporting the efficiency wage and strategy literature (Gerhart & Milkovich, 1990).

Whether such an approach is taken with respect to variable pay is not clear. Employers who pursue employer-of-choice strategies to gain the benefits suggested by efficiency wage theory, would seemingly undermine their goals if they did not provide market-leading salaries *and* variable pay. Consistent with this, approximately 80 percent of companies participating in a recent survey (Overman, 1998) provided variable pay as an add-on rather than a substitute for base pay. In contrast, firms pursuing defender strategies (Miles & Snow, 1978) may both lag the market in base pay and make small payouts relative to those of other organizations using incentive systems. Defenders attempt to preserve a secure niche in a relatively stable product or service area (Gomez-Mejia & Balkin, 1992). Neither leaders nor laggards would necessarily maintain highly leveraged systems, because the total compensation package rather than the relationship among the components operationalizes these strategies. However, if the entire package is competitive or better, the leader may offer high incentives to attract and keep superstars.

Proposition 7. After the effects of other compensation are controlled, incentives will be larger, where the base pay strategy is to lead rather than lag the market.

The Organization's Characteristics

Structure and Process.   Previous research has shown that compensation strategies for managers can vary depending, for example, on ownership structure (Werner & Tosi, 1995). A case analysis of Lincoln Electric (Milgrom & Roberts, 1995), long a model of successful management of highly leveraged pay, suggested that incentive program success may result in part from other structural features of the organization. For example, the firm is "largely owned by its employees and managers, and the company has long had both an open door policy for its top executives and institutionalized channels for direct communication between the two groups" (Milgrom & Roberts, 1995, p. 201). Incentive pay plan effectiveness may be harmed when unilateral management practices are followed (Lawler, 1990). Specifically, if the performance standards are raised when management perceives that the employees are making too much money, mistrust and counterproductive behavior follow. Opportunities for genuine participation may be useful in preventing these problems.

The quality of participation may be important. Interestingly, Lincoln Electric requires that two rules be followed during employee-management discussions. First, employees must base inputs on facts, rather than hearsay. Second, the overriding concern must be for the best interests of the organization. Thus, comments based on rumors or suggestions for changes that serve the interests of the speaker rather than the organization are considered out of bounds (Sabo, 1997).

Obviously, many variables are confounded here. Structural factors other than participation may account for Lincoln's success. Where employees are owners of the organization, they have additional incentives to perform effectively. Ownership, rather than participation, may be key. Research is needed to sort out which organizational characteristics will affect which plan characteristics, and which these in turn determine success.

Proposition 8.   Plan characteristics will vary with ownership and quality of employee participation.

Size.   Larger organizations may provide larger variable pay payouts for two reasons. First, they have greater ability to pay and tend to pay higher wages and salaries and may then adopt similar practices with respect to variable pay (Heneman, von Hippel, Eskew, & Greenberger, 1997). However, the incentive proportion in the pay mix may decline with organizational size because smaller organizations cannot compete without putting relatively more pay at risk. Second, variable pay may have greater impact in a small firm. In one study, variable pay for "average employees" was related to organizational performance in small firms but not in large firms (Rayton, 1997).

Research testing these notions has yielded inconclusive results. In one study of managers' pay, the proportion of variable (vs. fixed) pay costs in the total package, and the variable pay plan strategy's effectiveness, decreased with organization size (Balkin & Gomez-Mejia, 1987). In another study (Roth & O'Donnell, 1996), there was no relationship between corporate or subsidiary size and pay plan leverage. Obviously, research is needed to clarify the relationship between size and leverage.

Size may influence pay strategy as reflected in the basis for payouts. In one study, variable pay plans in smaller organizations were more likely to base payouts on attendance measures, and less likely to reward quality enhancement (Miceli & Heneman, 1997). Finally, larger firms are more likely to base payouts on profitability (Cheadle, 1989; Gomez-Mejia & Balkin, 1992).

Proposition 9.   Organization size will affect a variety of plan features, including the size of the bonus, leverage, and the payout formula.

Product Life Cycle. By leveraging highly, i.e., by putting relatively large amounts at risk and making them contingent on some measure of performance (individual, group, unit, or organizationally-based), organizations may be able to support a strategy of attracting and motivating high-performing employees at a lower cost than might organizations with more traditional pay systems. Research on product life cycles (Balkin & Gomez-Mejia, 1987) provides evidence that start-up companies, or those in an industry where such plans are common, may be likely to use such strategies. In very early stages, however, there may be no incentives because of the critical need to raise capital. In contrast, organizations in more mature stages would choose smaller payouts (Balkin & Gomez-Mejia, 1987).

Proposition 10.   Beyond the earliest stage of company start-up, leverage is an inverse function of product life cycle maturity.

Age.   Institutionalization theory predicts that the age of an organization will be related to the strategy chosen (Eisenhardt, 1988). As noted earlier, organizations tend to mimic common practice at the time of founding. Although organizations may update practice somewhat as the environment changes, perhaps simply to appear legitimate (Wright & McMahan, 1992), there is a tendency to rely heavily on taken-for-granted ways of doing things (Pfeffer, 1982). Doing so allows people to save decision-making resources for novel situations (Cyert & March, 1963; Eisenhardt, 1988). On the other hand, some evidence suggests that pay traditions may interfere with economically rational thinking (Conlon & Parks, 1990; Taras, 1997). As variable pay plans moved in and out of vogue over the past 50 years, it was predicted and found that the age of a retail store would relate to the adoption of incentive plans (Eisenhardt, 1988). If the plan is added after an organization is begun, institutionalization suggests that the plan founding date (plan age) would be more pertinent than the organization age. The plan champions would likely benchmark other organizations when making the case for plan adoption, though these would be adapted to fit with organizational tradition in order to enhance acceptance. This reasoning would suggest the proposition below.

Proposition 11.   Organizational pay traditions, and pay practices popular at the time of variable pay plan inception, will be reflected in variable pay plan characteristics.

Organizational Culture.   The organizational culture can influence the characteristics of variable pay plans. Organizations wanting to encourage long-term relationships with their managers put greater emphasis on behaviors than on outcomes; consistent with this, such organizations pay a higher proportion of total pay in the form of salaries (Stroh et al., 1996).

Similarly, the organizational culture may support full or permanent employment policies to encourage commitment to the organization (Klaas & Ullman, 1995). Highly leveraged pay systems can make full employment policies more feasible because downturns can be managed through means other than layoffs. At Lincoln Electric, workers are guaranteed at least 30 hours per week and there is no history of layoffs even in severe recessions (Milgrom & Roberts 1995). This suggests a positive relationship between leverage and full employment policies (articulated or enacted). On the other hand, organizations could substitute high leverage for layoffs-they may lay people off but pay the survivors well so that output will stay the same. Highly leveraged systems could also enable organizations to replace low performers with higher performers (Klaas & Ullman, 1995). Thus, one might expect a negative relationship between leverage and employment security. Yet large payouts may seem highly inappropriate and illegitimate to employees where layoffs are necessary. Further, if the plan formula is based on organizational performance, payouts may not be allowable under the plan under the circumstances that create both opportunities to reduce pay and reduce employment. Obviously, research is needed to determine which reasoning is supported.

Proposition 12. Full employment policies will be related to plan characteristics.

Union Representation. Unions may influence or constrain the payout size and other characteristics (Gomez-Mejia & Balkin, 1992; Heneman et al., 1997). Traditionally, union leaders and members have resisted variable pay because it may be subject to management manipulation, particularly where subjective measures of individual performance are used. On the other hand, unions may support the provision of large payouts where base pay is relatively high and the formula for earning the payouts is clearly specified, i.e., not discretionary with management, and based on group performance. Such plans formalize the principle of management's sharing the wealth generated by the extra efforts of the workforce. These plans may be seen as adding to the pie and financed out of funds that otherwise might not benefit workers.

Proposition 13. Greater union coverage will be associated with higher variable pay but lower leverage, where variable pay does not substitute for base pay.

The Nature of the Work Performed. Agency theory (Fama & Jensen, 1983; Jensen & Meckling, 1976) suggests that one variable that may be associated with the size of payouts is the nature of the work performed (Eisenhardt, 1988). Indeed, one central assumption of this article is that plans for

employees in general may be different from those of plans covering executives and perhaps, middle or lower level managers, because the nature of
their responsibilities differs.

Another work variable shown to be related to plan establishment or
characteristics is job or task programmability—the extent to which behaviors can be precisely defined. In programmable jobs, it may be easier to
monitor and reward desired behaviors. Many support jobs and non-pro-
duction jobs, which may be highly programmable, do not lend themselves
to variable pay (Lawler, 1990). Task programmability was associated with
the use of salaries rather than commissions (measured dichotomously) for
retail salespersons (Eisenhardt, 1988). Task programmability is influenced
by turbulence in the organization, and it was also inversely related to the
proportion of total pay in the form of incentives, for middle managers
(Stroh et al., 1996).

Proposition 14.   The higher the job programmability, the smaller
the variable pay as a proportion of total pay.

CONCLUSIONS

Here, we attempted to describe more explicitly than has been done in the
past, a basis for linking contextual factors and variable pay plan characteristics. We offered specific propositions based on extensions of efficiency
wage theory, institutional theory, and agency theory, and on existing variable pay research. It is our hope that our article helps to further the development of theory and to stimulate research on variable pay systems. We
hope ultimately that research will resolve issues pertaining to the extent to
which contextual factors should be considered in evaluating which plan
features to adopt, and under which circumstances variable pay plans are
likely to be effective.

REFERENCES

Balkin, D.B., & Gomez-Mejia, L.R. (1987). Toward a contingency theory of com-
    pensation strategy. *Strategic Management Journal*, 8, 169–182.
Banker, R.D., Lee, S.-Y., Potter, G., & Srinivasan, D. (1996). Contextual analysis of
    performance impacts of outcome-based incentive compensation. *Academy of
    Management Journal*, *39*, 920–948.
Becker, B.E., & Huselid, M.A. (1996). *Managerial compensation systems and firm perfor-
    mance.* Paper presented at the annual meeting of the Academy of Manage-
    ment, Cincinnati.

Becker, G. (1975). *Human capital: A theoretical and empirical analysis, with special reference to education* (2nd ed.). Chicago: University Chicago Press.

Belcher, J.G., Jr. (1996). *How to design and implement a results-oriented variable pay system.* New York: AMACOM.

Belcher, J.G., Jr, Butler, R.J., Cheatham, D.W., Goberville, G.J., Heneman, R.L., & Bloom, M.C., & Milkovich, G.T. (1998). Relationships among risk, incentive pay, and organizational performance. *Academy of Management Journal, 41,* 283–297.

Campbell, C.M., III. (1993). Do firms pay efficiency wages? Evidence with data at the firm level. *Journal of Labor Economics, 11,* 442–469.

Cheadle, A. (1989). Explaining patterns of profit sharing activity. *Industrial Relations, 28,* 387–401.

Conlon, E., & Parks, J.M. (1990). Effects of monitoring and tradition on compensation arrangements: An experiment with principal-agent dyads. *Academy of Management Journal, 33,* 603–622.

Cyert, R.M., & March, J.G. (1963). *A behavioral theory of the firm.* Englewood Cliffs, NJ: Prentice-Hall.

Delaney, J.T., & Huselid, M.A. (1996). The impact of human resource management practices on perceptions of organizational performance. *Academy of Management Journal, 39,* 949–969.

DeMatteo, J.S., Eby, L.T., & Sundstrom, E. (1998). Team-based rewards: Current empirical evidence and directions for future research. In B. Staw (Ed.), *Research in organizational behavior* (pp. 141–183). Greenwich, CT: JAI Press.

Dess, G.G., & Beard, D.W. (1984). Dimensions of organizational task environments. *Administrative Science Quarterly, 29,* 52–73.

Eisenhardt, K.M. (1988). Agency- and institutional-theory explanations: The case of retail sales compensation. *Academy of Management Journal, 31,* 488–511.

Eisenhardt, K.M. (1989). Agency theory: An assessment and review. *Academy of Management Review, 14,* 57–74.

Fama, E., & Jensen, M.C. (1983). Separation of ownership and control. *Journal of Law and Economics, 26,* 301–325.

Gerhart, B., & Milkovich, G.T. (1990). Organizational differences in managerial compensation and financial performance. *Academy of Management Journal, 33,* 663–691.

Gerhart, B., & Milkovich, G.T. (1992). Employee compensation: Research and practice. In M.D. Dunnette & L.M. Hough (Eds.), *Handbook of industrial and organizational psychology* (pp. 481–569). Palo Alto, CA: Consulting Psychologists Press.

Gerhart, B., Trevor, C., & Graham, M.E. (1996). New directions in compensation research: Synergies, risk and survival. In G.R. Ferris (Ed.), *Research in personnel and human resources management* (pp. 143–203). Greenwich, CT: JAI Press.

Gomez-Mejia, L.R., & Balkin, D.B. (1992). *Compensation, organizational strategy, and firm performance.* Cincinnati, OH: South-Western.

Heneman, R.L. (1992). *Merit pay: Linking pay increases to performance ratings.* Reading, MA: Addison-Wesley.

Heneman, R.L., Ledford, G.E., Jr., & Gresham, M. (in press). The effects of changes in the nature of work on compensation. In S. Rynes & B. Gerhart

(Eds.), *Compensation in organizations: Progress and prospects.* San Francisco: Jossey-Bass.

Heneman, R.L., von Hippel, C., Eskew, D.E., & Greenberger, D.B. (1997, Summer). Alternative rewards in unionized environments. *ACA Journal,* pp. 42–55.

Jackson, S.E., & Schuler, R.S. (1995). Understanding human resource management in the context of organizations and their environments. *Annual Review of Psychology,* 46, 237–264.

Jensen, M.C., & Meckling, W.H. (1976). Theory of the firm: Managerial behavior, agency costs, and ownership structure. *Journal of Financial Economics,* 3, 305–360.

Jereski, L. (1996, September 10). At a high-tech firm, the daily stock price is everyone's business. *Wall Street Journal,* pp. Al, A8.

Katz, L. (1987). Efficiency wage theories: A partial evaluation. In S. Fischer (Ed.), *NBER macroeconomics annual* (pp. 235–276). Cambridge, MA: MIT Press.

Kidwell, R.E., Jr., & Bennett, N. (1993). Employee propensity to withhold effort: A conceptual model to intersect three avenues of research. *Academy of Management Review, 18,* 429–456.

Klaas, B.S., & Ullman, J.C. (1995). Sticky wages revisited: Organizational responses to a declining market-clearing wage. *Academy of Management Review, 20,* 281–310.

Lawler, E.E., III (1990). *Strategic pay: Aligning organizational strategies and pay systems.* San Francisco: Jossey-Bass.

Lawler, E.E., III, Ledford, B.E., Jr., Mohrman, S.A., & Ledford, G.E.J. (1995). *Creating high performance organizations.* San Francisco: Jossey-Bass.

McAdams, J.L., & Hawk, E.J. (1994). *Organizational performance and rewards.* Scottsdale, AZ: American Compensation Association and Maritz, Inc.

Miceli, M.P., & Heneman, R.L. (1997). *Group rewards: Differences among large and small businesses.* Paper presented at the annual meeting of the Southern Academy of Management, Atlanta, GA.

Miles, R.E., & Snow, C.C. (1978). *Organizational strategy, structure, and process.* New York: McGraw-Hill.

Milgrom, P., & Roberts, J. (1995). Complementarities and fit: Strategy, structure, and organizational change in manufacturing. *Journal of Accounting and Economics.*

Mitchell, D.J.B. (1997). If *this is a new era of flexible pay systems, can anyone explain why aggregate pay is so sluggish?* Paper presented at the Industrial Relations Research Association, New Orleans.

Overman, S. (1998, June 7). Reich: Peg pay to company performance. *HR News.*

Pfeffer, J. (1982). *Organizations and organization theory.* Boston: Pitman Publishing.

Rayton, B.A. (1997). Rent-sharing or incentives? Estimating the residual claim of average employees. *Applied Economics Letters, 4,* 725–728.

Roth, K., & O'Donnell, S. (1996). Foreign subsidiary compensation strategy: An agency theory perspective. *Academy of Management Journal,* 39, 678–703.

Sabo, R. (1997). *Compensation at Lincoln Electric.* Presentation at Ohio State University.

Schuster, J.R., & Zingheim, P.K. (1992). *The new pay: Linking employee and organizational performance.* New York: Lexington.

Smith, A. (1937). *An inquiry into the nature and causes of the wealth of nations.* New York: Random House.

Stroh, L.K., Brett, J.M., Baumann, J.P., & Reilly, A.H. (1996). Agency theory and variable pay compensation strategies. *Academy of Management Journal, 39,* 751–767.

Taras, D.G. (1997). Managerial intentions and wage determination in the Canadian petroleum industry. *Industrial Relations, 36,* 178–205.

Weitzman, M.L., & Kruse, D.L. (1990). Profit sharing and productivity. In A.S. Blinder (Ed.), *Paying for productivity: A look at the evidence* (pp. 95–142). Washington, DC: Brookings Institute.

Welbourne, T.M., & Gomez-Mejia, L.R. (1995). Gainsharing: A critical review and a future research agenda. *Journal of Management, 21,* 559–609.

Werner, S., & Tosi, H. (1995). Other people's money: The effects of ownership on compensation strategy and managerial pay. *Academy of Management Journal, 38,* 1672–1691.

Wilson, T.B. (1995). *Innovative rewards for the changing workplace.* New York: McGraw-Hill.

Wright, P.M., & McMahan, G.C. (1992). Theoretical perspectives for strategic human resource management. *Journal of Management, 18,* 295–320.

Yellen, J. (1984). Efficiency wage models of unemployment. *American Economic Review Proceedings, 74,* 200–205.

CHAPTER 10

REWARD SYSTEM ALIGNMENT

Robert L. Heneman and Katherine E. Dixon

Source: Heneman, R.L. & Dixon, K., *Compensation and Benefits Review* (in press), copyright © 2001 by Sage Publications, Inc. Reprinted with permission of Sage Publications, Inc.

Reward system design and implementation is most often guided by best practice surveys (e.g., McAdams & Hawk, 1994) or by normative models established by the compensation profession (e.g., Milkovich & Newman, 2000). This practice of imitating the reward systems of other organizations benefits those organizations that intend to use reward system practices to move company performance from below average industry performance to average industry performance (Barney, 1997). On the other hand, companies need to create unique reward systems (as well as other HR practices) in order to use reward systems to drive company performance above the industry average (Barney & Wright, 1998).

One critical element in designing and implementing a unique reward system is to carefully tailor the design and implementation of the reward system to the business strategy, organizational structure, and organizational culture of the organization. The effectiveness of creating an alignment between these organizational systems has been clearly established in the practitioner (e.g., Lawler, 1990) and academic literature (e.g., Gomez-Mejia & Balkin, 1992). Missing from both the practitioner and academic literature, however, is guidance on how to align these organizational systems. The objective of this chapter is to describe, and illustrate with case examples, an expert system that can be used to align reward systems with the business strategy, organizational structure, and organizational culture of organizations. The phrase "expert system" in the context of this objective refers to recommended reward system design and implementation practices for various forms of business strategy, organizational structure, and organizational culture.

In order to accomplish this objective, the chapter will be organized in the following manner. First, four major systems of the organization will be described: business strategy, organizational structure, organizational culture, and rewards. Second, the alignment of these systems with one another will be described. Third, recommended reward systems for each configuration of business strategy, organizational structure, and organizational culture will be presented.

ORGANIZATIONAL SYSTEMS

Many different frameworks of systems that comprise organizations have been advanced over the years. Common to many of these frameworks are the following systems in organizations: business strategy, organizational structure, organizational culture, and rewards. Then, adding further complexity, each of these three systems of the organization have been operationalized with a variety of models. In this section, each one of these systems will be described using the most well known models in the literature. By using the most well known models, the reader will be able to link this chapter on reward systems to the broader literature on these organizational systems and their relationships with organizational effectiveness.

Business Strategy

According to Miles, Snow, and colleagues (Miles & Snow, 1978; Miles, Snow, Meyer, & Coleman, 1978; Snow & Hrebiniak, 1980), organizations differ from one another by the business strategies that they pursue. Organizations may be prospectors or defenders depending upon their business strategies. Figure 1 shows the business strategies of prospector and defender strategies. Prospector firms are proactive in their interactions with the environment. They actively seek out new business opportunities to expand upon or redefine their existing line(s) of products and/or services. Defender firms are more reactive in their interactions with the environment. These businesses act to enhance and fortify existing product or service lines through increased quality, changing prices, and other activities.

Defender
- Located in stable product or service markets
- Offers a narrow range of products or services
- Protects product or service market from competitors
- Competes on the basis of low cost and/or high quality

Prospector
- Located in changing product or service markets
- Offers a wide range of products or services
- Locates and exploits new product and service markets
- Competes on the basis of innovation

Figure 1.   Defender versus prospector business strategies

Since organizations often have multiple business strategies rather than a single business strategy, a traditional, bureaucratic organization may or may not have a defender business strategy for all of its business units. A traditional bureaucracy might, for example, have new start-up firms to enhance their offerings.

Public as well as private sector organizations have business strategies. Given the bureaucracy associated with government, it is tempting to assume that all public sector organizations follow a defender strategy. While this often occurs, there are exceptions. For example, in the State of Ohio, a new agency was created to help the K-12 school system wire all classrooms in the state for internet access as well as to learn how to best use this technology. Legislation was passed to, in essence, make this new agency independent of the bureaucratic ground rules found in many state government agencies. As a result, this new agency was able to pursue a prospector strategy.

As a last cautionary note, sometimes people assume that unionized organizations are all defender-type organizations. As a general rule, this belief holds true; however, there are exceptions to this rule. Increasingly, unions organize employees in companies with prospector strategies including information systems and health care.

Given that traditional stereotypes regarding business strategy may not hold, designers and implementers of reward systems must carefully assess the business strategy of each part of the organization. In order to do this, they must collect data from the organization including mission and vision statements and operational plans. From this information, they can make an assessment about which segments of the organization follow which business strategy.

Organizational Structure

Burns and Stalker (1961) made an important distinction in the different ways that work can be organized to achieve the organizational goals spelled out in the business plan. Figure 2 shows the two major ways to organize, or structure, work.

Mechanistic
- High formalization
- High centralization
- Narrow span of control
- High standardization

Organic
- Low formalization
- Low centralization
- Wide span of control
- Low standardization

Figure 2.   Mechanistic versus organic organizational structures

When work is organized in a mechanistic structure, it resembles a bureaucracy. Customers of an organization with a mechanistic structure are likely to encounter service representatives that can only play a limited role in resolving problems. Customer service providers must escalate any problems that fall outside standard scripted responses to their managers for resolution; front-line personnel have almost no latitude to exercise discretion. Although this mechanistic approach is slow and not very responsive to customer needs, it does ensure predictable and consistent products and services.

By contrast, customers of organic organizations are likely to find much more tailored responses to their problems. Employees have a wide range of latitude in performing their jobs and can operate across organizational boundaries to resolve problems. Although service providers may be quick to respond in organic organizations, customers may not receive predictable or consistent services.

ORGANIZATIONAL CULTURE

Business strategy and organizational structure are formal systems of organizations can be verified through formal statements such as mission statements and organizational charts. Organizational culture, a system that reflects the values and benefits held by the organization, tends to be a less

Traditional
- Clear division of labor
- Vertical communications
- Top-down decision making
- Turf protection
- Allegiance to employer
- Control systems

Involvement
- Loose division of labor
- Lateral communications
- Shared decision making
- Risk taking
- Allegiance to profession
- Feedback systems

Figure 3.   Traditional versus involvement organizational cultures.

formal system. As such, culture is much more difficult to assess using archival records. Instead, surveys and unobtrusive measures need to be used to assess the culture of the organization. For example, at NCR, employees completed upward appraisals about their supervisors as to how empowered they feel. At Xerox, anthropologists have conducted participant/observer studies to describe employees' beliefs and values.

One way to view culture in an organization is by whether it is a traditional culture or an employee involvement culture. Figure 3 shows differences between a traditional and an involvement culture. Traditional cultures are grounded in a military command and control model where orders come from the top of the chain of command and are communicated down through the organization for execution by employees. Control systems exist to ensure that the plans are executed in the intended manner. Involvement cultures are grounded in the concept of clans where people bond together to do whatever it takes to get the goal of the clan accomplished. Members of clans share in the decisions on what needs to be done to further the goals of the clan. Feedback from the job itself, rather than control systems by managers, is used to ensure that the goals of the organization are met.

Rewards

It has long been known that: (a) reward systems are multidimensional and, (b) the process used to determine rewards can be as important as the amount of the reward received. Given these long-standing premises of reward systems, Figure 4 shows the important characteristics of reward systems.

Reward Form
- Monetary
- Nonmonetary

Unit of Analysis
- Job
- Person

Value Comparison
- Internal
- External

Reward Measures
- Behaviors
- Results

Reward Level
- Individual
- Business unit

Pay Increase
- Fixed
- Variable

Administrative Level
- Centralized
- Decentralized

Timing
- Lead
- Lag

Communications
- Open
- Closed

Figure 4.   Pay system design and implementation dimensions.

Reward Form.   There are two types of rewards that organizations can use for goal achievement: monetary and nonmonetary. Monetary rewards refer to those rewards with a recognized cash value like base pay, pay increases, bonus pay, stock options and benefits. Nonmonetary rewards are those rewards with less well-known cash value such as recognition, training, and psychological characteristics of work.

Unit of Analysis.   Organizations can allocate rewards either on the basis of the employee's duties and responsibilities or by the employee's qualifications. When duties and responsibilities determine rewards, it is referred to as job-based pay. When rewards are allocated for the qualifications (i.e.,

Knowledge, Skills, Abilities, and Others) that an employee brings to the job, it is referred to as person-based pay.

Value Comparisons.   In determining the value of the rewards to offer employees, the organization must establish a value benchmark. Organizations can assess value either through an internal or external comparison. Companies use work evaluation to establish the internal value of jobs and people to the organization. Organizations conduct market surveys to assess the external value of jobs and people (i.e., the amount of reward provided for a comparable job or person in a similar organization).

Reward Measures.   In order to issue rewards, an organization must assess how well the employee is performing the job. In order to make this assessment, some sort of measure is needed to assess performance. Performance standards typically include both behaviors and results. Behaviors measure what the person does while results measure what the person accomplishes. At General Electric, behaviors are referred to as the "how" and results are referred to as the "what."

Reward Levels.   An employee is a member of a number of groups in an organization. Different types of groups include teams, departments, divisions, sectors, and the entire organization. Collectively these groups are often labeled as business units. Organizations must decide whether to deliver rewards based on individual employee performance or business unit performance.

Administrative Level.   Decision rules and reward system administration can be managed at a centralized level (i.e., corporate) or at a decentralized level (i.e., business unit).

Timing.   A reward system can either lead or lag the implementation of other organizational systems (i.e., business strategy, organizational structure, and organizational culture). That is, the reward system can be designed and implemented before (i.e., lead) or after (i.e., lag) the design and implementation of other organizational systems.

Communications.   Organizations can communicate information about the design and implementation of a reward system in an open fashion whereby all employees have access to the information or in a closed manner whereby only some employees (usually managers) have access to the information.

ALIGNMENT OF ORGANIZATIONAL SYSTEMS

In order for organizations to perform successfully, the business strategy, organizational structure, and reward systems must align with one another. The ideas and practices within each system must be consistent with those of the other systems as depicted in Figure 5.

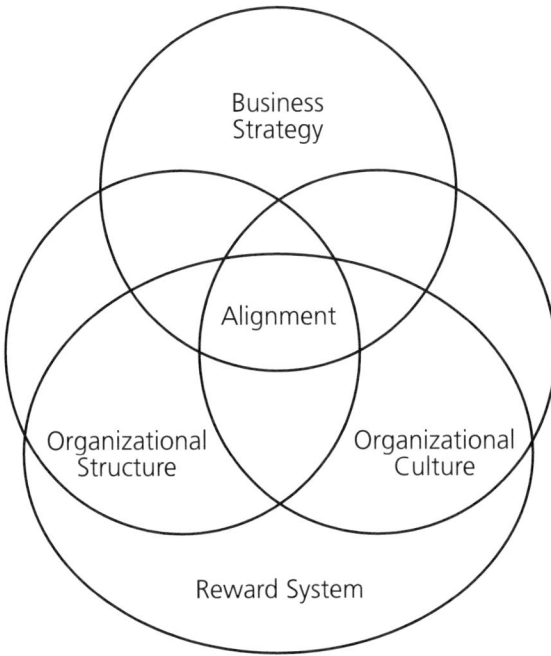

Figure 5.   Alignment model.

Strategy and Structure

The business environment surrounding an organization drives the alignment of strategy and structure. In a stable business environment, organizations have the luxury of time to react to changes in the environment because they do not occur frequently. As a result, a stable environment is consistent with a defender business strategy and mechanistic organizational structure. Infrequent changes in the business environment along with a stable strategy also allow time for organizations to develop mechanistic structures to withstand the test of time. Although there still are some examples of stable business environments in the world (e.g., paper clips, shoe laces), the business environment for most organizations is becoming much more turbulent.

Misalignment between strategy and structure usually occurs when an organization adopts a new prospector strategy but retains its mechanistic structure. Under this common scenario, a new CEO hastily enacts a new business strategy in response to changes in the business environment. Because of the length of time it takes to create a new structure, the old structure may be left intact and decrease organizational effectiveness. Alternatively, the old structure may be retained because there is fear that employees will not have the skills or willingness to work under a new structure.

Strategy and Culture

Both an organization's formal strategy as well as its informal culture must align with its structure. This alignment between culture and strategy contributes much to organizational effectiveness. Among other things, a willing culture provides energy to overcome the formal structure that may require change.

Alignment of strategy with culture takes place when a defender strategy is coupled with a traditional culture and when a prospector strategy is aligned with an involvement culture. In the former example, people expect to perform rigid roles and the strategy allows them to because of a stable business environment. In the latter case, people expect to develop new roles, and the strategy requires them to do so because the rapidly changing business environment no longer provides role stability.

A common misalignment between business strategy and organizational culture takes place when an organization imposes a prospector business strategy on a traditional culture. If people are not ready or capable of adjusting to new roles required by the formal business strategy, the traditional culture may thwart efforts at change. A less common misalignment happens most frequently in corporate mergers or acquisitions. If a company with a defender strategy acquires a group with an involvement culture, employees may become frustrated at the parent company's bureaucracy and inward-focused practices.

Strategy and Rewards

Rewards can encourage employees to carry out a business strategy. By providing rewards for producing results consistent with the business strategy, organizations can use new forms of rewards such as competency or skill-based pay to motivate employees to learn new behaviors.

In order for reward systems to align with the business strategy, each component of a pay system must be consistent with the business strategy. Pay system components include job analysis, job evaluation, market surveys, pay structures, and performance measures. Heneman (2001) provides theory and case studies that indicates that prospector strategies are more likely to be successful when the business strategy is supported by a competency-based job analysis and job evaluation systems, when broad pay ranges are used, and when performance measures are used at all levels of the organization. Alternatively, defender strategies succeed more often when the business strategy is supported by a job-based job analysis and job evaluation system, when pay ranges are narrow, and when incentives emphasize cost and quality performance measures.

Structure and Culture

Organizational structure describes what employees *should* do while culture describes what employees *actually* do. In order for organizations to be effective, what employees should do and what they actually do should align with one another. Mechanistic structures work well with traditional cultures while organic structures work well with involvement cultures.

A common form of misalignment that can detract from organizational effectiveness is when an organic structure is imposed upon a traditional culture. Employees may be very fearful of new roles because they may not have the skills required to operate in an organic structure. Also, they may not be interested in doing the new things required by an organic structure, like being more flexible, working longer, and exhibiting creativity.

Structure and Rewards

Many organizations in today's business environments are attempting to move from mechanistic to organic organizational structures. Reward systems can help motivate employees to welcome organic structures. One type of organic structure receiving recent attention is the virtual organization. A virtual organization usually has the following characteristics: team-based, temporary, alliances across functions or companies, and a technology backbone. To encourage employees to perform in these new work environments, virtual organizations use nontraditional forms of pay including stock options, profit sharing, and variable pay plans (Heneman, Tansky, & Tomlinson, in press). Moreover, as an organization evolves to become more virtual, it may offer pay forms that change to support that evolution (Heneman, Tansky, & Tomlinson, in press).

An example of virtual organizations can be seen with new product development and operations team in a computer storage company with whom the authors have consulted. These highly effective teams, composed of members from different departments, work together for approximately 18 to 36 months and are then disbanded. The teams have evolved over time to become more highly functional and more virtual; as the teams' structure and culture evolved, so have their reward systems.

The first reward program, developed for novice, non-virtual teams, added team members to a discretionary cash bonus plan designed for senior managers and key employees. The next iteration of team rewards corresponded to the intermediate stage of the teams' development and "virtual-ness." This separate team incentive plan used business results and team development as the main measures and scored each using individual and team components.

The company, with consulting from the authors, designed the third reward system to address the needs of the newly advanced and high-functioning virtual teams. The team-based incentive program uses both strategic and competency measures. With guidance from senior management, the teams themselves develop, review, and revise their own incentive plans. While their plan currently pays out in cash, the company plans to move to a flexible; cafeteria-style menu of payout options as the program and the teams themselves evolve.

Culture and Rewards

Rewards can also help hasten change from traditional to involvement cultures. For example, Figure 3 shows risk taking is an element of an involvement culture. In order for people to take risks, they sometimes need rewards to justify the risks. New forms of rewards, such as bonuses and stock options, provide incentives for risk taking.

Even organizations with traditional cultures that have been in place for a long period of time can move toward a more involvement-type culture. The first author has worked with several unionized organizations where it would be unthinkable to arrange for mutually agreed upon terms of employment outside those agreed upon at the collective bargaining table. However, when a pay for performance was used to supplement traditional seniority-based pay, the unthinkable happened. The conditions for the pay-for-performance plan were agreed upon by consensus outside of the collective bargaining process. Moreover, other issues (e.g., grievances) also started to be resolved outside the formal labor-arbitration process. Hence, changes in the pay system helped provide a change in the culture from one of formal conflict resolution procedures to less formal problem solving between the parties without the assistance of a third party arbitrator.

INTEGRATION OF THE ALIGNMENT MODEL AND
REWARD SYSTEM COMPONENTS

In order for reward systems to add value to the organization, the components of the reward system shown in Figure 4 must be integrated with the alignment scenarios between the business strategy, organizational structure, and organizational culture. Figure 6 shows an expert system of reward system integration with business strategy, organizational structures, and organizational culture.

Table 1 shows each reward system component required by various alignment scenarios. Each compensation system will now be described in turn.

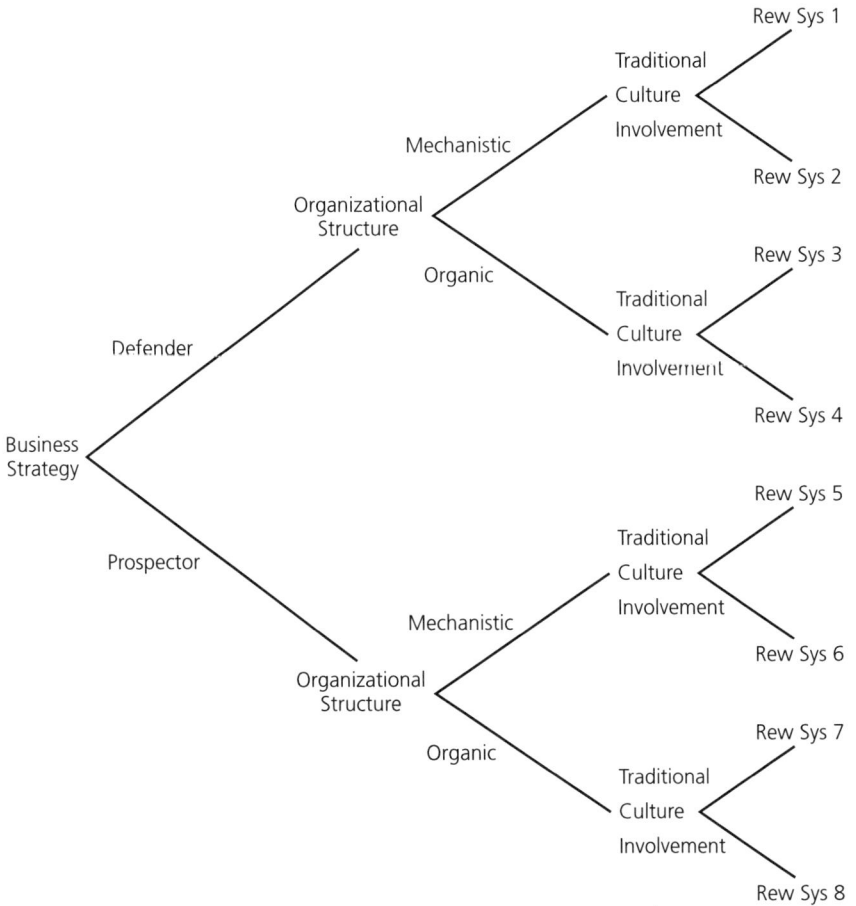

Figure 6.   Expert system of recommended reward systems by various alignments of business strategy, organizational structure, and organizational culture.

Table 1. Recommended Reward System Characteristics for Each Reward System Type

Reward System Characteristic	Reward System Type (Figure 10.6)							
	1	2	3	4	5	6	7	8
Unit of Analysis	Job	Job/Person	Person/Job	Job	Job	Job/Person	Person/Job	Person
Value Comparison	Internal/External	Internal/External	Internal/External	External	External/Internal	External	External	External
Reward Measures	Behaviors/Results	Behaviors/Results	Behaviors	Results	Results	Results/Behaviors	Results/Behaviors	Results
Reward Levels	Individual	Individual/Business Unit	Business Unit/Individual	Business Unit	Business Unit/Individual	Business Unit	Business Unit/Individual	Business Unit
Pay Increase	Fixed	Fixed	Fixed/Variable	Variable	Fixed/Variable	Variable/Fixed	Variable/Fixed	Variable
Adm. Level	Central	Central	Central/Decentralized	Central	Central	Central	Decentralized	Decentralized
Timing	Lag	Lag	Lead	Lead	Lead	Lead	Lag	Lag
Communications	Closed	Closed/Open	Open/Closed	Open	Closed/Open	Open/Closed	Open/Closed	Open

Reward System One

Reward system one requires a very traditional compensation system for a traditional business organization. Examples here include public sector agencies that have defender strategies, are bureaucratic in design, mechanistic in operation, and staffed by unionized employees. Under these circumstances, the reward system lags the business strategy, is developed and administered by a central group, and focuses on rewarding individuals on the basis of the successful completion of work activities spelled out in a job description. For example, one of the authors has worked with a large, state agency and with a large, county agency. Both agencies had a large number of unionized employees. The reward systems developed had a heavy emphasis on the job and individual contributions to the job. In the case of the state agency, the successful completion of job duties was evaluated by evaluators in a merit pay system while in the county agency, both seniority and performance counted toward pay increase decisions. Performance, often not used in unionized settings, was recommended by the consultant and accepted by the union because they could see that the changing demands of the business environment would eventually translate into a new business strategy, structure, and culture more consistent with rewarding performance rather than membership in the organization (seniority).

Reward System Two

A more fluid approach to rewards is required under reward system two than under reward system one because the involvement culture of the organization demands it. However, because the organization's strategy (defender) and its structure (mechanistic) are highly disciplined, rewards in this system are still relatively conservative.

One author worked with a unionized team within an old-line industrial manufacturing organization to implement a small, team-specific profit-sharing plan. This plan, negotiated with the union, rewarded employees for saving energy and increasing production. Since the affected employees all had long tenure with the company and had developed a high degree of trust and teamwork, the profit-sharing program was implemented easily and showed positive results quickly. Because this new reward program was limited to the part of the organization with an involvement culture, it did not cause issues with the more traditional culture of the company at large.

In order to fit an involvement culture together with a defender strategy and mechanistic structure, the reward system needs to comprise elements of a traditional reward system and a more fluid reward system. By having elements of both, the command and control culture does not overwhelm the involvement culture or vice versa.

Reward System Three

Reward system three is appropriate for an organization with a defender strategy, an organic structure, and a traditional culture. The type of situation appropriate for reward system three is one where a traditional organization realizes that it must change, and to do so uses the organizational system as the platform for change. For example, one of the authors developed a reward system for a new state agency changed with developing the information technology capabilities of all primary and secondary schools in the state. This task was highly complex because it required integrating state-of-the-art computers and learning methodologies with a large number of traditional school districts with almost no technology. Initial funding was extremely large, so the business strategy adapted was a defender position. Most employees hired for the project came from state agencies with a traditional culture. In order to adapt to the constantly changing needs of the client base, the structure was very organic and changed often.

Presented with this set of contingencies, a type-three reward system was designed and implemented. In order to support the command and control culture, elements of traditional reward systems were retained including a job, internal equity, and individual emphasis. In order to support desired changes in the business strategy from defender to prospector and organizational culture from traditional to involvement, new pay elements were also put in place including an emphasis on the person, internal equity, and business unit measures. Lastly, to warm the organization to a new business strategy and culture, the leading reward system emphasized variable pay and a focus on behaviors rather than results. This approach showed employees that pay increases would not always be permanent and to show them how to behave under a new business strategy, culture, and structure (e.g., customer service orientation).

Reward System Four

Reward system four is appropriate for organizations that have an involvement culture, organic structure, and a defender business strategy. Like the examples for reward systems two and three, the organizational systems do not align; however, the reward system can guide the alignment of the organizational strategy with its culture and structure.

An example of this type of situation for a reward system four, is a national educational products distribution company that used an organic structure to work with highly involved in business-decision making employees coupled with a defender business strategy. The company used a defender business strategy because it was the only one-stop location for primary and secondary school teachers to buy supplies. Senior management failed to recognize that their competitors could copy their business model and that a smaller company might eventually buy out the company.

At this organization, the consultant installed reward system number four. It was implemented as a lead rather than lag system in hopes of showing senior management how they needed to be more sensitive to possible changes in the business environment. To make the point, greater emphasis was placed upon external than internal equity, on results rather than behaviors, on business unit performance than individual performance, and a variable pay rather than fixed pay. Also, data about the market (e.g., salary data) were made accessible to employees as well as managers to sensitize them to market realities.

Reward System Five

In the situation most appropriate for reward system five, the business strategy (prospector) is not in alignment with the structure (mechanistic) or culture (command and control). Again, the reward system can be used in a lead fashion in order to bring about alignment. For example, one of the authors consulted with a gourmet food packager and distributor. Owned by an industrial engineer in a rural, Midwestern community it utilized a mechanistic structure with a command and control culture. Out of fear of competitor organizations, the company diversified their product lines and adapted a prospector strategy.

Compensation system five recommended in this situation had several elements of a traditional reward system to help support the current structure and culture. These elements included an internal value comparison, an individual level of rewards, and fixed payments. In order to get the organization to think about the need to develop a more fluid structure and culture in alignment with the prospector strategy, the company implemented new reward system components as well. Critical elements of reward system five included an emphasis on results as well as behaviors for reward measures, rewards at the business unit level, variable pay, and open communications about the new reward system. The company involved employees in the design and implementation phases to teach the organization about the value of employee participation in decision making.

Reward System Six

Reward system six is appropriate for a situation where a prospector business strategy is coupled with a mechanistic organizational structure and an involvement culture. Such was the situation encountered by one of the authors when consulting with a large computer company. Because the company was so large, it used a mechanistic structure to control its business processes. Employee involvement had long been a hallmark of a strong human resource function in the organization. As competition escalated in the computer industry, the company used a prospector strategy to avoid price warfare over traditional product lines.

The company's solution, critiqued by one of the authors, was reward system number six. The organization used rewards were used as a lead system to transform the company's structure into a more organic one salient to senior management. To do so, reward system six emphasizes the person as well as the job. The new reward system reinforced skill sets needed in a more flexible organizational structure. Similarly, business performance was emphasized over individual performance; for example, rewards were higher for employees who figured out ways to organize the business more effectively, than for individuals who simply performed the duties spelled out in their job descriptions.

Reward System Seven

Reward system seven is intended for fairly progressive companies that have adopted a prospector strategy, an organic structure, and have a traditional culture that emphasizes command and control. As an example, one of the authors worked with a telecommunications company. Given radical transformations in the telecommunications industry, new leadership was brought in to transform the organization and its systems. The new president decided to lead with a new business strategy (prospector) and a new structure (organic). In order to change the culture of the organization to one of involvement, consistent with the new business strategy and structure, reward system six was used to support (lag) the desired cultural change. Several elements of reward system seven emphasized that employees needed to shift to a new set of beliefs and values. First, the company rewarded employees for enhancing their skills as well as performing their job duties. Second, in order to sensitize employees to new skills valued in the market and by their current employer (like leadership), the company emphasized market competitiveness over internal equity. Third, the company stressed business unit performance over individual performance to motivate employees to perform work that would benefit their entire business unit. The company placed less emphasis on individual results to encourage behaviors consistent with an empowered culture (e.g., teamwork).

Reward System Eight

Reward system eight is to be used with progressive organizations that have alignment between organizational systems. That is, system eight is to be used in an organization with a prospector strategy, an organic structure, and an involvement culture. In this progressive context, organizations need significant departures from traditional reward systems.

Many start-up and "dot com" companies show alignment between their strategy, structure and culture. One author has worked extensively designing compensation systems for high-tech startup companies. These organizations, highly concerned with expenses, tend to view rewards as "return on investment" items; each piece of employee rewards must show a payback for the organization.

While a certain level of base pay is required for any company to compete for talent, rewards beyond base pay in reward system eight vary widely. Non-traditional benefits like the ability to bring pets to work and giving "bonuses" of sports cars instead of cash allow companies to showcase their unique "deal" for employees and capture the attention of employees in a highly competitive, ultra-prospector environment. Rewards developed in direct response to employee needs (such as concierge services and support of non-traditional work hours) reflect both the organic structure and the involvement culture of these organizations.

Reward system eight also promotes less-traditional reward administration. An organization might pay a company-wide bonus (or give stock options) without a formal program to recognize a business milestone. Reward systems are highly fluid and dynamic; timing, amounts, and forms of rewards can vary from business unit to business unit and reward period to reward period. Many organizations reward employees heavily with stock options early in the startup phase and move toward bonuses as the organization matures.

SUMMARY AND CONCLUSIONS

As shown in the models and case studies presented, reward system design and implementation work most effectively when they align with business strategy, organizational structure, and organizational culture. Organizations may use defender or prospector strategies, mechanistic or organic structures, and traditional or involvement cultures. Elements of reward strategy include reward form, unit of analysis, value comparisons, reward measures and levels, administrative processes, timing, and communications. Each combination of business strategy, structure, and culture is best served by a unique reward strategy.

While research and academic literature clearly show the effectiveness of creating alignment between these organizational systems, no guidance exists on the process of making this alignment. Reward design and implementation plans should include tactics for aligning with (or driving) desired strategy, structure, and culture. Organizations need to create innovative rewards to drive (and maintain) company performance above industry averages, and the expert system described in this chapter allow designers to select appropriate rewards strategies to enable desired business results.

REFERENCES

Barney, J. (1997). *Gaining and sustaining competitive advantage.* Reading, MA: Addison-Wesley.

Barney J.B., & Wright, P.M. (1998). On becoming a strategic partner: The role of human resources in gaining competitive advantage. *Human Resource Management, 37*(1), 3146.

Burns, T., & Stalker, G.M. (1961). *The management of innovation.* London: Tavistock publications.

Dessler, G. (1980). *Organizational theory: Integrating structure and behavior.* Englewood Cliffs, NJ: Prentice-Hall.

Gomez-Mejia, L.R., & Balkin, D.B. (1992). *Compensation, organizational strategy and firm performance.* Cincinnati, OH: South-Western.

Heneman, R.L. (in press). Compensation in virtual organizations. In R.L. Heneman & D.B. Greenberger (Eds.), *Human resource management in virtual organizations.* Greenwich, CT: Information Age Publishing.

Heneman, R.L. (2001). *Business-driven compensation policies: Integrating compensation systems with organizational rewards.* New York: AMACOM.

Heneman, R.L., Dixon, K.E., & Gresham, M.T. (2000). Team pay for novice, intermediate, and advanced teams. In M.A. Byerlein, D.A. Johnson, & S. Byerlein (Eds.), *Advances in interdisciplinary studies of work teams: Team development* (Vol. 7). New York: Elsevier.

Heneman, R.L., & Gresham, M. (1998). Performance-based pay plans. In J.W. Smither (Ed.), *Performance appraisal: State-of-the-art methods for performance management* (pp. 496–536), Society for Industrial and Organizational Psychology Professional Practice Series. San Francisco: Jossey-Bass.

Heneman, R.L., Ledford, G.E., & Gresham, M. (2000). The changing nature of work and its effects on compensation design and delivery. In S. Rynes & B. Gerhart (Ed.), *Compensation in organizations: Current research and practice* (pp.

195–240), Society for Industrial and Organizational Psychology Frontiers of Industrial and Organizational Psychology Series. San Francisco: Jossey-Bass.

Heneman, R.L., Tansky, J.A., & Tomlinson, E. (in press,a). Compensation in virtual organizations. In R. Heneman & D. Greenberger (eds.) *HRM in virtual organizations*. Greenwich, CT: Information Age Publishing.

Heneman, R.L., Tansky, J.W., & Tomlinson, E.C. (in press,b). Hybrid reward systems for virtual organizations: A review and recommendations. In R. Heneman & D. Greenberger (Eds.), *HRM in virtual organizations*. Greenwich, CT: Information Age Press.

Lawler, E.E., III (1990a). *Strategic pay*. San Francisco: Jossey-Bass.

Lawler, E.E., III (1990b). *Strategic pay: Aligning organizational strategies and pay system*. San Francisco: Jossey-Bass.

McAdams, J.L., & Hawk, E.J. (1994). *Organizational performance and rewards*. Scottsdale, AZ: American Compensation Association.

Miles, R.E., & Snow, C.C. (1978). *Organizational strategy, structure, and process*. New York: McGraw-Hill.

Miles, R.E., Snow, C.L., Meyer, A.D., & Coleman, H.J. (1978). Organizational strategy, structure, and process. *Academy of Management Review, 3*, 546–562.

Milkovich, G.T., & Newman, J.A. (2000). *Compensation*. New York: McGraw-Hill.

Snow, C.C., & Hrebiniak, L.L. (1980). Strategy, distinctive competence, and organizational performance. *Administrative Science Quarterly, 25*, 317–336.

CHAPTER 11

HOW TO FIND, SELECT, AND EVALUATE PAY SURVEYS TO MEET YOUR ORGANIZATION'S NEEDS

Robert L. Heneman and Kate Dixon

Source: Reprinted from *Salary Survey Guidebook: Finding and Evaluating Compensation and Benefits Data.* Copyright 1998 by American Management Association and American Compensation Association. Used with the permission of the publisher, American Management Association International, New York, NY. All rights reserved. http://www.amanet.org.

Pay surveys are available to employers in ever increasing quantities and forms as a result of advancements in information technology. Their increased availability, however, is both a blessing and a curse. On the positive side, it is much easier for organizations to price their jobs relative to the market. On the negative side, however, wide-scale availability can lead to the careless selection of market data. Inappropriate data selection can be as dangerous as too little data in pricing jobs in the marketplace.

To avoid collecting a large amount of meaningless data, a thorough staffing needs assessment should be conducted before finding, selecting and evaluating survey data. This helps target which surveys to use and how to best use them to make compensation decisions. In assessing needs, organizations need to answer three primary questions (see Figure 1).

1	What kind of compensation data do you need to gather?
2	For which jobs do you need survey data?
3	From which labor markets do you need survey data?

Figure 1.   Questions to answer in assessing needs.

WHAT KIND OF DATA TO GATHER

To answer the first question, think of pay in terms of total compensation, which includes base pay, incentives, stock and benefits. Depending on the organization's needs, you may decide to concentrate on one or more elements of total compensation.

Along with looking at the competitive value of each pay category, you may wish to collect data on pay practices and types of programs that support each category. Another significant purpose is employee communications. Employees are concerned about forms of compensation besides base pay and about the procedures used to allocate pay. If organizations are insensitive to these issues, pay programs may have limited effectiveness in attracting, retaining and motivating employees.

WHICH JOBS TO SELECT

To answer the second question, you will want data on both benchmark and nonbenchmark jobs. Benchmark jobs are those jobs common to many organizations because they are easily recognizable and the job content is well known and stable. Benchmark survey data are typically used to form the backbone of the compensation structure and are useful to observe compensation trends from year to year.

The nonbenchmark jobs you may select would include any positions that are strategically important to the organization and for which you can make meaningful survey matches. These jobs may be ones for which there is great demand, such as software engineers, or which have changed significantly since they were last surveyed, such as librarians.

WHICH LABOR MARKETS TO EXAMINE

The third question deals with selecting labor markets (or competitor companies) from which you need survey data. Companies to survey are those from which you are likely to recruit employees or to which you are likely to lose employees.

In many cases, the survey participants should be approximately equal in size to your company. If they are too small or too large, the pay levels may not be appropriate for your company. At lower organizational levels, your competitors may be in your own industry and in others, and are more likely to have a local or regional market. At higher organizational levels, most of your competitors may be in your own industry, and the market for talent may be more national or global. In short, depending on the types of jobs and seniority levels you have, different organizations and geographical areas may need to be surveyed for different types of jobs.

FINDING SURVEYS

After a needs assessment is conducted, then it is a straightforward task to research surveys and to find the relevant ones. Surveys are available from a wide variety of sources. Federal, state and even local governments provide a large amount of survey data that are usually free or very inexpensive. Unfortunately, the data may not be available in a timely manner or be very specific.

Compensation consulting firms are another large source of compensation data. Although costly, consultants' surveys are usually current and offer very specific job, industry and geographic breakdowns of data. Many consulting firms also can provide additional analysis of survey data for an extra cost.

Professional and industry associations are an excellent source of job-specific surveys that are available at a nominal cost to members. Increasingly, survey data are also available on the Internet. These data tend to be highly accessible, somewhat costly, and many capture market rates on somewhat unique jobs.

Colleges and universities usually collect market data on entry-level pay rates. Increasingly, the pay rates of alumni are tracked as well. Usually, these data are available to employers at no cost, but the information available is usually not very specific, especially regarding industry breakdowns.

Unions also collect market data that tend to be more useful for nonsupervisory jobs. *Note:* An overlooked source of information is employees themselves. Some may have knowledge of good industry or profession surveys.

SELECTING SURVEYS

An organization's needs assessment will guide the selection of the most appropriate surveys. This appraisal shows what data need to be in the survey, what jobs need to be reported, and what industry and regional breakdowns are needed. Often multiple surveys are needed because seldom are all of the relevant data reported in one survey.

Three technical issues also need to be considered in the selection of surveys:

- *Quality of the job matching process.*   What steps have the survey provider taken to ensure that the jobs surveyed were comparable from one organization to the next? Matching jobs on the basis of job titles alone can be highly misleading. Jobs with the same or similar titles may have different meanings or levels of responsibilities. Most surveys include brief job summaries. Even so, different interpretations can result in differing matches. The best, most rigorous matches often are made in survey matching sessions where participants come to a shared understanding of surveyed positions. Unfortunately, matching sessions are not always available or practical. In any case, the better participants match jobs, the more reliable the survey data.
- *Statistics used to report the data.*   Ideally, the survey should report the mean, median, mode and standard deviation. Unfortunately, the mean (simple average) is often reported without a median (central data point). While both statistics are valuable, the median is often more appropriate because it is less susceptible to very high or low pay rates, which can bias the mean upward or downward.

  Another statistic often not reported is the standard deviation, a measure of dispersion of pay rates around the average. It is a useful statistic because it shows the consistency (or lack thereof) of pay rates across organizations in the survey. Percentiles (10th, 25th, 75th and 90th) of the distribution of pay may also be helpful in measuring the range of pay levels for a particular job.
- *Size and number of respondents to the survey.*   When surveying management jobs, it's especially important that the companies in a survey should be approximately equal in size to your company. If the survey participants are too small or too large, the pay levels may be overestimated or underestimated. If there is a small number of respondents to the survey as a whole or to certain critical jobs within the survey, it can indicate that the results are unlikely to be stable. That is, had a different small set of organizations responded to the survey, the results may have been significantly different. As a general rule of thumb, be wary of survey results for fewer than 20 organizations

unless, of course, these 20 organizations constitute a majority of the population that should be surveyed for the job in question. The same rule of thumb may be applied to the number of incumbents in any particular job in a survey.

EVALUATING SURVEYS

Evaluating surveys requires assessing whether your needs are being met. Again, this clearly points to the importance of defining needs before, rather than after, the purchase of a survey. Not only should you have done your needs assessment before purchase, but also you should make an effort to assess other clients' reactions to the survey. Reference checks should be used with promotional materials before purchasing any survey Organizations should evaluate the survey content by following a checklist (see Figure 2).

By carefully identifying your organization's needs and researching the wide variety of available surveys, you can efficiently and effectively select pay surveys to deliver appropriate market data to your company.

☐ What information was collected? Is it consistent with your needs?
☐ What companies were surveyed? Do they match your list?
☐ What jobs were surveyed? Do they match your needs?
☐ Are the appropriate statistics reported? (Ideally, this will include mean, median more, and standard deviation)
☐ What is the effective date of the data included in the survey? Is it current enough for your needs?
☐ How expensive is the survey? Can you minimize your costs by being a participant in the survey? Is it possible to purchase the survey without participating in it?
☐ Can the survey organization provide you with any additional data analysis you may require?

Figure 2.   Content checklist

CHAPTER 12

COMPENSATION:

A Troublesome Lead System In Organizational Change

Gerald E. Ledford Jr. and Robert L. Heneman

Source: Reprinted by permission of Harvard Business School Press from Ledford, G.E. & Heneman, R.L. Compensation: A Troublesome Lead System in Organizational Change. In M. Beer & N. Noria (Eds.), *Breaking the Code of Change* (pp. 307–322). Cambridge, MA: Harvard Business School Press. Copyright 2000 by the Harvard Business School Publishing Corporation; all rights reserved.

While preparing this chapter, we heard the following story from a consultant. The CEO of a Fortune 500 firm was a turnaround specialist, and he had plenty of work to do in his new company. The firm he now headed was losing money and market share while its peer companies were not. The firm's strategy was ill defined, tentative, and ineffective. The previous chief executive had badly overpaid for a major acquisition, causing financial problems, then compounded the difficulty by overhyping the deal, which gave the firm a bad reputation in the business press. The organizational culture was toxic: highly political, bureaucratic, full of meaningless turf battles. There was no shortage of organizational and human resource problems. After surveying the landscape, the new CEO decided that the place to start in changing the organization was the compensation system. He decided that his first change had to be big enough to capture the attention of managers and employees to shake things up in a rigid, political, uncreative organization. Was the pay system a wise place to begin in changing the company? The story is still unfolding, so the case does not yet give us a definitive answer to our question. This paper explores the question and takes the position that the CEO was mistaken to begin organizational change with pay.

Issues of change sequencing and timing are basic to change strategy. No one undertaking a major organizational change effort can avoid these issues. Yet the question of whether the pay system should lead or lag other types of change is unresolved and largely ignored in the organizational change and compensation literatures. This is clearly a blind spot in our thinking about change. It is not difficult to see why there is little research on the topic. Large-scale survey studies based on samples large enough to be used for statistical analysis are very difficult to conduct, and data collected at one point in time about long-term patterns of organizational change is often suspect. On the other hand, solid case studies of major, complex organizational change efforts are relatively rare. Understanding even one case requires long-term, relatively intensive, and privileged relationship with the organization that is the subject of the research. The database of cases good enough to allow us to draw strong research-based inferences about the most effective timing and sequencing of changes simply does not exist.

What is more surprising is that there is so little speculation in the practitioner and academic literatures about the timing and sequencing of changes in compensation systems. In a scan of major recent trade books and academic works on organizational change, we found almost no discussion of these issues. The compensation literature is equally silent. There have been a number of books about compensation strategy, design, and innovation in recent years, but we know of none that have given the lead-lag issue serious, consideration. The only observer we have found who explicitly discusses in some detail the advantages and disadvantages of compensation as a lead system and as a lag system is Edward Lawler (e.g., Lawler, 1981). We draw upon his arguments later in this chapter.

The possible role of compensation as a lead system is becoming an increasingly important consideration. For decades the issue was relatively unimportant because there was so little change in compensation systems, whether as lead incentives or as lag rewards. Until about 1990 compensation systems simply changed less than technology, operations, and human resource systems such as training, selection, or labor relations. During the 1990s, however, base pay, pay for performance, benefits, and virtually all other aspects of compensation changed dramatically (Heneman et al., in press; Lawler et al., 1998). An important strategic issue becomes whether such changes should precede or follow other organizational changes.

We both confess to being conflicted about the answer to our question. In this paper, however, we will take a strong stance for purposes of the debate that this paper joins. Our hope is that a sharp dialectic discussion can advance our thinking about an important but neglected issue.

CAN PAY SYSTEMS CHANGE EMPLOYEE BEHAVIOR AND PERFORMANCE?

Before we consider the arguments against pay as a lead system, it is important to deal with one argument in opposition that is becoming popular in some quarters but is, in our view, flatly wrong. Some would argue that pay system changes should not lead organizational change because pay system changes are usually ineffective, counterproductive, or both. It is altogether fitting that we address this argument in a book published by the Harvard Business School, because the Harvard Business School has been more responsible for the propagation of this argument than any other academic institution.

The argument that pay changes are ineffective or counterproductive has been made at least since the beginning of the human relations movement the better part of a century ago, and it regains currency every decade or so. Human relations theory, an outgrowth of the famous Hawthorne experiments, argued that social relationships—especially work group relationships—are primary in determining employee motivation, satisfaction, and productivity, whereas objective conditions such as pay are much less important (Mayo, 1933; Roethlisberger & Dickson, 1939). We may note for the record that Mayo, Roethlisberger, and Dickson, who conducted the Hawthorne research, were faculty members from the Harvard Business School.

Herzberg (1966) added a different argument in the 1960s, claiming that intrinsic sources of motivation arising from the design of work are much more important than extrinsic sources in determining the employee motivation. Extrinsic motivation is the result of rewards that are external to the individual, such as pay, recognition from peers, or praise from a supervisor. Intrinsic rewards are internally rewarding experiences, such as a feeling of accomplishment, that derive from behavior such as performing the job. Herzberg's most famous and influential statement appeared in the *Harvard Business Review* (1968). In Herzberg's view, extrinsic sources are "hygiene" factors that can have a negative effect but not a positive effect on motivation, whereas intrinsic sources are true "motivators."

The distinction between extrinsic and intrinsic rewards has great practical importance. The major approaches to increasing and directing employee motivation tend to be oriented primarily toward one of these types. Compensation systems, for example, offer extrinsic rewards for performance; job design approaches are designed to increase intrinsic motivation. Contrary to Herzberg's argument (although not contrary to his data), contemporary scholars overwhelmingly concur that extrinsic rewards are motivating. In a metanalysis of thirty-nine studies of financial incentives, Jenkins and colleagues (1998) found a .34 correlation between the use of financial rewards and job performance. Moreover, the vast majority of authorities on motivation conclude that motivation from extrinsic sources is complementary and additive to motivation from intrinsic sources. That is, total motivation is greater if both extrinsic and intrinsic motivation are high (Scott et al., 1988). Also, low extrinsic motivation reduces total motivation reduces total motivation even if intrinsic motivation is high, and vice versa. In practical terms this means that managers should create both extrinsic rewards (such as pay) and intrinsic rewards (e.g., through job design) that are congruent and consistent.

A more recent point of view has achieved considerable prominence in the practitioner literature through the work of journalist Alfie Kohn (1993). His polemic received a flood of attention after an article summarizing Kohn's book was published in the *Harvard Business Review*. Based on a highly selective review of the research literature, Kohn argues that extrinsic rewards cannot work for several reasons. For example, he maintains that extrinsic rewards such as pay must be pr continually to be effective, whereas sources of intrinsic rewards, such as work design, by their nature continue to be available to employees without continuous management action. Of course, no serious observer would disagree with the point that pay and recognition need to be available continually for them to be effective. In addition, Kohn rehashes Herzberg's arguments about motivators and hygiene factors. Although Kohn's work aspires to be a serious review of the literature, it somehow misses the many criticisms of Herzberg's theory over the years—not the least of which is that Herzberg's own data did not support it. Researchers appreciate Herzberg's work because he helped draw attention to the importance of intrinsic motivation and job design, but the hygiene-motivator distinction is no longer considered credible by scholars in the field. As Dipboye and colleagues (1994) noted, Herzberg's theory is only "of historical interest" today.

Kohn also makes an argument based on work of Deci and his colleagues (Deci, 1975; Deci & Ryan, 1985). Deci contends that extrinsic and intrinsic motivation are not additive, and that in fact extrinsic rewards (including pay, praise, and recognition) undermine intrinsic motivation. Deci's theory is based primarily on laboratory research, in which he typically measures intrinsic motivation by the amount of time subjects voluntarily spend working on artificial tasks. It is important to note that Deci's work is not well accepted by motivation researchers. For example, Locke and Henne (1986) point to flaws in of Deci's theory and research. They conclude that studies in tradition do not meaningfully test the theory, and that Deci's conclusons are misleading interpretations of the available results. In a comprehensive review of ninety-six studies, Eisenberger and Cameron (1996) found that "detrimental effects of reward occur under highly restricted, easily avoidable conditions" (p. 1154). The only consistent negative effect occurred when an expected reward was presented only once regardless of the quality of performance. Indeed, the reviewers found that extrinsic rewards are more likely to have a positive than a negative effect on both intrinsic motivation and creativity. To repeat, then, extrinsic and intrinsic rewards should be considered as complementary, and managers need to make use of both types of rewards to motivate employees.

In summary, we can find no compelling arguments or data to support the argument that compensation systems should not be used as lead systems because compensation systems in themselves are ineffective or counterproductive as motivators. Hence, contrary to some who oppose compensation as a lead system, we will not oppose compensation as a lead system on these grounds.

We will argue, however, both from the perspective of human resource strategy and from the perspective of emotions typically attached to compensation, that compensation as a lag system is superior to compensation as a lead system.

STRATEGIC COMPENSATION DESIGN

If compensation systems can have powerful, positive effects, should they lead or lag other organizational changes? We argue first that pay should be a lag system on strategic grounds: Compensation must be aligned with other organizational systems that must be designed first in order for it to be effective.

In reviewing the compensation design literature, we are struck by the degree to which the alignment perspective has become almost universal among authors in both academic and trade media. This perspective argues that no particular pay system design is effective or ineffective in the abstract. Rather, a given compensation design is effective to the extent that it is aligned with business needs and with other organizational systems. This perspective makes several assumptions. It suggests that different pay systems may be effective in different contexts. It argues that compensation system changes must be part of a web of mutually reinforcing systems, all pulling employee behavior in the same direction. Finally, and most important for our purposes here, it indicates that no pay system is effective unless it meets business needs. Figure 1 is our version of an alignment model.

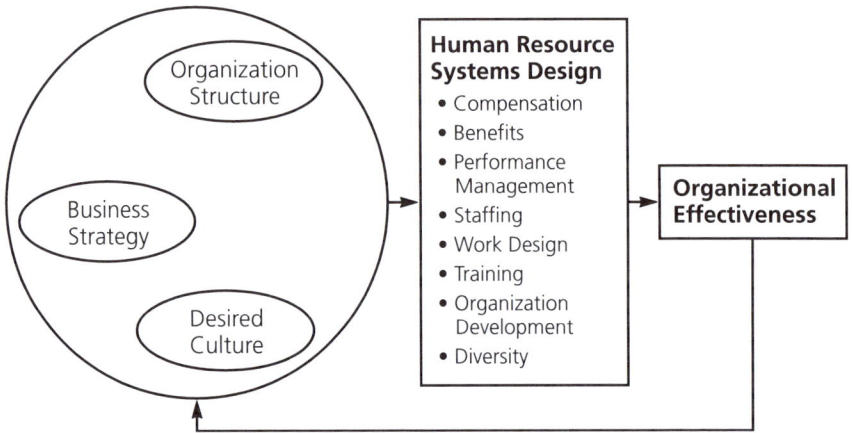

Figure 1.   A compensation alignment model.

The alignment perspective explains why compensation cannot truly by a lead system. The question we might ask is, "Leading what?" The compensation system cannot provide its own direction. It must follow at least some organizational changes if it is to be designed effectively. Using compensation as a lead system is like launching an unguided missile. It may hit the target, but it also may circle back and do damage to the place from which it was launched. For a compensation system to impact its intended targets, it must be given direction. Figure 1 suggests that the direction for compensation systems is derived from the business strategy of the organization, the manner in which the organization is structured, the culture of the organization, and other human resource systems. We consider these in turn.

Business Strategy

An organization's business strategy provides considerable guidance about the types of reward systems that will be most appropriate for that organization. The strategy indicates how the organization will gain competitive advantage in the marketplace. Will the organization emphasize lower prices than those of competitors, higher quality, better customer service, or faster new-product innovation? A strategy helps give direction to the compensation system by indicating the types of employee behaviors and abilities that the company needs to be successful in the marketplace. For example, 3M famously rewards product innovation through significant rewards and penalties for managers; this system supports the 3M goal stating that each business must derive 30 percent of its sales from products introduced within the previous four years. Similarly, in high-technology startups the heavy use of broad-based stock options and company wide performance bonuses helps reinforce entrepreneurial behavior by rewarding risk taking and extraordinary effort.

True lead pay systems can be based only on generic business strategies that do not offer competitive advantage. Lead pay systems also tend to be stand-alone programs unrelated to the strategy of the organization, because designers of the systems do not know where to start. For example, generic job evaluation systems that emphasize general factors like skill, effectiveness, responsibility, and working conditions may have little relationship to the core capabilities the organization wishes to develop in order to support the business strategy. For business strategies to lead to sustained competitive advantage, decision makers must identify the core competencies of the organization, that will be difficult for competitors to imitate (Barney, 1996). Compensation systems need to support and reinforce these core competencies, but a generic compensation system is unlikely to do so.

Organizational Structure

The compensation system, intentionally or unintentionally, sends strong messages to employees about what organizational units and levels are most important. Unless management has first defined what units and levels it wishes to emphasize, the pay system is likely to send the wrong messages to employees. For example, does management wish to stress the team, plant or unit, division, or sector level of performance in the organization? Incentives can be designed that reinforce any level of performance, but they cannot be designed effectively reinforce all levels simultaneously. Unless management has defined the levels of performance that have the highest priority, compensation systems are likely to follow fashion or whim but not organizational needs. For example, team-based rewards are widely used today and have received considerable attention in the compensation community. We have witnessed organizations that have prematurely developed team incentive plans without carefully considering organizational structure issues. Many organizations with team incentives should be reinforcing the plant or unit level, both because there are no adequate metrics for managing performance at the team level and because employees do not work in discrete teams.

Organizational Culture

Organizational culture expresses the organization's most deeply held values, beliefs, and assumptions. The culture helps define for employees what is good, proper, and sensible. Once management has defined the kind of organizational culture that it wishes to encourage, virtually any, desired organizational culture can be reinforced by means of compensation systems. For example, a cultural variable that has long been shown to be important in pay system design is the degree to which management wishes to emphasize employee involvement (Lawler, 1981). Involvement-oriented cultures tend to look systematically different and to be accompanied by such pay innovations as skill-based gainsharing, profit sharing, and open communication about pay. These pay plans tend to be more effective in involvement-oriented cultures, which are able to make use of the greater skills and sense of responsibility that these systems encourage.

But an existing organizational culture can be a key detriment of the effectiveness of compensation (Beer & Katz, 1997). Lead pay systems are sometimes used to help bring about changes in culture. Stories abound, however, about the resistance created by such a strategy. This is especially true when a pay-for-performance plan is used as lead system to promote a shift from an egalitarian culture to one of a meritocracy. Research clearly shows that people in blue-collar occupations, women, and labor union members prefer an egalitarian method reward distribution over a performance-based system (see Heneman, 1992 for a review). In the absence of other systems needed to support a pay-for-performance culture, a lead compensation system may create a culture of dissension rather than high performance. Compensation as lag system, in contrast, allows time for people to adjust to the need for a new plan. Moreover, it allows employees the opportunity to be educated on how the system works and to upgrade their capabilities to take full advantage of the new compensation plan.

Ideally, organizational structure and culture follow from the business strategy. Together these three factors give business direction to the organization. Without such direction, designing compensation system changes that meet the organization's needs is simply a matter of luck. We cannot imagine how one could responsibly design the compensation system for a given organization without the kind of understanding of organizational needs that an analysis of strategy, structure, and culture provides.

Alignment with Human Resource Systems

Although we are firmly convinced, and we believe that most authorities would agree, that compensation system design should lag behind the definition of business needs, there remains the question of whether compensation design ought to lead or lag the design of other human resource systems. Here authorities are not unanimous. Some (e.g., Beer et al., 1990) argue that pay system change is most appropriately used as a lag system after other systems, such as training, communication, and appraisal have changed. Others (e.g., Galbraith, 1995) argue that once business direction is set, other changes can be adopted in essentially any order, recognizing that eventually all will have to change to support the new business direction. The research to resolve these differences of opinion does not exist, so we must determine the answer as best we can.

We argue that compensation should be a lag system even among human resource systems, because communication, training, and, other changes are needed to make any reward system change effective. Compensation systems usually are complex and require extensive communication to help employees understand them and understand the differences between the old and new systems. Training is also required, to give employees an understanding of how the system works and to provide them with new skills that may be needed. Installing pay system first and hoping to create the supporting infrastructure later is a recipe for disaster. Employee confusion and resistance are likely, and changes in the pay system are unlikely to produce changes in behavior.

For example, a well-developed method of performance assessment is critical for the effective functioning of a compensation system. We may look at the experience of the federal government with the implementation of merit pay as a lead system aimed at changing the culture form one based on seniority to one based on performance. This change was made prior to, rather than after, the creation of a sound method of performance management. According to all documented accounts, the change had disastrous results. Another example concerns labor relations. Petty and colleagues (1992) reported on an electric utility where a very well developed and effective incentive plan was abandoned because of a conflict between labor and management officials. Both of these illustrations show the need to lag compensation behind the development and integration of complementary human resource systems.

EMOTIONS AND PAY SYSTEMS

Another major reason to view compensation as a troublesome lead system for organizational change is that compensation changes tend to provoke intense and counterproductive emotional responses from employees and managers. Although any organizational change has the potential to provoke negative emotional reactions, compensation changes tend to be particularly loaded with affect.

Researchers have rediscovered emotions as an important effect and cause of behavior in organizations (George & Brief, 1996). One of the most important reasons to be concerned about intense emotional responses among employees is that managers, like other human beings, tend to deal with such reactions poorly. When possible, they avoid making changes that may provoke emotional outbursts. Managers' defensiveness and fear can lead to inappropriate choices during an organizational change. On the other hand, employees who react with a high level of emotion to an organizational change may react defensively as well, failing to deal constructively and effectively with problems surrounding the change.

Several factors increase the emotional reactions of employees to organizational changes. Emotional responses increase to the extent that a change has a direct and tangible impact on perceived employee well-being. Changes in business strategy, for example, often provoke little emotional response from employees, because the effects of the changes seem remote and difficult to interpret. Conversely, changes in seemingly inconsequential personnel policies often lead to extreme emotional reactions. Emotional responses also increase to the extent that more employees are affected by the change. Shutting down an entire business unit has a greater emotional impact than scattered layoffs, and layoffs carry more emotional impact than the firing of a single poor performer.

Pay systems in organizations are emotionally loaded relative to other human resource systems, as indicated by Figure 2. Please note initially that this figure does not attempt to suggest the objective importance or organizational impact of different human resource systems, only the degree of emotion invested in each system by employees.

External selection tends to be low in the emotionality that employees attach to it, because this system affects people who are not yet in the organization. Indeed, selection matters most to people who *do not* become members of the organization, rather than to current employees.

Employees and managers alike almost universally value *training*. However, the value of training compared to that of pressing daily activities usually is ambiguous. The payoffs of training to the organization and the

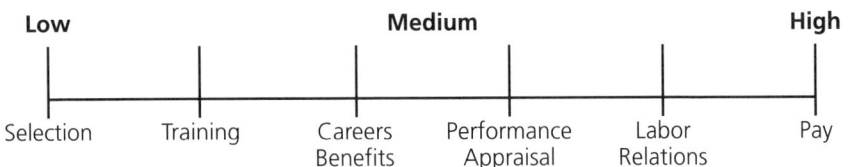

Figure 2.   Emotion attached to HR systems.

individual are usually long-term and less concrete than the opportunity cost of trainees' inability to complete day-to-day tasks while enrolled in a training program. This explains why an activity that is so universally appreciated is so routinely deferred without incident. Thus, the emotions attached to training are positive but not strong.

Changes in *careers, benefits,* and *work design* tend to create a moderate emotional response. Career issues, including promotion, can affect the self-interests of many employees. However, not all employees expect or want career advancement; and changes in career patterns are often ambiguous and remote, because they are long-term. Benefits have a direct impact on employee well-being, and sometimes (as in the case of changes in health care benefits in recent years) changes can provoke an intense employee reaction. However, employees usually have a limited understanding of the pros and cons of different benefits and benefit options. In addition, changes in many benefits have remote consequences. For example, few employees need to make use of life insurance benefits, and retirement benefits tend to be so long-term that they are of limited concern to many workers. Work design changes can have a direct effect on employee emotions, but changes in work design rarely affect a large number of employees at one time. Thus, all of these changes tend to have a moderate emotional content, either the changes tend to affect few employees or because the changes have limited or ambiguous effects on employees interests.

Performance appraisal tends to be a relatively emotion-laden human resource subsystem. Appraisals have a direct impact on employee pay for many employees, and the appraisal event itself can be a highly emotional event. Yet not all employees receive performance appraisals. In many organizations, moreover, the performance appraisal event typically is handled in a perfunctory and ineffective way. In such organizations managers and employees conspire to keep the emotional content to a minimum. Finally, changes in performance appraisal systems often have little emotional effect, because changes often are relatively trivial (such as changes in the appraisal form).

Labor relations can have high emotional content. Labor relations often are extremely contentious in unionized settings. However, a relatively small percentage of people in the U.S. workforce are members of unions so relatively few employees are directly affected by this system.

Compensation, on the other hand, has the highest emotional content of any human resource system. It directly affects all employees, all the time; and almost all employees greatly value their compensation. Employees value compensation for many reasons: as a means of meeting basic needs, as a source of status, as a signal of success, and so on (Lawler, 1981). Employees closely monitor the pay system and tend to show a level of awareness and concern about pay system changes that is absent for other types of changes.

The research literature shows that as emotion increases, attention focused on the source of that emotion increases as well (George & Brief, 1996). Consequently, employees become very focused on changes in pay systems. Not only do people have global reactions to the pay system; they also form reactions to components of the pay system (Heneman & Schwab, 1985). Because of this attention, a high level of scrutiny is given to outcomes from the compensation system as well as to the design, implementation, and administration of the system (Greenberg, 1987).

The intense scrutiny that pay system changes receive is a double-edged sword for organizational change. Changes in pay systems emphasize for employees that management is serious about organizational change. However, concerns about changes in pay may drown out interest in other changes. The organization's expectations of getting to other organizational changes sometime later may never be realized if problems with the pay system are too severe. We know of several instances in which pay changes were intended to be the first in a series of organizational changes but led to the failure of the entire organizational change effort—because the pay system changes failed and poisoned the atmosphere for related changes.

It takes time to carefully craft a pay system that is likely to be acceptable to employees. When a company designs and implements a pay plan as a lead system, often the time needed to develop a successful plan is not available. Moreover, the event is extremely salient to employees, as it is placed in the forefront of change and it concerns their income. Expectations regarding the plan may therefore be inflated and errors in the plan magnified. By contrast, a compensation plan that is a lag system can be more carefully crafted and can be kept out of the limelight until it had been successfully scrutinized.

SUMMARY

We began this chapter by reviewing the possible argument that compensation should not be a lead system in organization change because it is ineffective at changing employee behavior. We dismissed that argument based on considerable research evidence: Compensation system changes can indeed be powerful. But the question of whether compensation changes should be a lead or a lag system remains. We have offered two arguments for making compensation a lag system. First, the alignment perspective, now the dominant theoretical perspective on compensation design, requires that business direction be set first. Compensation cannot lag business strategy, structure, and culture, and probably should not lag the adoption of other human resource systems either. Second, we have argued that compensation is a highly emotional topic. It makes a poor candidate for leading organizational change, because it is more likely than other kinds of changes to generate employee resistance and thus to cause management to abandon the entire change effort rather than developing necessary supporting systems.

REFERENCES

Barney, J.B. (1996). *Gaining and sustaining competitive advantage.* Reading, MA: Addison-Wesley.

Beer, M., Eisenstat, R., & Spector, B. (1990). *The critical path to corporate renewal.* Boston: Harvard Business School Press.

Beer, M., & Katz, N. (1997). *Do incentives work? The perceptions of senior executives from thirty countries.* Unpublished manuscript, Harvard Business School.

Deci, E.L. (1975). *Intrinsic motivation.* New York: Plenum.

Deci, E.L., & Ryan, R.M. (1985). *Intrinsic motivation and self-determination in human behavior.* New York: Plenum.

Dipboye, R.L., Smith, C.S., & Howell, W.C. (1994). *Understanding industrial and organizational psychology: An integrated approach.* Fort Worth, TX: Harcourt Brace College.

Eisenberger, J., & Cameron, R. (1996). Detrimental effects of rewards: Reality or myth? *American Psychologist, 51,* 1153–1166.

Galbraith, J.R. (1995). *Designing organizations: An executive briefing on strategy, structure, and process.* San Francisco: Jossey-Bass.

George, J.M., & Brief, A.P. (1996). Motivational agendas in the workplace: The effects of feelings on focus of attention and work motivation. In B.M. Staw & L.L. Cummings (Eds.), *Research in organizational behavior* (Vol. 18, pp. 75–110). Greenwich, CT: JAI Press.

Greenberg, J. (1987). Reactions to procedural justice in payment distributions: Do the ends justify the means? *Journal of Applied Psychology, 72,* 55–61.

Heneman, H.G., III, & Schwab, D.P. (1985). Pay satisfaction: Its multidimensional nature and assessment. *International Journal of Psychology, 20,* 129–141.

Heneman, R.L. (1992). *Merit pay: Linking pay increases to performance ratings.* Reading, MA: Addison-Wesley.

Heneman, R.L., Ledford, G.E., Jr., & Gresham, M. (In press). Compensation and the changing nature of work. In S. Rynes & B. Gerhart (Eds.), *Compensation in organizations: Progress and prospects* (Society for Industrial and Organizational Psychology Frontiers of Industrial and Organizational Psychology Series). San Francisco: New Lexington Press.

Herzberg, F. (1966). *Work and the nature of man.* New York: World.

Herzberg, F. (1968, January-February). One more time: How do you motivate employees? *Harvard Business Review.*

Jenkins, G.D. Jr., Mitra, A., Gupta, N., & Shaw, J.D. (1998). Are financial incentives related to performance? A meta-analytic review of empirical research. *Journal of Applied Psychology, 83,* 777–787.

Kohn, A. (1993). *Punished by rewards.* Boston: Houghton Mifflin.

Lawler, E.E., III. (1981). *Pay and organizational development.* Reading, MA: Addison-Wesley.

Lawler, E.E., III, Mohrman, S.A., & Ledford, G.E., Jr. (1998). *Strategies for high performance organizations: The CEO report.* San Francisco: Jossey-Bass.

Locke, E.A., & Henne, D. (1986). Work motivation theories. In C.L. Cooper & I. Robertson (Eds.), *International review of industrial and organizational psychology* (pp. 1–35). Chichester: Wiley.

Mayo, E. (1933). *The human problems of an industrial civilization.* New York: Macmillan.

Petty, M.M., Singleton, B., & Campbell, D.W. (1992). An experimental evaluation of an organizational incentive plan in the electric utility industry. *Journal of Applied Psychology, 77,* 427–436.

Rothlisberger, F.L., & Dixon, W. (1939). *Management and the worker.* New York: Wiley.

Scott, W.E., Farh, J.L., & Podsakoff, P.M. (1988). The effects of "intrinsic" and "extrinsic" reinforcement contingencies on task behavior. *Organizational Behavior and Human Decision Processes, 41,* 405–425.

Part V

FROM JOB EVALUATION TO WORK EVALUATION

A fundamental building block of reward program development is the nature of the work being performed. Although this statement has been true for a long period of time, currently there is debate as to the best way to describe the nature of work. At the extremes, one group argues that job evaluation defines work and a second group argues that market value defines work. The conclusion reached here is that both job evaluation and market surveys are important, but that the concept of job needs to be expanded to work in order to include roles, competencies, and teams in the definition of work.

Heneman, R.L. (in press). Job and work evaluation: A literature review. *Public Personnel Management.*

Heneman, R.L. (in press). Work evaluation: Current state of the art and future prospects. *WorldatWork Journal.*

CHAPTER 13

JOB AND WORK EVALUATION

A Literature Review

Robert L. Heneman

Source: Heneman, R.L. (in press). Job and Work Evaluation: A Literature Review. *Public Personnel Management.* Reprinted with permission from Public Personnel Management and the International Personnel Management Association.

INTRODUCTION

Classification and job evaluation systems have come under attack in the public sector. A literature review was conducted to help public sector human resource professionals make informed decisions about whether or not to change or even abandon traditional classification and job evaluation systems for compensation purposes. It is concluded that traditional classification and job evaluation procedures continue to have relevance in public sector settings. However, current classification and job evaluation systems need to be broadened to adapt to the changing nature of work in public sector organizations. Recommendations to shift the focus from "job" to "work" evaluation are offered.

Classification and job evaluation procedures have come under attack in the public sector in recent years (Risher & Fay, 1997). Criticisms range from charges of favoritism and politics being used to make job value decisions to the reinforcement of bureaucratic thinking (Lawler, 1990). Arguments have been made that market pricing and skill and competency pay are needed to assess job worth rather than traditional classification and job evaluation practices (Heneman, 2000; Risher & Fay, 1997).

While the debates concerning classification and job evaluation systems are informative, they may be misleading. Often missing from those debates is reference to the voluminous body of scientific and practical literature that has been amassed on classification and job evaluation systems. The purpose of this review is to help public sector human resource professionals make informed decisions about whether or not to change or even abandon traditional classification and other job evaluation systems for compensation purposes. In order to accomplish this objective, a literature review is conducted on job evaluation over the years, and more recently, the literature that has been conducted more broadly on work evaluation. Work evaluation is a broader concept than job evaluation and allows for the evaluation of roles, competencies, and teams as well as the evaluation of tasks and duties associated with traditional job evaluation systems (Heneman, 2000). As will be shown in this review, job evaluation is most certainly not gone nor should it be forgotten. However, current job evaluation approaches need to be broadened to adapt to the changing nature of work in public sector organizations.

This report will be organized in the following fashion. First the procedures used to generate the articles reviewed in this report will be summarized. Second, major methods of work evaluation identified in the literature will be briefly described. Third, the major perspectives that emerge from debates regarding the usefulness of job evaluation will be summarized and discussed. Fourth, a framework to categorize the literature will be set forth. Fifth, the literature will be reviewed using this framework. Sixth, a series of guidelines will be offered.

LITERATURE SELECTION

The starting point to identify job and work evaluation articles was the reference lists in popular compensation texts (Bergmann, Scarpello, & Hill, 1998; Henderson, 1997; Martocchio, 2000; Milkovich & Newman, 1998). A library search was also conducted using various search engines. A comprehensive search was made of articles from the WorldatWork (formerly the American Compensation Association) and building block series, research reports, and WorldatWork Journal. Upon gathering this information, the final part of the search was to secure other articles referenced that had not yet been collected. The net result is a fairly comprehensive list of articles from about 1980 to the present. Judgment was applied, however, in order to ensure that the articles described added value above and beyond existing knowledge. In the same spirit, articles prior to 1980 were included as well. Lastly, emphasis in the selection of articles and the literature review is more heavily weighted toward empirical than conceptual articles.

Work Evaluation Methods

Although some methods of job evaluation are commonly known (e.g., classification), others are less well known (e.g., market pricing). Hence, a brief review of job and work evaluation methods is needed prior to the rest of the review. The most common approaches to work evaluation reported in the literature can be categorized by two dimensions as shown in Figure 1. One dimension is the type of comparisons made. Jobs, people, and teams can be compared against other jobs, people, or teams, respectively, or they can be compared to written standards in order to gauge value. The second dimension is the number of standards used to assess value. Some approaches use a single standard while other approaches use multiple standards. The most common methods of work evaluation will now be described along with a listing of the strengths and weaknesses of each approach.

Number of Standards	Comparison	
	Other Jobs	Written Standards
Single	• Ranking • Market Pricing • Banding	• Classification • Single Factor Plans
Multiple	• Factor Comparison	• Point Factor System • Competencies

Figure 1.   Work evaluation taxonomy

Ranking

Ranking is the most straightforward method of work evaluation. Jobs, people, or even teams can be ranked from the ones adding most value to least value to the organization. Criteria for the ranking are not made explicit. Jobs rather than people are easier to rank when there are a large number of people in jobs. Teams can be ranked in a team-based environment as a substitute for or addition to the ranking of jobs and people. When a larger number of jobs, people, or teams are to be ranked, the method of paired comparisons can be used. With this approach each entity is compared to every other entity in terms of value to the organization. Overall value of the entity is determined by the number of times that the entity is evaluated as being of greater value then the entity being compared against. If an extremely large number of comparisons needs to be made, statistical formulas are available to reduce the number of comparisons required using sampling theory.

Advantages

1. Simple to use if there is a small number of jobs, people, or teams to evaluate.
2. Requires little time.
3. Minimal administration required.

Disadvantages

1. Criteria for ranking not understood.
2. Increases possibility of evaluator bias.
3. Very difficult to use if there is a large number of jobs, people, or teams to evaluate.
4. Rankings by different evaluators are not comparable.
5. Distance between each rank is not necessarily equal.
6. May invite perceptions of inequity.

Market Pricing

Market pricing relies on the external market value of jobs, people, and teams as the comparison to be made for internal jobs, people, and teams. For jobs, careful comparisons must be made to ensure that jobs are comparable. For people, comparisons are made on the basis of competencies (i.e., knowledge, skills, abilities, and other factors). For teams, careful comparisons must be made to ensure that teams are comparable. For example, members of self-directed work teams perform different functions than do members of teams guided by a supervisor or team leader.

Advantages

1. Market value has face validity to employees.
2. Market value appears to be more objective than other work evaluation approaches.
3. Increasingly there is a large amount of market data on jobs available to employers.
4. It is a quick procedure to follow for some jobs.

Disadvantages

1. Market data is susceptible to sampling error.
2. Market data is susceptible to measurement error.
3. Market data for people and teams is extremely hard to locate.
4. Market data may reflect discriminatory practices by employers against minorities and women.

Banding

A banding procedure takes place when jobs are grouped together by common characteristics. Characteristics used to group jobs follow: exempt versus nonexempt, professional versus nonprofessional, union versus non-union, key contributor versus non-key contributor, line versus staff, technical versus non-technical, value-added versus non-value-added, and classified versus non-classified. Often these groups are then rank ordered and each group is then placed in a pay band.

Advantages

1. Quick and easy procedure.
2. Has initial face validity to employees.
3. Allows for organizational flexibility.
4. Minimal administration required.

Disadvantages

1. Subtle, but important, differences between groups ignored.
2. Subtle, but important, differences within groups ignored.
3. May invite inequity perceptions.

Classification

Classification systems define the value of jobs, people, or teams with written standards for a hierarchy of classification level. Each classification level may be defined by a number of factors that need to be present for a job, person, or team to be slotted into a particular classification level. These factors are usually blended together resulting in one standard for each classification level.

Advantages

1. Jobs, people, and teams can be quickly slotted into the structure.
2. Classification levels have face validity for employees.
3. Standards to establish value are made explicit.

Disadvantages

1. Many jobs, people, or teams do not fit neatly into a classification level.
2. Extensive judgment is required because standards used to define each factor are blended together.
3. Differences between classification levels may not be equal.
4. Creates status hierarchies within organizations.
5. Extensive administration required.

Single Factor Plans

Single factor plans select one standard to be used to differentiate the value of different jobs, people, or teams. One of the following standards is selected to differentiate work: ability, (e.g., Position Analysis Questionnaire), skill (e.g., skill-based pay), knowledge (e.g., maturity curve), or job characteristic (e.g., team leader). Using these standards as examples, a pay system can be constructed such that there are different pay ranges based on whether the job or person is characterized as high ability/skill or low ability/skill. Different pay ranges can be constructed on the basis of knowledge where the highest pay range is for a Ph.D., and the lowest pay range is for a bachelor's degree, for example. In team environments, the salary range for the team leader position may be higher than the pay range for team members.

Advantages

1. Easy to follow.
2. Minimal administration required.
3. Face validity for professionals and managers.
4. Allows for more flexible definitions of work.

Disadvantages

1. Incomplete measurement of value.
2. Limited applicability to jobs that do not vary by the selected standard (e.g., homogeneous skill sets).
3. Complicated measurement systems need to be developed.
4. Market data is very difficult to locate in this format.

Competencies

Unlike single factor plans, competencies are defined in terms of knowledge, skills, abilities, *and* other attributes of people related to high performance rather than knowledge, skills, abilities, *or* other attributes of people related to high performance. Competencies are also defined in terms of specific and observable behaviors that manifest themselves as a result of having the requisite knowledge, skills, abilities, and other attributes (e.g., motivation) needed to perform the work. For example, teamwork is a competency increasingly required by work. Teamwork can be defined by specific and behavioral statements like the following:

1. Attends team meetings on a regular basis.
2. Completes assignments for the team in a timely and accurate manner.
3. Is an active participant at team meetings.
4. Offers constructive criticism when necessary.
5. Provides useful ideas to the team.

In order to demonstrate these behaviors that define teamwork, assumptions are made about the level of knowledge, skill, ability, and other attributes required of the team member. For example, in order to provide useful ideas to the team, the team member may have to have certain level of education in order to generate ideas germane to the goals of the team.

As can be seen from this explanation, competencies look very similar to behaviors evaluated in performance appraisal. In fact, some organizations use competencies as performance appraisal standards while other organizations treat competencies as work evaluation standards.

Advantages

1. Allows for very flexible definitions of work.
2. Face validity for professional and managerial positions.
3. May decrease status differences between people.
4. Makes criteria for advancement and development more explicit.

Disadvantages

1. Incomplete measure of value.
2. Complicated measurement systems need to be developed.
3. Market data is difficult to locate in this format.
4. Extensive administration required.

Point Factor System

While competencies tend to focus on the jobholder rather than the job, point factor systems tend to focus on the job rather than the jobholder. Written standards, known as "factors," are used to define units of compensable worth to the organization. Examples of traditional factors include difficulty level, experience required, supervision performed, knowledge required, and working conditions. Examples of more contemporary factors include fiscal accountability, leadership, teamwork, and project accountability. Each factor is defined in terms of levels with a "point" value associated with each level. For example, a scale may be used to define the factor experience and range from level 1 equals 1–2 years of experience to level 5 equals 10 or more years experience. The point value associated with each level might range from 1 point to 10 points for level 1 and level 5 requirements, respectively.

Advantages

1. Comprehensive measurement of value.
2. Used extensively in industry for years.
3. Value assessment standards are very explicit.
4. Market data are readily available.
5. Minimize inequity perceptions between jobs.

Disadvantages

1. Associated with inflexible work.
2. Extensive administration required.
3. Creates status differences.

Factor Comparisons

Factors are again used with factor comparison systems. Rather than have a scale to rate each job relative to each factor, however, each job is instead rank ordered from highest to lowest for each factor.

Advantages

1. Comprehensive measurement of value.
2. Ranking is easy to do.

Disadvantages

1. Associated with inflexible work.
2. Extensive administration required.
3. Creates states differences.
4. Difficult to explain rankings to employees.

Major Perspectives

Major perspectives on job and work evaluation presented in the literature are summarized in Table 1. A more detailed description and comparison of each perspective follows.

Table 1. Summary of Major Job and Work Evaluation Perspectives

Perspective	Representative Authors	Descriptions
Traditional	Plachy (1987)[53] Mays (1997)[54]	Job evaluation is an excellent procedure when done right, problem is implementation not the concept; "An engineer still does engineering."
Realists	Lawler (1990)[55] Risher (1984, 1997)[56]	Job evaluation does not fix with contemporary organizational characteristics (e.g., fast change, fluid structure, teams); political "gamesmanship" define scores
Market Advocates	Beatty and Beatty (1984)[57] Schwab (1980)[58] Lawler (2000)[59]	Both explicitly and implicitly the factors used in job evaluations are meant to be substitutes for market pay; market pay is in better alignment with business strategy than job evaluation scores
Strategists	Murlis and Fitt (1991)[60] Heneman (2000)[61] Zingheim, Ledford, and Schuster (1996)[62]	Job evaluation should be designed to reinforce the business strategy; job evaluation gives the organization a source of sustained competitive advantage
Organizational Development	Schwab and H. Heneman (1986)[63] Milkovich and Newman (1999a,b)[64]	Job evaluation is a consensus building activity to bring about change in the organization
Social Reality	Quaid (1993)[65] Sandberg (2000)[66]	Job evaluation is a symbol in the organization that is socially constructed by its participants
Contingency Theory	Mahoney (1991)[67] Wolf (2000)[68]	Job evaluation is a neutral process; needs to be matched appropriately with organization and environment
Competencies	Hofrichter and Spencer (1996)[69] O'Neal (1993–94, 1995)[70]	The job is the person as assessed by knowledge, skills, abilities, and other factors related to effective performance
Cognitive Decision Making	Campion and Berger (1990)[71] Huber and Crandall (1994)[72]	Work evaluation ratings are influenced by the cognitive ability of the rater to process work information and the social factors that influence these cognitions

Traditionalists

Traditionalists believe that the basic methods of work analysis just reviewed can be adapted to organizations and people as they change over time. In addition, traditionalists believe that while work has indeed changed dramatically in recent times, it has not eliminated jobs as the basic building block of work. As stated by Mays (1997): "An engineer still does engineering." According to traditionalists, while job evaluation does have its problems as a method of work evaluation, these problems stem from poor implementation rather than poor conception.

Realists

Realists point to the problems of both job and person evaluation as methods of work evaluation. In particular, attention is focused on the limited circumstances that exist in organizations where job evaluation can be used (i.e., in bureaucracies). They also point to the politics involved in the process of determining work hierarchies. Similarly, they point to the very limited circumstances where competencies work (e.g., high skill technical jobs). Most realists are instead in favor of market pay.

Market Advocates

According to this approach, job evaluation is a poor substitute for the market value of jobs. Job evaluation systems are either explicitly designed or implicitly designed to measure segments of work having market value (e.g., skill, effort, responsibility, working conditions). Moreover, these factors detract from actual market values that are closer in alignment with the business strategy of the organization.

Strategists

Strategists are like realists in that they believe that common work evaluation systems can be adapted to the changing nature of people and organizations. To do so requires that the work evaluation factors used be based directly on the business strategy, which is internally focused rather than externally focused. That is, organizations gain competitive advantage by doing unique things in the business that their competitors cannot copy. While pay survey amount strategies can be matched by competitors, it is very difficult for competitors to develop work evaluation factors that rein-force the goals of the business.

The position of strategists is well stated by Murlis and Fitt (1991), "Job evaluation, properly implemented, remains the way that organizations place value on parts of their structure through which employees carry out their business strategies and purpose. However flexible and fast-moving an organization may be, job evaluation provides the essential link between business direction and individual rate value" (p. 43).

Organizational Development

The organizational development perspective focuses in on the process whereby work evaluations are conducted. In many organizations, this is a consensus building activity that is critical to the effective functioning of the organization. Effectiveness is increased as a result of the common mutual expectations developed for people and jobs by discussing the nature and value of work. Moreover, synergies may be created between people and jobs through these discussions.

Social Reality Perspective

Closely allowed to be realist perspective and the organizational develop-ment perspective is the social reality perspective. All three of these perspec-tives focus on the process used to develop work evaluations. Unlike the realist and organizational development perspectives, however, the social reality perspective believes that work evaluation is a socially constructed phenomenon. That is, it is more a symbol of the organization than it is an actual measurable value of work to the organization. The attention paid to the symbolism of work evaluation is similar to the strategic perspective.

Contingency Theory

According to the contingency perspective, the type of work evaluation approach used must be carefully matched to the organization and to the business environment faced by the organization. As such, there is no one "best" way to conduct work evaluation. Many of the problems pointed out by the realists can be accommodated by the contingency perspective. As such, work evaluation is a neutral procedure until it is designed. In contrast to traditionalists' views, contingency theorists focus in on the importance of design more than implementation for the effective use of work evaluation.

Competencies

Most job evaluation methods focus on the job rather than the person (ACA, 1989). People in the contingency school of thought reject the notion of the job for reasons set forth by some realists. Unlike realists that often advocate a market-based perspective as well, advocates of competencies instead argue that the person makes the job and that the focus should be on people rather than jobs or markets. Although people are very important to social reality theorists, people operating from the competency perspective focus on actual rather than perceived characteristics of jobs.

Cognitive Decision Making

The cognitive decision making perspective view work evaluation as a series of judgments made by evaluators about work. This perspective recognizes the inherent biases brought to this process as a result of the limited cognitive abilities of people as evaluators. In addition, this perspective recognizes how social factors also influence these cognitions in decision making. The cognitive approach is similar to the society reality approach in that it views job evaluation decisions as being embedded in the social milieu of organizations. Unlike the social reality approach, however, the cognitive perspective does consider work independent of the social situation as well.

Assessment

As will be shown in the next section, there is supporting evidence for all of these perspectives. No one perspective is sufficient to explain the outcomes of work evaluation in and of itself. By comparing these various perspectives, several important themes emerge:

1. Work evaluation is an ongoing rather than static process.
2. Both perceived and actual evaluations of work are important.
3. Work evaluation sends a very important message to employees.
4. Successful work evaluation processes are both difficult to design and difficult to implement.
5. Work evaluation can be a source of competitive advantage for work organizations.
6. There is no one best way to conduct work evaluation
7. Jobs still exist.
8. People make the place.

Work Evaluation Framework

A work evaluation framework that emerges from the literature is shown in Figure 2. This framework will be used to categorize publications reviewed. Before doing so, a brief description of the framework is presented.

The focal point of the framework is the middle box and it depicts the dynamic process known as work evaluation. In turn, work evaluation is a function of four sets of variables: Evaluator characteristics, evaluatee characteristics, environmental conditions, and organizational conditions. Evaluator and evaluatee characteristics include their respective attitudes, behaviors, and background characteristics. Environmental conditions refer include laws and regulations, labor and product markets, and the pressure of unions and professional associations. Organizational conditions include the structure of the organization and business strategies. The end outcomes that emerge from the work evaluation process include the measurement properties of the system and the behavioral and attitudinal reactions of those parties involved in decision making and affected by the work evaluation process.

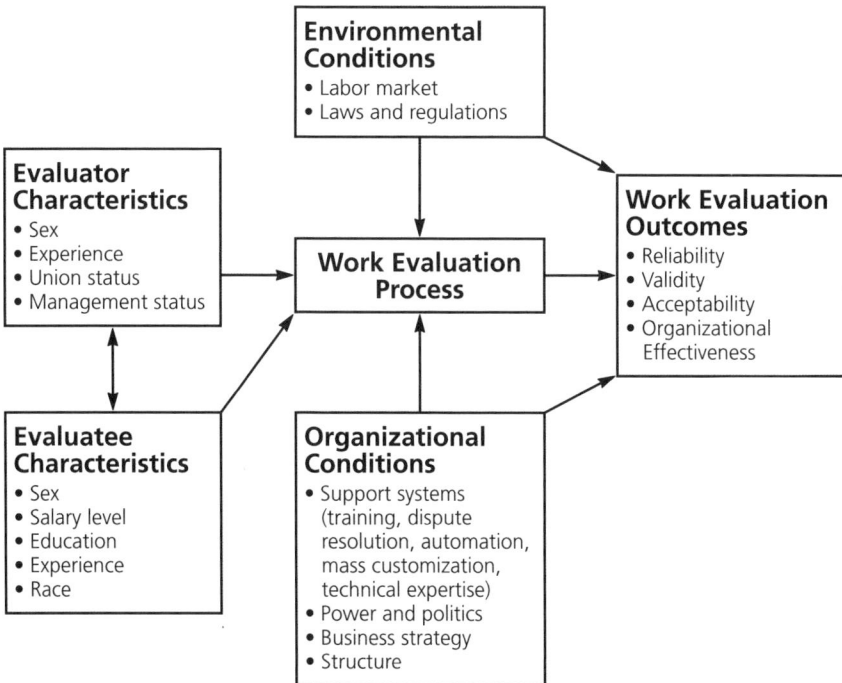

Figure 2.   Work evaluation framework: Variables identified in the literature to date.

Work Evaluation Process

The work evaluation process mentioned in the work evaluation framework is depicted in Figure 3. It begins with the work being performed and ends with a work hierarchy that is an array of work (e.g., people, jobs, teams, occupational, by value to the organization (Campion & Berger, 1990). It is this work hierarchy that is eventually priced by the organization to determine pay rates.

The first step in the translation of work to a work hierarchy is to conduct a work analysis. This analysis provides a detailed assessment of the person performing the work, the nature of the work, and/or the context in which work is performed (Heneman, 2000). This step may be carried out by questionnaires, interview, and/or observation. Several constituencies may be consulted including the job incumbents, superiors, and job analysts.

The next step is to summarize the job analysis information into a work description. The work description may take the form of a job description, role profile, and/or competency model.

Once the work data have been summarized, the next step shown in Figure 3 is to evaluate work descriptions in order to attach an assessment of value to the organization to each work description. A direct approach may be taken as shown by the straight line in Figure 3 or an indirect approach may be taken as shown by the dotted lines in Figure 3.

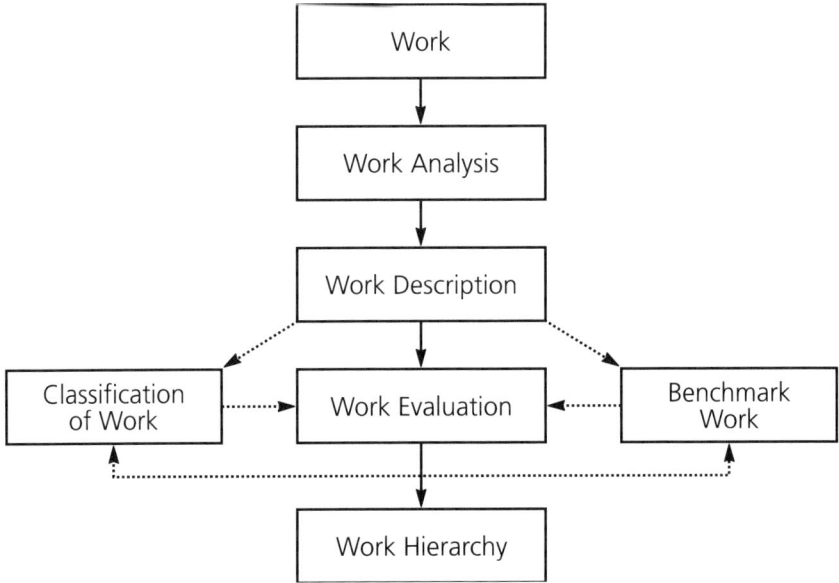

Figure 3.   Work evaluation process.

With the direct approach, each work description is evaluated against the criteria included in the work evaluation. These criteria maybe grouped by single or multiple standards and a job to job or job to written standard comparison (Heneman, 2000). These grouping of criteria yield the following job evaluation methods that may be used to assess the value of each work description: ranking, market pricing, banding, classification, single factor plans, factor comparisons, point factor systems, and competencies.

With the indirect approach, as indicated by the dotted lines in Figure 3, work descriptions may be aggregated to a higher level (e.g., job to an occupation) as indicated by the box labeled classification of work. Alternately, or in addition, to the classification of work, some representative work descriptions rather than all work descriptions may be evaluated as indicated by the benchmark work box. In either event, work descriptions receive these treatments (i.e., classification or benchmarks) prior to being assessed for value with the work evaluation procedures.

Because of the complex process associated with work evaluation, difficulties can arise at each stage due to the judgments required. Difficulties are especially likely to arrive when the indirect path is followed in the third step. For example, difficult statistical techniques used to determine the similarity of jobs for purposes of classification yield different classifications of work (Ash, Levine, & Sistrunk, 1983; Arvery, Maxwell, Gutenberg, & Camero, 1981; Lee & Mendoza, 1981).

Evaluator Characteristics

Many different evaluators may be involved in the work evaluation process including job incumbents, superiors, and analysts. Although participation by all of these sources is recommended by several authors in the literature (Lawler, 1990; Risher & Fay, 1997), most of the research to date has focused on superiors and analysts as evaluators. The only characteristics of evaluators studied to date are the sex of the evaluator and the union status of the evaluator.

The sex of the evaluator has been examined in several studies. Well-designed empirical studies find no impact of evaluator sex on job evaluation ratings (Rynes, Weber, & Milkovich, 1989; Schwab & Grahams, 1985). However, when another facet of the work evaluation process is considered, job analysis, there is at least one study that shows the impact of the sex of the evaluator has an effect on work analysis ratings with females giving lower scores than males (Arvey, Passino, & Loundsbury, 1987). Also, at least one qualitative study has provided evidence of the impact of the evaluators sex on job evaluation ratings with raters, especially males, having deep-seated feelings about the value of means versus women's work (Shimmin, 1987).

In terms of the background of the evaluator, an early study by Lawshe and Farbo (1948) found that the reliability of job evaluation scores was higher for management than union evaluators.

Evaluatee Characteristics

As with characteristics of the evaluator, characteristics of the ratee studied have primarily centered around sex, as well as sex in conjunction with salary level, education level, and experience level of the evaluatee. According to Schwab and Grams (1985), there can be either a direct or indirect effect of sex of the evaluatee on work evaluation ratings. A direct effect means that men systematically undervalue the work of women. An indirect effect means that men undervalue the work of women because women have on average lower salaries and less experience and education than do men. As with the sex of the evaluator, the sex of the evaluatee appears to have little impact on the work evaluation ratings in well-designed studies (Rynes, Weber, & Milkovich, 1989; Schwab & Grahams, 1985). Also, in these same well-designed studies, the indirect impact of sex had no effect. When job analysis was considered as a part of the evaluation process, in at least one study, the indirect impact of sex on job analysis ratings by way of experience was reported (Doverspike & Barrett, 1984).

In one study, the race of the job incumbent did have an impact on job evaluation scores with blacks receiving lower scores than whites (Treiman, 1984). In another two studies, one in a university setting with actual evaluates and evaluatees (Mount & Ellis, 1987) and one in a laboratory study with undergraduate evaluators, there was a significant impact for salary level. That is, high salary jobs received higher ratings than lower salary jobs. If the salary level is free from bias, then these two studies show that the job evaluation systems used are valid. If the actual salary levels are biased, then these two studies show that salary level may be a rating error.

Environmental Conditions

Very little research has been conducted on the impact of environmental conditions on work evaluation. Hence, we know for example, virtually nothing about union reactions to job evaluation in contemporary times. Also, we have little systematic knowledge as to employer practices in regards to work evaluation in response to government regulations (e.g., equal pay act). One notable exception is the review of court decisions by

Cooper and Barrett (1982). In this review they found that many organizations had no job evaluation system and when this was the case, the court had to infer the value of jobs. Also, as would be expected given the equal pay act, job evaluation systems that measured factors related to skill, effort, responsibility and working conditions fared better as a business defense to discriminating pay practices.

Another area that yields very little research is the impact of labor markets on work evaluation decisions. Back in 1926, Lott recognized the importance of labor markets to job evaluation decision making by suggesting that scarcity of labor should be a job evaluation factor (Lott, 1926). Given today's tight labor markets, it might not be a bad idea to include a factor of this nature to reflect the strategic value of labor to the goals of the organizations.

More recently, Olson, Schwab, and Rau (2000) reported evidence that if the scarcity of labor is not explicitly considered, then it will be considered implicitly. They found in a study of the General Schedule system that GS administrators assigned new employees to higher-grade levels than deserved as a result of wage levels in the local labor market.

Organizational Conditions

Of all the determents of the work evaluation process shown in Figure 2, the one most studied is organizational conditions. Variables studied can be clustered into the following categories: support systems, work evaluation design, power and politics, organization and job design, and business strategy.

Support Systems

Given the elaborate nature of work evaluation shown in Figure 3, it is no surprise that a considerable number of support systems need to be in place for the system to function effectively.

One critical support system is training. Hahn and Dipboye (1988) found that the reliability and validity of job evaluation ratings generated by undergraduate subjects was increased with a one hour training session devoted to defining the job evaluation factors and giving to student examples of work at various factor levels. Reliability and validity increased because the trained evaluators were less likely to commit halo and leniency error than untrained evaluators.

Along with training, another support system is dispute resolution procedures. A procedure to resolve disputes is needed when multiple evaluators are used and they cannot reach a consensus on evaluation values. Blood, Graham, and Zedeck (1987) provided a case study showing how disputes were settled in a unionized, international shipping company using industrial psychologists as mediators.

Automation is another important support system. Risher and Wise (1999) present a case study of an automated job evaluation system being used in Dade County, Florida. Pearlman and Barney (2000) describe an automated job analysis system being used at Lucent. The system at Lucent is very advanced in that it relies upon artificial intelligence. A similar system could be created for job evaluation whereby the operating system would look for key words in job descriptions to match the job to the appropriate job evaluation level. Certainly this feature would be a very useful support system for large organizations.

Another important feature that could be integrated into an automated system when a large number of jobs need to be evaluated is mass customization (1997). Under this approach, each part of the organization would select those standards to be used to assess work value (e.g., factor bank) that are consistent with the strategy, structure, and operating processes of their part of the business. In order to ensure some consistency across the parts of the organization, so that there are some common goals across the organization, a core set of standards could be required for all parts of the organization with the option to select additional standards more specific to the needs of various parts of the organization. By allowing for custom-made standards in each part of the organization, there is more participation in the process than is usual in large organizations. As such, it may help overcome the resistance common to changes in work evaluation practices that have been in place for many years such as the U.S. Government (Gupta, 1997; Holley & O'Connell, 1997). A good case study of a mass customization strategy at ABB is reported in Eyes (1999).

As part of an automated system, there is also a need for a knowledge management system especially in large organizations. This type of system would fulfill several roles. First, it would develop work evaluation processes (e.g., factor bank). Second, it would store work evaluation processes in a central location. Third, it would distribute work evaluation knowledge (e.g., demonstration projects) to other parts of the organization not involved in demonstration projects.

A high level of technical expertise is also required as a support system. In particular, individuals with strong psychometric skills are needed. Psychometricians can add immense value to the project. Some of the findings of psychometrician of value to date include the points that a large number of evaluators (e.g., 360 degree review) are not needed for reliable ratings (Doverspike, Carlisi, Barrett, & Alexander, 1983), that a large number of items for each factor may not be needed (Lawshe & Fabro, 1948; Doverspike,

Carlisi, Barrett, & Alexander, 1983), that the rational weights for factors developed by subject matter experts are sometimes just as good as statistical weights (Davis & Sauser, 1991), that bias can be partially controlled for using statistical analyses (Doverspike & Barrett, 1986), that jobs grouped into higher aggregates (e.g., occupation) are difficult to evaluate accurately (Beatty & Beatty, 1984) and that a small number of factors (e.g., 3–5) works just as well as a large number of factors (Gerhart & Milkovich, 1992).

Power and Politics

Two interesting studies have been conducted on the role of power and politics in job evaluation settings. Benson and Hornsby (1988) reported on the influence tactics used by evaluators in the job evaluation process: "Rationality (the use of reason, logic, and facts to persuade others), Integration (the use of flattery and the enhancement of others self-esteem to persuade others), Blocking (the use of stubborn behavior to convince others that it is not worth the effort to change the influence's position), Expertise (the appeal to expert knowledge, especially that of the external consultant, to convince others to change their positions). Threat (the use of perceived potential political problems and coercion to convince others to change their positions), and Exchange (the use of reciprocity, or the trading of favors)." The use of these tactics was shown to be related to self-esteem, need for dominance, and need for affiliation of 44 job evaluation committee members using the FES in city and county governments in the southeastern United States. Welbourne and Trevor (2000) examined departmental and position power is job evaluation in a university setting. Their results indicated that greater departmental power resulted in a greater number of positions approved, upgraded, and requested pay levels. Department power influence was even greater when the position power of the evaluatee was high.

Business Strategy

The linking of work evaluation standards is critical to the effectiveness of work evaluation systems (Heneman, 2000). In support of this view, several case studies describes the positive effect of taking this approach (Liccione, 1995; Heneman, 2000) while another case study, using the FES in the State of Montana, shows the negative effects of not taking this approach. Weinberger (1992) developed an interesting method of job evaluation based on the concept of the "strategic centrality" of jobs to the organization.

Structure

The last and certainly not least important organizational condition is the structure of the organization. It has been clearly demonstrated in the competencies literature of case studies that person-based work evaluation systems work best in organizations that are flat rather than hierarchical, static rather than stable, and organized by teams rather than individuals (Heneman, Ledford, & Gresham, 2000). Unfortunately, no empirical studies have been conducted to verify these conclusions to date.

Work Evaluation Outcomes

Ultimately, the major issue with work evaluation processes is the resulting reliability and validity of the system. That is, to what extent does the work evaluation system produce a set of consistent results (e.g., point values) that measures what was intended to be measured. To answer these issues, Huber and Crandall (1994) did an excellent job of reviewing all the major studies conducted. Their conclusions will be reviewed here and supplemented with articles omitted in the review, more recent articles, and case studies and laboratory studies not included in the review. One omission in their review and in the present one is the many studies on Elliot Jacques' single factor job evaluation plan known as Time Span of Discretion. The research clearly shown that this approach is neither reliable nor valid (Gordon, 1969).

It should also be noted that while a considerable amount of evidence has been amassed on outcomes associated with work evaluation, the vast majority of the research has been on job evaluation and point-factor systems in particular.

Reliability

Considerable evidence has been amassed that point-factor systems are reliable. This finding is very robust as it has held up across a variety of reliability measures. In particular, point factor systems have proven to be reliable when the evaluations of one evaluator are correlated with the ratings of another evaluator, when the evaluations of one evaluator are correlated with a composite evaluation of other raters, when the evaluations of evaluators at one point in time are correlated with the evaluations of the same evaluators at a later point in time, and when the variance of evaluations is partitioned into job and evaluator impact. Typically, as would be expected given reliability formulas, the reliability of total point values is greater than the reliability of point values for individual factors. Factors with high reliability include skills, experience, and education. Factors with lower reliability include responsibility, effort, and working conditions.

Validity

In work evaluation, validity is very difficult to establish as it varies by work evaluation perspective. For example, the strategic perspective validates factors against the business plan, while an organizational development perspective validates evaluations against evaluator and evaluatee effectiveness. The measure that has primarily been used in the published literature is "hit rate" which refers to the correct classification of jobs using the work evaluation system into the pay grade it has actually been assigned. The results here are less encouraging than the results for reliability in that validity is usually lower than reliability. Moreover, it is very difficult to interpret what hit rate means when there is usually no indication in the research as to how actual grade assignments have been made. They may have been made, for example, on the basis of rating errors (e.g., leniency) in which case it is nonsensical to validate job evaluation ratings against an error filled criterion measure.

Acceptability

Affective reactions to job evaluation plans have simply not been studied. At best, they are mentioned in passing with anecdotal evidence as part of case studies. This situation is very unfortunate because one would hypothesize that the survival rate of work evaluation systems is in large part dependent upon the acceptability of the work evaluation system to the affected parties.

Organizational Effectiveness

Descriptive surveys and case studies represent another approach to evaluate the effectiveness of work evaluation plans. Typically, compared to reliability and validity studies, much broader indicators of success are used (e.g., productivity) and a more qualitative approach is taken.

In terms of descriptive surveys, the two that have been conducted center around skill and competency-based pay. A study of 97 different skill base pay plans was conducted by Jenkins, Ledford, Gupta, & Doty (1992). It was reported that at least 80 percent of the 97 organizations found their skill-based pay plan to be moderately successful. Benefits cited included greater employee motivation, flexibility, and versatility as well as lower labor costs and turnover. Although the results are positive, bear in mind that these data are self-report and may have been aggrandized.

In a survey of competency-based pay (ACA, 1996), 32 competency pay plans were evaluated. Self-report data was again used and the majority respondents indicated that competency based HR programs had a "positive effect" on behavioral measures of organizational effectiveness such as communications and customer focus. Interestingly, of the 217 companies studied (not all had a plan in place for a year, so only 32 were in the effectiveness survey), none of them used competencies for compensation purposes. Instead, they were used for staffing, training, and development purposes. A survey of several case studies on competency-based pay in the United Kingdom was reported by Armstrong and Brown (1998). They reported that competency base pay plans worked best when they were used in conjunction with existing pay systems rather than as replacements for existing pay systems. Hence, the authors suggested that the title of competency pay systems be changed form "competency-based" to "competency-related."

Three of the most interesting case studies on work evaluation report situations where work evaluation was ineffective. Negative results are infrequently reported in the literature and much is to be gained from the learning points that come from negative as well as positive outcomes. Parent and Weber (1994) found that in the Ford Motor Company plant with knowledge-based pay system, that productivity was less for the plant with knowledge-based pay system than for the plant with not knowledge based pay system. The authors speculated that the results may be due to differences in age and gender between the two plants.

Tompkins, Brown, and McEwen (1990) conducted a case study of the FES in the State of Montana in order to eliminate gender bias in pay. Due to "political and administrative realities" and "technical or methodological shortcomings" it was not implemented. Interestingly, the greatest determinant of non-implementation was the political and administrative realities rather than the technical issues.

Quaid (1993) conducted an elaborate qualitative study of the introduction of the Hay plan to one of Canada's ten provincial governments. The Hay plan replaced the classification plan that had been previously used. According to the authors, from a social reality perspective, while the plan was adopted by the government, it had developed "mystical" properties that institutionalized inequities in the pay system. The author showed how this social reality developed through a three-stage process.

An excellent case study using an experimental design evaluated the effectiveness of skill-based pay (Murray & Gerhart, 1998). When one plant with skill-based pay was completed over time to a comparable plant with skill-based pay, the plant with skill-based pay has 58% greater productivity, 16% less labor costs, and more favorable quality outcomes.

SUMMARY AND CONCLUSION

Although there has not been an abundance of research conducted on work evaluation, the work that has been conducted has many applied implications to guide policy makers and implementers of work evaluation systems. These implications are summarized in Figure 4. Hopefully, these implications will be of help to public sector human resource professionals as they make alterations to existing job evaluation systems.

Perspectives
- Work evaluation is an ongoing rather than static process
- Both perceived and actual evaluation of work are important
- Work evaluation sends a very strong message to employees
- Successful work evaluation processes are difficult to design and implement
- Work evaluation can be a source of competitive advantage for work organizations
- There is no one best way to conduct work evaluation
- Jobs still exist
- People make the place

Process
- It is very difficult to accurately group jobs into aggregate levels for job evaluation purposes
- Gender bias does not appear to be a problem in job evaluation
- Rating errors exist in job evaluation as well as performance evaluation
- Training can eliminate rating errors in job evaluation
- Labor market indicators (e.g., salary levels) influence job evaluation scores
- A variety of support systems are needed for job evaluation to be effective
- Large numbers of evaluators (e.g., 360 degree reviews) are not needed for accurate job evaluation ratings

Figure 4. Major findings from literature review.

- A small number of factors (3-5) works as well as a large number of factors
- Rational weights for factors are probably as good as statistical weights in most situations
- Power and politics influence job evaluation ratings

Outcomes
- Point-factor systems are very reliable
- Total point values are more reliable than point values for each factor
- The validity of work evaluation systems is not well known
- The affective reactions of people to work evaluation systems is not well known
- Competency pay is not used very often
- Skill-based pay works well under certain conditions
- Most work evaluation systems have not been evaluated

Source: Adapted from Heneman (in press).

Figure 4.   Major findings from literature review (Continued).

ACKNOWLEDGMENT

The research underlying this article was commissioned by the U.S. Office of Personnel Management (OPM), as part of its comprehensive review of job and work evaluation. OPM's Office of Performance and Compensation Systems Design has undertaken that review as part of a larger effort to determine ways in which the federal government's compensation systems can be improved. The views presented here are those of the author and do not necessarily reflect the views of the U.S. government in general or the Office of Personnel Management in particular.

REFERENCES

ACA (1996).

Armstrong & Brown (1998).

Arvey, R.D., Maxwell, S.E., Gutenberg, R.L., & Camero (1981). Detecting job differences: A Monte Carlo study. *Personnel Psychology, 34.*

Arvey, R.D., Passino, E.M., & Lounsbury, J.W. (1977). Job analysis results as influenced by sex of incumbent and sex of analyst. *Journal of Applied Psychology, 62*(4).

Ash, R.A., Levine, E.L., & Sistrunk, S. (1983). The role of jobs and job-based methods in personnel and human resources management. In K.M. Rowland & G.R.

Ferris (Eds.), *Research in personnel and human resources management* (Vol. 1). Greenwich, CT: JAI Press.

Beatty. & Beatty. (1984).

Benson, P.G., & Hornsby, J.S. (1988). The politics of pay—The use of influence tactics in job evaluation committees. *Group & Organization Studies, 13*(2).

Bergmann, T.J., Scarpello, V.G., & Hills, F.S. (1998). *Compensation decision making.* Fort Worth, TX: The Dryden Press.

Blood, M.R., Graham, W.K., & Zedeck, S. (1987). Resolving compensation disputes with three-party job evaluation. *Applied Psychology: An International Review, 36*(1).

Campion, M.A., & Berger, C. (1990). Conceptual integration and empirical test of job design and compensation relationships. *Personnel Psychology.*

Cooper & Barrett (1982).

Davis, Jr., K.R., & Sauser, Jr., W.I. (1991). Effects of alternative weighting methods in a policy-capturing approach to job evaluation: A review and empirical investigation. *Personnel Psychology, 44.*

Doverspike, D., & Barrett, G.V. (1984). An internal bias analysis of a job evaluation instrument. *Journal of Applied Psychology, 69*(4).

Doverspike, D., & Barrett, G.V. (1986).

Doverspike, D., Carlisi, A.M., Barrett, G.V., & Alexander, R. (1983). Generalizability analysis of a point-method job evaluation instrument. *Journal of Applied Psychology, 68*(3).

Eyes, P.R. (19??). Streamlining compensation management in a decentralized environment—Merging technology and process. *ACA Journal.*

Gerhart, B., & Milkovich, G.T. (1992). Employee compensation: Research and practice.

Gordon (1969).

Gupta, N. (1997). Rewarding skills in the public sector, new strategies for public pay rethinking government compensation programs.

Hahn, D.C., & Dipboye, R.L. (1988). Effects of training and information on the accuracy and reliability of job evaluations. *Journal of Applied Psychology, 73*(2).

Henderson, R.I. (1997). *Compensation management in a knowledge-based world.* Upper Saddle River, NJ: Prentice-Hall.

Heneman, R.L. (in press). Work evaluation: Current state-of-the art and future prospects. *WorldatWork Journal.*

Heneman, R.L. (2000). *Work evaluation: Strategic issues and alternative methods.* Alexandria, VA: Human Resources Research Organization.

Heneman, R.L., Ledford, G.E., & Gresham, M. (2000). The changing nature of work and its effects on compensation design and delivery. In S. Rynes & B. Gerhart (Eds.), *Compensation in organizations: Current research and practice* (pp. 195–240). San Francisco: Jossey-Bass.

Hofrichter, D.A., & Spencer Jr., L.M. (1996). Competencies: The right foundation for effective human resources management. *Compensation & Benefits Review.*

Holley, L.M., & O'Connell, J.R. (1997). Job classification—The support system for personnel decision making. *New strategies for public pay—Rethinking government compensation programs.*

Huber, V.L., & Crandall, S.R. (1994). Job measurement: A social-cognitive decision perspective. In G.R. Ferris (Ed.), *Research in personnel and human resources management* (Vol. 12). Greenwich, CT: JAI Press.

Lawler, E.E., III (2000). *Rewarding excellence.* San Francisco: Jossey-Bass.

Lawler, E.E., III (1990). *Strategic pay: Aligning organizational strategies and pay systems.* San Francisco: Jossey-Bass.

Lawshe, Jr., C.H., & Farbo, P.C. (1948). Studies in job evaluation: The reliability of an abbreviated job evaluation system. *Journal of Applied Psychology, 33.*

LeBlanc, P.V. (1997). Mass customization: A rewards mosaic for the future? *ACA Journal.*

Lee, J.A., & Mendoza, J.I. (1981). A comparison of techniques which test for job differences. *Personnel Psychology, 34.*

Lott, M.R. (1926). *Wage scales and job evaluation—Scientific determination of wage rates on the basis of services rendered.* New York: The Ronald Press Company.

Ledford, Gupta, & Doty (**????**).

Liccione, W.J. (1995). Evaluate the strategic value of jobs. **HR Focus.**

Mahoney, T. (1991). Job evaluation: Endangered species or anachronism? *Human Resources Management Review, 1*(2).

Martocchio, J.J. (2001). *Strategic compensation.* Upper Saddle River, NJ: Prentice-Hall.

Mays, J. (1997). Why we haven't seen "the end of jobs" or the end of pay surveys. *Compensation & Benefits Review.*

Milkovich, G.T., & Newman, J.M. (1999a). Person-based structures. *Compensation.*

Milkovich, G.T., & Newman, J.M. (1999b). Evaluating work: Job evaluation. *Compensation.*

Milkovich, G., & Newman, G. (1998). *Compensation.* New York: McGraw-Hill.

Mount, M.K., & Ellis, R.A. (1987). Investigation of bias in job evaluation ratings of comparable worth study participants. *Personnel Psychology, 40.*

Murlis, H., & Fitt, D. (1991). Job evaluation in a changing world. *Personnel Management.*

Murray & Gerhart (1998).

Olson, C.A., Schwab, D.P., & Rau, B.L. (2000). The effects of local market conditions on two pay setting systems in the federal sector. *Industrial and Labor Relations Review, 38*(2).

O'Neal, S. (1993–94). Competencies: The DNA of the corporation. *ACA Journal.*

O'Neal, S. (1995). Competencies and pay in the evolving world of work. *ACA Journal.*

Parent & Weber (1994).

Pearlman, K., & Barney, M.F. (2000). Selection for a changing workplace, managing selection in changing organizations. *Human Resource Strategies.*

Plachy, R.J. (1987). Compensation management: Cases and applications—The point factor job evaluation system: A step-by-step guide, Part 1 and 2. *Compensation & Benefits Review, 19.*

Quaid, M. (1993). Job evaluation as institutional myth. *Journal of Management Studies, 30*(2).

Risher, H. (1984). Job evaluation: Problems and prospects. *Personnel.*

Risher, H. (1997). Competency-based pay: The next model for salary management. *New strategies for public pay—Rethinking government compensation programs.*

Risher, H., & Fay, C.H. (1997). *New strategies for public pay.* San Francisco: Jossey-Bass.

Risher, H., & Wise, L.R. (1997). Job evaluation—The search for internal equity. *New strategies for public pay—Rethinking government compensation programs.*

Rynes, S.L., Weber, C.L., & Milkovich, G.T. (1989). Effects of market survey rates, job evaluation, and job gender on job pay. *Journal of Applied Psychology, 74*(1).

Sandberg, J. (2000). Understanding human competence at work: An interpretative approach. *Academy of Management Journal, 43*(1).

Schwab (1980) not found

Schwab, D.P., & Grahams, R. (1985). Sex-related errors in job evaluation: A "real-world" test. *Journal of Applied Psychology, 70*(3).

Schwab, D.P., & Heneman, III, H.G. (1986). Assessment of a consensus-based multiple information source job evaluation system. *Journal of Applied Psychology, 71*(2).

Shimmin, S. (1987). Job evaluation and equal pay for work of equal value. *Applied Psychology: An International Review, 36*(1).

Thompkins, Brown, & MeEwen (1990).

Treiman, D.J. (1984). Effect of choice of factors and factor weights in job evaluation, comparable worth and wage discrimination: Technical possibilities and political realities.

Weinberger (1992).

Welbourne, T.M., & Trevor, C.O. (2000). The roles of departmental and position power in job evaluation. *Academy of Management Journal, 43*(4).

Wolf, M.G. (2000). Compensation: An overview. *The compensation handbook.*

Zingheim, P.K., Ledford Jr., G.E., & Schuster, J.R. (1996). Competencies and competency models: Does one size fit all. *ACA Journal.*

CHAPTER 14

WORK EVALUATION:

Current State of the Art and Future Prospects

Robert L. Heneman

Source: Reprinted from Heneman, R.L. (in press). Work Evaluation: Current State of the Art and Future Prospects. *WorldatWork Journal,* with permission from WorldatWork (formerly American Compensation Association); 14040 N. Northsight Blvd., Scottsdale, AZ 85260; phone (877) 951-9191; fax (480) 483-8352; www.worldatwork.org. (copyright) 1997 WorldatWork. Unauthorized reproduction or distribution is strictly prohibited.

Job evaluation, a fundamental building block of traditional compensation systems, has come under attack recently, despite companies using its methods for more than 50 years. In particular, some critics believe that job evaluation is an anachronism because traditional systems fail to adapt to the rapidly changing nature of work. These same opponents propose to abandon traditional job evaluation systems and instead, focus solely on market pricing to determine wages and salaries.

A better solution to this criticism of traditional job evaluation would be to:

- Review what has been learned about traditional job evaluation over the years.
- Assess whether all or some components of job evaluation should be abandoned by organizations.

- Show how the traditional methods might have relevance under certain circumstances, while more contemporary approaches might be used under other circumstances.

This article's objective[1] is to show that the wholesale abandonment of job evaluation is not warranted and that the concept of job evaluation needs to be broadened to work evaluation. The concept of work evaluation, rather than job evaluation allows us to draw upon the strengths and discard the weaknesses of traditional job evaluation, while accommodating the changing nature of work faced by organizations.

To accomplish this objective, this article will:

- Summarize and review 200-plus articles[2] on job and work evaluation.
- Present a view of leading company practices and thought leaders.
- Draw conclusions regarding the future need to move from job to work evaluation.

LITERATURE REVIEW

It is now common practice to debate the usefulness of job evaluation to contemporary organizations. Missing from the debates, however, are the many studies on job evaluation that have been conducted over the years.

The broader term "work," rather than "job," allows for the evaluation of roles, competencies, and teams. Figure 1 offers a summary of findings on job evaluation and indicates that current job evaluation approaches need to be broadened to adapt to the changing nature of work in organizations.

Processes
- It is very difficult to accurately group jobs into aggregate levels for job evaluation purposes
- Gender bias does not appear to be a problem in job evaluation
- Rating errors exist in job evaluation as well as performance evaluation
- Training can eliminate rating errors in job evaluation
- Labor market indicators (e.g., salary levels) influence job evaluation scores
- A variety of support systems are needed for job evaluation to be effective
- Large numbers of evaluators (e.g., 360 degree reviews) are not needed for accurate job evaluation ratings

Figure 1.   Summary of major findings from the literature review.

- A small number of factors (3-5) works as well as a large number of factors
- Rational weights for factors are probably as good as statistical weights in most situations
- Power and politics influence job evaluation ratings

Outcomes
- Point-factor systems are very reliable
- Total point values are more reliable than point values for each factor
- The validity of work evaluation systems is not well known
- The affective reactions of people to work evaluation systems is not well known
- Competency pay is not used very often
- Skill-based pay works well under certain conditions
- Most work evaluation systems have not been evaluated

Figure 1. Summary of major findings from the literature review (Continued).

LEADING COMPANY WORK EVALUATION CHANGES

Table 1 demonstrates a survey of changes in company work evaluation practices. Consistent with the observations of thought leaders, point-factor systems continue to exist, but are being replaced in many cases. One company has used a point-factor system for 40-plus years; it communicates to employees the company's culture and its unions are very comfortable with this approach. But for some companies and thought leaders, point-factor systems are burdensome to administer and are disliked by managers because they are perceived as an administrative control system.

Replacement systems most often include market pricing and classification systems. Market pricing is viewed as a business strategy to ensure that the "best and brightest" are attracted and retained. Classification is viewed as a business strategy to minimize the "cost of doing business" because it is a less cumbersome system to administer. Also, classification systems work well when it is easy to classify jobs (i.e., the job sets are homogeneous) and the business environment is too unstable to match factors to the constantly changing business strategy. A problem noted with classification systems is that internal equity issues arise when standards used to classify jobs are not clearly defined and consistent across jobs and business units.

Table 1.   Summary of Leading Company Work Evaluation Methods

Company	Previous Work Evaluation	Current Work Evaluation	Reason for Change
Auto Manufacturer	Point-factor system	Point-factor system	No change, system in place for 40 years, part of labor-management culture
Chip Manufacturer	Classification	Classification	No change, classification works well for constantly changing business environment and homogenous job sets
High Technology Conglomerate	Point-factor system	Classification	Point-factor system too cumbersome to administer
Services and Manufacturing Conglomerate	Point-factor system	Classification	Point-factor system places too much control over managerial decision-making.
Computer Services and Manufacturer	Point-factor system	Market Pricing	Need to attract and retain best people

THOUGHT-LEADER PERSPECTIVES

Total Pay

Less elaborate methods of work evaluation are being used because base pay is being de-emphasized in the total pay package, according to one thought leader. That is, organizations are attempting to accomplish their compensation goals by increasing the amount of variable pay while decreasing the amount of base pay.

The irony is that the de-emphasis on work evaluation also impacts variable pay. The amount of variable pay granted by most organizations is determined by the base pay level of the person; employees with higher base pay levels usually receive a larger amount of variable pay than employees with lower base pay levels. Hence, work evaluation issues influence not only base pay, but variable pay. Often this point is overlooked. Because variable pay, in addition to base pay and benefits are dependent upon work evaluation, one might argue that *more*, not less elaborate and costly work evaluation systems should be used. Contrary to this argument, most companies are placing less rather than more emphasis on work evaluation, as more emphasis is placed on variable pay than base pay.

Competencies

All of the thought leaders interviewed agreed on the limited role that competencies should play in compensation decision-making. Competencies should only be used in two situations. First, they should be used as performance standards to determine pay increases for exempt employees. However, in doing so, the accomplishment of results should be weighted more heavily than competency mastery. Second, competencies can be used for skill-based pay plans in manufacturing plants with well-defined skill sets. Other than these two situations, competencies for pay should not be used because of the resources needed to develop sound evaluation standards and the difficulty of pricing the value of competencies on the external market for jobs.

These conclusions reached by the thought leaders are remarkable for two reasons. First, there was a consensus of opinion. Second, many of these experts were in a position where they could generate considerable personal income if competency-based pay systems were used more often by companies.

Broadbanding

A critical point raised by one thought leader is the fact that broadbanding is not a work evaluation method. It is instead a pay structure development method. Broadbanding is a complement to, not a substitute for work evaluation. Work evaluation is used to determine which jobs and people belong in which bands. Work evaluation, not broadbanding makes this determination.

For broadbanding to be effective, it must be coupled with career management systems. Promotions are valued by employees and it is very difficult to develop a substitute for promotions. As a result, broad bands may become less broad. Microsoft, for example, recently added bands to its pay system. While most companies are reducing the number of bands, in time, the amount of pay band reduction by broadbanding may be reversed.

Market Pricing

All of the thought leaders agreed that there is a very large movement by companies to place more emphasis on the value of work as determined by the market, and less emphasis on the value of work as determined by work evaluation. Some thought-leaders saw this as a positive step because it resulted in less emphasis on work evaluation systems viewed as too rigid to meet the fluid nature of today's organizations. All agreed that because of technology, there is an unprecedented amount of data available on external rates and that this trend is likely to continue. Employees, as well as employers, are increasingly likely to have these external data because they are now being posted by various groups (e.g., employee associations) on the Internet.

Several thought leaders voiced concerned about the accuracy of data available from the external market. Research has clearly shown that there is sample, measurement and evaluator bias in market data (Heneman, 2001). That is, the results that one obtains from a market survey is biased by the sampling procedures used, the measurement instrument used (e.g., job matches) and the person interpreting the data (e.g., supervisor vs. HR analyst). As a result, much care must be taken if "pure" market pricing is to be used without any work evaluation.

Another concern with market pricing viewed by one thought-leader was the "living wage" arguments being voiced again by public opinion groups. In particular, concern is being expressed about the pay differential between the "have" and "have-nots" in our country. To the extent that the market alone drives pay decisions, it may exacerbate the differential and create more negative reactions to pay systems by employees.

Legal Issues

Three legal issues, in particular, concerned the thought leaders. One legal concern has to do with the decreased use of elaborate methods of work evaluation with known reliability and validity properties (e.g., point-factor system). The concern is, that when jobs are grouped together to form bands, these bands are used to determine not only base pay, but incentive pay and benefit levels as well. If these pay levels are challenged by employees, how can they be defended in the absence of reliable and valid methods of grouping jobs? During economic downturns, people realize that:

- Their base pay has been previously reduced over time to grant more variable pay.
- Variable pay no longer is available due to the downturn.
- The base and variable pay level received depends on how the job is classified.

A second issue of concern raised is the Office of Federal Contract Compliance Program (OFCCP) concern about "comparable worth," the "glass ceiling," and "pay equity." The OFCCP has begun to audit pay systems of firms in terms of pay equity for minorities and women. This trend is likely to continue, but only by the OFCCP and at the state levels because there is no national comparable worth act. One thought leader believes that those firms facing challenge by the OFCCP are much more likely to be able to defend their pay decisions to the extent that they have a validated work evaluation system.

Another legal concern is the need to develop new methods of validation procedures for work evaluation systems. Traditional methods of validity assessment take a considerable amount of time. Given the turbulent business environments faced by many organizations, by the time the work evaluation systems is validated, it is sometimes obsolete because the business place has changed in response to the changing business market. One possibility suggested is that there needs to be a new form of validation, "future-state," to supplement the traditional forms of validity (content, criterion-related, and construct). With this approach, the standards developed for work evaluation are evaluated relative to a future state of the company (e.g., strategic plan).

Pay Plan Design and Administration

Two issues arise in the development and administration of pay plans that are likely to be more salient in the future. First, companies are providing for much more participation by employees and managers in pay plan design and administration. This is especially true of work evaluation. Decisions made about the value of work are increasingly being made by managers rather than the HR department. Work descriptions used to make work evaluation decisions are increasingly being made by the employee instead of HR. By involving managers and employees in the process, there is a greater sense of ownership to the system by the affected parties, as well as a greater willingness by the affected parties to commit to the work evaluation decisions made.

Second, as technology becomes increasingly sophisticated in human resources, it will become possible to design pay systems around the individual as the unit of analysis rather than collections of individuals, (e.g., jobs, occupations) as the unit of analysis. This approach will place tremendous pressure, especially on larger organizations, to custom design and administer pay plans to the level of the individual. Equity considerations will become particularly salient to employees under these types of arrangement.

Figure 2 is a summary of likely future trends based on the author's extrapolation of comments received by company representatives and thought leaders as part of this project.

- Point-factor systems will continue to be used for work evaluation in the old economy companies.
- New economy companies will use classification systems for work evaluation.
- Greater emphasis will be placed on variable pay than base pay is compensation design and administration.
- Broadbanding will be used by all organizations, but in conjunction with career development, and with less broad bands.
- Market pricing will be used by all organizations, most in conjunction with work evaluation.
- Employees will have access to pay data with or without company permission.
- Managers and employees will have more emphasis in pay decisions than HR analysts.
- Compensation packages will eventually be tailor made for each employee rather than groups of employees.
- A lack of attention to measurement issues in pay system decisions, especially work evaluation, will result in many legal challenges by employees when the economy turns down and pay increase levels are reduced.
- New forms of "validation" will need to be developed for pay system decisions to supplement traditional validation designs.

Figure 2.   Summary of future trends by thought leaders.

CONCLUSION

The current controversy surrounding job evaluation is very healthy for the compensation profession. It forces us to reexamine traditional job evaluation practices. As asserted in this article, traditional job evaluation practices should not be abandoned, but instead refined, expanded upon, and used appropriately. Overall, "work" needs to be viewed more broadly than a "job." The phrase "work evaluation" is more appropriate than "job evaluation" because work not only includes jobs, but people, competencies, and roles performed by individuals or teams.

It seems premature to abandon work evaluation in favor of strict market pricing given the legal concerns about not having work evaluation systems found in literature, company practice, and/or subject matter expert material. Moreover, work evaluation data can be perceived as an instrumental tool in verifying market data and supporting business strategies.

ACKNOWLEDGMENT

Special thanks to the company representatives and thought leaders that spoke with me.

NOTES

1.   The research underlying this article was commissioned by the U.S. Office of Personnel Management (OPM), as part of its comprehensive review of job and work evaluation. OPM's Office of Performance and Compensation Systems Design has undertaken that review as part of a larger effort to determine ways in which the federal government's compensation systems can be improved. The views presented here are those of the author and do not necessarily reflect the views of the U.S. government in general or the Office of Personnel Management in particular.

2.   A list of the 200 articles is available upon request from the author as well as a lengthier literature review.

REFERENCES

Heneman, R. (2001). *Business-driven compensation policies: Integrating compensation systems with corporate strategies.* New York: AMACOM.

Murlis, H., & Fitt, D. (1991, Spring). Job evaluation in a changing world. *Personnel Management,* 4–20.

Rynes, S., & Milkovich, G. (1986). Wage surveys: Dispelling some myths about the market wage. *Personnel Psychology, 39,* 71–90.

.

Part VI

TEAM PAY

The focus of this part of the book is a particular type of strategic reward program known as team pay. The intent of the readings in this section was to further develop the theory of team pay so that it might be more effectively implemented in organizations. In particular, it is shown how team pay may need to vary as teams develop over time from novice to advanced teams. Also, it is argued that teamwork as a performance measure can be used in organizations *without* formal, intact work teams. In many organizations, team pay is in its infancy and may require further development before it is more widely used.

Heneman, R.L., & von Hippel, C. (1995). Balancing group and individual rewards: Rewarding individual contributions to the team. *Compensation and Benefits Review, 25*(4), 63–68.

Heneman, R.L., Dixon, K.E., & Gresham, M.T. (2000). Team pay for novice, intermediate, and advanced teams. In M.A. Byerlein, D.A. Johnson, S. Byerlein (Eds.), *Advances in interdisciplinary work teams* (Vol. 7). Greenwich, CT: JAI Press.

CHAPTER 15

BALANCING GROUP AND INDIVIDUAL REWARDS:

Rewarding Individual Contributions to the Team

Robert L. Heneman and Courtney Von Hippel

Source: Heneman, R.L. and von Hippel, C. *Compensation and Benefits Review,* 25(4), pp. 63–68., copyright © 1995 by Sage Publications, Inc. Reprinted by permission of Sage Publications, Inc.

> *Through instituting team-based merit pay, traditional organizations can move closer to the new pay, and innovative organizations can foster the development of skilled team players.*

Workplace redesign continues to shift emphasis away from individual performance, placing greater importance on the role of teams and work groups. To support this new emphasis, many organizations have designed group-based reward systems, such as team-based pay, gainsharing, and goal sharing, to reward employees for a group's success in contributing to the organization's strategy. While various studies have documented the effectiveness of these plans, issues still remain on how best to use them. One such issue centers on whether the organization's pay systems support alignment between individual behaviors and group goals or frustrate group cohesiveness.

GROUP AND INDIVIDUAL GOALS

Group-based reward plans measure group performance and reward individuals on the basis of how well the group performs. This approach generally proves to be very functional, directing group members' efforts toward common goals consistent with the organization's strategies and critical success factors. Unfortunately, group-based plans may also create the opportunity for low-performing employees to earn the same reward as high performers. Troublesome issues of inequity come into play.

Social loafing occurs when employees withdraw their individual efforts, in the hopes that other group members will ensure the group meets its goals. The dysfunctional behavior of these "free riders," as K.L. Bettenhausen (1991) called them, adversely affects the organization's strategy because group goals typically require maximum effort from all employees, not just a few. Moreover, high performers may withdraw their group efforts because the group-based pay plans do not recognize their individual accomplishments relative to the free riders. Another reason some employees may withdraw their efforts is because they feel their individual contributions do not really affect the group's performance. Thus, why bother exerting much effort when the costs of contributing outweigh the benefits?

Peer pressure may resolve some of the problems with free riders. For example, other group members may exert social pressure on the free riders to improve their performance, so that the group can accomplish its goals more easily. However, peer pressure may also create animosity and other problems that limit group effectiveness. Animosity works against the supportive culture that groups need to operate effectively.

REWARDING INDIVIDUAL CONTRIBUTIONS

Providing both group and individual rewards creates a more viable solution for the free rider problem than peer pressure. This approach rewards employees for behaviors consistent with the norms of the team, rather than punishing employees for not conforming to those norms. Such an approach requires the organization to use team-based merit pay—which rewards individual contributions to the team—either alone or in conjunction with the group-based rewards.

Compared to traditional merit pay plans, with pay increases based on the individual's contribution to the organization (individual quality and quantity measures), team-based merit pay provides rewards on the basis of individual contributions to the team (Heneman, 1992)). Critics of traditional merit pay plans charge that they decrease cooperation among group members because they reinforce the accomplishment of individual goals at the expense of group goals. Group-based merit pay plans overcome this criticism by directly rewarding individuals for their contributions to the group, including their cooperation with other group members.

The pay plan at Johnsonville Foods, Inc. illustrates how a team-based merit pay plan works. This organization makes teamwork an important standard for the determination of merit increases. Team leaders and associates rate each associate's contribution to team goals, communication effectiveness with other team members, willingness to work with other team members, and attendance and timeliness at team meetings (Stayer, 1990).

Supporting this example from Johnsonville Foods, Inc., Figure 1 summarizes the critical competencies required of group members for effective group functioning, identified through years of research (Katzenbach & Smith, 1993; Stevens & Campion, 1994). These competencies have many similarities to those needed in self-directed work teams. Roles traditionally played by the supervisor (planning, task coordination, etc.) now belong to members of the group. However, simply setting group goals does not ensure that individuals will have the knowledge or willingness to perform these critical roles. Too often in a workplace redesign, organizations assign employees to "teams," but the employees have little knowledge of what constitutes a good team player. To ensure that group members perform their roles, the organization must specify the roles and train employees in these competencies, so they know what is expected of them. The organization also must provide appropriate rewards.

- Dedication to a common purpose
- Sense of mutual accountability
- Mutual respect and support
- Technical and functional expertise
- Collaborative problem-solving skills
- Interpersonal skills
- Cooperation
- Trust-based relationships
- Conflict resolution
- Communications
- Goal setting and performance management
- Planning and task coordination

Figure 1.   Individual competencies critical to effective team functioning.

DEVELOPING A TEAM-BASED MERIT PAY PLAN

A three-step process—illustrated in Figure 2—can help an organization establish a team-based merit pay plan to reward individual contributions to the team. The steps are summarized below:

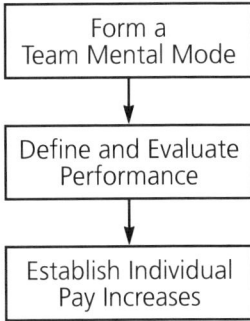

Figure 2.   Steps to develop a team-based merit pay plan.

Form a Team Mental Model

A team mental model—a shared set of values and beliefs held by group members regarding the effective operation of the group (Klimoski & Mohammed, 1994)—outlines how group members should operate in order to accomplish group goals. Implicit in the functioning of the group, although rarely even spoken about, the shared understanding underlying team mental models needs to be documented in order to work effectively to link individual behaviors to group goals. Through the documentation process, the group can discuss and validate their beliefs. Figure 3 presents examples of written team mental models.

> - We are committed as individual team members to putting the goals of the team before our own personal interests by openly sharing information, actively airing our differences, supporting one another, and making decisions on the basis of consensus.
> - We believe that it is an honor to be a team member and, out of respect for our fellow team members, we pledge to provide support to one another, resolve our differences through mutual problem-solving, and seek out the

Figure 3.   Examples of team mental models.

opinions of other group members before taking action.
- In order to meet our production goals as a team, we agree that as individual team members we will initiate action when required, take full responsibility for the accomplishment of goals, and encourage a free exchange of ideas in a non-threatening environment.

Figure 3. Examples of team mental models (Continued).

A variety of factors, including those shown in Figure 4, can influence the formation of team mental models. In order for team mental models to contribute to the goals of the organization, they must align with its overall strategic business plan and critical success factors. For example, the team mental model may not include decision making by consensus if an organization needs speed in bringing a new service to market. On the other hand, if the organization competes in the service market on the basis of quality decisions, the importance of consensus to the team mental model increases.

The capabilities of the group greatly influence the development of a team mental model. To function effectively as a group, the individual members need to have the knowledge, skills, and abilities to fulfill the required behaviors in the team mental model. In forming the team mental model, therefore, team members need to realistically assess the strengths and weaknesses of the current team. The model then serves as a blueprint to guide the team in the training and selection of members.

Length of group membership also influences the formation of a team mental model. The model for an intact work team, for example, may include specific language addressing the need to overcome obstacles that have historically hindered the effectiveness of the team. On the other hand, newly formed teams in a start-up operation may establish a set of general principles until each team has a history to draw upon.

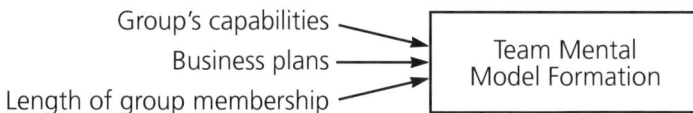

Group's capabilities
Business plans → Team Mental Model Formation
Length of group membership

Figure 4. Factors influencing team mental models.

Define and Evaluate Performance

After establishing a team mental model, the next step in developing a team-based merit pay plan is to define individual performance consistent with the team mental model. By defining performance using behavioral standards, team members can make the link between what they do on a day-by-day basis and what the team mental model requires.

To help specify the desired behaviors, for example, members would extract key phrases or themes from the team mental model. For example, one key phrase in the first model in Figure 3 points to the value that the team places on "supporting one another."

Then, for each key phrase or theme extracted, members would write behavioral statements defining the phrase or theme in terms of day-to-day operations (Latham & Wexley, 1994). Figure 5 shows examples of behavioral statements defining "supporting one another," along with a scale that

---

1. Encourage team members to make suggestions

Almost never	Seldom	Sometimes	Frequently	Almost always
0	1	2	3	4

2. Mediates team member conflicts

Almost never	Seldom	Sometimes	Frequently	Almost always
0	1	2	3	4

3. Praises team members for valuable ideas

Almost never	Seldom	Sometimes	Frequently	Almost always
0	1	2	3	4

4. Makes self available for consultation with other group members

Almost never	Seldom	Sometimes	Frequently	Almost always
0	1	2	3	4

5. Helps other team members when own work is completed

Almost never	Seldom	Sometimes	Frequently	Almost always
0	1	2	3	4

Figure 5.   Behavioral items for "Supporting One Another" dimension of a team mental model.

will help the job incumbent, supervisor, and peers assess the extent to which each team member makes that specific contribution to the team.

Team members should participate in the process of defining team-oriented performance. By participating, they gain a better understanding of the process and a sense of "ownership," which in turn makes them more committed to meeting the behavioral standards of the team mental model. If it is necessary to create standards across teams for purposes of fairness, team members can elect a member or two from each team to serve on a task force charged with defining behavioral standards consistent with team mental models.

Multiple evaluators will prove valuable for assessing actual contributions using these standards. For example, job incumbents should rate themselves for developmental purposes. By comparing those self-ratings to other ratings, they can assess whether they have a firm understanding of the team mental model. Team-leaders should rate contributions also, since they may have an advanced understanding of the team process based on previous experience, and because they are ultimately accountable for the team's success or failure. Peers should participate in the rating process since they may have much more day-to-day contact with the job incumbent than the team leader. In addition, peers "own" the team mental model and, therefore, should have responsibility for its administration. Multiple evaluators, rather than a single source, will provide a more accurate and complete picture of actual performance, enhancing the validity of the evaluations. Any single source, in contrast, may bring biases to the evaluations and provide an incomplete picture of the job incumbent's relevant performance as a team member.

When using multiple sources, the team leaders should coordinate the process by gathering the ratings, weighting the information, and providing feedback, including pay increase decisions, to the job incumbent. The team leader can eliminate ratings and comments that have no bearing on the team mental model. The leader can also meet with other team members to reconcile inconsistent ratings. The team leader should weight the ratings by two important factors: knowledge and opportunity to observe. Thus, they should give more weight to ratings assigned by individuals with a better understanding of the team mental model and more opportunity to see the job incumbent perform. So, for example, the leader gives more weight to ratings from a peer who has hour-by-hour contact with the incumbent and less weight to self-ratings from a job incumbent new to the job who may have little knowledge about the team mental model. To remove personalities from negative feedback, the supervisor can summarize ratings and keep them anonymous.

Establish Individual Pay Increases

The final step in implementing team-based merit pay is to provide pay increases to those individuals who contribute the most to the team. There are several approaches to this:

- Perhaps the most straightforward approach to establishing individual pay increases treats teamwork as one criterion for determining rewards in a traditional merit pay plan. That is, pay will be allocated on the basis of traditional performance measures, such as quality and quantity of performance, along with more innovative measures of performance based on team mental models. This approach may work best in organizations with traditional pay practices (see Lawler, "*The New Pay: A Strategic Approach*," in this issue). Using team-based merit pay can serve as a transition toward the new pay based on employee empowerment. Team-based increases, developed by and evaluated with the help of employees, supplement the pay increases based on traditional top-down ratings.
- Another approach couples team-based merit pay increases with group-based pay plans such as gainsharing and goal sharing. With this approach, organizations reward the achievement of both group and individual goals because both sets of goals contribute to the overall goals of the organization. This approach works well in organizations that already have these forms of new pay in place but have concerns about the free rider issue and want to further reinforce teamwork by rewarding individual contributions to the team.

This approach has a potential downside: it may add to total payroll costs in the form of direct costs (team-based merit increases) and indirect costs (development of team mental models and measures). Organizations can allay such cost concerns in two ways. First, they can make the group-based plan a funding gate. If the group meets goals such as labor cost reductions, then the organization rewards team members for these accomplishments on the basis of team-based merit. Second, by marginally reducing the amount of rewards allocated to team members for the accomplishment of group goals, the organization can use the excess to fund a separate account for team-based merit awards.

CONCLUSION

Some leaders assume that the use of group-based pay plans automatically leads to improved teamwork among team members in the form of cooperation, collegiality, and the like. Unfortunately, group-based pay plans sometimes create the opportunity for social loafing and a place for free riders to hide. These unintended consequences can lead to friction in the group, as members attempt to manage one another through peer pressure and other social sanctions. Providing rewards for individual contributions to the team addresses this problem by increasing motivation for improved teamwork among all team members.

The use of team-based merit pay to recognize individual contributions to the team helps create a better balance between group and individual goal accomplishment. Effective teamwork develops under team-based merit pay with the use of team mental models, but it also requires the development of valid measures of the individual's contribution to the team. In turn, developing valid measures requires participation by employees in setting standards as well as the use of multiple rating sources. Through instituting team-based merit pay, traditional organizations can move closer to the new pay, and innovative organizations can foster the development of skilled team players.

REFERENCES

Bettenhausen, K.L. (1991). Five years of group research: What we have learned and what needs to be addressed. *Journal of Management, 17,* 345–381.

Heneman, R.L. (1992). *Merit pay: Linking pay increases to performance ratings.* Reading, MA: Addison-Wesley.

Katzenbach, J.R., & Smith, D.K. (1993). *The wisdom of teams.* New York: Harper-Collins.

Klimoski, R., & Mohammed, S. (1994). Team mental model: Construct or metaphor? *Journal of Management, 20,* 403–437.

Latham, L.P., & Wexley, K.N. (1994). *Increasing productivity through performance appraisal* (2nd ed.). Reading, MA: Addison-Wesley.

Stayer, R. (1990). How I learned to let my workers lead. *Harvard Business Review, 68*(6), 65–72.

Stevens, M.J., & Campion, M.A. (1994). The knowledge, skill, and ability requirements for teamwork: Implications for human resource management. *Journal of Management, 20,* 503–530.

CHAPTER 16

TEAM PAY FOR NOVICE, INTERMEDIATE, AND ADVANCED TEAMS

Robert L. Heneman, Katherine E. Dixon, and Maria T. Gresham

Source: Reprinted from Heneman, R.L., Dixon, K.E., & Gresham, M.T. (2000). Team Pay for Novice, Intermediate, and Advanced Teams. In M.A. Byerlein, D.A. Johnson, & S. Byerlein (Eds.), *Advances in Interdisciplinary Work Teams* (Vol. 7). Greenwich, CT: JAI Press with permission from Elsevier Science.

ABSTRACT

There is no one best type of team pay plan. In order for team pay plans to be effective, they must be carefully matched to the development stage of the team. To further develop this argument, a three-stage model of team pay is advanced (novice, intermediate, and advanced), and each stage is defined by several dimensions (strategic focus, individualism/collectivism, team composition, plan owner/developer, and autonomy). Furthermore, the dimensions used to differentiate between various types of team pay plans are articulated (measures, measurement levels, evaluators, and pay form). The general hypothesis advanced is that team effectiveness is better explained by the interaction of team development stage and type of pay plan, than by the main effect for type of team pay plan alone. A case study of a Fortune 500 company is used to illustrate the importance of different types of team pay at different stages of team development. Implications for theory, research, and practice are discussed.

INTRODUCTION

Several authors have argued that in order for teams to perform effectively, team pay plans need to vary as a function of the type of team (e.g., Gross, 1995; Wageman, 1995). Intact work teams, for example, have different characteristics than product development teams which in turn necessitates a different type of reward system for intact work teams than for product development teams (Janz, Colquitt, & Noe, 1997). Overlooked in the pay and organizational development literature, however, is the need for team pay plans to vary as a function of the stage of development of work teams in organizations. In particular, attraction, retention, and motivation issues are different in advanced as compared to newly created teams (Gersick, 1988). Team pay systems must evolve to match the maturity level of the team in order to successfully attract, retain, and motivate team members.

In a recent review of team-based rewards, DeMatteo, Eby, and Sundstrom (1998) comment on the lack of theory development and research with regard to team pay and the stage of team development:

> In sum, team-based rewards may only be effective to the extent that they can be tailored to address changing needs at different development stages. Unfortunately, most research on group incentives has not examined the effects of the stage of group development. While current research does not indicate the extent to which group development gives rise to shifts in the responses of team members, it may be wise to assume that an incentive system well suited for a newly formed team may not be optimal for a mature team. (p. 163)

In response to this underdeveloped line of inquiry, our first objective is to contribute to the literature on advanced teams by developing a model on how teams develop over time and in turn, which types of pay systems are appropriate at each stage. This model is grounded in previous research which shows that team member preferences for different types of pay systems varies as a function of the stage of team development (DeMatteo et al., 1998), and that pay systems should vary as a function of the life cycle of the organization in order to be associated with organizational effectiveness (Balkin & Gomez-Mejia, 1987).

Our second objective is to add to the literature on advanced teams by providing a case study of a Fortune 500 company that has used teams for 18 years to illustrate the utility of the models presented for organizations. This company provides a unique opportunity to provide a longitudinal, qualitative assessment of the model because teams have been used for such a long period of time. Current case study research on teams and team pay (Tonkin & Ellis, 1997) primarily examine how team pay is provided at one point in time, and because most of theses teams are relatively new, they do not address team pay for the advanced team. The models we present can be used by organizations to develop reward systems that will support the advancement of teams as shown in the case.

In order to accomplish these two objectives, first we provide a brief review of stage models of group development followed by our own stage model. Second, we provide a brief review of team pay systems followed by our model of the characteristics of team pay needed at each stage of our stage model. Finally, we illustrate both of our models with a case study.

TEAM DEVELOPMENT STAGES

There have been many attempts to define phases of group development, however Tuckman (1965) reviewed many of these, and he pointed out the similarity of the various analyses. He concluded that four phases, which he called forming, storming, norming, and performing, could describe the typical sequence of group development. In the forming phase, groups are concerned with orientation through testing, which serves to define both interpersonal and task behaviors. Essentially members are determining what types of behavior are acceptable. This stage is complete when members have begun to think of themselves as part of a group. Storming centers around conflict and polarization with respect to interpersonal issues, which is also reflected in task behavior. Members accept the existence of the group, but resist the constraints the group imposes on individuality. Further, there is conflict over who will control the group. The third stage, norming, is reached when the group begins to resolve conflicts and establish new standards, and roles, cohesiveness, and in-group feelings. Finally, the performing stage is one in which the interpersonal structure serves the achievement of group goals. Roles are flexible and energy is devoted to task activities. Group energy has moved from getting to know and understand to performing the tasks at hand. Researchers such as Heinen and Jacobson (1976) and Tuckman and Jensen (1977) concurred, but also added a final stage: adjourning for teams those that are temporary, or have limited tasks to perform. Other examinations of stages of development have shown results that can be interpreted as partially supporting, or at least not disconfirming, the modified Tuckman five stage model (McGrath & O'Connor, 1996).

One interesting application of the Tuckman (1965) model to team pay has taken place at Motorola (Gedvilas, 1997). At Motorola, team development is conceptualized as a four-stage process similar to Tuckman's. At stage one, starting, skill-based pay and gainsharing is provided to give direction to the team. At stage two, establishing itself, and stage three, performing the task, emphasis is placed on non-cash awards and celebrations to provide support and recognition for the team. At stage four, ending, individual and team based merit pay is provided to celebrate the end of the project.

Many interpreters of the five-stage model have assumed a group becomes more effective as it progresses throughout the first four stages. While this is generally true, what makes a group effective is more complex than the model acknowledges. Other studies have confirmed that groups do not develop in a universal sequence of stages, but the timing of when groups form and change the way they work is highly consistent.

For example, Gersick (1988) studied the life spans of eight naturally occurring teams. Her research indicates that those groups' attention to time and pacing is an important catalyst of progress through creative projects. Specifically, she found that the first meeting sets the groups' direction, and the first phase of group activity is one of inertia. That is, once a group determines its direction, it tends to stand still or become locked into a fixed course of action. Even if it gains new insights that challenge the initial patterns and assumptions, the group is incapable of acting on these new insights. A transition takes place at the end of the first phase, which occurs exactly when the group has used up half its allotted time. As a result, the transition initiates major changes. This transition ends phase one and is characterized by concentrated burst of changes, dropping of old patterns, and adoption of new perspectives used to revise the direction for phase two. However, a second phase of inertia follows the transition and the group's last meeting is characterized by markedly accelerated activity.

In summary, the punctuated equilibrium model characterizes groups as exhibiting long periods of inertia interspersed with brief revolutionary changes triggered primarily by their members' awareness of time and deadlines. Gersick's model suggests that uncertain and shifting deadlines for interdependent organizational units and synchrony in group members' expectations about deadlines may be critical to the groups' ability to accomplish successful transitions in their work. She further argued that environmental events might be especially powerful at the very beginning and midpoint of the groups' life span.

Gersick's (1988) model presents a new model of viewing group development, which is beneficial for organizations. However, it does have an important shortcoming. Similar to the five-stage model, Gersick's model fails to address organizational factors—such as the compensation system—which may impact the effectiveness of the group. Pay is one of many support systems critical to the effective functioning of the team (Mohrman, Cohen, & Mohrman, 1995). As groups develop over time, members may respond differently to group bonuses. For example, members of new groups may be satisfied with an incentive system that provides an equal distribution of rewards. As groups mature, however, members may notice differential contributions by individuals within the group and may want differential allocation of group rewards to reflect those contributions. In effect, group development may bring rise to a norm shift in the group from one of equality to one of equity (DeMatteo, Eby, & Sundstrum, 1998). Thus, while groups become more effective over time, they may only be effective to the extent that they can be tailored to address changing needs at different developmental stages. Issues of pay, along with the time and deadline variables mentioned by Gersick (1988), may also trigger revolutionary changes in the stage of group development.

A THREE-STAGE DEVELOPMENT MODEL

Table 1 presents a stage model of group development. Each of the three stages (novice, intermediate, advanced) is described using a typology of teams adapted from DeMatteo et al. (1998). Each stage is discussed below. We will discuss the developmental stages of teams using the following dimensions: Strategic focus, individualism/collectivism, team composition, leadership, plan owner/developer, and autonomy. Strategic focus is the goal or mission of the team. Individualism/collectivism is the likelihood that team members will operate dependently rather than as independent members. Team composition goes to the size of the group and its relative homogeneity or heterogeneity. Leadership is the style and source of leadership that the team uses. Plan owner/developer is the group responsible for developing, administering, and revising the plans associated with the team (e.g., goal setting, performance, and compensation plans). Sources of leadership include appointed supervisors, elected or appointed team leaders, outside facilitators, or regular team members on a rotating basis. Autonomy is the degree of freedom to act that senior management gives the team in its ability to make decisions on its mission, performance assessment, and rewards.

Table 1.   Team Development Stages

Dimension	Developmental Stage		
Strategic Focus	Novice	Intermediate	Advanced
Individualism/	Process	Tasks, Goals	Innovation
Collectivism	Individualistic	Individualistic/ Collectivistic	Collectivistic
Team Composition	Large, Homogeneous	Medium, Moderately Heterogeneous	Small, Highly Heterogeneous
Leadership	Formal, Autocratic	Consultative	Ad hoc, Egalitarian
Plan Owner/ Developer	Management	Management with Team input	Team with Management Oversight
Autonomy	Low	Medium	High

Novice Teams

In novice teams, team development has just begun. Group norms, values, and expectations are not yet determined. As a result, individuals operating within the group are still focused on individual needs, since, at this stage individual team members tend to evaluate how team activities and goals impact individual needs and expectations. Thus, team members tend to be more individualistic in their thoughts and actions. In situations where there is team conflict, personal interests supersede any team objectives in the individualism situation. Wagner (1995) refers to this notion as individualism collectivism—a construct that explains the level of cooperation among team members. Wagner and Moch (1986) define individualism as the condition in which personal interests are accorded greater importance than are the needs of groups. As a result, personal goals have priority over group goals in individualism, but they are subordinated to the collective goals in collectivism (Triandis, 1995). While members accept the existence of the group, they resist the constraints the group imposes on individuality. As a result, group cooperation is minimal at best. Thus, at this stage it is expected that individualism for each team member is at its highest.

In novice teams, members lack objective information that can be used to make inferences about team members in terms of shared interests, goals, values, and skill sets. Research from both organizational behavior (Schneider, 1987) and social psychology (Newcomb, 1961) supports the idea that group members base initial categorization of other group members on surface level diversity, such as race, gender, ethnicity and disability. Initial categorizations are accompanied by perceptions of similarity or dissimilarity. Thus, surface level characteristics are critical for novice teams. Novice teams, lacking great detail concerning teammates, rely on these initial categorizations for the deeper level information needed to make judgments about similarity of attitudes among group members.

Novice teams, most often seen in organizations where teams are new, are those in their earliest stage of development. The novice team is characterized by a strategic focus on establishing team processes. Because the team is new, its members must build a model for behavior and ask itself, either formally or informally, how to accomplish its tasks. The novice team is, in many ways, a collection of individuals. These teams have low levels of task interdependence since their members are learning the functions and abilities of the other team members and are inefficient at using the resources of the team across functional lines. Novice teams are typically larger and have more single-function members than more mature teams, again since they are relatively unfamiliar with other team member functions and team processes. Due to the inexperience of these teams, they often adopt an autocratic leadership style with the designated team leader or outside manager making decisions for the team. Management keeps tight controls on novice teams and allows minimal autonomy in determining performance goals, assessment, or rewards.

Intermediate Teams

As the team develops and moves to the intermediate stage, team goals, values, and expectations are formed. Teams become more task oriented. Group effort is directed toward accomplishing the established objectives. It is during this time period when individuals realize *how much* effort is required. Team members attune to factors such as group size, task type, and the degree of shared responsibility to determine their level of effort (Wagner, 1995). Thus, it is during this stage that the group becomes diverse in individual efforts. More individualistic members may decide to *free ride*. That is, these individuals may choose to avoid cooperating in the pursuit of rewards to be shared by the members of a group, but expect to obtain personal benefit from those rewards, acquired through other's efforts. This decision is a result of perceived low shared responsibility, and low ability to identify individual effort in the task. In spite of such circumstance, other individuals may choose to cooperate. Those team members who are collectivists fully identify with team values, norms and expectations, and give group well-being priority over individual goals.

Intermediate teams, having increased their level of interpersonal interaction, have a deeper understanding of team members. Researchers such as Stangor, Lynch, Duan, and Glass (1992) and Harrison, Price, and Bell (1998) argue that over time these perceptions change when deep level information is obtained. Over time, as people acquire more information, their perceptions are based more on observed behavior and less on stereotypes prompted by overt characteristics (Miliken & Martins, 1996). As a result, knowledge of attitudinal, belief, and value similarity between individuals form the basis for continued attraction and affiliation. Time provides the opportunity to acquire interpersonal information and the amount of information acquired is a function of the length of shared experience for group members (Harrison et al., 1998).

Intermediate teams have mastered the rudiments of team processes and are focused on meeting specific customer or business goals with a strong task orientation. Intermediate team members are more comfortable with team processes, and they are more aware of the functions and abilities of other members of the team. Because team members are able to understand more fully the interdependence of the different functions within the team, they are able to identify redundancies within the team and become more multifunctional. This allows the teams to reduce the number of members and increase team efficiency. Leadership in intermediate teams is more team-oriented with ad hoc functional leadership arising conjointly with formal leadership and many decisions made using a team vote process. These teams are able to operate more autonomously than novice teams as their efficiency increases and the organization's experience with teams is expanded. These teams may assist in the development of their performance goals, the assessment of those goals, and designing reward plans.

ADVANCED TEAMS

Advanced teams, those teams that have reached the final stage of development, focus less on factors that concern the individual and focus more on continuous improvement of the team and the organization. Collectivism is defined as an orientation toward group interests. Collectivists look out for the well-being of the groups to which they belong, even if such actions require that personal interests be disregarded. During this stage team members determine the needs, and innovations necessary to improve group and organizational effectiveness. As a result, advanced teammates are less diverse in their level of individualism collectivism characteristic. In advanced teams, team members realize that their individual effectiveness stems from the success of the group. As a result, collectivism (and, thus, cooperation) is highest for team members during this stage. This is supported by research by Chen, Chen, and Meindl (1998). These authors argue that reward allocation preferences for collectivists depend on the time frame of the cooperative relationship. When no long-term relationship is expected, collectivists at best, expect equity-based reward allocations. In circumstances where long-term interactions are expected, collectivists are more willing to compromise equity to ensure a harmonious relationship.

Advanced teams, because they have in-depth knowledge of their teammates, rely on information from past work experience, past team performance, current goals, and the knowledge, skills and abilities of team members to make decisions. In short, advanced teams' negative affective outcomes that are based on surface level factors tend to decrease as the amount of time that the group stays together increases (Miliken & Martins, 1996). As a result, team members rely more on objective factors to assess factors such as similarity and individual capability (Harrison et al., 1998).

Advanced teams, already effective at team processes, have moved from a reactive task orientation to the proactive, strategic focus in the areas of innovation, anticipation of customer needs, and continuous improvement. These teams have the minimum number of members required to perform all functions of the team. Because these efficiencies require team members to be more mufti-functional, their interdependence increases dramatically. Team leadership in advanced teams tends to be more informal and to shift from member to member as the functional focus of the team changes. These teams are sometimes allowed a higher degree of autonomy from their management because the teams are well established and are sometimes allowed greater flexibility in order to provide innovative solutions. This autonomy is demonstrated by the ability of advanced teams to not only participate in the design of performance goals, reward plans, and assessment process but also the proactive ownership of these key areas.

TEAM PAY

Different types of team pay systems have been described in a variety of different places. Gross (1995) presents different categories of team pay. Tonkin and Ellis (1997) present different organizational examples of team pay. Although these approaches are interesting and informative, they confound the different components of team pay with one another. As a result of these confounds, it is difficult to recommend different types of team pay for different types of development. A team pay plan such as "team-based merit pay" may have components some of which are applicable in one stage of development and some of which are more applicable in another stage of development. Hence, rather than labeling different types of team pay plans, we instead offer a list of the dimensions of team pay in Table 2 along which team pay plans can vary. We describe each dimension in Table 2 and then show how the levels within each dimension are best suited for the stages of team development in Table 3.

Table 2. Dimensions of Team Pay

Dimension	Level
Measures	• Results, e.g., quantity, sales • Process, e.g., teamwork • Competencies, e.g., interpersonal
Measurement Levels	• Leader • Member • Team
Evaluators	• Customers • Team members • Leaders • Management • Self

Table 2.   Dimensions of Team Pay (Cont.)

Dimension	Level
Pay Form	• Bonus • Pay Increase • Base Pay • Stock • Time-off
Owners	• Management • Business Unity • Team
Developers	• Management • Business Unit • Team

Table 3.   Team Pay Components for Different Stages of Team Development

Dimension	Team Stage		
Measures	Novice Process	Intermediate Results	Advanced Process Results Competencies
Measurement Levels	Leader Team	Team	Team Member
Evaluators	Management Leaders	Team Members Self	Team Members Self Customers
Pay Form	Bonus	Bonus	Bonus Stock Base Pay
Owners	Management	Management Team	Team
Developers	Management Business Unit	Management Business Unit Team	Team

Measures

Organizations measure teams along three basic dimensions: Process, results, and competencies. Process measures focus on the way the team works and include such dimensions as teamwork or team effectiveness. Although important to assess, these measures are difficult to design and, unless they are clearly defined, can be dependent on the discretion of the raters.

Results measures include the majority of measures being used by teams today and include task-oriented, team-specific measures of quantity or quality (e.g., sales figures or time to market). When designed appropriately, these measures can focus the team on specific outputs that are important to the organization.

Competency measures are measures of team and/or individual behavior and reflect organizational values. These measures may include such things as interpersonal skills, technical expertise, or ability to provide creative solutions. Competency measures are more stable over the long term in an organization and need to be reviewed and revised far less frequently than do results measures. The effectiveness of competency measures depends on the organization's ability to communicate those values or competencies well enough to provide a shared understanding among team members and raters.

MEASUREMENT LEVELS

Process, results, and competency measures may be evaluated for differing levels within the team. Performance of the team's leader, the individual members of the team, and the team as a whole may be measured singly or in combination.

Organizations measure team performance based on leader performance when the leader's results have a high impact. For instance, at the novice stage, the competence of the team's leader is more important to team performance than in the advanced stage, when the team is largely self-managed.

When the organization wishes to evaluate individual contributions, it uses the team member level. If the organization feels that contributions differ significantly among team members, using this level affords the organization the ability to reward based on individual performance. This level of measurement is most effective when the individualism of the team is high (novice or intermediate stages).

Measuring the team as a whole is appropriate for those measures achieved by team performance. Team process measures are always best assessed using the team as a whole; however, since the stage of team development determines its relative collectivism, results and competency measures may or may not be appropriate to evaluate using the team dimension in novice or intermediate stages.

Evaluators

Many sources, including management, team leaders, customers, and team members can provide feedback and assessment of team performance measures. Management always provides assessment of teams, whether formal or informal. By allowing funding for team incentive plans or simply allowing teams to exist within the organization, management provides a more passive evaluation of teams. In more formal settings, management evaluates teams directly on their performance.

Team leaders may also provide direct or indirect feedback of team member performance. With direct feedback, team leaders give ratings of individuals or the team; with indirect assessment, their input may be provided to management or another evaluator as anecdotal or supporting information.

Additional evaluations of team or team member performance may be provided by customers or team members. Customers may be either external or internal customers and evaluate the team's delivery of products or services. Team members may rate one another or provide data to another source (team leader or management) on their performance as a team.

Pay Form

Several categories of rewards are discussed in compensation: Base pay, incentive pay, long-term rewards, and benefits. The base pay, or salary category is not typically considered in and of itself in team reward strategy, although it can significantly affect team pay. Most incentive plans target a certain percentage of salary to pay out (depending on performance), so base pay differences among team members can result in markedly differing payouts even when performance remains constant.

Incentive pay is the most commonly used method for rewarding team performance. These incentives are paid in addition to base pay and benefits, and payouts may be in any of several forms including cash, stock, and benefits. Although incentive plans can be designed to incorporate a multitude of corporate goals, plan types typically vary by the evolutionary stage of the team, as illustrated in Table 3.

Long-term incentives include stock options and deferred compensation. Traditionally offered to only the most senior executives in the organization, this form of reward is becoming more prevalent in lower levels of companies. Long-term incentives are particularly attractive in key strategic sections such as product development, engineering, and production—all areas in which team development and incentives are common. In addition to offering stock options or deferred compensation opportunities to these employees, employers are starting to incorporate long-term incentives into a menu of payout choices (instead of cash only) for team incentive plans.

Benefits include health and life insurance, paid time off, and a host of perquisites that varies widely with the type of industry and location of the employer. As team incentive plans grow increasingly sophisticated, they are including choices in the benefits arena (such as paid time off) as payouts for team incentive plans.

TEAM REWARDS FOR TEAM DEVELOPMENT STAGES

The aforementioned dimensions of team reward plans, measures, measurement levels, evaluators, and pay form should reflect the needs appropriate to the team's developmental stage (see Table 3).

Novice Teams

Novice teams, with their strategic focus on team development, need to concentrate on process measures to evaluate their performance. In order to move from the novice stage to the intermediate stage of team development, novice teams must move from an individualistic point of view to a more collective, mufti-functional one. Process measures, with their focus on team development, make the most sense for these groups. Frequently, organizations attempt to artificially accelerate team evolution by using results-oriented measures for novice teams. Unfortunately, since the team must go through the process of development before it can become effective, focus on results at this stage is not appropriate. The novice team is unable to direct itself effectively or assess its own performance, so management and team leaders make the most appropriate performance evaluators. Team rewards at the novice level often take the form of discretionary bonuses based on individual team member results achieved within the team; however, in order to reward team process achievements appropriately, organizations would be well served to base at least a portion of the bonus on team development. Using cash as the form of payout is appropriate at this stage, because it is the easiest form of pay to communicate to team members. With so many other areas for participants to learn and focus on, making the plan simple and easy to communicate increases the chances of its success, especially at the novice stage.

Intermediate Teams

Intermediate teams focus on results and task completion, so results-oriented measures are the best type to use. Results measures tend to be detailed and team-specific, and as such, must be re-evaluated and often extensively revised after each performance cycle. Although these teams have mastered the basics of functioning interdependently, including a measure of team effectiveness would continue to focus the team on its behavior and development. Intermediate team members have the knowledge to assist in establishing performance measures as well as participating in their performance assessment. At this developmental stage, we would expect management to provide oversight of the performance evaluation process to ensure consistency between teams, as well as adherence to organizational strategy. Incentive plans for intermediate teams usually have a team level measurement and a team member level measurement, reflecting the individualism-collectivism typical of this stage of team development. Cash payouts for intermediate teams again make sense as they do for Novice teams; however, as intermediate teams continue to develop, adding other payout options such as paid time off gives team members additional flexibility.

Advanced Teams

Advanced teams require the highest degree of sophistication and flexibility in their team rewards. At this stage, competency measures are the biggest focus, but team process and results measures are also included. Advanced teams focus on innovation and continuous process improvement, so customers are often the best source of performance assessment. Because customer evaluations can sometimes be difficult to obtain, surrogate measures of customer satisfaction (e.g., customer returns, complaints, or renewals) may be the best way to assess the team's performance. Collectivism in these teams is high, so evaluation of team performance by the team itself can be extremely effective, as well. Members of advanced teams, with their focus on innovation and creative solutions, are best served with a full menu of choices for payouts. Because advanced teams understand team development and performance well, their incentive plan payouts can offer a higher degree of complexity with a strong likelihood that team members will comprehend them. Cash, stock options, stock grants, paid time off, and other perquisites may be assembled in any combination or left as a choice for the plan participant.

CASE STUDY

Company X, a $6 billion manufacturer of computer storage products, has used teams for product development for the past 18 years. Senior management at Company X is of the belief that teams are a source of sustained competitive advantage for the company. That is, team effectiveness developed at Company X over eighteen years would be very difficult to replicate by others (Barney, 1997). As a result of Company X's success with teams, we will necessarily need to be somewhat general in the presentation of this case in order not to divulge some of the details critical to this core capability of the organization. Because team performance is such an integral part of Company X's corporate culture, we were able to observe its team evolution, as well as the development of compensation systems to accommodate team changes. Currently, Company X uses portions of both the intermediate team and advanced team models, but it plans to fully adopt the advanced team model over time.

Team Evolution at Company X

Company X, founded in 1980, has used teams since its inception. From 1980 until 1989, teams at Company X were in the novice stage. The company used project managers to lead product development efforts. These project managers were charged with the task of developing a particular product and bringing it to market. Team participation was ancillary to functional responsibility, so no employees were assigned to teams full-time. As is the case with most novice teams, Company X's operated as a collection of individuals within functional silos. Because team members did not adequately understand their roles, conflicts within the teams were high. Designated project managers had little knowledge of team development or leadership, and decisions were frequently escalated to senior management. As issues were raised to management, it became clear that there was little cross-functionality of the teams. And because senior management was forced to intervene in team decision making, it was unwilling to give the teams autonomy.

In 1988, two functional managers, one from marketing and one from engineering, unofficially ushered in the intermediate stage of team development at Company X. They elected to work together, cross-functionally, in their project manager roles to develop a new product. Since their efforts were so successful, the company decided to formalize the team process at Company X in 1989. These new product teams were assigned members from six functions within the company, and a sponsor from senior management was assigned to both coach the team and act as liaison with senior staff. As these teams became more prevalent within the company, cross-functional knowledge increased, and team roles became increasingly clear, Teamwork skills were enhanced intentionally by assigning an organizational development consultant to each team to help with process issues and to provide the necessary training to develop the skills needed to operate in a cross-functional environment. Because the staff had a liaison with each team, it was comfortable giving the teams more authority to make decisions.

In 1997, teams at Company X moved to the highest developmental stage, advanced teams. Team processes were reassessed to further define team roles and responsibilities. Focus shifted away from a list of specific, task-oriented deliverables and toward providing innovative solutions for customers and anticipating their needs. These new teams are highly cross-functional, and they are considerably smaller than those of Company X's intermediate teams. The teams have some members who participate in team activities part time and some whose sole function is team activity. With their increased efficiency, Company X's product teams have designed an effective method for interacting with another group of teams within the company. Because teams had been in place at Company X for many years, senior management felt comfortable with the role of teams within the organization, and gave teams the freedom to define their own processes, goals, and assessment. In addition, members of these teams played a key part in the design of a new compensation plan. Company X's goal is to continually improve the functionality of these teams, to make them more self-managed and nimble so that they may not only respond quickly, but also anticipate market needs. Advanced teams at Company X now more closely resemble 'heavy weight' product development teams (Clark & Wheelwright, 1992) or "well trained, mature teams," (Manz & Newstrom, 1999).

Using the theory developed in Table 1, it can be why some teams at Company X are more intermediate and advanced in nature. The strategic focus has shifted from learning to use teams (process) to expecting specific, innovative accomplishments from the teams. In terms of individualism and collectivism, there is a decided mix of the two in intermediate teams. While most team members still report to their individual functions there is much more knowledge about, appreciation of, and use of other team members functions. Moreover, some team members now have full time duties as members of the team which is symbolic of the increasing recognition of the importance of collectivism. Composition of the teams has changed in two ways. The size of the teams has decreased while the heterogeneity of the teams has increased. Team leadership is less authoritarian based on position power and is more consultative with leadership based more on knowledge held by the team member. While the senior management of Company X closely monitor the results of teams, they provide the teams with more autonomy as to how they operate and are consultative in terms of the measures used to set goals.

Team Rewards at Company X

To compensate novice teams, Company X added team members to a general bonus plan designed for senior managers and key employees. The payouts were in cash only, and there were no measures tied to team performance. These payouts were essentially discretionary bonuses with plan design and performance assessment by senior management.

As Company X's teams moved into their second iteration, intermediate teams, team rewards became more sophisticated. A separate team incentive plan was created to replace the bonus plan used for Novice team members. While the payout remained cash only, measures focused on both business results and team development. Company X used team performance, as well as individual performance, within the team to determine plan payouts. This plan was designed using input from team members with oversight from senior management.

Company X's approach to team rewards changed again to reflect the need for increasing flexibility as its teams evolved to the advanced stage. There is a separate team incentive, but the measures are more strategic and competency-based. These strategic measures reflect Company X's core values, and are unlikely to change in the short term. The measures are supported by more detailed and results-oriented sub-measures that are modified for each team. The team owns development, review, and revision of the plan with the support and input of senior management.

Using Table 3, it can be seen from this description how the variations on team pay have changed to support intermediate and advanced as opposed to novice teams. Measures focus on team results and competencies rather than team process alone. Evaluation of results is done by the team and customers rather than by senior management. This approach to team pay for immediate and advanced teams is consistent with the more collectivist orientation of intermediate and advanced teams and less of a perceived need by top management to closely manage team activities.

In the future, more teams at Company X are likely to be advanced in orientation. That is, the teams will be accountable for even more innovation in product development which is sensitive to the needs of the customer. Still greater autonomy from senior management will be granted because of the well-defined results measures that can be used to monitor performance and because teamwork competencies (Heneman & von Hippel, 1995) will be further developed through experiences as team members. Additional development will occur through competency building development activities by the organizational development group. As teams become more advanced, they are rewarded for competency mastery as well as the accomplishment of team goals. In the future, they are more likely to receive rewards other than cash such as stock options and paid time off. Additional rewards, such as these are needed to motivate star performers to continue to be active on teams over extended periods of time even in the face of time consuming duties with their functional assignments.

CONCLUSIONS

As shown in the models and case study presented, team pay plans must be heterogeneous with respect to the different stages of team development in order to be effective. Unique characteristics at each stage of group development may require different team pay characteristics. Characteristics of the team to be assessed include strategic focus, individualism/collectivism, team composition, leadership, plan owner/developer, and autonomy. Characteristics of team pay include measures, measurement levels, evaluators, and pay form.

The models presented here have implications for theory, research, and practice. In terms of theory, the team pay literature treats teams as a static phenomenon over time. That is, the same form of team pay is viewed as appropriate regardless of team development stage. Compensation models need to be changed to accommodate the changing nature of teams over time. While the organizational development literature does acknowledge the changing nature of teams over time, compensation is omitted, as a critical variable needed to make the transitions in team development. Team development models need to consider the role that compensation plays in effective team functioning over time.

In terms of research, the interaction of team development stages and team pay needs to be empirically verified. Although we do present some qualitative information about team pay at Company X to verify our claims, rigorous empirical research needs to be collected to validate over models. The general model to be tested can be thought of in terms of the following equation. The dependent variable is team effectiveness. Independent variables include the stage of team development, type of pay system, the interaction of stage of team development by type of pay system, and control variables. The hypothesis to be tested is that the stage of team development by type of pay system interaction effect will explain more of the variance in team effectiveness than the main effect for type of pay plan.

In terms of practice, two issues stand out. First, the design of teams must factor in compensation as a critical component of team process that must be planned as teams change. Second, the process by which team pay systems are developed must also conform to the appropriate stage of team development. Advanced teams, for example, are much more likely to be able to design their own incentive plans. They have the maturity, perspective, process, and experience to design team pay plans in alignment with the goals of the team, organization, and individual team members. In addition, they can develop alternative payouts that may heighten the motivational effectiveness of the team pay plan.

REFERENCES

Balkin, D.B., & Gomez-Mejia, L.R. (1987). Toward a contingency theory of compensation strategy. *Strategic Management Journal, 8*, 169–182.

Barney, J.B. (1997). *Gaining and sustaining competitive advantage.* Reading, MA: Addison-Wesley.

Chen, C.C., Chen, X.P., & Meindl, J.R. (1998). How can cooperation be fostered? The cultural effects of individualism and collectivism. *The Academy of Management Review, 23*, 285–305.

Clark, K.B., & Wheelwright, S.L. (1992, Spring). Organizing and leading 'heavyweight' development teams. *California Management Review*, 9–28.

DeMatteo, J.S., Eby, L.T., & Sundstrom, E. (1998). Team-based rewards: Current empirical evidence and directions for future research. In B.M. Stow & L.L. Cummings (Eds), *Research in organizational behavior* (Vol. 20, pp. 141–183). Greenwich, CT: JAI Press.

Gedvilas, C. (1997). Recognizing and rewarding team performance at Motorola. *ACA News*, 5–9.

Gersick, C.J. (1988). Time and transition in work teams: Toward a new model of growth. *Academy of Management Journal, 31*, 9–41.

Gross, S.E. (1995). *Compensation for teams.* New York: AMACOM.

Harrison, D.A., Price, K.H., & Bell, M.P. (1998). Beyond relational demography: Time and the effects of surface- and deep-level diversity on work group cohesion. *The Academy of Management Journal, 41*, 96–107.

Heinen, J.S., & Jacobson, E. (1976). A model of task group development in complex organization and a strategy of implementation. *Academy of Management Review, 1*, 98–111.

Heneman, R.L., & von Hippel, C. (1995). Balancing group and individual rewards: Rewarding individual contributions to the team. *Compensation and Benefits Review, 25*(4), 63–68.

Janz, B.D., Colquitt, J.A., & Noe, R.A. (1997). Knowledge worker team effectiveness: The role of autonomy, interdependence, team development, and contextual support variables. *Personnel Psychology, 50*, 877–904.

Manz, C.M., & Newstrom, J. (1999). Team performance at Lake Superior Paper Company. In G.L. Stewart, C.C. Manz, & H.P. Sims, Jr. (Eds.), *Teamwork and group dynamics* (pp. 126–137). New York: John Wiley.

McGrath, J.E., & O'Connor, K.M. (1996). Temporal issues and work groups. In M.M. West (Ed.), *Handbook of work group psychology* (pp. 25–52). New York: John Wiley & Sons.

Miliken, F.J., & Martins, L.L. (1996). Searching for common threads: Understanding the multiple effects of diversity in organizational groups. *The Academy of Management Review, 21,* 402–433.

Mohrman, S.A., Cohen, S.G., & Mohrman, A.M. Jr. (1995). *Designing team-based organizations.* San Francisco: Jossey-Bass.

Newcomb, T.M. (1961). *The acquaintance process.* New York: Holt, Rinehart & Winston.

Schneider, B. (1987). The people make the place. *Personnel Psychology, 40,* 437–1153.

Stagnor, C., Lynch, L., Duan, C., & Glass, B. (1992). Categorization of individuals on the basis of multiple social features. *Journal of Personality and Social Psychology, 62,* 207–218.

Tonkin, L.A.P., & Ellis, C.M. (1997). Team performance and rewards: Building responsibility for results. *Target, 13,* 1–4

Triandis, J.W.H.C. (1995). *Individualism and collectivism.* Boulder, CO: Westview.

Tuckman, B.W. (1965). Developmental sequence in small groups. *Psychological Bulletin, 63,* 384–399.

Tuckman, B.W., & Jensen, M. (1977). Stages of small group development revisited. *Group and Organization Studies, 2,* 419–427.

Wageman, R. (1995). Interdependence and group effectiveness. *Administrative Science Quarterly, 40,* 1445180.

Wagner, III, J.A. (1995). Studies of individualism-collectivism: Effects on cooperation. *Academy of Management Journal, 38,* 152–168.

Wagner, III, J.A., & Moch, M.K., (1986). Individualism collectivism: Concept and measure. *Group and Organization Studies, 11ll,* 280–303.

Part VII

MERIT PAY REVISITED

Merit pay is seldom mentioned along with strategic reward programs. The reason for this has to do with the fact that merit pay has never been focused on the accomplishment of well-measured business results. It has been used in a sweeping manner by organizations to be the reward program for most employees. Coupled with a lack of focus on business results, it has also been implemented with poorly designed measures. In this part of the book it is argued that merit pay can be made strategic and can be implemented with well-developed measures of employee performance.

Heneman, R.L., & von Hippel, C. (1996). The assessment of job performance: Focusing attention on context, process and group issues. In D. Lewin, D.J.B. Mitchell, & M.A. Zaidi (Eds.), *Handbook of human resource management* (pp. 587–617). Greenwich, CT: JAI Press.

Heneman, R.L. (2001). Merit pay. In C. Fay (Ed.), *The executive handbook of compensation* (pp. 447–464). New York: Free Press.

Eskew, D., & Heneman, R.L. (1996). A survey of merit pay plan effectiveness: End of the line for merit pay or hope for improvement? *Human Resource Planning, 19*(2), 12–19.

CHAPTER 17

THE ASSESSMENT OF PERFORMANCE:

Focusing Attention on Context, Process, and Group Issues

Robert L. Heneman and Courtney von Hippel

Source: Reprinted from Heneman, R.L. & von Hippel, C. (1996). The Assessment of Job Performance: Focusing Attention on Context, Process and Group Issues. In D. Lewin, D.J.B. Mitchell, & M.A. Zaidi (Eds.), *Handbook of Human Resource Management* (pp. 587–617). Greenwich, CT: JAI Press with permission from Elsevier Science.

Since the early 1980s there have been two profound shifts in the manner in which job performance is assessed in organizations and is studied by organizational researchers. Specifically, there is now less emphasis on the performance assessment instrument and greater emphasis has been placed on measurement of group rather than individual performance. Prior to the 1980s organizations were primarily concerned with trying to develop the best possible instrument with which to make performance assessments (Patten, 1982). In a complementary fashion, researchers focused on making instruments reliable and free from bias (Landy & Farr, 1980). The focus today is no longer on the performance assessment instrument, but has instead shifted to understanding the processes used in making assessments of performance (Ilgen, Barnes-Farrel, & McKellin, 1993) and the context in which these processes take place (Murphy & Cleveland, 1991).

The current focus indicates that in order for assessments of employee performance to be effective, it is not sufficient to have only a well-developed assessment instrument. Rather, the instrument itself is only one part of the system needed for effective performance assessment (Lawler, 1994). While a well-developed assessment instrument is a necessary condition for effective performance assessment, an understanding of how the assessment instrument is used under various circumstances is also required. By having this understanding, a complete system can be developed for effective performance assessment.

Additionally, prior to the early 1980s emphasis was placed by organizations on measuring the performance of the individual rather than of a team, business unit, or organization to which the individual belongs. Today many organizations continue to assess individual performance, but increasingly also assess the performance of the team, business unit, or organization. The reason for this shift in measurement from the individual to the group has to do with the design of work in organizations. In the past, work was designed primarily to be centered around the individual. Increasingly, today's organizations are shifting toward work design around the group. For example, in automobile assembly plants, employees used to be responsible for placing certain parts on an engine. Today, in some auto plants, employees are responsible as a team for assembling the entire engine together.

In order for assessments of employee performance to be effective, it is critical that performance of the group be measured along with performance of the individual. By making assessments of the group, organizations can make strategic decisions regarding the direction of the organization and resource allocations. That is, financial, technological, and human resources can be allocated in such a manner that the groups operate in accordance with the desired direction of the organization. Unfortunately, there is very little research on the assessment of performance at the group level, and thus, there is a crying need for performance assessment researchers to turn their attention to this important topic. As will be shown in this chapter, most of the research on performance of the group thus far has simply been descriptive. This state of affairs leaves us with many questions regarding which practices are effective and why they are effective at the group level.

The objective of this chapter is to show how an understanding of the assessment process and the context of the assessment can be used to make more effective assessments of performance. In order to meet this objective, current research illustrative of this new focus will be reviewed. Specifically, we will address issues dealing with context followed by issues addressing process. The literature will be introduced with a discussion of the purposes of performance assessments in organizations and the criteria used to gauge the effectiveness of performance assessments. Because of the limited amount of research conducted on the assessment of group performance, most of information presented will center around performance assessment at the individual level.

PURPOSES OF PERFORMANCE ASSESSMENT

Performance assessment refers to a formal evaluation of an employee's contribution to the organization, usually conducted on a yearly basis. These assessments, often referred to as performance appraisals, performance reviews, or performance evaluations, are used in a variety of different ways in organizations. Some of the more important purposes of these assessments include management decisions, developmental feedback, and staffing and training support.

Management Decisions

Evaluations of employee performance are used to make management decisions. These decisions include rewards, promotion, demotions and terminations, and job assignments. In order to motivate continued good performance, rewards are allocated on the basis of performance on both an informal and formal basis. On an informal basis, praise is provided on the basis of good performance during day-to-day coaching. On a formal basis, rewards are allocated for good individual and group performance. Individual performance is most often formally recognized in organizations with a merit pay increase whereby pay allocations are made on the basis of one's performance assessment and position in the pay range (Heneman, 1992). Group performance is often rewarded through gainsharing plans which make pay increase allocations to individuals on the basis of the productivity of the work group or the entire organization (McAdams & Hawk, 1994; Mitchell, Lewin, & Lawler, 1990). In order to retain the best performers, promotion, demotions, and terminations should also be made on the basis of performance assessments. Job assignments are made on the basis of performance to ensure that assignments are successfully completed. The quality of these decisions regarding rewards and the movement of employees in the organization is highly dependent on the effectiveness of the performance assessments made.

Developmental Feedback

Performance assessments are an important source of developmental feedback to employees. In order for employees to maintain and improve upon present performance, it is important that specific and challenging goals be set. The research clearly shows that when specific and challenging goals are set and accepted by employees, performance is improved (Locke & Latham, 1990). Performance assessments are the vehicles used by managers to set specific and challenging goals for and with employees (Latham & Wexley, 1994); the more effective the assessment, the more likely that employee development will occur.

Performance assessment is one component of the developmental process in organizations known as *performance management*. Managers use the performance management process to help employees develop in ways which are consistent with the goals of the organization. Stages and steps involved in the performance management process are shown in Figure 1.

The first stage in the process is the development of a performance plan which consists of setting goals for the employee. Goals define standards for good performance and typically are jointly set by the manager and employee. Along with goals, performance plans also contain action plans which are developed to specify the activities that must be undertaken to accomplish the goals. Both goals and action plans are linked to organizational goals by the first step in the performance planning stage, which is to

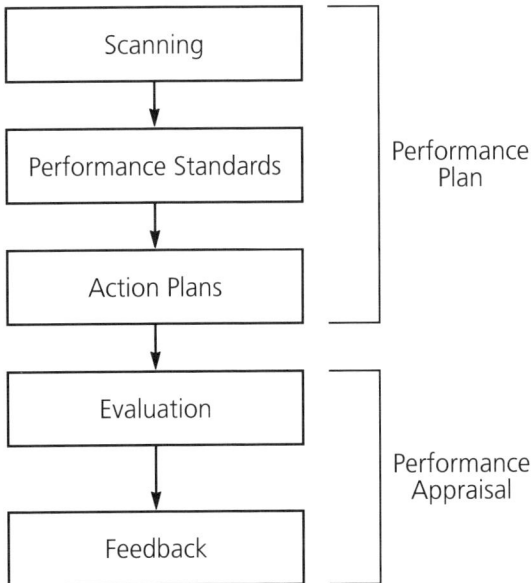

Figure 1.   Performance management process

scan the organization for business planning documents that can be used to develop goals for the positions which are consistent with the goals of the organization. The second stage of the process is actually to appraise employee performance once a plan has been developed. The initial step here is the assessment of performance where the employee's actual performance is compared to the organization's standards. The next step is to provide the employee with feedback on how well he has done relative to the standards and what must be done to improve on or maintain job performance. Also, a discussion of additional resources needed by the employee to facilitate goal accomplishment, such as training, is provided as a part of such feedback.

Staffing and Training Support

Performance assessments help to facilitate the recruitment, selection, and training of employees. In terms of recruitment, performance assessments can be used as a "realistic job preview" to inform job applicants of the type of work and the levels of performance they would be expected to perform at as an employee. When realistic job information is presented to current employees, it gives them the opportunity to decide whether the organization's expectations are consistent with their own. To the extent these expectations are consistent, job applicants who become employees are more likely to be satisfied with their jobs and remain with the organization (Wanous, 1992).

In terms of selection, tools such as interviews and tests are validated against employee performance. A valid selection device is one which allows managers to predict actual performance by the job candidate should the person be hired. In order for actual performance to be predicted, it is important that an effective performance assessment system be in place.

In terms of training, performance assessments are used by managers to assess the need for training and evaluate the effectiveness of training. One reason to provide training is to correct performance deficiencies; performance assessments can be used to show who is in need of training due to deficiencies in performance. It is also important to determine if the training actually affects job performance. Performance assessments should be made before and after training and compared to employees who do receive training to determine if the training actually affects job performance.

As can be seen from these three sets of purposes, performance assessment plays a critical role in helping organizations manage human resources. The old stereotype, namely, that performance appraisals are "...just another stupid form to be filled out for the Personnel Department," is clearly incorrect. Performance assessments are an important part of the total management process; in order to be useful, however, they must be effective. The criteria used to gauge the effectiveness of performance assessments will now be reviewed.

EFFECTIVENESS CRITERIA

The quality of decisions made by managers regarding human resources using job performance as the criterion are only as good as the quality of their assessments of employee performance. In order to make high quality or effective performance assessments, it is important to know how effectiveness is gauged, which is typically measured via multiple indicators (Austin, Villanova, Kane, & Bernardin, 1991). These indicators serve as the goals of effective performance assessment and will be used to judge the effectiveness of recommended performance assessment practices in subsequent sections of this chapter. A brief summary of these indicators from a variety of sources (Heneman, 1992; Latham & Wexley, 1994; Smith, 1976; Thorndike, 1949) follows, and are arranged from the micro to the macro level of analysis.

Reliability

Reliability refers to the consistency of assessments across raters, measures, and time. If multiple evaluators are assessing the same person or group, using the same form, after observing the person or group perform the same work, their evaluations should be similar; this is known as inter-rater reliability. If two measures of the same concept are used by the same evaluator, the evaluations should be correlated; this is known as internal consistency reliability. For example, if customer ratings of "courtesy" and "friendliness" are designed to measure an aspect of customer service, then these ratings should be correlated with one another. If an assessment is completed twice at different points in time (when actual performance is not expected to change), then the evaluations should be similar; this is known as test-retest reliability. For example, output should be correlated at two different points in time if the same person is using the same machine set at the same pace. Consistency is essential to the performance assessment process. If performance assessments are not consistent, then the wrong employees may be targeted for rewards, promotions, and dismissals.

Validity

Validity refers to the degree to which the assessment measures what it actually purports to measure. In order to be valid, a performance assessment should be accurate and free from bias. Accuracy refers to the extent to which the assessment captures all dimensions of actual job performance. That is, the assessment instrument should contain all of the relevant components of the job, as spelled out in a job analysis. For example, simply measuring an individual employee's productivity in a team setting would be a deficient measure. It would ignore another important element of the job, which is the need for the team to work together to accomplish team goals. Freedom from bias refers to the extent to which the assessment measures actual performance rather than nonperformance related factors.

Examples of nonperformance factors that bias performance assessments are known as rating errors. Halo error takes place when an evaluator generalizes from one aspect of an employee's performance to other aspects of an employee's performance without regard to the employee's actual performance. An example of halo error is when it is automatically assumed that just because a professor is a good researcher he or she is also a good teacher. Some professors are good at both, but some are better at one dimension of performance than another; hence, it is an error when they are automatically assumed to be good at both. A similar example arises when examining a supervisor's performance on the technical versus managerial aspects of performance. Halo error can also occur in group settings; if one division of a large organization is profitable, and a customer automatically assumes that other divisions are profitable too, then halo error has occurred.

Leniency, a specific type of halo error, occurs when employees are always rated very high or very low on all aspects of their performance. While it is true that some employees are particularly good or bad in all aspects of their performance, most employees, like professors, are good in some aspects and not so good in other aspects. In contrast, central tendency error takes place when employees are rated average in all aspects of their performance. Again, as with leniency, there is little variance in the ratings of different aspects of performance. This tendency is an error given that this lack of variance is at odds with the greater variance in the several aspects of performance usually exhibited by many employees.

The rating process is not only contaminated by the "cold," computer-like rating errors that may occur with the cognitive processing of performance information, it is also influenced by the "hot" affect or "states of feeling" held by the evaluator (Cardy & Dobbins, 1994). Conventional wisdom in organizations suggests that in order to make valid performance assessments, raters should be in a "good" mood. The reality seems to be that when raters are slightly depressed, rather than elated, they tend to be more thorough in their processing of performance information, resulting in more valid appraisals (Harris, 1994; Sinclair, 1988). This finding is a robust one and holds up in certain areas of social judgments (e.g., self-assessments) other than performance assessments (Isen, 1987).

Bias in performance assessments is not simply a function of the mood of the assessor, is also a function of "perverse incentives" built into the assessment system (Lewin & Mitchell, 1995). In many organizations, for example, performance ratings are skewed toward the positive end of the rating scale. That is, almost everyone is rated above average or better. A skewed distribution of this nature may not reflect actual performance levels and, hence, reduce the validity of the assessments. The reason for this bias is that the performance assessment system may have incentives built into it that reward the supervisor for skewed ratings which are perverse to the organization. Incentives for the supervisor/manager to give high ratings include not having to feel the discomfort associated with confronting a poor performing subordinate and being able to garner a larger raise due to the good performance of the manager's subordinates.

Fairness

In order for managers to be willing to make performance assessments and for employees to be willing to act on the results of the assessment, they must believe that the system is fair (Dickinson, 1993). Perceptions of fairness regarding performance assessments can be conceptualized in terms of *distributive* and *procedural justice* (Greenberg, 1987). Distributive justice refers to whether the outcome of the assessment (e.g., positive, negative) is viewed as fair. Procedural justice refers to whether the procedures used to make this determination are seen as fair. Both distributive and procedural justice perceptions are essential for effective performance assessment.

Distributive justice is established on the basis of equity considerations (Adams, 1965). Individuals performing the same job at the same level of performance should receive the same evaluation. Procedural justice is established on the basis of several rules (Leventhal, Karuza, & Fry, 1980). According to these rules, assessments should be consistent across evaluators and over time, be made using accurate information, be correctable, and reflect the concerns of the participants. In addition, bias should be suppressed and evaluations should comply with ethical standards.

Legality

Many laws and regulations govern what can and cannot be done in the context of performance assessments. Two of the major laws, the Civil Rights Act of 1964, 1991, and the Age Discrimination in Employment Act of 1967, make it illegal to assess performance on the basis of age, race, sex, color, religion, and national origin. An effective performance assessment procedure in an organization will not show any statistical pattern of discrimination or discriminatory treatment of an individual in performance assessments for members of these protected groups relative to nonprotected group members.

Practicality

An effective performance assessment system must also be practical to be effective. A practical performance assessment is one that is understandable to the person conducting the evaluation and the person being evaluated. It also has "face validity," which means that the results of the assessment seem plausible to both parties. Additionally, an effective performance assessment will be "user friendly." That is, the assessment procedure will provide clear instruction and the process will not be overly cumbersome to either party.

This list of criteria used to evaluate the effectiveness of performance assessments is an imposing one and reflects the attention that must be devoted to performance assessments by organizations if sound decisions are to be made on the basis of performance. Although it is not possible to develop a system of performance assessment that perfectly meets all of these criteria, these criteria can nevertheless be used to guide system development. Moreover, as will be shown in the next section of this chapter, it is becoming more possible than ever before to meet these criteria with the new emphasis in performance assessment on context and process, rather than focusing solely on the rating instrument.

CONTEXT

A considerable amount of performance assessment research has been conducted in laboratory studies. While this type of research has added to our knowledge of the assessment process, concerns have been expressed over the generalizability of laboratory study results to the "real world" (Ilgen & Favero, 1985). In recognition of this limitation, designers and users of performance assessment must go beyond laboratory research to develop effective performance assessments. In order to do so, fortunately, it is possible to learn from business strategists, legal experts, labor relations specialists, and organizational behavior theorists about real-world variables that must be dealt with in assessing employee performance. Four of these sets of variables—business strategy, organizational culture, unions, and laws and regulations—will now be addressed.

Business Planning

In order for performance assessments to be effective they must be consistent with the business plans of the organization. By aligning business plans with performance assessments, the goals of the individual and organization are brought into alignment with one another. Operationally, alignment is accomplished by having the performance standards used to assess employee performance developed after business plans of the organization and business units within the organization are established. Not only should performance standards be formed after the formation of the business plan, rather than before, they should also be carefully shaped to be consistent with the core competencies or critical success factors contained in the business plan. These competencies or factors spell out the actions that must be taken by the organization to be effective in their product or service markets. To develop performance standards consistent with core competencies, inferences must be made about job behaviors and results that will contribute to each core competency.

An example of this process comes from Ameritech. At Ameritech one of the critical success factors is customer service. In order to be more successful than competitors in their markets, it is the company's belief that they must offer more effective customer service than their competitors. In order to do so, they have developed customer-based performance standards for their service representatives. These standards spell out a number of dimensions of good customer service, and each dimension is defined by specific behavioral indicators. For example, one dimension is "Personalizes Customer Contacts" and behavioral indicators include "Treats each customer as an individual with individual needs," "Incorporates customer information in conversations," and "Recognizes different personality types and responds appropriately."

One methodology available to strengthen the link between individual and organizational goals is to develop "competency platforms" (Tucker & Cofsky, 1994). A competency platform establishes the underlying competencies needed by employees to accomplish the goals of the business plan. Competencies refer to those characteristics of the employee that predict superior performance consistent with the business plan of the organization. Hence, it links individual employee capabilities to organizational strategies. As such, competency platforms not only spell out desired performance, they go one step further and show the underlying characteristics of employees that are needed to meet these standards. Underlying characteristics of competency plans include knowledge, skills, and abilities. These competencies can then be used to select and train employees as well as to monitor their performance. An example of a competency model is shown in Table 1.

Table 1. Example of a Competency Model for Plant Supervisors and Managers

The following is an example of the competencies that predicted success for the plant supervisors and managers of a large food-processing company:

Leveraging Technical and Business Systems

Using expertise to solve operational problems, optimize systems and plan for future requirements

Leading For Results

Using initiative and influence to drive results and promote continuos improvement

Building Work-Force Effectiveness

Coaching individual development and building capability of operational project or cross-functional teams to achieve business results

Understanding and Meeting Customer Needs

Working with customers to meet overall business objectives

Source: Reprinted from Tucker and Cofsky (1994), with permission from the American Compensation Association (ACA).

More and better performance assessment theory and research is needed to guide the development of competency platforms. A theory of competency that shows considerable promise is presented in Figure 2. This model holds promise as it incorporates current developments in organizational psychology, but has not yet been empirically tested. Other competency models that have been tested were done in military settings, and thus may

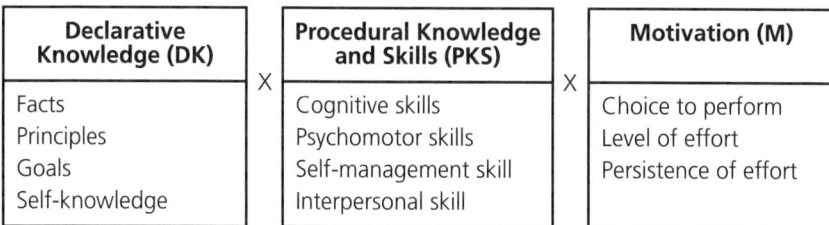

Declarative Knowledge (DK)		Procedural Knowledge and Skills (PKS)		Motivation (M)
Facts Principles Goals Self-knowledge	X	Cognitive skills Psychomotor skills Self-management skill Interpersonal skill	X	Choice to perform Level of effort Persistence of effort

Figure 2.   Determinants of job performance components (Adapted from Campbell et al. [1993]).

not be generalizable (e.g., Borman, White, Pulakos, & Oppler, 1991). The modeling of human performance obviously needs to be further developed and tested in nonmilitary settings.

Organizational Culture

In order for performance assessments to be effective they must not only be consistent with business plans, but must also be consistent with the culture of the organization. The culture represents the shared set of beliefs and values held by members of the organization (Ott, 1989). Different types of cultures support different types of performance assessment systems. Hence, the performance assessment system must be carefully matched to the culture. Two different cultures can be used to illustrate this point (Walton, 1985).

A "control" culture is one that characterizes many large bureaucracies such as the military where jobs are strictly defined and highly specialized, many layers of management prevail, there is little lateral communication, and authority is top down. A "commitment" culture is typically found in smaller organizations that must respond to a rapidly changing business environment. In this type of culture, jobs are broadly defined with few specific duties, there are few layers of management, much lateral communication occurs, and authority resides at all levels of the organization. Table 2 shows the type of performance assessment system appropriate in each of these two cultures.

Table 2.   Culture and Performance Assessment System

	Culture	
Performance Assessment System Characteristics	*Control*	*Commitment*
Purpose of Evaluation	Evaluation	Development
Unit of Analysis	Individual	Team and Individual
Source of Evaluation	Superior	Superior Self Peers Subordinates Customers
Performance Standards	Quantity	Quantity Quality Teamwork Customer Service
Appraisal Period	Yearly	Ongoing

The importance of organizational culture can be highlighted with the case of self-directed work teams whereby such teams are formed to be more responsive to the needs of the customer. These teams are directed by the employees so that decisions traditionally made by management are made by employees. Such an approach enables issues raised by the customer to be dealt with immediately rather than having the customer wait for an extended period for the issue to be resolved by management. Self-directed work teams are also formed to take advantage of ideas for better business performance held by employees. Because employees are closer to day-to-day operations than managers, employees have many good ideas not thought of by management which can be immediately used in self-directed teams. The culture with self-directed work teams is one of commitment. If a control-oriented performance assessment system were used here, it could lead to disastrous results. It would suggest to employees that they cannot be trusted to be a part of the appraisal process by rating their own performance and that of their peers. A mistake made by many companies is to tell employees that they are empowered to make decisions as a self-directed team, but then are not given the authority to be part of the performance assessment process. Similarly, customer evaluations should be used to reinforce the customer service focus of service-based teams, and team assessments should be conducted to reinforce this concept of a work team.

Unionized Settings

Many organizations with workforces represented by labor unions do not have performance assessment systems. Instead of making human resource decisions on the basis of performance, managers are sometimes required to make decisions on the basis of seniority as specified in a labor contract negotiated and agreed on by labor and management.

Some unions do allow performance assessments to take place. They may be in favor of performance assessments because it helps members become developed and promoted. It also may help the union to decide which grievances are meritorious and should be processed by the union. Acceptance of a performance assessment system by the union is more likely to take place when it is developed jointly by labor and management. Performance assessments are also more likely to be acceptable to a union when they are used solely for developmental reasons and not used to make pay or promotion decisions.

On the whole, union resistance to performance assessment is strong as evidenced by the fact that only about 15 percent of unionized organizations have incentive pay plans, where pay is made contingent on performance (U.S. Department of Labor, 1981). Even in those organizations that do have performance assessment systems, research suggests that unionized employees are less satisfied than nonunionized employees with the performance assessment process (Gaertner & Gaertner, 1987).

Unions are resistant to performance assessments for several reasons (Balkin, 1989; Barkin, 1948; Freeman, 1982). First, there is an overriding concern that assessments are not conducted fairly because of the subjectivity involved in the assessment process. Concern is often expressed, for example, about how the evaluations are biased by personality conflicts. Second, performance assessment is very costly in terms of the time required by the union to monitor the results of performance assessments to be sure that they are not biased. Third, concern is expressed that when performance is assessed, union members will be in competition with one another, which defeats the goal of solidarity among union members.

Laws and Regulations

As previously noted in this chapter, various laws and regulations govern permissible practices with regard to performance assessments. The laws and court cases ruling on these laws have been subject to narrative (Latham & Wexley, 1994; Martin, Bartol, & Levine, 1987; Nathan & Cascio, 1986) and empirical reviews (Feild & Holley, 1982). Based on these reviews, the following steps should be taken to ensure that performance assessments are legally defensible:

- Performance standards should always be based on a sound job analysis.
- Personality traits should not be evaluated as it is difficult to show their relationship to the job.
- Instructions and training on how to make effective performance assessments should be given to all assessors.
- An appeals procedure should be in place for employees who feel that they have not been fairly treated in the assessment process.
- The completed assessment must be reviewed with the employee being assessed and a signature indicating that a review was conducted with the employee should be given by the employee.

It should be noted that these guidelines do not impose an undue hardship on employers. To the contrary, they are very consistent with sound business practice and research, as will be shown in the next section of this chapter on process issues.

PROCESS

Along with a consideration of contextual issues, another issue that must be considered if effective performance assessments are to be formed is the process used to formulate performance assessments. In the past, this has meant considerable attention being given to the cognitive processes used by evaluators to make performance assessments. While cognitive processes are important, they should not be considered at the expense of organizational processes, which are as important, or perhaps more important, than cognitive processes in determining performance assessments (Ilgen, Barnes-Farrel, & McKellin, 1993; Murphy & Cleveland, 1991).

One way to view process issues that incorporates both individual and organizational processes is shown in Figure 3. According to this perspective, performance assessment is a three-step process that is required as a part of the evaluator's or rater's role. The rater must formulate standards, gather data on how the employee performs, and compare the employee's performance to the standards in order to make final ratings of performance. In executing these steps, the rater draws on two sets of resources: individual and organizational. Individual resources include the ability and motivation to make performance assessments. In order to make an assessment of performance, the rater must be able (Feldman, 1981) and motivated (Dickinson, 1993) to observe performance, store the observations, recall the observations, and integrate them into a summary judgment (DeNisi, Cafferty, & Meglino, 1984; Wexley & Klimoski, 1984). Organizational resources can also be drawn on to perform the rater's role. Organizational resources include the time needed to complete the tasks, training on how to conduct the tasks, being placed in a situation where performance can be observed, being provided with information about the nature

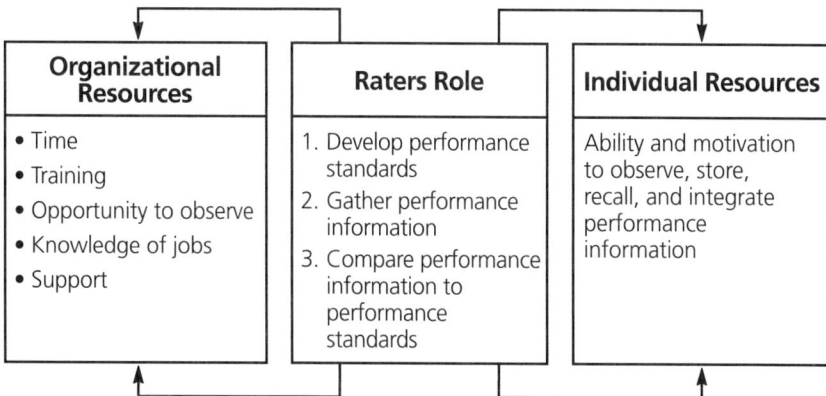

Organizational Resources	Raters Role	Individual Resources
• Time • Training • Opportunity to observe • Knowledge of jobs • Support	1. Develop performance standards 2. Gather performance information 3. Compare performance information to performance standards	Ability and motivation to observe, store, recall, and integrate performance information

Figure 3.   The performance assessment process.

of the job, and having the support of subordinates, peers, and superiors necessary to complete the three-step rating process. A variety of forces have been identified in the literature as impacting raters as they undertake this process. These factors will now be described as it is these factors that must be managed if effective performance assessments are to be made.

Most of the research that will be reviewed has focused on the ability of the rater to acquire resources needed to make effective assessments. Whenever possible, the motivation to acquire needed resources will also be examined. Motivation is a very important part of the rating process, as it affects even the most basic issues underlying the rating process. For example, one such factor is willingness to complete a performance assessment. In an organization studied by Fried, Tiegs, and Bellamy (1992), about 30 percent of the ratees did not even receive scheduled performance assessments, let alone valid ones. Most of the research conducted regarding motivation has examined the motivation to provide valid ratings. Researchers need to take a step back and consider the willingness of and incentives for managers to even use performance assessments.

As indicated throughout this chapter, the assessment instrument or measure is not a panacea for effective performance assessment. The measurement process or steps used to develop the instrument do, however, play a critical role in the effectiveness of performance assessment. Important issues related to the measurement process will now be reviewed.

In order to ensure that performance assessments are accurate and reflect critical elements of the job, a process-flow analysis should be conducted to develop the standards used to assess performance (Zigon, 1994). A process-flow analysis involves identifying the inputs, transformations, and outcomes required to complete major work assignments (Noe, Hollenbeck, Gerhart, & Wright, 1994). Performance standards should be developed at each stage of the work process whereby inputs are transformed into outcomes (e.g., materials are manufactured into products). To make work consistent with the goals of the organization, emphasis should first be placed on the desired outcomes followed by an assessment of activities and inputs required to achieve these outcomes. Desired outcomes should be based on the business plan of the organization. When outcomes are measured in relation to the activities and inputs needed to produce these outcomes, organizational productivity, an important source of competitive advantage, is being assessed (Pritchard, 1992).

Outcomes are often measured in organizations with standards known as objectives. These objectives measure specific products or services provided by employees and are usually calibrated in terms of quality (e.g., scrap rate) or quantity (e.g., sales). Systems used to measure outcomes at the individual or group-based level are usually labeled "Management by Objectives." Although they are frequently used by organizations, little is known about the reliability and validity of these systems. These objectives are quite important, however, as they are related to the "bottom line" of the organization. On the other hand, the bottom-line results may not be under the control of employees because such results are influenced by other factors such as capital, technology, and the economy. Consequently, behaviors that are under the control of employee also need to be considered.

Transformations to inputs are often measured in terms of employee behaviors. These behaviors refer to the manner in which employees carry out their work activities or duties. Behavioral standards that should be emphasized are those which are highly effective for goal accomplishment (Latham & Wexley, 1994). Performance appraisal systems that capture these critical behaviors include behavioral observation scales (BOS) and behaviorally anchored rating scales (BARS), both of which have acceptable levels of reliability and validity. An assessment of these behaviors is important because they help employees learn about the relationship between their activities at work and the goals of the organization. Conflicting opinions abound as to how, when, and where to measure group-level performance. As a result of this confusion, it is very difficult to specify appropriate group-level measures.

Fortunately, there is now the beginning of some theory to end this confusion and provide organizations with guidance to measure performance at the group level. One stream of thought that provides some assistance in formulating group measures of job performance comes from the business planning literature. As reviewed in the section of this chapter on context, group-level measures should be consistent with the strategic objectives of the organization.

A second stream of thought concerning organizational effectiveness is helpful in designing organizational level measures of effectiveness. This perspective suggests that there is no one best conceptualization or measure of organizational effectiveness. Rather, the appropriate measure depends on the purpose of the measure and the situation. Furthermore, it should not be assumed that the goal-directed strategy of the organization solely defines performance at the organization level (Whetten &Cameron, 1994). An example of this perspective comes from Scott (1992), who argues that different stakeholders in the organization look to different measures of organizational performance: stockholders tend to emphasize the accomplishment of strategic objectives; clients and customers focus on outcomes such as quality and quantity; employees look at the accomplishment of activities needed to accomplish outcomes; and staff administrators are most concerned with structural capabilities of the organization to be effective. This perspective indicates that multiple measures, not a single measure, of group performance are needed. This perspective recognizes that organizations have multiple goals, based on multiple constituencies, resulting in multiple outcomes (Whetten & Cameron, 1994).

A third stream of thought comes from consultants involved in work design. For example, Zigon (1994) takes a multilevel view of the organization which leads to a method of developing performance measures at the team and individual level. His system of developing performance measures is shown in Table 3, and examples of team and individual performance measures are shown in Tables 4 and 5, respectively.

Table 3.   How To Develop Team Measures

1. **Review and revise organizational and business-unit measures.**
   Do business-unit measures flow from and support corporate strategy? If only financial measures are being used, ask why. Identify measures to evaluate both strategic success and market results.

2. **Review and revise business operating system measures.**
   Are there measures for customer satisfaction? Flexibility or innovation? Productivity?

3. **Map the business process.**
   Identify the teams customers and the products/services the customers need. Identify all major process steps and handoffs that lead to the final product. Change the process to simplify it and increase value to the customer.

4. **Identify team measurement points.**
   Always measure the final product. Decide with process steps and handoffs are worth measuring. Measure processes by waste and cycle time. Measure handoffs by delivery and quality.

5. **Identify individual accomplishments that support the team's process.**
   Build a role-result matrix with team members down the left column, key process steps across the top row and accomplishments needed to support each process step inside each cell.

6. **Develop team and individual performance measures.**
   For each accomplishment, select the general measures that are important (quantity, quality, cost and/or timeliness). For each general measure, answer the question, "How can (quantity, quality, cost and/or timeliness) be measured?" If an accomplishment can be measured with numbers, record the units to be counted (or tracked by percentage). If performance only can be described, list who will judge the work and what factors they will consider.

7. **Develop team and individual performance objectives.**
   The goal is verifiability. If the measure is numeric, ask, "For this measure, what number would represent 'meeting expectations'?" Establish a range of performance above which recognition is warranted and below which a performance problem exists. If the measure is descriptive, ask, "For each factor the judge will look at, what would this person see that means a good job has been done?" List the judge, factors, and what constitutes a good job for each factor. Ask, "If this description equals 'meeting expectations', what would 'exceeding' look like?" Write what the judge would see happening if these expectations were exceeded.

Source: Reprinted from Zigon (1994), with permission from the American Compensation Association (ACA).

Table 4.   Examples Of Team-Performance Objectives

Category	Team-Performance Objectives
Customer	• 90 to 95 percent of customers say they are "likely" or "very likely" to purchase the product. • 50 to 75 percent of customers say they are "likely" or "very likely" to repurchase. • There is a 10 to 15 percent sales increase that occurs during the first 90 days.

Operations	• There is no negative impact on customer satisfaction scores.
	• Restaurant managers are satisfied that:
	    • The labor standards are accurate.
	    • They have enough storage capacity and the product is easy to store.
	    • The complexity of the procedure does not prevent them from selling within required service and hold times.
	    • They are able to handle all customer questions about the product.
	    • All needed supplies are received on time and to specification.
	    • The procedure is simple enough to allow the food to be prepared consistently.

Financial	• There is a 45 to 70 percent return on investment.
Project Management	• There is a $5,000 to $10,000 national average capital per store. • The test is completed by September, 1994. • There is no more than a $26.7 million capital project investment.

Source: Reprinted from Zigon (1994), with permission from the American Compensation Association (ACA).

Table 5.

Team Member	Individual-Performance Objectives

Operations Person in Charge of Restaurant Modifications	• 90 to 95 percent of customers say they are satisfied with the following:
	    • Utility hookups are in the right location.
	    • Utility service levels meet the equipment's needs.
	    • There is no negative effect on restaurant operation.
	    • Modification scheduling is coordinated with the restaurant's schedule.
	    • The vice president of operations is satisfied that the modifications support the project's goals.
	    • Modifications are completed by agreed-upon deadlines.
	    • Installation is no more than 10 percent above the estimate.

Table 5.   (Cont.)

Team Member	Individual-Performance Objectives
Marketing Person in Charge of Product Design	• Customers want to buy the product based on multiple-market research test data. • Store managers say the product is doable in the restaurant environment during the single-store test and multiple-store market test. • The design meets or falls below product-cost targets.
Procurement Person in Charge of Equipment	• Restaurant services and research-and-development function sign off on equipment specifications. • Specifications and prototypes are created by agreed-upon deadlines. • Equipment costs are 10 percent or less above budget for capital cost per store. • Installation is completed by agreed-upon deadlines. • Equipment has 99.5 to 99.8 percent up-time. • No retrofits are required. • 90 to 95 percent of service calls are responded to within 24 hours or within the time specified by the service contract. • 88 to 92 percent of repairs are completed correctly during the first visit.
Information Systems Person	• Restaurant managers are satisfied that cash-register changes have resulted in the following: • Keystrokes are minimized. • Keyboard overlay matches data. • Download to cash registers occurs in time for training or the night before product rollout.
Training Representative	• Procedure produces a consistent product • Restaurant managers are satisfied that the training package: • communicates the procedures clearly • is complete (e.g., includes job aids, procedures) • fits the restaurant environment • arrives two weeks prior to product rollout date.

Source: Reprinted from Zigon (1994), with permission from the American Compensation Association (ACA).

Sources

The rating process is also influenced by those individuals who conduct the assessments. Traditionally, the usual source for assessments was the employee's immediate supervisor. Clearly, supervisors should play a role in assessment as they have knowledge of organizational goals and are ultimately accountable for their subordinate's performance. Increasingly, however, they do not have the resources to be effective by themselves in this role. Recently, organizations have reduced layers of management to cut costs as a source of competitive advantage for the organization (Shaw & Scheiner, 1994). In doing so, supervisors have many more people reporting to them along with more job responsibilities themselves. Also, technology has made it possible for employees to work at locations separate from their supervisor. When there is more to do, more subordinates to appraise, and more subordinates in remote locations, opportunities for the supervisor to observe performance are decreased. This decreased opportunity to observe performance reduces the accuracy of performance ratings (Heneman & Wexley, 1983). Consequently, organizations with effective performance assessments will need to move toward multisource or 360-degree performance assessment. With this approach, performance assessments are not made only by the supervisor, but made also by peers, subordinates, the job incumbent (self), and customers who may have more or different opportunities to observe the employee in action than does the supervisor. Each of these sources of performance assessment will be addressed next.

An excellent, but often overlooked, source of performance information in traditional organizations is peer assessment. Under this approach, members of the organization at the same level provide ratings of peers. Reviews of the literature show that the reliability and validity of peer ratings are as good or better than supervisory ratings (Latham & Wexley, 1994). The correlations between supervisory and peer ratings are fairly strong (Harris & Schaubroeck, 1988), so they can be used as a check on supervisory ratings. On the negative side, employees tend to dislike peer ratings (Love, 1981). One way to minimize this dislike may be to have peers provide anonymous ratings or to use peer ratings for developmental rather than for other human resource decision making. Peer ratings appear to have high potential in modern-day work organizations in which work is designed for work teams with a minimum of supervision. Importantly, peer assessments are consistent with the self-directed and managed philosophy underlying these teams. It should be noted, however, that there are opportunity costs associated with peer ratings in the form of downtime from work. This is especially true if the person works in a large work group requiring many ratings. In order to minimize this cost and to increase the validity of peer ratings, peers should only rate other peer's work with which they are very familiar.

A small, but increasing number of organizations are using subordinate ratings of managerial performance. These ratings have been primarily used for the purposes of team-building in organizations (Latham & Wexley, 1994) and as a way to diagnose training deficiencies of managers. That is, they are used for gathering data on how well managers perform the duties most closely observed by employees (e.g., delegation). Little is known about the reliability, validity, or acceptability of these ratings, however. As with peer ratings, they may be best introduced into organizations by being conducted in an anonymous fashion and for developmental purposes only, in order to gather support for this process. Subordinate ratings seem to lend themselves well to innovative organizational arrangements that have empowered self-directed teams to complete the work. Subordinate ratings could be used in this type of context to assess whether managers are providing subordinate teams with the necessary resources (e.g., time, direction, equipment) to get the tasks accomplished properly. As with peer ratings, subordinate ratings are likely to be used more frequently by organizations in the future (Cardy & Dobbins, 1994).

On the face of things, self-ratings seem to be an excellent source of performance information. After all, who knows the job better than the employee herself? While many managers have tried self-appraisals, many have abruptly stopped using them. The reason managers are no longer using them is that they are often inflated as a result of positive leniency, and are not as closely correlated with supervisory ratings as are peer ratings (Borman, 1991; Latham & Wexley, 1994). These problems are correctable, however. One method to decrease leniency is to provide job incumbents who are expected to make self-ratings with instructions on the rating process. Often job incumbents are expected to conduct self-ratings with no preparation. Another way to decrease leniency with self-ratings is to use the ratings for developmental purposes only. Employees should also be encouraged to provide self-ratings because it gives them the opportunity to be part of the performance assessment process. By being a part of the process, they are more likely to be committed to the outcomes of the process (Mohrman, Resnick-West, & Lawler, 1989).

Customer assessments have been used frequently for many years in some sectors of the economy (e.g., hotels and restaurants). Unfortunately, virtually no empirical data have been reported as to their effectiveness (Cardy & Dobbins, 1994). There is a great need for research in this area of performance assessment. Given the focus of most organizations on the customer in the business planning process, these ratings would seem to be a very important source of information for performance assessments. Using customers to help assess the performance of employees is evidence of a strengthened link between performance assessment systems and business plan objectives. Caution should be exercised in using customer ratings, however, as there are both direct and indirect costs to the organization of their use. Customers expect a response from the organization when they take the time to rate employees and, hence, not only must the ratings be processed, but acknowledgments in the form of letters to the customer must be sent which add indirect costs. Direct costs include any actions that must be taken as a result of a letter from a customer to remedy the situation if poor service was provided (e.g., a free meal).

A critical question faced by organizations in the performance assessment is "Which rating sources should be used?" The answer is threefold. First, in most cases multiple raters should be used as multiple ratings are likely to be more reliable than single ratings (Latham & Wexley, 1994). Second, multiple raters should be very carefully selected. In particular, only those raters who have the opportunity to observe and are knowledgeable about the job of the person being evaluated should be selected (Borman, 1991). Third, raters should be asked only to rate those aspects of the job which they are knowledgeable about (Cardy & Dobbins, 1994). For example, subordinates may be knowledgeable about their manager's performance in delegating assessments, but have little knowledge about their budgeting performance.

Administration

The effectiveness of performance assessments is also dependent on administrative practices, such as how and when ratings are conducted. Often what is required by the organization in terms of making assessments is in conflict with the capabilities of the rater cognitively to process performance information (Heneman, 1992); as a result, the validity of ratings is diminished. Therefore, to increase the validity of ratings, attention must be devoted to making administrative practice more consistent with cognitive processes. Fortunately, recent research in the area of cognition as it applies to performance appraisal provides some guidance about how to make administrative practice congruent with cognitive processes.

The most promising avenue for organizations to pursue in increasing the effectiveness of performance assessments is to provide raters with training. Smith (1986) reviewed 24 studies of performance assessment training and found it effective in increasing the validity of performance assessments under two important conditions. First, the more active the raters are in the training process, the better the outcomes. Raters should be given the opportunity to discuss issues of concern and participate in practice and feedback sessions. Second, raters should be put in practice sessions with the actual performance standards they are expected to use. These standards help structure the observation and judgment of performance which, in turn, leads to more valid ratings. Not only do these two steps help to increase the abilities of evaluators, they motivate raters to make valid assessments as well (Bernardin, Cardy, & Abbott, 1982). Unfortunately, most training programs do not build these steps into the program and instead simply focus on how to fill out and route forms associated with the appraisal process (Bretz, Milkovich, & Read, 1992). Organizations need to devote more resources to these proven training techniques for increasing the validity of performance assessments. These approaches are costly, how-ever, and they may not be possible in smaller organizations.

Another way to increase the validity of ratings, which has received less empirical study thus far but appears to hold great promise, is to hold raters accountable for the results of their ratings. If rewards are provided for valid ratings and announced in advance, then raters do a better job of cognitively processing performance information, which results in more valid ratings (Salvemini, Reilly, & Smither, 1993). Unfortunately, most organizations cur-rently do not generally follow this practice. A study of employer practices in the banking and newspaper industries by Napier and Latham (1986) found that not only do raters not receive tangible rewards for valid ratings, they do not even receive a word of appreciation from the boss!

A notable exception here is Pratt & Whitney which ties rewards for man-agers directly to how well they conduct performance assessments of their subordinates (Schneier, 1989). This practice can also be followed in the public sector and with smaller organizations as well. For example, in the municipal government of Columbus, Ohio, managers' appraisals include a measure of how well they conduct performance assessments of their subor-dinates. Criteria evaluated to make this determination include whether they turn the ratings in on time, the level of documentation provided to substantiate their ratings, and whether they provided feedback to the employees. In turn, their performance on these criteria serve as one of sev-eral measures used to determine the size of their merit pay increase.

An additional body of literature indicates that raters should keep diaries of critical performance ratings. One reason for this recommendation is that a delay between the observation and recording of performance infor-mation reduces the validity of assessments due to memory decay over time (Heneman & Wexley, 1983). Furthermore, demands on memory are less-ened with a diary. A second reason for the use of diaries is that the validity of ratings is lower when raters do not have comparative data on how other employees are performing (Heneman, 1986); this is especially true with self-appraisals (Farh & Dobbins, 1989). Diaries can be used so that compar-ative performance data are available on demand. The effectiveness of dia-ries was reported in a study by DeNisi, Robbins, and Cafferty (1989). They found that raters who keep a diary were more valid than raters who did not keep a diary. Also, they found that raters who organized their diaries by the ratee, rather than by the task performed by the ratee, were more accurate. This finding indicates that a separate file should be kept on each employee to record critical performance incidents.

The keeping of diaries requires extra time by the evaluator in the rating process. Hence, it may be seen as a cost by the evaluator. In order to mini-mize the cost, only critical incidents of highly effective or ineffective per-formance should be recorded, rather than recording everything the employee does. From the organization's perspective, the time cost may be offset by the increased validity of the assessments. Hence, organizations may be willing to provide incentives for diary-keeping by managers. To do so diary-keeping maybe one standard that evaluators are held accountable for in the assessment of the evaluator's performance.

A final administrative issue that needs to be addressed in order to produce effective performance assessments concerns the parties to be involved in the development of performance standards. Traditionally, performance standards were developed by the human resource department for everyone or by managers for their direct reports. Neither practice is recommended, given current theory and research. Managers and employees, not human resource departments or managers alone, should develop performance standards. Friedman and Cornelius (1976) found that when managers participated in the development of performance standards, the ratings were more valid than ratings made when managers were not involved in the process of setting standards. Employees should also be involved in the development of standards being used by their managers to rate their performance. By participating in the process employees are likely to feel that there is greater fairness (procedural justice) than when they do not participate (Greenberg, 1986); another result is likely to be improved motivation on the part of the employee. Silverman and Wexley (1984) reported that employees involved in the setting of performance standards for their positions were more satisfied with the appraisals and more willing to improve their performance than were employees not involved in the setting of standards for their positions.

Incentives may need to be provided by the organization to get managers to undertake participation in standard-setting. Involving employees in the setting of standards takes a considerable amount of time by the manager to teach employees how to do this and to review the standards being set by the employee. Hence, there is a disincentive (the time required) for managers to use participation. From the organization's perspective, however, this cost in the form of time may be offset by the increased validity and acceptability of the assessments. Consequently, the organization may formally require managers to use participation by making it apart of the manager's performance assessment. In turn, the incentive of a pay increase can be tied to this part of the manager's performance assessment.

Social Influence

Although much research has been conducted on characteristics of the rater and ratee which influence the effectiveness of performance ratings, little attention has been directed to the influence of social interactions between raters and ratees (Wexley & Klimoski, 1984). This lack of research has been a problematic oversight in that social interactions have a potentially important influence on the motivation of the rater (Harris, 1994) and affective states of the rater (Wayne & Kacmar, 1991). One promising area of research is the influence of impression management techniques on the effectiveness of performance assessment.

Employees engage in behaviors intended to manage the impressions of the rater (i.e., impression management). The hope, of course, is to create positive impressions of one's self which in turn result in a favorable performance assessment. The available research indicates that there is general support for this intention. Impression management tactics by employees lead to a positive affect ("liking") by the manager, which in turn results in favorable performance ratings (Ferris, Judge, Rowland, & Fitzgibbons, 1994). Not all impression management tactics by employees are successful, however. While being politically connected produces more favorable ratings (Bartol & Martin, 1990), as does the threat to use such connections, using ingratiation or flattery is not effective (Gould & Penley, 1984; Martin, 1987). Clearly, politics play a very important, but often overlooked, part of the performance appraisal process (Longnecker, Sims, & Gioia, 1987).

Impression management techniques are not only undertaken by the person being evaluated, they are undertaken by the evaluator as well (Harris, 1994). These tactics are used by the evaluators to influence both the people that report to them and the people they report to. Evaluators may give out high rating with positive leniency to impress their boss—a "perverse incentive" (Lewin & Mitchell, 1995). By having a staff of high performing subordinates, evaluators can boast to their bosses about what a good job they have done at developing their subordinates. In contrast, evaluators may give low ratings with negative leniency to protect themselves from the wrath of their bosses. By having a staff of subordinates with low ratings, the evaluators can attribute their own failures to the staff rather than to themselves. Finally, evaluators may give average ratings with central tendency (error) in order to maintain work group cohesion. By evaluating everyone as average, evaluator's may believe that they have not created any friends (because no high ratings were given), but also have not created any enemies (because no low ratings were given). As can be seen from these examples, impression management techniques can be self-serving for the evaluator as well as the employee.

CONCLUSION

Managers and human resource specialists often become disenchanted with performance assessments. One response to this disenchantment is to eliminate performance assessments. The elimination of performance assessments is not an acceptable practice, however, as it ignores the much needed role that performance assessment plays in making management decisions, providing developmental feedback, and supporting staffing and training practices. Another response to this disenchantment with performance assessments is to attempt to develop an "ideal form" that will lead to performance assessments which are reliable, valid, legal, fair, and practical. Research and practice has clearly demonstrated that it is virtually impossible to create such a form, however.

A better approach to developing effective performance assessments is to come to an understanding of the *context* in which performance assessments are made and the *processes* used by evaluators to make performance assessments. An understanding of the *context* leads to the development of development of performance assessment systems that are linked to the goals of the organization, rather than merely a form based on the whims and fancies of managers and human resource specialists. Consideration of the context also promotes the development of performance assessment systems that are consistent with the law, the culture of the organization, and labor organizations, rather than a form that can be used in all situations.

An understanding of the *process* leads to measurement issues, sources of assessments, management practices, and social influences that must be accommodated by a performance assessment system. Attention should be devoted to using multiple measures of performance at both the individual and group levels, gathering performance data from multiple sources, recording performance incidents immediately in a diary, providing training to raters, holding raters accountable for their ratings, and involving employees in the development of standards. By taking these steps, we are confident that more effective performance assessments can be made, and that the disappointment associated with the creation of new performance assessment methods will be check.

We are still very concerned, however, about the lack of research being conducted on measuring performance at the level of the group. As shown in this chapter, there are some very important reasons to measure performance of the team, as well as the business unit and organization. At the same time, there are also problems with measurement at this level, especially the degree to which the performance of the group can be influenced by individual members of the group. More research is certainly needed here, and we hope that it will be directed at context and process issues concerning group performance rather than being directed at attempting to develop the "best" format to capture group performance.

REFERENCES

Adams, J.S. (1965). Inequity in social exchange. In L.R. Berkowitz (Ed.), *Advances in experimental social psychology* (Vol. 2, pp. 267–299). New York: Academic Press.

Austin, J.T., Villanova, P., Kane, J.S., & Bernadin, H.J. (1991). Construct validation of performance measures: Definitional issues, development, and evaluation of indicators. In G.R. Ferris & K.M. Rowland (Eds.), *Research in personnel and human resources management* (Vol. 9, pp. 159–233). Greenwich, CT: JAI Press.

Balkin, D.B. (1989). Union influences on pay policy: A survey. *Journal of Labor Research, 10,* 299–310.

Barkin, S. (1948). Labor's attitude toward wage incentive plans. *Industrial and Labor Relations Review, 1,* 553–572.

Bartol, K.M., & Martin, D.L. (1990). When politics pays: Factors influencing managerial cooperation decisions. *Personnel Psychology, 43,* 599–610.

Bernardin, H.J. Cardy, R.L., & Abbot, J.G. (1982). *The effects of individual performance schemata, familiarization with the rating scales and racer motivation on rating effectiveness.* Paper presented at the annual Academy of Management meetings.

Borman, W.C. (1991). Job behavior, performance, and effectiveness. In M.D. Dunnette & L.M. Hough (Eds.), *Handbook of industrial/organizational psychology* (Vol. 2, 2nd ed.). Palo Alto, CA: Consulting Psychologists.

Borman, W.C., & Motowildo, S.J. (1993). Expanding the criterion domain to include elements of contextual performance. In N. Schmitt & W.C. Borman (Eds.), *Personnel selection organizations* (pp. 71–98). San Francisco: Jossey-Bass.

Borman, W.C., White, L.A., Pulakos, E.D., & Oppler, S.H. (1991). Models of supervisory job performance ratings. *Journal of Applied Psychology, 76,* 863–872.

Bretz, R.D., Jr., Milkovich, G.T., & Read, W. (1992). The current state of performance appraisal research and practice: Concerns, directions, and implications. *Journal of Management, 18,* 321–352.

Campbell, J.P., McCloy, R.A., Oppler, S.H., & Sager, C.E. (1993). A theory of performance. In N. Schmitt & W.C. Borman (Eds.), *Personnel selection in organizations* (pp. 35–70). San Francisco: Jossey-Bass.

Cardy, R.L., & Dobbins, G.H. (1994). *Performance appraisal: Alternative perspectives.* Cincinnati OH: South-Western.

DeNisi, A.S., Cafferty, T.P., & Meglino, B.M. (1984). A cognitive view of performance appraisal: A model and research propositions. *Organizational Behavior and Human Performance, 33,* 360–396.

DeNisi, A.S., Robbins, T., & Cafferty, T.P. (1989). Organization of information used for performance appraisals: Role of diary keeping. *Journal of Applied Psychology, 74,* 124–129.

Dickinson, T.L. (1993). Attitudes about performance appraisal. In H. Schules, J.L. Farr, & M. Smith (Eds.), *Personnel selection and assessment* (pp. 141–161). Hillsdale, NJ: Lawrence Elsbaum.

Farh, J.L., & Dobbins, G.H. (1989). Effects of comparative performance information on the accuracy of self-ratings and agreement between self and supervisory ratings. *Journal of Applied Psychology, 74,* 606–610.

Feild,H.S., & Honey, W.H. (1982). The relationship of performance appraisal system characteristics to verdicts in selected employment discrimination cases. *Academy of Management Journal, 25,* 392–406.

Feldman, J.M. (1981). Beyond attribution theory: Cognitive processes in performance appraisal. *Journal of Applied Psychology, 66,* 127–148.

Ferris, G.R., Judge, T.A., Rowland, K.M., & Fitzgibbons, D.E. (1994). Subordinate influence on the performance evaluation process: Test of a model. *Organizational Behavior and Human Decision Processes, 58,* 101–135.

Freeman, R.B. (1982). Union wage practices and wage dispersion within establishments. *Industrial and Labor Relations Review, 36,* 3–21.

Fried, Y., Tiegs, R.B., & Bellamy, A. (1992). Personal and interpersonal predictors of supervisors' avoidance of evaluating subordinates. *Journal of Applied Psychology, 77,* 462–468.

Friedman, B.A., & Cornelius, E.T., III. (1976). Effects of rater participation in scale construction on the psychometric characteristics of two rating scale formats. *Journal of Applied Psychology, 61,* 210–216.

Gaertner, K.S., & Gaertner, G.H. (1987). Union membership and attitudes toward participation in determining conditions of work in the federal government. *Human Relations, 40,* 431–444.

Gould, S., & Penley, L.E. (1984). Career strategies and salary progression: A study of their relationships in a municipal bureaucracy. *Organizational Behavior and Human performance, 34,* 244–265.

Greenberg, J. (1986). Determinants of perceived fairness of performance evaluations. *Journal of Applied Psychology, 71,* 340–342.

Greenberg, J . (1987). A taxonomy of organizational justice theories. *Academy of Management Review, 12,* 9–22.

Harris, M.M. (1994). Rater motivation in the performance appraisal context: A theoretical perspective. *Journal of Management, 20,* 737–756.

Harris, M.M., & Schaubroeck, J. (1988). A meta-analysis of self-supervisor, self-peer, and peer-supervisor ratings. *Personnel Psychology, 41,* 43–62.

Heneman, R.L. (1986). The relationship between supervisory ratings and results-oriented measures of performance: A meta-analysis. *Personnel Psychology, 39,* 811–826.

Heneman, R.L. (1992). *Merit pay: Linking pay increases to performance ratings.* Reading, MA: Addison-Wesley.

Heneman, R.L., & Wexley, K.N. (1983). The effects of time delay in rating and amount of information observed on performance rating accuracy. *Academy of Management Journal, 26,* 677–686.

Hogan, R.T. (1991). Personality and personality measurement. In M.D. Dunnette & L.M. Hough (Eds.), *Handbook of industrial/ organizational psychology* (Vol. 2, pp. 873–919, 2nd ed.). Palo Alto, CA: Consulting Psychologists.

Hunter, J.E. (1986). Cognitive ability, cognitive aptitudes, job knowledge, and job performance. *Journal of Vocational Behavior, 29,* 340–362.

Ilgen, D.R., & Favero, J.L. (1985). Limits in generalizing from psychological research to performance appraisal processes. *Academy of Management Review, 10,* 311–321.

Ilgen, D.R., Barnes-Farrel, J.L., & McKellin, D.B. (1993). Performance appraisal process research in the 1980's: What has contributed to appraisals in use? *Organizational Behavior and Human Decision Processes, 54,* 321–368.

Isen, M. (1987). Positive affect, cognitive processes, and social behavior. In L. Berkowitz (Ed.), *Advances in experimental social psychology* (Vol. 20, pp. 203–253). New York: Academic Press.

Landy, F.J., & Farr, J.L. (1980). Performance ratings. *Psychological Bulletin, 87,* 72–107.

Latham, G.P., & Wexley, K.N. (1994). *Increasing productivity through performance appraisal* (2nd ed.). Reading, MA: Addison-Wesley.

Lawler, E.E., III (1994, May-June). Performance management: The next generation. *Compensation & Benefits Review,* 16–19.

Leventhal, G.S., Karuza, J., & Fry, W.R. (1980). Beyond fairness: A theory of allocation preferences. In J.M. Kula (Ed.), *Justice and social interaction* (pp. 167–218). New York: Springer-Verlag.

Lewin, D., & Mitchell, D.J.P. (1995). *Human. resource management: An economic approach* (2nd ed.). Cincinnati, OH: South Western.

Locke, E., & Latham, G.P. (1990). *A theory of goal setting and monetary incentives.* New York: Prentice-Hall.

Longnecker, C.O., Sims, H.P., & Gioia, D.A. (1987). Beyond the mask: The politics of employee appraisal. *Academy of Management Executive, 1,* 183–193.

Love, K.G. (1981). Comparisons of peer assessment methods: Reliability, validity, friendship bias, and user reaction. *Journal of Applied Psychology, 66,* 451–457.

Martin, D.C., Bartol, K.M., & Levine, M.J. (1987). The legal ramifications of performance appraisal. *Employee Relations Law Journal, 12,* 370–395.

Martin, D.L., (1987). Factors influencing pay decisions: Balancing managerial vulnerabilities. *Human Relations, 40,* 417–430.

McAdams, J.L., & Hawk, E.J. (1994). *Organizational performance and rewards: 663 experiences in making the link.* Scottsdale, AZ: American Compensation Association.

Mitchell, D.J.B., Lewin, D., & Lawler, E.E., III. (1990). Alternative pay systems, firm performance, and productivity. In A.S. Blinder (Ed.), *Paying for productivity: A look at the evidence* (pp. 15–87). Washington: The Brookings Institution.

Mohrman, A.J., Jr., Resnick-West, S.M., & Lawler, E.E., III. (1989). *Designing performance appraisal systems.* San Francisco: Jossey-Bass.

Murphy, K.R., & Cleveland, J.R. (1991). *Performance appraisal: An organization's perspective.* Boston: Allyn & Bacon.

Napier, N.K., & Latham, G.P. (1986). Outcome expectancies of people who conduct performance appraisals. *Personnel Psychology, 39,* 827–837.

Nathan, B.R., & Cascio, W.F. (1986). Technical and legal standards. In R.A. Berk (Ed.), *Performance assessment* (pp. 1–50). Baltimore, MD: John Hopkins.

Noe, R.A., Hollenbeck, J.R. Gerhart, B., & Wright, P.M. (1994). *Human resource management. Gaining a competitive advantage.* Burr Ridge, IL: Irwin.

Organ, D. (1988). *Organizational citizenship behavior: The good soldier syndrome.* Lexington, MA: D.C. Heath.

Ott, J.S. (1989). *The organizational culture perspective.* Chicago: The Dorsey Press.

Patten, T.H., Jr. (1982). *Performance appraisal: A manager's guide.* New York; Free Press.

Pritchard, R.D. (1992). Organizational productivity. In M.D. Dunnette & L.M. Hough (Eds.), *Handbook of industrial and organizational psychology* (Vol. 3, pp. 443–471, 2nd ed.). Palo Alto, CA: Consulting Psychologists.

Salvemini, N.J., Reilly, R.R., & Smither, J.W. (1993). The influence of rather motivation on assimilation effects and accuracy in performance ratings. *Organizational Behavior and Human Decision Processes, 55,* 41–60.

Schneier, C.E. (1989). Implementing performance management and recognition and reward (PMRR) systems at the strategic level: A line management effort. *Human Resource Planning, 12,* 205–220.

Scott, W.R. (1992). *Organizations: Rational, natural and open systems* (3rd ed.). Englewood Cliffs, NJ: Prentice-Hall.

Shaw, D.G., & Scheiner, C.E. (1994), Making organization change happen: The keys to successful delayering. *Human Resource Planning, 16,* 1–18.

Silverman, S.B., & Wexley, K.N. (1984). Reactions of employees to performance appraisal interviews as a function of their participation in scale development. *Personnel Psychology, 37,* 703–710.

Sinclair, R.C. (1988). Mood, categorization breadth, and performance appraisal: The effects of order of information acquisition and affective states on halo, accuracy, information retrieval and evaluations. *Organizational Behavior and Human Decision Processes, 42,* 22–46.

Smith, D.E. (1986). Training programs for performance appraisal: A review. *Academy of Management Review, 11,* 22–40.

Smith, P.L. (1976). Behaviors, results, and organizational effectiveness: The problem of criteria. In M.D. Dunnette (Ed.), *Handbook of industrial and organizational psychology.* Chicago: Rand McNally.

Thorndike, R.L. (1949). *Personnel selection: Tests and measurement.* New York: Wiley.

Tucker, S.A., & Cofsky, K.M. (1994, Spring). Competency-based pay on a banding platform. *ACA Journal,* 30–45.

U.S. Department of Labor (1981). *Characteristics of major collective bargaining agreements.* Washington, DC: U.S. Government Printing Office.

Walton, R.E. (1985, March-April). From control to commitment in the workplace. *Harvard Business Review,* 76–84.

Wanous J.P. (1992). *Organizational entry: Recruitment, selection, orientation, and socialization of newcomers.* Reading, MA: Addison-Wesley.

Wayne, S.J., & Kacmar, K.M. (1991). The effects of impression management on the performance appraisal process. *Organizational Behavior and Human Decision Processes, 48,* 70–88.

Wexley, K.N. (1984). Appraisal Interview In R.A. Berk (Ed.), *Performance assessment, methods, and applications.* Baltimore, MD: John Hopkins.

Wexley, K.N., & Klimoski, R.J. (1984). Performance appraisal: An update. In K.M. Rowland & G.R. Ferris (Eds.), *Research in personnel and human resources management* (Vol. 2). Greenwich, CT: JAI Press.

Whetten, D.A., & Cameron, K.S. (1994). Organizational effectiveness: Old models and new constructs. In J. Greenberg (Ed.), *Organizational behavior: State of science* (pp. 135–154). Hillsdale, NJ: Lawrence Erlbaum Associates.

Weirsma, U., & Latham, G.P. (1986). The practicality of behavioral observation scales, and trait scales. *Personnel Psychology, 39,* 619–628.

Wood, D.J. (1991). Corporate social performance revisited. *Academy of Management Journal, 16,* 691–714.
Zigon, J. (1994, Autumn). Measuring the performance of work teams. *ACA Journal,* 18–33, 30.

CHAPTER 18

MERIT PAY

Robert L. Heneman

Source: This chapter is from *The Executive Handbook of Compensation,* edited by Charles Fay (pp. 447–64). Copyright 2000 by The Hay Group. Reprinted with permission of The Free Press, a Division of Simon & Schuster, Inc.

In some compensation circles, it has become popular to proclaim that merit pay is "dead." The argument goes that merit pay is rapidly declining in the frequency of its use because it is no longer a viable reward option. While interesting, the conclusion that merit pay plans are dead is simply false. Surveys indicate that merit pay is frequently used by organizations, and the research clearly shows that merit pay can be successful in some situations. Motorola and Hewlett-Packard have used merit pay for many years. There are problems with merit pay, but that does not mean that the concept is no longer valid or that merit pay plans are no longer used.

The first objective of this chapter is to show that, when merit pay is issued for the right reasons, and when enough attention is paid to strategy and implementation issues associated with merit pay, it can be a viable reward program. Conversely, if the time and resources needed to address strategy and implementation are not allocated, then merit pay should be dead. The second objective is to suggest some new directions that merit pay should take. In particular, attention will be given to: (1) taking lessons from alternative reward plans (e.g., skill-based pay, gainsharing, profit sharing) and applying them to merit pay, and (2) how merit pay can be used to complement other strategic reward programs. In support of these two objectives, topics are organized as follows: process and philosophy, strategic considerations, integration with other pay and human resources programs, and summary and conclusions.

PROCESS AND PHILOSOPHY

By definition alone, merit pay is a very straightforward concept. In the *American Compensation Association Glossary*, a merit pay increase is defined as: An increase to an individual's base pay rate based on performance.

Although merit pay is straightforward in concept, it becomes much more complex in practice. Designing, implementing, and administering a merit pay plan is very complicated because of the many variables connected to the pay-for-performance relationship, as shown in Figure 1.

For example, in a study conducted with a local manufacturing company, I found that not only did non-performance-related factors (e.g., age, tenure) predict the size of the merit pay recipients' merit increases, but the non-performance-related factors of the *evaluator* also predicted the recipients' merit increases (Heneman & Cohen, 1988). Although the company had a strongly worded policy for merit pay increases, the policy in and of

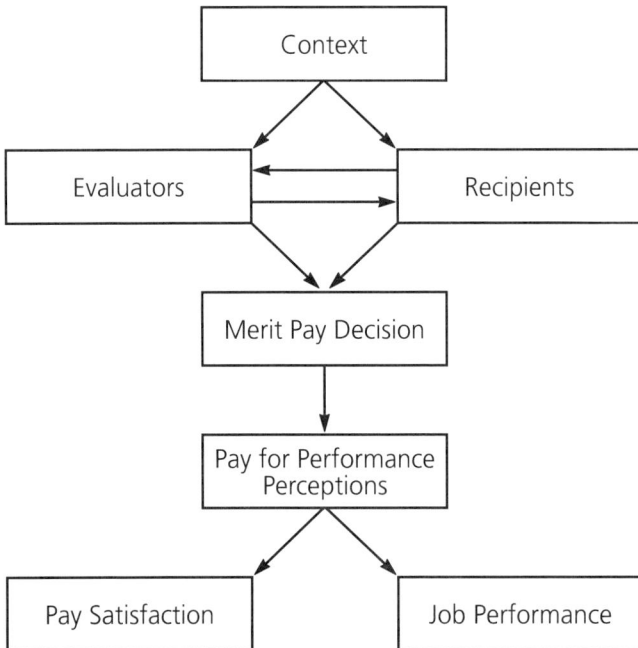

Figure 1.   The merit pay process.

itself was very ineffective, given the complexity of the criteria used to determine pay increases.

As another example, along with the evaluators' and recipients' characteristics, the context they operate in also influences the pay-performance relationship. Research has shown that merit pay increases are larger for employees who are in a "tight" labor market (demand for workers exceeds supply) than for employees in a "loose" labor market (supply of workers exceeds demands), even when employees in the two kinds of labor markets have the same level of performance (Heneman, 1990).

As a final example, pay-for-performance perceptions may be different from the correlation between actual performance ratings and actual merit increases. Research has shown this to be an actual relationship, but few studies have found a *perceived* relationship (Heneman, 1992).

Research also indicates that a perceived relationship is critical to the success of merit pay plans (Eskew & Heneman, 1996; Lowery, Petty, & Thompson, 1997). If merit pay is to be effective, establishing an actual relationship between pay and performance is simply not enough. Employees must *see* the relationship; too often, they do not.

Given the complexities associated with merit pay, creating an effective merit pay plan is a difficult process. An effective plan needs an actual and a perceived relationship between pay and performance. For these links to occur, there must be a substantial investment in the development of a sound merit pay strategy and a set of implementation procedures. The return on this investment, in terms of improved employee attitudes (e.g., pay satisfaction) and behaviors (e.g., attendance), is documented in the research (Heneman, 1990, 1992).

Ultimately, one must decide whether to use or not use merit pay. Organizations without merit pay often do not have slack resources for experimentation with merit pay, so they must decide whether to adopt a merit pay policy prior to knowing the actual effectiveness of the plan. Organizations with merit pay often have not monitored its effectiveness, and no data are available to support or reject the continued usage of a merit pay plan. In these companies, decisions regarding the use of merit pay are often made on a philosophical basis. Unfortunately, as shown in Table 1, misconception is the real basis of this philosophical decision. Fortunately, some factual information does support the philosophical decision to use or not use merit pay (see Table 1).

Should merit pay always be used? No, it should not; but neither should it be automatically excluded as the basis for a reward program because someone has pronounced merit pay as being "dead." It is very difficult to reject merit pay on philosophical grounds when one considers how frequently it is used, how much it is desired by employees, and the impact that it may have on the organization. The appropriateness of merit pay for an organi-

Table 1.   Myths and Realities Concerning Merit Pay

Myth 1	Organizations have abandoned merit pay
Reality	Merit pay is the most frequently used reward program; over 80 percent of employers use it.
Myth 2	Merit pay programs are ineffective
Reality	Merit pay is almost always related to improved employee attitudes (which, in turn, are related to attendance and retention), and merit pay is sometimes related to improved job performance.
Myth 3	Merit pay decreases satisfaction with work.
Reality	Merit pay adds to satisfaction with work.
Myth 4	Employees prefer team and organization based rewards over individual rewards such as merit pay.
Reality	Employees prefer individual rewards over team and organization based rewards.

Note: Data from LeBlanc and Mulvey (1998) and Heneman (1992).

zation is very difficult, if not impossible, to assess on a philosophical level. Consideration must also be given to the organization's strategic design and implementation issues.

STRATEGIC CONSIDERATIONS

To design and implement an effective merit pay plan, many key strategic issues must be considered. The strategic areas for consideration are presented in Figure 2. Their organization shows the steps that are needed to develop a merit pay plan (Seltz & Heneman, 1993). The steps also form an audit checklist for organizations with an existing merit pay plan.

Business and Compensation Strategies

Perhaps the biggest problem with existing merit pay programs is failure to tie them to the business strategy of the organization. Merit pay is then mistakenly viewed as entitlement. Employees often fail to see a link between merit pay and the accomplishment of business goals because no link is being made.

Business strategies help the organizations to define who they are (mission statement) and to state their long-term (vision statement) and short-term goals (operational plans). Merit pay should be used to help organiza-

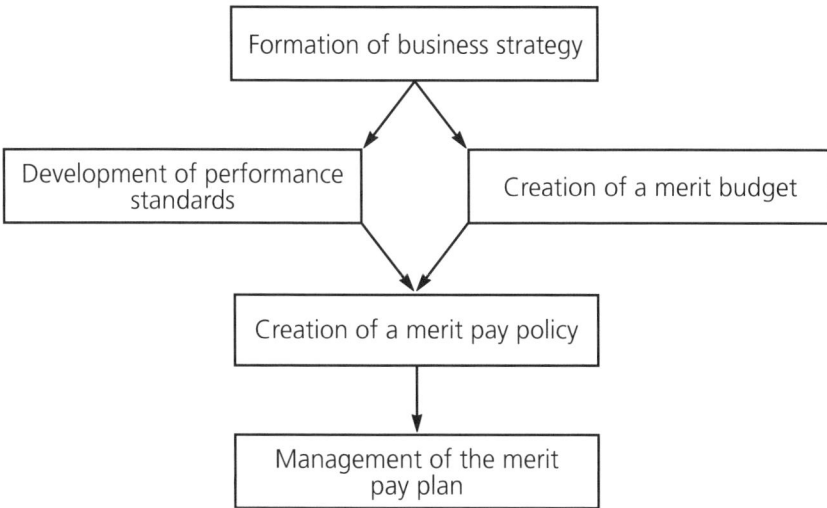

Figure 2.   Merit pay programs: strategic considerations.

tions accomplish these objectives. Merit pay can support business strategies in one of the three following ways:

1. Merit pay can be used as a stand-alone reward program, that is, as the sole platform for linking pay to performance in the organization. This is a very common approach where the only pay-for-performance plan is merit pay. Unfortunately, merit pay often fails as a stand-alone program because too much is being attempted with just one pay plan (Eskew & Heneman, 1996). Organizations have multiple strategic objectives, and multiple pay-fox-performance plans are often needed to support these objectives. Lincoln Electric and Motorola have used merit pay in conjunction with other reward plans to successfully achieve their business objectives.

2. Merit pay can be used as a "transitional" reward program, while the organization is moving from one type of culture to another. For example, many organizations retain a reward system designed to reward individuals while work to be performed in teams is being designed. If team pay immediately replaces merit pay, it may be too much of a "shock" to the culture of an organization that has emphasized individuals rather than teams as rewards recipients. If the individual reward plan continues in use, however, efforts to develop a team culture may be thwarted. Instead, team-based merit pay can be used during the organization's transition to team emphasis. With

this approach, reward for performance is defined in terms of team-work. If employees demonstrate individual behaviors consistent with being good team players (e.g., preparing for and attending team meetings, helping other team members when their own work is completed), merit pay is granted. Teamwork has been successfully used as a criterion for individual rewards by Johnsonville Foods. Team pay can more easily be implemented after this transitionary use of merit pay.

3. Merit pay can be a complement to other reward programs. Merit pay can support some strategic objectives while other reward programs support other strategic objectives. (Ways of accomplishing this approach are described later in this chapter.) In general, merit pay would seem to work best in rewarding the "soft" criteria for effective organizational functioning. Soft criteria measure *how* goals are accomplished (e.g., teamwork, customer service). "Hard" criteria measure *what is* accomplished (e.g., productivity, profit). If organizations are to learn and develop the most effective ways to produce the *what,* then the *how* must be clearly articulated and rewarded. Quantum is a successful organization that rewards both the *what* and the *how.* The *how is* rewarded with merit pay.

Performance Standards

The measurement of performance is sometimes said to be the "Achilles' heel" of merit pay plans. Theories of motivation, borrowed from psychology, indicate that there must be a clear link between pay and performance if merit pay is to be motivational. For this link to occur, attention must be given to the measurement issues in Table 2.

Table 2.   Measurement Issues for Merit Pay

1. What sources should be used to develop performance standards?

- Organizational competencies
- Organizational values
- Job duties

2. At what level should performance standards for merit pay be measured?

- Individual
- Team

3. What types of performance measures should be used?

- Results
- Behaviors

Table 2.   Measurement Issues for Merit Pay (Cont.)

4. Who should evaluate performance?

- Superiors
- Supervisor
- Self
- Peers
- Subordinates
- Customers

The performance standards used in a merit pay plan should be closely linked to the business strategy of the organization. Unfortunately, this is often not done. Too many organizations use personality characteristics (e.g., temperament), which are difficult to observe, or generic standards (e.g., quality, quantity), which are too general to measure accurately. The relationship between subjective measures such as these and the business plan is not clear.

What performance standards are appropriate for purposes of merit pay increases? Some critical strategic assessments are required. One set of assessments revolves around defining the core competencies or capabilities of the organization. The organization must be clear about what it does best—what differentiates it from its competitors; for example, some organizations attempt to distinguish themselves by delivering extraordinary customer service. In a company that is competing on such a basis, merit pay standards should reinforce these competencies. Traditional measures of personality or generic standards are not specific enough to capture a competency such as customer service. Instead, specific customer service strategies must be first formed and then captured on the merit pay rating form.

Another critical assessment involves values. The values of the organization articulate the philosophy to be used by members of the organization as they make decisions about the business. Merit pay standards can give life to the value statements of organizations. They can be used, along with competencies, as a source of performance standards.

A final source of performance standards is the job itself, as documented in a job analysis. Some observers have argued that "jobs" no longer exist because work is constantly changing and organizations need as much flexibility as possible. Extending this logic one step further suggests that specific tasks and duties do not form good sources of performance standards. This is a dangerous extension of the idea that work is "jobless." Our legal system clearly draws on the concept of jobs in pay discrimination suits, so to ignore the job is a recipe for potential legal disaster. The more difficult question to answer is: What should the relative balance be among competency-based, values-based, and job-based standards for merit pay decisions? Job-based standards are most prominent in the final equation, but the competencies and values of the organization are also present. The degree of their relationship is still open to deliberation.

Another balancing act with regard to performance standards has to do with the level of performance measurement. All of the standards previously reviewed can be measured at the level of the individual contributor, or the level of the team, or both. If only individual assessments are made, a competitive environment among team members may be created. Hence, the use of only individual standards is probably best where there are no interdependencies between jobs. If only team assessments are made, a "freerider" problem may result. Individuals may shirk their assignments because they know that the team's capabilities will make up for the loss of one person's performance. Team assessments alone should probably be used only for high-performance work teams in which shirking is not likely to be an issue. To ensure that both the team and the individuals thrive, it may be desirable to have both individual and team measures.

Performance standards can also be measured as results, behaviors, or competencies (knowledge, skills, abilities, and other performance attributes of the person). Results focus on what was accomplished, in very specific terms. The measurement of results is desirable because they can be used to set specific and challenging goals that will motivate employees. The downside to results is that they may be outside the control of the individual.

Behaviors are more difficult to measure, but they are critical for developmental purposes. They show employees how goals are to be accomplished. Because of the relative merits and drawbacks of each type of performance standard, organizations increasingly use both results and behaviors for performance standards in merit pay systems.

The use of competencies in merit pay is new. Emphasis is on the critical capabilities an individual must have, in order to exhibit effective behaviors and achieve desired results. Used along with behaviors and results, competencies more completely map the total performance domain. More controversial is the use of competencies to the exclusion of behaviors and results. Under this approach, merit pay would be allocated solely for potential, rather than demonstrated, performance. The potential that competencies guarantee to organizational flexibility is important, but only in extremely limited circumstances could organizations pay for this luxury without regard to demonstrated performance.

A final issue regarding performance measurement in merit pay systems is: Which individuals will rate performance? Traditional merit pay plans relied solely on ratings by immediate supervisors. Additional raters now being used in multirater or 360-degree performance reviews include superiors, subordinates, peers, self, and customers. For validation, additional raters are welcome. Multiple raters offer a more complete profile of performance, and the biases of raters may cancel each other, creating more accurate ratings for merit pay decisions. Two problems exist, however, when multirater assessments are used for purposes of merit pay decisions:

1. Having more raters is not always better. Raters should only be part of the process if they are knowledgeable about the job and have a reasonable opportunity to observe the person perform.
2. There is a potential for acrimonious behavior to occur. For example, peers may rate others low, to get a larger raise themselves; subordinates may "gang up" on the boss, and so on.

For a 360-degree approach to rating to be successful, raters need to be carefully selected. Evaluations should be first used as a developmental tool for a period of time, to get people comfortable with the system before it becomes the basis for merit pay decisions, and ratings should be kept anonymous.

In making decisions concerning performance measurement, a process issue must be considered: Who will make decisions regarding the performance measures to be used? Allowing some job incumbents to make these decisions is likely to result in standards that are better understood and more likely to be accepted by all job incumbents than if senior managers make these decisions alone. On the other hand, the use of job incumbents is more time-consuming than if senior managers alone decide. As a compromise, many organizations assign a team of managers and job incumbents to deliver, in a timely manner, a set of standards related to the business strategy and acceptable to employees. Although not all employees and managers are directly involved in creating the standards, they at least know that they have a "voice" in the process.

Merit Budget

Determining the merit budget requires attention to both the size and the distribution of the budget. Among the factors used to determine the size of the budget are: the financial performance of the organization, its competitive position in the market, and the current cost of living. Distribution of the budget is usually based on a uniform percentage of payroll dollars for each business unit. Although this basis is easy to administer and not likely to raise equity issues, a uniform percentage for each business unit fails to recognize that some business units are more successful than others. Instead, consideration should be given to a non-uniform budget size for business units, based on each unit's performance. Although this approach will raise the issue of inequities across business units, it will force the organization to justify any inequities by carefully tracking each business unit's performance. An early effect will be that employees become more aware of the finances of the business. Merit pay may then gain some of the positive features of gainsharing, goal sharing, and profit sharing, wherein employees are taught the basics of the business through the reward plan.

Merit Pay Policy

Three strategic issues arise in the creation of a merit pay policy: (1) the size of the merit increase, (2) the form of the increase (cash bonus or base pay increase), and (3) the timing of the increase (anniversary vs. common review date). There does not appear to be any magic number for the size of a merit increase, but several guidelines have emerged front practice. Increases for high performers should be high relative to low performers. To accomplish this objective, employers can actively manage low-performing employees out of the organization or grant them no increases. At a minimum, the average merit increase should be at the level of the cost of living, to keep employees whole with the economy. Ideally, high performers should receive a greater increase than average performers: (1) to have a noticeable impact on the behaviors and attitudes of average employees aspiring to higher levels of performance, and (2) to motivate higher performers to maintain this level of performance.

Many organizations now use lump-sum increases; cash is paid out as a yearly bonus for merit and must be re-earned each year. This approach contrasts with traditional merit increases that are paid as a permanent adjustment to base pay. Payroll costs are lessened for organizations using a lump-sum approach, and employees that are at the limit of their pay range can be given a merit increase because it does not cause their base salary to exceed the maximum. The downside to this approach is that total compensation for employees will be less in organizations with lump-sum rather than traditional merit plans. Although a lump sum is desirable from a cost perspective, it may limit the organization's ability to attract, retain, and motivate quality employees.

Regarding the timing of the increase, the traditional approach is to pay it out on the employee's anniversary date with the organization. This approach spreads the administrative burden of merit reviews over the length of the entire year, and managers can focus more attention on each review. The downside to the traditional approach, however, is that relative performance information about other employees may not be available. Research indicates that managers can do more accurate performance evaluations when relative data are available (Heneman & von Hippel, 1996). A common review date for all employees provides for relative performance evaluations, and, increasingly, organizations are moving toward that policy.

The downside is that busy managers have a larger number of evaluations to complete at one time, and the budgetary impact is felt all at once rather than being spread out over the entire year.

Merit Pay Management

After a merit pay policy has been established, managing the system requires careful attention to ensure delivery of the intended results. Two important issues here are pay secrecy and evaluation. Pay secrecy refers to the degree of concealment surrounding merit decisions within the organization. Secrecy is characterized by two dimensions: (1) outcomes, the actual merit increases received by employees, and (2) process, the factors (e.g., budget and performance ratings) used to determine actual merit increases. Organizations can range from being "open" to "closed"; most organizations are somewhere in between. Open merit pay plans are used at many public universities. At Ohio State University, public record laws allow not only employees, but the public as well, to access state employees personnel documents, including merit pay decisions. Information available to the public is both outcome and process in orientation. In a closed system, the only pieces of information available to employees are their individual performance ratings and their merit increase amounts. Most organizations let employees know the minimum and maximum values for pay increases, but not individual values other than the employees' own increase.

A dilemma here is that both open and closed merit systems have desirable features. Open systems allow employees to better understand the process and the outcomes and, as a result, feel a sense of ownership toward the system. Such an approach is desirable with participative systems of management. On the other hand, closed systems make it easier for supervisors to differentiate between employees on the basis of performance, because they do not have to defend the ratings to all employees. This approach is consistent with a managerial philosophy of pay for performance.

A compromise between the two systems allows organizations to become more open about the process and remain more closed about the outcome. To most employees, including managers, the merit budget process is a "black box" in the organization. Much more can and should be done to teach all employees about the budgetary process behind merit pay. As previously stated, this is a virtue of other reward programs such as profit sharing, and should be a part of merit pay as well. Employee representatives should sit on a merit budget committee to learn about the process and to be ambassadors of the process for the committee. Similarly, employee representatives should be made part of a committee to develop and oversee the performance assessment process. Better communication of the plan can also be reached by having a merit pay newsletter, a solution that was very successful for McDonnell Aircraft Company (Heneman, 1992). In the newsletter, employees were updated on matters such as the merit pay process and the performance evaluation process.

Another component of merit pay management is the process of evaluation. It is an embarrassment to our profession how few well-designed empirical studies have ever been conducted to assess the impact of merit pay, given the overwhelming number of companies that use merit pay and the huge direct and indirect costs involved. At an absolute minimum, companies should routinely collect data on the attitudinal impact of merit pay. Standardized measures of employees' attitudes toward pay, with sound reliability and validity properties, are easily accessible from the research literature (Heneman, Eskew, & Fox, 1998). Better yet, employers might assess using controlled designs to measure the impact of merit pay on performance and productivity. Unfortunately, the number of studies of this type can literally be counted on one hand.

INTEGRATION WITH OTHER PAY AND HUMAN RESOURCES PROGRAMS

Merit pay is too often viewed as a stand-alone program that is independent of other elements in a total compensation system and of the larger human resources subsystem of the organization. Direct linking with merit pay needs to be made in several areas: base pay, recruitment, performance appraisal, training, labor relations, and alternative reward programs.

Base Pay

When setting the level of merit pay, attention must be paid to base pay, which is a potential funding source for merit pay. In essence, an organization can choose to pay more or less base pay, in order to provide less or more merit pay. The ratio of merit pay to base pay is the amount of leverage in the system. Leverage can be higher when there is a well-developed performance evaluation system. Leverage should be lower when there is not a well-developed evaluation system, because the accuracy of the decisions reached will be lower, as will the employer's confidence in the system.

The amount of leverage for merit pay is also dependent on the capital heeds of the organization. If the capital needs are severe, the organization may not even have a merit pay plan and may instead offer, for example, stock or phantom stock to be converted to cash at a point in time when cash becomes readily available. Another strategy when cash is needed for capital is to increase the leverage in merit pay and pay for it with a reduction in base pay. There are, of course, trade-offs with a low base-pay strategy, including difficulty in attracting and retaining talent.

Performance evaluation and capital needs also work in concert with one another. Merit pay is disastrous in situations where the organization is in a start-up phase with high capital needs and little time to devote to the development of a sound performance evaluation system. Similarly, problems arise with merit pay in declining organizations. Again, capital needs are great, for survival, and the organization doesn't have the luxury of time to develop a sound evaluation system.

Recruitment

As odd as it may seem, traditional merit pay can be a source of competitive advantage in recruiting employees, especially during times such as pay and competencies are merged (Heneman & Thomas, 1997). Merit pay increases are granted to senior managers for what they know and do and for the results they produce. As another example, Cinergy Corporation uses a combined merit and skill-based pay plan for some of its unionized employees. Rather than just paying for skills or potential, Cinergy also pays out for the demonstration of these skills in the form of critical behaviors back on the job (Dalton, Stevens, & Heneman, 1997).

Rothschild Gourmet Foods uses team pay with a goal-sharing plan. Funding for the plan comes from the achievement of goals in cost, quality, and sales areas. Distribution of the funds is based on ratings of individual performance. Merit Resource Group combines profit sharing and merit pay. Profit serves as the funding gate, and distribution to employees is based on an assessment of their individual performance. Quantum combines team pay and merit pay. Pay increases are based on individual performance as well as team performance. As can be seen in these examples, merit pay can supplement pay for potential performance with pay for actual performance. Merit pay can also supplement rewards for team and organization-level performance with rewards for individual performance. The new pay programs being used by employers are not necessarily alternatives to merit pay. The new pay and merit pay can be complementary to one another.

SUMMARY AND CONCLUSIONS

Contrary to popular belief, merit pay programs are not dead. They continue to be used extensively and can add value to an organization if used appropriately. Many new strategies and techniques are available to enhance the value of merit pay plans and should be considered. Abandonment of merit pay is appropriate for organizations that are unwilling to reconfigure their merit pay plans to be in line with these new strategies and techniques.

Two objectives were advanced for this chapter. The first objective was to show the conditions under which merit pay is a viable pay program for organizations to use. It was shown that merit pay works best when it is directly linked to the business strategy of the organization rather than being viewed as a stand-alone compensation plan, as has been the case traditionally. Of equal importance is the relentless pursuit of a performance evaluation system that is reliable, valid, and acceptable to the affected parties. In and of themselves, written strategies and standards will do little good. Attention must also be paid to the merit pay process, including the budget, the review process, communication of merit pay, and integration with other pay and human resources systems. Specific techniques that seem to work were discussed in all of these areas.

A second objective was to show the possible synergy between merit pay and other strategic reward programs such as skill-based pay, goal sharing, and profit sharing. Merit pay should follow the lead of these programs in three ways:

1. Participation in the design and administration of the pay plan is needed.
2. The pay plan must be directly linked to the business strategy.
3. Rewards should include rewards for team-based contributions.

Merit pay can contribute to other strategic reward plans by helping to keep a focus on individual performance as well as potential performance, team performance, and organizational performance. Individualism is very strong in the United States, and employees expect the reward system to acknowledge this important aspect of our culture.

REFERENCES

Dalton, G.L., Stevens, J., & Heneman, R.L. (1997). Alternative rewards in union settings. *Journal for Quality and Participation, 27*(5), 26–31.

Eskew, D., & Heneman, R.L. (1996). A survey of merit pay plan effectiveness: End of the line for merit pay or hope for improvement? *Human Resource Planning, 19*(2), 12–19.

Heneman, R.L. (1990). Merit pay research. In G.R. Ferris & K.M. Rowland (Eds.), *Research in personnel and human resources management* (Vol. 8, pp. 203–263). Greenwich, CT: JAI Press.

Heneman, R.L. (1992). *Merit pay: Linking pay increases to performance ratings.* (Addison-Wesley HRM Series.) Reading, MA: Addison-Wesley.

Heneman, R.L., & Cohen, D.J. (1988, Summer). Supervisory and employee characteristics as correlates of employee salary increases. *Personnel Psychology, 41*(2), 345–360.

Heneman, R.L., Eskew, D., & Fox, J. (1998). Using survey data to evaluate the effectiveness of a profit sharing and performance management system in a high technology firm. *Compensation and Benefits Review, 30*(1), 40–44.

Heneman, R.L., & Thomas, A.L. (1997). The Limited, Inc: Using strategic performance to drive brand leadership. *Compensation and Benefits Review, 29*(6), 33–40.

Heneman, R.L., & von Hippel, C. (1996). The assessment of job performance: Focusing attention on context, process and group issues. In D. Lewin, D.J.B. Mitchell, & M.A. Zaidi (Eds.), *Handbook of human resource management* (pp. 587–617). Greenwich, CT: JAI Press.

LeBlanc, P.V., & Mulvey, P.W. (1998). How American workers see the rewards of work. *Compensation and Benefits Review, 3*(1), 24–28.

Lowery, C.M., Petty, M.M., & Thompson, J.W. (1996). Assessing the merit of merit pay: Employee reactions to performance-based pay. *Hunan Resource Planning, 19*(1), 26–37.

Seltz, S.P., & Heneman, R.L. (1993). *Linking pay to performance: An approach to designing merit pay plans.* (Building blocks in total compensation.) Scottsdale, AZ: American Compensation Association.

CHAPTER 19

A SURVEY OF MERIT PAY PLAN EFFECTIVENESS:

End of the Line for Merit Pay or Hope for Improvement?

Don Eskew and Robert L. Heneman

Source: Reprinted with permission from *Human Resource Planning, 19*(2), 1996. Copyright 1996 by The Human Resource Planning Society, 317 Madison Avenue, Suite 1509, New York, NY 10017, Phone: (212) 490-6387, Fax: (212) 682-6851.

The widespread use of merit pay plans by organizations is a continuing source of debate, with some arguing for and others against the effectiveness of merit pay plans. A survey of senior compensation professionals in 72 organizations was conducted to examine the effectiveness of merit pay in achieving organizational objectives. The results indicate that merit pay is seen as being "marginally successful" in influencing employee attitudes (e.g., pay satisfaction) and behaviors (e.g., performance) which represents a decrease in effectiveness compared to a survey conducted 10 years ago where merit pay was seen as "moderately successful." Merit pay practices shown to be related to improved merit pay plan effectiveness include clarifying the link between pay and performance for the employee by increasing the frequency of appraisals, establishing developmental action plans, and developing a formal merit pay policy with safeguards to ensure employee perceptions of fairness. It is concluded that unless improvements are made to existing merit pay plans they are likely to cease to exist due to a failure to add value to organizational effectiveness. It is recommended that merit pay play a more limited role in organizations and be used to support alternative reward strategies such as gainsharing, team-based pay, and profit sharing.

Human resource executives wrestle with the decision to continue to use merit pay plans or to abandon them. Surveys show that while the number of organizations that continue to use merit pay is declining, merit pay plans are still the most frequently used method of determining pay increases for exempt employees (Heneman, 1992). Merit pay plans continue to be controversial with some arguing for and others arguing against the effectiveness of merit pay plans in achieving organizational objectives. Unfortunately, there is not much research evidence to help human resource executives decide whether to use merit pay. The available evidence is case study in orientation and very organization specific. Unless one faces similar circumstances as those in a particular case, the data from the case are of limited value in making a strategic decision regarding the use of merit pay.

Extensive survey data that is more applicable to a wide range of organizations is available regarding forms of reward strategies other than merit pay (e.g., McAdams & Hawk, 1994). Only one such survey, however, is available regarding merit pay (Peck, 1984). The purpose of the present study was to generate additional data that may be useful to human resource decision makers in deciding whether merit pay adds enough value to the achievement of organizational objectives to be continued to be used and to identify practices that can be used to increase the effectiveness of merit pay plans.

The Peck (1984) survey found that across about 370 organizations in many different industries merit pay was on average judged to be "moderately successful." One objective of the present study was to update these data, as they are now about 10 years old, and see to what extent merit pay was continued to be seen by organizations as being "moderately successful." A second objective of the present study was to determine what criteria are used by organizations to define the "successfulness" of merit pay plans. Peck (1984) did not specify on what basis this determination was made. A third objective was to update current merit pay practices to provide some benchmark data for human resource executives to compare the merit pay plans in their organizations against. Rather than simply repeating the characteristics reviewed by Peck (1984), new practices were added based on new theoretical developments and practices in merit pay since 1984. The final objective was to provide some data on "best practices" with regard to merit pay. This was accomplished by correlating benchmark practices with a measure of overall merit pay plan effectiveness.

THE SURVEY

A survey was conducted by the authors in 1993 and 1994. In an attempt to begin to establish the causality of merit pay practices influencing merit pay plan effectiveness, the survey asked for 1992 data on merit pay plan practices and asked for 1993 data on merit pay plan effectiveness. The survey was sent to a sample of 700 organizations with members in the American Compensation Association (ACA). The survey was sent to the most senior compensation official (usually a compensation manager) listed on the ACA membership roster. Seventy-two usable surveys were returned for a response rate of 12 percent. The average size of the organization was 9965 employees and about 33 percent of the surveys came from manufacturing, 33 percent came from the services, and the remaining 34 percent came from miscellaneous other industries. Although the response rate was rather low and is a limitation to the conclusions reached in the present study, it is not uncommon to have a low response rate when conducting compensation surveys because most compensation departments are flooded with requests for compensation surveys to be completed and there is not enough time to complete all the surveys.

OVERALL EFFECTIVENESS OF MERIT PAY

Like the Peck (1984) survey, one question on the present study asked the respondents to indicate the overall effectiveness of their plan. The majority of the respondents in the Peck survey indicated that their merit pay plan was "moderately successful" while the majority of the respondents in the present study indicated that the merit pay plan in their organization was "marginally successful." Although these data are from two different samples and not directly comparable, they are suggestive of a downward trend in the perceived effectiveness of merit pay over the past 10 years. This trend is consistent with the anticipated decreased use of merit pay plans (O'Dell, 1986). This trend indicates that unless merit pay plans are improved and in turn judged to be more "successful," they are unlikely to be used nearly as much in the future.

THE MEANING OF SUCCESS

In the Peck (1984) survey it was not at all clear on what basis "success" was defined. The survey used in the current study was designed to show on what basis merit pay success was determined. Analysis of this determination is shown in Table 1. Several features stand out in this table. The first and second column shows that respondents were undecided or in slight disagreement with the statements that merit pay would lead to improved employee behavior (performance) and employee attitude (satisfaction). There was stronger disagreement that merit pay led to decreased absenteeism and turnover. The third column shows that the overall success of merit pay plans was gauged by respondents in terms of performance and satisfaction improvements rather than absenteeism or turnover improvements.

Table 1.   Merit Pay Plan Contribution to Organizational Effectiveness

Statements Merit Pay Leads to:	Agreement[1]		Rank[2]	Correlation[3]	Significance[4]
	X	SD			
Increased performance	3.30	1.20	1	.63	.001
Increased pay satisfaction	3.29	1.28	2	.67	.001
Positive attitudes and behaviors	3.28	1.17	3	.69	.001
Increased job satisfaction	3.08	1.13	4	.65	.001
Decreased turnover	2.81	1.24	5	.47	.001
Decreased absenteeism	2.71	1.17	6	.36	.002

1. Mean rating and standard deviation by survey respondents to each statement with a scale rating from 1 = strongly disagree to 7 = strongly agree
2. Rank order of statements by agreement score
3. Correlation of agreement rating with a statement measuring overall merit pay plan effectiveness
4. Shows the level of statistical significance

The results from Table 1 indicate the success is evaluated very broadly by senior compensation professionals to include more general (e.g., performance) rather than specific behaviors (e.g., attendance). The results also show that merit pay is not seen as being particularly useful in achieving these broad-based objectives. One conclusion to be reached here is that merit pay plans are unlikely to continue to be used because they do not contribute to the broader business results of the organization.

Another interpretation of the results from Table 1 is that merit pay plans are being used to try to accomplish too much. It is doubtful that any one reward plan or human resource intervention, yet alone merit pay, can significantly influence employee performance in and of itself (Huselid, 1995). In order for human resource programs to be effective, they must be targeted to achieve specific objectives and to work in concert with other human resource programs. Unfortunately, neither condition typically holds true for merit pay. It is often used as the major reward program and used as a standalone program. With this approach, merit pay plans may be doomed to fail. A better approach may be to target merit pay only to improve specific aspects of performance and be used in conjunction with other reward programs. For example, Heneman and von Hippel (1995a) show how merit pay can be used along with gainsharing. While gainsharing is targeted to meet business unit productivity and financial objectives, merit pay can be targeted to improve the teamwork among business unit employees. In the absence of merit-based rewards to encourage teamwork, a dysfunctional consequence of gainsharing may be the creation of "free-riders" who only exert enough effort to retain their job and let others exert maximum effort to achieve the bonus that all share equally including the free-riders. Heneman and von Hippel (1995) show how merit pay can be used to motivate all individuals in the group to be good team players and contribute as best they can to the team. Merit pay plans may be more effective if they reinforce one specific aspect of performance like teamwork rather than all aspects of performance.

MERIT PAY PLAN PRACTICES

Table 2 shows current practices used by the majority of survey respondents. These practices are grouped by performance appraisal, merit pay, and fairness issues. Recent theory development in each area along with current practice will be reviewed.

Table 2. Merit Pay Plan Characteristics

Performance Appraisal

- Supervisors are expected to evaluate employee performance formally twice a year.
- Employees are evaluated by two evaluators.
- Evaluators are trained on how to conduct performance appraisals and receive written instructions on how to make ratings.
- Results and behaviors are usually evaluated, rather than traits, and the results and behaviors are sometimes based on job analysis.

Merit Pay

- There is a formal merit pay policy.
- Employees are uncertain whether there is a relationship between pay and performance under the merit pay plan.

Fairness Procedures

- Employees usually have the opportunity to find out why they received certain merit increases.
- Employees seldom have the opportunity to appeal the size of their merit increases.
- Employees usually discuss how their performance was evaluated, but seldom feel free to express their feelings about a merit decision.
- Employees sometimes develop with their supervisors an action plan for future performance.

PERFORMANCE APPRAISAL

Performance appraisal is a critical component to the merit pay process as pay increases are based upon the ratings from performance appraisals. Although the performance appraisal form itself is important, current theory and research show that it is the process whereby the form is used rather than the form itself that generates valid ratings (Heneman & von Hippel, 1995b). Valid ratings are critical if pay is to be truly linked to performance under a merit pay plan.

The data presented in Table 2 indicate that organizations are taking steps consistent with current theory and research to generate valid ratings for purposes of merit increase decisions. In particular, raters are being coached through training and written instructions on how to make ratings. Validity is increased with rater coaching as common performance rating errors like "halo" can be minimized (Latham & Wexley, 1994). Employees are being evaluated more than once a year and by two evaluators or more rather than one evaluator. These practices should improve the validity of ratings as more complete data about employee performance are gathered with multiple observations and evaluators. Results and behaviors are being evaluated rather than personality traits which should improve validity as traits are very subjective and subject to misinterpretation. In short, the results of this survey show significant improvements by organizations in the rating process. An earlier survey regarding organizations' performance appraisal practices (Bernardin & Klatt, 1985) questioned the validity of performance ratings because organizations failed to pay attention to process issues such as multiple raters, multiple evaluations, and rater training.

One area where organizations continue to appear to fall short in the performance appraisal process is the limited practice of linking the standards on the form to a job analysis. Failure to use job analysis in the performance appraisal process may indicate that employees are not being consulted on the development of performance standards for their jobs. If this is the case, then employees may not completely understand or accept the standards used to evaluate their performance (Heneman, 1992).

MERIT PAY POLICY

The survey results in Table 2 indicate that explicit guidelines are being developed by organizations regarding merit pay. A formal policy, as opposed to ad-hoc procedure should be helpful to establish the link between pay and performance in the eyes of the employer. Unfortunately, a policy alone does not appear to be enough to establish a perception of pay-for-performance. The survey results indicate that employees are still uncertain about the link between pay and performance even in the presence of a merit pay policy. As previously indicated, in order for employees to see a link between pay and performance, they may need to be involved in the standard setting process. In the absence of job analysis, it is doubtful that this participation is taking place.

FAIRNESS PROCEDURES

An important new theory in the social sciences is known as organizational justice (Greenberg, 1987). According to this theory, employees are concerned with the fairness of two aspects of organizational decisions. One aspect is the fairness of the outcomes; this aspect of fairness is labeled "distributive justice." Another aspect is the fairness of the procedures used to determine outcomes and is labeled "procedural justice." In the context of merit pay, this theory indicates that employees are concerned about both the amount of merit pay they receive and the fairness of the procedures used to determine the amount they receive. If merit pay is to lead to improved employee attitudes and behaviors, then not only must the amount of the increase be seen as fair, but so too must the procedures.

Fairness procedures used to establish perceptions of procedural justice are shown in terms of actual organizational practice in Table 2. For the most part, organizational practice is beginning to be consistent with the general principles of procedural justice. In particular, organizations are explaining why employees received the merit raise they did. On the other hand, less attention is given to showing employees what they need to do to earn a merit increase or to providing employees with an appeals mechanism should they feel that their merit was not accurately assessed. Current research shows that employees are more committed to performance improvement with merit pay when procedural justice rules are followed by employees (Folger & Konovsky, 1989).

INCREASING THE EFFECTIVENESS OF MERIT PAY

Although all of the merit pay practices just received should improve merit pay plans somewhat, some practices may be more effective than others. In order to test this possibility in the present study, merit pay practices were correlated with the measure of overall merit pay plan effectiveness. The results are shown in Table 3. From this table it can be seen that only a few correlations are statistically significant at a conventional level (significance level less than .05), but this is to be expected given the small sample in the

402   D. ESKEW and R.L. HENEMAN

present study. That is, the lack of statistical significance may be a statistical artifact rather than a true indication of the importance of each practice.

Table 3.   Effective Merit Pay Plan Practices

Practice	Correlation[1]	Significance[2]
Performance Appraisal		
More than one appraisal by supervisor per year	.21	.10
More than one evaluation used	.12	.33
Evaluators receive training	.00	.97
Evaluators receive written instructions	.06	.59
Evaluation standards based on job analysis	.14	.25
Merit Pay Plan		
Formal merit pay policy used	.20	.10
Employees perceive a relationship between pay and performance under the merit pay plan	.64	.00
Fairness Procedures		
Employees have the opportunity to find out why they received a certain merit increase	.23	.06
Employees have the opportunity to appeal the size of their merit increases	.18	.13
Employees have the opportunity to discuss how their performance was evaluated	.13	.30
Employees feel free to express their feelings about a merit decision	.14	.25
Employees develop an action plan for future performance with their supervisors	.26	.01
Several of these fairness procedures are used	.29	.05

1. Correlation between merit pay plan practice and overall merit pay plan effectiveness
2. Statistical significance

From a practical standpoint, the magnitude of the correlation shown in the first column of Table 3 indicates the relative importance of merit pay plan characteristics. Using this criterion, two practices stand out of critical importance. First, employers must perceive a relationship between pay and performance. Second, employees must see the system as being fair in terms of the procedures that are used.

The remaining correlations, which are of smaller magnitudes, indicate what can be done to accomplish these objectives. The perceived link between pay and performance can be strengthened by having a formal merit pay policy and by making evaluations more than once a year. Both practices communicate the importance of the pay for performance relationship. Perceptions of fairness with the system can be enhanced by carefully explaining to employees why they received a particular merit increase and what they can do to continue to receive merit increases. These practices imply a forward-looking orientation to the merit pay program. Unfortunately, many merit pay programs have a backward-looking orientation that rewards employees for previous accomplishments but fails to promote future accomplishments. The data presented here suggest that successful merit pay plans promote the accomplishment of goals in the coming evaluation period.

CONCLUSIONS

A survey was conducted to answer four basic questions for those executives involved in making strategic decisions regarding the use of merit pay: How successful are merit pay plans? What criteria are used to gauge success? What are current merit pay practices in organizations? How successful are these merit pay practices? The data collected in this survey indicate that the successfulness of merit pay plans has diminished somewhat in recent years. Merit pay plans are now viewed as marginally significant. Success is gauged in terms of improved employee attitudes and behaviors. Merit pay practices, especially in the performance appraisal arena, have improved somewhat in recent years. The successfulness of merit pay plans is dependent upon a clearly perceived link between pay and performance and the perceived fairness of the procedures used. While all of these conclusions are tentative given the small sample in the present study, the data do provide a much needed update on the Peck (1984) survey and bring forth some evidence on the latest theoretical developments regarding merit pay.

These data can be used by human resource executives to begin to analyze the successfulness of merit pay in their own organizations. For some decision makers, these data may be further evidence of the need to eliminate merit pay plans. In making the decision to begin to use or to eliminate merit pay, organizations must also consider the fit of a merit pay to the business objectives of the organization along with benchmarking data (Greene, 1995). For other decision makers, these data may suggest areas of improvement for their merit pay plans. It is the authors' belief that the results of this survey point to the need for merit pay plans not to be eliminated, but to instead have a much narrower focus in organizations. Merit pay plans should be used to support very specific behavioral objectives (e.g., teamwork, customer service) not covered by other more results-oriented reward programs that emphasize the accomplishment of specific results (e.g., labor cost reductions, productivity). In addition to planning a more limited and targeted strategic role in the total compensation program, merit pay plans need to be reengineered to be more effective. Steps that can be taken to improve upon existing merit pay based on the survey results are shown in Table 4.

Table 4.   Steps to Increase Merit Pay Plan Effectiveness

1. Reward the accomplishment of specific behavioral objectives such as teamwork and customer service.

2. Base the development of performance standards on a job analysis process with employee participation.

3. Use multiple raters and review performance data with employees several times a year to establish the link between performance and rewards clearly.

4. Enhance employee fairness perceptions by having supervisors clearly explain why ratings were granted and what can be done by employees to improve upon these ratings in the future.

ACKNOWLEDGMENT

The authors would like to thank the Greater Cincinnati Human Resource Association for providing a Dupee-Olsten research grant to conduct the research. The views presented here are those of the authors and do not necessarily reflect the views of the sponsoring organizations.

REFERENCES

Bemardin, H.J., & Klatt, L.A. (1985). Managerial appraisal systems: Has practice caught up to the state of the art? *The Personnel Administrator, 30*(11), 71–86.

Folger, R., & Konovsky, M.A. (1989). Effects of procedural and distributive justice on reactions to pay raise decisions. *Academy of Management Journal,* 270–272.

Greenberg, J. (1987). A taxonomy of organizational theories. *Academy of Management Review, 12,* 9–22.

Greene, R.J. (1995, July-August). Merit pay may be a 'best-fit' strategy. *ACA News,* 10.

Heneman, R.L. (1992). *Merit pay: Linking pay increases to performance ratings.* Reading, MA: Addison-Wesley.

Heneman, R.L., & von Hippel, C. (1995a). Balancing group and individual rewards: Rewarding individual contributions to the team. *Compensation and Benefits Review, 27*(4), 63–68.

Heneman, R.L., & von Hippel, C.(1995b). The assessment of job performance: Focusing attention on context, process, and group issues. In D. Lewin, D.J.B. Mitchell, & M.A. Zadi (Eds.), *Handbook of human resource management.* Greenwich, CT: JAI Press.

Huselid, M. (1995). The impact of human resource management practices on turn-over, productivity, and corporate financial performance. *Academy of Management Journal, 38*, 635–672.

Latham, G.P., & Wexley, K.N. (1994). *Increasing productivity through performance appraisal* (2nd ed.). Reading, MA: Addison-Wesley.

McAdams, J.L., & Hawk, E.J. (1994). *Organizational performance and rewards.* Scotts-dale, AZ: American Compensation Association.

O'Dell, C.O. (1987). *Major findings from people, performance, and pay.* Scottsdale, AZ: American Productivity Center and American Compensation Association.

Peck, (1984). *Pay and performance: The interaction of compensation and performance appraisal* (Research Bulletin No. 155). New York: The Conference Board.

Part VIII

COMPETENCY PAY

The most recent innovation in strategic rewards is competency pay. Because of its newness, it is subject to much debate. In this part of the book, elements of this debate are described including the definition of competencies, and competencies versus job based systems of rewards. Also, an example of an actual competency-based pay system is described in a case study.

Ledford, G.E., & Heneman, R.L. (2000). Pay for skills, knowledge, and competencies. In L. Berger & D. Berger (Ed.), *The compensation handbook: A state-of-the-art guide to compensation strategy and design* (4th ed.). New York: McGraw-Hill.

Heneman, R.L., & Thomas, A.L. (1997). The Limited Inc.: Using strategic performance management to drive brand leadership. *Compensation and Benefits Review, 27*(6), 33–40.

Cohen, D.J., & Heneman, R.L. (1994). Ability and effort weights in pay level and pay increase decisions. *Journal of Business and Psychology, 8,* 327–343. Reprinted in *Personnel Research Highlights, 1994.* Washington, DC: Office of Personnel Management, 1995.

CHAPTER 20

PAY FOR SKILLS, KNOWLEDGE, AND COMPETENCIES

Gerald E. Ledford, Jr. and Robert L. Heneman

Source: Ledford, G.E., & Heneman, R.L. (2000). Pay for Skills, Knowledge, and Competencies. In L. Berger & D. Berger (Ed.), *The Compensation Handbook: A state-of-the-art Guide to Compensation Strategy and Design* (4th ed.). New York: McGraw-Hill. This material is reproduced with the permission of The McGraw-Hill Companies.

Compensation systems that pay for *skills, knowledge, and competen*cies (SKCs) use a logic different from conventional job-based pay systems. More familiar, job-based pay systems compensate for the *job* that an employee is performing at a particular time. In contrast, systems that pay for skills, knowledge, and competencies reward the employee's repertoire of capabilities. Moreover, compensation typically follows a formal certification that the employee has acquired SKCs. In contrast, the trigger for a change in job-based pay is a change in the employee's job, not a demonstration of accomplishment. In the extreme, the employee's job-base compensation level may change during the course of the workday as the person temporarily changes jobs.

It is important to recognize that, by definition, pay for SKC plans are not reward for performance. Rather, these plans seek to provide employees with the SKCs that *enable* greater performance. Thus, these plans are not complete pay systems by themselves. They need to be supplemented by performance incentives. Group or unit incentives such as gainsharing or goalsharing often make a potent combination with pay for SKCs. The pay for SKCs encourages increased potential and almost always rewards individuals. Group or unit incentives help overcome the centrifugal force of the individualistic SKC plan and encourage a balance between immediate performance requirements and developmental needs.

In recent years, there has been a tremendous growth in the use of systems that pay employees for their skills, knowledge, and competencies. For example, surveys by the Center for Effective Organizations (CEO) at the University of Southern California indicate that 62 percent of Fortune 1000 firms used such pay plans for at least some employees in 1996, up from 40 percent in 1987. The users of these plans consistently report a high level of satisfaction with them. For example, the CEO study found that firms were four times more likely to rate these pay plans as successful than unsuccessful. (Perhaps because so many plans are new, however, almost half reported that they were undecided about the success of the plans.) Similarly, a study of 97 skill-based pay plans sponsored by the American Compensation Association found that two-thirds to three-quarters of skill-based pay users found these plans to be successful on a wide range of outcome measures.

This chapter will consider two major issues concerning these plans. First, we will examine different types of plans and consider whether the differences in plan labels reflect real or surface differences. Second, we will consider the major issues in the design of these plans, including the infrastructure needed to support them.

VARIETIES OF PLANS TO PAY FOR SKILLS, KNOWLEDGE, AND COMPETENCIES

Plans discussed in this chapter have many names. Are they basically similar, or are skill-based pay plans fundamentally different from pay-for-knowledge plans; competency pay plans, or plans that pay for strategic competencies? In our view, these plans are more alike than different. They share the key characteristic of paying for the employee's repertoire of SKCs rather than for the job the employee is currently performing. However, plans with different names have origins at different places in the organization and tend to be applied to different groups of employees. Figure 1 depicts three major approaches that we consider here.

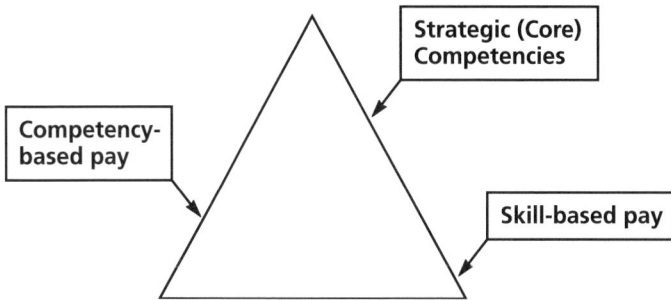

Figure 1.   Targets and constituencies for different forms of pay for skills, knowledge, and competencies.

Skill-Based Pay

Skill-based pay originated as a way to reward nonexempt employees for cross skilling. These plans are also called *pay for knowledge, knowledge-based pay, pay for skills,* or *pay for applied skills.* Although versions of this approach are ancient, we can trace the modern approach to high-involvement manufacturing plants that Procter & Gamble built in the 1960s. Line managers developed skill-based pay plans to incent employees to learn the multiple jobs necessary to support self-managed teams and business involvement. Compared to the other forms of pay for SKCs, skill-based pay systems stick very closely to the specific tasks that employees perform. Characteristics of the original Procter & Gamble plans describe the classic skill-based pay plan still commonly found today. The *classic skill-based pay plan* has the following characteristics.

Compensation Approach.   The classic system is pure base pay, not a set of bonuses or add-ons to job-based pay.

Design Methodology.   The classic system is based on a relatively exhaustive analysis and cataloguing of all the skills necessary to do the work of the organization. The skills identified through this analysis are then packaged into skill blocks that represent compensable units of skill and employees are rewarded for mastering these blocks. Assessment procedures are developed to test whether employees have mastered new skill blocks and training systems are established to make it possible for employees to learn new skill blocks.

Most Common Settings.   Classic plans are most commonly found in manufacturing or manufacturing-like service settings, such as back-office operations in insurance and financial services. The term *skill-based pay* continues to be applied primarily to plans that cover employees at the lower levels of the organizational hierarchy.

Implicit Assumptions.   Classic skill-based pay plans require a significant start-up investment, and typically 6 to 18 months are required to complete the entire design process in a large plant or similar unit. These plans depend on having enough organizational stability to realize a payback on the investment in the design process.

We have far more experience with such skill-based pay plans than with other types of plans that pay for SKCs. The available research suggests that the clear majority of these plans are successful in encouraging multi-skilling and in increasing organizational performance, notwithstanding some well-publicize failures (such as one at Motorola). A relatively strong finding in the literature is that these plans work best and are found most often in settings that encourage a high degree of employee involvement and indeed involve employees in the design and administration of the pay plan. In addition to the typical advantages of employee involvement in the process of organization change, a high-involvement system is more likely than a traditional bureaucratic management system to take good advantage of the new skills that employees acquire. A system that adds skills but does not take advantage of new employee abilities simply adds cost without gaining offsetting advantages.

Competency Pay Plans

Competency pay plans evolved from the work of psychologist David McClelland and others on the importance of competencies in determining individual job performance. *Competencies* are demonstrable characteristics of the person; including knowledge, skills, and behaviors, that enable performance. Most of the work in this tradition has focused on the exempt workforce, specifically managers and professionals. In keeping with the nature of the work of these populations, the competencies rewarded in these systems tend to be more abstract and less closely tied to the specific tasks of those on the plan. Cognitive skills (such as analytical thinking), values, self-image (such as self-confidence), motivational patterns, and even personality traits have been used as competencies that are rewarded in pay plans.

Writings about competency pay often include lengthy discussions about what constitutes a competency and about distinctions among different types of competencies. Each author tends to apply his or her own classification scheme. A common distinction is between those competencies that are necessary to perform the job but are not the source of competitive advantage and those that are more difficult to achieve and more strategic in nature, offering the hope of competitive advantage. The former are called, for example, *requisite* or *threshold competencies*, while the latter are called, for example, *strategic* or *differentiating competencies*. Common characteristics of competency pay systems include the following.

Compensation Approach. The typical competency pay system is pure base pay, not a set of bonuses or add-ons to job-based pay.

Design Methodology. The most common approach to designing competency pay systems is to study a group of performers who are judged superior on specified performance criteria and to collect extensive data to determine how top performers are different from average or poor performers. An extensive battery of tests, interviews, observations, and ratings may be used to discover such differences. The differences are packaged into competencies that are then tied to human resource systems, including compensation.

Most Common Organizational Settings. The term *competency pay* is most often applied to systems that cover managers, supervisors, professionals (including human resource professionals), and technical personnel. Often, these systems are applied to large numbers of personnel in different positions and locations within a company. When this occurs, the system may not be closely tied to the specific work of covered employees.

Implicit Assumptions. Competency pay plans require considerable design and installation effort, and thus these plans make the same assumptions as skill-based pay plans about the organizational stability needed to realize a return on the up-front investment in the plan. These plans also make a strong assumption that performance at the organizational level will increase if more employees emulate the behavior and values of superior individual performers. This assumption is rarely tested, even though a fair amount of research suggests that organizational performance is not merely the sum of individual performance. The problem is that collective behaviors (such as setting a good performance strategy and coordinating effort) may be needed to generate good organizational performance but not to generate the superior individual performance captured by the competency-modeling process.

There is relatively little research about the effectiveness of competency pay systems in increasing organizational as opposed to individual performance. A 1996 American Compensation Association survey study found too few competency pay cases to draw conclusions about the organizational effects of these plans. A great many validation studies, similar in methodology to industrial psychology tests of the validity of hiring tests, offer encouragement, but these usually validate against individual rather than organizational performance.

A particular concern with competency pay plans is the risk of legal jeopardy for poorly conceived and validated competency pay systems that may illegally discriminate against minorities and other protected groups. This is a special concern with competencies that are based on personality traits and other abstract competencies far removed from the actual work. These may not pass the *face-valid test* and may invite court challenges.

Plans Based on Strategic Competencies

The third approach is the most embryonic. It has been the subject of considerable discussion because of the intense interest in *core competencies* in the business strategy literature and among senior executives during the 1990s. The *core competencies* approach argues that a small set of technological and organizational skill complexes are a more stable and effective source of competitive advantage than superiority in particular markets or products. Market leadership is fleeting and products evolve rapidly, but competencies remain. For example, Sony's core competencies in miniaturization and precision manufacturing, Toyota's prowess at manufacturing, and Wal-Mart's core competencies in distribution, marketing, information technology, are underlying sources of competitive advantage that remain despite rapidly shifting markets and products.

In many companies, human resource managers and consultants have used executive interest in core competencies as an opportunity to introduce competency-based pay plans. However, it is important to recognize that the "core competencies" of the strategy literature bear no relation to those found in many pay systems. It takes extensive analysis and effort to discover the handful of core competencies that business strategists have in mind. In the competency pay literate "core" often means basic or requisite—the opposite of the meaning in the strategy literature. Worse, simply selecting competencies from a consultant's menu of prepackaged choices, a procedure that is far too common, invites ridicule from strategists and executives interested in discovering the unique competencies that gain competitive advantage for the firm.

One of the most positive aspects of the focus on strategic competencies is that it encourages forward thinking. In contrast, the focus in the competency pay approach on identifying why some are superior performers is essentially backward looking in that it identifies the competencies that have made some people successful in the past. For companies that are about to undergo fundamental change in response to business conditions, reinforcing old successful habits can be a recipe for disaster. Consider IBM or AT&T in 1980s, at the dawn of the PC and telecommunications revolutions. If they had paid for competencies, would they have been better served by a forward-looking or backward-looking system? Many companies believe that their situation today is analogous to that faced by IBM and AT&T 20 years ago.

There are relatively few examples of pay systems based on strategic competencies. Business leaders and authors have devoted relatively little attention to how this approach might be applied to human resource systems, as opposed to business strategy. However, some characteristics of this approach seem clear.

Compensation Approach.   The typical system is a base pay compensation system.

Design Methodology.   The design methodology is top down, evolving from the top executive group's identification of the core competencies of the corporation rather than from the current work of employees. This permits identification and rewarding of forward-looking competencies that have not received significant prior attention in the corporation.

Most Common Settings.   Although experience is limited so far, it seems likely that the pay of managers and professionals is most likely to be touched by these plans.

Implicit Assumptions.   An important assumption is that highly abstract strategic competencies that may not be within the experience of most employees can serve as the basis for an effective pay plan. This places a heavy burden on management to explain their reasoning and persuade employees of the merits of the strategic competency approach.

There is no published research about this type of plan. The first author has conducted an unpublished study of a plan that fits the strategic competency definition. The plan covered nearly 1,000 managers from a variety of functions and levels within a large food company. All were rewarded by movement within a broad band for their mastery of just four competencies that applied to all those covered on the plan. The competencies were closely linked to the business strategy of the firm. For example, one competency supported the customer focus that was important to the company's then-new total quality management (TQM) initiative. The study found that across the company, the regions that were most effective in implementing and supporting the competency pay plan were the most effective on hard measures of performance (productivity, cost, and quality).

SKC Bonuses

So far, we have considered three kinds of base pay systems for rewarding the acquisition of SKCs. In general, base pay systems are advantageous.

Adoption of a base pay system tends to force a relatively thorough analysis of needed SKCs rather than the casual adoption of a new pay plan. Base pay plans also are relatively difficult to remove arbitrarily. Finally, employees tend to view base pay increases as desirable and meaningful rewards. However, one-time bonuses are an underused alternative to base pay increases, and they make a great deal of sense in two situations.

First, bonuses may help preserve a competitive wage position in the market. If an existing organization is converting to a pay-for-skills plan, and if base wages are already over market, the organization may not be able to offer additional base wage increases without becoming uncompetitive. It is difficult to see how existing plans in the auto industry, for example, can offer meaningful base wage incentives for skill acquisition, but one-time bonuses may offer an attractive alternative. This is because bonuses do not have the recurring annuity cost of base wage increases.

Second, bonuses are attractive when the organization is experiencing rapid changes in the types and mix of skills, knowledge, and competencies that it needs to be successful. In high technology, for example, the competitive landscape changes so frequently that long-term planning is difficult. The rate of technical obsolescence may be so great that the organization does not have the luxury of devoting a year or two to creating a competency pay plan. The plan might be largely obsolete before the design is complete. Bonuses are an attractive option because they can be developed and implemented very quickly. Such plans can be modified frequently. For example, a new set of bonuses can be adopted each year, changing as business conditions change.

Bonuses have other advantages—and problems. They can be targeted to a select few competencies without upsetting the base pay system. Administrative support is much less than it is for a base pay system. Sloppy or even poor design in any given year have fewer negative consequences because of the absence of an annuity feature. On the other hand, bonuses may have more limited incentive value to employees. Also, these plans are probably more difficult to sustain over time because management tends to feel more comfortable about terminating bonus plans than terminating base pay plans. A quickly executed plan may lack credibility with employees if the company fails to support it with an adequate communications and training infrastructure.

There is no research about SKC bonus plans, but such companies as Monsanto and Rockwell have used them. Anecdotal evidence is highly encouraging. One engineering-intensive company placed thousands of employees on a competence pay bonus system. All exempt employees negotiated learning contracts with their supervisors in an appraisal cycle set off by 6 months from the performance review cycle. The plan offered employees a $750 bonus for meeting the negotiated learning contract. The company experienced a fivefold increase in the amount of development activity in the company at a relatively modest cost in bonuses. The tuition reimbursement budget actually-experienced a windfall, as technical person stopped taking classes that were not directly relevant to their work (and their learning contracts).

THE DESIGN CONTEXT

In designing plans that pay for skills, knowledge, and competencies, managers often seem to have an irresistible urge to jump into the details of skill block design. The first lesson from research and experience is that the fit of the system with its organizational context is far more important than any choice about the design of particular skill blocks. In particular, the system must be carefully married to the business context. Specifically, this means that designers should attend to the following issues.

Business-Based Objectives

Skill-based pay plans, for example, can be especially helpful in increasing employee flexibility, encouraging training, and reinforcing self-management skills. Designers need to think through what specific patterns of behavior are required of employees, whether the proposed pay plan is able to reinforce those skills, and how the intended benefits will be realized. A very important business issue to consider is how much flexibility the organization has to increase average wages levels, which will affect the availability of meaningful incentives in exchange for mastering new skills, knowledge, and competencies.

Organizational Structure and Technology

Plans that pay for skills, knowledge, and competencies can reinforce or undermine organizational structure. For example, if the organization is emphasizing the use of employee teams, cross-skilling within teams may be more appropriate than cross-skilling throughout the entire organization. The organization's technology often acts as an important constraint, and in some cases it may need to be modified to support training needs. For example, in customer service organizations, new technology can provide fully trained customer service agents with all the information they need to fully service a customer so that they do not have to make inquiries of many departments.

Organizational Culture

As we have indicated, organizations that adopt plans that pay for SKCs should have or be moving to an open, participative culture. This is one of the strongest predictors of success in part because cultures with such characteristics are far more likely to take advantage of the new capabilities employees develop through the plan.

THE DESIGN OF COMPENSABLE SKILLS, KNOWLEDGE, AND COMPETENCIES

Whatever form the pay system takes, it will be constituted of certain units of skills, knowledge, and competencies that the organization is willing to compensate. There are three major issues that must be addressed in the design of compensable units. These are depicted in Figure 2.

Compensation Management

First, the architecture of the overall compensation system requires attention. The nature of the SKC blocks will be determined primarily by the type of plan being implemented. A number of questions arise after the basic blocks are defined. How will SKC blocks or units be ordered, indicating career paths and minimum and maximum advancement opportunities? Decisions about these matters will give employees messages about the sequence of actions necessary to advance and to remain an employee in

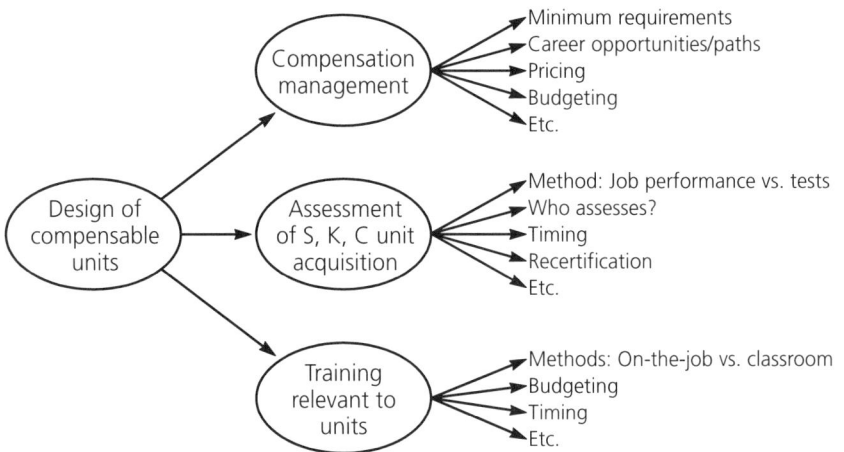

Figure 2.   Elements of a system paying for skills, knowledge, and competencies.

good standing. In general, it is best to err on the side of conservatism in these decisions early in the history of the plan. Employees rarely complain, if they end up with more career opportunities; easier minimum requirements, and greater maximum earning potential later, but the opposite condition feels like a loss.

An important issue concerns the pricing of plans that pay for skills, knowledge, and competencies. Often, it is impossible to price each competency or skill block to the market, in the way that each job in a job-based system can be priced. Rather, the typical procedure is to price the overall system rather than each element of it. The entry rate is set at the level just high enough to entice talented people to join the organization. The top rate is set based on market conditions as well. For example, in skill-based pay plans for semiskilled factory workers, the top end of the range may be placed appropriately near the bottom of the skilled worker classification. Finally, in some cases an average-rate pay rate is also set to market, based on labor market or industry benchmarks. Within these anchor points, skill blocks or competencies are assigned values based on their relative degree of difficulty. To take a simple example, assume that the entry rate is $10 per hour and the top rate is $20 per hour, both determined by the market. If there are 10 skill blocks of equal difficulty (as indicated by learning time or some other metric), each block an employee masters might be given a value of $1 per hour.

Employees need to have some idea of how long it will take to master competencies or skill blocks. The amount of time required to master a block or competency can vary tremendously, from a few months to several years. In general, it is desirable to break very complex blocks or competencies into several pieces so that at least annual advancement is possible within the system. If the blocks or competencies require only a few weeks to master, on the other hand, it is better to group them into a longer and more meaningful grouping or reconsider whether the plan really fits the skill requirements of the organization. The organization does not want too many blocks or competencies because this makes the plan difficult to administer and communicate and because it sets up the expectation that employees will receive compensation every time they learn something.

Assessment of SKC Acquisition

Any system requires some way of determining whether an employee has mastered skill blocks or competencies. The methods and procedures for assessment can be quite contentious if they are not thought through well. The assessment step has no counterpart in job-based pay systems. Unless it is done well in SKC pay plans, however, the plan will deteriorate into a *de facto* time-in-grade system, and the organization will receive no value for the increased wages provided under the system.

Part of the design of each skill block or competency is the specification of the standards for determining how to verify that an employee has mastered it. In skill-based pay plans for nonexempt employees, the process can be fairly elaborate, involving measurement of on-the-job performance, testing, and other methods. In general, management should rely on work samples whenever possible. Work samples are *face valid*, meaning they have natural credibility with employees. However, work samples may need to be supplemented with oral testing, written testing, or live demonstrations, if it is important to know, for instance, how the employee would respond to rare or hazardous conditions that are not likely to be encountered during the work sample of a few weeks or months.

In skill-based pay systems, certification may become one of the most time-consuming supervisory duties. Thus, it is important to think through the scheduling of certifications and the procedures for handling those who fail the tests. For example, how soon will they be allowed to retest? Is there any queuing of certification opportunities in the work unit?

Periodic recertification, perhaps annually, seems to be an increasing trend in skill-based systems. This ensures that employees maintain the skills for which they receive compensation. Without recertifications, the pay plan can result in increased wages that are attached to skills long lost through disuse.

Competency pay plans tend to incorporate competency assessments into the performance appraisal system. By their nature, most competencies are demonstrated on the job over a long period of time. Increasingly, assessments have a *360-degree component*, with reviews by peers, subordinates, supervisors, and customers who have relevant knowledge of the employee's demonstrated competency.

Training

Unless employees have the opportunity to develop the skills and competencies that make up the pay system, they will be frustrated by the incentives they have no opportunity to earn. Experience and research clearly indicate that demand for training greatly increases once employee pay is attached to the mastery of skills and competencies.

It is desirable to create a solid training plan in advance of the installation of the pay system. The starting point of the plan is the assessment of the training required to master each skill block or competency in the system, together with an estimate of the likely speed and path of progression of employees through the system. A menu of training courses relevant to the system, a specific schedule offerings, and the assignment of instructors (which may be peers, vendors, managers, or trainers) are part of the plan. An adequate training budget is essential.

Job rotation is a critical part of the acquisition of many skills and competencies, especially in skill-based pay systems. No classroom training can take the place of the experiences on the job that are needed for mastery of most skills included in the typical system. Rotation issues can become very contentious, and it is best to anticipate the problems and plan for rotation ahead of time. Many issues need to be determined. Who will decide when to rotate, and according to what timetable? How will the organization balance production needs with employee desires for training? How will it handle slow learners and those who refuse to rotate, which can lock up the whole rotation system? Competency systems for exempt employees may require new assignments rather than something analogous to job rotation. However, the same types of issues are relevant.

CONCLUSION

Since publication of the third edition of this handbook, systems that pay for skills, knowledge, and competencies have gone from a rarity to an increasingly standard tool of compensation practice. We expect the use of these plans to continue to increase because they meet the needs of so many contemporary organizations. The need for ever-increasing employee skill and knowledge, the increasing use of work systems emphasizing employee self-management, the decline of the conventional job and the job-based pay systems that went with it, and the general pressure for improved corporate performance that drives innovation of many kinds, all will encourage greater use of these systems.

We will conclude with four summary lessons drawn from our experience and research:

1. The design of the system is important, but the quality of the infrastructure needed to support it (certification, training, communication, etc.) is a stronger predictor of success than the elegance of the design.

2. All things being equal, simpler is better. One of the major problems with SKC pay plans is that they tend to become unnecessarily complex, and sometimes they are abandoned because management comes to feel that the administrative hassle outweighs any benefit.

3. Communication is even more important than for job-based pay systems. SKC systems are inevitably unfamiliar to most employees, they are complex compared to job-based pay systems, and they are

dependent on employee understanding of certification and training requirements that add complexity.

4. Any SKC pay plan will change over time, or it will be abandoned, because of its inflexibility and lack of fit with changing conditions. A complete design includes provisions for periodically revisiting the design and its infrastructure and making revisions as necessary. This provision should be very explicit, to increase the chances that employees will greet changes with interest and appreciation rather than resistance.

ADDITIONAL READINGS

A recent, relatively comprehensive review of research on the management of (including pay for) skills, knowledge, and competencies is E.E. Lawler III and G.E. Ledford, Jr., "New approaches to Organizing: Competencies, Capabilities, and the Decline of the Bureaucratic Model," in C.L. Cooper and S.E. Jackson (Eds.), *Creating Tomorrow's Organization: A Handbook for Future Research in Organization Behavior* (New York: Wiley, 1987).

The American Compensation Association-sponsored study of 97 skill-based pay plans is reported in a monograph G.D. Jenkins, Jr., G.E. Ledford, Jr., N. Gupta, and D.H. Doty, *Skill-Based Pay: Practices, Payoffs, Pitfalls, and Prospects* (Scottsdale, AZ: American Compensation Association, 1992). At this time, the best academic case study of skill-based pay is by B. Murray and B. Gerhart, "An Empirical Analysis of a Skill-Based Pay Program and Plant Performance Outcomes," *Academy of Management Journal*, 1998, *41*, 68–78. Three case studies of skill-based pay were reported in a special issue of *Compensation and Benefits Review*, 1991, *23*(2).

The competency pay (and more generally, competency management) approach is outlined in L.M. Spencer and S.M. Spencer, *Competence at Work* (New York: Wiley, 1993). The ACA-sponsored survey study of competency management is *Raising the Bar: Using Competencies to Enhance Employee Performance* (Scottsdale, AZ: American Compensation Association, 1996). Skepticism about the similarity of competency systems in many different types of organizations is expressed in P. Zingheim, G.E. Ledford, Jr., and J. Schuster, "Competencies and Competency models: One Size Fits All?" *ACA Journal*, 1996, *5*(1), 56–65.

Most writing about the strategic or core competencies approach is oriented toward business strategy rather than pay and other human resource practices. The original and seminal description of this approach was C.K. Prahalad and G. Hamel, "The Core Competence of the Corporation," *Harvard Business Review*, May-June 1990, pp. 79–91. A rare application of this approach to human resource management, albeit in highly academic language, is A.A. Lado and M.L. Wilson, "Human Resource Systems and Sustained Competitive Advantage: A Competency-Based Perspective," *Academy of Management Review,* 1994, *19*, 699–727.

Data cited about the incidence of the use of pay for skills, knowledge, and competencies were from a study at the Center for Effective Organizations, by E. Lawler III with S.A. Mohrman and G.E. Ledford, Jr., *Strategies for High Performance Organizations: Employee Involvement, TQM, and Reengineering Programs in Fortune 1000 Corporations* (San Francisco: Jossey-Bass, 1998).

CHAPTER 21

THE LIMITED, INC.:

Using Strategic Performance Management to Drive Brand Leadership

Robert L. Heneman and Andrea L. Thomas

Source: Heneman, R.L. and Thomas, A.L., *Compensation and Benefits Review,* 27(6), 33–40, copyright © 1997 by Sage Publications, Inc. Reprinted by permission of Sage Publications, Inc.

Today's management practices bring a new complexity to the way work is organized and managed. Companies are asking employees to become team players, rather than individual contributors. Managers are expected to relinquish their positions as authority figures with command and control responsibilities to become leaders, coaches, facilitators, and strategists. And executives are advised to temper their obsessions with quarterly numbers so as to develop a balanced focus on both short- and long-term results.

Many managers are not adequately prepared—or are perhaps unwilling—to deal with these complexities. In this regard, a company's performance management system *should* serve as a catalyst for helping them assume these new roles. This is not always the case. And while some companies are creating performance management systems to support the new expectations of employees, relatively little attention is being devoted to developing similar systems for managers.

In theory, at least, the performance management system should be designed to emphasize competencies and results consistent with the company's overall mission and objectives. Results measure performance relative to the organization's financial goals, while competencies represent the means by which these results are attained. Both are important: the means—*how* results are achieved—are as important to the company's long-term viability as the results themselves.

The Limited, Inc., a $9 billion retailer headquartered in Columbus, Ohio, has successfully integrated competencies and results into a performance management system for managers. The Limited's story is worth telling, in that evidence to date suggests that the system is improving the company's overall organizational effectiveness.

GROWTH THROUGH BRAND LEADERSHIP

The Limited, Inc. operates with 14 retail and 4 nonretail strategic business units, including Victoria's Secret; Bath and Body Works; Abercrombie and Fitch, Co.; Structure; Express; Limited; Galyans; Henri Bendel; Lane Bryant; The Limited Too; Mast Industries, Inc.; and Lerner New York.

Led by founder Leslie Wexner, The Limited, Inc., maintains a highly energized entrepreneurial spirit. Fueled by brand extensions, new brand development, and acquisitions, the company has transformed itself from a $400 million single-brand retailer to its current size and diversity within the past 15 years. Although The Limited, Inc., is 30 years old, the average business unit is only eight years old.

The Limited now operates more than 6,000 stores in the United States plus global catalogue operations. Employment is variable, with typically 33,000 salaried employees, 180,000 total employees, and 380,000 W-2 forms processed in a year.

FINDING THE ADVANTAGES

During its planning sessions in the early 1990s, The Limited management looked for a strategy that would be difficult for competitors to imitate. These strategy sessions came at a time when expert advice emphasized "running lean" (downsizing and restructuring were in vogue). The company's management recognized, however, that such tactics can be easily imitated by competitors and would thus yield only a temporary advantage (see Barney, 2001).

Instead, management focused on brand leadership (defined as an integrated system that includes brand management, merchandise process redesign, sourcing and production, and change management) as a more powerful source of competitive advantage. To support this brand leadership capability, the company implemented an active and multifaceted change agenda. This included the following:

- creation of a new governance model;
- leveraging of core capabilities in the business;
- investment in core processes and business disciplines;
- vertical integration of business disciplines to support the strategic business units; and
- the internationalization of the business.

Developing successful leaders throughout the company would be a critical success factor in implementing this change agenda.

NEEDED: A NEW PERFORMANCE MANAGEMENT SYSTEM

The Limited's entrepreneurial environment had emphasized "survival of the fittest" in the managerial ranks. A manager's accomplishments were measured almost entirely on the basis of business results. Those managers who survived over time were indeed talented, each with a proven track record in meeting operational and financial objectives.

This way of running a business can easily become unbalanced, especially when a company is seeking long-term growth. Just as it would be ludicrous to expect a pilot to steer an aircraft using only one instrument, say an altimeter or air speed indicator, it is equally unwise to ask managers to run a business using only short-term financial gauges. Robert S. Kaplan and David P Norton use this airplane analogy in their introduction to *The Balanced Scorecard* (Harvard Business School Press, 1996), a book that has sparked considerable interest in recent years. Kaplan and Norton argue that activities in four areas—financial, customer service, internal business processes, and learning—drive business success. Thus, these are the areas that should be monitored and used to steer business strategy.

The Limited adapted a variation of the balanced scorecard concept as an initial component of its management system, shown in Figure 1. The strategy team set three-year objectives in each of the four areas on the scorecard. Then, by identifying the "critical few" activities that would provide a foundation for success in the longer term, individual managers were able to formulate a one-year development plan.

The Limited's management wanted to put a greater emphasis on learning and growth as key strategic objectives. To do so, the design team created the *Strategic Leadership Development Model* shown in Figure 2. Note, first, that the model supports a very ambitious long-term goal—the creation of a $20 billion portfolio of brands. Second, note that the model emphasizes a cyclical process of identifying core leadership competencies, developing

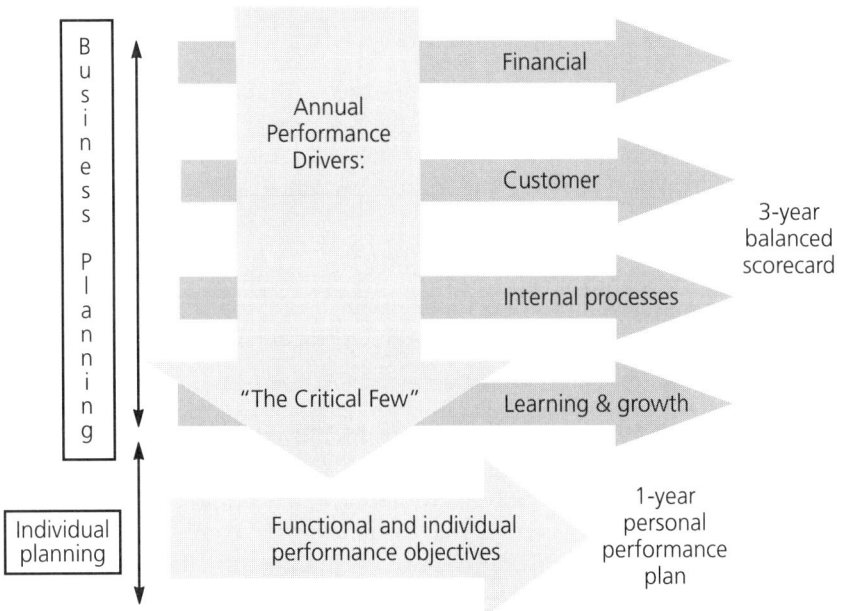

Figure 1.   Alignment of objectives. *Source:* The Limited, Inc.

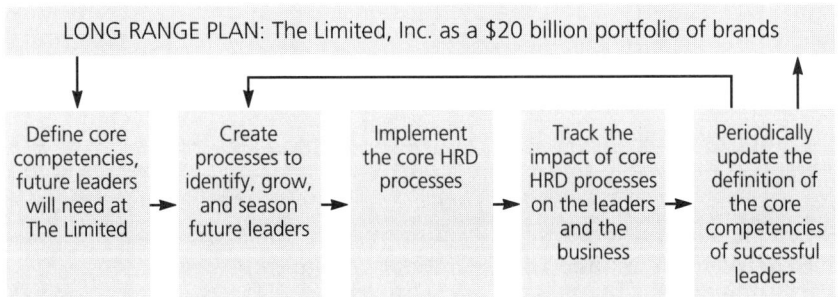

Creating a
common
understanding
so we can . . . . . .talk the talk. . . . .walk the talk. . . . . .listen effectively . . . . . .and learn.

Figure 2.   A strategic leadership development model for The Limited, Inc.

future leaders, monitoring success, and revising core competencies. Again, the emphasis is on creating a sustainable competitive advantage by developing the organizational leaders who can build brand leadership.

ASSESSING PERFORMANCE

Previously, each of The Limited's 14 business units had developed its own unique performance management system. But corporate management felt that the company needed a common method of performance assessment to ensure that leadership skills were transferable across strategic business units (SBUs). Moreover, a common assessment device would ensure a degree of consistency in the evaluations of managers in different SBUs.

Before designing a new performance management system, the development team established goals that would guide the process and serve as criteria for evaluating the success of the system. According to these goals, the system should:

- create a common yardstick to assess performance across business units;
- drive the alignment of individual and strategic business unit objectives;
- improve feedback quality; minimize administration detail;
- be accepted across all of the business units; and
- be integrated with other core human resource processes (selection and orientation, coaching and mentoring, education and training, developmental assignments, succession management, compensation).

DEVELOPMENT AND IMPLEMENTATION

Figure 3 provides an overview of the performance management system that evolved. Self-evaluations, performance appraisals, and performance reviews are based on standards that gauge competencies as well as business results. This leads to performance planning, with the balanced scorecard used as a means to focus development plans on the success drivers. Let's take a closer look at the system's components and how they developed.

Phase 1 of the project focused on the development of performance standards. To accomplish this task, the design team drew on assistance from outside resources. The Renaissance Group helped the team to develop standards for business results, and Personnel Decisions International aided with the development of competencies. (For more information on developing leadership competencies, see Davis et al., 2000.) In the process, the consultants engaged a wide range of management personnel, conducting both in-depth interviews with senior management and focus groups with other managers. A cross-business advisory group, led by the organization and leadership development team, was formed to oversee the work.

Figure 4 provides examples of standards used to measure results.

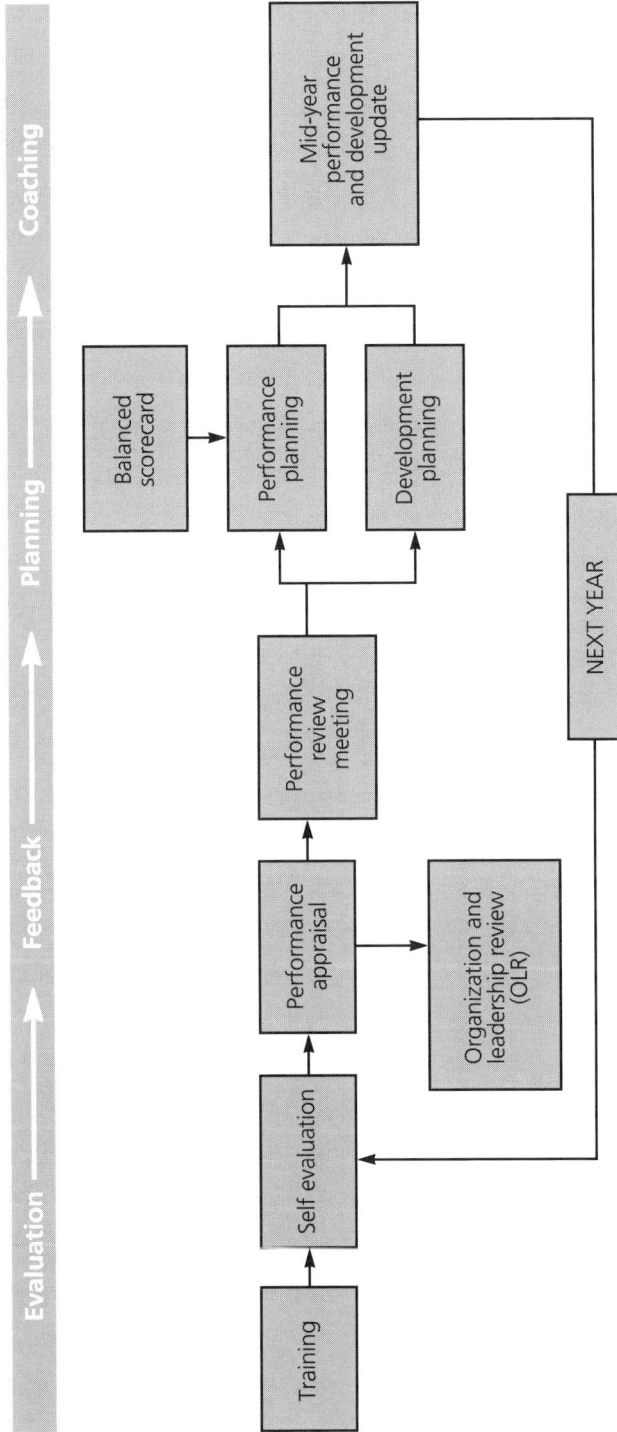

Figure 3. Overview: The annual performance management cycle.

- Total sales
- Total sales per store
- New store size
- Average store size
- Pre-tax profit growth rate
- Market share
- Expense/Sales growth ratio

Figure 4.   Results to measure performance.

Figure 5 shows the leadership competencies. Note that the competencies are truly "centered" on The Limited's business and are markedly different from the generic competencies often cited in discussions of leadership. To maintain brand leadership, The Limited's managers must

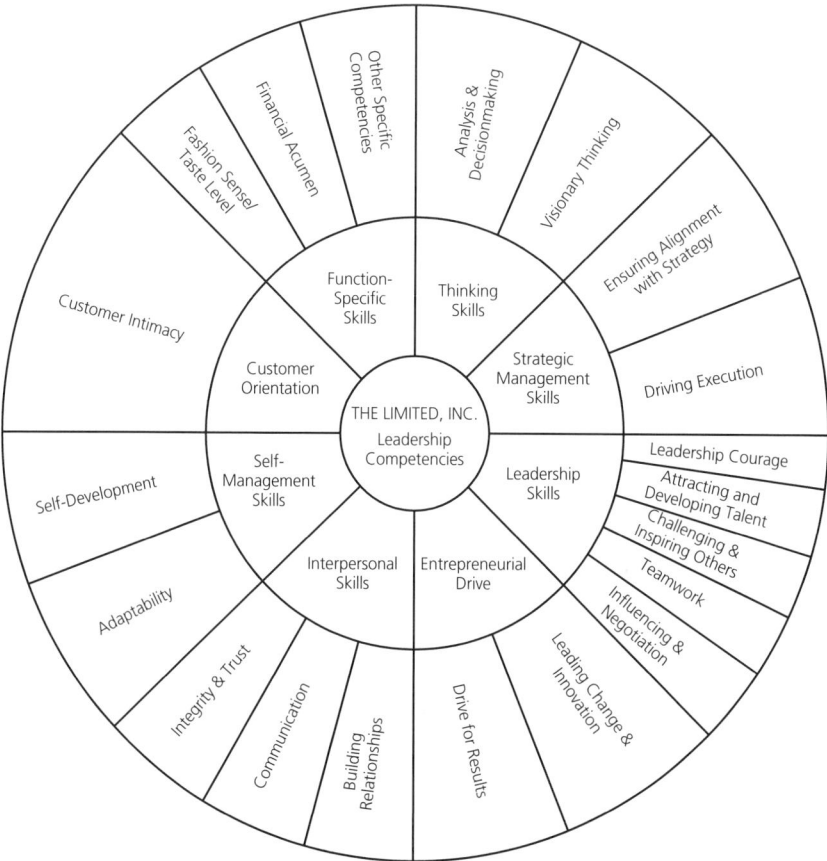

Figure 5.   The Limited, Inc. leadership competencies.

	Towering Strength	O.K./Effective	Ineffective/Needs Improvement	Overused Strength
IDENTIFY ISSUES	Identifies or recognizes the key issues, trends, and/or opportunities when confronted with complex or ambiguous problems.	Identifies or recognizes the most importance issues, trends, or opportunities; may miss or overlook some importance points.	Identifies or recognizes the obvious issues, trends, or opportunities; often misses or overlooks important points.	Concentrates so much on issue identification that implementation plans are not developed.
MAKE TIMELY DECISIONS	Consistently makes timely decisions that balance systematic analysis with decisiveness.	Timing on decisions is appropriate for some issues; delays too long or moves too quickly on some issues.	Makes snap judgments without necessary information or delays too long on decision.	Unwilling to halt programs due to always meeting decision milestones.

Figure 6.   Behavioral anchors analysis and decision making. *Source:* The Limited, Inc.

develop a "fashion sense," "financial acumen," "entrepreneurial drive," and the like. Each of the competencies is defined by a series of performance anchors (i.e., behavioral examples of performance within a particular competency). Figure 6 provides one example: the performance anchors for the competency labeled "analysis and decision-making."

Similar rating scales were developed to assess performance relative to each of the business results and leadership competencies. Averages on each of these dimensions come together in the matrix shown in Figure 7. For example, a manager rated as "highly effective" on the leadership criteria and "greatly exceeds expectations" on the business results would receive an overall performance assessment of "greatly exceeds."

Phase II consisted of piloting the new assessment tool. Five strategic business units volunteered to participate in the pilot test. To ensure that the new tool would yield accurate and useful information, the design team developed a survey to assess the reactions from 100 participants in the pilot study. These participants were asked to compare the new tool with the prior tool in such areas as:

- accuracy of ratings;
- consistency of ratings across associates;
- efficiency;
- quality of feedback on both competencies and results; and
- usefulness in formulating meaningful development plans.

RESULTS

LEADERSHIP

	Greatly exceeds expectations	Exceeds expectations	Meets expectations	Does not meet expectations	Failed to perform
Highly effective	Greatly exceeds	Exceeds	Meets	Does not meet	Failed to perform
Highly effective	Exceeds	Exceeds	Meets	Does not meet	Failed to perform
Highly effective	Does not meet	Does not meet	Does not meet	Does not meet	Failed to perform

Figure 7. What and how: The overall performance rating. *Source:* The Limited, Inc.

The new tool proved superior. Based on these results and the written comments, the instrument was further refined before implementation.

Phase III consisted of training and implementation. The design team assembled a performance management reference guide to steer the training and implementation effort. The guide explained:

- the purpose of the process;
- the stages of the process;
- performance and development planning;
- development feedback and coaching;
- evaluation and feedback; and
- performance standards.

These components formed the integrated performance management process shown in Figure 3.

The initial performance management system was developed for approximately 500 managers at the level of director or above. Implementation took approximately two years. This may seem like a long time, but the development team consciously pursued the longer time line for two reasons. First, by "going slow" initially, it would be possible to go much faster in the latter stages. By building a credible system that top management not only verbally supported but also actually used to guide their day-to-day decision making, the development team would avoid the need to revise later.

Second, this period allowed opportunity for management participation in the project and the development of valid performance measures. In terms of fairness perceptions about the new system by end users, both participation and validity are critical components.

RESULTS AND CHALLENGES

The newly developed performance management system is currently being used at the director level and above for all strategic business units at The Limited, Inc. In addition to serving as a developmental tool, it is also being used for compensation decisions, including merit increases and eligibility for stock. In some strategic business units, the system is being cascaded to lower levels of the organization. There is also some experimentation with the use of 360-degree reviews to assess leadership competencies.

On the whole, The Limited has been pleased with the results of this process. Specifically, by linking individual objectives to balanced scorecard objectives and measures, the new process has helped the organization to align individual performance with business strategies. Additionally, raters have found that the performance anchors are quite helpful because they provide clarity with regard to the competency definitions. Another positive outcome is the managers' frequently expressed appreciation for concern with *how* things are done (as opposed to a strict focus on *what is* done, or a results-only focus).

On the other hand, The Limited still faces some challenges with this system. For example, some individuals have expressed concerns about the overall evaluation of someone who is rated as being "effective" in terms of leadership competencies and "exceeds expectations" in terms of business results.

According to the matrix shown in Figure 7, this person should receive an overall assessment of "exceeds" standards. This assessment gives greater weight to business results than to leadership competencies. Interestingly, the pilot model labeled this cell in the matrix as "meets" overall performance standards, indicating that competencies are weighted more heavily than business results in the final assessment. While the "meets" designation would certainly put teeth into the leadership competency model, it may be too soon to use this designation in an entrepreneurial culture that places such heavy emphasis on business results.

Perhaps The Limited, Inc., will put greater emphasis on leadership competencies in the future as senior management becomes more familiar with and confident in the processes. Continued experimentation will be required to further refine the system-which is true for many organizations. Continued experimentation with performance management systems is also needed to help managers assimilate their new roles as coaches, leaders, and strategists.

CONCLUSIONS

Fierce competition in domestic and international product and service markets has brought about fundamental changes in the way companies structure and organize work. As organizations navigate their transition from traditional to contemporary management practices, they will likely find, as did The Limited, that not all managers are prepared to take on these new duties. Training and rewards must be provided to motivate traditional managers to change and to encourage junior employees to aspire to these newly created, more difficult managerial roles. Managers are key players in the transition to new forms of work arrangements for employees and executives. Without the support of managers, it is very difficult for organizations to align the goals of their higher and lower levels.

Consequently, there is a critical need to align performance management systems for managers with the changing nature of managerial work. Experiences at The Limited show how leadership competencies can be measured, rewarded, and integrated with business results to contribute to improved organizational effectiveness.

REFERENCES

Barney, J.B. (2001). Looking inside for competitive advantage. *Academy of Management Executive, 9*(4), 49–61.

Davis, L., Skube, C.J., Hellervik, L.W., Gebelein, S.H., & Sheard, J.L. (2000). *Successful manager's handbook.* Minneapolis, MN: Personnel Decisions, Inc.

CHAPTER 22

ABILITY AND EFFORT WEIGHTS IN PAY LEVEL AND PAY INCREASE DECISIONS

Debra J. Cohen and Robert L. Heneman

Source: Cohen, D.J., & Heneman, R.L. (1994). Ability and Effort Weights in Pay Level and Pay Increase Decisions. *Journal of Business and Psychology, 8,* 327–343. Reprinted in *Personnel Research Highlights, 1994.* Washington, DC: Office of Personnel Management, 1995.

ABSTRACT

It was hypothesized that ability, effort, and the interaction between ability and effort would influence pay level and pay increase decisions. An experiment was conducted with 66 human resource professionals to test this hypothesis. The results indicate that pay level decisions are influenced primarily by ability, and pay increase decisions are influenced primarily by the interaction between ability and effort. The results are discussed in the context of the traditional compensation model which suggests that ability should influence pay level, but not pay increase, and that effort should influence pay increase, but not pay level. It was concluded that the distinction currently being made between person and job based pay plans may not be meaningful.

A familiar prescription in the compensation literature is that pay levels should to be established on the basis of the worth of the job to the organization, while pay increases should be based on the contributions of the employee to the organization (Milkovich & Newman, 1987; Wallace & Fay, 1988). In support of these prescriptions, job evaluation and salary survey procedures have been developed to assess the worth of the job to the organization, and procedures such as performance appraisal have been developed to measure and rate the contribution of the person to the organization. Using these procedures, total direct compensation received by employees should be a function of the worth of the job they hold, and individual contributions to the job such as performance.

This distinction between the worth of the job versus the worth of the person has led to debate as to whether the job *or* the person *should* be used to make initial and subsequent compensation decisions (Porter, Barrett, Mahoney, Gupta, Jenkins, & Lawler, 1990). Recently this debate was the focus of an entire issue of *Human Resource Management Review* (Kane, 1991). Regardless of whether one sides with the job or the person as the unit of compensable value to organizations, the assumption is that a clear separation can be made between the job and the person. While a clear separation can be made between the job and the person in organizational policy, it may not be possible, or pragmatic, to make this distinction in practice. For example, person-oriented information is used to evaluate both the worth of the job and the person to the organization. Person-oriented information includes the knowledge, skills, and abilities needed to perform a job (McCormick, 1979). These factors or KSAs are commonly used to establish the worth of the job through job evaluation and to establish the contribution of the person through skill-based reward systems.

The purpose of the present study is to *question* whether the age-old distinction between the person and the job in compensation policy is meaningful. This study is responsive to the call by Gupta and Jenkins (1991a) for researchers to critically examine the assumptions made in pay policies. As stated by the authors: "It is easy for us to forget what was once considered infallible, does not necessarily stand up to subsequent scrutiny" (p. 94). It is argued here that under current practice there is no separation between the person and the job in compensation decision-making. Regardless of the pay decisions (initial pay level or subsequent pay increase), both person and job attributes enter into the decisions.

The issue of whether the job and person are treated separately in compensation decision-making is an important one for purposes of both research and practice. From a research perspective, we clearly need to specify the pay criteria in compensation decisions. For example, structural equation modeling is sometimes used to model compensation decisions (Witting & Berman, 1991). Erroneous results may be received if decisions are modeled on the basis of person or job characteristics only when decision makers actually use both person and job characteristics. By only including one characteristic, the model being developed will be deficient which is a limitation to the construct validity of the model (Witting & Berman, 1991).

From a practice perspective, the separation of the person and the job is also important (Gupta & Jenkins, 1991b; Lawler, 1991). In terms of human resource strategy, organizations may wish to emphasize pay for the job or pay for the person. For example, organizations that wish to emphasize cost minimization may pay for the job while those wishing to pursue the goal of high output from employees may pay for the person (Gupta & Jenkins, 1991b). Or as another example, pay for the job may work well in bureaucratic organizations with well-defined jobs and little room for individual discretion. On the other hand, pay for the person may work well in organic organizations with loosely defined jobs and a great deal of room for individual discretion in performing work (Lawler, 1991). The problem, however, with the distinction between the job and the person is that while organizations may have a policy to pay the person or the job, in practice they may be paying for both the person and the job. As a result, their strategic goals may be thwarted.

Some might think we are presenting an overly simplistic "straw man" argument. However, we do not think so. A fundamental shift appears to be occurring, in which organizations are moving more toward person-based compensation systems (e.g., pay-for-knowledge). Hence, we clearly need to understand why, how, or if, the distinctions between the person and the job in compensation decision-making have been made. These two perspectives are clearly present in the literature. They are clearly present in organization policies and in compensation decision-makers themselves. Therefore, a study examining how the distinction is or is not handled in practice is warranted.

Under traditional models of compensation, one would expect to find that pay level assigned to a particular job is determined on the basis of the worth of the job to the organization as well as the worth of the job in the external labor market (Mahoney, 1991; Schwab, 1980). One way to define the worth of the job to the organization is to look at the level of ability that is required to perform a job. Ability is a common factor used in many job evaluation plans. While one finds ability as a factor in many job evaluation plans, one finds effort as a factor less frequently. The traditional model suggests, therefore, that ability to perform the job should be more strongly related to the pay level received than will effort. Also under traditional models of compensation, pay increases are often awarded on the basis of merit. Merit pay is allocated in hopes of motivating improved effort by the employee (Heneman, 1990). Motivational theories suggest that organizations are attempting to influence effort rather than ability in the allocation of pay increases (Vroom, 1964). Pay increases therefore should be more strongly related to effort than to ability.

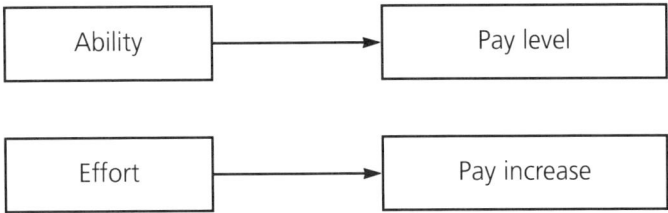

Figure 1.   Traditional model.

The traditional model is depicted in Figure 1. Under the traditional model, pay level is determined by characteristics of the job. One characteristic of the job is the level of ability required to do the job. Pay increase is determined by characteristics of the person. One characteristic of the person is the level of *effort exerted* by the person.

The argument advanced here is that Figure 2 is a more realistic model which better captures actual compensation practice. As can be seen, it is argued that both pay level and pay increase decisions are influenced by characteristics of the job (e.g., ability) and characteristics of the person (e.g., effort). More specifically, it is hypothesized that:

H1. Main effects for ability and effort on pay level will both be significant.

H2. Main effects for ability and effort on pay increase will both be significant.

H3. The interaction effect between ability and effort will be significant for pay level and pay increase.

H4. For pay level decisions, ability will exhibit significantly greater beta and correlation values than effort.

H5. For pay increase decisions, effort will exhibit significantly greater beta and correlation values than ability.

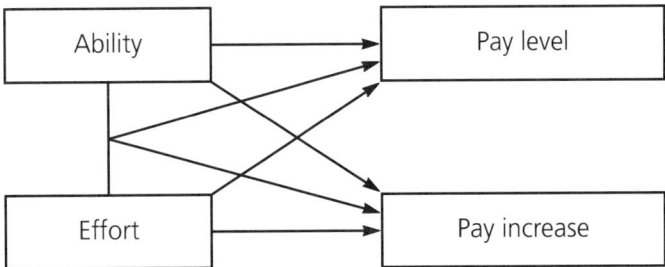

Figure 2.   Hypothesized model.

The rationale for these hypotheses is twofold. First, attribution theory (Heider, 1958; Weiner, 1985) suggests that evaluators pay attention to both ability and effort in making compensation decisions. Attribution theory is seen in practice when one individual observes a behavior and then tries to determine whether it was intentional or accidental behavior. If the behavior is believed to be intentional, then the decision maker will try to assess whether the cause was determined by the situation (e.g., ability) or because of the individual's personality (e.g., effort). Hence, compensation decision makers may consider both ability and effort in deciding the level of pay to provide employees.

Second, Heneman (1990) reviews several studies which indicate that pay increases are not solely based on the determination of employee effort. Instead, ability is given a heavy emphasis. Peck (1984) reported the results of a survey of 25,000 employees by Opinion Research Corporation. These employees perceived little relationship between effort and pay increases. Heilman and Guzzo (1978) provided evidence that pay raises were viewed as appropriate rewards regardless of whether success was attributed to ability or effort. Dugan (1989) found that salary increases were larger when performance was attributed to ability rather than to effort. Fossum and Fitch (1985) found that merit increases were larger for employees perceived to have more, rather than less capability, even after performance was controlled. Leventhal, Michaels, and Sanford (1972) found that when effort was controlled, the amount of merit allocated to higher performers was significantly larger than the amount of merit pay allocated to lower performers.

To show that compensation decisions are made on the basis of both ability and effort weights, a laboratory study was conducted. By conducting this study in the laboratory, it was possible to hold performance and the job constant. By holding performance and the job constant, it was possible to show the impact of a characteristic of a job requirement (ability) and a person attribute (effort) on compensation decisions. The job was held constant by having compensation decisions made for one job only. Performance was held constant by having the same performance rating for each incumbent.

METHOD

Design

In order to investigate the hypotheses an exploratory study was conducted and, a 2 × 2 factorial with complete within-subjects design was used. The factor was ability and consisted of two levels (high and low). The second factor was effort and was defined by two levels (high and low). The dependent variables were pay level and pay increase.

Subjects

Subjects were 66 Human Resource professionals and represented a convenience sample of human resource professionals in a large Mid-Atlantic metropolitan area of the United States. Sixty percent (40) were females, and the average age of the subjects was 36. Overall education of the sample was fairly high. High school and two-year degrees were held by 12 percent, 47 percent had four-year degrees, 38 percent held masters degrees and 3 percent had Ph.D.s. Subjects had an average of 10 years work experience with a range of 1 to 34 years. Seventy percent had supervisory responsibility, and on average supervised 13 employees. Sixty-nine percent had performance appraisal responsibilities and 61 percent had salary allocation responsibilities. Eighty-six percent of the sample was white while the remaining 14 percent fell into minority categories.

Procedures

Each subject was given a study instrument and told that their participation would take no more than 20 minutes to help the researcher with a study on compensation. Subjects were provided with a written set of instructions, a job description for the position of Personnel Clerk (including the salary range), a written job evaluation for the position of Personnel Clerk, and four scenarios describing four incumbents in the position of Personnel Clerk. Each incumbent had a different last name preceded by a single initial so that the descriptions remained gender neutral. Each incumbent worked for the same organization and each received an overall performance rating of 5 out of 7 possible points. These procedures were followed to hold the job, organization, gender of the incumbent, and rated performance of the incumbent constant across experimental conditions.

The job of Personnel Clerk was chosen and developed for a specific reason. This position was chosen because it was believed that this study should involve respondents who were familiar with the task of salary administration and allocation. Hence, it was decided that Human Resource Professionals would be a wise population from which to draw the sample. It was believed that even if these individuals did not have salary allocation responsibility, that they would at least be familiar with the task by virtue of their link to the Human Resource profession. As it turned out, the majority of respondents (61 percent) did have such responsibilities.

The job description and completed job evaluation for the position were developed using information from the *Dictionary of Occupational Titles* (U.S. Department of Labor, 1977) as well as several sample job descriptions obtained from published textbooks. Key points about the task, education level, and job requirements, were blended together to describe a generic entry-level position in Human Resources, with which most HR professionals would have been able to identify, and hence, feel comfortable making salary level and increase decisions.

Subjects were given three worksheets. The first worksheet asked them to make salary allocations for each incumbent and to allocate a raise to each incumbent. The second worksheet, an incumbent evaluation form, was a manipulation check to verify that subjects saw differences in ability and effort and no differences in performance levels. The third worksheet collected demographic and background information about each subject. A pilot study was conducted using a separate sample of students to insure that the instructions were clear.

The respondents in this study represent a convenience sample. Subjects were contacted in a variety of ways. First, human resource professionals attending a state human resource professional society conference were asked to voluntarily participate and return their worksheets. Second, a group of human resource professionals attending a local professional society workshop were asked to voluntarily participate. Finally, a small mailing was sent to a local human resource professional society chapter. An exact response rate cannot be determined since it is likely that there was overlap in attendance at the conference, the workshop, and in the chapter membership. Hence, the respondents represent a convenience sample.

Manipulations

Within each scenario, ability and effort were manipulated with written descriptions so that one incumbent had high ability and high effort, one had high ability and low effort, one had low ability and high effort, and one had low ability and low effort. The ability and effort characteristics used in the manipulations were chosen based on the commonalities found in a variety of published job descriptions such as the *Dictionary of Occupational Titles*.

Ability.   High ability was coded as 2 and low ability as 1. High ability incumbents possessed a Bachelors degree in Human Resource Management from a local 4-year university, had a typing speed of 70 words per minute with no errors, and were described as being accurate and having excellent mathematical skills. Low ability incumbents possessed a liberal arts degree from a local 2-year community college, had a typing speed of 40 words per minute with approximately 5 spelling errors on average, and were described as being less accurate and as having little mathematical skills.

Effort.   High effort was coded as 2 and low effort coded as 1. High effort incumbents were never late with any work and often completed work before required by management. They completed work accurately and presented it in a logical fashion without error. The high effort incumbent was described as well liked and hence, often sought after by coworkers for information (over other equally accessible clerks). This incumbent kept files up-to-date, and was highly trusted. Finally, this individual came to work early and was always willing to stay late if necessary. The low effort incumbent was described in exactly the opposite fashion.

The effort manipulation was difficult to operationalize because effort, if combined with the appropriate ability, will typically lead to higher performance. In addition, as one might expect, raters may have a difficult time distinguishing effort from performance. Hence, the effort manipulations may have been confounded with performance. However, performance was specifically held constant by providing the same performance rating for each incumbent. Thus, while a subject may have interpreted the effort manipulations as indicators of performance, they were told that performance was at a specific level.

Measures

Manipulation Checks.   Manipulation checks were built into the study to verify that subjects perceived the incumbents as either high or low in ability and either high or low in effort. This was accomplished through the use of an evaluation sheet that asked for subjects to rate each of the four incumbents on a 7-point scale for each of the 3 variables: performance, ability, and effort. The scale ranged from 1 = unacceptable to 7 = exceptional. Performance was also included in this evaluation so as not to sensitize subjects that the manipulations were directed solely at ability and effort and to see what extent performance was indeed constant across conditions.

Dependent Variables.   Subjects determined the pay level for each incumbent. A pay range was provided on both the job evaluation and on the initial worksheet to guide the subjects' allocations. Subjects were simply asked to make a base salary allocation (dollars per year to be received) for each of the four incumbents and were asked to keep that allocation within the stipulated range of $12,500 and $18,000 per year. Respondents were then asked to total all four salaries and multiply the total by 8 percent to arrive at the raise pool they would then use in allocating merit increases. For pay increases (measured as dollars per year to be added to base pay), subjects were told that they could allocate raises in any way they saw fit.

Only one condition was given, that they did *not* exceed the allotted raise pool. Beyond these instructions, subjects were given free rein to make pay level and pay increase decisions.

Analysis

The hypotheses were tested using multiple regression (cf. Cohen & Cohen, 1975), with a SAS program. Differences in pay level and pay increase means between conditions were assessed using Scheffe's a posteriori comparisons (cf. Kirk, 1972). Manipulation checks were done using overall *t*-tests to check for significant differences.

RESULTS

Table 1 presents the results of the manipulation checks. The results of the manipulation checks indicated that subjects did discriminate between high and low effort and between high and low ability. Using an overall t test for each variable, the results indicate significant differences. All manipulations except one were significant at the $p \leq .001$ level. High vs. low effort with ability held constant was marginally significant at the $p \leq .10$ level.

Performance was included in the study so that subjects would not guess the purpose of the study. It was also included in the manipulation check analysis to determine if subjects complied with the stated performance rating (constant across conditions) or made their own judgment. In both cases, high versus low ability ($t = 3.89$) and high versus low effort ($t = 30.99$), difference in performance was significant at the $p \leq .001$ level. This indicates that subjects ignored the stated rating and made judgments of their own based on the scenario descriptions of ability and effort. As a result, performance was entered into the analysis as a control variable.

The results of the correlation and regression analyses are shown in Tables 2 and 3 respectively. These results were used to test hypotheses one through five. Hypothesis one predicted that the main effects for ability and effort on pay level would both be significant. The main effect for ability was significant at the $p \leq .05$ level, but was not significant for effort. Hypothesis two predicted the same for pay increases. Ability was negatively correlated at the $p \leq .10$ level but was also not significant for effort. Hypothesis three stated that there would be an interaction effect between ability and effort for both pay level and pay in creases. The interaction was not significant for pay level, but was significant ($p \leq .001$) for pay increases. Results for the regressions can be found in Table 3.

Table 1. Manipulation Checks

	Manipulations															
	Ability							Effort								
Measures	$\overline{X}$ High S.D.	N	$\overline{X}$	Low S.D.	N	t		$\overline{X}$ High S.D.	N	$\overline{X}$	Low S.D.	N	t			
Performance	4.43 2.26	132	3.44	1.81	132	3.89***		5.80 1.02	132	2.07	.92	132	30.99***			
Ability	5.84 1.30	132	3.25	1.20	132	16.71***		5.25 1.49	132	3.84	1.80	132	6.93***			
Effort	4.21 2.46	132	3.68	2.21	132	1.83+		6.12 .85	132	1.76	.85	132	40.52***			

Note: *** $p \leq .001$; ** $p \leq .01$; * $p \leq .05$; + $p \leq .10$

446

Table 2. Means, SDs, and Intercorrelations Between Independent and Dependent Variables

Variables	$\overline{X}$	SD	(1)	(2)	(3)	(4)	(5)
(1) Ability	1.5	.50	—				
(2) Effort	1.5	.50	.00	—			
(3) Pay Level	14906	1860	.47*	.36*	—		
(4) Pay Increase	980	836	.27*	.79*	.48*	—	
(5) Performance	3.94	2.10	.23*	.89*	.48*	.84*	—

Note: *$p \leq .001$

Table 3. Multiple Regression Results

	Dependent Variables			
	Pay Level		Pay Increase	
Independent Variables	Understandardized Beta	Standardized Beta	Understandardized Beta	Standardized Beta
Ability (A)	1321.42* (585)	.35	−291.88+ (166)	−.17
Effort (E)	180.14* (636)	.05	98.46 (180)	.06
Performance	269.67* (114)	.31	170.63*** (32.61)	.43
A × E	97.04 (385)	.06	384.32*** (109)	.50
R^2	.36***	.36***	.75***	.75***

Notes: Standard errors in parentheses. ***$p \leq .001$; ** $p \leq .01$; * $p \leq .05$; + $p \leq .10$

Although not hypothesized, performance was included in the regression equation as a control measure since it was determined, by the manipulation check, that subjects were not holding performance constant as was intended in the scenarios. The main effects for performance on pay level and pay increases were both significant at the $p \leq .05$ and .001 levels respectively.

Hypothesis four states that for pay level decisions, the beta and correlation values with ability will be greater than the beta and correlation values with effort. This hypothesis was supported with correlation values for ability and effort of .47 and .36 respectively as shown in Table 2. Moreover, the standardized beta values for ability were greater than for effort under pay level with values of .35 and .05 respectively. Hypothesis five stated that for pay increase decisions, the beta and correlation values with effort will be greater than the beta and correlation values with ability. This hypothesis was also supported with correlation values for effort and ability of .79 and .27, respectively. The regression results did not support hypothesis five. The magnitude of the standardized beta values for effort was less than for ability with values of .06 and –.17 respectively.

DISCUSSION

A summary of the results is shown in Figure 3. It can be seen that elements of both the traditional and hypothesized models received support in the actual results. Perhaps the most important finding in the present study is the strong influence that ability plays in compensation decisions. As indicated by the standardized betas which are comparable, ability was the strongest predictor of pay level. Ability in interaction with effort was the strongest predictor of pay increases. Effort, on the other hand, did not add much predictive power. The standardized beta of effort for pay level was small and not significant. The same was true for effort as a predictor of pay increases. Effort was only a significant predictor through its interaction with ability in predicting pay increases.

The importance of ability can be seen at a pragmatic level. Being high, rather than low in effort resulted in about a 7 percent $(((1321 - 18000) - 18000) \times 100)$ to 11 percent $(((1321 - 12500) - 12500) \times 100)$ larger base salary. For high effort incumbents, pay raises for those with high ability were about 36 percent $(((2000 - 1270) - 2000) \times 100)$ larger than for those with low ability. For low effort incumbents, pay raises for those with high ability were about 42 percent $(((412 - 237) - 412) \times 100)$ larger than for those with low ability. See Tables 4 and 5 for a 2×2 depiction of the mean differences of salary levels and increases for various combinations of effort and ability. As can be seen from these figures, substantial differentiation is made between incumbent compensation on the basis of ability.

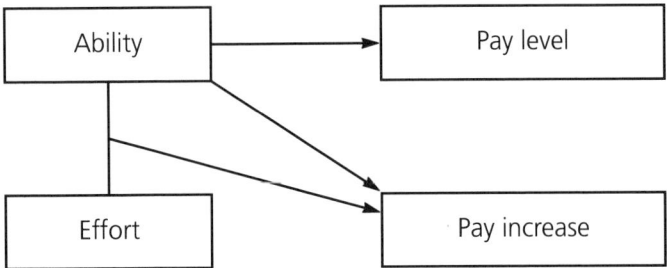

Figure 3.   Actual results.

Table 4.   Means and Standard Deviations and Pay Increase by Experimental Condition

	Ability	
Effort	High	Low
High	X̄ = 2000.50 SD = 600.96	X̄ = 1270.38 SD = 395.42
Low	X̄ = 412.09 SD = 422.53	X̄ = 236.92 SD = 313.65

Note: Minimum significant $(p \leq .05)$ difference between means = 108.02 using Scheffe's a posteriori comparisons.

Table 5.   Means and Standard deviation for Pay Level by Experimental Condition

	Ability	
Effort	High	Low
High	X̄ = 16529.56 SD = 1565.66	X̄ = 14613.63 SD = 1562.36
Low	X̄ = 15015.35 SD = 1686.78	X̄ = 13466.14 SD = 1173.67

Note: Minimum significant $(p \leq .05)$ difference between means = 365.89 using Scheffe's a posteriori comparisons.

Large differences in compensation due to ability might be expected for several reasons. First, current research shows that ability differences are predictive of productivity (e.g., Hunter & Hunter, 1984) and utility (e.g., Schmidt, Hunter, McKenzie, & Muldrow, 1979). To the extent that organizations wish to be competitive, productivity can be enhanced by paying for high rather than low ability employees. Second, effort is a very difficult concept to define and measure (Mitchell, 1982). Given the importance of ability to organizations and the difficulty involved in measuring effort, it may be no surprise that human resource professionals weight ability more heavily than effort in compensation decisions. Third, attribution theory may account for the ability effects. Under attribution theory, ability is treated as a stable attribution while effort is treated as an unstable attribution. Human resource decision makers probably follow a rational model and pay for ability which is perceived to be constant over time rather than paying for effort which is variable over time.

Although not necessarily surprising, compensation differences due to ability may be disconcerting. It suggests that relatively less attention is given to effort by human resource decision makers. The limited role played by effort in compensation decisions may call into question the large resources devoted to the study of motivation by academics and to the arrangement of work conditions to facilitate motivation by practitioners.

In order for our motivational theories to be effectively used by organizations, we may need to provide better systems for matching up compensation allocation with desired person-oriented goals. Merit pay is meant to reward past performance in order to motivate greater effort by employees in the future. Although this is the intent, even human resource professionals do not seem to follow this system. In the present study, ability in conjunction with effort was a better predictor of merit pay increases than was performance or effort alone. If we want to motivate effort expenditures, then we may need to better measure this construct. Moreover, individuals who work in such an environment must be made aware that *effort* will be rewarded and that generally, such effort must be linked to actual performance ratings. What we may need to do is to develop pay-for-effort reward systems to supplement current pay-for-performance reward systems.

The heavy use of ability in the present study both supports and *questions* the traditional model of compensation which separates the person from the job. As one would expect under the traditional model, ability was the strongest predictor of pay level. This is to be expected because ability is one of the major factors used by organizations to evaluate the worth of the job to the organization. In turn, the worth of the job is used to establish pay levels under the traditional model.

While the use of ability to establish pay level supports the traditional model, the use of ability to determine pay increase questions the traditional model. This finding suggests that it may not be possible in practice to separate out the person from the job in compensation decisions. Ability may be both a characteristic of the job and the person. In policy, how much ability is required may be used to determine pay levels and how much ability one has may be used to determine pay increase. In practice, these differences in the treatment of ability may break down with both decisions being based on a general ability factor.

These findings should be interpreted in the context of the limitations associated with the sample, design, and measures. Compensation in most organizations is quite complex. Setting salaries and allocating increases involves multiple and varied factors. The current design may not capture all the complexities of consequences that would occur in most organizations.

One problem with the present sample is the small size. It may be that subjects believed the instrument would take longer to complete. In the pilot test, subjects completed the instrument in 12 to 20 minutes. To be on the safe side, subjects were told to plan 20 minutes. The instrument, however, was rather thick and it may have appeared to subjects that more time would actually be needed. This factor may have played a part in the lower response by the human resource professionals and the need for a convenience sample.

Given the small sample, it was not possible to create a hold-out sample in order to cross-validate the results. As a result, the stability of the present findings may be open to question. Another problem is the sampling of subjects. The subjects in this sample were selected on a convenience basis. Hence, it is not known to what degree this sample is representative of the population. Finally, the sample is comprised of human resource professionals. It is difficult, therefore, to know to what extent the results would extend to nonhuman resource professionals.

Although limited, the sample was used because it represents a conservative test of the hypotheses. One would expect human resource professionals, compared to untrained managers or students, to be less likely to break from the traditional compensation model when making compensation decisions. Had nonhuman resource professionals been used as the sample, then the effects of ability and effort on both pay variables may have been more pronounced. This discussion of the sample suggests that the findings reported here are tentative, yet promising, and need to be further tested with better samples.

Another set of limitations, has to do with the design. One problematic design feature was the lack of a counterbalanced presentation of scenarios. The order in which scenarios were analyzed was left up to the discretion of the subjects in order to maximize the realism of the situation. An additional problematic design feature was the lack of independence among scenarios. As a result of this feature, the assumptions of homogeneity of variance and covariance may have been violated. Nonindependence of scenarios was retained as a design feature for the study, however, in order to maximize the realism of the study. Another design feature which may be problematic is the use of performance as a control variable in the analysis. It may have caused some multicollinearity among the predictor variables.

Yet another design limitation has to do with the use of fixed factor design rather than the use of continuous data. While using more continuous data in the rating of ability and effort would seem logical, the initial study was not designed this way. Future research would be wise to capture this component of continuous data rather since it uses more of the information about the independent variables and might create more variability.

A final design limitation in the present study is the use of "paper people." By using written scenarios rather than actual employees for purposes of compensation decisions, this design feature may limit the degree to which these results will generalize to compensation decisions regarding actual employees. Reviews of laboratory research, however, indicate that the problem of "paper people" may not be severe (Locke, 1986). Nevertheless, the current study should be replicated with actual, rather than paper employees.

These design limitations are problematic in that they may have increased the probability of the results being due to Type I error rather than the manipulations. Some care was taken against this threat by using Scheffe's a posteriori comparisons which are very conservative in rejecting the null hypothesis. In terms of the measures, one-item measures were used. As a result, the reliability of the measures is open to question. Future research in this area should use multiple item measures.

These findings regarding the traditional model also have implications for practice. At a general level, the results suggest that organizations need to carefully design and monitor pay systems to insure that the actual criteria being used to make compensation decisions are in line with the desired criteria spelled out in organizational policy. Other implications have to do with the role ability appears to play in merit increases. An unexpected result of the present study was the negative beta for ability under pay increases. Apparently, ability was held against people in increase decisions. This raises the question of fairness when a high ability employee has to work harder than a low ability employee to get the same pay increase.

At a more specific level, the results have implications for job evaluation and performance appraisal systems. If pay level decisions are based on performance as well as ability, and this is a desirable practice, then organizations may need to consider adding a factor for performance in the evaluation of jobs to be sure that it is being applied in an appropriate manner. If it is not a desirable practice, then efforts may need to be taken to get decision makers to minimize the use of performance in job evaluation decisions.

Similar arguments can be made about ability as a criterion in performance appraisal and merit decisions. If ability as well as effort is to be rewarded in merit pay plans, then the standard being used to evaluate ability, needs to be clearly specified in the performance appraisal system. On the other hand, if ability is to be solely rewarded upon entry into the organization, then steps need to be taken to insure that ability is not used as the basis for performance appraisal decisions.

In summary, traditional models of compensation make a distinction between the person and job in compensation decisions. As shown in the present study, this distinction may not be followed in actual pay decisions. Two characteristics of the person, ability and effort, were found to have separate and combined effects on pay increase and pay level decisions. Consistent with the traditional model of compensation, ability had an impact on pay levels. Consistent with the hypothesized model, ability and effort had an impact on pay increases. Contrary to both models, ability had a strong impact on pay increases. This pattern of findings indicates that a clear separation of the person from the job in compensation research and practice may not be possible.

ACKNOWLEDGMENTS

Portions of this paper were presented to the PHR division of the Southern Management Association, Atlanta, November 1991.

The authors wish to thank Marcia Miceli, Eileen Hogan, and Don Eskew, for their helpful comments on earlier drafts.

Address *all* correspondence to Debra J. Cohen, Management Science Department, George Washington University, School of Business and Public Management, Washington, DC 20052.

REFERENCES

Cohen, J., & Cohen, P. (1975). *Applied multiple regression/correlation analysis for the behavioral sciences* Hillsdale, NJ: Lawrence Erlbaum Associates.

Dugan, K.W. (1989). Ability and effort attributions: Do they affect how managers communicate performance feedback information. *Academy of Management Journal, 32,* 87–114.

Fossum, J., & Fitch, M., (1985). The effects of individual and contextual attributes on the sizes of recommended salary increases. *Personnel Psychology, 36,* 587–602.

Gupta, N., & Jenkins, G.D., Jr. (1991a). Job evaluation: An overview. *Human Resource Management Review, 1,* 91–96.

Gupta, N., & Jenkins, G.D., Jr. (1991b). Practical problems in using job evaluation systems to determine compensation. *Human Resource Management Review, 1,* 133–144.

Heider, F. (1958). *The psychology of interpersonal relations.* New York: Wiley.

Heilman, M., & Guzzo, R. (1978). The perceived causes of work success as a mediator of sex discrimination in organizations. *Organizational Behavior and Human Performance, 21,* 346 -357.

Heneman, R.L. (1990). Merit pay research. In G.R. Ferris & K.M. Rowland (Eds.), Research in personnel and human resources management (Vol. 8, pp. 203–262). Greenwich, CT: JAI Press.

Hunter J.E., & Hunter, R.F. (1984). Validity and utility of alternative predictors of job performance. *Psychological Bulletin, 96,* 72–98.

Kane, J.S. (1991). Alternative perspectives on job evaluation. *Human Resource Management Review, 1,* 91–162.

Kirk, R.E. (1972). *Statistical issues.* Montery, CA: Brooks/Cole.

Lawler, E.E. III. (1991). Paying the person: A Better approach to management? *Human Resource Management Review, 1,* 119–132.

Leventhal, G.S., Michaels, J.W., & Sanford, C. (1972). Inequity and interpersonal conflict: Reward allocation and secrecy about reward as methods of preventing conflict. *Journal of Personality and Social Psychology, 23,* 88–102.

Locke, E.A. (1986). *Generalizing from laboratory to field settings.* Lexington, MA: D.C. Heath.

Mahoney, T.A. (1991). Job evaluation: Endangered species or anachronism. *Human Resource Management Review, 1,* 155–162.

McCormick, E.J. (1979). *Job analysis applications and methods.* New York: AMOCOM.

Milkovich, G.T., & Newman, J.M. (1987). *Compensation* (2nd ed.) Plano, TX: Business Publications.

Mitchell, T.R. (1982). Motivation: New directions for theory, research, and practice. *Academy of Management Review, 7,* 80–88.

Peck, C. (1984). *Pay and performance: The Interaction of compensation and performance appraisal.* New York: The Conference Board.

Porter, L.W., Barrett, G.V., Mahoney, T.A., Gupta, N., Jenkens, G.D., Jr., & Lawler, E.E., III (1990). *Perspectives on job evaluation.* Symposium presented at the 50th Annual Meeting of the Academy of Management, San Francisco.

Schmidt, F.L., Hunter, J.E., McKenzie, R.L., & Muldrow, T.W. (1979). Impact of valid selection procedures on work-force productivity. *Journal of Applied Psychology, 64,* 609–626.

Schwab. D.P. (1980). Job evaluation and pay setting: Concepts and practices. In E.R. Livernash (Ed.), *Comparable worth: Issues and alternatives* (pp. 49–78). Washington, DC: Equal Employment Advising Council.

U.S. Department of Labor. (1977). *Dictionary of occupational titles* (4th ed.). Washington, DC: U.S. Government Printing Office.

Vroom, V.H. (1964). *Work and motivation.* New York: Wiley.

Wallace, M.J., & Fay, C.H. (1988). *Compensation theory and practice.* Boston: PWSKENT Publishing Company.

Weiner, B. (1985). An Attributional theory of achievement motivation and emotion. *Psychological Review, 92,* 548–573.

Witting, M.A., & Berman, S.L. (1991). A set of validity criteria for modeling job-based compensation systems. *Human Resource Management Review, 1,* 107–118.

Part IX

PAY SYSTEM EVALUATION

Given the large amount of money associated with strategic reward management, in the form of both direct (e.g., bonuses) and indirect (e.g., administration) costs, it is disconcerting how little systematic evaluation of strategic reward programs takes place. In this part of the book it is shown how evaluation can be done at low cost in even small companies. It is also shown how the evaluation of strategic reward programs needs to be improved to reflect the changing nature of work and pay practices, and to reflect more sophisticated statistical modeling.

Heneman, R.L., Greenberger, D.B., & Fox, J.A. (2001). Pay increase satisfaction: A reconceptualization of pay raise satisfaction based on changes in work and pay practices. *Human Resource Management Review.*

Heneman, R.L., Porter, G., Greenberger, D.B., & Strasser, S. (1997). Modeling the relationship between pay level and pay satisfaction. *Journal of Business and Psychology, 12*(2), 147–158.

Heneman, R.L., Eskew, D.E., & Fox, J.A. (1998). Using employee attitude surveys to evaluate a new incentive pay program. *Compensation and Benefits Review, 28*(1), 40–44.

CHAPTER 23

PAY INCREASE SATISFACTION:

A Reconceptualization of Pay Raise Satisfaction Based on Changes in Work and Pay Practices

Robert L. Heneman, David B. Greenberger, and Julie A. Fox

Source: Reprinted from Heneman, R.L., Greenberger, D.B. & Fox, J.A. Pay Increase Satisfaction: A Reconceptualization of Pay Raise Satisfaction Based on Changes in Work and Pay Practices. *Human Resource Management Review,* Copyright © 2001 with permission from Elsevier Science.

ABSTRACT

A new perspective on pay raise satisfaction, termed pay increase satisfaction, is conceptualized and used to guide the development of measures to supplement the widely used Pay Satisfaction Questionnaire (PSQ) [*International Journal of Psychology, 20,* (1985), p. 129]. The need for this new conceptualization lies in the nature of contemporary work and pay systems, particularly to those organizations adopting new strategic pay practices. Six dimensions of pay increase satisfaction are proposed: pay increase amount, pay increase opportunity, pay increase form, pay increase requirements, pay increase personal control, and pay increase rules. These dimensions are necessary to capture elements of the pay satisfaction domain not currently being captured by the PSQ. Implications for future research are discussed.

INTRODUCTION

Pay satisfaction continues to be one of the more frequently studied attitudinal constructs in human resource management research and these efforts have resulted in the development of an important body of knowledge (see H. Heneman, 1985; H. Heneman & Judge, in press; Miceli & Lane, 1991 for recent reviews). Given the ad hoc measures of pay satisfaction used prior to 1985, the prevailing knowledge that was developed up until that point should probably be deemed as tentative ongoing validation to the literature in this empirical study (H. Heneman, 1985). Since that time, however, with the development of the Pay Satisfaction Questionnaire (PSQ; H. Heneman & Schwab, 1985), the literature in this area has become cumulative (i.e., H. Heneman & Judge, in press, located 29 studies that have been conducted on pay satisfaction since 1985). Most importantly, pay satisfaction results can now be compared across studies because of the widespread use of the PSQ and its sound psychometric properties (H. Heneman & Judge, in press). As a result, in a most recent review of pay satisfaction studies, Heneman and Judge conclude, "In some cases, substantial studies have been made in pay satisfaction research in the past 13 years."

Although promising, H. Heneman and Judge (in press) also point to some troublesome issues regarding pay satisfaction research: "In another sense, however, we have fallen way behind. Organizations' pay practices have changed dramatically and forcefully, and our research has simply ignored or paid scant attention to these changes when viewed against this backdrop, our pay satisfaction research seems meager, misguided, and myopic." Recommendations for the future by Heneman and Judge include a call for a moratorium on PSQ factor analyses and instead, they call for careful development of new scales to supplement the PSQ.

The objective of the present writing is to begin the conceptual development of a new perspective on pay satisfaction that can be used to guide the careful development of measures to supplement the PSQ. Our fear is that the recommendations of Heneman and Judge (in press) could set off a wave of new ad hoc pay satisfaction scales being developed. Without careful conceptual development occurring first, we could easily return full circle to a situation similar to that described by H. Heneman (1985); i.e., one in which our body of knowledge regarding pay satisfaction was not cumulative due to the ad hoc nature of pay satisfaction measures.

In this chapter, we attempt to provide the conceptual underpinnings for the development of a new set of integrated measures of pay satisfaction and to do this prior to the evolution of new scales. By doing so, we will have a common starting point to further explicate the content domain of the pay satisfaction construct.

The conceptual domain that we draw upon for these ideas comes from changes in pay practices and theories. In particular, we will contrast the administrative perspective used previously with a more contemporary strategic perspective that we advocate for further advancements in pay satisfaction. Finally, we provide reflections on a new measure of pay increase satisfaction consistent with the strategic perspective.

CHANGES IN THE WORK AND PAY CONTEXT

The roots of the pay satisfaction construct lie in both theory and practice. The principle models of pay satisfaction are based upon equity theory (H. Heneman & Judge, in press). The PSQ pays homage to Adams' (1965) equity theory as well as to Lawler's (1971, 1981) discrepancy model. Both theories conceptualize pay satisfaction in terms of the fairness of the amount received relative to comparison of others, including self. More recent refinements to the pay satisfaction construct (such as by Miceli & Lane, 1991) are also grounded in equity theory, but rather than emphasizing pay outcomes, they emphasize the processes used to create pay outcomes (Folger & Konovsky, 1989; Greenberg, 1987).

Practice was also used to guide pay satisfaction model development. H. Heneman and Schwab (1979) first dimensionalized pay on the basis of how pay systems were administered and this 1979 conceptualization of pay, in turn, guided the 1985 development of the PSQ. Also, Dyer and Theriault (1976) refined the pay satisfaction concept by paying attention to pay policy administration. Miceli and Lane (1991) added to the model through their attention to components of the pay system.

This emphasis on equity and on administration would seem to be natural developments given pay practices that existed in the 1970s and 1980s. During this period, the textbook models used to guide pay plan design were heavily grounded in equity theory and tended to focus on the creation of pay structures that were not administratively complex for the human resource department to administer (e.g., Hills, 1987; Milkovich & Newman, 1984). A common element to equity theory, pay satisfaction models, and pay practice was the job and its associated characteristics. Actual job characteristics were used to determine pay amounts by the organization and the perceived value of the job was used by employees to gauge their satisfaction with pay.

While a residual focus on administration remains in theory and practice, a new strategic pay perspective is emerging in the 1990s and has the potential to shift theory and practice dramatically. In terms of theory, a shift is taking place in the study of pay away from the individual as the unit of analysis and toward the organization. Rather than focusing on the design of pay systems from an equity perspective, attention is being paid to the design of pay systems to be responsive to the needs of the business. These needs may include equity considerations, but are more likely to be concerned with fitting the pay system to the changing business environment, to the goals of the organization, and to the goals of other human resource subsystems in the organization (R. Heneman, Ledford, & Gresham, in press). Pay decision making is studied from the perspective of agency theory (Gomez-Mejia & Balkin, 1992) which focuses on pay rules being established to further the interests of the organization rather than the equity perceptions of recipients to pay decisions. Evidence of the change in orientation can best be seen in the market for both a strategic compensation research book (Gomez-Mejia & Balkin, 1992) and text (Martocchio, 1998).

In terms of practices, fundamental changes are taking place in the nature of work (Howard, 1995). These include changes in: organizational structure, with a greater focus on the use of teams; the employment relationship, with the declining use of permanent employment relationships; technology, with one effect being the monitoring of employees and pay system administration; and jobs, with the unit analysis shifting from jobs to people in roles (R. Heneman et al., in press). Consistent with these changes in the nature of work is the development of new pay systems such as skill-based pay, broadbanding, team pay, and employee ownership (R. Heneman et al., in press). Interestingly, reports on actual practices for these new pay systems indicate that while they are developed in direct response to business objectives in the organization, equity is seldom mentioned, or if it is, is of limited concern as a business objective (McAdams & Hawk, 1995).

As will be shown, pay systems have begun to shift from an administrative to a strategic focus. Pay theory has begun to focus on the pay system as the unit of analysis rather than the individual in the pay system. Pay practice has begun to focus on the person as the unit of analysis rather than the job. We believe that shifts in the unit of analysis used for research and practice constitute fundamental changes in pay rather than superficial ones and that these fundamental changes are likely to make traditional measures of pay satisfaction incomplete in the short run and possibly obsolete in the long run.

FUNDAMENTAL CHANGES IN THE NATURE OF PAY

As we have stated, changes in the nature of work have brought about changes in the compensation systems. Underlying these changes in types of pay are some common features which are fundamental because they both impact a variety of pay systems and can serve as the conceptual basis for further development of pay satisfaction measures (R. Heneman et al., in press). Identification of these common features is critical because developing different pay satisfaction measures for different pay system types limits the generalizability of results in empirical research and sacrifices parsimony in theoretical development. These two perspectives were initially conceptualized by Gomez-Mejia and Balkin, and then further refined by R. Heneman et al. (in press).

Pay systems characterized as administrative in focus can be summarized in the following way. Pay was provided to individuals on the basis of the job they held. In turn, the job was evaluated on the basis of value to the organization as determined by a job evaluation and by a market survey. The focus typically was on internal equity, especially in unionized settings, rather than external equity, and rewards were usually provided for time-on-the-job measures, such as seniority. Pay plans were centralized, having been developed by top management in conjunction with the human resources department, and seldom changed. The pay system usually lagged changes in the business and pay increases were built into base pay rather than being given in a bonus. In short, rigid order was imposed on employee pay with administrative pay systems.

By comparison, flexibility is emphasized with the more contemporary strategic pay systems. Pay is provided for characteristics of the person (i.e., KSAs) rather than the duties of the job. Pay is also provided for output rather than time spent in the job. Moreover, output of the team is assessed more than the contribution of the individual. Pay systems are dynamic and are designed to bring about change in the business. External equity is emphasized over internal equity. The creation of pay systems is done in a participative, rather than topdown, manner. Finally, pay decisions are decentralized and awards are often in the form of a bonus rather than being built into base pay.

CRITIQUE OF EXISTING PAY SATISFACTION MEASURES

The original measures of pay satisfaction have been critiqued by a number of individuals. H. Heneman (1985), for example, argued that pay satisfaction was treated as unidimensional when, in reality, it has multiple dimensions. Early attempts at assessing pay satisfaction were also criticized because they were often ad hoc, which rendered the results of a study idiosyncratic to that measure.

It is no surprise that the PSQ is better suited for organizations with an administrative focus as it was originally designed from the administrative perspective. But while it was intended to assess pay in the context of an administrative perspective, it should not be abandoned in strategic pay environments. Specifically, base pay (pay level), benefits, and process variables (structure/administration) continue to be of importance in most organizations including those with a strategic pay focus.

Nevertheless, in a number of ways, the PSQ fails to capture elements of the pay construct domain associated with strategic pay. First, pay raise satisfaction implies an increase to base pay. In organizations with a strategic focus, pay increases are more likely to be issued in the form of cash bonuses that are not built into base pay and, hence, cannot be considered as raises. Second, the form of pay issued may not be cash, but may instead be in the form of stock or paid time off. Third, with team and organizational measures used to determine rewards, in strategic pay environments, there are many influences on pay other than the supervisor such as internal resources and the state of the economy (R. Heneman & Gresham, 1998). Fourth, the PSQ does not recognize interdependencies between pay systems in strategic pay environments. Multiple reward systems may be used and in order for the organization to minimize costs, trade offs between pay systems are more salient than in administrative environments. For example, some organizations use variable pay where the amount received varies by performance of the organization. In some limited cases (e.g., Saturn), at-risk pay is used where pay is taken away from base pay and put at risk for employees on the basis of performance. Sixth, the development of pay plans is crucial in strategic pay environments because they may change often (Ledford, 1995) and be developed by employees as well as managers and human resource professionals (R. Heneman & Gresham, 1998). The PSQ fails to capture the dynamic nature of pay system development and the means used to develop the pay plan.

We have been able to locate only one effort to revise the PSQ to be in alignment with a strategic perspective. Sturman and Short (1999) developed a new measure labeled contingent pay satisfaction and provided some preliminary construct validity evidence to support this new measure. The intent of this measure was to develop a supplemental dimension to the PSQ which could be used to measure satisfaction with pay-for-performance plans other than merit pay. That is, the PSQ focused on pay satisfaction in the context of merit pay while the contingent pay satisfaction measure was developed in the context of variable pay plans such as gainsharing, goalsharing, piece rate, and profit sharing. To create this measure, they simply changed the language of the pay raise items in the PSQ to bonuses rather than raises. Although the initial construct validity evidence for this supplemental measure of contingent pay satisfaction is promising, it appears to be deficient in several areas as well because evidence in the fifth section of this article where we describe changes in the nature of pay systems which include not only a change in the type of pay granted (raise vs. bonus) but other important changes as well are not captured by the contingent pay satisfaction measures.

RECONCEPTUALIZATION OF PAY RAISE SATISFACTION

As can be seen, the pay raise dimension of the PSQ is limited in its applicability in strategic pay environments. As a result, it is time to reformulate the pay raise dimension to be consistent with changes in pay systems. As a start, it is first recommended that pay raise satisfaction be labeled pay increase satisfaction to acknowledge that additions to pay may not constitute a permanent pay raise but may instead be a cash bonus. Raises and bonuses can both be grouped under pay increase; hence, we favor the phrase pay increase rather than contingent pay.

In particular, we believe that the aspects of pay increases salient to employees in strategic pay environments include the following:

1. What is the size of my increases?
2. What opportunities do I have for pay increases?
3. In what form will my pay increase be?
4. How much will my increase cost me in terms of time, effort, difficulty, and time away from leisure?
5. How much influence do I have over the payout standards?
6. What rules do I have to follow to receive increases?

More formally, these aspects of pay translate into the following five hypothesized dimensions of pay increase satisfaction:

1. Pay increase amount;
2. Pay increase opportunity;
3. Pay increase requirements;
4. Pay increase personal control; and
5. Pay increase rules.

Each of these dimensions will be described in turn and grounded in relevant theory and practice. A summary of each dimension is presented in Table 1.

Table 1.   Pay increase satisfaction

Pay increase amount

Size of pay increases
Size of increase relative to income and payroll taxes on increase
Size of increase needed to make a difference in attitudes and behavior
Size of increases received relative to others
Size of increases received relative to cost of living.
Size of increases received relative to base pay

Pay increase opportunity

Eligibility for stock
Possibility of cash bonuses
Total earnings possibilities
Opportunity for time off with pay
Permanent increases to my base pay
Promotional pay increases
Cost of living increases
Pay increases for seniority

Pay increase form

Total amount of increases to base pay
Total amount of increases as cash bonuses
Total amount of increases in the form of time off with pay
Total amount of increases in the form of stock

Pay increase requirements

Reduction in base pay
Fluctuations in size of increase
Extra effort required
Longer work hours
Difficulty of the work
Develop new skills

Pay increase possibility

Ability to influence performance standards
Helpfulness of others in achieving goals
Resources to do the job
Time to complete the job
Performance standards under own control
Influence of team on own performance
Influence of company on own performance
Influence of economy on own performance
Understanding of performance standards
Ability to monitor own work

Table 1.   Pay increase satisfaction (Cont.)

Pay increase rules

Being able to help set pay increase rules
Being able to help set performance standards
Understanding of rules for pay increases
Availability of information regarding pay increase rules
Difficulty level of pay increase rules
Communication of pay increase rules
Frequency of payout
Opportunity to appeal pay increase decisions
Changes to pay plan design
Opportunity to select people to evaluate performance

Pay Increase Amount

Pay increase amount refers to the perceived size of pay increases received. Because there are few pay increase benchmarks, size in and of itself is difficult for employees to assess. Benchmarks that do exist can be derived from equity theory (Adams, 1965) and just noticeable difference theory (H. Heneman & Ellis, 1982), and include such salient items as cost of living, other employees, and base pay as shown in Table 1. That is, in order to gauge satisfaction with the pay increase amount, the employee must compare the increase to a standard. Standards identified in the research literature include other employees inside the organization, other employees outside the organization, the self over time, and the size of the increase relative to the size of the base pay amount (pay level) received.

Pay Increase Opportunity

Pay increase opportunity refers to the perceived opportunities to receive pay increases. These opportunities relate to the sources of earning as shown in Table 1. The importance of this construct to employees comes from the concept of valance in expectancy theory (Vroom, 1964). Individual reactions to the attractiveness of outcomes influences the level of satisfaction with pay (Lawler, 1971, 1981). Opportunities for pay increases used to include only merit pay, piece-rate plans, and sales commissions in administrative pay systems. In strategic pay systems, the list of opportunities expands to include stock, cash bonuses, and time off. In addition, seniority and cost-of-living increases may also be present especially in unionized environments.

Pay Increase Form

Pay increase form refers to the form of currency used for the pay transaction. Distinctions often made in strategic pay environments often include cash vs. stock, cash vs. time off, cash vs. pay raise to base salary (Lawler, 1990). Different currency forms may have different levels of valance to people that in turn affect their feelings of satisfaction (Lawler, 1971).

Pay Increase Requirements

Pay increase requirements refer to the perceived costs to employees that are associated with strategic pay in a variety of different forms. These costs, shown in Table 1, can be in the form of reduction to base pay (i.e., at-risk pay), fluctuations in pay increases (variable pay), and personal sacrifices in terms of more difficult work (such as work requiring more effort, more time-consuming work, and additional time in the job away from leisure and/or family pursuits). Both classical economic theory and psychological theories such as equity theory (Kauffman, 1989) assume that satisfaction with work, pay in this situation, is a function of the balance between outcomes (pay increases) and inputs (pay increase requirements). Increasingly, strategic pay systems require greater effort by employees in order to achieve the desired results. For example, skill-based pay plans may require learning and certification off the job. Hence, expectancy perceptions are also likely to be altered (R. Heneman et al., in press).

Pay Increase Personal Control

Pay increase personal control refers to the sources of contamination, bias, and deficiency in performance standards linked to pay which serve to constrain employee expectancy perceptions. For example, performance measures used to determine increases may be both contaminated and deficient for a number of reasons, such as those shown in Table 1 and derived from the work of Peters, O'Connor, and Eulberg (1985). In turn, these sources of contamination and deficiency are likely to result in dissatisfaction with pay increases when employees come to perceive themselves as not having personal influence over performance objectives (Greenberger & Strasser, 1991). Practitioners often refer to these sources, which undermine personal control over meeting prescribed performance standards, as the problem of line of sight (R. Heneman et al., in press). For example, a lower-level employee may have very little influence over profit as a performance standard for reasons shown in Table 1. That is, they may be dissatisfied with profit sharing because profit is a function of factors other than performance (e.g., economy), the profit measures may be biased (Loomis, 1999), and the employee's performance may be dependent on higher-level employees and the work team.

Pay Increase Rules

Pay increase rules refer to the perceived ways in which individuals are paid. Recall that the PSQ looked at pay procedures from the perspective of how employees perceived the pay structure and pay administration. Although pay structure and pay administrative were treated as separate constructs, empirically, they were collapsed together (Heneman & Schwab, 1985). Pay increase rules are conceptualized to include the basic structure and administrative issues, but also such pay-related factors as: fixed vs. variable increases, appeals mechanisms, participation in pay plan design, timing of payouts to individual employees, and timing of changes to the pay system. These other factors are strategic considerations in the design of contemporary pay systems (Belcher et al., 1998) and are likely to influence employees' procedural justice perceptions (R. Heneman et al., in press).

FUTURE RESEARCH

The five new dimensions of pay raise satisfaction merely represent a start to the reconceptualization of pay raise satisfaction to be more aligned with contemporary pay practices and compensation theory. Additional work is needed and Heneman and Judge (in press) provide guidance in this area. Their call has led us to propose this new, more contemporary conceptualization. However, they also point out that more qualitative research needs to be conducted as well: We must enter the field, rather than merely survey it, in order to fully appreciate its content and change.

A systematic and strategic approach appears most relevant to achieve this next step. First, the dimensions proposed must meet the test of face validity. Employees, executives, and compensation professionals need to be approached to discuss the meaningfulness of the proposed dimensions. Second, items need to be generated and submitted to confirmatory tests. Third, construct validation procedures need to be undertaken. Fourth, pay raise satisfaction using new measures should vary systematically in predictable ways by individual differences and organizational variables. For example, Cable and Judge (1994) found that college students preferred individual pay over team-based pay. Hence, pay increase satisfaction in team-based environments should be lower for younger employees, rather than more senior ones. Fifth, substantive hypotheses can be tested. Strategic pay theory, for example, suggests that participation in pay plan design is critical to employee pay satisfaction (Lawler, 1990). Hence, one might expect to see employees at moderate, rather than low, levels of pay increase rule satisfaction even when pay increase amount satisfaction is low (Folger & Konovsky, 1989). Finally, new hypotheses can be set forth and tested. As shown in Table 1, changes in the nature of work have an influence on changes in pay practices as documented by Heneman et al. (in press). In turn, changes in pay practices are likely to have a multitude of effects on pay increase satisfaction that are described in the current paper. These links await future hypothesis development and empirical testing.

Two categories arise with our conceptualization of pay increase satisfaction that may need to be resolved with additional research.[1] The first criticism has to do with our combining raises and bonuses together under the category of pay increases. Employees may be very sensitive to these differences because a pay raise is a permanent increase to pay that compounds in value over the course of time, while a bonus is a one-time cash allotment that does not compound over time because it is not built into base pay (R. Heneman, 1992). Whether and when employees make this distinction in terms of their reactions to pay is an empirical question in our minds. Anecdotal data exist on both sides of the issue. We have added the dimension pay increase form to reflect differences that may exist in reactions to different forms of pay (e.g., pay raise vs. pay bonus). Variables such as education may produce differential affective reactions to the various types of currency in our pay increase type dimension (i.e., base pay raise, cash bonus, stock, time off). That is, we would expect higher-educated employees to make these distinctions more often than less-educated employees.

The second criticism is that five of our dimensions are actually determinants of pay increase satisfaction (i.e., opportunity, form, requirements, possibility, and rules). Again, we think that this is a question best resolved in an empirical fashion. In at least one large company that we are familiar with, pay increase amount is fairly uniform and high while there is considerable variability as to reactions to the other dimensions of pay increase satisfaction that we detail. Also, it is our belief that if structure/administration is a dimension of pay satisfaction for the PSQ, then our other dimensions are very analogous to structure/administrative decisions for strategic pay purposes.

CONCLUSION

Considerable change has taken place in compensation systems from 1985 to the present. New systems are gaining in popularity and are likely to continue to grow (Lawler, Mohrman, & Ledford, 1998). In order to capture employee satisfaction with these new pay systems accurately, new pay satisfaction measures need to be created. Before jumping into large-scale survey development procedures, however, care must be taken to carefully chart changes in the nature of compensation systems and the likely impact on the dimensionality of pay satisfaction. Our paper represents an attempt to move the pay satisfaction research further in this direction. Additional work is needed to verify and begin to operationalize the six new dimensions of pay raise satisfaction we have developed.

NOTE

1. We would like to thank a reviewer for bringing these criticisms to our attention.

REFERENCES

Adams, J.S. (1965). Inequity in social exchange. In L. Berkowitz (Ed.), *Advances in experimental social psychology* (Vol. 2, pp. 267–299). New York: Academic Press.

Belcher, J.G. Jr., Butler, R.J., Cheatham, D.W, Goberville, G.J., Heneman, R.L., & Wilson, T.B. (1998). *How to design variable pay plan*. Scottsdale, AZ: American Compensation Association.

Cable, D.M., & Judge, T.A. (1994). Pay preferences and job search decisions: A personorganization fit perspective. *Personnel Psychology, 47*, 317–329.

Dyer, L.D., & Theriault, R. (1976). The determinants of pay satisfaction. *Journal of Applied Psychology, 61*, 596–604.

Folger, R., & Konovsky, M.A. (1989). Effects of procedural and distributive justice on reactions to pay raise decisions. *Academy of Management Journal, 32*, 115–130.

Gomez-Mejia, L., & Balkin, D.B. (1992). *Compensation, organizational strategy, and firm performance*. Cincinnati, OH: Southwestern.

Greenberg, J. (1987). Reactions to procedural injustice in payment distributions: do the means justify the ends? *Journal of Applied Psychology, 72*, 55–61.

Greenberger, D.B., & Strasser, S. (1991). The role of situational and dispositional factors in the enhancement of personal control in organizations. In L.L. Cummings & B.M. Staw (Eds.), *Research in organizational behavior* (Vol. 13, pp. 111–146). Greenwich, CT: JAI Press.

Heneman, H.G., III (1985). Pay satisfaction. In K.M. Rowland & G.R. Ferris (Eds.), *Research in personnel and human resources management* (Vol. 3, pp. 115–140). Greenwich, CT: JAI Press.

Heneman, H.G., & Ellis, R.A. (1982). Correlates of just-noticeable differences in pay increases. *Labor Law Journal, 34*, 533–538.

Heneman, H.G., & Judge, T A. (in press). Compensation attitudes: A review and recommendations for future research. In S. L. Rynes & B. Gerhart (Eds.), *Com-*

pensation in organizations: Progress and prospects. San Francisco: New Lexington Press.

Heneman, H.G., & Schwab, D.P. (1979). Work and rewards theory. In D. Yoder & H.G. Heneman, Jr. (Eds.), *ASPA handbook of personnel and industrial relations* (pp. 6(1)-6(22)). Washington, DC: Bureau of National Affairs.

Heneman, H.G., III, & Schwab, D.P. (1985). Pay satisfaction: Its multidimensional nature and measurement. *International Journal of Psychology, 20,* 129–142.

Heneman, R.L., & Gresham, M. (1998). Linking appraisals to compensation and incentives. In J.W Smither (Ed.), *Performance appraisal: State-of-the art methods for performance management. Society for Industrial and Organizational Psychology Professional Practice Series* (pp. 496–536). San Francisco: Jossey-Bass.

Heneman, R.L., Ledford, G.L., & Gresham, M.T. (in press). Compensation and the changing nature of work. In S. Rynes & B. Gerhart (Eds.), *Compensation in organizations: Progress and prospects. Society for Industrial and Organizational Psychology Frontiers of Industrial and Organizational Psychology Series.* San Francisco: New Lexington Press.

Hills, F.S. (1987). *Compensation decision making.* Fort Worth, TX: Dryden Press.

Howard, A. (1995). *The changing nature of work.* San Francisco: Jossey-Bass.

Kauffman, B.E. (1989). Models of man in industrial relations research. *Industrial and Labor Relations Review, 43,* 72–88.

Lawler, E.E., III (1971). *Pay and organizational effectiveness.* New York: McGraw-Hill.

Lawler, E.E., III (1981). *Pay and organizational development.* Reading, MA: Addison-Wesley.

Lawler, E.E., III (1990). *Strategic pay: Aligning organizational strategies and pay systems.* San Francisco: Jossey-Bass.

Lawler, E.E., III, Mohrman, S.A., & Ledford, G.E. (1998). *Strategies for high-performance organizations.* San Francisco: Jossey-Bass.

Ledford, G.E., Jr. (1995). Designing nimble reward systems. *Compensation and Benefits Review, 27,* 46–54.

Loomis, C.J. (1999). Lies, damned lies, and managed earnings. *Fortune, 140*(3), 74–94.

Martocchio, J.J. (1998). *Strategic compensation.* Upper Saddle River, NJ: Prentice-Hall.

Miceli, M.P., & Lane, M.C. (1991). Antecedents of pay satisfaction: A review and extension. In K.M. Rowland & G.R. Ferris (Eds.), *Research in personnel and human resources management* (Vol. 9, pp. 6–19). Greenwich, CT: JAI Press.

Milkovich, G.T., & Newman, J.M. (1984). *Compensation.* Chicago: Irwin.

Peters, L.H., O'Connor, E.J., & Eulberg, J.R. (1985). Situational constraints: Sources, consequences, and future considerations. In K.M. Rowland & G.R. Ferris (Eds.), *Research in personnel and human resources management* (Vol. 3, pp. 79–114). Greenwich, CT: JAI Press.

Sturman, M.C., & Short, J.C. (1999). *The construct of contingent pay satisfaction: Adding and validating a new pay satisfaction dimension.* Paper presented at the Annual Academy of Management Meetings, Chicago.

Vroom, V.H. (1964). *Work and motivation.* New York: Wiley.

CHAPTER 24

MODELING THE RELATIONSHIP BETWEEN PAY LEVEL AND PAY SATISFACTION

Robert L. Heneman, Gayle Porter, David B. Greenberger, and Stephen Strasser

Source: Heneman, R.L., Porter, G., Greenberger, D.B., & Strasser, S. (1997). Modeling the Relationship Between Pay Level and Pay Satisfaction. *Journal of Business and Psychology, 12*(2), 147–158.

ABSTRACT

The relationship between pay level and pay satisfaction was modeled in a field study with 456 employees of nursing departments in a large hospital. After controlling for person, job, and pay system characteristics, pay satisfaction variance was better explained by treating pay level as a power function rather than a linear function. This result was expected given the low wage rate relative to the market, the lack of a formal rewards system, and the high level of tenure in the workforce. Implications of this finding for theory, research, and practice were discussed.

INTRODUCTION

Many criteria are used by organizations to gauge the effectiveness of their compensation plans. These criteria include improved performance, compliance with laws and regulations, cost reduction, and contribution to the strategic plans (Hills, Bergmann, & Scarpello, 1994; Gomez-Mejia, 1992). Employee attitudes are also used to gauge the effectiveness of compensation plans. Attitudes are important to gauging compensation plan effectiveness because it is believed that they can be used to predict important organizational outcomes. This is certainly the case for pay satisfaction which has been shown to be related to attendance, turnover, and union vote (Heneman, 1985).

Because pay satisfaction is related to important organizational outcomes, a considerable amount of research has been devoted to predicting and explaining pay satisfaction. A consistent finding in the literature is that there is a positive relationship between pay level and pay satisfaction (Heneman, 1985). Actual pay can be used, therefore, by researchers and administrators to explain and predict pay satisfaction. In order to model the precise relationship between pay level and pay satisfaction, however, care must be taken to consider characteristics of the person and job (Lawler, 1971) and pay system administration (Dyer & Theriault, 1976) which may also influence pay satisfaction. The inclusion of these variables is now becoming more of a common practice in pay satisfaction research (e.g., Judge, 1993).

Another consideration, which unfortunately has not been common practice, is to look for the possibility of a nonlinear relationship between pay level and pay satisfaction. It is argued here that the use of a nonlinear function between pay level and pay satisfaction may improve upon the precision with which pay satisfaction can be predicted and explained. It is also argued here that taking a 'blind-empirical' approach to specify the form(s) of the nonlinear function is inappropriate. Instead, a contingency approach should be used to guide the choice of a nonlinear function.

Traditionally in pay satisfaction research, a linear relationship between pay level and pay satisfaction is tested. Application of a linear function suggests that incremental increases in pay will be matched by proportional increases in employee satisfaction with pay. This application may be associated with a philosophy that the best pay level strategy is to pay as much as possible, limited only to the budget constraints of the organization.

A preferable approach to pay level strategy is to use pay as a source of competitive advantage (Lawler, 1990). By knowing the potential return on pay level dollars in the form of satisfaction, organizational planners can better see to what extent the pay portion of the reward system will support the strategic agenda of the organization. Under this more strategic approach to determining pay level, it will no longer be sufficient to know that, in general, pay level relates positively to pay satisfaction. Instead, knowledge will be needed as to the likely levels of satisfaction at varying pay levels being considered by the organization. For example, decision makers may need to know if pay satisfaction increases at a constant rate, increasing rate, or decreasing rate with increasing salary rates. Fortunately, a number of disciplines offer theories which show possible nonlinear relationships that can be considered in making strategic pay level decisions.

Possible nonlinear relationships between pay level and pay satisfaction were reviewed by Porter, Greenberger, and Heneman (1990). Economic theory suggests that, based upon the principle of decreasing marginal utility, the relationship between pay level and pay satisfaction is best characterized as a logarithmic function (Bernoulli, 1964). A logarithmic function corresponds to decreasing marginal utility. The rate of increase in pay satisfaction diminishes as pay level increases. Psychophysics theory suggests that a power function best captures the relationship (Stevens, 1959). The power function implies that the rate of increase in pay satisfaction accelerates as pay level increases. Psychological theory suggests that the function should be quadratic (Adams, 1965). That is, there is a curvilinear relationship between pay level and pay satisfaction. There is an initial positive relationship between pay level and pay satisfaction, leveling off at some point, and then changing into a gradual decline of pay satisfaction as pay level continues to increase.

In addition to reviewing these theories, Porter et al. (1990) also tested each theory versus the linear model. The results provided support for each of the nonlinear models when general satisfaction was used as the department variable. The nonlinear models accounted for additional variance in general satisfaction not accounted for by the linear model. The authors concluded that there was support for nonlinear functions and that the selection of which function to use in modeling pay satisfaction using pay level depended upon the match between the focal organizations characteristics and the theoretical constructs associated with each theory.

Although suggestive, the results of the Porter et al. (1990) study can be improved upon in two ways to strengthen the modeled relationship between pay level and pay satisfaction. First, a set of variables containing person, job, and pay system characteristics should be entered along with pay level as independent variables. As indicated in the Heneman (1985) review, many previous studies have failed to incorporate these important predictor variables when modeling pay level and pay satisfaction. Second, theoretical rationale should be given as to which function should be tested given particular organizational conditions. Previous research, reviewed by Porter et al. (1990), identified alternative nonlinear relationships, but failed to describe under which conditions each is likely to occur. Theory needs to be used to describe the appropriate nonlinear function in particular situations. Both of these steps will be taken in the present study in order to improve upon the amount of variance in pay satisfaction explained by pay level alone.

The present study was conducted in a large midwestern hospital. Based on previous research reviewed by Heneman (1985), several person, job, and pay system characteristics were believed to be related to pay satisfaction and were included in the analysis. Age was expected to have a positive relationship with pay satisfaction as older workers were expected to have more seniority and pay. Supervisors were expected to have less satisfaction with pay. Due to overtime and shift differentials, the pay of supervisors could be compressed by their subordinates pay. Tenure was predicted to be negatively associated with pay satisfaction. More tenured individuals were likely to be up against the maximum for their pay grade. Job tier was included and it was expected that higher level jobs would receive higher wages than lower level jobs and hence, satisfaction would be greater. Employee type was another variable of concern. It was expected that non-regular employees (supplemental and contingent) would be more satisfied with pay, than regular (part-time and full-time) because of the larger wages paid to non-regulars. The compa-ratio or comparative salary ratio was also used. It was expected that there would be a positive relationship with pay satisfaction as individuals with higher compa-ratios have, by definition, higher rates of pay relative to others.

Like many hospitals, the present hospital did not have a well-defined compensation plan for pay level determinations. While they did have pay grades, movement within pay grades was not systematically determined. Performance ratings were only sporadically made and communicated. Pay increases were not large and pay levels were below the market average. Most employees were full-time and had considerable tenure with the organization. Given these circumstances, it was hypothesized that a power function would better model the relationship between pay satisfaction and pay level than would the linear relationship. With the power function, it was expected that the rate of increase in satisfaction would be at an increasing rate as pay levels increased. That is, each additional dollar in pay level would provide increasing levels of pay satisfaction as shown in Figure 1.

This prediction was made for several reasons. First, the slope of the function should be positive because these were not high paying jobs. The employees were no where near being satiated with pay. Had they been satiated with pay, then the slope may turn negative as other rewards such as leisure take on more importance (Heilbroner & Thurow, 1982). Given the below market wages this was not believed to be the case here. Second, the slope should steepen with additional pay levels because of a poorly administered rewards system. Little performance feedback or recognition was

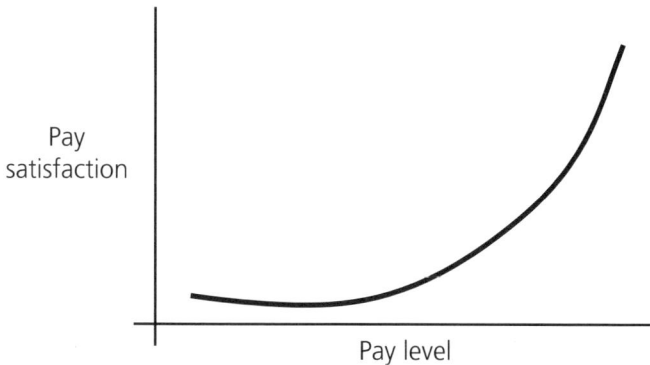

Figure 1.   Power function.

provided. Under these circumstances, employees may derive added satisfaction from pay increases because pay increases serves as a source of feedback to the employee not available elsewhere (Krefting, 1980; Krystofiak, Newman, & Krefting, 1982). The slope may not steepen until higher levels of wages because it may take a substantial salary to be perceived as anything other than a market adjustment.

Third, previous research (Giles & Barnett, 1971) had found support for a power function over a linear or quadratic function when pay increase was the independent variable with pay satisfaction as the dependent variable. In the present study it was expected that the power function would be even more pronounced because differences in pay levels are usually greater than differences in pay increases.

Fourth, the high levels of tenure in the organization should also contribute to a steeper slope at higher pay levels. Large salaries would not be expected given budget constraints. To be extent large salaries were awarded, satisfaction would be higher because salary exceeds expectations.

Fifth, given the somewhat low pay levels in the hospital, it is doubtful that employees would feel overpaid. Hence, the curve is not expected to turn downward at higher pay levels as might be predicted from equity theory (Adams, 1965).

METHOD

Setting

Data were collected at a large Midwestern hospital in a metropolitan area. The hospital had a nonunion workforce. The hospital consisted of 33 different departments including surgery, intensive care, pediatrics, oncology, psychiatry, burns, and chemical dependency. There were a total of 44 job classifications including a variety of registered nurses, therapists, technicians, technologists, and aides. Each classification corresponded to a pay grade. There were up to five levels within each pay grade. Pay rates were on average below market. Performance appraisals were not routinely completed. Pay increases were made annually and made on the basis of market considerations. Pay increases were sometimes adjusted on the basis of supervisory ratings of performance if available.

Subjects

Through voluntary participation, 456 employees of 33 nursing departments provided data for a response rate of about 50 percent. These data were collected as a part of a lengthy survey distributed to all hospital employees, which they were asked to complete on their own time. The modal age category was 26–45 and 94 percent of the subjects were female. Seventy-one percent were full-time employees, 20 percent part-time, and 9 percent contingent or supplemental. About 11 percent were in supervisory positions. Twenty-five percent of the sample had worked at the hospital less than three years, 31 percent from three to 10 years, and 44 percent more than ten years. The sample obtained was similar in demographics to the total employees of these 33 departments, described as: 89 percent between the ages of 26 and 45; 82 percent female; 68 percent full-time employees; and 12 percent had tenure of less than three years, 52 percent from three to ten years, and 35 percent more than ten years.

Measures

The dependent variable was pay satisfaction and was measured using the pay satisfaction questionnaire (PSQ; Heneman & Schwab, 1985). The psychometric properties of this measure are very good, well established, and reported in detail elsewhere (Heneman & Schwab, 1985; Judge, 1993; Scarpello, Huber, & Vandenberg, 1988).

Pay satisfaction was modeled against seven independent variables: pay level, age, supervisory responsibility, tenure, job tier, employee type, and compa-ratio. Pay level was measured as current hourly wage.

Age responses were by ranges and coded as 1 = under 26, 2 = 2634, 3 = 35–45, and 4 = over 45. For supervisory responsibility a yes response was entered as 1 and included administration, department heads, head nurses, and supervisors. A no response was entered as 2. Tenure also was reported by ranges of time with this employer: 1 = less than 1 year, 2 = 1–3 years, 3 = 3–7 years, 4 = 7–10 years, and 5 = more than 10 years.

Job tier was a representation of job level. The only indication of job level supplied directly was the hourly wage, and in this organization pay grades overlap. Therefore, the only cut off between levels that eliminated possible misclassification was to determine breaks where the highest level of one pay grade did not overlap the lowest level of the next. Among the 44 pay grades in this sample, there was only one such break, at approximately $10.80 per hour. Above this point (coded as tier 2) are 16 pay grades including head nurses, nurse specialists, program coordinators, clinical therapists, surgeon's assistants, and registered nurses. The pay grades below this point (coded as tier 1) included jobs such as technicians, technologists, aides, surgical attendants, secretaries, clerks, and transcriptionists.

Employee type differentiates 1 = non-regular employees (supplemental and contingent), and 2 = regular employees (full-time and part-time). Examination of t-tests indicated no significant difference in responses between full- and part-time employees but significant differences between regular and non-regular.

The term *compa-ratio* (comparative salary ratio), refers to the employees salary relative to a midpoint for that employee's pay grade. Because pay grades were not individually identified within the current study, this concept was adapted to the available information. Pay grade midpoints were calculated as an average value using the highest and lowest level possible within each pay grade of each nursing department. The mean of pay grade midpoints for each job tier was then used as the overall midpoint to calculate a compa-ratio, the employee's salary compared to the overall midpoint for the job tier.

Analysis

Hierarchical regression was used with pay satisfaction as the dependent variable. Two sets of independent variables were entered. The first set consisted of the person and job characteristics (age, supervisory responsibility, tenure, job tier, employee type, and compa-ratio). The second set consisted of one variable-pay level. Two hierarchical regressions were conducted. In both cases, the personal and job characteristics were entered first followed by pay level. The two regressions differed from one another by the form of the function used with pay level. In the first regression, a linear function was used by analyzing the data using ordinary least squares. The second regression involved a nonlinear transformation of pay level using a power function. In order to do so, pay level was squared in the regression equation.[1]

Age, supervisor status, tenure, job tier, employee type, and compa-ratio were included in the analysis as control variables. Therefore, the linear assumptions of prior research were accepted as adequate for our purpose. The focus of the analysis was to test the form of the relationship between pay level and pay satisfaction, so only pay level was transformed into an alternate representation.

RESULTS

The reliability of the PSQ was .94 for the present sample. Means, standard deviations, and zero-order correlations are shown in Table 1. The results of the hierarchical regressions are shown in Table 2. As can be seen in Table 1, person and job characteristics did account for a significant amount of pay satisfaction variance. For each variable in the set, the sign for both was in the predicted direction. Also, as can be seen by the adjusted R^2 values, a significant amount of additional pay satisfaction variance was explained using a power rather than linear function. The adjusted R^2 for personal and control variables was .068. When pay level was added as a linear function the adjusted R^2 increased to .082. When pay level was added as a power function, the adjusted R^2 was .093.

Because the power function appeared to be the better representation, a second hierarchical regression was performed. The pay level was added to step one, along with the other independent variables to control for the linear component of the relationship (Cohen & Cohen, 1983). The power function was added in step two, in order to test whether it was a significant improvement. The resulting change in R^2 was .01 ($F = 4.28$, $p < .04$). The significant change in R^2 indicates the power function was a better model of the relationship.

DISCUSSION

In the present study, it was shown that the best fit of the data showing the relationship between pay level and pay satisfaction was a power function rather than a linear function. The power function accounted for a significant variance in pay satisfaction above the linear function even after controlling for person, job, and pay system characteristics. The results of this study have implications for theory, research, and practice. These issues will be addressed in turn.

In terms of theory, the results of the present study provide support for a power function derived from psychophysics. Changes in pay level were associated with increasing rates of pay satisfaction. The reason for the

Table 1. Descriptive Statistics and Intercorrelations

Variable	Mean	SD	(1)	(2)	(3)	(4)	(5)	(6)	(7)	(8)
1. Pay Satisfaction	2.79	.71								
2. Pay Level	14.51	2.65	08							
3. Age	2.42	.83	-03	14**						
4. Supervisor	1.89	.31	-11*	-40***	-15**					
5. Tenure	3.54	1.42	-01	24***	40***	-15**				
6. Job Tier	1.87	.33	25***	77***	-07	-11**	-02			
7. Employee Type	1.914	.28	14*	10*	02	-08*	05	12**		
8. Compa-Ratio	96.11	11.13	05	53***	29***	-47***	38***	-20***	-01	

Notes: Decimals omitted in correlation matrix. * $p < .05$ ** $p < .01$ *** $p < .001$

Table 2. Results of Hierarchial Regressions

Step	Variables entered	Beta
1	Age	.12
	Supervisory	-.15
	Tenure	-.25
	Job Tier	.01
	Employee Type	-.02
	Compa-Ratio	.10

						df
			F	AdjR²		
Results of Step 1:	TOTAL R^2 = .083		5.46**	.068		6,360

| | | | Change | | Total | |
Step	Variables Entered	Beta^a	$R^2$2	F	AdjR²	Df
2	Current Hourly Wage: LINEAR	2.10	.017	6.67*	.082	7,359
2	Current Hourly Wage: POWER (2)	1.25	.027	10.94**	.093	7,359

Note: * $p < .05$ ** $p < .01$ *** $p < .001$

increasing rate in pay satisfaction may be due to the symbolic nature of pay level (Krefting, 1980). Pay level may serve as a proxy measure in the eyes of the employees as to how well they are doing in the absence of a well-developed appraisal system in the studied organization. Higher levels of pay may also be seen as a vote of confidence or signal of appreciation. This vote of confidence would seem to have particular value in the health care setting where there is tremendous pressure to contain costs by keeping salaries low. Both of these explanations need to be tested with further research as we did not collect data on the psychological meaningfulness of pay in the present study.

Also, in terms of theory, the results of the present study suggest that in specifying the expected relationship between pay and satisfaction, a contingency approach is more useful than a blind empirical approach. Factors to be considered in deciding which function is most likely to fit the data include the amount of pay relative to others, the type of reward system, and characteristics of the workforce. These contingency factors and others need to be studied in the context of different forms of pay and the different facets of pay satisfaction. The type of function which best models the relationship between pay increases and pay satisfaction may, for example, be different than the function which best models the relationship between pay level and pay satisfaction. As another example, the type of function which best models the relationship between pay level and pay level satisfaction may be different from the function which best models the relationship between pay level and benefits satisfaction. As demonstrated by several authors (Heneman et al., 1988; Judge, 1993), the same predictor variables may have differential effects on various pay satisfaction facets. It may also be the case that the best fitting function may depend upon the facet of satisfaction being studied.

The results of this study also have implications for research. As shown here, it should not be automatically assumed that the relationship between pay level and pay satisfaction can be modeled with a simple linear function. Instead, care must be taken in modeling this relationship to include characteristics of the person, job, and pay system. Moreover, possible nonlinear relationships need to be examined. Rather than simply testing alternative nonlinear functions, theory should be used to select these alternative forms. The first theoretical consideration is which form of pay is being examined (level, increase, benefits). The second theoretical consideration is which facets of satisfaction are of importance (level, raise, benefits, structure, administration, overall). The third consideration is what variables are likely to mediate the relationship between the chosen pay variables and pay satisfaction variables. The three mediating variables considered in the present study were pay level relative to others, type of reward systems, and characteristics of the workforce. Based upon these three sets of considerations, a choice can be made as to the most likely functional form for the pay form variable. In the present study, the power function emerged and was supported. Other possibilities which can be considered include logarithmic and quadratic functions (Porter et al., 1990).

In terms of practice, the results of this study have implications to those administrators making strategic decisions regarding pay levels. In making these decisions, criteria can be applied as to the likely return to the organization from various pay levels. These criteria, noted earlier, may include the likelihood of better attendance, less turnover, cost minimization, better performance, and accomplishment of the strategic plan. Another criteria is pay satisfaction and was examined in the present study. It was found that if pay satisfaction is treated as one return to the hospital, then an increasing return rate in pay satisfaction could be expected for increasing levels of pay. This fact may, for example, have large relevance for decision makers if the goal of the hospital is to remain union free. In order to meet this objective, higher pay levels may need to be offered. But they may not need to be as large as was perhaps assumed because of the increasing rate of satisfaction returned for each pay level dollar allocated.

Pay satisfaction is one important measure of organizational effectiveness. Rather than speculating about the impact of pay on satisfaction, organizations should routinely measure pay satisfaction using a standardized measure like the PSQ used in this study and many others. Better strategic decisions can then be made as they are based upon actual data. The process of surveying employees is very consistent with the practice in hospitals of surveying customers. By using the PSQ, employees are being treated as internal customers with a stake in the success of the organization.

NOTE

1.   Squaring the pay level was an initial estimate. To improve on this we modeled the relationship in the SPSS/PC nonlinear regression procedure which uses Levenburg-Morquardt algorithms to determine the best fitting parameters from initial estimates (SPSS/ PC + V3.0 Update Manual). This modeling function was unable to derive an improved estimate. Therefore, we used the power of 2 in our analysis.

REFERENCES

Adams, J.S. (1965). Inequity in social exchange. In L. Berkowitz (Ed.), *Advances in experimental social psychology* (pp. 267–299). New York: Academic Press.

Bernoulli, D. (1964). Exposition of a new theory on the measurement of risk. In G.A. Miller (Ed.), *Mathematics and psychology*. New York: Wiley.

Cohen, J., & Cohen, P. (1983). *Applied multiple regression/correlation analysis for the behavioral sciences.* Hillsdale, NJ: Erlbaum.

Dyer, L., & Theriault, R. (1976). The determinants of pay satisfaction. *Journal of Applied Psychology, 61,* 596–604.

Giles, B.A., & Barrett, G.V (1971). Utility of merit increase. *Journal of Applied Psychology, 55*(2), 103–109.

Gomez-Mejia, L.R., & Balkin, D.B. (1992). *Compensation, organizational strategy, and firm performance.* Cincinnati, OH: South-Western.

Heilbroner, R.L., & Thurow, L.C. (1982). *Economics explained.* Englewood Cliffs, NJ: Prentice-Hall.

Heneman, H.G., III (1985). Pay Satisfaction. In K.M. Rowland & G.R. Ferris (Eds.), *Research in personnel and human resources management* (Vol. 3, pp. 115–139). Greenwich, CT: JAI Press.

Heneman, H.G., III, & Schwab, D.P. (1985). Pay satisfaction: Its multidimensional nature and measurement. *International Journal of Psychology, 20,* 129–141.

Heneman, R.L., Greenberger, D.B., & Strasser, S. (1988). The relationship between pay-for-performance perceptions and pay satisfaction. *Personnel Psychology, 41,* 745–760.

Hills, F .S., Bergmann, T.J., & Scarpello, VG. (1994). *Compensation decision making.* Fort Worth, TX: Dryden.

Judge, T.A. (1993). Validity of the dimensions of the pay satisfaction questionnaire: Evidence of differential prediction. *Personnel Psychology, 46,* 331–355.

Krefting, L.A. (1980). Differences in orientations toward pay increases. *Industrial Relations, 19,* 81–87.

Krzystofiak, F., Newman, J., & Krefting, L. (1982). Pay meaning, satisfaction and size of a meaningful pay increase. *Psychological Reports, 51,* 660–662.

Lawler, E.E., III (1971). *Pay and organizational effectiveness: A psychological view.* New York: McGraw-Hill.

Lawler, E.E., III (1990). *Strategic pay.* San Francisco: Jossey-Bass.

Porter, G.P, Greenberger, D.B., & Heneman, R.L. (1990). Pay and pay satisfaction: A comparison of economic, political, psychological, and psychophysical predictions. *Academy of Management Best Paper Proceeding, 50,* 289–293.

Scarpello, V., Huber, V., & Vandenberg, R.J. (1988). Compensation satisfaction: Its measurement and dimensionality. *Journal of Applied Psychology, 73*(2), 163–171.

SPSS/PC+ V3.0 Update Manual. (1988). Chicago: SPSS.

Stevens, S.S. (1959). Measurement, psychophysics, and utility. In C.W Churchman & P. Ratoosh (Eds.), *Measurement: Definitions and theories.* New York: Wiley.

Zedeck, S., & Smith, PC. (1968). A psychophysical determination of equitable payment: A methodological study. *Journal of Applied Psychology, 52*(5), 343–347.

CHAPTER 25

CASE STUDY:

Using Employee Attitude Surveys to Evaluate a New Incentive Pay Program

Robert L. Heneman, Don E. Eskew, and Julie Fox

Source: Heneman, R.L., Eskew, D., & Fox, J. *Compensation and Benefits Review*, *28*(1), 40–44, copyright © 1988 by Sage Publications, Inc. Reprinted by Permission of Sage Publications, Inc.

It is becoming increasingly common for senior managers to ask compensation professionals to provide economic data to justify the need for new pay systems. Such requests are certainly not unexpected, given the large direct and indirect costs of compensation to organizations. Ideally, management would like to see how the investment in pay systems directly translates to the bottom line in terms of productivity and economic value added.

Making this link, however, can be very difficult—for several reasons. First, some jobs (e.g., support staff) lack objective measures of profitability because they do not directly touch the final service or product. Second, profitability is often subject to external forces, such as the state of the economy, that are outside the control of individual employees. Third, most organizations are undergoing massive change and restructuring, and it is very difficult to disentangle the impact of a new pay system on organizational performance from the impact of other changes taking place simultaneously.

The need for economic justification for pay plans and the difficulties of measuring economic impact pose a dilemma for compensation professionals. How can one overcome the measurement difficulties inherent in this process and thus provide an accurate assessment of a pay program's economic impact? One solution, described here, is to assess the direct impact of pay systems on employee attitudes toward the pay system.

At first blush, the use of employee attitude surveys to measure this impact appears to be unacceptably "soft"—not the kind of data that will impress senior management. After all, people can feel good, but business performance can be lousy.

In response to this criticism, one can argue that "hard" data may also be misleading. For example, profitability may be more a function of cutting costs than a new pay plan. More importantly, however, various studies have shown a direct relationship between soft and hard data. In particular, studies on pay satisfaction clearly show that positive attitudes toward pay are associated with better attendance, less turnover, and a lower probability of employees voting for a union (H. Heneman, 1985; R. Heneman, 1992).

The point here is that neither soft nor hard data are perfectly objective. Obviously, hard data are preferable, but for some occupations it is difficult if not impossible to obtain. Because research has established a link between soft data and behaviors, there is some basis to use soft data as a measure of effectiveness. Moreover, when multiple changes are taking place in an organization, pay satisfaction data may arguably be preferable because attitudes toward pay can be directly linked to the pay system rather than to other interventions going on simultaneously.

Fortunately for compensation professionals, the measurement of employee attitudes toward pay is a straightforward process. The remainder of this article presents a case study from a high technology firm on how pay satisfaction can be measured and used to guide strategic pay decisions. The objective is to show a rigorous approach to the assessment of attitudes toward pay.

Although straightforward, such a process is not easy. Hastily constructed measures of attitudes toward pay will likely lack reliability and validity. As such, they can be more problematic than no assessment of the effectiveness of pay plans because they may send a false signal to senior management. On the other hand, the vigorous assessment of employee attitudes toward pay can provide a very useful barometer on pay plan effectiveness.

NEED FOR A NEW PAY SYSTEM

Simcom is a small, privately held, 10-year-old company with locations in Orlando and Phoenix. It is in the business of building flight simulators and training pilots on twin propeller planes as well as small jets. The company's approximately 80 employees are organized into teams based on functional units: production, marketing, sales, training, computer services, and clerical.

Growth has been rapid. In 1990, Simcom trained only 54 pilots; in 1997, approximately 2,650 pilots received Simcom training. The company is recognized as a leader in its industry, as evidenced by a "Best of the Best" Award from *Flying Magazine*.

In 1992, Simcom's senior management asked the lead author of this article to assess the need for an incentive pay plan. At the time, the organization was in a start-up/growth phase with a large investment in technology. The pay system then in place was based on market pricing with seniority-based increases.

The company's new president expected associates to act like owners and placed heavy emphasis on customer service as a business strategy. The president and the company's owner wanted to examine the possibility of incentive pay as a method to emphasize performance within that framework.

PHASES OF THE PROJECT

In response to this situation, Simcom implemented a three-phase project. In Phase One, the company developed a survey to assess the need for incentive pay. In Phase Two, it developed and implemented an incentive pay system. In Phase Three, management assessed the effectiveness of the incentive pay system by comparing the survey results prior to pay system implementation with survey results after implementation.

THE SURVEY

The initial survey aimed at assessing the readiness of employees for an incentive pay plan. An internal survey of all associates was chosen over an external survey of similar-company incentive practices because senior management valued employee input and wanted to develop an incentive system unique to its business and culture. Rather than viewing incentive pay as a separate system, management took a more holistic approach in which it viewed incentive pay as part of the larger system of compensation and rewards (both monetary and nonmonetary). The results of the survey were validated in both Phase One and Phase Three by conducting focus groups with a sample of employees and by statistically calculating the reliability of the survey measures each time.

The survey measured attitudes in four areas:

- job satisfaction,
- pay satisfaction,

- performance ratings, and
- pay-for-performance.

Figures 1, 2, 3, and 4 show the dimensions covered in each area. For job satisfaction and pay satisfaction (Figures 1 and 2), the instrument used multiple statements to define each dimension. Survey participants responded using the 5 to 1 scale shown. The pay and pay-for-performance measures (Figures 3 and 4) were shorter and consisted of the statements and rating scale shown in the exhibits. All of these measures had been used in previous research and their statistical reliability had been documented (see notations for each figure).

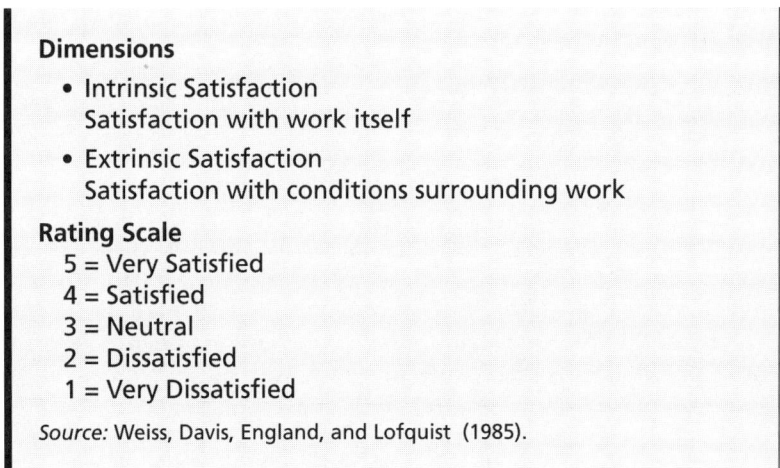

Dimensions

- **Intrinsic Satisfaction**
  Satisfaction with work itself
- **Extrinsic Satisfaction**
  Satisfaction with conditions surrounding work

Rating Scale
5 = Very Satisfied
4 = Satisfied
3 = Neutral
2 = Dissatisfied
1 = Very Dissatisfied

Source: Weiss, Davis, England, and Lofquist (1985).

Figure 1.   Job satisfaction measure.

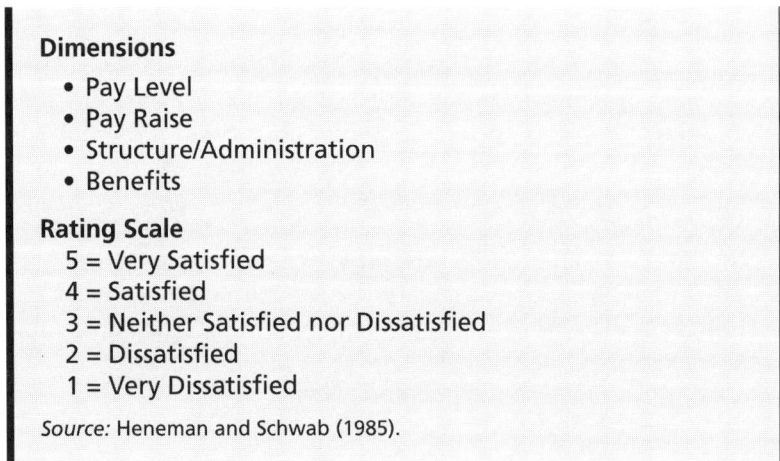

Dimensions

- Pay Level
- Pay Raise
- Structure/Administration
- Benefits

Rating Scale
5 = Very Satisfied
4 = Satisfied
3 = Neither Satisfied nor Dissatisfied
2 = Dissatisfied
1 = Very Dissatisfied

Source: Heneman and Schwab (1985).

Figure 2.   Pay satisfaction measure.

Statements
- Quality
- Quantity
- Following of Procedures
- Ability to Help Others
- Ability to Get Along with Others
- Productivity Under Pressure
- Acceptance of Responsibility
- Adaptation to Different Situations
- Overall Performance

Scale
5 = Excellent
4 = Above Average
3 = Average
2 = Below Average
1 = Poor

Source: Heneman, Greenberger, and Ananyou (1989).

Figure 3.   Performance ratings measure.

Statements
"If I perform especially well on my job it is likely that I will get a pay raise."

"The best workers in the company get the highest pay raises."

"The pay raises that I receive on my job make me work harder."

"High performers and low performers get the same pay raises."

Scale
5 = Strongly Agree
4 = Agree
3 = Neither Agree Nor Disagree
2 = Disagree
1 = Strongly Disagree

Source: Heneman, Greenberger, and Strasser (1988).

Figure 4.   Pay-for-performance measure.

INITIAL SURVEY RESULTS

The first column in Figure 5 shows the survey results for Phase One of the project. As the data show, associates had favorable job satisfaction scores, especially with regard to the work itself (intrinsic satisfaction). Satisfaction with pay, however, was somewhat low, especially for benefits. In addition, the link between pay and performance was not clear to employees nor was administration of the pay system.

Measure	Pre-Plan 1992	Post-Plan 1997
Job Satisfaction	3.55	3.99
Extrinsic Satisfaction	3.64	4.36
Intrinsic Satisfaction	3.80	4.05
Pay Satisfaction	2.80	3.27
Benefits	2.58	3.19
Level	2.87	3.35
Raise	2.90	3.22
Structure/Administration	2.73	3.21
Pay for Performance	2.69	3.02
Performance	4.07	3.84

Scale: 1 = Low, 5 = High

Figure 5.   Employee attitude survey results.

The focus groups confirmed these results. For example, researchers heard a consistent theme related to the need to tie pay to performance. One employee, for example, indicated that associates should have the opportunity to "earn what they deserve." A manager indicated that employees at the company were very "dedicated and committed and should be rewarded accordingly."

THE REWARD PLAN

Based on the results in Phase One, senior management decided that a new reward plan would, indeed, be appropriate. Phase Two consisted of the development of the plan. Goals for the reward system included providing a share in company success, rewarding customer service, establishing above-market salaries, and providing job security. The reward plan consisted of three components: clarification of role expectations, a new performance management system, and profit sharing.

Role expectations were clearly communicated through a written, personalized document for each employee. The document lists required tasks, core competencies needed to perform each task, and employee and team leader expectations. The performance management system spells out the performance competencies on which employees will be assessed. The system measures a number of dimensions believed to be critical to customer service. These include:

- understanding and support of company goals,
- relationships with supervisors and coworkers,
- doing "whatever it takes,"
- creativity,
- self-improvement, and
- communications.

Ten percent of operating profit is set aside for the profit-sharing plan. The plan pays out twice a year and is administered by a management-associate committee. The amount an individual receives depends on his or her performance rating, pay level, and seniority. All employees and managers are eligible. Due to a downturn in business conditions at the start of the plan, the first payout came in 1996 with another payout anticipated for 1997.

EFFECTIVENESS OF THE REWARD PLAN

Prior to the 1997 payouts, Simcom readministered the survey conducted in Phase One (in 1992) to assess the effectiveness of the plan to date. The second column of Figure 5 shows the results. As with Phase One, the lead author conducted a series of focus groups to confirm the numerical results from the survey.

As the data show, scores increased in all categories except performance. Although the increases are not large, they are statistically significant and take on additional meaning when we consider that the plan had only paid out once. At the same time, however, score increases cannot be totally attributed to the pay plan because there was also turnover among employees during the five-year period. Although the performance scores dropped somewhat, this may actually be a positive event if we interpret it as meaning that supervisors now take the evaluation process more seriously because pay is involved and are thus less lenient in their ratings.

The pattern of scores also underscores the effectiveness of the plan. For example, in 1992 intrinsic satisfaction was greater than extrinsic satisfaction. In 1997, extrinsic satisfaction was greater than intrinsic satisfaction. Moreover, the increase in pay satisfaction was greater than the increase in job satisfaction. These sets of data show that pay as a source of satisfaction at work had grown relative to satisfaction with other aspects of work.

Based on the results of the survey and focus groups, senior management plans to continue to use the reward plan. In the future, the plan will be further refined by several ideas currently under consideration. Multiple raters may be used to gather a more complete picture of employee performance. Training may be provided to raters to ensure that accurate ratings are being made. In order for the process to lead to the development of new skills, learning contracts may be established with employees through the performance management process. To make the performance management process a "living, working" document for employees, personal mission statements may be used to supplement the company mission statement. Care must be exercised in refining the system because associates expressed concern during the focus groups about changes taking place too frequently with the plan.

DISCUSSION AND CONCLUSIONS

The results of this case study suggest that "soft" data in the form of employee attitudes toward pay can be successfully used to assess the effectiveness of a pay system. In this instance, senior management accepted soft data as a basis for deciding whether to use a new pay plan, how to design and refine the plan, and whether to continue the plan.

As shown in this case, well-developed measures of employee attitudes toward work already exist and can be readily used. To develop a comprehensive understanding of these surveys, the numerical results should be supplemented with focus group data, as in the present case. As new forms of reward plans are developed, additional measures will be needed and are being worked on at universities like The Ohio State University. However, in the meantime, the currently available surveys provide a good starting point.

Taking this approach to assessing the economic impact of pay in the organization is critical because of the established link between pay satisfaction and absenteeism, turnover, and union vote. Senior management cannot ignore the potential costs associated with these three indicators of organizational effectiveness.

REFERENCES

Heneman, H.G., III (1985). Pay satisfaction. In K.M. Rowland & G.R. Ferris (Eds.), *Research in personnel and human resources management* (Vol. 3). Greenwich, CT: JAI Press.

Heneman, H.G., III, & Schwab, D.P. (1985). Pay satisfaction: Its multidimensional nature and measurement. *International Journal of Psychology, 20*, 129–141.

Heneman, R.L. (1992). *Merit pay: Linking pay increases to performance ratings.* Reading, MA: Addison-Wesley.

Heneman, R.L., Greenberger, D., & Ananyou, C. (1989). Attributions and exchanges: The effects of interpersonal factors on the diagnosis of employee performance. *Academy of Management Journal, 32*, 466–476.

Heneman, R.L., Greenberger, D.B., & Strasser, S. (1988). The relationship between pay for performance perceptions and pay satisfaction. *Personnel Psychology, 41*, 745–759.

Weiss, D.J., Davis, R.V, England, G.W., & Lofquist, R.H. (1985). *Manual for the Minnesota Satisfaction Questionnaire (Minnesota Studies in Vocational Rehabilitation: XXII).* Minneapolis: University of Minnesota Industrial Relations Center, Work Adjustment Project.

Part X

CONCLUSIONS & THE FUTURE OF
STRATEGIC REWARD MANAGEMENT

I n order for strategic reward programs to be effective they must be carefully managed. This means that the design, implementation, and evaluation issues raised in this book need to be carefully considered. Moreover, the management of reward programs must be integrated with the larger business context in order to be effective. Reward programs are doomed to fail when they are taken off the shelf and simply "administered" rather than developed specifically to the needs of the organization and then managed.

The available research on strategic reward programs, reviewed in several places throughout this book, clearly shows the positive impact of these plans on organizational effectiveness. However, much remains to be done to further improve the effectiveness of these plans. Practitioners need to place more emphasis on the management of these plans and scholars need to do more and better evaluation of these plans. The initial research is very promising and provides us with incentive to undertake these activities. Strategic reward programs are now and will continue to be the most powerful human resource interventions that we can undertake.

As shown in the last reading, however, more work remains to be done. Execution is equally as important as the design and implementation of reward plans. Hence we must work hard at administering plans in a manner consistent with their intent. In addition, strategic reward management holds great promise as a method of compensation for nontraditional reward environments (e.g., public sector, not-for-profit, unionized organizations).

Heneman, R.L., & Schutt, W. (in press). Total rewards management. In S. Chowdhury (Ed.), *Organization 21C: Someday all organizations will lead this way.* London: Financial Times; Prentice-Hall.

CHAPTER 26

TOTAL REWARDS MANAGEMENT

Robert L. Heneman and Wendy K. Schutt

Source: Heneman, R.L., and Schutt, W. (in press). Total Rewards Management. In S. Chowdhury (Ed.), *Organization 21C: Someday all Organizations will Lead this Way.* London: Financial Times; Prentice-Hall. Reprinted with permission from Prentice-Hall.

During the twentieth century, a significant body of knowledge regarding reward systems was developed. Basic principles were established such as the need to link pay to performance in order to increase productivity.[1] Research was conducted that clearly showed the positive impact of reward systems on employee and organizational performance (Jenkins, Mitra, Gupta, & Shaw, 1998). New forms of reward systems such as variable and skill-based pay were created (Jenkins, Ledford, & Gupta, 1987; McAdams & Hawk, 1995). The importance of linking reward systems to business strategy in order to align the interests of employees and owners was emphasized (Heneman, 2001, in press, a).

Much of this progress took place during unstable, rather than stable, business periods such as the turmoil of two World Wars and a Great Depression. For example, many job evaluation methods that are currently used by employers (e.g., Hay System) were developed during or shortly after World War II (Heneman, in press, b).

Turmoil also is likely to exist in the twenty-first century and this turmoil is likely to further hasten advances in reward systems. Current turmoil faced by employers is the rapidly changing nature of work. Elements of this change include changes in the nature of the employment relationship from permanent to contingent employment, changes in technology that have made it easier for organizations to monitor vast amounts of data about employee and organizational performance, changes in organizational structures from bureaucracies to virtual organizations, and changes in the design of jobs from strict to loose role definitions for employees to follow (Heneman, Ledford, & Gresham, 2000).

The purpose of this chapter is to propose some fundamental issues that need to be addressed by executives in order for basic reward principles developed in the twentieth century to be successfully applied to the rapidly changing nature of work in the twenty-first century. More importantly, the issues addressed in this chapter need to be considered if further progress is to be made at developing new principles of compensation applicable to organizations in the twenty-first century. Issues to be explored in this chapter include the following: Moving from compensation to total rewards, focusing on execution as well as strategy, integrating reward systems with organizational learning systems, revisiting the concept of equity, public sector rewards design, and extending reward systems to new business environments. These topics will be covered in turn.

MOVING FROM COMPENSATION TO TOTAL REWARDS

The portfolio of reward programs used by most managers in the twentieth century consisted primarily of compensation (wages, salaries, and incentives) and benefits. The "portfolio" of compensation and benefits was usually homogeneous for occupational groups and controlled by the human resource management department. This approach worked relatively well with stable business environments that characterized much of the twentieth century.

Radical changes in the nature of work in the twenty-first century require a shift in the paradigm from two forms of rewards to multiple forms of rewards, from homogeneous rewards to heterogeneous reward programs, and from human resource management control to line manager control. In the absence of this shift to total rewards, it is unlikely that managers will be able to successfully align the interests of employees with the interests of the organization.

In terms of the forms that rewards take, they need to be expanded to include learning opportunities and job design. Learning opportunities are now needed given the changing nature of the employment relationship from permanent employment to contingent employment. Learning opportunities help employees to broaden their skill sets to take on multiple roles in the organization. When roles cease to exist temporarily or permanently, employees are then equipped to shift from one role to another role that is still being performed in the organization. Ultimately, when the employee no longer works for a particular organization, learning opportunities help employees to develop their human capital so that they are desirable to other employers.

In addition to learning opportunities, job design is another aspect of total reward systems for the twenty-first century. Dynamic rather than static job assignments can be used as a selling point by the organization to align employee and owner interests. Research has clearly demonstrated that for many, but not all employees, work that is characterized as high in autonomy, feedback from the work itself, skill variety, and work significance, is more likely to lead to employees committed to their work. These characteristics of work promote a sense of psychological meaningfulness to work for employees and are more likely to be present with dynamic rather than static work (Hackman & Lawler, 1971).

The mix of base pay, incentives, benefits, learning opportunities, and meaningful work needs to be carefully matched to the finances of the organization and to the needs of employees at various stages in their lives. Flexible or "cafeteria" style rewards plans will be needed to match the interests of employees with owners. Employees are much more likely to perform in a manner commensurate with organizational goals when they have input into the mix of rewards they receive (Lawler, Mohrman, & Ledford, 1998). While the amount of total rewards that they receive may remain homogeneous by occupation and performance, the forms that pay is delivered in may be very heterogeneous.

In terms of control over pay decisions, the human resource department will not be able in the twenty-first century to retain the tight control over pay decisions that they had in the twentieth century. Work will be changing so rapidly that line managers, those closest to the changing nature of work, will be the only ones close enough to the changes to be able to make the rapid-fire adjustments in pay that will be required. Certainly, human resource management departments still play a role in setting pay parameters for line manager to follow (e.g., market value), but much more discretion will need to be given to line managers in total reward decisions (Ulrich, Losey, & Lake, 1997).

FOCUSING ON EXECUTION AS WELL AS STRATEGY

In the latter parts of the twentieth century, compensation professionals became obsessed with strategic compensation. The focus was on what types of compensation systems work best under certain business circumstances. While this is an extremely important issue, many lost track of the assumption that is made with strategic compensation; namely, that the compensation strategy selected will be properly designed, implemented, administered, and evaluated. Unfortunately, gains made by strategic thinking in the twentieth century were often lost due to poor execution. An example of this gain and subsequent loss is the use of employee competencies as a basis for pay. From a strategic perspective, this approach to compensation is very much in strategic alignment with contemporary organizations such as virtual organizations (Heneman & Greenberger, in press). Unfortunately, the use of competencies as a compensation strategy has fallen into disfavor. In order to pay on the basis of competencies, many organizations simply copied competencies from a competency catalog made available by consultants and then added these competencies to the merit pay system. No concern was given to the reliability and validity of these competencies in a particular organization. Not surprisingly, many competency pay systems failed, not because of strategy, but because of execution.

In order for human resource professionals to add value to organizations, they must do a better job at execution than in the twentieth century. Basic analytical concepts such as reliability and validity have slipped from the tool kit of human resource professionals and need to be replaced as we go forward in the twenty-first century. In the absence of basic analytical knowledge by human resource professionals, it is very doubtful that new compensation strategies will be successfully implemented.

INTEGRATING REWARD SYSTEMS WITH ORGANIZATIONAL LEARNING SYSTEMS

As reward systems become more fluid and flexible in response to the changing nature of work, organizations will be forced to develop, store, and disseminate knowledge about how reward systems most effectively operate. Never has the need for this integration of reward systems and organizational learning ever been stronger because not only is the changing nature of work impacting compensation systems, but so too is the current decline in compensation knowledge. Due to the changing nature of the labor force, subject matter experts in rewards will continue to retire at a rapid rate as the baby-boom generation ages (Drucker, 2001). In addition, compensation scholars are retiring for similar reasons and unfortunately, fewer and fewer of the new generation of scholars are doing research in reward systems.

An important technological advancement should be very useful for the integration of reward systems and organizational learning. The advancement is expert systems that capture subject matter expert's ideas, codify them, and develop them into a software program that can be used after the subject-matter expert moves on. An example of this approach was undertaken by one of the authors. An expert system was created that shows the appropriate reward system to use depending upon the business strategy (prospector versus defender), organizational structure (organic versus mechanistic), and organizational culture (high involvement versus low involvement) of the company. Depending upon the configuration of these three variables for a company, the system provides the most appropriate reward system to follow. The system is defined by the reward form (monetary versus nonmonetary), unit of analysis (person versus job), value comparison (internal versus external markets) reward measures (behaviors versus results), reward level (individual versus business unit), pay increase (fixed versus variable), administrative level (centralized versus decentralized), timing (lead versus lag), and communications (open versus closed) (Heneman & Dixon, in press). Subject matter experts used to create this expert system included practitioners and scholars.

Alliances will also need to be formed to create additional rewards knowledge. One example here is the Consortium for Alternative Reward Strategies Research (CARS) that was formed to investigate the effectiveness of incentive plans in over 663 companies for up to a five-year period. Consortium members included private sector companies and the advisory board and research sponsors consisted of consultants, academics, and professional association staff. This monumental undertaking produced a wealth of best practice information on incentive plans.

A similar approach is currently underway and is called the Knowledge of Pay study. This study, coordinated by WorldatWork and the LeBlanc Group, has 25 leading private sector companies in the United States and Canada that are having their white-collar employees surveyed regarding the extent to which their employees are aware of, understand, and believe in their compensation systems. The hypothesis being tested is that employees most knowledgeable about their pay systems are more likely to be engaged in their work as evidenced by greater commitment to their work organizations. For practitioners, this study will provide ideas on how to best communicate pay plans for maximum impact on employee attitudes and beliefs.

The major point being made here is that organizations in the twenty-first century will have to be proactive in generating reward system knowledge for their organization. Expert systems can be created for internal benchmarks and alliances can be formed for external benchmarks. Because of the death of information being created by organizations and by scholars with the retirement of the baby-boom generation, increasingly the knowledge being created about reward programs in the twenty-first century will become proprietary and a source of competitive advantage for those organizations that actively integrate reward systems with organizational learning.

REVISITING THE CONCEPT OF EQUITY

In order to ease the administrative burden associated with reward decision making, organizations in the twentieth century focused on developing pay systems around the job as the unit of pay rather than the person as the unit of pay. This practice dates back to the world wars. In order to aid the war efforts, it was far easier to design reward systems for thousands of jobs than for millions of people. Job evaluation systems that were created during the world wars became the method that was used to link jobs to pay rather than people to pay. This approach was adopted by industry right after World War II and was used throughout the rest of the twentieth century.

This job-based approach focused employees on the description of their jobs, as the job, rather than the person, was the unit of pay priced by the organization. Comparisons between similar jobs both within the organization and between organizations became the basis for employee equity perceptions. Given the rapidly changing nature of work, and the demise of fixed duties in jobs, equity issues become far more complex to manage. Unfortunately, one common response by employers has been to ignore internal equity issues and use the demise of job descriptions as an excuse.

Equity perceptions remain regardless of whether there is a formal job description and they actually may become more salient rather than less salient to employees in the absence of a job description. Inequity perceptions are correlated with withdrawal attitudes and behaviors (e.g., turnover). As a result, work still needs to be defined and categorized in order for equity issues and subsequent withdrawal behaviors to be successfully managed.

One of the authors is working on a new procedure to evaluate the worth of work rather than the worth of jobs in organizations. In this new system, attention is given to the many different types of work including jobs, roles, competencies, and teams. In addition, evaluation standards are being developed that take into account the changing nature of work for many employees and give employees credit for those changes on an ongoing basis. Hopefully, efforts such as these will help managers in the twenty-first century.

Scholars are also developing new ways to manage equity perceptions. The most well known effort here is to look at what has become to be known as "procedural justice" (Greenberg, 1987). This concept and the supportive research behind it indicates that "how" people are paid is just as important as "what" people are paid in forming equity perceptions (Folger & Konovsky, 1989). Research shows that procedural justice procedures are strengthened when work is clearly defined for employees, employees have an opportunity to say what work they will perform, and employees have a chance to appeal decisions about their work. Employees are more likely to feel equitably paid, even if their pay is low, when these components of procedural justice are followed. In the twenty-first century, the process used to pay people will be as important as the amount that is paid.

PUBLIC SECTOR REWARDS DESIGN

Much of the focus on compensation research and design during the twentieth century has been on private sector businesses, with less attention paid to public sector organizations. This may be due to the fact that traditionally the public sector has been viewed as a desirable place to work and "exempt" from the usual woes of rewards system design and implementation. This perception is fueled by several components including the perception of "lifetime employment" (i.e., employment stability with little risk of layoffs, downsizing, or performance-based terminations), consistent and scheduled wage increases, a sound benefits package including guaranteed retirement funds, an environment uninterrupted by global change, and reasonable work hours.

As the working world continues to change and adequately skilled employees are increasingly difficult to attract and retain, the public sector has been forced to review and update its rewards practices. In addition to the factors just mentioned, increased accountability and public scrutiny have also fed into the need to examine public sector compensation systems and their effectiveness.

In a recent study conducted by the authors at a large state agency, several themes were noted in the structure, implementation and effectiveness of the rewards system. First, the human resources function continues to be the "ruling force" in compensation design and decision-making, practically eliminating feedback and decision-making authority from line management employees. Second, pay ranges and practices were outdated and inflexible and therefore not meeting recruitment and retention needs (i.e., no practices in place to address the need for employees with skills in "hot technologies" in the information technology arena). Third, the public sector is just beginning to understand the meaning and importance of total compensation. And fourth, the compensation expertise in labor market trends and basic labor market data is lacking as the focus continues to be internal, rather than external.

The consequences of these four themes are varied and substantial. As a survival technique front-line managers are forced to manipulate position descriptions to escalate the pay range of an employee to increase pay. The trust of the human resources function is low, and therefore the functional impact is minimal. Attraction and retention are difficult as salaries are not competitive and the environment is undesirable to many in the labor market.

Although this is just one example of public sector rewards system readiness and effectiveness, the authors have been involved in several other studies with public sector organizations that confirm these findings are indeed trends, rather than exceptions.

Public sector organizations are beginning to realize that rewards system design is critical. Therefore, many organizations are commissioning studies to analyze and design skill-based pay plans, knowledge-based pay plans, bonus systems, and pay-for-performance rewards programs. Although this is a positive first step in modernizing public sector pay practices and improving their effectiveness, the acceptance, viability and sustainability of these concepts is yet to be established.

EXTENDING INNOVATIVE REWARD SYSTEMS TO NEW BUSINESS ENVIRONMENTS

Traditional reward systems in the early twentieth century placed an emphasis on base pay and benefits. A major determinant of the level of pay and benefits was seniority. This approach was developed in private unionized companies and extended to nonunion companies, public sector organizations, and not-for-profit organizations.

At the end of the twentieth century, private nonunion companies began to use more innovative reward programs. A common theme to these programs was to focus on pay *increases* based on *performance*. Performance was defined in a multitude of ways ranging from performance ratings to output measures at the individual, team, and organizational level. In the twenty-first century, private unionized companies, public sector organizations, and not-for-profit organizations are likely to also use innovative reward programs. Resistance to performance rather than seniority as a primary determinant of pay is down in unions because they realize that pay-for-performance results in greater productivity and in turn, greater productivity leads to more job security (Heneman, von Hippel, Eskew, & Greenberger, 1997). The public sector is more receptive to pay-for-performance because they realize that they must compete with private sector organizations to deliver services to the public. In this new twenty-first century environment, measures of performance such as customer service are critical to public sector organizations (Alge, Gresham, Henneman, Fox, & Smith, in press). Not-for-profits in the twenty-first century will be not only responsible for delivering services, but also for doing it at the lowest level of cost possible. Innovative reward strategies such as gainsharing are critical to not-for-profit organizations as they provide rewards on the basis of cost reductions to the organization.

SUMMARY AND IMPLICATIONS

As we move into the twenty-first century and face a diverse and changing labor market, continuous global transformation, an increasingly fast work pace, mounting technological enhancements and demands, and a shift away from bureaucratic work structures, organizational rewards systems *must* have the ability to meet these challenges and enhance organizational success and achievement. This article has addressed several of the components needed to meet these demands, as follows:

- Moving from a strict compensation only viewpoint to a total rewards philosophy, including integrating learning opportunities and job design. Learning opportunities allow employees to broaden their skill and knowledge base thereby increasing employees internal mobility and external marketability. Job design refers to the dynamic make-up of positions and job assignments and is characterized by high levels of autonomy, skill variety, work significance, and so on.
- Shifting the focus to include both strategy and execution. This focus should include a rewards system that is both strategic in nature (i.e., the system is in alignment with, and feeds into, organization strategy and goals) and reflective of sound compensation design (i.e., properly designed, implemented, administered and evaluated).
- Integrating reward systems with organizational learning systems so that the development, storage and dissemination of compensation system knowledge are an integral part of the organization and are rewarded accordingly.
- Managing equity perceptions by shifting the focus from a job-based only approach to a dual job-based and person-based method. This allows organizations to assess and address both internal and external equity issues while enhancing employees perceptions of fairness and proper compensation levels.
- Revisiting public sector rewards system design and enhancing their effectiveness by implementing contemporary compensation practices, educating employees and line management about pay practices, equity issues, and so on, implementing skill-based, knowledge-based and bonus driven pay systems, and ensuring that a system of supports is in place to make certain these changes are successful.
- Extend innovative reward systems to new business environments by implementing performance based pay systems into private businesses, public sector organizations as well as not-for-profit agencies and shift away from seniority driven rewards systems.

To assist professionals in determining if an organization's reward system is ready for the unique challenges of the twenty-first century, a comprehensive checklist may be found in Figure 1 at the conclusion of this article.

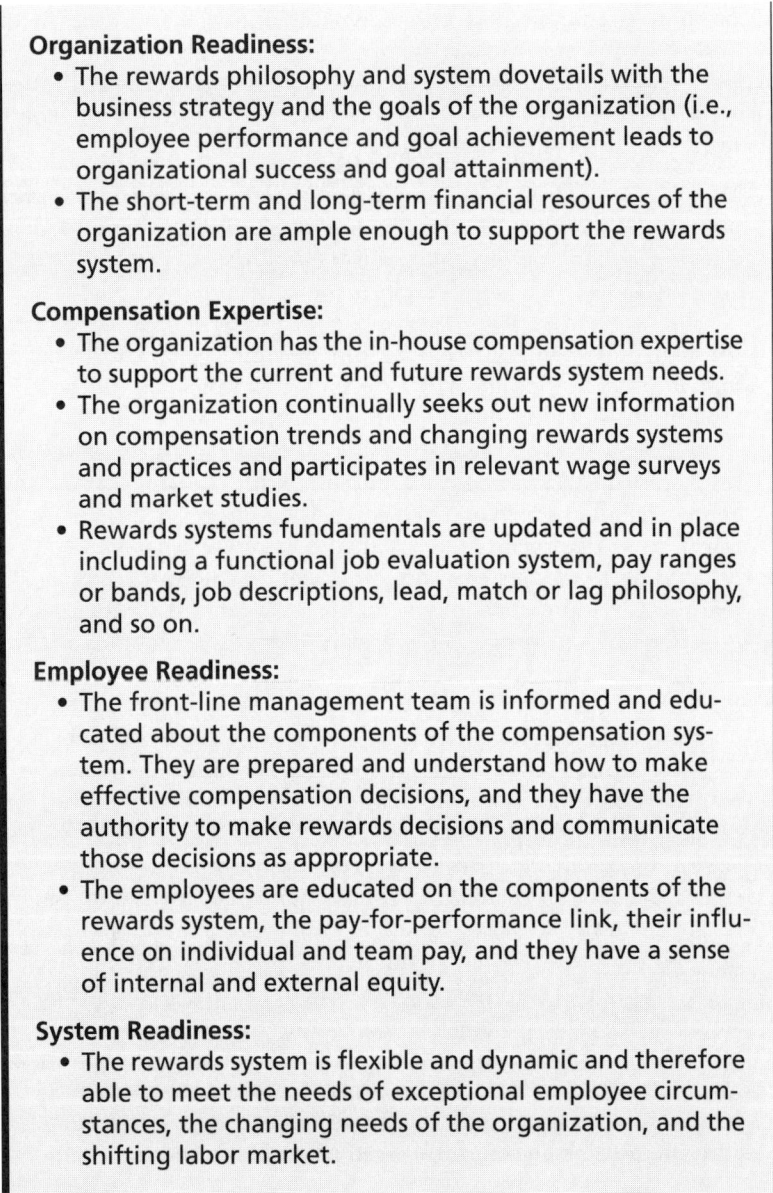

Organization Readiness:
- The rewards philosophy and system dovetails with the business strategy and the goals of the organization (i.e., employee performance and goal achievement leads to organizational success and goal attainment).
- The short-term and long-term financial resources of the organization are ample enough to support the rewards system.

Compensation Expertise:
- The organization has the in-house compensation expertise to support the current and future rewards system needs.
- The organization continually seeks out new information on compensation trends and changing rewards systems and practices and participates in relevant wage surveys and market studies.
- Rewards systems fundamentals are updated and in place including a functional job evaluation system, pay ranges or bands, job descriptions, lead, match or lag philosophy, and so on.

Employee Readiness:
- The front-line management team is informed and educated about the components of the compensation system. They are prepared and understand how to make effective compensation decisions, and they have the authority to make rewards decisions and communicate those decisions as appropriate.
- The employees are educated on the components of the rewards system, the pay-for-performance link, their influence on individual and team pay, and they have a sense of internal and external equity.

System Readiness:
- The rewards system is flexible and dynamic and therefore able to meet the needs of exceptional employee circumstances, the changing needs of the organization, and the shifting labor market.

Figure 1.   Reward system readiness checklist for the twenty-first century.

> • An auditing process is in place to periodically assess if the rewards plan is meeting the needs of the business and tracking with labor market demands.
> • A scalable rewards plan is in position that adapts as the company grows and diversifies.

Figure 1.   Reward system readiness checklist for the twenty-first century (Cont.).

NOTE

1. See Milkovich & Newman (2002) for a review of basic reward principles. The first compensation book was D.F. Schloss (1892).

REFERENCES

Alge,B., Gresham, M., Heneman, R.L., Fox, J., & Smith, R. (in press). Measuring customer service orientation using a measure of interpersonal skills: A test in a public sector organization. *Journal of Business and Psychology.*

Drucker, P. (2001, November 3). The next society: A survey of the near future. *The Economist,* special insert.

Folger, R., & Konovsky, M.A. (1989). Effects of procedural and distributive justice on reactions to pay raise decisions. *Academy of Management Journal,* 270–272.

Greenberg, J. (1987). A taxonomy of organizational justice theories. *Academy of Management Review, 12,* 9–22.

Hackman, J.R., & Lawler, III, E.E. (1971). Employee reactions to job characteristics. *Journal of Applied Psychology, 55,* 259–286.

Heneman, R.L. (in press, a). *Strategic reward management: Design, implementation, and evaluation.* Greenwich, CT: Information Age Press.

Heneman, R.L. (in press, b). Job and work evaluation: A literature review. *Public Personnel Management.*

Heneman, R.L. (2001). *Business-driven compensation policies: Integrating compensation systems with corporate strategies.* New York: AMACOM.

Heneman, R.L., & Dixon, K.E. (in press). Rewards and organizational systems alignment: An expert system. *Compensation and Benefits Review.*

Heneman, R., & Greenberger, D. (in press). *Human resource management in virtual organizations.* Greenwich, CT: Information Age Press.

Heneman, R.L., Ledford, G.E., & Gresham, M. (2000). The changing nature of work and its effects on compensation design and delivery. In S. Rynes & B. Gerhart (Eds.), *Compensation in organizations: Current research and practice* (Society for Industrial and Organizational Psychology Frontiers of Industrial and Organizational Psychology Series) pp. 195–240. San Francisco: Jossey-Bass.

Heneman, R.L., von Hippel, C., Eskew, D., & Greenberger, D. (1997, Summer). Alternative rewards in unionized environments. *American Compensation Association Journal*, 42–55.

Jenkins, Jr., D.G., Ledford, Jr., G.E., Gupta, N., & Doty, D.H. (1987). *Skill-based pay: Practices, payoffs, pitfalls, and prescriptions*. Scottsdale, AZ: American Compensation Association.

Jenkins, Jr., D.G., Mitra, A., Gupta, N., & Shaw, J.D. (1998). Are financial incentives related to performance? A meta-analysis review of empirical research. *Journal of Applied Psychology, 83*, 777–787.

Lawler, III, E.E., Mohrman, S.A., & Ledford, Jr., G.E. (1998). *Strategies for high performance organizations*. San Francisco: Jossey-Bass.

McAdams, J.L., & Hawk, E.J. (1995). *Organizational performance and rewards*, Scottsdale, AZ: American Compensation Association.

Milkovich, G.T., & Newman, J.M. (2002). *Compensation* (7th ed.). Boston: McGraw-Hill/Irwin.

Schloss, D.F. (1892). *Industrial remuneration*. London: Williams and Norgate

Ulrich, D., Losey, M.R., & Lake, G. (Eds.). (1997). *Tomorrow's HR management*. New York: John Wiley & Sons.

ABOUT THE AUTHOR

BIOGRAPHY FOR ROBERT L. HENEMAN

Rob Heneman is a Professor of Management and Human Resources and Director of Graduate Programs in Labor and Human Resources in the Max M. Fisher College of Business at the Ohio State University. Rob has a Ph.D. in Labor and Industrial Relations from Michigan State University, an M.A. in Labor and Industrial Relations from the University of Illinois at Urbana-Champaign, and a B.A. in Economics and Psychology from Lake Forest College. Prior to joining the Ohio State University, Rob worked as a Human Resource Specialist for Pacific Gas and Electric Company. Rob's primary areas of research, teaching, and consulting are in performance management, compensation, staffing, and work design. He has over 70 publications. He has received over $1 million in funds for his research from the Work in America Institute, AT&T Foundation, Ford Motor Company, World at Work, State of Ohio, Society for Human Resource Management, and the Kauffman Center for Entrepreneurial Leadership. He is on the editorial boards of *Human Resource Management Journal, Human Resource Management Review, Human Resource Planning, Compensation and Benefits Review,* and *SAM Advanced Management Journal.* He has been awarded the Outstanding Teacher Award in the Masters in Labor and Human Resources Program numerous times by the students at Ohio State University and is recipient of the first WorldatWork Distinguished Total Rewards Educator Award. He has written or edited seven books including, *Merit Pay: Linking Pay Increases to Performance Ratings, Staffing Organizations* (3rd ed.), *Business-Driven Compensation Policies: Integrating Compensation Systems With Corporate Business Strategies, Human Resource Management in Virtual Organizations* and *Strategic Reward Management: Design, Implementation, and Evalua-*

tion. He has consulted with over 60 public and private sector organizations including IBM, Owens-Corning, BancOne, Time Warner, American Electric Power, Whirlpool, Quantum, AFL-CIO, Nationwide Insurance, the Limited, Worthington Industries, Borden, ABB, POSCO, U.S. Government Office of Personnel Management, and the states of Ohio and Michigan. Rob is past Division Chair, Program Chair, and Executive Committee member for the Human Resources Division of the Academy of Management. He is also a member of the certification program faculty of the World at Work and has served on the research, education, and academic partnership network advisory boards of the World at Work. He has made over 60 invited presentations to universities, professional associations, and civic organizations. He has worked with business organizations and universities in North America, Europe, Russia, Asia, and Africa. His work has been reported in the *Wall Street Journal, USA Today, Money Magazine, ABCNEWS.COM,* and he is listed in *Who's Who in the World, Who's Who in America,* and *Outstanding People in the 20th Century.*

Rob Heneman may be contacted at: Department of Management and Human Resources, Fisher College of Business, The Ohio State University, 2100 Neil Avenue, Columbus, OH 43210; (614) 292-4587; Heneman.1@osu.edu

INDEX

509